D070752

We Can Be
Who We Are

Movie Musicals of the 1970s

Lee Gambin

WITHDRAWN

BearManor
Media

Albany, Georgia

We Can Be Who We Are: Movie Musicals from the 1970s

Copyright © 2015 Lee Gambin. All Rights Reserved.

No part of this book may be reproduced in any form or by any means, electronic, mechanical, digital, photocopying or recording, except for the inclusion in a review, without permission in writing from the publisher.

Published in the USA by
BearManor Media
P.O. Box 71426
Albany, GA 31708
www.BearManorMedia.com

ISBN: 1-59393-855-1

Library of Congress Control Number: 2015912139
BearManor Media, Albany, GA

Printed in the United States of America

For my beautiful dogs: Dotty, Scruffy, Molly and Buddy.

And for the lovers, the dreamers and you.

Table of Contents

Introduction

"We're Not in Kansas Anymore"

The Changing Face of the Movie Musical

MUSICALS ARE NOT FLUFFY, AND IF A DECADE EVER PROVED THIS IT WAS the 1970s. There has been an unwarranted and completely inaccurate idea floating around that all musicals are light hearted romps where fun and frivolity unfold and joyous escapism is assured. The notion that musicals—in all their complicated and varying forms—are by their very nature cheery and bright is not only ludicrous but also remarkably inaccurate. Airy and halcyon musicals do exist, of course; one must only look to the endless slew of musicals to come out of the 1930s and early 1940s to validate that broad point. These beautifully crafted (if somewhat incredibly simple) films were pieced together by standards from the Great American Songbook, fundamentally delivering a "boy meets girl, boy loses girl, boy gets desperate and regains girl" plot. See, for example,

Cheer Up and Smile (1930), *Love Me Tonight* (1932), and *Down Argentine Way* (1940). But the American musical film has also provided powerful commentary on American history, and social and personal struggles. Musicals from the Great Depression that weren't glitzy, glamorous fairy tales usually told the story of a young girl clawing her way out from the gutter and trying to make ends meet and trying to survive. What made these scenarios romantic and idealistic is that this Depression-era heroine always did so with a sparkle in her eye, as seen in such films as *Sally, Irene and Mary* (1938) and *The Girl Said No* (1937). In essence, what the musical of yesteryear did was take a grim situation and offer a sense of optimism that elevates the grit and introduces hope to despair. This is epitomized in the songs of the era which were written with incurable bittersweet melancholy, as heard in the beautiful standards "Singin' in the Rain," "Life Is Just a Bowl of Cherries," "Brother, Can You Spare a Dime?" and then later with "The Surrey with the Fringe on Top" from Richard Rodgers and Oscar Hammerstein II, all of which offer a sense of longing and simple hope in a world that cannot truly escape dark times, or plagued with the humdrum.

Dark and bleak themes have always permeated the American musical film, and this has been the case from the dawn of the genre itself. Musicals are of course descendants of the opera, and what great opera doesn't feature sex and violence and a grandiose bloody death just before the curtain call? In the grips of World War I and II and the Depression, American audiences needed entertainment more than ever, and the musical—along with its genre relatives, the horror film and the western—provided this escapist bliss, giving people who could barely afford to eat some much deserved hope. But even in the throes of giving an audience "a good time," it wasn't all frills, feathers and Busby Berkley visual flair: musicals had a lot to say, and they got louder and angrier as time went by.

Most movie musicals were, of course, born from the stage, be it on the Great White Way or in some experimental theatre in some slum or ghetto. However, during the Golden Age of the movie musical, many also sprouted from the studio system itself, bought to life by the hordes of immigrants working hard to deliver a new form of escapist entertainment. While Universal Studios delivered the goods with their movie monsters (starring horror film icons such as Boris Karloff and Bela Lugosi, as featured in the likes of *Frankenstein* and *Dracula* (1931), MGM was triumphant with endless movie musicals showcasing an array of talented artists such as Judy Garland, Gene Kelly, Mickey Rooney, Carmen Miranda, Esther Williams, Alice Faye, Anne Miller, Fred Astaire, Ginger Rogers and many more. MGM was the musical movie making machine, and with directors such as Vincente Minnelli with his incredible *Meet Me in St. Louis* (1944) and Stanley Donen with the outstanding *Singin' in The Rain* (1952), MGM lead the way for musicals to become originally conceived products, starting life in celluloid form rather than being adapted from the boards.

Of course, for the most part musicals *did* step off the stages of Broadway and beyond, and made their transition to the movie houses: sometimes successfully and with changes that worked (such as in the Rodgers and Hammerstein musicals) and sometimes unsuccessfully (where ideas and formulas that looked and sounded great on stage just didn't translate well on screen). Musicals that originated in film form started to become recognized as integral and important artistic expressions of filmmaking, for example, the aforementioned Minnelli film became one of the first notable integrated musicals, where numbers arose from plot and situation rather than being presented in a diegetic form where they were treated as staged "performances." Donen's masterpiece was an incredibly insightful look at the transition of cinema from silents to sound, while utilizing already-established numbers born in Tin Pan Alley. Landmark cinema was slowly being born, and the musical, in all its Technicolor glory, was instrumental to this revolution.

Musical films based on established stage shows were also inspiring movie going audiences as well as ruffling feathers along the way. During the height of the Hayes Production Code, sexuality and violence had to be handled with meticulous care from screenwriters and directors. Taboo topics such as rape, suicide, murder, interracial relations and so forth had to be constructed in a way that wouldn't jeopardize a film's release. What was acceptable on the Broadway stage was scrutinized in film. Major changes were made to endless musicals in their transition from stage to screen including *Carousel*, *Oklahoma!*, *West Side Story*, *Kiss Me Kate* and many others. Themes were heavy in these musicals and, thankfully, the creators of these great filmic adaptations were exceptionally clever and worked around the oppressive Production Code in order to deliver something truthful and also irresistibly engaging.

For instance, in *Oklahoma!* (1955) there is suggested rape, addiction to pornography, emotional abuse and hushed violence. When Jud Frye (Rod Steiger) is killed, there is really no remorse or mourning, it's as if this cretin with his constant lecherous leanings over the flirtatious and naïve Laurie (Shirley Jones) is presented as a pest, and being the pest that he is, has to be taken care of and exiled from the newly founded state of Oklahoma. In *Carousel* (1956), one of the darkest and most sexually complex of the Rodgers and Hammerstein canon, domestic violence sits at the heart of the story. Billy Bigelow (Gordon MacRae) is the quintessential anti-hero, with emphasis on the anti. Here is a man who is a Lothario wooing and charming women, seducing them and also stealing from them. But when he manages to be wrangled into a monogamous strained romantic partnership with millworker Julie Jordan (Shirley Jones), he lashes out and beats her. The violence in *Carousel* is something that fuels the story, but it's not only the violence that exists within the confines of a household between husband and wife; there is the violence of sex and sensuality, the decay of familial morality and the endless pursuit of redemption that comes at a heavy hand. *Carousel* is ultimately a masterpiece of writing and storytelling, but it also has the guts to disturb; which is something that many more musicals inspired by raw and honest emotionality will soon do as well.

These examples are not rare. Gang warfare, rape, knife fights, racism and desperate passions are examined in *West Side Story* (1961), miscegenation and sub-sequential xenophobia propels *Show Boat* (1936), and the misogynistic attitudes from the brothers is palpable and at times jaw-drop inducing in *Seven Brides for Seven Brothers* (1954) (a musical inspired by "The Rape of the Sabine Women"). The dark seedy underbelly of show business is often presented as a nasty entity: sometimes the drug and booze riddled lifestyle is displayed in ground breaking films such as *42nd Street* (1933) and *A Star is Born* (1954), while suicide, mental illness and overcoming the sorrows brought upon by physical deformity are all found in *Lili* (1953). Race becomes yet another sore thumb in the terrific *Cabin in the Sky* (1943), *South Pacific* (1958) and the controversial but elegant Disney film *Song of the South* (1946), which also dissects themes of poverty and class, while at the same time providing some of the greatest mixed animation with live action ever put to screen.

The 1930s, 1940s and 1950s were truly a Golden Age of musical movies, but there was a progressive change happening from decade to decade. Audiences and filmmakers alike were far more interested in solid storytelling and character driven drama, and the integrated musical became a much welcomed cinematic offering rather than the musical driven by a wafer-thin plot stringed together by exciting and enjoyable, but ultimately non-plot serving musical numbers. By the 1950s, musicals finally shook the shackles of non-linear performance pieces tacked-on in favour of more story heavy outings in the tradition of *Show Boat* and headed by the wildly successful musicals of Rodgers and Hammerstein. Musicals such as *Hollywood Canteen* (1944), *Stage Door Canteen* and *Stormy Weather* (1943) were rapidly disappearing, until finally *Summer Stock* (1950) became the last of the heavily diegetic musicals; from here on in, exquisite films such as *An American in Paris* (1951), *Gigi* (1958) and then just into the 1960s, the biographical *Gypsy* (1962), which told the story of famous burlesque superstar Gypsy Rose Lee and her domineering stage mother, became the type of musical to watch out for. These are perfectly realized films that would excite the senses for decades to come.

Musicals were changing, and artists were playing with the form, and by the 1960s, auteurs were experimenting with standard formulas. *The Umbrellas of Cherbourg* (1964) was a unique take on the sung-through musical, while *Stop the World I Want to Get Off* (1966) was an oddity of allegory and very much presented as a filmed play. Some musicals were purely created just to showcase an artist's work and promote record sales as seen in *Summer Holiday* (1963), while animated films became less formal and more liberal, for example, *Gay Purr-ee* (1962) and *Hey There, It's Yogi Bear!* (1964), and at the same time, diegetic musicals turned into sombre outings with Judy Garland giving her last performance in *I Could Go on Singing* (1963). Additionally in the 1960s, prostitutes, zombies and the British invasion featured and influenced wildly entertaining, but not always perfect, movie musicals such as *Sweet Charity* (1969), *The*

Incredibly Strange Creatures Who Stopped Living and Became Mixed-Up Zombies (1964) and *A Hard Day's Night* (1964).

However it was on stage where things were really shaken up, and to quote legendary film critic Pauline Kael, creators began "frightening the horses." Rock musicals sprang into action with the accessible and also rather classicistic *Bye Bye Birdie* leading the way, which in 1963 became a very stylistic, almost cartoon-like, movie starring the stunning Ann-Margret. Following that were a number of intelligent and not-so-intelligent musicals that crept up onto the boards, some ready to say something profound and others simply there to shock.

For example, *Hair* was one of the most important musicals of the American theatre, and it stunned some audiences with its graphic depiction of sex, nudity, drug use, profanity and anti-establishment ideologies. The vignette-bodied *Oh! Calcutta!* came out not long after and did the same thing with its blunt statement on the diversity of sexual practice. *Hair* got a film treatment more than a decade later, in 1979. While in 1972 (while the musical was still being performed on stage) *Oh! Calcutta!* was shot in a theatre and presented as a filmed live performance piece.

The 1960s continued to push boundaries on stage and screen, with many films employing intriguing ideas and cinematic devices that were highly inventive and also remarkably influential. The art direction in *How to Succeed in Business Without Really Trying* (1967) influenced architecture on a national level, while Asian leading characters populated the world of *Flower Drum Song* (1961). Biographical (and semi-biographical) musicals flourished and received praise, such as in *The Singing Nun* (1966), *Funny Girl* (1968) and *Star!* (1968), showcasing the incredible talents of artists Debbie Reynolds, Barbra Streisand and Julie Andrews. The idea of the motion picture blockbuster was generated by the enchanting and hugely successful *The Sound of Music* (1965), once again starring the lovely Andrews, which—along with films such as *Planet of the Apes* (1968), *Butch Cassidy and the Sundance Kid* (1969) and *2001: A Space Odyssey* (1968)—paved the way for ground breaking blockbusters such as *The Godfather* (1972), *The Exorcist* (1973) and *Jaws* (1975) the following decade, all which revolutionized the way movies were made and marketed.

During the 1960s, movie musicals that had no history on the Broadway stage also came to the fore. Youthful wackiness and the sexual preoccupations of the younger generations germinated in films from low budget maestros American International Pictures with the multiple rock'n'roll heavy "beach blanket" movies such as *Bikini Beach* and *Muscle Beach Party* (1964). There were also the endless hit-and-miss Elvis Presley movies, and of course the whimsically wonderful world of Walt Disney musicals such as the animated *The Jungle Book* (1967) and the non-animated *Babes in Toyland* (1961). It is significant that Disney himself passed away in the 1960s, allowing a dramatic transition in the shift in his studio's films come the 1970s.

Broadway in the 1970s was one of the most electric periods in the history of the American musical, with dramatic changes in tone and themes. Musicals became gritty and edgy, and with the push from the angry *Hair*, bleaker and dirtier stage shows were welcomed by hungry theatre goers.

For instance, *A Chorus Line* cut right through the fabricated glamour of being a dancer on Broadway and delivered a painfully honest, gritty portrait of people in the heart of the recession needing a job. This story didn't receive a filmic adaptation until the early 1980s, where this great work of theatrical art was completely watered down and turned into a grotesque, poor excuse for a film directed by Richard Attenborough. The amazing musicals from brilliant lyricist and composer Stephen Sondheim examined the human condition like never before, tackling concerns such as singlehood and marriage in *Company* through to the disenchantment and anxiety of former performers in *Follies*. He closed the decade with the violent blood sport of revenge at the heart of the Industrial revolution in turn of the century London in the horror-musical masterpiece *Sweeney Todd: The Demon Barber of Fleet Street*, which eventually got a flawed but relatively enjoyable movie adaptation in 2007 by popular director Tim Burton. Only *A Little Night Music* received a movie deal in 1977, and as flat and as uninspired the movie is, it does feature some lovely musical moments thanks to the incredible Stephen Sondheim.

Although Sondheim's musicals were very adult in tone and theme, the 1970s was a decade consumed by youth culture and a celebration of their ideologies. The movie musical shifted gears and had something very new, and at times very angry, to sing about. As Bob Dylan had noted in 1964, "the times they were a changin'" and movie musicals were no exception. Films like *Doctor Doolittle* (1967) and *Hello, Dolly!* (1969) were completely out of step with what audiences were interested in seeing, and in many cases these lavish big budget films began to lose major dollars for studios such as 20th Century Fox. However, the musical wasn't a completely bankrupt genre. *Oliver!* (1968), based on the Lionel Bart musical adaption of Charles Dickens's *Oliver Twist* was an incredible success and swept the Academy Awards, taking home the coveted prize for Best Picture in 1968. *Chitty Chitty Bang Bang* (1968) was an outstanding achievement and proved to be a great success both financially and critically and of course before that was the superlative *Mary Poppins* (1964), which revolutionized the animated/live action hybrid which would soon become a staple for Disney Studios in the years to come.

Traditions were changing, as masterfully explored in *Fiddler on the Roof* (1971). The concept of what made a great Hollywood musical started to come under scrutiny, and by the time it got to the 1970s, musical tastes (diverse and complex) started to imprint a major influence in the structure, themes, writing and direction of how the movie musical will prosper. Long gone was the romantic whimsy of those charming Arthur Freed musicals starring Mickey Rooney and Judy Garland, but their core idea of "let's put on a show" continued to flourish as far as the work ethics of young filmmakers coping with minimal budgets and working on an empty belly. Obviously there were major studio efforts that had money pumped into their products, however since the disastrous *Hello, Dolly!* and *Doctor Doolittle*, producers were now nervous when a musical came their way.

But at the dawn of the Age of Aquarius, and with new and exciting styles brewing and rapidly seducing the young such as heavy metal, punk rock, glam rock and disco, the movie musical was seen as an ideal vehicle to celebrate and exploit these newfound and newly forming genres of popular music. Soon enough, cynical musicals started to surface, rock operas became a successful trend, the concept album sparked a major interest in musical acts from Frank Zappa to ABBA, and television musical specials flourished. The traditional integrated musical became angrier, edgier and reflective of exploitation cinema, and the arrival of the docu-musical and concert film landed with brilliantly executed films such as *Woodstock* (1970), *Gimme Shelter* (1970) and *Ziggy Stardust and the Spiders from Mars* (1973) setting amazing standards.

The 1970s was a wonderful decade of excesses and rock'n'roll ecstasy. Its sounds could be inspiring, apathetic and a war-cry for outsiders. Visually, the era was also exciting as noted by the creepy monstrosities and garishly coloured makeup and costumes of rock'n'roll bands such as KISS and The New York Dolls, as well as the visceral violent energy of punk rock and the bizarre melting pot of soul, R&B and disco. The counter culture became a multiple subdivision of stadium rock fans right through to silk-shirt-wearing club hoppers, and the musicals of the decade reflected that. *Jesus Christ Superstar* (1973), *Tommy* and *The Rocky Horror Picture Show* (1975) among many others paid tribute to rock'n'roll in its purest and most raw form, some of them employing a legitimate analogy of the rock industry itself, others celebrating the chaotic excess of stirring youth angst and many of them revelling in the fresh and alluring sexual revolution. Paying homage to yesteryear came thick and heavy with musicals such as *Grease* (1978) and *Xanadu* (1980), while completely integrating modern sensibilities within the structure and layout as well. Musicals such as *Funny Lady* (1975), *Song of Norway* (1970) and *Mame* (1974) clung to traditional principles and for the most part fumbled in the dark, losing audiences who were screaming for Alice Cooper, not Alice Faye.

Much like Dorothy Gale and Toto in *The Wizard of Oz* (1939), audiences (and the movie musical) weren't in Kansas anymore. But this is not to say that non-rock musicals of the period weren't artistically and commercially effective and profitable, in fact some of the most important and eclectic musicals were made during the decade. A major portion of this success was due to the subject matter such as the torment and sorrow bought on from the Russian Revolution in *Fiddler on the Roof*, the rise of Nazism, abortion and sexual politics in *Cabaret* (1972) and mortality, artistic integrity, drug abuse and promiscuity in *All That Jazz* (1979).

From the quirky and clever *On a Clear Day You Can See Forever* (1970) to the nonsensical lunacy of *Can't Stop the Music* (1980), from the critically panned atrocities *Lost Horizon* (1973) and *Sgt. Pepper's Lonely*

Hearts Club Band (1978) to acclaimed cinematic gems *Saturday Night Fever* (1977) and *New York, New York* (1977), the 1970s movie musical is a diverse, free thinking wild animal that deserves your full attention! So, to quote the wonderful British actor Charles Gray in *The Rocky Horror Picture Show*: I would like, if I may, to take you on a strange journey...

1970

"Hurry! It's Lovely Up Here"
Reincarnation, Charles Dickens and the Hills Are Not So Alive in Norway

BY THE END OF THE 1960S, THE HOLLYWOOD MOVIE MUSICAL WAS the epitome of hit and miss. Some worked and garnered critical and box office acclaim (such as *Oliver!*), while some hindered studios such as *Hello, Dolly!* At the dawn of the 1970s, sensibilities and artistic expression were evolving: the American cinema was exploring a world outside of the studio system and youthful, energetic filmmakers were taking a new, unique approach to storytelling. Most of the directors to come out of the early 1970s were dedicated cinefiles and revelled in the history and artistry of the motion picture industry from yesteryear, but their voices were now different. Although auteurs like Vincente Minnelli and Stanley Donen were still making movies throughout the decade, their much younger contemporaries were challenging pre-established standards and breaking all kinds of taboos. Gifted visionaries like Martin

Scorsese, D.A. Pennebaker, Michael Wadleigh, Ken Russell and the more seasoned Blake Edwards took the cinematic musical and injected it with freshness. Their innovative energy at many times resulted in the creation of something totally original.

The birth of the concert film had come before the start of the 1970s, however it was not until then that the concept of the "rockumentary" (rock 'n' roll documentary) and the onstage/backstage performance piece flourished. These incredibly candid films showcased raw talent from bands such as The Rolling Stones (*Gimme Shelter*, 1970) and *Cocksucker Blues*,1972) and iconic musicians from Elvis Presley (*Elvis: That's the Way It Is*, 1970) to David Bowie (*Ziggy Stardust and the Spiders from Mars, 1973*). These films also captured the essence of an era that truly belonged to the young: the longhaired, disenfranchised, free loving, drug taking youth that had also heavily influenced a whole range of movies that celebrated (and also maligned) the idealistic and sometimes even aggressive countercultures of hippiedom, biker gangs, street thugs, punks and so forth. The movies of Roger Corman, Russ Meyer, Andy Warhol and American International Pictures expressed a more than healthy interest in youth subcultures, and this influence was of course also introduced to the musical film.

A majority of young people (and filmmakers) during this time were not responding positively to movie musicals such as the ill-fated and misdirected *Paint Your Wagon* and *Oh! What a Lovely War* (1969). Because of this, narrative-driven movie musicals in the tradition of the integrated book musical established by pioneering composers, librettists and lyricists took a back seat at the transition from the 1960s to the 1970s. In their place came an increasing interest and hunger for rockumentaries and the filmed live concert. Kicking off the decade in 1970 was a feature documentary film that chronicled the three days of love, peace and music from the year before, Michael Wadleigh's spectacular *Woodstock*.

WE ARE STARDUST, WE ARE GOLDEN: Rockumentaries

Woodstock is an innovative and incredibly engaging excursion into the culmination of 1960s youth counterculture and the anti-war movement. It boasts an outstanding array of musical talent including Joan Baez, Crosby, Stills, Nash and Young, Janis Joplin, The Grateful Dead, Canned

Heat and many more. Jefferson Airplane was a stand out, marked by front woman Grace Slick's sensual bellowing and incredible harmonies with her fellow musicians. When "Won't You Try" bleeds into "Saturday Afternoon," it is an incredible psychedelic moment, not just as a musical performance but as something even bigger that grabs hold of your attention. Slick's piercing blue eyes, dirty, messy hair, and her face bronzed by a combination of suntan and mud is an image of both earth mother and bestial temptress. This a soulful siren delivering her sermon to alien outsiders completely preoccupied with sex, drugs and rock'n'roll. Director Wadleigh's crafty use of split-screen and his fantastic handle on sound captures all of this with a fiery determination.

The "rockumentary" is born in *Woodstock* (1970)

Woodstock's most interesting moments, however, are Wadleigh's interviews with young people themselves. One scene depicts a young girl talking to her mother on a telephone as she frets for her safety amidst the maddening crowds (people died at the festival, so her concerns were justified). She explains to her mother that the locale is now considered a "disaster zone," swarming with people of whom most were on mind-altering drugs. Another classic moment of *vox pop*-style *cinema verite* is where a young couple discuss their estrangement from their parents and from their family. They lament that they have had to create their own community and their own familial structure, a reflection of the hippie movement condensed into a personal anecdote of middle class teenage struggle. *Woodstock* does not only celebrate youthful exuberance and passion as kids yell "fuck the rain!," or a young nude lady talking about the merits of the human body in its purest forms, it also documents something much bigger—something mournful and maudlin. It marks the end of something that could have been and could have sustained idealistic and spiritually fulfilling ideologies, but instead what is left is a filthy farm littered with garbage. This is *Woodstock*'s brilliance.

Another rock'n'roll extravaganza is the fantastic—although much darker—*Gimme Shelter*. As the spindly and ghostly Mick Jagger sings "Gonna get us a little satisfaction!," kids go wild in this incredibly bleak portrait of the death of idealism and the slaughter of the spirit encapsulated by the "smile on your brother" doctrine. The film chronicles the last weeks of The Rolling Stones 1969 American tour leading up to the unbelievable tragedy that was the Altamont Free Concert, where eighteen-year-old Meredith Hunter was stabbed to death by Hells Angel Alan Passaro.

Gimme Shelter is one of the all-time favourite documentaries of author and film journalist Kier-La Janisse, who draws comparison to this violence-drenched historic moment in rock'n'roll to the later horror/musical hybrid *Phantom of the Paradise* (1974, which shall be explored in a later chapter). Janisse says:

> It wasn't just a concert film, it is a document of the utopian ideals of 1960s being subverted and destroyed, it depicts that event which, along with the murders at Cielo Drive, soured the whole decade for good. It captures a murder onscreen. It captures a million bad decisions all exploding at once. It was an event that not only determined the course of the whole next decade, but became a keystone in the decade's self-referential films *Phantom of the Paradise*, another of my favourites, would not exist without *Gimme Shelter*.

Pioneering documentary filmmaker D.A. Pennebaker had already directed *Monterey Pop* (1968), a film that read like a companion piece to Woodstock and was a prime example of film capturing the peace and love generation. In 1970, Pennebaker delivered two rock'n'roll movies and offered an interesting take on a brand new kind of Broadway musical. The rock show *Keep on Rockin'* featured Little Richard amongst others, and is a magnificent examination of a legendary 1950s rock'n'roll artist working years after his prime, when iconic songs like "Tutti Fruitti" and "Reddy Teddy" were now considered relics and depressingly shunned in favour of psychedelic rock and the folk ramblings of Bob Dylan. Thankfully, all the energy, sheer enthusiasm and passion of the fabulously talented Little Richard is captured in this amazing film that truly makes a loud and proud statement—uncompromised and authentic, rock'n'roll is here to stay! Thank God for artists like this enigmatic showman for keeping it healthy and strong, and for D.A. Pennebaker for confirming his legend. But the film was not without its problems, as Pennebaker recalls:

> When we went out to Toronto to do *Keep on Rockin'*, I thought well there will be these four great rock'n'roll musicians such as Little Richard and Jerry Lee Lewis, and we'll shoot it and it will be great. But the problem was trying to distribute it theatrically even though we had a Dolby track and had this really wonderful stereo track. Nobody really wanted to screen it, it was very hard. And everyone who was interested in these musicians would rather see them live then watch a movie about them. But I couldn't have been happier with the people involved. Little Richard was just great. I took the film out for him to see it at MGM. He was so terrific about it, he couldn't have been nicer. And Bo Diddley liked it as well and when I met with him he asked if I would like to see him play a full house, and I of course said yes, and he wired up his front porch and went out front and played in front of his house! He had such an incredible sound, such a distinct sound and back then when an artist had a specific and very unique sound it meant a lot, you could build a career out that.

Another Pennebaker concert film arose from the success *Keep on Rockin'* that introduced the world to the Grand Guignol of rock'n'roll. *Alice Cooper* is an exhilarating theatrical monster show, and Pennebaker recalls:

> We were up in Toronto doing *Keep on Rockin'* which was all about the four guys who carried the weight of rock'n'roll, and then this particular act suddenly appeared and someone told me about it and I thought, "well let's just film it while we're here!" And it was a surprise for me and for anyone who was in that audience waiting to see Little Richard and Jerry Lee Lewis and so forth. First of all when I heard the name Alice Cooper I thought it was a woman and then when I saw him up there on stage I thought it was the ugliest woman I'd ever seen in my life. So I was sort of intrigued by all that. And then of course when he threw the chicken out into the audience I thought "well this is terrific, you can only make a film about this, you couldn't tell about it!"

IN THE COMPANY OF SONDHEIM: *Company: Cast Recording*

Stephen Sondheim's musical *Company* (1970) marks an interesting time in Broadway where the Great White Way metaphorically grew up. This musical dissected relationships, scrutinized the concept of the middle classes, and was ambitious, innovative and emotionally complicated. The non-linear narrative was told through a series of snapshots that were strung together through the songs, stories and situations experienced by its protagonist Bobby, a dedicated promiscuous bachelor surrounded by married friends. Much like the terrific *You're A Good Man Charlie Brown* (1967), *Company* is a vignette-heavy exploration of the human condition. But unlike the *Peanuts* comics musical adaptation, *Company* is interested in the very adult human condition under both the great stress and joy of coupling-up and succumbing to marriage and monogamy, as opposed to the freedoms that a Peter Pan-syndrome fuelled ideal of promiscuity and eternal singlehood promises. The charismatic and attractive Bobby is surrounded by his overbearing but loving in their own weird way married friends, and while his female friends worry about the perpetually single

Bobby (lamenting over every single choice of girlfriend), his male friends live vicariously through this sexually active bachelor as he indiscriminately sows his seeds. As the musical progresses, however, the men too secretly begin to see Bobby as ultimately a lonely and disconnected figure.

The musical has never had a filmic adaptation (arguably because it is far too high concept, and would struggle to translate well on screen), but it eventually had a couple of filmed stage versions in the 2000s. However, it is D.A. Pennebaker's incredible film *Company: Cast Recording* where we get an amazing fly on the wall insight into the creation of the original Broadway cast album.

**Elaine Stritch struggles with "The Ladies Who Lunch"
with Hal Prince in *Company: Cast Recording* (1970)**

Pennebaker recalls:

> I knew Steve (Sondheim) slightly, not well, but slightly, and the guy who was the producer of this film asked me to shoot the recording of the cast album. In those days there was an effort to make a record of Broadway musicals because back then the record industry wasn't quite dead yet, and they wanted to bring out a film to come out with it that you could play on television to help sell the record. So we had three synced cameras so that all three camera people could shoot and be in synch with what we recorded. The cameras were small and handheld and we had a great control over what we

7

were filming. They had not been able to sell it to a network, so what they did was sell it individually to different parts of the country and different areas of television in the county so it was put together in parts and since different areas had different sponsors I knew it had to be made as three different acts, that is that it had to have spaces between the acts in order for the networks to put in their ads in between those. So it turned it into a three act play unto itself. Steve was just great and the man recording producing was just great as well. It turned out to be a lucky draw.

Pennebaker's *Company: Cast Recording* is an incredible look at the long, gruelling recording of the soundtrack album and it is in every way just as mesmerizing as Sondheim's ground breaking musical itself. Unlike recording the songs of standard musicians, working on a musical requires a lot of acute direction—both musically and dramatically—and composer and lyricist Stephen Sondheim, with his genius cemented on both fronts, completely runs the show and conjures up magnificent performances from a very talented cast. There are some spectacular moments showcasing Sondheim's almost supernatural connection to music, lyric, rhythm and wordplay: here is a wordsmith and musical mathematician at work outside of creation, but completely devoted to ensuring the immortal cast recording is done to pinpoint perfection. One incredible sequence depicts Sondheim's meticulous skill at knowing exactly where actress Pamela Myers (who plays one of Bobby's girlfriends) drops a single note in the delectable number "You Could Drive A Person Crazy." Another is where Sondheim overlooks the insanely fast patter song "Getting Married Today," and the image of him practically pulling his hair out and wiping his weary eyes while Broadway legend Elaine Stritch belts out "The Ladies Who Lunch" over and over again is priceless.

Elaine Stritch is so much fun to watch throughout Pennebaker's film, and at the same time she is a perfect example of an artist plagued with personal torment and completely disabled by the notion and suffocating stress of "not getting it quite right." Her battle with hitting the right notes, getting the right personality across and managing the emotional nuances of "The Ladies Who Lunch" is something that every single dramatic performer (most notably those involved with musical theatre) simply has to watch: Stritch's personal demons and long-time struggle with alcoholism somehow come across during her endless takes.

Pennebaker remembers:

> I had known Elaine and in the end she came through, but she got very, very boozey throughout the performance. It was all done in one night and it was about four or five in the morning when we finished, it was a late night enterprise. Elaine was an alcoholic, she had drank all her life, and she would get alcohol wherever she could. She needed it, and that's what it was alcoholism quite simply—booze helped her get through performing.

Stephen Sondheim and Pamela Myers go through "You Could Drive a Person Crazy" in *Company: Cast Recording* **(1970)**

This making-of film was set to be the first in a whole line of documentaries chronicling the formation of a musical's soundtrack recording, however budget and audience appeal killed the idea.

Pennebaker explains:

> The problem is that when you're dealing with a new musical there isn't an audience for it, so it's hard to get theatrical distribution for a film about the recording of an album based on the songs from a new musical. Also it can get very expensive to pay for the rights to use the songs.

But *Company: Cast Recording* was an extraordinarily positive and eye-opening moment in the career of this phenomenal documentary filmmaker.

He says:

> It was an amazing experience, there was a point where we had been told at the beginning that if we ever got in the way or ever hit a microphone where there was some kind of objectionable sound we would be thrown right out. I liked that energy, that aspect of the filming, to make sure we were stealthy enough just observing. I remember when I was filming Elaine I was very nervous about hitting a mic, but luckily I didn't. Also, Steve is just amazing. It's so great when he picks up on the G that the actress misses in "Another Hundred People," I mean he's such an incredible musician and I've always loved that about him. I saw *Company* on stage and I was actually quite nervous as to getting my head around how we were going to film what we filmed and get the story of the play across, but then when we decided to just film the recordings of the songs, that actually fed a narrative of sorts. Also, it helped that the cast were all relatively young and just starting out. That was a massive advantage in that we could almost do anything we really wanted. I used to go to a lot of stuff on Broadway and I was raised on Broadway by my mother. I loved plays because a lot of them taught me what entertainment could be, that it could say something, that it could be an insight into the times.

BLAKE EDWARD'S DARLING: *Darling Lili*

Artists such as Joni Mitchell and The Carpenters also had TV specials made for them through major networks such as the BBC, but the traditional musical film (traditionally presented as either book/integrated or diegetic musical) was still hanging on for dear life during the explosion of making-of cast recordings, rockumentaries and concert films. Much like the motion pictures of the late 1960s, some were as great and as endearing as the fabulous *Funny Girl* (1968) and some were just as cringe-worthy as Clint Eastwood (in P*aint Your Wagon*) attempting to sing in that musical western that nobody wanted to see.

The ridiculously talented Blake Edwards had already made an incredible impression as a director turning out the playful romance of *Breakfast at Tiffany's* (1961) as well as the astoundingly good and heartbreakingly harrowing *Days of Wine and Roses* (1962), to name two very different but equally romantic films. He was also a writer whose versatility and insight into the human condition was perfect, as illustrated by his take on Holly Golightly and the devastating effects of alcoholism in the two aforementioned films. Edwards' screenplays boast a cavalcade of characters that have depth and warmth while also being completely plagued with insecurities and fraught with social and personal anxieties. His writing can also be swiftly comic and it catered to the talent he usually acquired. His musical *Darling Lili* was a vehicle for his wife Julie Andrews to shed her goodie two shoes persona—unfairly bequeathed to her from the terrific *The Sound of Music* and *Mary Poppins*—by giving her the opportunity to play a racy, sensual and comic World War I burlesque performer. However, even with the combined efforts of Edwards and the magnificent Andrews, the film just does not swing in the right direction and most of the efforts get lost in lengthy airplane dogfights sequences.

Rock Hudson and Julie Andrews take a break on location for
***Darling Lili* (1970)**

11

Unfortunately *Darling Lili* was not as well received or admired as previous works such as Edwards' popular comedies *The Pink Panther* (1963) and *The Party* (1968). The ill-conceived film is a rather bland and flat excursion into the spy and espionage genre and the comic elements of the film are sadly its worst attribute.

Screenwriter William Peter Blatty was already working with Edwards at the time of the conception of the film:

> I was co-writing a screenplay called *Gunn* (1967) with Blake Edwards when he approached me with a problem. He had a concept for a World War I comedy that was structured around the male lead. He had Jack Lemmon in mind but Jack wasn't interested. At this point Blake had started up a relationship with his future wife Julie Andrews, and he asked me if I could figure out a way to restructure the story for a female lead. After some thought (overnight, I seem to recall) I came up with a couple of pages in which Julie would play a type of Gracie Fields, the legendary British musical comedy star, who would in fact be a German spy, sleeping with the enemy in order to extort secret information from them, the "kicker" being that she is repelled by sex and believes herself to be either a lesbian or, more likely, sexually cold and dead.

Julie Andrews of course falls in love with the man she is meant to manipulate—played by Rock Hudson—but the romance is remarkably stilted and overly formal: there seems to be no passionate exchange whatsoever.

Blatty explains:

> The fun in the idea comes when she (Julie Andrews) is assigned to extract secret information from the leader of the Lafayette Escadrille which was played by Rock Hudson, though we wanted James Coburn who said to me famously when I was about to start writing the screenplay, "Just give me two balls and let me swing." Along the way she finds herself actually jealous of a suspected liaison between the

aviator and a French café beauty. That much you know. What you do not know is that when Blake did a rewrite, in reel one he introduced a hot sexual clinch between Lili and her German "control," a *guy!* I never got to see this draft for I wasn't asked to join the company for the shoot in Europe, but to this day I feel this scene totally destroyed the unique premise that first attracted Paramount to make it. My next shot came when, returning from a film research trip to Japan, I ran into then Paramount chief Bob Evans who informed me "Bill, you're going to love it. We've added a dozen songs." I believe I awoke in ER!

Julie Andrews discusses character with director and husband Blake Edwards on the set of *Darling Lili* (1970)

Diegetic musicals are by their very nature far more palpable for non-musical film (and theatre) lovers. The idea of musical performances arising as just that—as performances—is something that cynical audiences who do not buy into escapist fanfare like genre cinema can easily and readily swallow, so perhaps this works for *Darling Lili*...or perhaps it doesn't? The songs are set pieces that do not particularly move the story forward in any way, nor do they comment on the action of the film: instead, they are just plotted into the spy romantic-comedy hybrid and give Julie Andrews an opportunity to break into various kinds of show tunes.

Perhaps Edwards should have introduced an integrated musical formula where the plot could move ahead with interesting character driven songs or, like William Peter Blatty suggests, not musicalize it at all.

Creative differences between Blatty and Edwards rose rather early in the process of writing the film:

> There was the scene in which Rock Hudson makes a harrowing, bullet and explosive riddled escape on their attack on a German encampment and in my script that was to be followed immediately by a limping, injured Hudson coming to see Lili. And he needs a cane to help him walk. Lili is icy, totally disbelieving he had an encounter with The Red Baron but rather had a sexy weekend with the café dancer. But it doesn't work because between the battle scene and the encounter with Lili. So Blake, or the studio, inserted a sultry dance number in which Lili is working off her aggression and jealousy by being "sexy," thus pre-empting the theme of the following scene. Before I saw it, Julie, although I wasn't sure what she was talking about, mentioned a "new scene" that troubled her and for which she wanted my opinion. But I never did get to see it prior to the film's release.

Working on *Darling Lili* reinforced an opposition to writing collaborations for Blatty:

> I wrote the first draft entirely on my own, then Blake did a second draft rewrite. That was my preference. I've never been able to collaborate since I co-authored a humor column in high school. I learned from Bob Evans that songs had been added after I'd turned in my script. Blake must have done the lead-ins and outs.

Darling Lili seems to have all the right elements going for it—an incredible director, a very talented screenwriter and two legends of the silver screen. However, it never gets off the ground. Although there are some lovely musical moments and some refined singing from the impeccable Andrews, the film is dull and dreary. Thankfully, Blatty would go on to write (and win the Academy Award for) the masterpiece that is *The Exorcist* (1973). Edwards and Andrews would combine efforts again in the 1980s with the superlative *Victor/Victoria* (1982) which became one of the best movie musicals to come out of that decade.

Co-star Lesley Ann Warren reminisces about the gender bending *Victor/Victoria*:

> *Victor/Victoria* was a huge moment in my life. It was just an incredible opportunity and a really great triumph for everyone involved in that film. It will never go out of style. And when I signed on to do it there was no musical number for my character Norma, and one day I was sitting next to Blake Edwards in the dailies and he said "Do you still sing?" and I said "I do" and he said "Well I'm not seeing enough of Norma, I want to see more of Norma, I'm going to write you a number!" and so a number was written and the rest is history. What I saw Blake doing with that musical, and you have to remember that he had done two more previously that had not been received as well, they were still of another time like *Darling Lili*, so what he did with *Victor/Victoria* is that he utilized these numbers to speak about themes of transsexualism and homosexuality and identity and a lot of things that had never really been dealt with in a musical film. And he wrote those numbers in a lot of ways to explore that, and it was so smart and such a visionary thing to do. As well as being totally entertaining. It was phenomenal to be a part of that. And very revolutionary for the musical film.

STREISAND'S SECOND COMING:
On a Clear Day You Can See Forever

Released the same month as the flatliner that is *Darling Lili* came one of the greatest (and strangest) movie musicals of the 1970s, and its star was not unlike Julie Andrews in that she was not only a naturally gifted phenomenon but someone who took risks and made interesting career choices as an actress and singer. Barbra Streisand came from two very important musicals of the 1960s; one being the very good bio-musical *Funny Girl* (1968), where she played the vaudevillian sensation Fanny Brice, and the disastrous, widely panned *Hello, Dolly!* Her next musical venture would prove to be far more captivating than both. *On a Clear Day You Can See Forever* is Vincente Minnelli's secondto last film and if it was his last it would have been an incredible high note to end a brilliant career. Minnelli is an artist, a remarkably talented auteur who manages to gracefully capture the heart and soul of his stories while not sacrificing a visual flair that has become signature of his films. This musical released right at the beginning of the 1970s is a testament to Minnelli's sheer brilliance as not only a director but as a fine artist, a storyteller and a man completely devoted to his characters. It is an oddball movie musical, completely strange in tone and structure and it never loses steam; instead it draws you in rapidly and successfully.

Barbra Streisand on the set for *On a Clear Day You Can See Forever* (1970)

Another stroke of genius is the fact that the film plays with the musical form. There are songs that are performed through soliloquy and others that are performed as an extension of internalized dialogue, and then finally others are an insight into the situation and sung over the scene acting like an enchanting voice over: the latter can be heard in the incredible "Love with all the Trimmings." The majesty of this track is intoxicating and loaded with sexual prowess. This is a major highlight of the movie: Streisand, in a past life flashback, dolled-up in a glamorous and almost otherworldly white headdress with her cleavage on fine display, is outstanding in this moment, and utterly kooky.

The opening of the film is cinematic bliss, and a perfect symbol for the end of the 1960s and the birth of the 1970s. Images of flowers blossoming clearly deliver an effective visual of awakening and add to that the bouncing elegance of Barbra Streisand's booming voice singing "Hurry! It's Lovely up Here" as she welcomes budding roses and other flowers to the world, and all of this is a thing of magic. That is ultimately what this movie is—complicated and very adult magic. This is musical fantasy at its most intriguing, most weird and most irresistibly romantic. Vincente Minnelli's lush vision is pure and rich, and there is an endless sense of wonder in this film that just has to be seen to be believed. Following Streisand's energetic homage to the bouncy musicals of yesteryear comes one of the jazziest title sequences of the 1970s, where a regressive psychedelic window zooms backwards as a chorus sings the title song.

Streisand's Daisy Gamble is a marvellous creation, a kooky misfit who seems to be alienated by her situation. She seems to go nowhere in her current life and her susceptibility to hypnosis is hilarious: she wakes in and out of it in a flash, and the stroke of genius in the writing is that she is more comfortable in herself when she is under. When she has to cope with her current life she is a mess, a neurotic chain-smoking freak. As Melinda, the character through whom she comes to know her past life through and feels empowered by, is commanding, self-possessed and hyper-sexual. But the nutsy Daisy is not without her merits: she is slightly psychic (she can tell when the phone is about to ring, she knows where the psychiatrist Dr. Chabot—played by Yves Montand–keeps certain notes, etc.), and she also has the supernatural ability to make flowers and plants grow at incredible speed. These "gifts" seem to torment poor Daisy, and they most certainly add to her alienation from her peers at college. She is far more interested in finding out about herself and channelling these quirks than fitting in with late 1960s teens. Her bond with Dr. Chabot begins with her wanting to quit smoking, and she asks that he hypnotise her to quit this filthy habit. Daisy's relentless attempts to convince Dr. Chabot to help her are pure cinematic gold ("I'm normal, I swear, I'm just an addict is all!") and this is where Streisand's comic timing is impeccable—her phrasing jumps from paranoia and extreme nervousness to subdued and exhausted with such precision and articulate elegance that she is completely hypnotising to watch!

Barbra Streisand adjusts her make-up on the set of *On a Clear Day You Can See Forever* **(1970)**

The art direction is just as exquisite with the 1960s literally fading and the 1970s dawning smoothly in an aesthetic sense, while simultaneously revolutionary in a social context. The babydoll dresses and mary-jane shoes, the painted wallpapers, the hairstyles and wood-panelled dens would slowly make way for 1970s sensibilities. But at the same time, a lot of it will stay, and the way Minnelli chooses to shoot his subjects sometimes look as if they are right out of the 1950s. It is remarkable filmmaking and with all its progressive attention and keen interest in the future of diversity in storytelling and movie making techniques, it also strangely holds onto the filmic style of the romantic comedies of the 1950s.

The songs are phenomenally good and not only do they showcase Streisand's talents as a singer, but as a formidable and versatile actress. She sensually belts out "Love with All the Trimmings," she wistfully plays with the melodic delicacy of "Go to Sleep," and when she lets loose on the title song at the end of the picture it is simply breathtaking. Streisand has ushered us into the 1970s movie musical, a place of weirdness, darkness, complexity and incurable diversity.

Yves Montand is fantastic as the perplexed psychiatrist who starts to believe in ESP through his practice of hypnosis. When he discovers Melinda (Daisy's past life from the turn of the century) he is drawn to her and—quite naturally—falls in love with her. Melinda, however, is a charlatan: she is not the aristocratic debutante that parades around grandiose galas, she is the daughter of a wash woman, a poor working class lady who uses her wits and sharp intellect to slip through the cracks of an oppressive system. Here is a young poor urchin who skilfully maneuverers her way to the top, and this impresses Dr. Chabot. It most definitely impresses him more than the wacky college student who smells of tobacco and fidgets and fusses. His anger and depression over the fact that reincarnation has been responsible for turning the resourceful Melinda into the fruity Daisy infuriates him, but Daisy is super likeable and sweet in a nutsy way. Daisy begins to like herself through the hypnosis sessions and through them, she begins to assert herself. When she finally comes to the realization that Dr. Chabot is in love with Melinda (she listens to one of the session recordings and hears him whine and complain about Daisy "If I have to hear another 'I mean' I will do up my tie so tight that I choke myself to death!"), it breaks her heart and she changes. She grows and blossoms just like one of the flowers she inspires to flourish at supernatural speed. Eventually, Dr. Chabot finds the charm in Daisy's progress, as he sings "Who would not be stunned to see you bloom?," continuing "You'll be impressed with you." Dr. Chabot's number "Come Back to Me" is a fun song with Daisy racing around New York City and finding herself being sung to by Dr. Chabot via a police officer, a cooking instructor, an elderly couple, a little boy and even a poodle! It is masterfully handled and truly a magical moment in musical fantasy cinema, a category in which this film comfortably finds itself.

Minnelli sets up some beautiful imagery, from the sumptuous imagery of the heavens coated in blood red lingering over Melinda in court, the zany jump cuts from past to present to future life to past life et al, to the stunning Royal Pavilion in Brighton at the turn of the century and flooding the production with exquisite costumes that are continually complimented by Harry Stradling Jr.'s rich cinematography. Minnelli has made majestic movies all his life, and all of his works have merit both artistically and socially. *Tea and Sympathy* (1956) examined gender and the concept of masculinity in comparison to latent homosexuality, *An American in Paris* (1951) questioned the importance of art over romantic union and paired the two, arguing that they are inseparable, and so forth. And here, in this strange fantastical musical, Minnelli treats us with lavish imagery and set pieces but also delivers an exceptionally intellectual and progressive story. We fall in love with at least one of Streisand's personas—the chatty neurotic student or the English working class daughter of a maidservant posing as a wealthy debutante; and the insanely talented songstress performs them with acute brilliance. Funnily enough, when Streisand falls into hypnosis and starts to transform into her previous life it is a thing of terror. It recalls the act of possession, significant because the 1970s were a period of mass interest in the occult and alternative religions (on this note, it was not long after *On a Clear Day You Can See Forever* that Streisand was in talks to play Chris MacNeil in the adaptation of William Peter Blatty's best selling horror novel *The Exorcist*, a story all about possession).

The rest of the cast are just as wonderful. Bob Newhart shines as Streisand's straight laced and ambitious fiancé who is clearly not at all the right match. Jack Nicholson plays Streisand's ex-step-brother Tad, and is very relaxed in this film, still fresh in the public's mind's eye from his great turn in the landmark counterculture opus *Easy Rider* (1969). Nicholson carries on his anti-establishment persona in Minnelli's musical: he is introduced playing the lute and sporting a paisley shirt, and with his cool smooth voice is an attractive addition to the film and is a perfect counterpart to Bob Newhart's stuffy, erratic and highly strung business minded fiancé. But this is Streisand's film and her performance is electric as opposed to her misguided turn in *The Owl and the Pussycat* (1970) where her likability is at an all-time low: here she is incredibly enigmatic and fun to watch. Her kookiness is palpable and beautifully realized, her artistic choices in the film are seemingly flawlessly delivered and when she announces "My name is Melinda!" you truly believe her.

"On a Clear Day You Can See Forever" is one of those great songs that cements the sentiment and moral of the story: with a clear head and heart, Daisy can learn to accept herself. She is not a diminished damsel in distress in a perpetual stressed state, but rather a grounded, blossoming young woman who is coming into her own. Melinda has been exorcised and Daisy can now grow. When Dr. Chabot explains this it exhausts her, and after the final hypnosis session where she tells him about being married to him in a future life, she comes out as a new person. That person is the same old, but new and improved, Daisy Gamble. The film closes with Daisy celebrating the fact that "On a Clear Day You Can See Forever."

Vincente Minnelli directs Streisand in *On a Clear Day You Can See Forever* (1970)

21

CALLING OCCUPANTS: *Toomorrow*

A musical completely different to Minnelli's masterpiece and not at all
nearly as lavish or intelligent as the Streisand reincarnation venture, is
a science fiction low budget diegetic romp starring someone who will
go on to star in two pivotal musicals of the 1970s and very early 1980s.
Toomorrow is quite frankly a bizarre film, not only conceptually but also
in its muted approach; however it is insanely engaging (up to a certain
point) and so weird that it simply demands your attention (again, up to a
certain point). The premise of the film is this: aliens from a distant planet
need to employ the assistance of a garage band headed by Australian pop
sensation-to-be Olivia Newton-John to save their doomed planet. Shot
at the famous Pinewood Studios in London, *Toomorrow*'s focus is on
a rather cartoon-like band comprised of a lothario handsome guitarist,
a jive-talking Black Panther reject drummer, a quirky keyboardist who
is dating a girl "who doesn't dig pop, she digs classical!" and the lovely
Newton-John as the featured "girl-singer" who seems to bounce through
the movie with great confidence and showcasing some inspired dance
moves. The band are reminiscent of a Hanna-Barbera cartoon act à
la Josie and the Pussycats (1970-1972), and more rock outfits from the
famous animation team would come to grace television sets across the
world throughout the 1970s. Their style, melodies, zealousness and the
idea of having them whisked up into space by aliens (who also look
like the numerous creatures that populated Saturday morning cartoons
like *Thundarr the Barbarian* ,1980-1982 and *The Herculoids,* 1967-1969)
makes the film even more like a 'toon that you would watch armed with
a bowl of sugar-coated cereal. This is a good thing and this is what makes
Toomorrow work.

Another thing that *Toomorrow* has going for it is that in a sense the
film is also a British response to not only the cult of American Saturday
morning cartoons, but it is most certainly a very late reaction to the beach
blanket craze of the 1950s and 1960s from the USA starring the likes of
Frankie Avalon and Annette Funicello. But being British, *Toomorrow*
does have its own distinct flair and tries to heavily rely on the sleekness
and hip sophistication of "swinging London" that had already passed by
1970.

The best thing about the film is the terrific songs. They are poppy, memorable numbers that feature some great garage twang and rather complicated and sweet harmonies. Newton-John's vocal ability will be represented in later movie musicals (*Grease* and *Xanadu*) as the years go on, however in *Toomorrow* she is possibly the most relaxed as you will ever see her. She thoroughly looks as though she is enjoying herself, singing her heart out and not being afraid to act or look silly. There is a completely nuanced performance here, and it's also seemingly effortless. Newton-John's talents as an actress come across through her naturalistic intentions, with her endearing softness and kittenishness. The rock'n'roll frivolity is addictive and even though the film touches on student unrest and political activism from college kids, it is a light-hearted launching pad to give Newton-John a chance to take the world by storm.

A lobby card for the sci-fi diegetic British musical *Toomorrow* (1970)

This is not to say that the film lacks moments of ingenuity. Take for instance the inspired moment where the lead alien (concealed in "earthling" attire) comes across the band playing joyous dance-inducing rock'n'roll in their school cafeteria. Here the alien, completely seduced by their music, approaches them and discusses their song writing and equipment while students protest the bureaucracy of the system and their rights to a free education holding up placards that say things like "Student Representation." This clever little juxtaposition shared between the angry students and the ultimate alien is a nice little commentary on what the film is ultimately saying: that music can change the world. Eventually, the band is taken aboard the alien's spaceship and told that their music will save their planet, and it is the idea of music bringing the world together that grants this obscure oddball sci-fi musical an unlikely similarity to *Woodstock* which realistically highlights the notion that all idealistic free thought can also lead to excess and cynicism. *Toomorrow* does not present any of that, instead it sings out with optimism and wacky joy. Structurally, the film has definite peaks and troughs: there are moments of great wit and silliness that are completely enjoyable, while at other times there are set pieces that go on far too long and do not deliver the punch when it is needed. For example, the sequence where the sex-crazed guitarist distracts the saucy music teacher in order for Newton-John to take a bass drum is an absolute dud that bogs down the already wafer-thin story. Moments before this, however, a gorgeous bimbette alien leads a fun comedic set up employing every single trick from the naughty British sex comedy lexicon. The bimbette alien herself is taken to grindhouse theatres in London town by her leader to see films such as the fabricated sexploitation parody *The Son of Fanny Hill* to learn about sex and seduction in order to manipulate the male members of the band, but she finds these films hilarious because apparently her race have stopped having sex and therefore see it as old fashioned and meaningless. This strange sub-plot serves no real purpose at all, but it is an effective stand-alone joke that does not get in the way of the fun pop music.

Toomorrow's music is also surprisingly wonderful. In a strange way, it embodies both the lounge-act sass and bourbon-drenched semi-sophistication of the early 1960s, and fuses it with off-the-cuff infectious pop sensibilities of the great garage rock bands of the same period. Of course, the enjoyable songs do not make *Toomorrow* a perfect film, and it is absolutely far from it. It is ultimately a flawed sci-fi protest diegetic musical, whose main problem is that it stops caring about the central premise about half way through (this is frustrating if you have taken the time to let the silliness take you on this weird ride).

Toomorrow brings a slice of rose-tinted optimism at the height of teenage angst and rebellion as even the authorities in this film are given very little screen time, just to remind an audience already in the throes of pure disdain and distrust in the oppressive forces that be that the real enemy does not have to make an impression if you block them out. *Toomorrow* says, "forget about the real worries be they real life ones such as universities and colleges run by fascist dictators or fabricated/ metaphoric woes such as alien beings being concerned about the state of their native planet, just close your eyes, pretend that everything is OK and listen to Olivia Newton-John sing." And sometimes—but not always—this can be enough. *Toomorrow* was meant to cash-in on the fictional band craze that was taking the world by storm with television shows such as *The Partridge Family* (1970-1974) and *The Monkees* (1966-1968), but the efforts of director Val Guest (who did some fantastic horror films with Hammer Studios) just did not work. And his movie musical did not garner much of an audience outside of Olivia Newton-John fans and cult cinema enthusiasts.

BAH HUMBUG: *Scrooge*

In the grand tradition of the cash-in, 1970 was a year that tried to capitalize on the major movie musicals that came before it, and one of these films took its lead from the winner of the 1968 Best Picture Academy Award. Riding on the success of the Oscar winning *Oliver!*, *Scrooge* is not nearly as rich and not nearly as beautifully crafted as Carol Reed's stunning musical adaptation of Charles Dickens classic. 1968's *Oliver!* is quite simply a masterpiece, whereas *Scrooge* is an uneventful disappointment. However, the film is satisfactorily staged and has some captivating moments. These stick out like sore thumbs, however, because the rest of the movie is rather bland and uninspired. *Scrooge* staggers along and does not hit the marks it is supposed to be hitting. The film seems to suffer from lack of genuine interest and investment from the production company (the independent Cinema Center) that made it, so from the get-go it falls flat and fizzles out on multiple occasions. Because of this, when a sequence looks, sounds or feels good (one of note is where

Scrooge's deceased business partner Marley—played by Alec Guiness—appears in a delightfully spooky manner) it is exceptionally good and you wish the rest of the movie will take heed and follow by example. Sadly, it does not.

The campaign art for *Scrooge* (1970), decrying the musical adaptation with its brave tagline

For some strange reason, Albert Finney does not really capture the cantankerous menace of Dickens' most famous grouch. He mumbles through the performance and seems slightly uncomfortable in the part. Finney was in his 1930s when he took on the role of Ebenezer Scrooge and although he has an uncanny knack to embody a crusty old man (with the help of very effective and highly convincing make-up), it seems a rather odd choice to have such a young actor to take on a role normally associated with a senior and more seasoned thespian. Of course, it works in his favour when we see a young ambitious Ebenezer Scrooge shunning the romantic advances of his fiancée when the Ghost of Christmas Past (Edith Evans) takes him back to his younger years. However, as an old man, Finney's is an extremely muted performance and there is nothing truly menacing about this miserable miser. This is even more problematic when the first half an hour of the film spends its time showcasing his disdain for people, his greed and most importantly, his hatred of Christmas and the Christmas spirit. Finney seems tired and almost disinterested in the role and it is distracting.

Throughout the years, Ebenezer Scrooge has always been presented as a caricature that goes through a spiritual transition but at both polar opposites and it is usually played simplistically and without much complex depth. The tragedy of this literary icon is something that many filmmakers taking on the story of *A Christmas Carol* fail to capture. However, luckily in this musical this overwhelming self-loathing and devastating loneliness is a palpable presence, and this is *Scrooge*'s strength. Much like the Muppet variant on the story, *The Muppet Christmas Carol* (1992), a musical adaptation of the story allows this exploration into the psychology of isolation and depressing misanthropy. The idea of melancholy and pathos is allowed to exist within the structure of symphonic and orchestral insight into character and tone. In *Scrooge*, Finney is at his best in the downbeat, sombre moments of the film. His comic talents are not at all put to use, unlike how they are later in his career where he takes on comic book billionaire Oliver "Daddy" Warbucks in John Huston's adaptation of the Charles Strouse musical *Annie* (1982). Unlike that brilliant filmic adaptation of a very good musical, the songs in *Scrooge* (a musical written specifically for the screen) are not at all memorable or enchanting: there is no moment in any of the melodies that soar or plummet, and nothing moves the heart with their ascending or descending notes. Instead, the songs are a chore and you find yourself wanting these characters to get on with it. At times you feel like yelling at the screen and telling these people to stop singing and this is quite frankly the worst possible thing you would want from a musical!

The film is also far too long and heavily repetitive. Even though Dickensian characters are clearly defined and established, director Ronald

Neame does nothing to alter their characterization or to exaggerate aspects of their personality to make them unique and enigmatic. Some of the most dreary characters populate this film, and this is partly to do with the writing, directing but most notably to an audience because of the performances—David Collings and Frances Cuka as the Cratchits are mind bogglingly dull and their children including Tiny Tim (Richard Beaumont) are hard to both watch and listen to. The ghosts are a little bit better, the most notably fun and powerful is Kenneth More as the Ghost of Christmas Present, who gets to sing a boisterous number called "I Like Life" which is a relative stand-out from the incredibly yawn-inducing score by Leslie Bricusse. Scrooge's early number "I Hate People" is also a highlight, but this does not say much about the overall film's music: the song itself is not incredible, but it is most definitely the most interesting and complicated. Scrooge's anger and disdain is obviously on show here but there are moments where his misanthropy might be warranted because the people he is surrounded by are obnoxious. The street urchins who look like leftovers from *Oliver!* (but not at all nearly as talented) shout out lyrics and act as tormentors to Scrooge, which at times seems so ruthlessly obnoxious that when Scrooge does lash out and attack the people he detests so much, it seems valid. This is something that you do not want from your Ebenezer Scrooge!

What *is* appealing about *Scrooge*, however, are its grotesque elements: there are ghosts that are truly terrifying, as are the ghastly images of monstrous entities that float by. This is something that works very well for the movie: without this element of gothic intrigue and its associated spooks, the film would be watery and silly. Finney shines when he is frightened and perplexed by the supernatural elements of the story. When he is dealing with poltergeist activity he is so believable and fun to watch, but everything else seems like a chore. Finney is great in the scene where the Ghost of Christmases yet to come confronts him—a hooded demon that does not speak. It is a quick but frightening scene as Ebenezer falls to his knees and is crippled with fear. It is a beautifully executed moment, and here is where the film starts to pick up, but sadly it is far too late. One nicely realized scene is where the "invisible" Ebenezer is plopped into a joyous crowd scene where he is greeted by the townsfolk celebrating his death, but the tragedy here is that Ebenezer himself has no idea what they are celebrating so instead he believes they are cheering his life and celebrating his celebrity. But as the hoard of crowds sing "Thank You Very Much" (a song nominated that year for Best Original Song at the Academy Awards) and dance on his grave, Ebenezer is left confused and slowly becomes aware of his delusions. Shortly after this, he realizes that Tiny Tim has died which acts as the turning point. When he sees his own grave he is literally tipped over and ready to begin his transformation. Ebenezer in hell is a comedic addition to the film, and reuniting with Marley, who is there to "show him to his quarters," is even more hilarious. The most interesting and dramatically innovative moments come very late in the piece, and sadly before these final moments the movie is a tedious watch. But with Ebenezer's descent to hell, the film picks up and sparks interest. There are some funny lines here delivered by Alec Guiness, for example when he explains that extra help had to be employed to make Scrooge's punishment chains that he will be burdened with wearing in the afterlife. He explains, "They had to take on extra devils at the foundry to finish it!" Guiness plays the role with camp glee, his mannerisms and walk are a sight to behold and refreshing in a movie littered with insipid supporting players.

The original ad campaign for *Scrooge* read: "What the Dickens have they done to Scrooge?," which is itself an insightful commentary on the musicalization of the classic yuletide story. It is almost as if even the campaign artists were not very confident with turning the story of Ebenezer Scrooge and his redemption and learning to love Christmas into a musical, which is indicative of the production company's conflicted interests. But if the film was not a musical, a lot of the complexity and layers of Ebenezer Scrooge's character would have been lost, and he would have been a cartoon meanie who becomes enlightened through an evening of learning. As a musical, the composition and scoring tells us all about his transgression and transformation and therefore Ebenezer's redemption and conversion is a wonderfully realized moment: here, Finney is given a lot to do. He is such a gifted actor and it is sad that he only really gets to enjoy the role in the last few moments of the movie.

The lush orchestrations are too grandiose for the singing. Or, more correctly, for the lack of singing: Finney bellows, and the rest of the cast are generic and sometimes so bland that you simply want the music to drown out the flatliner vocalizing and the dull, colourless lyrics. *Scrooge* also boasts the lengthiest redemption sequence ever used in a film based on *A Christmas Carol* with Ebenezer buying the biggest turkey, going crazy at a toy shop and buying multiple gifts for children, skipping around and singing a reprise of "I Like Life," as he is followed by a bunch of townsfolk and dancing through the streets, dolling up as Santa Claus and so forth. Unlike the rest of the movie, these joyous coda moments are entertaining. All in all however, the much later *The Muppet Christmas Carol* is a far more interesting musical adaptation of Charles Dickens's classic tale of enlightenment and spiritual awakening, with Michael Caine in the role of Scrooge.

MICKEY ROONEY'S HO-HO-HO: *Santa Claus Is Coming to Town*

In the same year as *Scrooge*, audiences were greeted with yet another Christmas themed musical, but this time the film was for television, and not one human being was to be seen anywhere in it. Writers/producers Arthur Rankin and Jules Bass were most definitely the go-to team to deliver festive television specials that generations of children (and adults alike) grew up loving. Their films featured some of the most enchanting stop motion animation (known as Animagic) ever put to screen and their work is legendary and iconic. Their first widely seen effort was the wonderful *Rudolph the Red Nosed Reindeer* (1964), which was simply based on the song by Johnny Marks and went on to become one of the most successful and much loved (and much screened) Christmas specials ever to air on network TV around the world. After that came more Christmas musical specials, such as *The Little Drummer Boy* (1968) and *Frosty the Snowman* (1969), featuring wonderful voice talents such as Greer Garson and Zero Mostel as well as incredible songs written by Maury Laws. Rankin-Bass's films began to get more sophisticated in tone and in story as the years went on and by the time of the early 1970s, their writing team headed by the gifted Romeo Muller dealt with informal themes and well-structured stories that fleshed out characters from folklore and festive mythology. Muller also had the distinct talent of taking a popular song like a Christmas carol and developing it into an exceptionally interesting plot that worked swiftly and with great ease, completely benefitting from some wonderful original songs that have since become lasting classics.

Their 1970 effort *Santa Claus Is Coming to Town* is no exception. Not only is it a smart little animated feature, it is also a fresh and very adult one. Where *Rudolph the Red Nosed Reindeer* dealt with the complexities of not fitting in and celebrated the notion of being a misfit, this feature—starring the vocal talents of movie musical legend Mickey Rooney—deals with the purpose of vocation and the meaning of existence outside of social norms. These themes reflect the cultural turning point that was the 1960s and 1970s, and although these films are geared towards entertaining children, they fundamentally are made by leftist idealists who want to ensure that newer generations understand and embrace individuality and freedom of expression.

Mickey Rooney gives voice to the leading man in Rankin/Bass's animated feature *Santa Claus Is Coming to Town* (1970)

The film opens with a sweet newsreel featuring a very serious newscaster explaining that children everywhere are waiting for their presents from Santa Claus. It is a great opening, but not at all as charming as the animated opening where a spindly mailman named S.D. Kluger (Fred Astaire) breaks the fourth wall and begins to tell the story of Santa Claus's origins. For a film based on a song introduced to the world by entertainer Eddie Cantor, the animated TV gem is meaty and rich and right away as soon as we get into the story of Santa it is as intriguing and as captivating as any fairy tale.

Much like the Disney princesses of the early days, such as Cinderella and Sleeping Beauty, Kris Kringle's (Rooney) best friends and confidants are the forest dwelling animals. He strikes up a lovely friendship with a penguin he calls Topper, an easily frightened little critter who becomes a surrogate son to the handsome and proactive Kringle, soon to be known as Santa Claus. Kringle is compassionate and nurturing, and this is embodied in his relationship with this fretful penguin. As the film's central protagonist, Kringle is the youthful bearer of gifts to children the world over, and he is a representative of new-wave masculinity as much as any other heroic 1970s movie male. He is sensitive but quietly strong and this kind of enlightened but tough man will start to pop up in mainstream (and non-animated) cinema from Kris Kristofferson in *Alice Doesn't Live Here Anymore* (1974) through to Beau Bridges in *Norma Rae* (1979). The idea of masculinity is something that the 1970s playfully complicates, and in this Rankin-Bass stop motion festive treasure, this gender dissection is not ignored.

Mickey Rooney's exuberance from yesteryear as a young musical and theatrical geniuses with his endless plight (along with the equally talented Judy Garland) of saving the farm house or music room in the endless slew of terrific Arthur Freed musicals is by 1970 a senior ex-hoofer who is set to remind us of a bygone era via the vessel of a stop motion animated puppet. Unlike many of his peers, Rooney can also deliver a contemporary fragile hero who is an extension of a youth culture that even children watching would be well aware of. Rooney will continue to present these kind of roles throughout the decade, carefully dancing between a sentimental and necessary reminiscence of a simpler and supposedly cheerier time and the fevered freshness of a complicated 1970s America. His character is a young and energetic (and remarkably ambitious and seriously hard working) Santa Claus, and he even manages to reform and recruit the clear villain of the piece the Winter Warlock (voiced by Keenan Wynn).

**Animagic from Rankin/Bass as presented in *Santa Claus
Is Coming to Town* (1970)**

Musically, the film is bright and includes catchy and melodic songs. The first is sung by Tanta Kringle (Joan Gardner) who leads the toy sweatshop into a "difficult responsibility" in the great number "The First Toy Makers to the King." "One Foot in Front of the Other" is a classic Rankin-Bass number that reminds eagle eyed (an eared) audiences of the song "Stay One Step Ahead" from an earlier feature, the entertaining *Mad Monster Party?* (1966). These songs have a cheery joyous feel that is synonymous with Rankin-Bass, and "One Foot in Front of the Other" from *Santa Claus Is Coming to Town* also acts as the moment that binds the hero and the newly reformed clear visceral villain. Because the Winter Warlock lives outside society, it is easy to understand why writer Muller made him an acceptable and loveable freak: in the world of Rankin-

Bass, even the most hardened outsider is redeemable, and can turn into a hero. In fact, a lot of the heroes that populate the Rankin-Bass world are genuine misfits, whereas the real villains are upstanding citizens who are devoid of any childlike magic: they are shaped by the society in which they live, and in turn become stone-faced cretins. In *Santa Claus Is Coming to Town* the real bad guy is the Burgermeister (Paul Frees) who has banned all toys in town. He screams at the children "You will never, never play again!" This is upsetting to Kris Kringle, and with the help of school teacher Miss Jessica (Robie Lester), a beautiful creation and similar to the sexy Francesca who appeared in the aforementioned *Mad Monster Party?*, fights for the rights of children and expresses the importance of play. Miss Jessica, who in the beginning seems to be upholding the law of the Burgermeister is seduced by not only Kringle but also by the memory of toys and the importance of childhood. Her soliloquy "My World Is Beginning Today" is the epitome of 1970s musical bliss—you can almost smell the taffeta and the pastel lipstick and billowy hair! The film's whimsical sweetness is centred around the beauty of childhood and this number reflects this from an "adult" perspective. The physical representation of childhood is toys and if they are outlawed then our heroes become rebels and are literally labelled non-conformist. The idea of the hero standing up against authority is something of the times and the sensitive and perceptive hero becomes the new cowboy. When Kringle is under attack from the authorities he must go into hiding, and it is a masterful stroke of social commentary as Kringle grows a beard to conceal his identity (the bearded youth of the 1960s), retreats to the woodlands (dropping out of established society) and changes his name to Santa Claus (the rejection of formal identity). As great as *Santa Claus Is Coming to Town* is, it will be surpassed by another Christmas themed Rankin-Bass feature film, which would be a cinematic effort and not just relegated to the small screen, a complex masterfully composed character study *Rudolph and Frosty's Christmas in July* (1979), which we shall discuss in a later chapter.

YEARS BEFORE LLOYD WEBBER'S JELLICLES: *The Aristocats*

More traditional animated musicals (i.e., cel-animation, as opposed to stop motion works) continued to be made throughout the 1970s, but a lot of these suffered from massive audience-pull concerns and budgetary issues. Even the mighty Disney studios struggled to deliver films that drew fans young and not so young: although exceptionally talented artists such as the song writing team of Richard and Robert Sherman were attached to some of these animated films, they seemed to be out of step with an audience who were interested in a more Avant-garde form of entertainment instead of classicist feel good animated cinema. Far from their golden age, Disney Studios also entered the first decade without their master Walt. The affectionately known Nine Old Men (the original core animators who were there from day one of animated feature film since *Snow White and the Seven Dwarfs*, 1937) were taking matters into their own hands, as producers and directors coped with financial losses and the changing interest in the motion picture industry without the guidance from their industrious master. There was no need to wow audiences with their wonderfully constructed and truly magical features such as *Fantastia*, *Pinocchio* (1940) and *Cinderella* (1950) anymore: the 1970s was a period of changing ideas in theme and form for Disney, who were simply just not ready to make that transition.

This may possibly have been for the best. When the studio reached what was known as their Renaissance era (1985-1995), a new wave of talent who were exploding with ideas resurrected the much loved and admired institution. They took their tentative learning steps with *The Great Mouse Detective* (1986) and *Oliver & Company* (1988), who paved the way for the studio to produce endless hits starting with the magnificent *The Little Mermaid* (1989). But before this cavalcade of brilliance, Disney in the 1970s had some staggering learning curves to comprehend and sadly they delivered some underwhelming shortcomings.

The Aristocats was one of these. Walt Disney himself had approved the production of *The Aristocats* before he died in 1966, and it was the last film he oversaw before it went to the story's animators. He also developed *The Rescuers* around the same time, however that film would not go into production until the mid to late 1970s (again, more on that film will be discussed later). Both movies—the only two solely animated Disney features of the 1970s—were curiously preoccupied with kidnapping. Produced at polar ends of the decade, these movies delivered villains Roddy Maude-Moxby (voiced by Edgar Balthazar) as an opportunistic butler in *The Aristocats* and, in *The Rescuers*, Madame Medusah (voiced by Geraldine Page), a pawn shop owner and treasure huntress, as characters completely dedicated to gaining wealth at whatever cost and without any real effort in channelling some good honest hard work. These villains are a major factor in the narrative failure of these two films (more so in regard to *The Aristocats*), as most iconic and memorable of Disney villains were the grandiose and glamorous evil enchantresses as seen in such classic fare as *Sleeping Beauty* (1959). But these supernatural, barren harpies and crones of the golden age retired during the 1970s (they would not return until 1988's *The Little Mermaid* with the gloriously conceived Ursula the sea witch), and in their place came the struggling working classes: they not only appear in the animated *The Aristocats* and *The Rescuers*, but also in the semi-animated *Pete's Dragon* (1977, itself a tragically underrated film that works on all levels).

A splash sheet for *The Aristocats* (1970) showcases some artistic differences

All in all, *The Aristocats* does have some whimsy, however it is possibly the most unrefined of the Disney films on a purely aesthetic level. The equally sketchy and grimy *101 Dalmatians* (1961) and *The Jungle Book* (1967) are incredible films because the narrative is strong and the characters have personal and social arcs that are dynamic and interesting, so you forgive their flatness. To go from something lush and sumptuous like *Bambi* (1942) or *Dumbo* (1941), *101 Dalmatians* (1961) and *The Jungle Book* (1967) are not too much of a step down because their impressive stories take over from visual flair. *The Aristocats*, however, does not land on its feet story wise either, and although there are some charming elements to the film, it is most certainly one of the weaker of the second wave of Disney features.

The legendary Sherman brothers composed the songs for the picture and they truly elevate it, transcending the muffled plot and semi-crude animation with numbers such as "Scales and Arpeggios" and the electric "Everybody Wants To Be a Cat," a stand-out moment in the film. The latter provides the mandatory "fantasy" moment in a grounded Disney plot where the animators are free to let loose and explode with energy and artistic liberty (remember the fabulous "Pink Elephants on Parade" number in *Dumbo*?). Here in this scene a group of beatnik alley cats praise the joys of being free felines, headed by the cool and smooth Jazz loving Scat Cat (voiced by the wonderful Scatman Crothers): this scene provides a much needed detour from a labored story. The color palette is generally muted and stark, but in "Everybody Wants to Be a Cat" and its Jazz-fusion, we are treated to bright pinks and blues as the frenzy of "being a cat" goes wild and thrilling. Sadly for the most part, the film is underwhelming. It picks up when we meet the charismatic Thomas O'Malley, and his song "Thomas O'Malley Cat" is a brilliant example of the flawless writing of the Shermans. Delivered by actor Phil Harris, it is performed with such smooth honesty that it singlehandedly pushes the film along.

The ultimate focus in the movie is the central cat, glamourpuss Duchess (voiced by Eva Gabor). *The Aristocats* follows her introduction to a life beyond being a pampered pet to a wealthy old woman. O'Malley shows her the wonders of human-free life, and her kittens are also seduced by this supposed freedom. This is something that is much more beautifully and intelligently explored in the far superior *Lady and the Tramp* (1955), a masterpiece of storytelling and animation. Unfortunately, this feline flavoured flick is not as vividly enchanting as the romantic dog tale: even from the start, *Lady and the Tramp* greets us with a deeply romantic vision in its dedication: "So it is to all dogs, be they ladies or tramps, that this film is truly dedicated." With *The Aristocats*, we get a great title song sung by French cabaret singer and actor Maurice Chevalier (who came out of retirement to record the number), but it in no way does it compare to the majesty of its canine-centric predecessor. *Lady and the Tramp* is Disney's most naturally informal and sentimental romantic animated feature, and *The Aristocats* could have followed its lead but sadly does not because it lacks in the artistic superlativeness of the older doggy-pic.

The Aristocats is not one of Disney's crowning achievements. It is lacking in focus, and hosts some of the sloppiest animation in their normally visually stunning film canon. The best thing about it is the voice actors employed to give life to these unkempt and scratchy looking characters; most notably the character actors who play the animals. Hungarian glamour queen Eva Gabor voices Duchess, and she injects this feline beauty with such sexiness and elegance that it is impossible to not fall in love with her. Phil Harris as Thomas O'Malley, the stray tomcat who is decidedly untrusting of humans, is wonderful with his slight-Brooklynite droll that oozes generous amounts of streetwise sass.

Even more memorable are the small parts relegated to helpful geese Amelia and Abigail Gabble, who are very proper English birds, beautifully voiced by the exceptionally talented Monica Evans and a legend of the musical theatre stage, Carole Shelley. Shelley remembers lending her voice for the loveable goose Amelia:

> At the time I was just thrilled to be doing it the way it had always been done so I never got the sense of the studio changing come the 1970s. I did the work just as it had always been done and how it had been evolved which included animators Frank Thomas and Ollie Johnson sitting in the studio while you were recording your voice where they would do a thumbnail sketch of you as you were acting. That's how they got that sort of lookalike thing happening, but later at Disney they would film you so they would always have this record of what you were physically doing while you were speaking.

38

A model sheet from *The Aristocats* (1970)

Wolfgang Reitherman directed *The Aristocats*, one of the long-standing chief animators at Disney for many years. He famously conceived the incredible dragon in *Sleeping Beauty*, the crocodile in the gorgeous *Peter Pan* (1953) and the Headless Horseman in the fantastic short *The Legend of Sleepy Hollow* (1949). In *The Aristocats* and previous films such as *The Sword in the Stone* (1963), Reitherman introduced a reuse system in animation where previously animated sequences were cut and pasted into future scenes. This was a trademark of his, but something that fellow animators did not like. But his talented pool of voice actors never minded.

Caroles Shelley goes on:

> Wolfgang Reitherman was the director and he had done a lot of full length animated features and he was wonderful, they were all wonderful. He knew exactly what he wanted and he gave you free reign. Once he got what he wanted he would then let you do whatever came into your head just in case he found something better.

Shelley had been in a popular comedy feature film that spawned a television sit-com that may have inspired "Woolie," as he was affectionately known as by his peers:

> *The Aristocats* was being done not long after Monica Evans and I had done the movie *The Odd Couple* (1968) and in that we played the Pidgeon sisters and I think that struck a chord with Woolie. It struck him so much that we didn't really have to actually audition, he knew that we had funny little personalities from those funny little performances in that film and I am sure that there is some tie in between us playing the Pidgeon sisters and then being cast as geese in his animated film, Woolie had that sense of humour about him that I dearly miss. Giving a voice to Amelia the goose was quite simply a lovely job.

Carole Shelley would then go on to lend her incredible vocal talents to another animated bird in the astonishingly much better *Robin Hood* (1973), which was a massive improvement from *The Aristocats*, both narratively and artistically. *Robin Hood* (as which we shall discuss later) was a milestone of 1970s animation, breathing an exceptionally fresh, unique and lasting new life into the literary and filmic history of Sherwood Forest's most infamous thieves.

HOW DO YOU SOLVE A PROBLEM LIKE CAROL BRADY?: *Song of Norway*

Returning to the idea of musicals from 1970 taking off where earlier grandiose musicals left off in the 1960s, *Song of Norway* is an even more blatant attempt to capitalize on the astounding success of a wildly successful musical than *Scrooge* was to *Oliver!*, here the core influence is, of course, Rodgers and Hammerstein's final movie musical, the legendary and ground breaking *The Sound of Music*. That classic film here becomes the source of inspiration for an uneven and uneventful musical telling of the story of composer Edvard Grieg.

Song of Norway is based on the operetta by Andrew L. Stone, and while it keeps most of the (sometimes) good songs, the film is lost and detached. The dramatic elements are muffled and unclear, and the attempts at a satirical commentary on artists being complicated, cold and bizarre idealists is mishandled and sloppy. The story unfolds in an obvious manner, and there is nothing that comes as a surprise or as an inspired turn of events. However, in this clichéd storytelling where you would think the efforts would be smooth and steady, the film is loaded with awkwardness and troublesome sequences that seem to confuse this musical autobiography even further.

A newspaper ad for *Song of Norway* (1970)

The film has one element that makes it most definitely worth watching, and her name is Florence Henderson. Henderson is a star. An absolute godsend of a singer and actress and her work with Rodgers and Hammerstein on stage where she performed in glorious musicals such as *Oklahoma!* and *South Pacific* should have set her up for a long career in cinematic musicals. But television beckoned, and during the late 1960s Henderson took on her most remembered role as the loving matriarch of the mixed-family *The Brady Bunch* (1969-1974). While the series was a massive success and has one of the biggest hearts in small screen history, it swallowed up Henderson's musical talents. Although she was able to showcase her marvellous singing in some episodes (and then later on *The Brady Variety Hour* that ran from 1976-1977), her warm and rich vocals would be wasted on the silver screen. *Song of Norway* gave her an opportunity to return, and when she is on screen, you pay attention. Sadly, however, when she is not on screen, interest is lost. Henderson's performance of "A Rhyme and a Reason" is not only enchanting, but also haunting and eerie. Backed by a group of maudlin children who seem to sing in flat non-descript tones, Henderson carries the number with graceful ease but also channels a whimsical eeriness in her performance. It is a brief inspired moment in the film, and conceived in a cautious and careful manner—the slight lighting changes from the clock maker's domain to the drug store, the slow pans across the lush green fields of Norway, the unsteady zoom in on Henderson as she slowly and carefully finishes this bizarre song. This is a stand out point in a very average film and a perfect example of Henderson's complexity as an actress. She can manoeuvre quite swiftly from wide-eyed and gooey, totally in love with the composer protagonist to delivering the most haunting melancholy that throws an audience off in a very, very good way.

The director also handles Henderson's relationship with her mother, who forbids her to marry Edvard Grieg, the famous composer. But sadly, for the most part, the film lets Henderson down. It is so misdirected and shallow that her nuanced performance is wasted. Famed film critic Pauline Kael wrote: "The movie is of an unbelievable badness; it brings back clichés you didn't know you knew—they're practically from the unconscious of moviegoers. To criticize this movie is like tripping a dwarf." Although Henderson's singing is delicate and also at times magically transcendental, the film is insipid and messy. And despite endlessly stunning picturesque imagery of Norway as the camera zooms through valleys and climbs glorious mountain tops, the film is no way near as good as another period musical about a European classical composer, Ken Rusell's *The Music Lovers* (which shall be discussed shortly).

ROCK'N'ROLL SUPERVIXENS: *Beyond the Valley of the Dolls*

Not even Ken Russell's dark and hyper-sophisticated *The Music Lovers* is as entertaining as the wacky *On a Clear Day You Can See Forever*, so there was the possibility that it wasn't an entirely good idea to base an entire movie musical around a classical composer, even in 1970. Russell's *Listzomania* (1975) failed to make waves, and it would not be until Milos Forman's *Amadeus* (1984) that anyone would truly capitalise on the gimmick. Thankfully, rock'n'roll came along to save the day and became the central musical flavour of one of the most dynamic movie musicals of the year. Directed by a man who made a career out of finding the most beautiful women in America and putting them in sexually dangerous and provocative cult films, Russ Meyer's *Beyond the Valley of the Dolls* is both amazing and weird for many reasons. It is not only a psychotic hybrid explosion of every single genre under the sun; it is also a dynamic musical with a phenomenal soundtrack.

From the title card right at the start, we learn that this sexually charged rock'n'roll extravaganza has nothing to do with the infamous melodramatic "monster" movie that is *The Valley of the Dolls* (1967). But with Roger Ebert's script and Russ Meyer's direction combined, *Beyond the Valley of the Dolls* is just as delightfully depraved and delectably dirty as Mark Robson's classic frenzied film from the 1960s.

Actor John LaZar remembers:

> Russ was as large a character as the breasts he so fondly photographed. As a director, he trusted me as an actor. He wasn't from the method school. He never discussed the character. He cast you and he expected you to know your job. It was one or two takes at the most and don't you dare blink. He was great to work with.

The film tells the story of Kelly MacNamara (Dolly Read) and her all-girl rock'n'roll band who, along with their manager (and Kelly's lover) Harris (David Gurian), leave the suburban constraints of playing gigs at school proms and hit the road to Los Angeles. Here they transform into The Carrie Nations, who become a cult favourite amidst the underground world of pornography, sex-crazed fashion, drug culture and the gradual blossoming of psychotic, maniacal violence. The dialogue bites with satire and hyper-zeal and this is most prevalent during the first party sequence hosted by the enigmatic and ambiguous (in every sense) Ronnie "Z-Man" Barzell (John LaZar). The sequence, which introduces Kelly to the weird wonderful world of the decedent, is an incredible example of punch line writing. Among the fabulous freaks that populate Meyer's film are Ashley St. Ives, played by the incredibly sexy Edy Williams who delivers an outstanding performance. Here is this violently sexual beast of a woman, completely animalistic and unsentimental about her conquests, proudly using young men to get her kicks and quickly making her moves on Harris who she tells "You're a groovy boy, I'd like to strap you on sometime."

Some of the greatest lines come from "Z-Man" as he delivers lengthy descriptions of each party guest and introduces our protagonist Kelly (and us) to a cavalcade of free-loving, hyper sexual and excitingly well-conceived characters. These include a handsome young actor Lance Rocke (Michael Blodgett) who is described as an "Adonis with bedroom eyes and a firm body." However, sex is secondary to this character's interests, and as Kelly finds out he is more interested in money and social climbing then connecting to a fellow human being. And that is what this magnificent film plays with—the idea of human disconnection, from the spiritual and the meaningful. It toys with hedonism from its most joyous and rapturous state (Kelly's rock'n'roll band makes a massive impact and entertains) to the most soulless and damaging (illustrated when the drummer of the band is caught in bed with another man, leading her lover into a sorrowful depression and accident involving being run down by the "other man").

Beyond the Valley of the Dolls is a morality play with no morality in it whatsoever, and thank goodness for its free thinking, anarchic attitude and dirty fun! "This is my happening and it freaks me out!" announces

"Z-Man" as he leads Kelly into a boudoir where they discover two men ready to fool around.

LaZar recalls:

> Ah, Roger's screenplay was fabulous! On my first read, I thought it was a marvellously hip satire dealing with sex, drugs and rock and roll in Hollywood. "Z-Man" jumped out at me and we became co-conspirators at the very beginning. It was the role of a lifetime. The inspiration for my character was part mock-Shakespeare and part being raised in San Francisco during the Haight-Ashbury period and the demi-monde of North Beach. In short, "Z-Man" was Richard the Third on acid.

Edy Williams "straps on" David Gurian in *Beyond the Valley of the Dolls* (1970)

The sexual freedom of the film is thrilling and highly political—Ashley St. Ives's aggressive heterosexual advances, Harris's desire for monogamy juxtaposed/married with his sexual dullness and inability to be "a good lay" and the sexual ambiguity of "Z-Man" himself. The character of "Z-Man" comes from a long line of psychologically scarred transgender characters that kill. By the end of the picture, this gender bending character goes on a crazed killing spree.

LaZar recalls:

> My wardrobe test for Super Woman began at wardrobe and continued with me walking on the lot to where Russ was shooting a scene. I experienced, even for a major studio used to having people in costumes, glances of surprise and laughter. I thought to myself: "I'm in for it now!" and Johnny Chambers hadn't even slapped the breasts on me yet. I drew upon my classical training for the lengthy speeches. Delivering them "was my happening and it freaked me out! Also, I may be wrong, but I rarely am, but I believe my transgender teen tycoon of rock preceded other transgender psycho serial killers that came after me.

Along with sexually ambiguous men who dress like Pontious Pilate are the incredibly beautiful women. These classic, big-breasted Russ Meyer body types are done up in (and out) of some stunning costumes as well. With all this lovely flesh parading around and being celebrated and respectfully bought to screen with such intelligence and potent sensuality, the film is astoundingly feminist in many ways, mostly because its female characters are remarkably in charge politically, socially, intellectually, physically and most importantly narratively. As far as cinematic history goes, Russ Meyer is one of the 1960s and 1970s most interesting and complicated feminist filmmakers. His films are a subversive extension of both the sexual liberation and Women's Movement. The notion of his films being sexist is absolutely ludicrous and moronic, as Meyer is genuinely interested and exceptionally good at delivering female-centric stories and his women are smart, beautiful (and sometimes horrendous on the inside countering the external aesthetic), bestial wolf-women who possess a sexual prowess that is both endearing and empowering. Titillation is completely acceptable and presented in such fascinating ways in Meyer's films, and *Beyond the Valley of the Dolls* is certainly no exception. Here we have numerous women who are buxom and absolutely gorgeous but also complicated and interesting: even Ashley St. Ives who could be presented as a cartoon sexpot is given depth and darkness that an incompetent director could have misrepresented.

John LaZar loved working on this cult masterpiece:

> My fellow cast mates and I, you could say, were the young guns of the day except we were all well behaved. We all got along and had a blast working together. The film was part satire, part horror film and, definitely, part musical. The music was jamming! The combination of The Strawberry Alarm Clock and Lynn Carrey was right up there. It was my first film and has been my favorite part throughout my career until one came along to rival it. A totally opposite part from the award-winning horror short film: "Alice Jacobs Is Dead." I'm glad *Beyond the Valley of the Dolls* is seen as a living classic but I miss the passing of Russ, Roger, Charles, Michael, Cynthia and Haji.

The songs in *Beyond the Valley of the Dolls* are also magnificent. Its melodies are charged with youthful energy and a knowing sense of sexual bravado. They are garage rock sounds, raw and vibrant, in a sun-soaked Californian style. "In the Long Run" is a beautifully written song, where the strength in the sentiment of 1960s love songs comes crashing into the advent of the 1970s and explodes with a desperate sensuality. It is also a wonderful moment in the film as The Carrie Nations not only become a success, but also win the admiration of two very different boys—Harris and "Z-Man." Once again, the feminist aspect of this film pits these two male characters utterly transfixed and dwarfed by the magnitude and sheer rock'n'roll beauty and power of this all-female band. When the main theme from "In The Long Run" is used as a part of the score with its swift strings, it is romantic and whimsical and a very smart move in the film's musical direction. The sexy "Sweet Candy Man" is a great teenage

47

angst song about being sexually knowing too much for one's own good. "Find It" is a fast and fun garage rock number that shakes you into the film's driving plot, while "Come With The Gentle People" is a great folk number that plays with both parody and genuine gentility. Russ Meyer's *Beyond the Valley of the Dolls* is a phenomenal piece and its broad sexual exploration is like an overflowing banquet of visual and musical delights.

Russ Meyer on the set of *Beyond the Valley of the Dolls* (1970)

Australian rock'n'roll performer, front woman of seminal punk outfit Magic Dirt and solo artist Adalita Srsen remembers the influence of the film:

Beyond The Valley of The Dolls was one of those rites of initiation into a cool, secret world of sub-culture in the 90's alternative scene in Geelong where I grew up. Every cool kid had to have seen this movie. It was a must. There would always be a group of us slacker kids in flares and cardigans and op shop t shirts with old 70's surf logos sitting in someone's low lit lounge room with incense on, beanbags, a cloud of pot smoke and junk food of some sort. And we all just loved this movie. I think it was my first Russ Meyer film (*Faster Pussycat Kill Kill* was closely

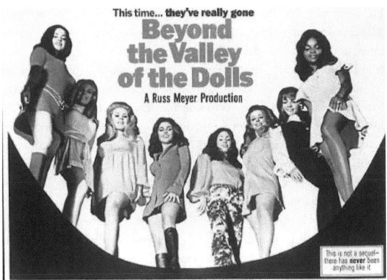

The poster art for *Beyond the Valley of the Dolls* (1970)

followed after *Beyond the Valley of the Dolls*). But I loved the weirdness and kooked out lingo, the women were beautiful and Amazonian and powerful in either their femininity or outrage or both. I loved Z-Man (everybody loved Z-Man!) especially in the final shocking scene where his secret identity is revealed. That bit always produced paroxysms of laughter in the room. I loved the 70's psychedelic look...something I guess us kids appropriated for ourselves and made it our own in the early 90's. But yes, this was such an influential film...we were often quoting memorable lines such as..."This is my happening and it freaks me out!," "I'd like to strap you on sometime..." and of course, "Don't bogart that joint."

THE LOVERS OF THE BIO-MUSICAL: *The Music Lovers*

Another film examined sexuality and gender in the context of the musical, albeit from a very different light as it zooms in on these elements with a finely tuned eye and ear. Ken Russell's *The Music Lovers* tells the story of famous composer Tchaikovsky and his inability to cope with

49

his homosexuality. Russell, normally the master of the monstrously garish and operatic consistently assaulting his audiences with a hyper-fantastical spectacle and broad strokes of sheer vibrant madness, reins it in here in this intimate portrait of a tormented artist and the woman he has chosen to share his life with. Instead of unleashing a screaming banshee, Russell introduces us to a soft-spoken soprano, who when she hits the high notes it will make the hairs on your arms stand high. The subtlety and quiet serenity in *The Music Lovers* makes the dramatic and highly charged erotica of the piece far more dynamic. The film itself is carefully and skilfully directed, its scenes paralleling music composed by the famous composer.

Richard Chamberlain plays the sexually conflicted Tchaikovsky with controlled stress, and focuses his energies in a direction that lends the right amount of restraint and repressed angst to give this real life character gravity and pathos. His violent outbursts and dark sexuality lift this musical biopic to an almost otherworldly state. The film is also proudly graphically explicit in its sexuality, as well as containing a deeply buried sensuality that successfully compliments the core theme of duality. There are times that the film's essence and multi-layered ideas reflect the staffs in musical notation: each note is plucked with intensity and passion and Ken Russell's visual flair never tramples on the story of a self-loathing man. It is a baroque, maudlin monster movie and its seductive sensuality is handled with both a fine toothcomb and sledgehammer. The darkness and the light are perfectly married in Russell's musical biopic and it is a saving grace when you consider this film in comparison to the treatment of composer Edvard Grieg in the awful *Song of Norway*.

The opening of the film is Ken Russell at his storytelling best—there is absolutely no dialogue spoken or lyric sung; instead it is a parade of drunken madness as we are introduced to Tchaikovsky and his male lover racing around Moscow only to have this frantic fun be severed by a sobering dose of harsh reality. Right from the opening, a dramatist insists that Tchaikovsky be more careful about being open about his homosexuality, the closet is a place that he has to live in begrudgingly but necessarily in fear of the conservative opinions of the music conservatorium and in fear of jeopardising his career as a professor of music.

Richard Chamberlain in *The Music Lovers* (1970)

Richard Chamberlain's performance of the famous musician is at its most captivating when he is playing the piano—there is ferocity in his tackling of his concertos, and Russell exploits this masterfully, as if suggesting that he is wrestling with his personal demons and in this case and in this film the demons are born from his conflicted sexual appetite. His romance with his wife is presented flowery and elegant, soft and whimsical (ten or so years later the token heterosexuality of director William Friedkin's *Cruising* (1980) would also be depicted in subdued serenity and accompanied by classical music as opposed to the rest of the film set to roaring punk rock whenever the film's star Al Pacino hit the streets or the gay leather bars). Ken Russell delivers beautiful elongated moments where Tchaikovsky comfortably revels in the company of his children and his wife—there is such a degree of romance and sweetness in these moments, so when we are presented with his wrestling with his homosexual leanings it is easy to become anxious seeing that his tender moments with wifey and kiddies are so pleasant and pretty.

For a musical where the musical numbers are not sung at all, instead set to the magnificent music of the famous Russian composer, it works as an exercise in pantomime and nightmarish frenzy—there is nothing subtle about the imagery or the way in which the story is told, but why on earth would you want there to be anything subtle in a Ken Russell musical? The scenes where characters run through the lush forests in slow motion are pure bliss—the sexual energy of every single character is dripping with whetted desire and Richard Chamberlain plays it to perfection. Glenda Jackson also dives into her role with an amazing amount of oozing sensuality—here Jackson is completely comfortable and at ease with her own sex appeal and vibrancy as an actress, she means everything she doesn't say. It is fundamentally a powerhouse performance and matches Chamberlain in its rawness and strict sultriness.

One of the strongest elements of the film is its ability to counterbalance the aggressive outbursts with the seductive beautiful elements—the soft focus that turns flowing white gowns into stars, the rich colors of the forests, the dreamlike quality of certain scenes and the surrealism of the film, add to all that the extremely creepy decadence that Russell enjoys assaulting his audiences with for example Tchaikovsky's flashbacks to his mother. All in all, if *The Music Lovers* is an incredible piece of filmmaking, storytelling and pantomime intertwined with biography, but more importantly, it shakes up the idea of the movie musical and is one of Russell's most subdued and yet one of the most engaging. It also can be looked at as a stunning warm up to more extreme musicals—the tribute to Busby Berkley in *The Boy Friend* (1971) and the rock opera masterpiece *Tommy* which we shall get to very soon.

THE DONKEYS ARE COMING, THE DOOMED MUSICALS ARE HERE: *Peau D'Ane*

Song of Norway and its conservative ideologies was not the only musical mistake made in 1970, and sometimes liberal and flamboyantly, unapologetically confronting musicals missed the point, too. *Peau D'Ane* could have been a haunting French musical based on a folkloric tale about a King who is unhealthily obsessed with his daughter to the point of wanting to marry her. But it just is not. One of its mistakes is that it clearly states the reasoning as to why the King has to marry his daughter: he promises his dying Queen that he will only remarry a woman as beautiful and as virtuous as she is, and the only woman like that is the Princess. Of course this is the legend, however it would have been far more interesting and far more complex if this prologue and set-up was held off for a while, so that this deliberately queasily made film could be even more unnerving and grotesque.

The Princess is played by the delicate and ethereal Catherine Deneuve, and she comes to understand that if she wears a magical donkey skin she can escape the incestuous marriage. The film is heavily influenced by Jean Cocteau's visually sumptuous *La belle et la bête* (1946) which is an astonishingly good film in style and substance. But this 1970s outing does not share the same elegance or sophistication. It also lacks Cocteau's driving and steady narrative. The main problem with *Peau D'Ane* is that it does not seem to have a solid direction and refuses to examine the intensity of the Princess's dilemma. This is a musical about incest, a tremendously grim and downbeat theme and yet director Jacques Demy does not seem to bother with exploring the horrors of this creepy theme. Musically the film is also uninspired and it positions songs without careful realization: these unmemorable ditties are plotted in all the wrong areas and not at all helpful to the story or characters. Its strength is Catherine Deneuve, but even this incredibly gifted actress is wasted in a dull and lazy film that does not expand on its themes either dramatically or musically. Deneuve was given an incredible opportunity in Demy's earlier film, the fantastic *The Umbrellas of Cherbourg* (1964), a mesmerising and innovative musical that is completely romantic and moody. Here, Deneuve has nothing to do but look gorgeous, and she looks bored doing that alone.

GOT MILK? (AND OTHER QUERIES) *Trouble in Molopolis, Racquel!, Myra Breckinridge* and *Jack and the Beanstalk*

Australian auteur Philippe Mora was just starting making films in 1970. With a string of shorts behind him, one of his first features was *Trouble In Molopolis*, a completely independent picture shot for minimal cost and starring Mora's friends, including feminist writer and activist Germaine Greer and cartoonist and pop-artist Martin Sharp. A musical highly influenced by comic books, gangster films, the Marx Brothers and Brecht, *Trouble in Molopolis* focuses on the rivalry of two gangs and their dealerships in "milkeasys" at a time where milk—as opposed to booze— has been banned. A musical about the prohibition of milk is not a far cry from what will come from Mora's incredibly diverse filmography: he would go on to direct two werewolf movies (one featuring Christopher Lee in sunshades and the other featuring were-marsupials), a fantastic horror film about a young man who transforms into a giant cicada and he will eventually pit Christopher Walken against aliens. Mora injects his films with a wry sense of humour and delivers exceptionally unpretentious socially aware films that boast a lot of artistic ingenuity and skill. This comes from his background as a fine artist, and *Trouble in Molopolis* with its bizarre premise benefits greatly from Mora's eye for inventiveness.

The opening for Australian underground musical *Trouble in Molopolis* (1970)

The film was co-produced by musician Eric Clapton who would later be seen as a cult-leader preacher in Ken Russell's phenomenal *Tommy* (1975) (which will be examined later). Clapton shared some insight into Philippe Mora's *Trouble in Molopolis* with newspaper *The Age* in 2008:

> Clapton said the document that best told the stories of their times together was the movie *Trouble in Molopolis*, which stars many of the protagonists of the period, including a saucy Germaine Greer who plays a cabaret singer. "Philippe's

movie that is showing downstairs ... that is the document of our time ... all those people in that movie for me, it was my first time producing, later, I got a go at producing sound tracks. He is a wonderful man, I'm the proud owner of three of his paintings and my kids love them ... they don't know the dark side, they think it's just naive wonderful, splendid art. Well, so do I. I am proud to be part of this opening. Enjoy the show," he said.

Underground films like *Trouble in Molopolis* adopted the traditional stylings of the movie musical, and soon enough, the complete polar opposite to punk rock DIY cinema, that of mainstream television, started to follow suit. The glamorous and gorgeous Raquel Welch had a fantastically fun TV mini-movie for NBC simply called *Raquel!* The forty-eight minute special featured the Amazonian beauty showcasing her flamboyance and varied talents from comedy to dance to singing "Aquarius" (a song made famous in the rock musical *Hair*). Welch is joined by singer Tom Jones, actor and comedian Bob Hope and most surprisingly (and wonderfully) the "Duke" himself, Mr. John Wayne. To have Wayne on a musical one-off variety show playing alongside the dazzling Welch is an absolute delight and a perfect example of how the 1970s was truly *the* era for spectacle, fun, zaniness and pure escapist bliss.

John Wayne, the epitome of the all-American tough guy and forever representative of the movie western, is a true legend. He is made even cooler by sharing (small) screen time with the supernaturally beautiful Welch on her kooky musical TV special. More legends of the silver screen would follow his lead such as Lauren Bacall. Welch also starred in the critically panned *Myra Breckinridge* (based on the novel by Gore Vidal) where she played the transgendered female counterpart to film critic Rex Reed. However, Welch never gets the opportunity to sing or dance in this film, all the musical numbers in the film (a total of two) belong to the imitable legend of the golden age of Hollywood (and the vaudeville stage) Mae West.

By 1970, West was well into her senior years but she gleefully plays Letitia Van Allen, a men's-only casting director, with a youthful playfulness that works on every level. She is a delight to watch and a perfect counterpart to the vivacious and strikingly beautiful Welch who delivers every line with burning intelligence and bite. West however casually glides through the film with ease and the perfect amount of nonchalance and her delivery of the songs is not only highly entertaining but utterly and completely bizarre. West is surrounded by dancing and prancing chorus boys and intercut with Carmen Miranda musicals of the 1940s, her numbers are gloriously garish and wonderfully crazy. There is nothing subtle or subversive about *Myra Breckinridge* and the musical numbers from Mae West are insane: thank God! The film is a messy montage, a masterpiece of manic movie masturbation and it works perfectly.

Mae West wardrobe test for *Myra Breckinridge* (1970)

Although it would not be considered a musical in the purest sense of the term, it does feature these diegetic numbers delivered by West and snippets from old wonderful musicals injected into its choppy fabric. Raquel Welch made this film around the same time as her TV special and although she shines as the transgender heroine of Hollywood she is far more comfortable on the small screen alongside Bob Hope, Tom Jones and a gun-tooting John Wayne. Both Racquel Welch vehicles seemed to channel youth interest by employing fun and energetic numbers and (in the case of *Myra Breckinridge*) playing with themes of varied sexualities, drugs and social rebellion.

Racquel Welch as the titular *Myra Breckinridge* (1970) shows John Huston and company what she's made of

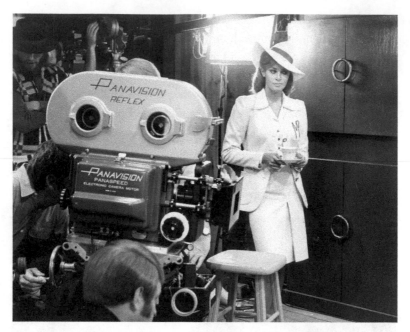

Behind the scenes on *Myra Breckinridge* (1970)

John Huston, Racquel Welch, Mae West and Rex Reed in Myra
Breckinridge (1970)

Mae West costume test for *Myra Breckinridge* **(1970)**

Another seldom seen independent movie musical that heavily relied on youth appeal was *Jack and the Beanstalk* which was a retelling of the famous fairy tale but riddled with "young person" speech. Jack would constantly say "groovy man" while the supporting players would cry "far out" and "wild man wild." The film is a relatively innocent feature but completely devoted to hipster lingo and spaced out silliness. It could have easily played on television and worked just as well, the idea of it being a theatrically released film is completely odd—it was not in the traditional

John Huston and Racquel Welch in *Myra Breckinridge* (1970)

realm of what would play at the inner city grindhouse theatres, it read like a clean cut (albeit for the incessant "youth talk") simple, even child-friendly, fairy tale musical.

Made for TV musicals were a relatively new invention in the 1970s, but they were not completely out of the ordinary. Many elongated selections from the musicals of Rodgers and Hammerstein made it on television in variety shows; scenes and numbers from musicals like *Carousel* and *South Pacific* were presented on the small screen and launched the careers of artists such as Florence Henderson. The 1970s was an incredible era for the variety television show: *The Sonny & Cher Comedy Hour* (1971-1974 and then 1976-1977), *The Carol Burnett Show* (1967-1978), *The Johnny Cash Show* (1969-1971) and *The Muppet Show* (1976-1981) were just a few television variety programs that acted as a fantastic platform for incredible artists to showcase their various talents from singing and dancing to comedy to dramatic readings.

CHEER FOR BACALL: *Applause!*

A full-fledged musical presented on the television screen was a rarity. However, in 1970 a Broadway musical based on the classic film and classic bitch-fest *All About Eve* (1950) was adapted for TV, starring a legend of the golden age of Hollywood who made her extraordinary mark in the *film noirs* of the 1940s: the glamorous Lauren Bacall.

The musical was *Applause!*, and it told the story of an aging actress named Margo Channing, who takes in a young upstart unaware that the young starlet has every intention of stealing her career and her man. The book was written by the legendary writing team of Betty Comden and Adolph Green who had great success with musicals such as *On the Town,* which was adapted into a very effective film in 1949. The witty lyrics for *Applause!* were written by the talented Lee Adams and the bouncy and incredibly hummable music was composed by legendary musical maestro Charles Strouse.

Says Strouse:

> Lauren Bacall was in London doing the show and was a great success in it and I thought she would have been exhausted, but she had agreed to do the TV special of it, and I gotta tell you something, Lauren loved to make a buck, so that's probably the main reason why she did it. I thought it was not the way to do it. The TV special just didn't have the same amount of glamour that it needed and the glamour that the stage show had. I only ever saw it once. My feelings about *Applause!* in general all have to do with my admiration and love for Lauren Bacall. She was a very strong and confident woman and she taught me a lot about confidence. She loved to work and she worked very hard and she was one of the last stars really. I mean real genuine article stars.

Applause! deals with aging in a very grounded and honest way: there is no dillydallying around the terrible reality that show business is a cruel mistress, favourable to the young and beautiful.

Strouse adds:

> The show is about an actress of a certain age who is having an affair with a man who is younger than she is and she is very frightened of losing him and her youth and this

is a problem that women face more than men. The original script, as well as the one by Betty Comden and Adolph Green is all about this and it's something that makes for a great story. We all fear aging and becoming obsolete. It's terrifying.

Lauren Bacall injects her Margot Channing with youthful gusto as she parades around singing and dancing up a storm through the television sets that come to represent different areas of New York City.

Strouse continues:

It's very difficult to find a star of the magnitude of a Bette Davis or a Lauren Bacall these days. Bacall is a very gutsy dame and she likes to take on challenges. She had a bad leg during *Applause!* but she kept working and working and had some therapy and did exercises. She never missed a performance and she gave me a great deal of respect. She had never sung before and she worked with me a great deal. She was very sharp and acerbic sometimes, if I had to correct her on a note she would give it to me! I was very fortunate to work with her. There aren't many actresses like Lauren Bacall. Bacall stayed vibrant all the way through doing *Applause!* And that show really requires that real star quality. One of the best was Anne Baxter who replaced Lauren Bacall, the original Eve from *All About Eve*, she wasn't as funny as Bacall but she was great.

The energy levels may not seem taxing while watching the frantically produced TV adaptation of the gutsy and tough musical, but composer Strouse felt that Bacall was being over worked having doing the stage show and then thrust into doing the on air special.

He says:

I wasn't asked to work on the TV special, but the fact is I thought that it should not have been done for a number of reasons and one of them being that I thought Lauren was just far too tired to do it. She was determined to do it though, she's such a work horse, and would never stop.

Lauren Bacall in *Applause!* (1970)

One of the stand out moments of the special became a very controversial and confronting moment in television history for a lot of American audiences. There is a scene in the musical where Margot Channing persuades her gay hairdresser Duane to take her and Eve out to Greenwich Village to the underground "queer" bar circuit for a night out of dancing and partying with adoring gay men. The song is "But Alive," where Margot Channing lists every single emotion she feels from bitchy and groggy and weary and tragic, but kills any conflict bought on from these feelings by claiming that she is alive. She leads Eve into the world of the flamboyant gay life in the East Village of New York and she is met with homosexuals racing toward her with arms outstretched and worshipping one of their goddesses of the theatrical stage. It is truly a sight to behold! Bacall is picked up and carried around, she delivers incredible athleticism as she dances alongside the chorus boys and she belts out the number with passion and high energy.

Strouse is very pleased with this sequence:

Lee and I credit ourselves that we were the first ever to use homosexuals not only in a musical but using them at all. Openly gay characters were never really used in musicals. This kind of taboo reminded us of our pride when we did *Golden Boy* (1964) where a black man and a white woman touched and kissed!

During the 1970s taboos were being broken, be it in *Applause!* by dealing head-on with aging in the arts industry, the cut-throat nature of the world of theatre, or homosexuality. With its oddball representation in a TV special, *Applause!* was a leading advocate, and although Bacall is a delight to watch and the lyrics and music are engaging and sophisticated, it still seems like a hurried elongated sketch on a variety show. The true essence of the musical is lost and the darkness and melancholy is whitewashed for stretched out dance sequences that are sometimes cluttered and not at all complimentary to the intoxicating score. Musically, *Applause!* is terrific but in this television treatment it is hard to truly hear the intricate use of horns and strings, and the edgy bombastic energy of the music is lost in an adaptation that misses the point.

Recalls Strouse:

I have to say that while we were writing *Applause!*, it was just at the same time of *Hair* (1967) opening. And that was a very, very different show. Critics were blown away by *Hair* and they all predicted that every musical from then on will have a full blown rock score. However, *Hair* was also extremely melodic however it was sung by a cast of people who weren't trained musical theatre people. And the attitude of that show was from outsiders, so I was very conscious of that, and that was something that possibly threatened *Applause!* which came from the legitimate American musical theatre.

Another Charles Strouse Broadway musical based on a comic book legend would get the television variety show style treatment some years later, which we shall come to later.

MAMMA CASS IS A WITCH: *Pufnstuf*

A musical based on a popular children's television show (conceived and released while the series was still in production) popped up out of nowhere financed by Universal Pictures and Kellogg's Cereal. The latter was a funding body because they also sponsored the TV show that the film was a spin-off from: the show was *H.R. Pufnstuf*, and the musical feature was simply called *Pufnstuf*. The wonderful Jack Wilde (who made a fabulous impression as the Artful Dodger in *Oliver!*) stars in this epitome of 1970s psychedelic bliss which is not only wildly manic and wacky but also made with such surprising gentle sweetness that it is hard not to be won over by its silly charms. It is also well directed and acted and the songs are great: not one of them is uninteresting or lacking in writing efforts. There are strange offbeat musical moments and pop sensibilities that are just as juicy and contagious as any hummable show tune.

Pufnstuf opens up the TV show and takes it beyond the restraints of the network studio. Universal Studios breathes new life into this kid's television show that was completely out of this world to begin with, born from 1960s counter culture. *H.R. Pufnstuf* was a television show that celebrated difference and gave a canvas for outsiders (including creators Sid and Marty Crofft) to paint upon and make their zany mark. Jack Wilde as Jimmy is an outsider from the beginning in this filmic extension of the television show. He is an English boy living in America and is picked on and considered a nuisance. He is also a dreamer as stated in the opening song "If I Could," and when his flute comes to life and talks to him it fulfils the wish fulfilment of every social misfit who comes into contact with the realm of fantasy cinema. Another brilliant addition to the film is the inclusion of rock'n'roll singer Cass Elliot from band The Mammas and the Pappas who plays Witch Hazel (a friend of Billie Hayes's iconic antagonist Witchypoo), and when Elliot sings and celebrates being "Different" it is an extraordinary moment as she leads a procession of witches who understand what it is like to be unlike others. This becomes a perfect condensation of the alienation of the young and also a clever reflection of the burgeoning Women's Liberation movement. These women are witches: scholars and philosophers and doctors and magicians who are creating their own world and embracing their sometimes lonely but completely honest and empowering difference. This subversive political edge makes the film a socially aware hallucination, but it remains thoroughly entertaining throughout. The art direction is splendid and the puppetry is so endearing that it is addictive to watch, almost like a drug. This is the kind of bizarre musical that truly reflects the 1970s mentality: loud, brash, bright, weird and completely enchanting.

There are also some subtle jokes that can completely go unnoticed, such as when H.R. Pufnstuf (Allan Melvin) first sees the talking flute (named Freddy and voiced by Hanna-Barbera legend Don Messick) and says "Oh it's a talking flute with a diamond skin condition!" This kind of oddball humour trickles through the film (in more extreme ways than the television show ever could), and most of the laughs come from the wonderful talents of Billie Hayes as Witchypoo. Hayes is fantastic and has such a marvellous energy about her that it is hard to not be in hysterics while she chews up the scenery. And may she eat it until her heart is content, she is simply terrific! There is a marvellous moment where Hayes is on the phone with Cass Elliot as these two witchy friends cackle and gossip like teenage girls, while one of the songs "Living Island" is just as joyous and insane. In this sequence, Jimmy has found home. Surrounded by a clock that has "time to spend," a hippy tree for "peace and love," a frog that leaps here and there and so forth—the sequence is a grandiose theatrical hyper-energetic moment that acts as both a showstopper but also a catalyst.

But as great as the art direction and sets look, something makes you want the film to spend more time in the real world. It would have been great to see the citizens of the Living Island run through the naturalistic sets and locations, but they are exclusively relegated to the fantastical realm of the film, and sadly that is a disappointment. But it certainly is the only one.

The year 1970 was dominated by the concert film and bizarre oddities that worked on many levels, such as *On a Clear Day You Can See Forever*, *Pufnstuf*, *Beyond the Valley of the Dolls* and *Santa Claus Is Coming to Town*. However, there were flops like *Song of Norway* and some tragic disappointments like *The Aristocats*, which were films that suggested the integrated movie musical was losing balance at the dawn of the 1970s. By the next year, the warm-up that was 1970 would prove to be beneficial with Disney delivering the goods and giving a platform for Angela Lansbury to sing some Sherman brothers gems, a classic children's book (dark in tone and completely adopting the "Ten Little Indians" motif) getting a musical adaptation and making a superstar out of Gene Wilder, and one of the most successful Broadway shows getting a much deserved extraordinarily brilliant filmic treatment with Oscar nominated director Norman Jewison at the reins.

1971

"The Age of Not Believing"

Jewison's Jews, Witches and Nazis, and Chocolate Factories

TRADITION. MUSICAL THEATRE AND FILM HAS RELIED ON A SENSE OF tradition where similar formulas, ideologies, narrative characteristics and structural elements have lasted a long time, ever since the book musical took over from vaudeville as one of the most popular and greatest forms of American entertainment. The lasting aspect of these traditions in the musical form has obviously been sustained throughout the years because they worked successfully, but that does not mean that the same traditions were also snubbed and altered for varying audiences and times. The 1970s were a perfect example of this, however one of the most successful Broadway musicals of the 1960s was a traditionally conceived and staged musical that adopted many old-style theatrical components (such as the breaking of the fourth wall), a rich and well-rounded score that reprised here and there and carried over themes from one scene to three or

69

four scenes later, and opera's sombre second act that became cemented into the traditions established by the musicals of Hart, Rodgers and Hammerstein.

This kind of musical—a traditional integrated book musical where story was the number one priority—was to quickly appear old fashioned when rock'n'roll angst-ridden musicals started to surface. But this did not mean that 'traditionally structured' and fundamentally 'traditionally scored' musicals weren't still speaking (and singing) to contemporary audiences. And the aforementioned success of the 1960s was a perfect example of this, so much so that when the film adaptation of this— "one of the last traditional American musicals"—opened, everybody watched and everybody listened. One of the main reasons why people paid attention and made it one of the biggest blockbusters of the early 1970s was because of the fact that this musical dissected the breakdown of traditions, something exceptionally fitting for the time: it addressed youth rebellion, the questioning of authority, organised religion and the law, societal change, and a number of other issues as well. The film I refer to is the majestic and superlative *Fiddler on the Roof.*

FOR PAPA MAKE HIM A SCHOLAR: *Fiddler on the Roof*

Put simply, *Fiddler on the Roof* is one of the greatest movie musicals of all time, and there are numerous reasons as to why. First, it is incredibly well made: the direction, the cinematography, the visually beautiful moments that clash dramatically with its starker and bleaker aspects all contribute to the creation of the perfect movie musical. Second, the score (orchestrated by soon-to-be phenomenally successful film composer John Williams) is divine. There are melodies, musical themes and arrangements that are elegant and eloquent, completely character and story driven and magnificently diverse. At the same time, they are structured so well that the entire score is a working fabric of themes that are magically reflective of the heart of the story, one all about the concept and the threat of change. Third, it is the writing of the story itself and the way these old Jewish folkloric tales are presented in relation to contemporary America that grants the film its unique magic. If the musical theatre (and film) is reflective of the times, then *Fiddler on the Roof* speaks volumes of the changing period of the late 1960s, and says it far more interestingly than a lot of rock'n'roll and folk musicians around the same period. *Fiddler on the Roof* states quite clearly that "change is happening and we both accept this and move along with it, or we remain unchanged and die off."

A publicity shot of the cast of *Fiddler on the Roof* (1971)

It is also interesting to note that not long after *Fiddler on the Roof* opened on Broadway, the extremely different but equally important *Hair* opened, which launched into the stratosphere the changing face of musicals, and showed that they could be a mirror on the western world (or at least the western world that were well aware of Broadway—and Off-Broadway—musicals). *Fiddler on the Roof*'s Marxist revolutionary Perchik (Michael Glaser) represents the youthful rebellion that was happening at the time of the musical's Broadway debut and subsequent film adaptation. He is instrumental in the course of change that the musical is actively interested in, successfully seducing the second eldest daughter Hodel (Michele Marsh) who eventually follows Perchik to Siberia, a testament of her loyalty to his political and intellectual insight. A famed Broadway critic said that when the curtain came up on *Fiddler on the Roof* it also came down on that type of musical with the advent of the aforementioned *Hair* and other musicals such as *A Chorus Line* and *Company* that were edgy new works taking over the Great White

71

Way. But there is regardless still much to be said about the revolutionary Jewish musical set at the time of the Russian revolution itself!

The film opens with protagonist Tevye (played by the magnificent Topol), an enigmatic and boisterous poor milk man living in an impoverished Russian town called Anatevka, as he breaks the fourth wall and explains what keeps this small Jewish town thriving: traditions that are held in high esteem and respected. From this pre-opening credits introduction we are hooked. This is masterful filmmaking at its most seductive and engaging. When those opening big broad notes for the first number "Tradition" drive in, we are completely and cordially invited into Anatevka and meet these people who we will soon learn to love (and in some cases, just tolerate). We let this fantastic cast, majestic music and exceptionally talented director Norman Jewison work their magic.

Jewison himself was baffled when United Artists approached him to direct the film. He remembers:

> I was shocked when they asked me to direct the film! I was totally dumbfounded because first of all I'm not Jewish! And coming with a name like Jewison which looks like it was originally a son of a Jew, but it's not! I found out it was an old English name. My mother was English and my father was also. So I just didn't understand when United Artists had called me up. I had done *In the Heat of the Night* (1967) and *The Russians Are Coming! The Russians Are Coming!* (1966) for them, and they were all pretty successful, I mean *In the Heat of the Night* had won the Academy Award, but I had never done a musical for them. But I had done a lot of musicals for television and musicals specials such as *The Judy Garland Show* (1963-1964) and *The Harry Belafonte Show* (1969) and a special on *The Danny Kaye Show* (1963), so I was very well versed in the musical form, but I was never out looking for a job—or looking out to direct a major musical film. I loved the stage production—I loved the score so much! I thought it was just fantastic. I was a big fan of Sheldon Harnick and Jerry Bock. But it was a curious thing when I was asked to fly into New York and meet with Arthur Krimm and they

Traditions slowly dissolve in *Fiddler on the Roof* (1971)

had kept it a secret, they told me not to tell my agent. I flew into New York and I guess that would have been 1969 and the stage show was a huge hit in New York and when they said, "What would you think if we asked you to produce and direct *Fiddler on the Roof?*" there was a long pause and my heart went into my mouth and I replied with "Well what would you say if I told you that I'm a Goy?" And they all sat there stunned—Bill Bernstein and Arnold Picker and David Picker and Bob Benjamin because I realized that they were all Jewish, and this is essentially a collection of Sholem Aleichem which is a major piece of Jewish history and heritage, I was just amazed. I watched all their faces fall but Krimm was very cool and he said "Why would we ask you to do the film? We don't want a piece of Yiddish kitsch. We want the film to play internationally to all people!" I asked about the stage director. He was brilliant and he had done the choreography. And they said that they had tried that with another musical and that didn't work out. They told me that they weren't using any of the theatre people. Not the director, not the choreographer, no one. So I said I'd think about! I was shocked! I loved the idea of *Fiddler on the Roof* on the screen. So I met with Joseph Stein who had written the book and we worked together. I asked if he wanted to do the screenplay. It meant we had to open this story up. I also suggested that we should shoot on location in Europe somewhere. I met with Harnick and Bock. And I was lucky enough to get John Williams. And then I was super lucky to get Isaac Stern to play the fiddle. It was an incredible group of people, a group of legitimate artists.

The opening number, "Tradition," is a finely pieced together montage of the hard working Jews in Anatevka, and it showcases each position of the family unit: the papa, the mamma, the sons and the daughters. Tevye, our central figure (who we will experience the story's overwhelming change through) also introduces us to the charismatic characters of Anatevka, such as Yente the matchmaker (Molly Picon) and Lazar Wolf the butcher (Paul Mann) to whom he has promised his eldest daughter to be wed. Anatevka is also seeing the growing anti-Semitism that is slowly surfacing, headed by the Christian church and the Russian Tsar, who will gradually become a violent and extreme threat.

Norman Jewison remembers directing the grandiose and complicated opening:

> To me "Tradition" sets up the piece physically so therefore I wanted to include as much as I could about that kind of life in Russian at the turn of the century. That was what I was trying to do with that number and extend it visually and make it more powerful and there I turned to John Williams and I said to him "Look, I'm going to construct this as a montage of all things and I am going to have to cut this all together." And I gave him a shot list and I explained to him in that list what each image would be about, such as women washing, men studying and so forth and it all worked out beautifully. We had control of everything and I was given

total creative control on the film, which I had in my contract and as long as I had that I felt secure that no one was going to come in and cut it all up and change everything. I had the freedom to cut the picture the way I wanted and I would submit the film to the studio and if they didn't like it there was conversation made, and because of that I had to be very, very sure of my production designer, editor and composers. As long as you're working with talented people there should be no problem. I didn't get any complaints from United Artists about length or anything, they didn't really ask for changes which was great.

The film truly opens up the original musical and the adaptation from stage to screen appeared to be an effortless task for the incredibly gifted Norman Jewison. But, as he recalls, the music itself dictated the transition:

> The film is very different to the play. It's the same as far as the music goes. I really loved the choreography in the play so I hired the assistant to the choreographer and I hired the lead dancer from the play and then hired dancers from all over the world. There is a similarity in the play and the film musically because we stayed with most of the orchestrations but then expanded them. As with a film, when you open it up you have to add music. So John Williams who is a brilliant composer and conductor made it possible to sit down and work it out with the actors what I had in mind and how I was going to stage it.

Thankfully the film does not omit the breaking down of the fourth wall. It intelligently keeps Tevye talking to us, the audience, and to God so that we get a theatrical sense of insight that works splendidly. It is handled with care and makes perfect sense so that when we first see Tevye looking directly into camera and talking to us, we understand that we have entered the realm of a very, very real fantasy (or, at least, a genre that relies heavily on escapism, the motion picture musical).

Jewison had to juggle this theatrical element and make it work swiftly for film, he recalls:

> The main problem was when Tevye has the scenes with his daughters and we have to go into his mind and his daughters don't hear what he's saying, they're not supposed to hear his torment. I didn't want to get an extreme close up of his eyes and do a voice over, because I didn't want to rob the actor, rob Topol, of having that opportunity to play it, I mean in the theatre you can isolate these characters purely by a lighting design, you know, everybody freezes and someone else goes ahead and talks, and you accept that in theatre. But in a film you can't do that, I mean films are realistic, they're the closest things we have to real life, it's the photography of life so everything has to be very believable. So I decided that I had to remove the daughters from Tevye and move them yards and yards away, so the audience would believe that he was now on his own while he sings his soliloquy. Separating them physically made it ok for him to then have his chat to God and so forth then he could look back at them and they'd be there, I could jump them back again. There is a lot you can do in film that you can't do in theatre.

Besides Tevye's talking to God and the breaking of the fourth wall, the theatricality of the film is subdued, which makes the musical numbers appear organically and feel unforced. There is such a perfect naturalism to the presentation of each number and the staging, that the acting and delivery of each emotion is authentic and pure. Even in the fantastical dream sequence, where Tevye speaks of the dead accompanied by the startling image of white-faced, ghoulish zombies rising from their graves (mimicking a horror film from Mario Bava), there is an overpowering sense of grounded realism that makes this creepy but light hearted sequence (one of the only light moments in the film) appropriate to the thick plot.

Director Norman Jewison on location for *Fiddler on the Roof* (1971)

The beautiful, harmonious "Matchmaker" is a romantic and whimsical song where one of the film's finest moments appears with the second verse, where the third eldest daughter Chava (Neva Small) sings out the swelling moment of "...the envy of all I see!" This is where master musician John Williams comes along with his stunning orchestrations, lifting the moment (Chava's dream of finding a husband she loves and not one forced upon her by Yente the matchmaker) and elevating the already stirring and brilliant Jerry Bock score. When Tevye laments "If I Were a Rich Man" we get a full picture of this man: a loveable but stubborn schmuck with dreams, but someone completely aware of his situation (the lame horse, the frustrated wife, the soon-to-be rebellious daughters). Topol's performance—much like that of his fabulous co-stars—is inspired and completely his own.

Jewison recalls the stage to screen casting:

> I changed the obvious casting which was the Broadway
> casting which was all built around the actor that performed

in it on Broadway. Everybody wanted to play Tevye. I'd never seen anything like it when we were casting. When I said that we weren't casting the Broadway cast the shit hit the fan, because everyone expected me to go with the stage cast. I felt that the original Tevye was too big, and I felt his performance was far too American, he was too New York and he was too broad and kitsch! So I reached out and went out in a different direction, I went to Israel and that's where Chaim Topol came into my life. He had played Tevye in Jerusalem and played it in Hebrew. He was so good that the casting agents of the London production got him to perform on the West End. They trained him up on English. I saw him and thought that he was it! He's a second generation Russian Jew! Even though he is also Israeli. That gave him a strength and pride in the role. Leonard Frey as Motel the tailor was also delightful, he was wonderful. I had no problem with him at all. He was really exciting to work with and all the girls were just terrific as well. Neva Small and the others were just lovely. The girls were all carefully chosen and they all knew that they were going to be in a very important film, a film that will truly be the essence of Jewish culture. We had the opportunity to rehearse in London so we rehearsed very, very closely and diligently. We had the whole cast there and we did all the recordings in London and rehearsed all the musical numbers there. We even built the interior of a barn there so Topol would know how many steps he would go up while he sang "If I Were a Rich Man." The designer Bob Boyle would give me exact sketches in advance as we worked out the music and staging. The problem with musicals in the past I've found is that nobody knows how the director is going to shoot it so it becomes almost impossible to know how to score it or stage it. So I had built sets to work out how the numbers will be conceived. Once you lay down the music with the orchestra you are locked into it and it becomes very difficult when you come back to the studio and try and add things and change things. That becomes maddening, so I tried to add everything before.

The procession that was the basis of the lovely and melancholy hymn "Sunrise, Sunset" also proved to be troublesome for Jewison:

> The wedding procession was a difficult number because we had to extend all the music to the beautiful song "Sunrise, Sunset" and also we had to make sure that all the people coming to the wedding carrying candles had their candles lit. So we had to have a battery operator at all times. I love that music in that scene so much and I just fell in love with that whole scene. I spent a lot of time shooting that and getting that lighting perfect, that golden hue.

Jewison's film is an outstanding achievement of memorable set pieces, some of them so perfectly in tune with the core theme of the consequences of transition that at times the film lets you forget the joyous moments by casually delivering the dark moments (and vice versa) indiscriminately. For example, when the eldest daughter Tzeitel (Rosalind Harris) marries her lover Motel (Leonard Frey), their wedding is a strained but ultimately happy occasion. It is also the grounds for an internal mini-revolution as Perchik insists that the men dance with the women, which is something completely unheard of in their Orthodox Jewish culture. When Tevye grabs hold of his wife Golde's (Norma Crane) hand and dances with her, these become his first steps into the realm of experiencing change: and it is a frivolous and happy experience. However, moments later, Tzietel and Motel's wedding is crashed by violently aggressive soldiers of the Russian Tsar, who smash through the place, destroying everything around the Jewish congregation. The image of the Star of David smashed to pieces is both provocative and incredibly political. Left in the shambles of what was firstly a traditional event (albeit a wedding outside of Tevye's approval) and then a home to Perchik's introduction of joyful change is the distraught family, Golde huddling her daughters and Tevye left standing among the ruins looking up to a God that has let this happen. Here he does not speak (something he normally does so well), instead

79

he is given a magnificent piece of music to speak for him. Once again, John Williams works his magic, but this time outside of the Bock score. Williams composed a specific piece of incidental music to close the first act of the film and it is one of the greatest pieces of music the man has ever written—it says everything that Tevye wants to express to God: sadness, defeat, anger and the question of "Why?"

Writer Joseph Stein was open to John Williams and his musical additions to the film adaptation of his work. Williams not only wrote this dramatic piece of music, but he also constructed something that would prove to be the film's signature, as Jewison recalls:

> John Williams wrote a brilliant cadenza at the beginning of the film that grows from the violin! It takes off and that writing is just so beautifully inspired and perfect for Isaac Stern. We also had the London Symphony behind him so the opening was exceptionally brilliant. Then he extended the fiddler scenes with Tevye that occur throughout the film and also he changed the arrangement a bit and inserted a lot of beautiful incidental music for the second half of the film when it gets very dark and takes on a more grim and dark tone. Making the film made it possible to bring in the Russian priests on screen and do very different things that was impossible to do on stage which enhanced the very dark stuff that goes on in the latter half of the film. Joe Stein was great! He was not overly protective of his work and was very open to change and opening up the film. The composers were also very easy to work with, they were happy with the change of direction and staging of certain scenes and musical moments.

Cinematically, the film works on all levels. It consistently looks and sounds superb, and the dramatic elements are well balanced with the dry comedy that permeates the film early on. Most of the comic elements come from the banter shared between Tevye and his long suffering wife Golde, who bicker like people who have been married for more than a lifetime. However, in the midst of all the social and political change that surrounds them, their relationship is the only true stable institution within the story. Their duet "Do You Love Me?" is a quiet, tender moment (one of the only softly sung songs in the entire libretto) that questions their marital union. Theirs is a relationship that is so secure in its complacency that once it's questioned it's shocking. "It's a new world Golde, a new world..." mournfully says Tevye as he leads into "Do You Love Me?," and it's a perfect condensation of a musical devoted to questioning the complexities of change, and at the heart of this change lies the idea of love and commitment. It is a beautiful moment and completely truthful to these two feisty characters. Even through the loving lyrics and moving sentiment they still argue, a testament to the brilliant authenticity of the film's characterizations and writing.

Norman Jewison directs Topol for "If I Were a Rich Man" from *Fiddler on the Roof* (1971)

As far as a songs go, "Far from the Home I Love" is one of the most beautifully realized moments in the film. It is a haunting and deeply sad moment where Hodel decides to leave Russia to join her exiled husband

Perchik, who is being detained in Siberia. Inspired and elegant lyrics such as "Oh what a melancholy choice this is…wanting home….wanting him" magically capture this young girl's worry and woe being forced into an uncertain adulthood. Topol's sad eyes watching Hodel leave sums up the entire moment and his lasting words to God asking that she simply keeps warm are magical stuff. Even more magical is the extraordinarily moving "Chava's Ballet." This incredibly emotionally stirring moment comes late in the piece (in the mournful and downbeat second act) where Golde tells Tevye that Chava has married a young Christian boy (the most extreme act of tradition-breaking). Tevye angrily proclaims that Chava is "dead to us" and Golde races off in tears. As Tevye saddles himself to his cart (now without his lame horse, adding to the misery of the piece) and begins to plough the dead fields he starts to remember Chava and his other daughters and reminisces of simpler times, when they were his "little birds." The music in this sequence—the gorgeous fiddle ringing out such sorrowful tunes—is outstanding, and the staging of this dance, set in silhouette and dreamlike in its approach is sheer movie magic as each girl is seduced and taken away by a suitor, one serenaded by the elfin Fiddler character (Tutte Lemkow) who opens the film and comes to represent the unsteadiness of cultural change.

Jewison remembers both "Chava's Ballet" and the role of the Fiddler:

> That was the choreographer Sammy Bayes who saved that because he was the assistant to Jerome Robbins who had worked on the stage show and I was in awe of Jerome's work in the theatre and I never quite realized why he didn't push to direct this film. He had done *West Side Story*, but I think he felt that that was such a mess of a film production with all the studio and creative politics, where they had to bring in another director to help him, so he may have turned off directing another film. I had Sammy Bayes who knew every step and every move, so I was able to make the transition from the choreography and I was able to explain to Sammy that I wanted to do this number in silhouette and on top of a hilltop, and that we would have to build a tiny stage and set that behind the hill so that the audience wouldn't see it but

the actors could possibly dance without it looking awkward. The Fiddler himself is the heart of the piece; he represents this change that Tevye has to deal with. He also becomes synonymous with Tevye because he is always following him and he's always there. I played him like an elf, like a strange creepy looking fellow who had to work until his fingers bled trying to match the fingering from Isaac Stern. The Fiddler wasn't a musician, he was an actor and a dancer and a mime that I found and who I fell in love with physically. I thought he was perfect for the part. I never paid too much attention to the fact that he had to mimic the work of Isaac Stern! That was hard work! A huge problem! The poor guy would get up on the roof and he would he standing way up high waiting for start that shoot for the opening title sequence. He never had a problem with the choreography or even the height but as soon as we would hit the playback which of course started off with the count in, the poor guy would start playing the violin and almost always immediately Johnny Williams would angrily scream "He's not bowing right! You can't bow like that! That's not spot on!" And this went on over and over again! It was just painful and this was hours and hours after rehearsal. The poor guy was just exhausted and bleeding from his fingers and my goodness I have never put an actor through that much strain or hardship before or since! John Williams is a genius and also an absolute perfectionist, so even when the Fiddler is up there on the roof and set in silhouette, he really, really wanted him to make sure that his fingering and bowing was perfect and completely matching Isaac Stern's tremendous violin playing. Williams wrote an exceptionally beautiful cadenza and extended that music so well that I think he was very proud, as he should have been, of it and this may have contributed to him wanting this Fiddler character to play it correctly. Talk about the sun going down, Jesus Christ! I should have hired a musician who could act and dance, but he had such a great look to him—he was so weird! And my God, I love that last moment of the film where Tevye gives him the nod as if saying "Alright come on! Come with us to the new world."

"Chava's Ballet" in *Fiddler on the Roof* **(1971)**

The last moments of the film follow the mass exodus from Anatevka as a result of the Tsar's command for the Jews to evacuate, and is understandably depressing, letting the mood of the film completely grind to a standstill. The number that leads the procession out of Russia, named after the small town itself, is consciously shot differently to the other musical moments of the film. Here the camera stays stagnant and steady, there are no sweeping shots or quick cuts.

Norman Jewison remembers the staging of "Anatevka," and the choice of locale for his story:

> I wanted it to be very still and very moving and have a visual impact. I wanted to take my time with it whereas normally I move my camera a lot more. Essentially I had done so much television and I had shot so many different numbers, I mean I did *Hit Parade* (circa. 1960s) where I had to shoot ten songs in one hour! So I was used to keep the camera moving and taking it all in. I think I drove the British cameraman mad, but he won the Oscar for it, so there you go! Telling your story in a musical form is the most exciting

thing you can do in film and I think I learned so much on *Fiddler* that when I did *Jesus Christ Superstar* it was possible to take on far more wilder images and crazier movements. Choosing a location was a massive problem firstly. The studio originally wanted me to shoot in America, in Sasquatch Ian which they thought would look like Russia in Spring time with sweeping cornfields and meadowlands, and I thought to myself there was no way it would look like Russia at all. It's too important a picture to fake authenticity, so I went out on a search for locations, I went everywhere I went to Israel and in Romania, but I found a wonderful place called Bausch which was exactly like walking into Anatevka and that was on the border of Russia and Romania, but the London production company wouldn't insure us if we went to Romania. I think politically everyone was kind of pleased to have us there because they thought we had bought a tremendous amount of money there in the shooting, and I had a Yugoslav production manager who later worked with Steven Spielberg and he was very brilliant at handling government problems. But we got along very well with the local people and they were excited to be in a movie because we did a lot of local casting.

Tevye is a loveable buffoon, but also someone whose paralysing fear of change makes him less unlikeable than frustratingly human. The film cleverly paints a picture of very real and very honest people under the great stress of having their heritage destroyed, the ultimate insult. *Fiddler on the Roof* executes all the ideologies of transformative progress and the dilemmas that come with it in a skilful and intelligent manner, making it impossible not to be swept away with the drama as well as the majestic musicality of the piece. Norman Jewison's keen insight into the foundation of the story comes across vividly and directly, but he never upstages the human drama and sweeping spectacle. He says:

> It's really about the agony of Tevye, because he is suffering the most with the breakdown of traditions. We discussed this

and essentially all my life I've been a rebel. I was marching in Los Angeles anti-Vietnam war demonstrations, so I was very aware of the politics of Fiddler, but essentially most of the traditions in the film are religious ones and social ones cemented in the Jewish tradition, and in that way it probably hits home to more contemporary times and young people.

The closing moments of *Fiddler on the Roof* are grim, its darkness intensified when we speculate what will eventually happen to a lot of these Jewish travellers heading towards Eastern Europe. Will Tevye's grandchildren eventually face the horrors of Adolf Hitler and the Holocaust? This is something that the musical leaves us with in the final moments, where the Fiddler is finally allowed to go along with Tevye and his cavalcade, and as they roll on by the final note rings out. A very realistic terror has surfaced in Jewison's film, and this continues throughout many of the movie musicals to come from the 1970s (as seen in equally brilliant films such as Bob Fosse's 1972 picture *Cabaret*). But more fantastical darkness will weave its way into the musical genre of the decade, and the integrated song-and-story exercise will borrow from a related escapist movie genre in its methods and madness.

DON'T CARE HOW, I WANT IT NOW:
Willy Wonka and the Chocolate Factory

Horror movie tropes exist within many other film genres, from straight-down-the-line, character-driven melodramas right through to family entertainment geared towards children. And of course, when these family films concentrate on the plights, struggles and lessons taught to children, then the horror can be used to heighten the fragility of the young, as represented by the masked, faceless men in black in *ET: The Extra Terrestrial* (1982). Alternatively, they can even be at the heart of childish, selfish evil, as *Willy Wonka and the Chocolate Factory* handles beautifully.

Willy Wonka and the Chocolate Factory is a musical fantasy based on a book by Roald Dahl, with songs by Anthony Newley and Leslie Bricusse. Five children are the focal point of the story, one good, while the remaining four are "bad eggs." Charlie Bucket (Peter Ostrum) is a sweet boy who is fatherless but in a loving but poor household surrounded by bedridden grandparents and a laundress mother who worries about the downtrodden but caring boy. Charlie's difference is not only marked by his poverty and loneliness, but by his goodness and kindness. He is an honest and good-natured boy, but not completely flawless either. Like Pinocchio, little Charlie Bucket is capable of going off the straight path. Of course, by the end of the picture, he stays true to good form and triumphs.

Gene Wilder as the enigmatic Willy Wonka in *Willy Wonka and the Chocolate Factory* (1971)

Charlie's peers in the film that are not the four central "bad eggs" exist at a distance from Charlie: they don't interact with him, leaving our likeable hero to really only have two central connections: the first is his Grandpa Joe (Jack Albertson), a whimsical old fool who even though is deep down good hearted and loving towards Charlie, is careless and opportunistic. The other is the titular Willy Wonka (Gene Wilder), an eccentric but elusive confectionary mogul who runs a beloved chocolate factory in the heart of an unnamed town (the film is shot in Munich, but this is clearly to establish the far away Neverland the film wants to convey). Wonka, in turn. is an untapped father figure for young Charlie Bucket much like the dewy skinned alien in *ET: The Extra Terrestrial* is to Elliot and The Terminator is to John Connor in *Terminator 2: Judgement Day* (1991). However, Willy Wonka is presented to us as a dark, almost sinister character. He sits in the middle of charm and elegance and downright menace and sickly kookiness. He also sits in the middle of truth and lies; he is the master of illusion and, much like Mary Poppins before him, is obsessed with firmly taking heed of rules and responsibility. Gene Wilder does wonders with all of this and it truly is an inspirational performance, where every single nuance and gesture is executed with idyllic flair and razzle dazzle. Wilder's comic abilities are so finely tuned that it is impossible to not watch him and smile.

Gene Wilder and Peter Ostrum take a break on the set of *Willy Wonka and the Chocolate Factory* (1971)

Charlie Bucket's trust is earned by the end of the film, but it is a rocky road. However, all turns out good for our sweet kid protagonist, but the four "bad eggs" are not so lucky. As the plot kicks in, the film introduces us one-by-one to these four vile children. Augstus Gloop (Michael Bollner) is a gluttonous, piggish boy whose dismissal and exclusion from the group comes early on. It is obvious that he will be the child first killed off as he somehow comes to represent the exact physical type that Darwinism teaches us will not survive. He is overweight, lazy and slow, a necessary pawn in the survival of the fittest. Violet Beauregard (Denise Nickerson) is a precocious brat obsessed with chewing gum, and even more unhealthily, obsessed with competition. Ignoring advice and instructions causes her to turn blue and blow up into a round human blueberry. Violet's crass competitiveness makes her an ugly child, and therefore her physical transition becomes an extension of such repulsive behaviour. Her bad habit (incessant gum chewing) consumes her. Veruca Salt (Julie Dawn Cole) is possibly the most horrible of the children. Veruca is a nasty piece of work, a self-involved brat whose greediness results in her demise.

Laying down the tracks for *Willy Wonka and the Chocolate Factory* (1971)

Actress Julie Dawn Cole remembers reading the character for the first time:

> When I first read the description of Veruca Salt, I thought she was absolutely despicable, but oh what fun it was

89

to be allowed to be that naughty and nasty. We went by what was on the page and that was what we actually shot. But Mel Stuart the director, was always encouraging me to be meaner and nastier. All of that wonderful pushing and shoving that went on between Denise who played Violet and myself was something we tentatively started to do. Mel spotted it and he pounced on it and made us take it a bit further.

A highlight of the film is Veruca's solo song "I Want It Now," a lively energetic number that begins as a list song where she lists the things she wants: a bean feast, ribbons in her hair, ten thousand tons of ice-cream. It gradually becomes a cry of dominance and relentless greed. Her grandiose desires go from performing baboons to wanting the world, today and tomorrow. This violent greed proves to destroy Veruca, and her descent into the furnace chute is quickly followed by her pathetic father (Roy Kinnear), whose life is completely empty without his daughter, diving in after her. Grandpa Joe states, "Well Mr. Salt finally got what he always wanted, Veruca went first." It is an odd comment, clearly in there for laughs (one of the many specifically adult-themed gags that pepper the script) but it holds a truth: Mr. Salt is so ruined by the demands of his monstrous daughter that after she has gone, there is no more need for him. He purely exists to serve her, like a manservant to a wicked powerful oppressor.

Cole recalls:

> I recorded my song before shooting started. I went out to Munich Germany and recorded it in an enormous studio. The orchestra had recorded separately so I sang along to the backing track with enormous headphones. When I originally auditioned for the part, the song had not been written so my audition song was "Happy Birthday." Then once it had been penned by Anthony Newley and Lesley Bricusse, I went to practice and audition with Walter Schaffe in his hotel on Park Lane. At this point they were still prepared to have me dubbed if I couldn't handle the arrangement. But after a very short while (and I was surprised how short!) Walter, said,

"Yes! I think you can sing it!" Back in Germany after the recording, they gave me a reel to reel tape recorder to practice the lip sync, in my hotel room, and I rehearsed on Saturdays with Howard Jeffrey, the choreographer.

In *Willy Wonka and the Chocolate Factory*, the film makes a clear statement about parent-child relations, commenting on the importance of limits and the power of saying "no." The final child of the group is Mike Teevee (Paris Themmen), a loud, brash little terror, devoid of any humanity. His obsession with television is unlike Carol-Ann Freeling's in *Poltergeist* (1982), who channels the "TV People" and is seduced by them, becoming victimized by evil forces; instead, Mike's love for television acts as a means of escape that makes him even more anti-social and self-important. Each of these children are monsters based in reality, and in this fantasy world of a brightly lit chocolate factory their awfulness is heightened.

The film can be read as another retelling of "The Twelve Little Indians," a story archetype used namely in slasher movies. Here it is used much in the same way as one by one kids are "killed off," either metaphorically or realistically. Either way, it is all done with style and class: it is an intelligent condensation of the importance of listening, taking advice and being honest and good like little Charlie Bucket, who eventually gets to inherit Wonka's factory. Charlie is so good that he even shows concern for the others: "What about the other children Mr. Wonka?" Even the most repugnant crass children such as Veruca and company are a cause of concern and worry for the innocent Charlie Bucket.

The vile children in *Willy Wonka and the Chocolate Factory* represent different aspects of the monstrousness of childhood: the unattractive, selfish and self-involved element of pre-adolescence, a world completely consumed by the benefit of the self. A violent end comes to these horrid children: Augustus's near drowning then being stuck in a piping system, Violet's painful transformation, Veruca's descent into a furnace and Mike's fragmentation and consequential shrinking all summarize the emptiness of these children's lives and the throwaway nature of their supposed evil. In *Willy Wonka and the Chocolate Factory*, the mean kids are not at all threatening, but they are rather more of a nuisance, like flies at a barbeque. Like flies, they need to be swatted in order for pleasantness to be maintained.

The core reasoning behind the children's demise is that they are consumed by emptiness, products of a world of materialism, bad habits and greed. Charlie is hungry for happiness, yet takes all woe in his stride and moves forward. His selfless acts (such as using the tiny bit of money he makes from doing a paper route to buy his family a loaf of bread) cements his difference from the others. He even teaches his Grandpa Joe a thing or two. Willy Wonka himself has a palpable dark side and shows little to no dismay at the consequences of the bad children, and is like the Pied Piper of lollipop land, but through the honesty of Charlie Bucket, even he learns that absolute goodness can come from children.

Jack Albertson and the "Oompa Loompas" on the set of *Willy Wonka and the Chocolate Factory* (1971)

Wonka has adopted childlike men in the form of green haired/orange skinned Oompa Loompas, who act as the film's moral majority.

These diminutive helpers to Wonka are refugees from a fabricated homeland that was under attack by violent creatures and throughout the movie they function as the Greek chorus of a morality play. At the coda of each child's (and respective parent's) dismissal, the Oompa Loompas sing short message sonnets, cautionary tales about over-indulgence, bad habits, greed and anti-social behaviour. In the song for Veruca's elimination, they state that it is "Mother and Father" to blame for a child's repugnant behaviour. These elders are pathetic and weasel-like fools, and just as repellent as the children: Violet's father is a shmuck completely obsessed with making a car sale even in Wonka-land, Mike's mother is pretentious and full of complaints, Mr. Salt is a pathetic simp under the thumb of his demanding daughter, and Mrs. Gloop (Ursula Reit) does not seem to mind her son overindulging.

Julie Dawn Cole remembers:

> I don't think I modelled Veruca on any one person that I knew, I just said the words and gave it as much oomph as I could. It was more like unleashing the bad side of myself that was always kept in check by my mother. I also strongly believe that Willy Wonka will always just be Gene Wilder to me. He was a lovely, patient, warm and funny human being. I will let others make up their minds as to what the character represents. But I do think that the children's fates weren›t so much punishments as they were consequences. The children were told not to do things, and they ignored the warnings which is a very good lesson! We all need to learn that there are consequences to our actions.

Willy Wonka and the Chocolate Factory is a masterfully played cautionary tale, transfixed on childhood cynicism and selfishness, treating ill-mannered children as disposable pests. In relation to the realm of the evil child subgenre of horror cinema, director Mel Stuart's musical take on Roald Dahl's offbeat creepy story truly hits home: it delivers mean spirited children, but unlike most cinema of the *les enfante terribles*, these children have no real sinister powers. Instead, they are at the mercy of someone who is completely insane and potentially violent: Willy Wonka himself.

Cole says:

> The film does have a sinister edge to it, but all kids like to be scared just a little. It was unusual for its time, as the only other children's films were Disney movies and killing kids off did not happen in Disney films. Of course it also shows the parents in a bad light. So it just shows what will happen to any child without proper parenting. If you think about it on a serious level it was not really the kids' faults that they were the way they were.

However, in all it is wonderfully delightful and refreshing darkness, and there is a lot of bright energy in there that is joyous and extremely moving. It is nothing short of perfect, and like *Fiddler on the Roof*, it does everything right. When Gene Wilder sings "Pure Imagination" you are swept into the romance of escapist cinema, which is exactly what you want.

Julie Dawn Cole remembers seeing the set where the "Pure Imagination" number was staged:

> The *pure imagination* room was beautiful. One of the nice things about being pre-CGI is that it was all "real." Mel Stuart was keen that we didn't see the set before the big reveal, but what I never let on was that before he made this pronouncement I had already been shown round it, by a studio hand. I kept my mouth shut and never said a word, pretending to be just as amazed as everyone else.

When the world is as dull and dreary as Charlie Bucket's, what you need is that brightly lit, mesmerizing chocolate factory and this is what the musical at its best can do: it lifts the spirits, takes you away for a moment and brings you pure joy. The very greatest examples also provide the darkness to counter and add texture to that experience. *Willy Wonka and the Chocolate Factory* masters this balancing act to perfection.

Film festival director Briony Kidd shares her own personal insight into the film:

> It's basically everything a child could want in one movie. A rags to riches story like *Oliver!*, but with a marvellous chocolate factory as well. It's scary. It's weird. It's fun. There's singing and dancing and burping. And there's absolutely no romance. It's not perfect of course, some scenes hold less interest. For example, it still feels odd to me to watch the song 'Cheer Up Charlie' minus the VHS tracking marks of my childhood, as I only ever watched that bit in fast forward. The Oompa Loompas singing and dancing the moral after each child does the wrong thing is one aspect that stands out now as almost revolutionary. Perhaps every child's conscience is like a singing and dancing Oompa Loopma, but the message to viewers is clear: You are free to be as naughty and selfish as you like. But be prepared to be the one we make fun of and sing means songs about. You won't be decent like Charlie Bucket, you'll be just another schmuck. It's an idea that allows children their humanity, paradoxically. Their actions do matter, they're just as capable as being "no good" as anyone. We're left with four children who are responsive, extroverted and driven by impulse, and one child who is introverted, thoughtful and who bides his time. The loudest voice doesn't win. Those who grab and grasp and struggle don't win. Intelligence and sensitivity are depicted as strength. I'm fairly idealistic about the 1970s but I really feel like this wasn't such a radical notion back in 1971. In the era of reality television and child pageants, it really is.

SUBSTITUTIARY LOCOMOTION: *Bedknobs and Broomsticks*

Disney's first great feature of the 1970s picked up from where *The Aristocats* failed, and it was also one of the studio's most surprisingly dark films, while also certainly one of the most complex in regard to themes and its narrative. Leaping off from the incredible success of *Mary Poppins*, the enchanting, elegant, intelligent and socially-aware *Bedknobs and Broomsticks* not only continued where *Mary Poppins* left with its marriage of live-action and animation, but also featured a very proper, very dignified and very magical leading female protagonist. Eglantine Price is a pragmatic Englishwoman with a mysterious secret—she's an apprentice witch! Not only that, this apprentice witch is about to take on the Nazis, who are set to invade England at the beginning of the 1940s! What a plot and what a brilliant musical!

After a great title sequence designed to look like a medieval tapestry (later the film will explore that historical period, emphasising its honor and nobility), the film opens with three young children being evacuated to Dorset in the south of the United Kingdom at the dawn of World War II. They are reluctantly taken in by Eglantine Price (played by the wonderful Angela Lansbury) who really has no time to look after children; she has more important things on her mind like learning the ancient art of witchcraft in order to defend England and fend off the vile Nazis. Lansbury's eloquence and sophistication as this motorcycle riding, no-nonsense, kooky little witch is just mesmerizing to watch as she flutters about making proud observations with bright and charming flair. There is also great warmth to this shut-off loner, who although does come across as stern and authoritarian (much like the Christ-figure that is Mary Poppins) is also at heart a woman completely damaged by her surroundings and personal experience. When she teaches the children all about "The Age of Not Believing" we get a sense of sorrow: here is a woman desperately trying to hold on to some kind of magic in a world that will soon be robbed of any semblance of childhood wonder. When she sings about this "age of not believing" she is truly singing out the lonely cry of someone who does not want the rest of the world to lose what she has: a sense of hope and enchantment. The song also acts as a perfect analogy of a period in which Disney films and other fantasy movies were losing audiences. Children—and children at heart—were losing interest, and had "stopped believing," and *Bedknobs and Broomsticks* seems to be well aware of this fact.

As Eglantine introduces the children to magic, they gradually accept that she is a witch and join her for the ride. Much like the magical nanny Mary Poppins and the children she governed, Eglantine enlightens these little evictees and with a steady and straight hand, teaching them the

"Bobbing Along" in *Bedknobs and Broomsticks* (1971)

value of believing in something beyond the harsh realities of a country about to be involved in the atrocities of war. The beauty of Lansbury's sensitive portrayal of the zealous witch lies in her ability to espouse an element of melancholic isolation: she is someone completely detached from other people and solely committed to a noble but ultimately lonely cause. Eglantine has no real understanding of children, and when she first takes in the three war orphans she is in over her head—and the tykes are completely aware of this fact—and she also has a strained idea of romance. However, both of these things will soon change as the film progresses, and much like the transformative developments that happen in *Mary Poppins* where characters grow, learn and become aware of others, in this film the changes occur far more subtly. But this works for both the film and the character of Eglantine herself.

This exploration into the character of Eglantine was originally neglected as the song "Nobody's Problems," which highlights her loneliness and suggests her growing need and desire to have Emelius (a con-artist and self-proclaimed professor played with delectable goodness by David Tomlinson) as her lover and the children as her fulltime wards, was originally cut from the theatrical version of the film. The cut was made because the studio felt the song slowed the film down, and that this sombre and introspective number came about far too late in the piece. Executives at Disney felt that it sidestepped the Nazi and the fun, magical animated elements and sequences of the film (the sugar that keeps the kiddies interested). "Nobody's Problems" is a beautifully written character-insight number, and song writing team the Sherman brothers insisted that it remain in the film stating that it fuelled the Eglantine character's motivation and story arc as she comes to acknowledge the merits of companionship. Sadly, the theatrical cut omitted this terrific soliloquy and it took many years for it to be restored with an anniversary DVD release of the movie released through Disney's vaults.

Bedknobs and Broomsticks counterbalances two kinds of magic: the literal magic bought upon by witchcraft and sorcery, and the magic of wonder and childhood belief. Like all the great Disney and family fantasy movies, these two kinds of magic are perfectly balanced and compliment characters and situations splendidly. There is not one moment in *Bedknobs and Broomsticks* where character is not the principal focal point, from Eglantine's obsession with perfecting her spells to Emelius's own strange misanthropy diminishing as he gets swept off his feet by Eglantine. This is a film that honors its characters and articulates their motivations through song and elegant storytelling. The literal magic of the film is magnificently handled: one of the children is turned into a rabbit, Eglantine wrestles with a broomstick as she tries to take off on it (a perfect sequence, like a child trying to get the hang of riding a bicycle) and in the fantastic climax, medieval armour comes to life and fights alongside the British Home Guard. The first song of the piece is sung by the old Home Guard (a troop of decrepit old men but still utterly devoted to defending England) and evokes the notion of the quiet strength of the United Kingdom. It suggests Germany should never underestimate ole' Britannia. The visual effects (the non-animated tangible practical effects) are impressive and well plotted, making the film thoroughly and consistently engaging. The film won the coveted Academy Award for Best Visual Effects in 1971 as well, and rightfully so. The dancing clothes that come to life and the armour going to battle are marvels of special effects. The armour itself was built in Spain and used in the epic *El Cid* (1961) and then later used in the musical *Camelot* (1967).

The romantic plotline of the film is also judiciously handled. When Emelius sings "Eglantine," it bounces with joy and frivolity. Here is a man who is childlike but alien, and his background in peddling is craftily used to "seduce" the headstrong Eglantine. In *Mary Poppins*, David Tomlinson had played the cantankerous, money loving Mr. Banks who learns to love his children, but here he plays a comic buffoon who learns to appreciate responsibility and the unselfish care for children (and his country). It is a wonderful polar opposite of his brilliant performance in *Mary Poppins* and suits him perfectly. When he leads "Portobello Road" we get an insight into his character's whimsical outlook on life as the citizens of the merchant village peddle their wares and dance up a storm. The sequence is electric, buzzing with energy and it bounces the film into a new direction: the first half of the picture is subtle and takes its time, but from the "Portobello Road" number the film speeds up and becomes action packed.

The Sherman brothers with Angela Lansbury and David Tomlinson on the set of *Bedknobs and Broomsticks* (1971)

The romantic "The Beautiful Briny" is a magnificent moment, where we enter the world where live-action and animation intersect. During this number, Eglantine and Emelius defy gravity under the waters of the island of Naboombu and dance amidst the seaweed and curious animated fish. Much like "It's a Jolly Holiday with Mary" from *Mary Poppins*, this number unites animated characters with human performers and adds to the romance. When the human characters are dragged onto the island of Naboombu, it is a masterful spectacle as we are greeted by talking bears, secretary birds and lions, and witness an entertaining soccer match. Superb films such as the ground breaking *Who Framed Roger Rabbit?* (1988) would take up where *Mary Poppins* and *Bedknobs and Broomsticks* left off in regard to the union of live-action and animation and deliver an even more incredible result—the lepine tribute to cartoons and *film noir* would go on to be one of the most important films of the 1980s.

Angela Lansbury's perfect diction and handle on the Sherman brothers' lyrics are her signature in the film. Her performance of the great "Substitutuary Locomotion" is divine, and she gives Eglantine so much depth and warmth that we care about what *she* wants, not so much what she can do for others. Throughout the entire film, Eglantine is determined to protect her country and defend those she has grown to love, but when she discovers that personal happiness is also something to be examined her character changes.

Along with all the great songs and engaging set pieces from the underwater dance sequence (one that foreshadows the Oscar-wining number "Under the Sea" from Disney's *The Little Mermaid* many years later) to the shootout involving the zombie-like medieval soldier uniforms, the epicene Roddy McDowall also makes a wonderful addition to the film as a nosey clergyman. He is a delight to watch as he fusses about trying to make sense of a world about to be in the throes of war.

The film also begs similarities to be drawn with the wonderful *Chitty Chitty Bang Bang* (1968), a musical film that features a tangible threat in the guise of the Child Catcher (played to creepy perfection by Robert Helpmann), there to eradicate the children acting as an extended arm of the metaphoric rise of Nazism that the film engages with. The magical car musical is set at the beginning of the 1900s but Ian Fleming's book upon which the film is based, was written in the late 1960s and heavily influenced by the concept of war and the idea of political upheaval being detrimental to the safety and wellbeing of children. Fleming himself wrote the book *for* his children, a departure from his famous James

Bond novels that were widely successful and the source for multiple film adaptations starting with *Dr. No* (1962). Many of *Chitty Chitty Bang Bang*'s themes turn up in *Bedknobs and Broomsticks*, but in this witchy Disney picture Nazism is made very real, and the threat of impending war is palpable. When Eglantine renounces her witchery and interest in witchcraft by the end of the film, this newly domesticated woman surprisingly becomes even more heroic, as if her efforts throughout the film are paid off by giving her a human connection.

Bedknobs and Broomsticks cements Disney's movie musicals as some of the greatest ever made, and it is a beautiful companion piece to the rich, perfect *Mary Poppins*. The two films were directed by Robert Stevenson, and he structures both films in distinctly different ways, but they are still well-fitted. His aesthetic for each movie is also different: *Bedknobs and Broomsticks* is, for the most part, painted with bleak and muted colours until the bed takes off with gloriously coloured opticals, or when the almost dreamlike Portobello Road with the soft focus and cloudy appearance, and of course when we enter Naboombu the animated colours take off with great gusto. *Mary Poppins* does not share this transitional multi-layered palette, but rather stays lush and rich ala classic Disney. *Bedknobs and Broomsticks* is indicative of the changing look of Disney: simple, direct and sharp. But regardless, both films are masterpieces, and *Bedknobs and Broomsticks* remains a much loved favourite, in large part due to its fearless acceptance of setting a musical fantasy children's film against a grim background.

The incredibly talented principal dancer Sonja Haney remembers the shoot and the process of making the film, and most notably recalls the famous "Portobello Road" sequence:

> Dancers, unless they are dancing in for a lead or assisting the choreographer, do not receive a script/screenplay. And, unless it's an historic book/story or has acclaim as a play or musical that is generally known, the story is not necessarily divulged, either. Rehearsals are generally with only piano, so unless the dancer is involved with the pre-record in some way, the fully orchestrated music is not heard until after the film's release. On the set, while filming, the dancer is

101

hearing the full orchestration for the dance number for the first time, and only for the dance number being filmed at that time. Orchestrations for dance numbers are usually (in my experience) developed during rehearsals, notated by the rehearsal pianist/dance arranger then fully orchestrated. I remember that it was shot in sections; the number calls for many different groups of characters in many different costumes and when it was your "turn" you had to make sure you were ready to dive right in! We rehearsed for weeks, and were quite prepared and I am quite sure at least some choreography was developed and tweaked during rehearsals. We had several weeks of rehearsal. Donald MacKayle the choreographer would give us class every morning, and then would disappear to work with the leads. He would return late in the day to rehearse with us, but while waiting for his return, the soundstage looked like an arts & crafts club; projects to do while waiting to rehearse. Most of us hooked rugs, did needle point, knitted, played cards or simply read. One dancer started her own business making Macramé, which later developed into a successful business designing dance clothes! I was fitted into a dress exactly like I had worn in high school! Sleeveless, tight waist with a belted full skirt and the red and white print was designed in squares. Great to dance in, and fun! Angela Lansbury was a peach! I did not work with her on camera, but she always went to the Commissary for lunch with all the dancers and the crew. She was consistently warm and friendly. Seems to me, she's the person who told us the Commissary at Disney actually served hot fudge sundaes! My belief is that David Tomlinson had a great time playing such a delightful fellow, but I don't remember being around him during shooting. I did have an opportunity to watch a rehearsal of the "under water" scene in which they actually were flown. Two wonderful dancers, Larri Thomas and Casse Jaeger, were the doubles for Angela and David. Sadly, both those wonderful dancers, whose resumes are filled with so many films and television shows, have passed. For me, I also think that this terrible history about World War II must be kept alive. Disney provides the truth but does it charmingly. But for me, the most memorable thing about working on the film was auditioning with the boys at their audition and being chosen to dance alongside so many brilliant dancers for the incomparable choreographer, Donald MacKayle and his incredible assistant, Carolyn Dyer. Dancing in a Disney musical and shooting on the Disney lot was frosting on the cake!

TWIGGY'S 1920s: *The Boy Friend*

The strange, spooky elements of *Bedknobs and Broomsticks* will soon become far more articulated as the years go on, and more malevolent monsters (rather than sweet natured apprentice witches) will surface, giving the musical motion picture a new and creepy edge. But before the very clearly defined marriage between horror and musicals found its way onto the silver screen, it is worth examining the English auteur who gave musical life to a sexually confused classical composer.

With 1970's *The Music Lovers* stirring some interest in semi-experimental musical films, Ken Russell channelled his keen interest in story with song when he adapted Sandy Wilson's musical tribute to the Roaring Twenties, *The Boy Friend*. Released the same year as Russell's controversial and very personal *The Devils* (1971), *The Boy Friend* is completely different than his previous musical venture: the Tchaikovsky saga was dense and confronting, whereas this musical is bright, energetic, fun and frilly. The film's tagline read: "A Glittering Super Colossal Heart Warming Toe-Tapping Continuously Delightful Musical Extravaganza" and it is: Russell's film does wonders with the original material and injects it with 1970s flamboyance and hyper-decadence.

Starring the iconic British model Twiggy, the film tells the story of young stage manager Polly (played with wide-eyed beauty by Twiggy herself), who is forced to understudy the leading lady of a play where a big time Hollywood director is watching, ready to cast his new film. Polly concocts grandiose fantasies in her mind's eye (she envisions an epic variant of the old British musical *The Boy Friend*) and here is where the film flourishes with visual flair, stylistic magic and quiet honestly. It is

103

a genuine article harkening to the golden age of musicals without losing track of its modern sensibilities.

Interestingly, Russell consciously neglects the original material's romance with screwball English musical comedies of the 1920s: after all, Sandy Wilson's original musical was a pastiche piece, completely indebted to these seldom appreciated wordy musicals (most of which were diegetic backstage musicals). Here in the filmic adaptation, Russell instead pays homage to the musicals of Vincente Minnelli and Busby Berkley, and he owes more tribute to Arthur Freed than the droll comic witticisms of British musicals of the ragtime period. Thankfully Russell chooses this route as the original musical is far too dry and bland for an audience ready to sink into "divine decadence." The ragtime period is also distinctly American, and would be lost in translation if he stuck to an English sensibility. The Americanisation of Russell's film is perfectly realized and skilfully handled, and there is nothing flat or uninteresting in his approach. Russell and his company deliver the pseudo-psychedelic wackiness with relentless gusto. The dizzying visuals are spectacular and extreme, elevating the simplicity of the plot.

And Twiggy is electric. By her very essence, she is *the* working class heroine—both in real life just as much as she is in Ken Russell's semi-experimental musical. She possesses a serene sense of bewilderment that is believable and at times heartbreaking. Her simple acting choices are an extension of her successes as a high fashion model, and her ability to connect and concentrate on the situations and the story's hyper-realism that surrounds her are not at all forced or phony. There is tangible working class intelligence to her, and it lends itself well to her sweet and straightforward performance in *The Boy Friend*. She bounces through the film with grace and silliness, allowing herself to be freethinking and feeling and every time she hits the screen. Whether in extreme close-up or dancing the Charleston on a glitzy staircase, she lights up the film with a fruity, feathery frivolity.

But the film is not without its depth and self-reflexive characteristics. There are moments where the satirical outlook on movie musicals as a piece of art and as a historical reference point come crashing down and introspective. There is a conflict and sense of nuisance in the break-out into song in some of the film's set pieces, and for Polly the dreams are

Twiggy and Christopher Gable in *The Boy Friend* (1971)

not without their heartbreak. The film bounces back and forth from lavishly staged musical number to reflective self-scrutiny, and Russell is a master at weaving in and out of these positions. One can't help think that Ken Russell may have been an interesting choice as director of the film version of the ground breaking therapy musical *A Chorus Line* which sadly got an atrocious movie adaptation way too late in 1985.

The very talented Twiggy remembers making the film:

> I'd actually been to see a revival of "The Boy Friend" in London around 1968, and absolutely loved it. As luck would have it, I was having dinner with Ken Russell and his lovely wife Shirley the next evening. I was telling Ken about the show, and how fabulous it was, and it was out of that conversation that Ken had the idea of making it into a film, with me playing Polly Brown. It's a wonderful stage musical. A pastiche on the 1920s, and I absolutely fell in love with it, as most people do when they see it. Ken had become a really good friend after I met him around 1967. I was a huge fan of his early work on TV in the UK. He did a series of films on "Omnibus" about classical composers, and one on Isadora Duncan, and they were ground breaking. He then

went on to making feature films, and my particular favourite then, and still, is *Women in Love*. So yes, I think you can say I was a huge fan. As you can see in the film *The Devils*, I was only in it for a nanosecond, we filmed my little piece in one day. Ken just wanted me to experience being on a big film set. As you can imagine, it was pretty awe inspiring, and a bit scary. But it was clever of him to let me experience it before we started filming *The Boyfriend*. Because of the way Ken re-wrote the script for the film, I was playing a young assistant stage director, for an amateur theatrical company, who suddenly gets thrown on to the stage to play the lead role, because the leading lady has an accident, and can't go on. So I played Polly as a rather naive, very scared young lady, who suddenly experiences the thrill of performing. I think the musical numbers are wonderful; Ken had such a brilliant flair and exuberance, and wanted to pay homage to the great Busby Berkley (the brilliant Hollywood choreographer from the 1930s). We also had Tommy Tune staging most of the big dance numbers, and he is brilliant. Again, Ken always had such a brilliant vision when it came to the art direction of his films. Also, Shirley, his wife, who did all the costumes, was a huge influence on all of his films, and definitely on the look of them. We also had the absolutely brilliant Tony Walton as our Art Director. He is one of the great Art Directors and designers, and I am lucky and proud to call him my dear friend. Tommy Tune and I got on like a house on fire from the moment we met. He is truly one of the great tap dancers of all time- so to have the chance to work with him, and learn from him, was fantastic for me. We became great friends, and it was from working on *The Boyfriend* together, that the idea for our Broadway show *My One and Only* came about. I had always thought I wouldn't have the courage to perform live on stage, let alone Broadway. But with Tommy at the helm as the director/ choreographer, I knew I was in great hands. He had already directed many Broadway shows, including the award winning, *Nine* and

The Best Little Whorehouse in Texas, among many others. The experience of doing *My One and Only* on Broadway was one of the highlights of my career, to sing all those wonderful Gershwin songs every night, and dance with Tommy, was a glorious experience. Probably the hardest scene to shoot was when Christopher Gable and myself had to dance on a huge replica of a phonograph record, because it rotated, and as we danced, the force of the rotation was pulling us to the outer edges of the record. It was very hard to keep our balance! Therefore, we had to do many many takes, but we got it in the end—and the result is a beautifully shot scene. I think it's always a great time for the movie musical, from the 1930s through to the present day. If done properly, and with the right cast, the movie musical is a wonderful genre.

ZAPPADU AND THE COWBOYS ON ACID:
200 Motels and *Zachariah*

Enigmatic and versatile musician Frank Zappa combined forces with visionary director Tony Palmer to give a nutsy visual voice to the long term romance rock'n'roll artists have had with "the road." *200 Motels* explores the madness and disillusionment of musical geniuses driven crazy by a small town mentality. While on the road (their road to freedom of expression and instigator of artistic creativity—and insanity) the surrealism of psychedelic rock, drug culture, sexual promiscuity and the chaotic anarchic social meshing of various freaks and weirdoes elevates the featured band, The Mothers of Invention, to a plane of higher learning, while at the same time they plummet down a Dadaist vortex. The film is a cartoon-like hyperactive nightmare, and is difficult to swallow at first watch. But during the course of multiple viewings and coming at the film from various angles (most notably from one as a musician or someone who fully comprehends the ideologies and almost folkloric properties of rock'n'roll life on the road), the film is a vibrant and engaging mess.

Zappa was not only a rock musician, but a composer, sound designer, producer and as *200 Motels* indicates, a filmmaker. He was an extraordinary auteur, and his interest in visually examining and dissecting the concepts of song writing and breaking down the notion of rock'n'roll clichés are vivid, if at times a little too bizarre to enjoy. But his work is important and it is thankfully more raw and energetic than self-indulgent and crass for its own sake.

Film historian Kier-La Janisse says:

> I think I was just the right age to appreciate *200 Motels* when I first saw it. I was a teenager and had accidentally eaten half a pan of hash brownies. But it was because of that film and its incredible visuals and music that I became interested in so many things, from Flo & Eddie to the GTOs. I was so obsessed with Miss Lucy from the GTOs that I even started wearing boy's underpants because she wears them in the film. And while many people find the film too lysergic to be anything but a curiosity piece, it actually works really well as a manic tour diary, and the kinds of in-jokes that come from spending long periods in close quarters with other creative types. It also was co-directed by Tony Palmer, who is music-doc royalty, and has animation by Murakami-Wolf who also did *The Point* (also 1971). It's an essential 1970s film as far as I'm concerned. Many years ago, I had the opportunity to have Pamela DesBarres in person because she was teaching a writing workshop related to her book "I'm With the Band"—as you know, Miss Pamela was a key member of the GTOs and featured prominently in the film—and so as a tie-in I suggested a screening of *200 Motels*. I found a 16mm film print of it with Swank Motion Pictures, who handled back-catalogue titles for many major studios, including Columbia who had rights on *200 Motels*. But apparently there was a legal dispute about who actually had the rights, and we got stuck in the middle of it. I got a call from Gail Zappa's assistant, who was telling me everything she said as she was screaming behind him (I could hear her just fine)—saying we had no permission to show the film, that Columbia didn't own the film, that it was disrespectful to Frank, that Pamela had no right to use his film to promote

herself. It wasn't even Pamela's idea, it was my idea and she unfortunately took some flak for it as well. Gail wanted us to hand the film print over to her saying that she technically owned it, and of course there was no way we could do this, because we had a legal contract with Swank, who had a legal contract with Columbia. So eventually Columbia stepped in and dealt with it but it was a bit of a nightmare.

200 Motels has been classed in the "surrealist documentary" subcategory and the incredible combination of the London Symphonic Orchestra, Ringo Starr, Keith Moon and choreographer Gillian Lynne (who would work on *The Muppet Show* and the 1980s hit musical *Cats*, 1981 on the West End) makes the film a bizarre cocktail of sexual frivolity, pseudo-biography about a band and their creation of an album, as Janisse points out, a perpetual in-joke.

More surrealist drug-induced concept work surfaced in the year with the pseudo-western *Zachariah*. Loosely based on the novel "Siddhartha" by Hermann Hesse, *Zachariah* is a diegetic musical featuring a Greek chorus called The Crackers, played by the band Country Joe and the Fish, who were instrumental in the formation of psychedelic rock. Much like the fellow acid-westerns to come out of the 1970s such as *Greaser's Palace* (1972), *Dirty Little Billy* (1972) and the remarkable *El Topo* (1970), *Zachariah* relies heavily on the deconstruction of the foundations of golden age westerns such as everything leading up to the magnificent *The Searchers* (1956), while fusing spaghetti-westerns of the same period and injecting it with a hippie agenda and a metaphysical edge. The musicality of the film is heavily satirical in that Country Joe and the Fish as the insane and "not-very-good" The Crackers play with the concept of isolation and self-reflection, treated with such profound seriousness in films such as Sydney Pollack's self-important *Jeremiah Johnson* (1972). This is what makes *Zachariah* watchable: it does not take itself seriously. It is creatively toying with the sometimes rigid and airy allegorical acid-westerns that came out around the same time, and having the film be a semi-musical also helped. With artists such as Joe Walsh and The James Gang, the film is a steadily enjoyable ride.

Surrealism and non-linear concept pieces would trickle into the following year in the movie musical form: Lewis Carroll would get a bizarre and unnerving treatment, and a collection of sexually provocative vignettes would shock Broadway and television viewers alike. But these would be overshadowed by story-heavy diegetic musicals about legendary songstresses with substance abuse problems and the rise of Nazism in Germany during the age of "divine decadence"...

1972

"The Happiest Corpse I'd Ever Seen"

Comic Strip Beagles, Nudists and More Nazis

THE SEXUAL LIBERATION OF THE 1960S FOUND A HOME IN THE VERY fabric of mainstream movie musicals of that decade, particularly in films such as the kittenish and playful *Bye Bye Birdie* (1963), which toyed with the "dangers of rock'n'roll" and its effects on horny young teenagers. The film starred the vibrant, sensual Ann-Margret as a young teen rock groupie pitted against the stuffiness and rigidity of her long-suffering father (played by the wonderful Paul Lynde). Of course, the 1960s were littered with a number of coy sex comedies from companies such as American International Pictures, who injected these teenage romps with great, raw rock'n'roll, right through to big budget fare such as the Doris Day and Rock Hudson films such as *Lover Come Back* (1961) and *Send Me No Flowers* (1964). These usually showcased a lush Day song to open

111

the film and at times would use her vocal abilities within the story with a musically diegetic function.

However, the blatantly sex-obsessed musicals from the underground theatres of New York and beyond never found their way onto the silver screen—Hollywood was just too frightened of them—and instead, these numerous "dirty" plays disappeared into obscurity and acted as filthy launching pads for the likes of gifted artists such as Bette Midler. One of the musicals that Midler performed in was a pseudo-pornographic oddity that deconstructed fairy tales, and the very idea of the film translating into a film to be released along the likes of *Sweet Charity* (a musical that had to downplay the core theme of prostitution) was inconceivable. However, these dirty plays (and musicals) did make it to both grindhouse theatres and—of all places—public television.

One of the dirtiest musicals to come from the stages of New York followed on the heels of the anarchic *Hair* and went well beyond with its graphic depiction of masturbation, rape and sadomasochism: the rock musical and explosion of sexual freedom that defined *Oh! Calcuttta!* It aired on television thanks to production company Elkins Entertainment who specialised in filmed plays for networks happy to take on the heavy subject matter.

HE LICKED OPEN MY CUNT WITH HIS BIG FAT HAIRY TONGUE: *Oh! Calcutta!*

Oh! Calcutta! is a theatrical revelation in that it leaves nothing to the imagination and reveals everything. Made up of sexually charged vignettes and extremely unapologetic in its graphic depiction of fornication in all forms, *Oh! Calcutta!* is a bright and dynamic theatre piece and its shocking nature and filthiness is completely organic: it is not at all forced, and in many moments it is genuinely sexy. There is nothing silly about it, but it is certainly playful. Thankfully, this is not the case for the entire show. There are many moments of severe darkness, and strangely enough the bleakest moment comes early on in the piece with the confronting "Jack and Jill" story sequence, which is fundamentally about rape trauma.

Two company members enter as Jack and Jill (they are dressed as little children at the turn of the century) bouncing into an oversized playpen complete with building blocks and a swing on ropes. They have just met each other and consider themselves "impossibly beautiful." The conversation is fraught with sexual anxiety and lives in the shadow of rejection as Jill is terrified that if she gives herself over to Jack's sexual dominance, she will lose him eventually to another potential lover. Jack promises this will not be the case, and introduces her to a "special game" he has made up. The game is an attempt to seduce Jill, and before explaining the rules he promises her that the game is about love, a notion that appeals to the naïve Jill. The game involves measuring the length of Jack's penis and the depth of Jill's vagina. The winner is the person with the most impressive measurement and the prize is sex (or the permission to deny sexual advances). The measurement competition is reflective of childhood games grounded in burgeoning sexual curiosity seen in playground games involving doctor and nurse role-play and the like, allowing this sophomoric goofiness to be presented in a cute manner. And although the duo talks about cocktail parties and orgies, they remain childlike and marked by pseudo-innocence.

But this innocence is never truly guaranteed or even genuine. The sexually frustrated Jack declares "I got my imagination and I got my cock," and as his sexual hunger grows rapidly as he resorts to the measurement game in an attempt to bed Jill. Jill, however, tells Jack that she is scared of him because "he is a boy" and she worries about him both using her for sex and about him deserting her after he has his way with her. Finally, Jack gains Jill's trust and persuades her to measure his penis—hence participating in the game. He then slides the measuring ruler into her vagina. First startled by the insertion Jill slowly eases into the sensation and begins to enjoy this penetration, but it's short lived and ignored. The measurements are compared and Jill wins by a few inches. Happy that she has won and relieved that she won't have to have sex with Jack (and potentially lose him to another girl), Jill races around cheering. However, the frustrated Jack gets violent and pins Jill down and the scene turns extremely nasty and ugly. Jack violently rapes Jill on one of the oversized building blocks. Jill screams in pain and then falls into a coma. Stunned by the results of this horrific rape, Jack desperately tries to get Jill to speak, but she remains silent, still and is completely catatonic. He continues to scream, trying to get a response, but to no avail. Finally, he resorts to forcing her to smile by moving her mouth and forcing a smile to stretch across her face.

This is a final insult and a brilliant condensation of male sexual dominance over a young girl, implying that she *will* enjoy what she is dealt and he will even force a smile on her face after the violent assault. Jack's misogyny is a slap in the face to the sexual liberties of the late 1960s and early 1970s, which is what the musical is singing—and stripping— about. That this brutal rape occurs in a child's playpen makes the scene all the more horrific, and it is a grim first story in a series of mostly comical and playful sexual vignettes.

Much like Stephen Sondheim's *Company*, *Oh! Calcutta!* is a look deep inside the complexities of human relationships; but where Sondheim's piece focused on anxiety-inducing coupling up, the supposed horrors of singlehood and the dread of marriage, this nudity-riddled musical has sexual interplay as its core. *Oh! Calcutta* is a musical driven by sexual liberation, diversity, experimentation, self-possession and a devoted commitment to the flesh. This is something that musicals like *The Rocky Horror Show* will explore in a more streamlined, straightforward manner years later.

The cast from a touring company of *Oh! Calcutta!* (1972)

The second major sequence in *Oh! Calcutta!* is confronting, but not as depressing. A line up of well-dressed company members read letters to a newspaper editor discussing their sexual desires: a man is interested in finding a woman that will dress in jewellery with him, a woman describes her thrill of licking a pick-up's anus, another man describes his sexual fetish for dogs, and so forth. The scene is played for laughs, but in many ways the song (both the melody and the intensity of the counterpart singing) makes the sequence both exceptionally intelligent and biting. As the cast climax by masturbating while describing their sexual desires (one woman ecstatically exclaims that "he then licked open my cunt with his big fat hairy tongue!"), 1970s-style Broadway rock 'n' roll captivates us completely: there is a seductive musical 'voice' to the piece, and the fact that five individuals in their elegant evening wear are aggressively masturbating before us makes it all the more intoxicating.

The film's interpretive dance is both elegant and attractive, and there are some inspired images created by these talented nudists. Margo Sappington's choreography is great art: she heightens the beauty of the naked female and male body, and celebrates youthful vigour with a sharp eye and a quirky sense of fun. There is a natural flow to the rhythm of her work, and her dancers are a talented mob. When the music stops and gives Sappington's work centre stage, it is captivating and in essence beautiful. For a show that could easily tip over into smut, the dance numbers (themselves very contemporary for the 1970s, with lots of free fall, ragdoll manoeuvres and balletic influence) are staged beautifully, and the bluesy rock music for "One on One (Clarence and Mildred)" is driving and sexually powerful.

Most of the sketches in *Oh! Calcutta!* are played for laughs and have a very energetic feel: this is an American sex comedy injected with social awareness and satire. There is a lot of profanity and vivid imagery to upset and provoke, but also a lot to laugh at and find endearing. For example, one of the stronger segments has a young couple bored with their sex life and who decide to invite another couple for a foursome. They reluctantly want to get involved with the swingers scene, however when they meet the other couple they are turned off the idea. In an interesting, refreshing twist, the young woman in the couple who was initially aggressive in her dislike of the idea, allows the swingers to satisfy her in ways she has never known with her husband, who by now has become uptight and sits back and watches. There is a marvellous moment where the swinger woman inserts her fingers into the uptight young man's anus and he ejaculates in his pants. The moment is crude but both comically and socially brilliant: a pleasure this young man never knew possible is bought to his attention by someone he is repulsed by. This is theatre and musical comedy at its most telling.

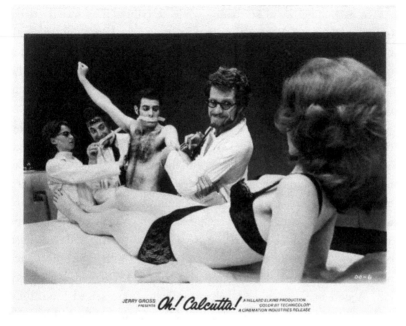

A publicity still for the televised production of *Oh! Calcutta!* (1972)

Oh! Calcutta! is a filmed stage production complete with sit-in audience, and even with its uneven presentation and sometimes confusing psychedelic expressions, the play and its dynamic songs are entertaining and shocking. Kenneth Tynan, a British drama critic who made his name in the pages of the long-running newspaper *The Observer*, conceived *Oh! Calcutta!* and collected works from playwrights Samuel Beckett, Sam Shepard, Leonard Melfi, Edna O'Brien, Jules Feiffer and Beatles guitarist John Lennon, who wrote the first draft of the short story "Four in Hand," which explored the complexities (and simplicities) of masturbation. This story seems to get the audience laughing comfortably, as opposed to other sequences such as Sherman Yellen's "Delicious Indignities" which features a lengthy monologue all about sadomasochism, child sexual abuse, rape and incest.

The audience within the film (seen in clear view right at the very beginning as they reluctantly take their seats) are clearly from high society: the wealthy New Yorkers who flocked to see avant-garde 'dirty' plays and musicals made by working class youngsters who were making unique and thought provoking work. The final moments in the musical features the cast in full frontal (and back) nudity echoing the thoughts of precisely this kind of an upper class audience. One girl says "I wonder what the girls do when they get their period" while another states, "This makes *Hair* look like *The Sound of Music*!" Someone else declares, "Most of these men are circumcised; this must be a Jewish show." Finally one of the cast members remarks "Who wrote this piece of shit?" These reflections by an audience perplexed by what they have just been subjected to is a palpable as a working piece of theatre: these sexually free youngsters have given a voice to the curious and the self-proclaimed theatre crowd. The absurdity of the show is subdued by breaking not the fourth wall, but another walls put up by the audience's own expectations and assumptions about what is acceptable. *Oh! Calcutta!* is an extremely dangerous show. There is nothing safe or particularly nice about it. It is a frenzied reflection and dissection of the sexual revolution, but also a comically nihilistic artistic expression of the ultimate solitude in promiscuity and obsession with the flesh.

Where *Oh! Calcutta!* is less successful is that it lets itself down and cuts itself short in that it doesn't trust that the audience to care about these people. And here is the tragedy: these characters are not presented as fully-formed people. Instead, they are cartoon nudists. The musical presents us with naked nubile young bodies performing fellatio, cunnilingus, bestiality and rape all set to a combination of lounge music and throbbing rock 'n' roll. With fuller character development, it could have been all that and more. The form is completely apropos (vignettes work here), but much like Sondheim's far more intellectually geared *Company*, it would not have hurt the piece to have some form of pathos and some solid characterizations. Interactions are engaging and fun, but they lack depth, and this is distracting and isolating.

Oh! Calcutta! is an incredible piece of working theatre, but it suffers by an unspoken attitude of 'where do I come in and enjoy the company of these people who seem to be completely enjoying each other's company as it is.' Its parade of endless nudity stops shocking eventually, and the genius of the show is when the nudity is used in different aspects and presented in different formats. A beautiful young girl stripping to sleazy rock music is tantalizing and powerful, but when the same girl has her childlike frock pulled up and her panties torn off and raped, there is something deeper going on. Whatever this musical is, its depiction and treatment of the nude body as living, breathing art is what makes it powerful and engaging, and most importantly confronting in a positive way. It is also a passable presentation in its form as filmed stage play: while certainly not as beautiful as Stephen Schwarz's *Pippin* (1981), the director here does his job and gives us a slice of America's obsession with sexual liberation and oppression.

EVERYBODY LOVES A WINNER, SO NOBODY LOVED ME: *Cabaret*

Sexuality and gender politics soon became a vital addition to the very dark and diverse storyline of the greatest movie musicals of the decade. This musical would be one of the very few that people who cried "I don't really like musicals" would use as their qualifying exception: this musical is *Cabaret*.

A ghastly, impish cretin appears on a dark and dingy stage, his face distorted by a reflective backdrop: he announces "Wilkommen," and is soon joined by equally ghoulish ladies of the night, vamping their way onto the stage and entertaining bloated beer swilling Germans. This opening moment ushers in one of the most perfectly realized movie musicals ever made. Much like the filmic adaptation of *West Side Story* before it, *Cabaret* is a grim and devastating musical that relies on character development and interaction. We care about the flawed and fruity people that populate the film and at the centrepiece is the aforementioned imp known as the Emcee (Joel Grey) who comments on the many bleak and also black comic situations that unfold through the story. His job is to musically make notes on the course of action in the film, from the social elements of the narrative including the rise of Nazism in Germany, to the personal elements of the tale involving the "divinely decedent"

Bob Fosse goes over the scene with Liza Minnelli and Marisa Berenson on the set of *Cabaret* (1972)

threesome of cabaret performer Sally Bowles (Liza Minnelli), journalist and English teacher Brian Roberts (Michael York) and wealthy playboy Maximilian von Huene (Helmut Griem).

Based on Christopher Isherwood's stories of pre-World War II Germany and namely from the ground breaking "I Am a Camera," *Cabaret* started its life on the Broadway stage, directed by musical theatre legend Hal Prince, with songs written by John Kander and Fred Ebb. It was an incredible hit and shocked audiences with its grim subject matter and bleak outcome. Nazism, street violence, political upheaval and the anti-Semitism of the piece covered major taboos, while themes of abortion, gender bending, bisexuality and homosexuality, sexually transmitted diseases and artistic nihilism took up the personal dimension and relentlessly refused to play any of these elements down. Most of these themes remained in the filmic adaptation (directed by legendary choreographer Bob Fosse), but he made one change to the stage to screen translation that had never really been done before: he completely cut out the book songs (songs integrated within plot and organically growing from dialogue) and only kept those performed diegetically inside the cabaret itself, the seedy and sleazy Kit Kat Klub. This ultimately left most of the songs for the Emcee and the ladies of burlesque headed by the iconic heroine of the piece Sally Bowles.

Bob Fosse and Liza Minnelli on location for *Cabaret* (1972)

Consequently, the supporting characters were left without songs, but most definitely not left without incredibly well written dramatic story. Screenwriter Jay Presson Allen's screenplay adaptation omits all the songs that occur within the world "outside" the Kit Kat Klub, so the musical is diegetic rather than a traditionally integrated book musical. The songs reflect the story and comment on the course of action rather than growing from the scenes presented to us. This drastic change initially worried cast members and those involved, but because of Allen and Fosse's genius, they soon realized it was a shrewd choice.

Joel Grey, who gave life to the creepy sinister Emcee remembers:

One is always reticent to mess with a classic and *Cabaret*
on Broadway was something very new and won all kinds of
awards. It was very original to begin with, so the idea that
somebody was going to come in and turn it upside and find
something or some way to make it more cinematic was a
curiosity to say the least. Of course once I read the screenplay
I thought it was phenomenal and really brilliant, plus I
thought the choices that they had made regarding the songs,
to make it cinematic, was very inspired. They decided to have
all the singing done inside the Kat Kat Klub and cut all of
the book songs. This was a really helpful way to make the
film a lot darker and more "real."

The violence and the uncertainty of a Nazi-era Berlin is presented
with brutal honesty in Fosse's film. The aggressive infiltration of right
wing extremists slowly contaminating bohemia and severing artistically-
inclined Germanics from their international peers (like American Sally
Bowles) is both palpable and scary. The distorted mirror opening and
closing the film is a perfect metaphor in *Cabaret* that art is reflective
of life, and that the ill-fated romance between Sally and Brian (and
the eventual threesome of Sally, Brian and Maximillian) as well as
the doomed relationship between the Christian and poor gigolo Fritz
Wendel (Fritz Wepper) and the Jewish and wealthy Natalia Landauer
(Marisa Berenson) is mirrored by the chaotic violence that eschews from
the formation of the Nazi Party and the fascist dictatorship soon to be
unleashed.

The genius of Bob Fosse and the musical itself is that the atrocities
of the rise of Nazism is summed up by a stirring number that paints
a picturesque image of good health and serenity. "Tomorrow Belongs
to Me" is a masterpiece of song writing: here are lyrics that present us
with the healthiest, most beautiful and most naturalistically spectacular
imagery such as a stag in the wilderness and all the majesty of nature in
all its poetic glory, masked as a propaganda song for a political agenda
that preaches hatred and violence against Jews and other groups. It is
also the only song sung outside the Kit Kat Klub, which elevates its other
worldliness. It is a terrifying image of Hitler Youth that will soon be

A threesome is born in *Cabaret* (1972)

propelling the dictatorship while the concerned elderly wipe their eyes with worry. This song comes late in the piece, where we have already been subjected to the violent brutality on the streets at the hands of the Nazis. This is more of the superlative structure of the musical—the song makes a terrifying opinion that the maliciousness that occurred earlier outside the Kit Kat Klub (while the Emcee gleefully spanks his chorus girls or referees an all-girl boxing match) is justified because "Tomorrow Belongs to Me" is presented as an elegant, graceful and healthy song. The Emcee appears right at the end of "Tomorrow Belongs to Me," but instead of taking to the stage and addressing a boozy audience, he simply looks up and shares a wickedly devilish wide grin.

Grey remembers:

> That was a beat that was in the Broadway show. But it needed to be put in another context for the film, so Fosse just had me backstage in my dressing room, knowing what was going on everywhere. Fosse knew exactly what he wanted, or at least he made you think he knew, but of course nobody

knows what exactly it is going to be because it is always adaption to the human element—he was open enough to allow things to be different and all of us did that, I mean he was such a great artist.

Cabaret does many wonderful things and one of them is providing an amazing character in Sally Bowles which proved to be a *tour de force* performance from Liza Minnelli. She is phenomenal in the role of the fragile but fun-loving nightclub singer. When she talks about her father ("the poor man, he tries to love me.") it is simply heartbreaking, and when she talks candidly about syphilis it is hilarious. The performance is nuanced and complicated, and yet at the same time miraculously controlled. Minnelli owns every single breath and moment of phrasing: she creates a nymphette of the burlesque stage, and does so with precise and beautiful sincerity. "Maybe I am just nothing..." she cries to Brian, and here we are presented with not only *Sally's* vulnerability and frail beauty, but also *Liza's*—an artist completely working from the heart and completely a slave to her craft. Everything both strong and fragile about Sally/Liza lives just under the surface and all the emotionality seeping through and undeniably truthful vulnerability comes out in fine display in Bob Fosse's film.

When she knocks out "Maybe This Time" it is simply breathtaking and completely tragic at the same time, and much like the aforementioned "Tomorrow Belongs to Me," the song comes through in a perfectly realized moment: when Sally (an absolute hopeless romantic plagued by loneliness) successfully seduces the homosexual Brian. "Maybe This Time" follows a wicked little comic moment that closes a scene where Sally looks down at Brian's erection. She raises her head and smiles at him. We then get into this incredible song (Minnelli at her most outstanding) and experience the power and desperation in her voice that is truly captivating. It is very hard not to applaud the song once she wraps it up. It is so incredibly moving that it shatters the fourth wall of the silver screen, and because it is so majestically directed it looks completely just like a theatre piece. The image of Sally on the blacked-out stage performing to three or four patrons and singing her heart out is what the musical is all about: rawness, honesty, showbiz-for-its-own-sake, and elements of desperation, fear, loneliness and delicate hope. Casting those great shadows on the backlit stage, Liza Minnelli looks and sounds like a genuine star. The scene comes close to matching her mother's iconic and very influential singing of "The Man That Got Away" from the ground breaking *A Star Is Born* (1954).

"Mein Herr," a number early in the piece, is treated exactly like a sleazy cabaret act in a seedy bar in Berlin and Fosse's choreography is remarkable. It is absolute controlled authorship: every single hip gesture, ever leg that stretches out to a fine point, every single finger that caresses the air or clicks to the frenzied beat is magnificently handled and yet not at all ever overstated, instead it is downplayed like a performance given by a group of dancers who aren't incredible chorus girls, led by Sally Bowles who is not the most remarkable performer ever to grace the Berlin stage. Fosse delivers an authentic creep show and Minnelli's immaculate talents are so finely tuned that she masterfully handles Sally's flawed but passionate performance.

Sally Bowles is a phenomenal creation, and Minnelli's performance is the much quoted "divine decadence" in its purest form. Sally is a fragile creature desperately hiding behind a hardened showbiz persona: she is her own creation, her own messy being and her quirks and slightly manic behaviour are completely intoxicating. When Sally races under a Berlin railway and waits for the train to cross over and screams with cathartic bliss, it is a strangely endearing moment. When she entices Brian to do the same it adds to her charm and the charm of the scene: it becomes a sweet oddball romantic interlude, but one that is suddenly bought to a halt as Fosse instantly assaults us with Nazi officers beating up a Jewish man on the streets. Fosse intercuts this with the Emcee presenting a traditional German comedy involving lederhosen-dressed girls being spanked.

Actor Joel Grey remembers the look and feel of the film and also the creation of the Emcee:

> I thought the look of the film was the epitome of perfection. I thought that the design team on both the set design and costume design were just phenomenal. And they went beyond from the stage, which were made by two iconic

designers, so it was not easy to top that, but they made it all their own and made it far more cinematic. The Emcee's look was essentially the exact make-up that was worn on stage. We didn't make any adaption at all, and the way it was developed in the first pace was Hal Prince and I discussing the character in depth—what he represented, what he wanted, what he was essentially there for. And then I started to experiment with various forms of make-ups, I had always been incredibly fascinated by make-up and make-up design. The Emcee's look became a matter of trial and error—"this one is too feminine, this one is too masculine" and so forth. It ended up being like a painting. When I was nine years old I was in this theatre in Cleveland, Ohio and I was very aware of Laurence Olivier, and I was in a repertory company and we didn't have any make-up artists, so every actor in order to do his job and play a part had to know how to do his own make-up: standard theatre make-up and character make-up. It was all learning on the spot. I was fascinated by watching the older actors take to the grease paint and create characters, and I would follow and then eventually create my own. The Emcee was never directly inspired by anyone I knew, I mean this was a character that was barely described on the page, so it became all about my imagination and my own creation. As I got into it I became very much influenced by the great music of *Cabaret* and I did a lot of research about Berlin nightclubs and Parisian nightclubs, I mean *Cabaret* was totally European, and I listened to a lot of the great music of that time. It all came form a bit from here and a bit from there and sometimes these things come together and create something brand new.

Along with the darkness comes moments of inspired hilarity. The scene where Brian first meets Fraulein Landau is cheeky comedy at its best. Liza Minnelli's comic timing and delivery is astounding, and her outspoken and saucy American showgirl plays well against Michael York's straight-laced, proper Englishman. When Sally tries to seduce

Brian very early in the film it is one of the most touching moments, and also one of the funniest. Here is a girl that at first is confused by Brian's lack of sexual interest in her, but when she finds out that he prefers the company of men, she completely understands it and accepts it. She goes from playing a jazz record to help the seduction to playing it to christen their newly formed friendship.

The film was one of the first movies to present homosexuality as a part of the sexual/social fabric, where nobody was concerned, no one cared and it was as natural as heterosexuality. But *Cabaret* is also a film that lends itself to the "cure them or kill them" motif that runs throughout cinematic representations of homosexuality. In *Cabaret*, Sally Bowles "cures" Brian by being the "right kind of girl" (albeit she is a girl that seems to attract bisexual men, seeing that Brian is eventually seduced by playboy Maximillian von Huene). The seduction scene also gives us an indication into Sally being a left over flapper of the Roaring Twenties stuck in a foreign land: when she shows Brian the wonders of her body ("it's a little flat here, not much here" etc.), she is presenting a body type that reflects the beauty ideal of the jazz age. Sally is also seduced by the rarity of having money spent on her, so when the wealthy Maximillian splashes out on her (and Brian) we get a sense of the appeal of decadence amidst the poverty stricken artistic community, but this is also fleeting as beautifully suggested in the number "Money." Here Sally is joined with the Emcee on stage frantically hyperventilating over the promise of material gain (even if it is for a brief moment).

Joel Grey reminisces:

> Liza and I laughed all the time! We had so much fun. We were like two bad little kids, naughty little kids looking for trouble. We had so many rehearsals and time spent on "Money." It was us against the world. I first met her when she was seventeen and she did a nightclub act at the Coconut Grove in Los Angeles and I remember seeing her and thinking "My God, this is an original! An original from an original!" it came from a tradition that we both understood. There was a sensibility there that was necessary for this film—the whole backstage element. We never discussed this,

by the time we got to work we just did it and we did it many ways and everybody found the right way. We had very similar work ethics because we both took as long as it took to get it perfect.

The rise of Nazism in *Cabaret* (1972)

The lives of the bohemian but doomed threesome of Sally, Brian and Maximillian are lush and very sexy, reflected on the stage by the Emcee, who sings the wonders of having "Two Ladies." The number was also very personal to Bob Fosse, who was famously hyper-sexual and enjoyed the company of many a woman, and who lived with two women for some time. The inner story of *Cabaret* being imitated on the stage at the Kit Kat Klub and then that being reflected in the life of the film's director is a thing of legend and is unique. Joel Grey's performance of numbers such as "Two Ladies" seem flawless, however having to present the performance pieces in front of a fabricated audience proved slightly tricky, as he recalls:

> We had exactly six weeks to shoot all the numbers, we had six weeks to rehearse them and six weeks to shoot. It was a lot of work with the audience, in terms of doing the numbers with them in front of us and then with the cameras behind me and then in front of them, I mean there was a lot

of work involved to make it look as if we were performing to these people and they were reacting the way they were.

"If You Could See Her Through My Eyes" is another brilliant production number: classic vaudeville shtick masking atrocities and horrendous horrors. The Emcee introduces the audience to a gorilla wearing a dainty hat and summer dress and explains what a perfect and elegant lady this ape is: "She doesn't smoke or drink gin, like I do…" The song is comical and whimsical, but the reality of the piece is that it is there to manipulate the audience and stick the knives in. The core essence of the song is stated explicitly in the Emcee's final line, the gag of the song: "You won't know she's Jewish at all!," followed by a wacky musical sting reminiscent of circus and clowning. The violent spit in the face from the Emcee, suggesting that if you conceal an ape in "civilian" gear then you can surely hide a Jew from the "chosen" race, is terrifying.

Joel Grey remembers:

> I thought it was one of the ugliest songs I had heard in my life. It was vicious and violently aggressive. To comprehend the notion that this trickster is making the audience believe that what he is performing and what he is singing about is light and fun and then by the end throwing in the shiv, I mean that is just vicious.

The supporting players (most notably Michael York as the stuffy Brian, who blossoms into a sexually confident and politically confident hero) and the sub-plot involving Fritz and Natalia (which begins blandly romantic and ends violently tragic) all add to the fantastic tapestry that is *Cabaret*. Add to that the way the film looks and sounds: shot in golden hues and a crisp chilly airiness when outdoors, there is also the smoky, gaudy garishness inside the Kit Kat Klub. The sound design is as rhythmic and enthralling as the score itself. Musically, the film is sheer perfection even when it is trying not to be, and when Sally belts out "Cabaret"— with lines like "I made my mind up back in Chelsea, when I die I'm goin' like Elsie"—it lifts your soul even though you have just been subjected to some of the most harrowing imagery and events ever put to screen.

Joel Grey wins his Oscar for *Cabaret* (1972)

Preceding the song of "Cabaret," Sally realizes that she is pregnant and decides to have an abortion, one of the film's darkest personal moments. But like all great musicals, it leaves a bittersweet fanfare represented by the title song. "What's good in sitting alone in your room? Come hear the music play" beckons hardened heroine Sally Bowles, and we can either live life carefully and comfortably or experience the seductive power of "divine decadence." The grotesquely enigmatic Emcee, the delicate but thriving Sally Bowles and *Cabaret* itself gives us that opportunity to choose, and it has since becomes one of the most important movie musicals ever made for it.

Joel Grey recalls seeing the film in Germany, where it received very different response to the way Americans saw the film:

Audiences were absolutely overwhelmed and often applauded the numbers in the middle of this very dark story. I was in Crete the year it came out holidaying with my family. We were at a spa, or more like a resort, and that was filled with all German people. I had a beard so nobody had any idea who I was. One night they showed the movie outside on a big screen for all the people staying there. And there was not a laugh to be had. These Germans did not find it one bit funny at all. It was eerie. They did not like that that story was being told again. It was shocking.

SAY YES: *Liza with a Z*

From the genius that was *Cabaret* came something remarkably unique that showcased the extraordinarily life affirming talents of Liza Minnelli. This songstress with tremendous amounts of vulnerability and tragedy as well as joy and glamour is a phenomenal talent born from two legendary artists, Judy Garland and Vincente Minnelli. Liza Minnelli always said that her mother gave her her drive and her father gave her her dreams, and in a brand new concert film directed by mastermind Bob Fosse, with songs by Kander and Ebb as well as featuring orchestrations by legendary, versatile composer Marvin Hamlisch, these gifts bestowed by her parents come to surface in one of the greatest filmed concerts of the 1970s (and of all time)—*Liza with a Z*.

Opening with the lyrical and empowering "Say Yes," Liza has such a natural command over the sheer essence of song: she thoroughly understands that delivery, timing and phrasing are all there to serve the point of the number. Much like Minnelli's insight into Bob Fosse's choreography, it is not about *how*, but about *why* and Minnelli's intent is so pin point perfect in its realization that its spellbinding to watch. Every move and every nuance is given all, and the energy and openness of Minnelli's performance is a delicate insight into an artist's life. Her booming voice and great control on her volume sums up her boisterous, humorous, joyous and fun self and then her softer, quieter and more introspective moments are a perfect parallel to Liza Minnelli as a beautiful oddity, as a sensitive soul who has not only show business running through her veins, but musicality, a supernatural understanding of the human condition and fragile tenderness. Minnelli's intrinsic theatricality is captivating, and it is all the more beautifully captured by Bob Fosse's direction and choreography. It is also given a broader and far richer canvas as Fosse decided to shoot this television special on 16mm film

Editor Alan Heim remembers the origins of *Liza with a Z*:

All of the cinematic elements to *Liza with a Z* is all Fosse. I was married to my second wife at the time and she had seen *Cabaret* when it opened and at that time I had no real interest in movie musicals. *Cabaret* had just opened and did massive business and then I got this call from Kenny Ott and asked if I would meet Bob Fosse and I said "Sure OK." I went to Broadway Arts which is the same place used in the opening cattle call sequence in *All That Jazz* which is actually a lot smaller than what it looks like on film, the stage we used was in fact a replica of the real place. I walked in and started talking to Fosse who was a vision in black! He was very serious, and he was always very serious, eventually thought the years we got over that and he would loosen up around me, but right from the beginning he was straight and direct and serious. So here I was standing there with him and looking at all these dancers who were sliding up to our feet and doing these incredibly athletic movements that just stunned me. I was just getting excited by the energy in the room. Now I was not a musician, I had never played an instrument at all, but I was a music editor, so I understood rhythm and I had a natural ear for tempo and timing but I was in no way a legitimate musician, so I got the feeling from Fosse when he looked me up and down and stared right into my eyes that he was thinking "Oh here we go again, they've sent me another ignorant non-musical editor to work with. Fuck me." So let's just say I wasn't really sure if I had gotten the job on *Liza with a Z*. Then I took the lead of my former wife and went and saw *Cabaret* and was blown away. I thought my God this man is a visual genius! So I anguished all night over whether or not I would get this job on *Liza with a Z*. I just wanted to connect to this man.

Much like artists such as Bette Midler, Cher, Barbra Streisand and her mother, Judy Garland, Minnelli can throw herself from comic genius to tragic songstress to deeply insightful social commentator not only throughout the duration of one song, but in a verse. The mastering of the patter of "Liza woth a Z" is fun to watch as Minnelli comically explains that "Lisa with an S goes Sssss not Zzzzz" and so forth and when she falls into the haunting trance singing the incredible number "It Was a Good Time" which chronicles the breakdown of a marriage as told through the eyes of a tormented child it is a fabulous performance. When Minnelli sings "Mamma wakes up and she's alone…" there is something completely profound and eerie. Minnelli's acting is so touching and raw that at times there is something fantastically terrifying in it. She is like a woman possessed, complicated by the demons of show business and her pure emotional exorcism would most certainly rival any rock'n'roll singer screaming their lungs out. Minnelli has an energy that is eerily devastating and yet so enchanting. Minnelli's cover of Dusty Springfield's "The Son of a Preacher Man" is given an almost schizophrenic musical theatre injection, and with the frantic tempo changes within the structure as well as being completely complimented by Bob Fosse's choreography it is a decidedly anarchic performance piece.

Alan Heim recalls Minnelli, Fosse and the shoot:

> Liza was most absolutely not involved in the editing process whatsoever. You just can't have an actor in the cutting room, because an actor's idea is what makes a good cut is a load of close ups of the actor and that just doesn't work. Not that Liza would think that way, but actors should never be involved in editing or even invited into the cutting room. I've had actors come into the editing suite and I would leave. I don't like them thinking they can sit over the editor or director's shoulder. The plan for it was to be a filmed concert at a disused theatre and the idea was that we were going to shoot with nine cameras and was all to be shot on 16mm

film and Owen Roizman who had shot films like *Network* and *The Exorcist* was filming it and he wanted to light it for film but Bob Fosse wanted to light it for stage, and there was a lot of discussion about this. There was an upstairs camera up on the top of the balcony, and up down the aisle were out second cameras, and the whole thing was shot in real time, there were no stops at all. No artificial stops at all. All the other cameras that were backstage and off to the side and low in front were all operated by terrific documentary cinematographers who rehearsed with Bob but I remember there was no real control between Bob and his camera men. The big issue was the synching, who had worked with me on *Godspell* as well. There was one point where they wanted to have a camera shoot the clock that was above the stage but I thought that was going to be more trouble than what it was worth. Trudy my assistant was a genius and she synched everything up from the stage, I mean we were dealing with a live orchestra and big band as well as Liza herself and we had cued everything up perfectly. Then it was just a matter of organising a lot of material. It was very labor intensive, we worked with a flatbed and there was a point where the tape went running off the reels and ripped and it went so fast that we couldn't stop it from happening. And Fosse walked in and told me that I looked terrible, and I had said oh I've never had my machines turn on me. Bob calmed me down and we talked about where to go from there. Fosse's brilliance as a choreographer which a lot of people didn't know was he knew where to pull your attention as an audience member. And he was incredible at directing me. I would do what editors do. People think "oh it's a dinner scene how difficult could it be?" but you have to decide where you want to pull your audience's attention, on the fork that's picked up or where someone takes a sip of wine and so forth, so in saying that, a lot of people who didn't understand dance always questioned my editing of Fosse's work. They think that there should be absolutely no cuts, and that everything should be shot like an old Fred Astaire movie in one big wide shot so you can see the whole body and God knows Fosse and I used a lot of wide shots but there is a lot of cuts. You see, Fosse loved hands and feet and fingers and white gloves and hats and really loved it when I cut these elements together that could really give his choreography and direction real authorship. *Liza with a Z* was shot to be cut as a film. It's a staccato shoot! It's there to entertain the audience and Bob knew how to do that.

The film also was lost for years until Liza Minnelli unearthed it from her personal vaults, as Heim recalls:

I didn't even know that Liza owned the rights to the film. We never could successfully get it onto video because of the way it was lit. In those days television images streaked because the whites would burn out the blacks and there was no clear movement. We went on the air with it and we were not at all happy with the sound quality because they supressed it and they did what they could with the technology they had but it was never releasable because of the state it was in. But Liza got a restoration on it and now it looks gorgeous.

STRANGE FRUIT: *Lady Sings the Blues*

Cabaret would be a revolutionary musical and much like *Gypsy* (1962) before it, one that so-called cinephiles who never gravitated towards musicals could accept and enjoy. This darkness continued to haunt seedy nightclubs in one of the most harrowing musical biopics ever made with one of the 1960s most notable songstresses playing one of the jazz age's most incredibly gifted (and equally tortured) divas.

Opening with a haggard, wafer-thin Billie Holiday (played to perfection by Diana Ross) being thrown into prison, *Lady Sings the Blues* is a gutsy musical biopic that covers a wide range of horrific subject matter such as racism, lynching, the Ku Klux Klan, and rape, but thematically tilts mostly towards the harrowing reality of heroin addiction. This is also the brilliance of the film in its commentary on the way drug addiction takes over beyond the realm of movies and storytelling, rendering everything else irrelevant to the substance abuser. Billie Holiday's rise to stardom and her ability to capture an audience's heart (both black and white) with a single breathy and sultry jazzy note become irrelevant as her desperate dependence on heroin grows. *Lady Sings the Blues* obsesses over the famous jazz singer's opiate addiction, but it does it with such grit that the audience is forced to vicariously "cut the pain" by watching the tortured Billie Holiday ram heroin up her arm.

Richard Pryor as The Piano Man and Diana Ross as Billie Holiday in *Lady Sings the Blues* (1972)

The story of Billie Holiday begins with her as a young teenager (delicately handled by the talented Diana Ross), introduced from the outset as a music lover. She obsesses over a jazz record, listening to it repeatedly at the brothel she cleans. The madam scolds her while a drunken, lusty john spots her and wishes to have his way with this underage jazz fan. Later, the repugnant john follows her to her aunt's house and rapes her. After the assault, Billie's concept of sex is distorted so that when she gets a job at an inner city Harlem brothel she is repulsed by the situation but also driven to work as a prostitute rather than a cleaner. The madam there mocks her appearance and is one of many characters throughout the film that tells the gawky youngster that she is no beauty queen. When Scatman Crothers as "Big Ben" comes to pay his way, Billie leaves the brothel, blossoming into a woman on a mission, and looking the part. She has her heart set on singing at a nearby blues bar, which she eventually does and takes Harlem by storm.

On her first time visiting the seedy underground mixed race jazz dive, she is driven out by the manager, but not before she watches the girls dance. The featured singer belts out some tunes and Mr. Louis McKay (Billy Dee Williams) walks down the stairwell decked out in a white suit and looking sharp. Here is how a man could look: unlike the sleazy johns that frequented the brothels, Louis is self-possessed, suave and remarkably handsome. Billy Dee Williams's sex appeal was a sensation around Hollywood, where he was renowned as 'the black Clark Gable'. Screenwriter Bill Kerby, who penned the script for a pseudo-musical biopic in *The Rose* (1979) (which we shall look at later) said of him:

> When Billy Dee Williams walked down that staircase in
> that Lady Day movie and walked in wearing that white suit,
> I swear to God everyone in Hollywood just held their breath.
> It was incredible.

Billie is smitten by Louis, literally swept off her feet as she is picked up by a heavy and tossed outside. When she returns, dolled up and looking like a peach, she auditions for a job as a dancer but does not impress. However, with the help of the messed up but compassionate Piano Man (Richard Pryor) she gets a job due to her vocal talents. Diana Ross's vocal abilities are divine: smooth and sultry, as well as terminally tragic. When she performs publically for the first time she is forced to grow up in one moment on stage. Before her is a performer that collects dollar bills with her vagina and Billie is expected to do the same, however the green artist simply cannot do it. Instead, she lets her heart sing out only to be greeted by a welcoming hand offering a dollar bill. It is a stunning image: Louis's well-dressed arm outstretched offering the talented Billie a helping hand. Once she collects it her confidence boosts and she loses herself in her vocal talents, the audience relaxes and enjoys it as well. Billie grows and becomes an overnight sensation in Harlem.

Billie and Louis spark a romantic union and their passionate love affair is treated as a secondary story element to what is essentially a film about a troubled artist. When Billie realizes that Louis is a strong and loving gentleman it frightens her: it is something that she is not used to. But Louis's dedication to Billie and support of her work is both real and stabilizing. Soon enough, more men enter Billie's life, this time white jazz musicians who wish her to join their band. Perplexed by the idea of a black woman fronting an all-white jazz band, Billie is nervous about the idea at first, but with some persuading she throws caution to the wind and joins.

Here Diana Ross truly shines, and seems the most comfortable as she roughhouses with her fellow band mates, completely holding her very own even as a black woman among white men. The scenes depicting her and her band on the road are possibly the most casual you will see Ross, and it works all the better when she really lets go and gets to perform: for example, the scene where she comes across a hanging black man after a Ku Klux Klan lynching is amazing. Ross wails and races off terrified by the situation, and the camera swivels around her emphasising her distressed state. Ross's acting in this film is revelatory, and her control of switching from tomfoolery to downright crazed is magical. When she sees the Ku Klux Klan and is forced to hide from them on the tour bus she angrily pushes through to make eye contact with the racist group. She is like a wild animal, ferocious and furious, ready to take on all the social injustices of the world. She screams and forces her way toward them, wanting to draw blood but is met with a violent blow from one of the Klansmen.

When Ross comes to perform the heroin-induced scenes, her performance is authentic and remarkably heartbreaking. There is such depth in her sadness and desperation that when she angrily screams at Louis and pulls a razor on him to get her fix we feel for her—some of us, like Louis, want to help her, and some of us (again like Louis in a state of "What else can I do?") just want to let her go and let the drugs win. This violent and harrowing scene is the heart of the film: Louis struggles to help Billie through her overwhelming addiction, and when he finally gives her the space to shoot up we feel his despair. Billy Dee Williams should have become a huge star after this performance, every single acting choice is in clear unison and responsive to Diana Ross's electric turn, be they coming from a place of hyper-masculinity or birthed from tenderness.

Richard Pryor is a living revelation in the supporting role of the Piano Man. Pryor is more than a capable dramatic actor and it is unfortunate that he didn't get a chance to do more straight work, as opposed to comedy. Although he injects The Piano Man with a great deal of his own unique brand of humour, his scene with Billie Holiday where she finds out that her mother has passed away is an awesome achievement and a perfect example of a heartbreaking performance. The scene opens with Billie getting her heroin fix from a dealer named The Hawk (Robert Gordy). Piano Man comes in and is concerned, and pleads with Billie to consider changing her drug habits. Billie tries to usher him out of the dressing room so she can be shot with her dose of heroin from The Hawk, but then receives a phone call. She finds out that her mother (Virginia Capers) has died, and her priorities immediately change. She storms back into her dressing room and screams at The Hawk to get out, leaving her a crumbling mess. Richard Pryor is painfully far too real in his performance, and the transition from fumbling, fearful shaky court jester to matching Diana Ross's portrayal of a crumbling mess is outstanding. Clearly his love for Mama Holliday was very real, and her death kills something in him: that last connection to what is good and wholesome in the world. This off screen death does the same thing to Billie, and she checks herself into a clinic to get clean. Diana Ross and Richard Pryor will reunite six years later on *The Wiz* (1978), and here Ross as Dorothy Gale delivers a very different, although equally frazzled performance. Pryor however is in a much smaller part as the titular character, and although he delves into very dark dramatic moments that are fleeting, they are most certainly there. But more on *The Wiz* later.

Lady Sings the Blues closes with Billie's triumphant performance at Carnegie Hall, completely enraptured and joyous, but still cursed by addiction and an overwhelming sadness. What you are left with is an artist in her public light: empowered, captivating, glamorous and luminous, a far cry from her dishevelled state, slumped on a toilet seat with track marks scattered across her arms. As depressing as the film is, it is also brilliant. The performances are pitch perfect, the way the story is plotted and told is effective and continuously engaging, and the look and feel of 1930s New York and the film's other locations feel authentic and appropriate.

A lobby card for *Lady Sings the Blues* (1972) featuring Billy Dee Williams checking for track marks on heroin addicted Diana Ross as Billie Holiday

The film is an absolute winner, and the bleak and very grim subject matter becomes all the more dark and devastating because you care about these people, especially this young woman who doesn't just *want* to sing, but *has to*. Billie Holiday is one of those tragic musical legends that we have come to know all too well, and the concept of fame being a hungry demonic entity that shreds through the artists serving its thirst for blood is a story that has been told many times before and afterward. But it is the great musical biopics such as this that transcend the exploration into personal demons, addiction and complicated relationships shared between artists and fame, and *Lady Sings the Blues* is one of them. Unrelenting, uncompromising, multi-layered and boasting a flawless cast headed by the astounding Diana Ross.

Director Sidney J. Furie recalls the production:

Well, a producer who is now a restaurant critic, named Jay Westman, who I knew, sent me an original screenplay and I said, 'We want to go after an actress named Diana Ross." I had just seen a Motown special, where Diana was acting in these comedy sketches, and I thought, 'Oh my gosh!" But a producer said "She can't act.' And I said, 'Oh, yes she can!' He saw the special and he said, "Well if she can do comedy, then she can do drama, because comedy is harder to pull off than drama." So, the next thing we know we got Diana. We got Billy, and we needed a studio. We got Paramount, and then we all decided—or I decided that I didn't like the script! So that became a very long process— to write a new screenplay. I think I wrote the beginning of this screenplay before we met anybody—something like that. But then, it never stopped being worked on. We basically shot the movie in sequence because we weren't sure where we were heading or what would change. Example: Richard Pryor came in for one's day's work. He plays a gentlemen in the club, when we first see him. And everyone was so blown away when we wrote him into the rest of the picture. Also, at least six or seven of the main scenes between Billy and Diana were totally improvised on the set. Actually, they were improvised while the cameras were rolling, and I would give them direction: change this, change that, go again. The best scenes are shared between them. Diana is one of the great improvisers I have ever met! You could just say, "Here is what this scene is about" and wham! While Billy is not a good improviser—he's a good actor and he would just play off of her. The big joke was that, when Diana read the script, she said, "Why are there so many scenes, can't we just talk? There are five numbers on an album, right?" Once we got over that she was unbelievable! The scene when they are in the bathroom, where she's trying to get her fix was pretty emotional. I don't think Diana had ever been on drugs

140

or anything like that in real life. I didn't ever really know the real person. You don't need too. You need to know the actors on the set. But I think it was a big stretch for her. And then the killing of Piano Man was pretty emotional as well. The audience has to care about the characters. And if they care about the characters—they care what they are going through. And the resolution of what they are going through is the end of the movie, you know. Also, the look of the film. We found streets in downtown L.A, that looked like Baltimore. But by today's standards it was a very inexpensive movie. I mean, twenty million dollars. A lot of the sets were standing sets that the art director found in a studio, and reconditioned. I don't even know if they keep old sets anymore in Hollywood, everything is changed. So, we have some incredible stuff that imported in the film. I had a very wonderful cameraman/director of photography, and he used light that gave a realistic look of light, coming through windows. He unfortunately died at an early age. By today's standards—it's a lower budget. I don't think I shot for more than 25-30 days a year. That's 40 days, so an extra 10 days or whatever helps. Although, it was a very leisurely pace on the set. I remember we went over budget and Paramount said, "We are not going to rush this!"

FUNDAMENTAL-FRIEND-DEPENDABILITY:
Snoopy Come Home and The Muppet Musicians of Bremen

Noted jazz composer Vince Guaraldi was a tremendous talent, and his work on the animated shorts based on the *Peanuts* comic strips by Charles M. Schulz was slick and memorable. He had also composed the music for the film *A Boy Named Charlie Brown* (1969) which was the first feature length *Peanuts* outing which was well received by critics and audiences alike. Guaraldi's music also garnered complimentary reviews, but when it came time for the next feature in 1972—*Snoopy Come Home*—Guaraldi's jazz fusion was put aside in favour of the whimsical wordplay and rich melodies of the Sherman brothers. *Peanuts* creator Shulz wanted the next feature length production to have a Disney 'feel' that the Sherman's could

141

certainly provide, seeing they had composed the songs for previous hits such as *Mary Poppins*, *The Jungle Book* and *Bedknobs and Broomsticks*. Does this work for the philosophising, slightly maudlin *Peanuts*? Absolutely!

Snoopy Come Home is a tender animated film that dissects friendship and the importance of togetherness the only way Charlie Brown, Snoopy and the rest of the *Peanuts* gang know how. The film introduces the character of Lila (voiced by Johanna Baer and singing voice by Shelby Flint) who was a minor player in the comic strips but a very important one as she was said to be the original owner of the forever cool beagle Snoopy. She adopted him from the Daisy Hill Puppy Farm but then later had to hand him over to Charlie Brown (here in this film voiced by Chad Webber with Todd Barbee as singing voice) when her parents moved to an apartment building that had a ban on dogs. The film reunites Snoopy with Lila but plays around with the original comic strip story elements. Here Lila is an ill child in the hospital who wishes to have Snoopy visit her to help with her recovery.

The film is surprisingly sorrowful and wistful for a *Peanuts* offering, and it deals directly with the notion of loss and grief. Within this quietly morose cartoon is a decidedly non-saccharine musical that is no way at all overly sentimental. Instead the Sherman brothers and Shulz simply tell it how it is: friendship can be forever but it is something that requires guidance and a lot of work. Musically the film explodes with thoughtful energy and subtle sweetness. "The Best of Buddies" has an overt bittersweet flutter to it, "Gettin' It Together" is classic Sherman brothers rejoicing in their love of rhythmic wordsmithery, and the title song plays with pensiveness in a reflective manner. Much like the live action *The Pied Piper* (which we will get to in a moment), *Snoopy Come Home* is painted with muted colours (reminiscent of the colour scheme you would find in a child care centre in the 1970s) and the simplicity of its iconic imagery is all the more laidback and strange in what essentially is a cartoon about loss. The best *Peanuts* stories work with vignettes woven together to give insight into these misfit characters: the bossy and super-egotistical Lucy, the introverted artist Schroder, the sweet playful Sally Brown and so forth. So when a feature is made with this quiet sadness built-in, even the wonders of a Sherman brothers tune (albeit a lot of those cast very dark and melancholy shadows) cannot elevate the mood.

Meanwhile, master puppeteer and up until this point at least, small-screen legend Jim Henson gave his Muppets a television special that would provide a taste of his more heartfelt genius that was still to come. *The Muppet Musicians of Bremen* is both a captivating and thought provoking little television special that played with the folkloric tale of "Town Musicians of Bremen." Although television shows such as *Sam and Friends* (1955-1961) and the long running children's educational series *Sesame Street* that began in 1969 (plus a number of commercials and TV appearances here and there) had introduced audiences to Henson's felt-and-foam, wacky and completely loveable Muppets—most notably the enigmatic and pragmatic central Kermit the Frog—it was this TV special that provided the foundations of what ultimately would become one of the greatest television events of the 1970s and early 1980s, *The Muppet Show* (1976-1981).

The special was an offshoot of an umbrella three-part series called *Tales from Muppetland* and followed another musical Muppet moment, *The Frog Prince* which aired in 1971. *The Frog Prince* was a gentle retelling of the classic fairy tale and featured songs written by *Sesame Street* mainstay Joe Raposo, who gave some lovely melodies and lyrical whimsy to characters such as Robin (Kermit's nephew, voiced by Jerry Nelson and puppeteered by Frank Oz) and the giant adorable ogre Sweetums (voiced and puppeteered by Carl Banas, who would later retire the character to Richard Hunt). This endearing Muppet mini-musical starring Trudy Young paved the way for a more elaborate and much more musically intricate special with *The Muppet Musicians of Bremen*. In this 1972 TV musical, Jim Henson's alter-ego Kermit the Frog narrates the story and introduces us to the swamplands of Louisiana: the tale unfolds here instead of the traditional Germany as depicted in the original folkloric tale. Already with the change in the setting, these very American Muppets have fun with the concept of the South and its signature musicality.

This is just a smidgen of the genius of Henson and his remarkably talented team that included his head writer of many years, Jerry Juhl. These gifted and sentimental artists would congregate over endless sleepless days and nights and discuss and plot and plan how they were to present their dear Muppets. The beauty underlying this fundamental groundwork was the actual work ethic and relationship Henson and his team had with these characters, soon to become a vital part of popular culture. Frank Oz (Henson's right hand) had stated that Henson was never precious about his Muppets, instead he had a healthy concept of what they were and what they represented and how they would work to serve the story or sketch or musical number the group were working on. For *The Muppet Musicians of Bremen*, Henson decided to let the musical numbers navigate the story and set the entire motif to cool rhythmic jazz. Jerry Juhl, a master craftsman of writing—not only short sketch comedy but also narrative-driven, humorous course runners injected with an incredible amount of sweetness—wrote the book and lyrics with a swift sensibility, bouncy punch lines and drove it with an emphasis on the idea of kindness. As the years went on, Henson, Oz, Juhl and the other men and women devoted to the Muppets would deliver funny and incredibly moving and poignant work, from TV specials such as this to a long running variety show in *The Muppet Show*, to feature films starting with *The Muppet Movie* (1979), the latter which we will also eventually get to.

The characters in this special include Catgut, a trumpet-playing feline whose singing voice was similar to Carol Channing's, a hound dog who plays trombone called Rover Joe, Leroy the donkey who is the only "player" to interact with narrator Kermit, and T.R. Rooster, who would be the only character from the special aside from Kermit who would go on appearing on *The Muppet Show* down the track. Catgut and Rover Joe would be remodelled and sometimes seen as background characters on the series, but Leroy would soon disappear into obscurity. These four animals run away from abusive humans and get caught up in a robbery, but the plot is the least of the special's absolute charm. The Muppets themselves do everything for you: they can be overwhelming, underwhelming, poignant, ridiculous, sweet or selfish. This is part of what Jim Henson and his colleagues bring to the fore: interesting complicated characters who are written for an audience wishing to *feel* something.

Henson and his team of dedicated artists—and Muppets—would make the 1970s their own. More television specials like *The Muppet Musicians of Bremen* would come, plus the successful variety show that the world would come to know and love as *The Muppet Show*, and finally

144

feature films. More on the incredible Muppets later, but first Peter O'Toole...

IT'S ALL THE SAME: *Man of La Mancha* **and** *The Great Waltz*

"To dream the impossible dream" is what *Man of La Mancha* sets out to do, but instead it spends most of its time unsuccessfully presenting us with nonsensical hope in the context of dire, horrific scenario of the Spanish Inquisition. This whistling-in-the-dark could have been interesting and engaging, but instead it is frustrating and tedious: when this terrible situation becomes too oppressive for even phony hopes to 'sing out', the audience tunes out and twiddles their thumbs waiting for the next dynamic but poorly plotted song. Most of the musical is set in the bleak arena where the dire results of the infamous Inquisition in Europe are awaited, and tries to distract us from the fact that its hero will be killed by presenting a number of laborious set pieces. Although the gritty realism of the film compliments its very good music (the grimy streets encrusted with mud is the perfect setting for some of the numbers), the story—as a movie musical, not so much in regard to its life as a Broadway musical—is not exactly well conceived for a musical. Additionally, the direction is all wrong and its casting is questionable.

Peter O'Toole is an extraordinary actor, but as a singer he is completely out of his element. He flutters through magnificent lyrics with unease, as if fluking every syllable, and sadly not hitting the notes necessary to lift the score to where it is supposed to be. But the main problem beyond this is in the film adaptation's orchestrations: there is no nuance, no effort in presenting the peaks and troughs that the score delivers and no sense of drama. The book and lyrics for *Man of La Mancha* are well written, especially the lyrics, but it is the score that elevates the material and could have been the highlight of this ultimately bland and seemingly offbeat adaptation.

If the very heart of *Man of La Mancha* is about wishful thinking in history's darkest moments, then this is a truly inspired piece of musical theatre and potentially musical film. However, this 1972 effort doesn't do this core theme any justice. A song like "Singin' in the Rain" (a Tin Pan Alley number written at the start of the Great Depression and, of course, used in the classic 1952 film of the same name) is a perfect condensation of taking an unpleasant situation—a rain storm, acting as a metaphor for the economic and social tumult of the time—and bringing hope and idealism to it, its "singin'." This is what the musical in a grand traditional sense has always managed to do: it can present a war and give it romance, delivering glamour, joy and a sense of freedom in an otherwise oppressive context. But musicals also relish in delivering downbeat endings and subject matter, especially musical dramas, the direct descendants of opera. This occurs just as much as the cheerier versions. By 1972, the grittiness of Hollywood cinema knew which kind of musical would be more palpable for movie-going audiences: bright and cheery musicals seemed out of place, and if it was to have an instrumental influence in movie musicals than it best be disguised as excessive, decedent and completely out of its mind. *Man of La Mancha* is a musical that is grey in tone, stained with the blood, sweat and tears of its situation and remarkably depressing in its method of storytelling and delivery. But it is these things for all the wrong reasons, and is poorly handled and executed. The endless image of the windmill representing perpetual turmoil and slavery becomes overstated and uninvited.

There is one attribute of *Man of La Mancha* that is a beacon of warmth and sincerity, as well as genuinely entertainment: Sophia Loren. Once again the incredibly sexy—almost bestial—Loren is cast as the whore with the heart of gold in the tradition of *Irma La Douce* (1956) and Nancy from *Oliver!*, but her performance as this downtrodden, soiled and hardened woman is nothing short of spectacular. She is the best thing in the film: her vocal abilities are strong and her presence is refreshing. Loren made a career playing animalistic sensual nymphettes, and here she is completely comfortable as Aldonza. But even Loren's fine turn does not save the film from being misdirected and uneventful. It is unfortunate seeing that the film is directed by the otherwise great Arthur Hiller, although admittedly there have been other boring and bland Hiller films such as *Making Love* (1980).

Just as insipid as *Man of La Mancha* is *The Great Waltz*, which does not succeed as a movie musical at all. Something is lost in its 1970s translation as the musical was originally conceived in the early 1930s and its chronicle of the well-documented feud between the Strausses (Johann the first and his son). The jealousy this musical genius father had

146

for his more gifted composer son is lost in this 1970s adaptation, made far too blatant and crass and therefore totally defying the subtle intention of the original musical. Instead of pacing the drama as the original stage production did, the film (directed by Andrew L. Stone, who incidentally also directed the poorly made *Song of Norway*) goes through the motions rather than proceeding with a steady pace. The emotional turmoil of the elder Strauss is diminished to the point of not being properly realized. The dramatic progression is so hurried that the film stumbles to the ground and comes crashing to multiple halts. There is something to be said in waiting forty odd years for a cinematic adaptation, and *The Great Waltz* would have been far more suited to a European New Wave sensibility of the 1960s rather than this, or even given over to a director such as Ken Russell who could have made something more carnival-esque, which would have suited it to a tea. But both Stones musical efforts from 1970 and 1972 were ill conceived, poorly executed and as a result, forgettable messes.

CURIOUSER AND CURIOUSER:
Alice's Adventures in Wonderland, The Pied Piper and *1776*

The idea of adapting a classic children's book into a musical is not a new concept, nor is it a rare one—think of all the Disney animated features alone. But the British musical *Alice's Adventures in Wonderland* does something with Lewis Carroll's material that adds a nightmarish element, while forcing 1970s unease and creepiness into an already weird and haunting novel. Directed by William Sterling and starring Fiona Fullerton as Alice, this 1972 musical is a gothic and super-stylized take on the famous story about self-discovery, psychedelic philosophy and overwhelming nonsense. It is also one of the most melancholy fairy tale musicals ever put to screen with every experience our heroine undertakes being one of despair.

Fullerton's Alice is a young girl blossoming into womanhood, rather than Disney's *Alice in Wonderland* (1951) and the original book's heroine, which gave us a pre-adolescent. This allows for a more complex take on the character: she is allowed to come into her own sexual awakening through her many experiences in Wonderland, and rather than being obsessed with good manners, Fullerton's Alice is interested in experience and making strong decisions (sometimes the right ones and sometimes not). She moves through this fantastical land with a fragility and comes out of each situation changed, but not necessarily for the better.

Fiona Fullerton behind the scenes on *Alice's Adventures in Wonderland* (1972)

The film opens semi-biographically with Lewis Carroll (Michael Jayston) and his friend Duckworth (Hywel Bennett) taking Alice and her young sisters out rowing. Already the subtle implication of paedophilia permeates (the idea that Carroll himself was attracted to much younger girls was and is forever up for speculation), as Carroll gives young Alice long lustful glares. Even though she isn't the age of Disney's Alice, Fullerton's character is so understandably and rightfully naive and

**Michael Crawford in his White Rabbit costume, taking a break with his
children on the set of *Alice's Adventures in Wonderland* (1972)**

The Mad Hatter's tea party in *Alice's Adventures in Wonderland* (1972)

innocent that Carroll's suggestive leanings are remarkably unnerving and inappropriate. To have a counterpart in the equally lustful Duckworth makes it even more concerning. But director William Sterling does not dwell on this prologue and keeps it quick, sending Alice down the rabbit hole in an instant. From here on, Alice goes through the legendary set pieces: chasing the White Rabbit (Michael Crawford), growing and shrinking, swimming in her own tears and so forth.

Fullerton plays Alice with a quiet sensuality that plays well against the buffoonery and maniacal freak show provided by character actors such as Peter Sellers as The March Hare, Dudley Moore as The Dormouse and Spike Milligan as The Gryphon. Robert Helpmann (who made a terrifying impression as the Child Catcher in *Chitty Chitty Bang Bang* a few years earlier) makes another unsettling impression as the Mad Hatter. The Mad Hatter's tea party sequence is frantic and frenzied—it is total anarchy—and when Alice is asked "Who are you?" continuously by the Caterpillar (Ralph Richardson) it is a reflection of youth self-worth. When he asks her "so you think you've changed, do you?" the musical magically transforms itself into something even darker and more menacing. Alice enters a dark forest, the camera following her much like any horror film set in spooky woodlands, and she encounters Tweedle Dee and Tweedle Dum (Fred and Frank Cox) who are infantile and violent, obese cretins. The song Alice sings that comments on Tweedle Dee and Tweedle Dum's battle is haunting and ushers in a violent storm. The slow motion sequences add to the unsettling mood, and the giant crow that lands at Alice's face is a thing of nightmares (and dark fantasies).

It should be noted that the film shares a lot of odd similarities with Neil Jordan's werewolf fairy tale anthology film *The Company of Wolves* (1984), based on feminist writer Angela Carter's works concerning the mythology surrounding "Little Red Riding Hood" in its imagery of burgeoning female sexuality: phallic crow's beaks, posturing doormen presented as frogs who could quite possibly turn into handsome prices and so forth. The most distressing scene in *Alice in Wonderland* is the sequence involving the Duchess (played by an aggressively manic drag queen in Peter Bull) and the violent Cook (Patsy Rowlands) who abuse a baby and smash plates.

The make-up design by Stuart Freeborn is the most outstanding aspect to the film: it is simply fantastic. The idea that he modelled each character's design on the original and iconic sketches from John Tenniel used in the original print run of Carroll's book and today synonymous with the story is sheer brilliance. Freeborn would later than go on to create beautiful make-up work on *Star Wars* (1977), with his creation of Yoda in *The Empire Strikes Back* (1980) a crowning achievement.

Musically the film is troubled, and although the magnificent score by John Barry is powerful and rich, the songs throughout the film are not completely realized. The intricate lyrics by Don Black are terrific and insightful (the conception of "It's More Like A Pig Than a Baby" is a work of genius, but the entire song is sung in two lines) but for some strange reason they are not structured properly and instead they lead into a scene and then suddenly and abruptly disappear. It is not as if the songs are just short, it is as if they just have not been finished.

The song "The Last Word Is Mine" is one of the best numbers. It is a duet between the White Rabbit and Alice and it is such a delicately written number with sweeping key changes and tempo changes that it could quite easily go for two more verses. This is the main problem with the film: the songs go nowhere. The best ones hook you in and then suddenly erode and take flight, never to be reprised or referenced again. This is something that the film could have benefited from. However, the bizarre design and creepy elements of the film are compelling and leave an unnerving sense of awe. It is a weird experience, and the drug culture of the 1970s would most definitely add its appeal. Thankfully however, countercultural references are left outside of the film and its non-monumental songs, but the shadow of LSD and other mind expanding drugs lingers, hovering over the film reminding us of the appeal.

The Pied Piper is an eerily effective counterculture variant on the legend of the famous literary rat/child catcher. Directed by French auteur Jacques Demy, who delivered the incredibly haunting *The Umbrellas of Cherbourg* in 1964, the film is a testament to the influence of youth subculture influencing classicist genres such as the musical film. *The Pied Piper* systematically examines the stressed relationship between the pious state and the church and the anti-establishment young in search of their own voice. Working alongside the music of pop folk artist Donovan and composer and jazz pianist Kenny Clayton, Demy's *The Pied Piper* is a carefully crafted film shot in muted colours, boasting some magnificent imagery of the English countryside. As opposed to his earlier French New Wave musical *The Umbrellas of Cherbourg*, Demy downplays the romance of *The Pied Piper* and keeps it subtle to non-existent. This is not to say that the film does not have a sense of airiness or sweetness, but it is most definitely a reflection of the angry cry of the outsider and does not present us with dewy love struck youngsters. Instead, these children are ready to picket and break down tradition. In opposition to the hyper-realism and saturated colours that lent an otherworldliness to *The Umbrellas of Cherbourg*, Demy here decides to revel in earth tones and naturalistic lighting to convey a sense of historical authenticity. The film looks and sounds like a traditional Anglo Saxon folkloric festival and with its theatrical set-up (theatrical in the sense that it is shot in stoic prolonged one-shots, making the film look like a staged event), it is as if the audience is witnessing a moment of English history.

The film stars a wide range of gifted actors and musicians such as Donald Pleasence, John Hurt, Jack Wilde and Diana Dors, and gives

Donovan a platform to showcase his talents as an actor as the titular character. He is an impish, elfin seducer and the camera seems to love him—there is nothing phony or crass about him, and his Piper is an enigmatic sideshow freak collecting the rebellious youth and giving them their much-needed voice. Youthful rebellion and anti-establishment ideals sit at the centre of the musical, and unlike the somewhat clumsy *Jack and the Beanstalk* from the year before, Demy does not rely on contemporising vocabulary of the musical. Instead, it reads like a grim political fairy tale.

Donovan leads the children in *The Pied Piper*

However, because musicals are by their very nature fantasy films or escapist fare, the should-be subversive ideologies in *The Pied Piper* sometimes come across too strong and blatant. Throughout the film the message of unity and understanding difference and alienation starts to become repetitive and to have it drummed into the audiences' head constantly becomes a nuisance. But beyond that, the film is a remarkable achievement. No way near as important *The Umbrellas of Cherbourg*, but an intelligent and compelling watch.

There are more connections to the folk-horror film *Blood on Satan's Claw* (1970) than there is something like *Peau d'Ane*, which has a similar feel and has its strange magical edge (but is no way near as good as Demy's film). In *Blood on Satan's Claw*, children are the monsters and congregate as Satanic cultists in order to resurrect the devil himself, and in *The Pied Piper* the young are angry at the pious state and the church and challenge the authorities. Both films examine youthful revolutionaries and the threat they are to their establishment elders. The film's central plot focuses on the marriage of the daughter of a Baron and the outbreak of a plague of rats that surface while the much discussed wedding comes to fruition, but the underlying heart of the film is its keen interest in youth culture and it makes no real effort in hiding this fact and Donovan is perfect in reflecting this.

Demy's musical adaptation of the Brothers Grimm fairy tale is a terrific, if not sometimes overstated, film and the music harkens back to *Ye Olde London* but with contemporary sensibilities. Another musical that chose to reject 1970s trends and musical aesthetic was based on a major historical event in the United States and garnered very mixed reviews on release.

1776 possibly suffers namely because of the time it was filmed. It is completely out of step with not only the 1970s and its sensibilities, but with itself and even its own direction. Unlike other musicals of the time, it does not possess a sense of whimsy or drama or fun, and although it has a solid straight-forward narrative that works, the songs are interruptive and bland. It is a dull history lesson that fails to do anything interesting with the material. A musical from the 1980s such as *Les Misérables* does give a historical event a dramatic, devastating and romantic flair while successfully utilising the decade's sensibilities and aesthetic (the 2012 film adaptation also successfully captures the grandiose and over the top material in a contemporary effort). However, *Les Misérables* comes from a legendary novel, a seminal classic that adapts well into pop-opera. *1776* does not have anything romantic or devastating to say, nor does it use the eclectic tones of the 1970s to push it along. Instead it simply burps away with overwhelming tedium.

Peter Stone is a wonderful book writer, and created some fantastic works, such as the musical *Two By Two* (1970). His screen adaptation of *1776* is to-the-point and steadily fashioned, and there are definitely some comic moments that would keep any old-fashioned musical farce fan happy. But Stone's words are lost with the poor direction, the badly executed visuals and the bloated performances from a mostly insipid cast. The cast is the biggest surprise: great actors such as William Daniels,

Howard Da Silva and John Cullum are dumped into a film that lacks depth and integrity, left to churn out uneven and clumsy performances.

One of the most fundamentally flawed aspects about *1776* is that it deviates from the notion of slavery that could have added much to the piece. Being a musical farce and a musical comedy, slavery would have lead the film into sombre territory, but perhaps this is something that it needed. Peter Stone certainly knew how to write drama and tragedy. This story about the Declaration of Independence would already struggle to find a mass audience, especially when presented as a light but ultimately pompous affair. But *1776* also suggests that there has been no attempt to make the score, the lyrics or the performances (once again, at the more than capable hands of great actors) workable or even remotely interesting.

At the premiere of *1776* (1972)

This results in what is really a musical high school lesson, but one that is excruciatingly and frustratingly dull and uninspired. What is worse is that instead of being a working piece of comedy, some of the sequences are laughable without intending to be, and the one-dimensional direction makes the transitions from scene-to-scene and from dialogue-to-song hard to swallow. The mood travels from light and silly to serious and political, and there is nothing make those shifts organic, and they instead comes across as if director Hunt is saying "Oh OK, here we'll have a song and now let's talk about Thomas Jefferson and his wife and maybe this can be where they share a number." Sadly, *1776*—not a great musical to begin with—does not do anything clever with its translation into film, and even though the source material may not be everyone's cup of tea, there was still room to make it accessible and entertaining.

Musicals with questionable subject matter would continue to flourish into the following year, and two of them would share the same protagonist: Jesus Christ. However, these two musicals would present the King of the Jews in remarkably different ways. One would depict him as a perplexed and angst-ridden rabble-rousing misfit, while the other would turn him into a minstrel clown parading around an emptied modern day New York City. These two musicals would also focus on different aspects of his life: one would deliver the last three days of his life, while the other would follow his teachings as told through vaudeville shtick. Both would prove to be equally controversial and brilliant…

1973

"I Shall Call the Pebble Dare"
The Christ Clown, Shangri-la, Sherwood Forest and Some Pig

By 1973, THE MOVIE MUSICAL HAD NOT YET MADE A STEADY COMEBACK. The genre was still on shaky ground. The early years of the decade were still haunted by the film flops of the 1960s, so many major players were hesitant to take on big budget motion picture musicals. But films such as *Fiddler on the Roof* and *Cabaret* suggested what the musical film could do and could deliver, as well as indicated how successful they could be critically and—more importantly—at the box office. This led certain studios (both major and minor) to take notice. On top of this, independent rock'n'roll extravaganzas such as *Woodstock* sparked a progressive interest from studio heads, who originally thought films featuring rock musicians performing were simply documentaries about youth culture. Over time, they began to realize that films such as *Keep on Rockin'*, *Alice Cooper: Live* and the made for TV *Liza with a Z* were seriously cinematic.

The fact that the movie musical was becoming more gritty and youth-oriented generated a healthy interest in funding more outlandish concepts, leading to the adaptation of Off-Broadway musicals that normally would have been sidelined or completely ignored. It also inspired adaptations of previous non-musical narrative driven stories into song and dance spectacles, as well as possibly the most innovative and freshest thing of all: breathing cinematic life into the concept album.

In 1973, the movie musical was given a new chance, as a new-wave of integrated and diegetic show-tune riddled films began to appear. The change in style was happening on the New York stage, and the silver screen was still catching up. However, it did so very quickly, and with an angry and cynical voice. Edgy musicals became the fad, and stylistic and eccentric choices became the norm in a year that introduced the world to the very first full-blown rock opera to come to the cinema screen, Norman Jewison's incredible cinematic adaptation of *Jesus Christ Superstar*...

COULD WE START AGAIN PLEASE?: *Jesus Christ Superstar*

Jesus Christ Superstar is a masterpiece, not only of song writing and performance, but of style, substance and innovation. Norman Jewison's filmic adaptation of the rock opera by Andrew Lloyd Webber and Tim Rice is so intelligently conceived and unique that it is most definitely a staple of the modern movie musical. If other filmic adaptations of musicals were like Jewison's film, then there would be laundry lists of genius motion pictures employing rock music that would flood the stages of musical theatre. It is an inspired, analogous rock opera that makes an insightful commentary on the record industry itself. At the heart of the film is the idea that Jesus Christ (Ted Neeley) is the first true or authentic rock star that appeals to the people. This threatens the priests and Pharisees, headed by Caiphas (Bob Bingham) and Annas (Kurt Yaghjian), who come to represent frightened "musicians" falling out of fashion and not so appealing to the energetic and passionate crowds lead by Mary Magdalene (Yvonne Elliman), the film's ultimate rock'n'roll groupie of Jesus. The concerned Judas Iscariot (Carl Anderson) therefore acts as Christ's worried manager, always watching and advising, questioning and scrutinizing Christ and his "band's" (the disciples) moves.

This metaphoric subtext is dwarfed by the film's spirited exuberance and unapologetic cynicism. This is a musical that does not want to paint a pretty picture: it is a bleak and angry rock'n'roll show that is dirty, dusty and sweaty. And thank Christ for that!

Director Norman Jewison washes the feet of Ted Neeley as Jesus, behind the scenes on *Jesus Christ Superstar* **(1973)**

The film opens with the beautiful image of a vast desert land, where you could expect to hear Middle Eastern instrumentation leading us into a lavish sandstorm epic. Instead, we are greeted by electric guitars that invite us into a bizarre and brand new experience in cinema. When the music crashes in, we are in dangerous territory. A large bus zooms through the desert and pouring out of it come a bunch of rock'n'roll youths with their long hair and soiled skirts and jeans. First, they are made up in stylized costumes that look like a cross between contemporary hippie garb and opera costume, and they then proceed to form a circle and finally present us with an incredibly holier-than-thou Jesus Christ in the form of the magnificently talented Ted Neeley. We have entered the world of players presenting a performance in the middle of the desert, but we are also experiencing what *Jesus Christ Superstar* is–a rock'n'roll show, but also an opera. The final image before the main title fades in is that of a prologue to an opera: spoken dialogue is not welcome here because the songs will set the scene. Andre Previn's phenomenal score boasts some fabulous musicians from contemporary rock acts such as Black Sabbath and Deep Purple, and is exhilarating and seductive.

Director Norman Jewison recalls how he wanted to approach the adaptation of what was originally a concept album that had gone onto stage not too long before Universal Studios picked up the film rights:

> It was a long discussion I had with Universal when they asked me to do the film. They said "Well how are we gonna do this?" and my answer was like this, "Well every story, every film I make, is based on an event that happened somewhere in the world" and what I wanted to do was recreate with some sort of authenticity in spite of it being a rock opera. I wanted to go on location scouts in the Middle East. And Universal reluctantly gave me permission to go to Palestine and to the Negev and so on. I called Melvyn Bragg, who was a young English writer and I went to him with the proposal that we have this rock opera which has taken off as a record and as a performance in London which was en route to New York and I said "I want to make this into a movie musical." So we sat down and we took two audio cassettes of the track and we took a couple of Walkman and put those in our ears and got on a plane to Tel Aviv. And literally, the two of us started to walk around to different areas such as the Dead Sea and all across the desert lands. While we were in the ruins of Navidad we saw a roaring bus come through and it had a lot of writing scrawled all over it and none of the writing was in Hebrew, and I thought "this is strange, this odd bus with a lot of Arabic writing on it coming into the middle of the desert" and out of this bus came a bunch of young students to look at these ruins, to do sketches. Then they piled on the bus and left. And I thought, that is just like *Jesus Christ Superstar* where a bunch of actors and dancers are going to arrive in the desert and perform this story and

then disappear again. So we thought of that as the seed for the idea. That is literally how it grew. And then I started to see different images there in Israel. I thought the lyrics of Tim Rice were so powerful that I got swept away with the message and with the distillation with trying to bring the biblical story into the present day, so that's when I started to work on the idea of the Roman soldiers would be dressed in modern tank tops and carry guns and wear heavy artillery boots. But they would also wear helmets that would be vintage of the time and they would reflect the sun. Then I got carried away and had these ideas for the whole production, for example I wanted modern military infiltration in some scenes, for example the scene where Judas played by Carl Anderson is chased down by large tanks and so forth. It became quite a musical spectacle and as I got more into the making of the film I got a bit looser with it. Richard MacDonald my production designer really deserves a lot of credit. He said "Just let your imagination go." And I thought yes, I will. And I said to him, "Look at that scaffolding that they have put up just next to the ruins!" and it was just some scaffolding that the workmen put up that went up about three stories. And it was sitting there silhouetted against the sky and I said "Send about three or four people up there, just to see how it looks." Then I turned to MacDonald and said "That looks great, why don't we put the high priests up there, in their high hats and big black robes?" That's how loose I was working! It was like I was back in television with five cameras doing a TV special with Gary Smith who used to be my designed in New York and we used to work with very minimal things. We worked with silhouettes and not much scenery. We worked with suggestion and you could do a lot with suggestion and get away with so much. And that's how Jesus Christ Superstar worked, we did it with very minimal sets and told the story and set up scenes through suggestion. And I must say, that MacDonald really helped me and he saw what I was doing and he worked much differently than other British designers who are usually very good at building scenery, they're usually very theatrical. I had Doug Slocombe as director of cinematography and he's very centric and I think I saved his life a couple of times! He was always stepping off scaffolding and I was always grabbing him and pulling him back. He was a little older than the rest of us and he was one of the best cinematographers from Britain. I had a young Canadian choreographer and that was really a big change for me and was a bit of a concern just because a lot of people working on the film challenged him, because he really wasn't an established choreographer. He came from Canada and he came from a television background. He was most definitely a rock'n'roll choreographer but he was also classically trained. Bob Iscove was his name and I brought him in. I had all this casting to do. The casting was done in London and in New York and in Toronto and in Tel Aviv. I mean it was the most incredibly mixed cast ever. And it was such an exciting thing for young actors and singers. We had no trouble in casting it really, I mean everyone wanted to be in it. I had fallen in love with Barry Dennen who played Pontious Pilate and I had picked him up from the British production. And I got Bob Bingham who played Caiphas, a great bass singer, and I gave that character a lot more and made him more three dimensional. When I found Ted Neeley in America, I auditioned him and he was inspired. Neeley was divine. And then I had the luck of putting he and Carl Anderson together in rehearsal in Los Angeles and a lot of people thought you can't test Carl Anderson because he is black and people will read into that as something negative. And that you're casting against type here. And I said, yes but what about the talent?! He's got the talent for the role! Why should I cast someone else because they're white? Anderson is brilliant and an amazing actor. He had everything I wanted for the part. And so I had my three, the good, the bad and the beautiful. I had Neeley, Elliman and Anderson. And those three were truly the important casting and then we you get the supporting players, and a lot of dancers from New York who had worked with me before; they were all real pros. And they knew all the moves very well. That's kind of the way the casting gestated.

Norman Jewison directs "What's the Buzz?" from *Jesus Christ Superstar*
(1973)

"Everything's Alright" is one of the most beautifully realized dramatic points of the film and sets up the three characters—the film's holy trinity—perfectly. Each character is written musically: Mary Magdalene has a soothing rock diva structure, Judas is given a brassy bluesy growl, and Christ represents the full-blown stadium rock of the 1970s. The musicality of these people, the dimensions of their performance through their voices, and their unique take on these characters is magical. Ted Neeley is a fabulous performer whose voice is a marvel, and Carl Anderson's portrayal of Judas Iscariot is nothing short of genius. Here is an actor whose raw passion, delivery and fine-tuned emotionality should have geared him towards an Oscar nomination. As fantastic as Ted Neeley is, Anderson is so phenomenally electric that his anger, rage, despair and loss is so recognizable and empathetic that Judas most certainly steals the show. Even when the angst ridden Judas interrupts the jazz fusion of "What's The Buzz?" with his sleazy "Strange Thing Mystifying" we fall under his spell: he is no killjoy, but simply second guessing Jesus's ideas and philosophies.

From song to song (and from scene to scene) we the audience experience the last three days of Christ's life in the most emotionally stirring manner. It is made all the more captivating by the inventive merging of the theatrical (the bizarre marriage of the contemporary with passion play operatics) with character driven drama. There are many phenomenally staged sequences throughout the picture: one scene depicts peddlers and whores selling their wares (including modern day artillery and cocaine) only to be banished by a screaming angry Jesus who is disgusted that they have turned his temple into a sleazy market place. This scene then shifts to the moment where Christ is met by the diseased and desperate lepers who claw at the reluctant messiah. The genius in the musicality of these two aforementioned scenes is that the score is completely the same—the melody drives to a frenzy and the stress levels rise in both our "enlightened" hero and in us, the audience. When Mary Magdalene belts out the iconic "I Don't Know How to Love Him," we feel her frustration and confusion. Here is a prostitute who has finally fallen in love, but with someone completely out of control and perplexed about his preordained power. "The Last Supper," explodes electrically and dramatically as Christ and Judas face off in an intense confrontation that elevates this rock opera from sensationalism to a pure, emotionally driven character study. When Christ ploughs through the amazing "I Only Want to Say (Gethsemane)," it is musical film at its greatest: a performance that not only embodies everything about the story we are experiencing, but also captures the very essence of the 1970s rock musical with all its rawness, anger, confusion, rage, passion, desperation and alienation. When Christ finally accepts his messianic influence, his grim fate, and his position of holy power, we hear a perplexed and terrified young man cry "I will drink your cup of poison...nail me to the cross and beat, bleed me, kill me, take me now...before I change my mind...." This is cynical lyricism at its finest.

"Peter's Denial" in *Jesus Christ Superstar* **(1973)**

In regard to the details of production itself, director Jewison continues:

Like most musicals of that time, everything was pre-recorded. It was a little bit more difficult for me because I was recording a lot of it in London before I had actually staged it. I had some problems with the staging. I had problems trying to stay with the music as it was originally recorded. I remember having a few problems that way. I had a lot of click tracks which would give me the tempo and then I could extend a lot of dance moves and movement strictly by staying in tempo. And then fix it later. Andre Previn who was an extremely experienced conductor, composer and arranger, happened to be the musical director of the London symphony. He had stopped doing movies and stopped playing jazz and gone legit. I had the opportunity of working with both the London Symphony Orchestra and with these wild rock musicians on Jesus Christ Superstar. And if you could have seen the first rehearsal when you had the London symphony sitting there and these rock musicians who had never seen a conductor in their life. And Andre Previn tapped the lectern and started. The orchestra played beautifully. And I was waiting for the rock musicians to kick off who were sitting in the front with their electric guitars and drums and so forth and I will never forget when it came to their cue they just sat there! They were stunned by the idea of a conductor and an orchestra! So when it came time to start playing, Andre angrily pointed his conductor's baton at them but they just sat there, playing nothing! He then stepped down from his pedestal and went at them! He said "Gentlemen do you know how to fucking count bars?!" It was hysterical; it was something I'll never forget from those recording sessions. And we had a great group, I mean we had some guys from Deep Purple and other bands, but it was a clash of cultures. When it came to taking a break, all the orchestral musicians would stop playing and just stand up and leave, while the rock musicians would stop and not know where they were going. They'd say "We're are they are off to?" We had to explain to them that they were taking their tea break. And they all just sat there staring at each other, I mean they all wanted to go and smoke a joint. It was hysterical. And Andre was just wonderful. When I bought the film back from Israel to London, to begin the editing process and got into those long scenes that I shot with no score at all, which I just laid some music on there, some scraps I had heard, and Andre sat down and composed a lot of material that was incidental, for example in the scene of the crucifixion, which was very jazzy. He didn't like Andrew Lloyd Webber very much! It wasn't a big fan of the score! It was a matter of really listening to the music and lyrics carefully and wandering around where the action that was travelling around the lyric would take place. It was so tactile, it kind of fell into place. I didn't find it a difficult thing, I mean we had to sit down and write it and describe it, like you do for all musical screenplays, they are broken down into segments—and of course we didn't have any dialogue, we had to simply just work with Tim Rice's lyrics. So it was really Rice's lyrics that guided us. I wasn't that difficult for me to open up as a musical from stage to screen. It flowed for me. Once I knew I could add eight bars here and sixteen bars there and a punctuation there, etc., once I knew I was free to do that with a click track I was fine. I also had a wonderful music editor at the time. I bought him in from Hollywood. And his knowledge of music was amazing and he had speakers with huge amps which filled the desert with sound! It was unbelievable the way we worked with this crew. I found this whole thing exciting. And it was the last film to be shot in Todd-AO. We had these huge Todd-AO lenses on tiny little Panaflex camera. So you would see this crane with this little camera and this huge lens and we would swoop all over the place. I was very anxious to keep the camera moving. At the time when you think back at it, at the time of its release in the early 1970s it was pretty avant garde. Now of course it's not that much at all. The growth of rock music and incredible energy in choreography is done to death now, but in those days it was very unique.

Dealing with the life and death of Jesus Christ sparked controversy, as Jewison remembers:

The film came under a lot of attack when it was completed. It was attacked by a group of very strong American Jewish rights groups who kind of tried to label it as anti-Semitic. And this really appalled me, because I had just finished doing *Fiddler on the Roof* so I couldn't quite understand where this attack was coming from. Then I found out that it was a small militant group that had also protested the stage production in New York. We had a problem with the Southern American Christian groups who protested against the film. When I finished the film my biggest fear was the organised power of the Catholic Church. So I approached the Vatican, the *Observartorio Romano*, which is the paper the Vatican controlled, and I said to somebody in there and explained to them that a film had been made of *Jesus Christ Superstar* and that I would invite someone from the Vatican to come and see it. We would pay their way and see what they thought. I'll never forget I did this with the blessing from Universal.

I told Universal, that if the Christian church disavows this film then you're in trouble. Tim Rice lyrics are very explicit and very cynical, and the film is filled with cynicism, so Universal said "OK show it to the Vatican" They thought it was very risky but eventually these people are going to see it. It's going to open in Rome! Let's see what happens here. They sent three guys over, a monsignor and two other priests from Rome and I sat them down in the screening room in Pinewood studios and said "Just let it happen!" I explained to them the story, that it was a group of young people working with rock music and a young composer, Webber was only in his 1920s, so was Rice, and these were young people trying to express themselves musically with Christ's story. And they had to take that into consideration. And I said this is going to be something that you've never seen before. And I said this is not religious music you're going to hear, it's totally polar opposite. Luckily these priests were fairly young and so they were aware of rock music. So they just sat there and were overwhelmed. After they saw it, the monsignor looked at me and said "Not since Leonard DaVinci and his innovative depiction of Christ have I been moved this much. You have made a work of art." And I thought, wow, if it works for him then maybe we'll get lucky here and get the blessing from the Catholic Church. But there were certainly religious groups who hated it and picketed it all across America.

Tim Rice's approach was incredible. Jesus was a young man in moments of insecurity and moments of "What am I doing?." He was depicted in a young twentieth century interpretation of Christ. And this was great because a lot of the young audience understood this and related. And that's where Ted Neely stepped in and just did so beautifully. That is a great soliloquy and that is the most important soliloquy that he has in the entire film and we spent a lot of time working it out and staging it. It was one of my favourite films I've ever made. I was bought up a Canadian Methodist, so I had to go to Sunday school and church and my folks bought me up as a fairly strong Methodist. For me, Superstar was a great blessing and I really poured my heart into it, I tried too hard to make it a film that would not just entertain but enlighten people.

Jewison recalls the film's characterizations, and the introduction of the add-on song "Could We Start Again Please?":

I think I felt that Yvonne Elliman, her character needed more gravity. I was always worried about Mary Magdalene, I felt like she needed a lot more. I always thought here was this woman who had this passionate devotion to this guy that was bigger than life itself and how does she deal with this? "I Don't Know How to Love Him" is an amazing song, and a true showstopper in the purest sense of the term, but I wanted more for her. So I approached the boys. It came out of a discussion that I had with Tim Rice and I remember Andrew playing a song for me called "Could We Start Again Please?" and it happened very early in the process. It was before we went on location and we were going through every aspect of the score and just decided we could use another number at that point in the musical. I was very, very enchanted by Yvonne's voice. It was really something. The song was kind of an extension of her character.

The film looks magnificent, and there are ingenious elements in Jewison's filmmaking. For example, in the "Simon Zealots" number, the disciples throw their nubile young bodies around deserted ancient ruins and temples, kicking up sand and exhaustively dancing around a frazzled and conflicted Christ. In the sequence involving King Herod (Josh Mostel), the Dead Sea is presented as a ragtime vaudeville number complete with comic shtick. Herod torments the fragile Christ with such nasty glee that the sequence is bright and funny but also mean-spirited and confronting. And when Christ is arrested and pushed through the crowds who interrogate him with questions, we enter the latter part of

169

the film knowing the outcome but not knowing how the outcome will be delivered.

The Simon Zealots number in *Jesus Christ Superstar* (1973)

Ultimately, *Jesus Christ Superstar* is a superbly directed rock opera film that never misses a beat and never sinks into cliché. Instead, it lifts itself from one mighty moment to another and sincerely symbolizes youthful angst and alienation in a well-informed and enlightened manner. There is a genuine angry cry of the outsider reflective in this film and the melancholy that permeates never outstays its welcome.

Jewison remembers further details about the film shoot itself:

> Tony Gibbs, my editor, was really into it! We had the opportunity to play with it. We were cutting it on an old moviola. It was a laborious task but the one good thing was bringing Tony Gibbs from London to Tel Aviv and put him in an editing suite in Israel with a moviola and editing track and that way I could see cut film maybe every three or four days. I could get into the editing room and look at some images and discuss them and talk about what I had seen, what idea I had, and if scenes would fit and he was so encouraging, he was like "Keep shooting! Keep shooting!" I think it was just one of those things that you try in the editing room and see if they work. I just tried it as an idea and then I liked the idea and then I could refine it. But these things were just tried as ideas that I had and Tony and I

experimented. As far as the freeze frame stuff I did that in television musicals. Which I worked on in New York. I had tried to freeze frame the dancers for two beats and in the end it was something you could do. In film however it's something you have to really work at until it becomes an optical. These are all television techniques. A lot of what I do with film comes from that. We did use the zoom lens and crane choreographically. The Last Supper is such a corny overused image to try to place everyone exactly as they're place in the painting and then to bring them to life. We had the sketch to work with. My biggest problem was to plant grass! Because I wanted them to sit on green grass, not on dirt or sand. I guess I was inspired by the painting, in that I wanted it to be kind of magical. So I planted grass. I had to water it every day. I realised one day that I had to get guards to stand around it and guard it because everyone wanted to bring their sheep down to eat it! It was hysterical! MacDonald protected it and we got the shot! In regard to Judas's suicide, the big thing is that you have to have a lot of confidence in the special effect guy! I had a long talk with Carl Anderson and let him know that if anything doesn't work I will grab his legs. We had a long cable so that when he actually hangs himself, when he throws his full weight off the tree, he would hit the cable and that saves him from actually being strangled. I promised him that I would be right there. It was quite a traumatic to do that. I said from the very beginning, I don't wanna portray Judas as a villain. He believes Christ is over stepping himself. He is challenging Christ's divinity. I tried to build Carl up and his belief in the character. He was such a great actor that he gave an outstanding performance. And for the last number, the title number, I got the biggest crane in Israel at the time to lower him down and bring him back to life for one more number! He was always hanging somewhere! That's a real rock stadium number and it has a lot of sexy ladies in it and we really got into it! That's where the rock music really cooks in that number. I just love that! And again it was an image I had in my mind, I had to question how to bring someone back to earth and I just thought bring him down by crane! Oh and Herod! Herod is such a fun character! I will never forget Josh Mostel. He was the son of Zero Mostel! I didn't use Zero in *Fiddler on the Roof*, so the rumour is, when I called Josh and he had auditioned for me in New York, I called him up and said "I thought about it and I just looked at the video of you and decided you should play Herod" and he was very happy and I heard someone carrying on in the background and I said "what's that?" and Josh said "Oh that's my dad!" and I heard his dad yell out "Why doesn't he call Topol's son!" I thought it was a camp moment, a very lascivious sissy role! They were always creepy those guys and lots of fun! A lot of those dancers and singers used in Herod's scene were from New York. Bayork Lee was someone I worked with. Some of them were bought in from Rob Iscove from Canada. He had certain dancers that he liked and wanted to cast. And then some of the apostles were cast in Israel because they happened to be available and they were English speaking actors. So we could save some money by hiring them. The four leads of the priests were from England, but there were some people that we used in Israel that lip synched to our score. Ah, I love the film. It was a real joy to work on and I love it a lot.

With Jewison's film, the rock opera presented as a motion picture was born. It all came from ingenious and risky ideas, as well as a healthy amount of controversy, angst and coolness. Eventually, director Ken Russell will follow up the rock opera film with his terrific *Tommy*, but before that frenetic odyssey, another religious themed rock musical would get the film treatment, and instead of a passion play enacted by rock'n'rollers, this one would borrow from American street theatre, vaudeville and clowning…

IT SAYS "KEDS": *Godspell*

In *Godspell*, New York City has never looked so picturesque. There is something irresistibly romantic and seductive about the way the color and spectacle of the Big Apple appears in David Greene's film. The cinematography is one of the movie's most magical features, and there are moments where the camera lifts you both physically and emotionally, then brings you into intimate close-ups with these clowns as the film showcases their emotive brilliance. Simultaneously, in the same scene the camera can distance you from them so they become like tiny ragdolls skipping through the emptied streets, dwarfed by their newfound Jerusalem. There is a sense of eeriness in *Godspell*, a strange kind of feeling aroused in both the senses and in the sensibilities of its audience. *Godspell* is not scared of taking risks, and it does it flawlessly.

The film opens on a piece of graffiti with a strange sound effect. Soon the voice of the Christ-clown (played by the wiry Victor Garber, who we shall soon meet) recites a small selection from a passage originally used in what was "The Tower of Babble" sequence in the original stage musical. The camera quietly glides across to our "new Jerusalem": New York City in the early 1970s. The title card travels towards us over the youthful and handsome David Haskell, who comes at us ready to deliver the word of the messiah and to introduce us to the world of *Godspell*. We then cut to the hustle and bustle of modern day New York, tossed into the heart of the rat race. People are angry, dissatisfied, impatient and ruthless, and we feel no need to understand them or care about them. But it is here we meet our cast of clowns-to-be, and they are enigmatic and interesting. One is a ballerina rehearsing, one a waitress trying to take in James Joyce's "Ulysses," another a taxi driver stuck in traffic, and so forth. All of them are magically greeted by David Haskell, a John the Baptist figure who leads them to Central Park to the iconic Bethesda Fountain and baptises them as they sing the popular song "Prepare Ye the Way of the Lord" (a contagious melody with the main title as the core of the song's lyric). These New Yorkers are christened and reborn as care-free loveable clowns, and they all soon meet their leader. He comes in the form of Victor Garber, with wildly huge afro hair, a Superman t-shirt and clown face, complete with a love heart painted on his forehead.

Robin Lamont in *Godspell* (1973)

The cast of *Godspell* (1973) visiting the White House

174

Joanna Jonas and Jerry Sroka play out the Good Samaritan parable in *Godspell* (1973)

Godspell is a high concept film. The idea of adapting a musical about a group of ragamuffins in a junkyard closed off from the world by a cyclone fence who re-enact the parables of the gospel according to St. Matthew was something that perplexed film executives and directors alike. The cast members also had reservations and concerns, as noted by original New York cast member Gilmer McCormick:

> I really couldn't have imagined it on film. I just couldn't picture how it could be played out on screen. At the same time *Jesus Christ Superstar* was being filmed and I remember there was a little bit of discussion about taking it over to Israel and filming it there, just like *Jesus Christ Superstar*, but that was completely discouraged because what *Godspell* is, is American street theatre, so it needed to be shot in America. Then the idea of closing off New York came about, which I thought was a great idea.

Producer Edgar Lansbury recalls the conception and creation of the film of *Godspell*:

> Back in the 1960s my partner and I, Joe Raposo, had been thinking about the spiritual renaissance that had been happening in America at the time, and we wanted to get something together that kind of fed into that feeling. And of course *Jesus Christ Superstar* arrived at about the same time, and we had heard of a small musical that had been playing downtown here in New York with a cast that was comprised of a bunch of drama students from Carnegie Technical College. It had been written and directed by John-Michael Tebelak. He came up with the concept and the show and he was really interested in religion and spirituality, especially Christianity. So my partner and I went down to see it at the Café La Mama and it was actually the last night of the play and we both decided that it would be a wonderful show to take uptown to the Cherry Lane Theatre. We had met Stephen Schwarz when he was trying to pitch an early rendition of *Pippin*. We weren't interested in *Pippin* but we thought he might be great to rewrite and create new songs for *Godspell*. *Godspell* was great but it needed a lot of work and both Joe and I thought that Stephen would be great for it; to give it new life. We then recast most of the roles from the original cast except for two, the other eight were completely recast. John-Michael, who wasn't very well at the time, directed, but Stephen was so good and so capable, I mean he was just starting his career out and we opened at the Cherry Lane and got tremendous reviews and sold out every night. At that time we had taken up a lease at a hotel and opened up a new theatre with a play called Promenade and we named the theatre after the show. The Promenade Theatre became a choice theatre in New York, it held three hundred seats and we moved *Godspell* there and then toured it all across American and it became a big sensation. Each time we did the show we had to recast it. That was quite a job

176

auditioning an ongoing project. There were people who would have liked to have made a film of *Godspell* but these were ideas that we didn't particularly like, so we decided to make it ourselves through Columbia Pictures. And when we got started to map out how we would film it, I bought in my friend and director David Greene and collaborated with him. David was an Englishman and also very talented and very inventive. He did a tremendous job and was very helpful in shaping the book and adapting it into a workable screenplay. He had that wonderful idea of setting the film in an empty city which was a very unique idea and it worked beautifully. We recast the movie where we felt it was necessary, but all the cast who were in it were in a production of *Godspell* in one place or another. Stephen was very busy with *Pippin* at the time of the filming of *Godspell*. He was involved but only just. He had written a new song for the film called "Beautiful City," which is a great song. As far as the concept of the film, it was mainly David Greene's idea to really use the city—he chose all these great locations to house the scenes and songs. The song "All for the Best" was staged on a billboard in Times Square which was very inventive. We never went outside of the city, everything we shot was in New York City. We were looking for a unique look to the city. Richard G. Heiman the photographer was incredible and our art designer who was another Englishman were just so brilliant in capturing the city and giving it that clean and fresh bright look. It was a meeting of minds and if Stephen felt it should have been grittier it would have been entirely possible, but I like the way it looked. Katie Hanley was in the road companies, she had also come from Carnegie. As did Robin, Gilmer, Jeffrey and Jerry Sroka was also in the original in the production, Lynne Thigpen was another one from the road company that we drew out. The only real new person was Merrell Jackson who sang "All Good Gifts." They were a great bunch of kids and all got along real well. The man who we namely dealt with at Columbia Pictures was a man called John Van Eisen who at that time was squiring Ingrid Bergman around town, he was an interesting fellow. He would have liked to have had David Essex in the role of Jesus who had played the role in England, I think he wanted someone with a bit of cache for the part. But we didn't use him. I only experienced a bit of backlash from the church. Interestingly enough when we did the revival recently there was support from religious groups who have finally come around to accepting the story and the show. I don't think the way we finally presented them was ever remotely close to hippiedom. They were most certainly minstrel clowns. That was the famous stage conception. Susan Tsu did the theatre design and was very influential in the film's look. She was not there a lot of the time as she had another job to do. The visual concept had really arrived with David Greene and our designer on the film and it was a joint agreement on how it should look. And the clown influence was a prevalent one. Although there are critics and movie fans out there that still think that these kids were a bunch of hippies. I never thought this was the case. Community was a very important idea to the film. The song "beautiful city" encapsulates that idea. It's a very positive message about humanity and cities in general. Of course Stephen wrote the song but it was done in partnership with David. I very much love the end of the film. That sadness. That's inherit in the play. It's an intense moment and a sombre moment. The character of John the Baptist who has now turned into Judas taking Jesus away to be crucified. I mean it's a terrible thing to happen especially when throughout the film you have these people having such a happy time together. In the case of improvisation, the scene in the Cherry Lane theatre with the old films was completely a novel and new idea and it wasn't something that we planned from the beginning, it was developed as we got into the film. Several of the songs including "All for the Best," that was a thought that came up one week and then we did it the next week. As far as emptying the city, that was just a matter of crowd control. We had stopped traffic on Park Avenue in that final moment when the city comes back to life. We had a lot of guys with walkie talkies running around controlling the crowds. There were several producers who would have liked to have bought the rights and we had decided to do it ourselves. The last time I saw David Greene he told me that it was the most important film he had ever done. David had worked in television which is where I met him, out in California at CBS so he had been thoroughly Americanizfor the bested—he was very inventive and there was no conflict there with his background—he was excited by the idea of doing it—Columbia approved him which was very wise instead of a blockbuster director and that's how it all happened. Also, Sammy Bayes was great—he was a choreographer whose speciality was working on the set and creating ideas and how it should be done—he was not a formulaic chore he was very inventive—there wasn't much choreography, it was very simple—it was his way of doing it—it grew out of the action of the scene. David and John and Stephen thought about doing the final's opening as it was presented in the play—the way the prologue works now is much more interesting and much more filmic—it was showing the city—it was showing the crowds and the action and the variety of jobs people have and how humanity fits in the city. The use of the World Trade Centre—one of the very few places on film where you can see it and get a view from it—yes it's a great monument to that building. The Cannes Film Festival was very exciting and very good for the film. It didn't win any prizes but it woke the world up to the movie. It really has proven its worth in time, however that wasn't the case originally when it was initially released. It was very important to me as a producer and as an individual. I made a lot of friends through it, wonderful relationships were born from it that have lasted my life. It is most certainly the most important film I ever made. And I appreciate how much it means to people.

Actress Gilmer McCormick recalls her legacy with *Godspell*:

John Michael-Tebelak did his master's thesis at Carnegie
and I had worked with him in a couple of summer stock
seasons in Ohio. We were great buddies. I graduated and he
stayed one more year and after he graduated he wanted to
mount that show. He called me, we rehearsed it and we had
a whole different score. What didn't please me was the
changing of the cast. I mean that really upset me. The
personalities from the stage show really made that show
what it was, and when they changed cast members for the
film. You know in the stage show we had established each of
our characters, there was the Gilmer character, the Peggy
Gordon character, the Sonia Manzano character and so
forth, and we all had very distinct personalities; very different
personalities. Sonja couldn't do the film because she was
committed to *Sesame Street*, so they got Joanne Jonas in there
but it wasn't the same. I was real disappointed. The original
chemistry was just so wonderful. I didn't think Victor was
successful in that role, I just wasn't convinced by him. He
wasn't the clown that Stephen Nathan was and if you go by
the idea that you become a child or at one with a child when
you enter the kingdom of heaven, then it stands to reason
that Jesus has to be the biggest clown or the biggest fool of
all. Being the daughter of a minister at first I thought the
show was completely sacrilegious, I just didn't get what John
Michael was getting at and when we got the script there
were no stage directions, it was just straight out bible with
Clown #1 though to Clown #10 written there on the page.
Eventually our names were used and they became the set
names of the clowns for the piece. When I first got it I just
didn't get it. But the more we worked it in the workshop the
more I got to understand it. I thought he was bringing the
joy of the gospel and the idea of "I have called you friend,"
which all struck a note in me. The idea of Jesus being a friend
really got to me and the notion of if you screw up Jesus is

gonna love you anyways, that message was great. And the parables, and performing them in a street theatre manner, gave the show a learning process and a transforming process. Originally John Michael wanted to make *Godspell* the first part of a trilogy. He was going to start with *Godspell* and then have the second part be the acts of the gospels, and he was going to call that *Gatherings* where the apostles were going to get together in the upper room and get their powers like language. And the third one which was going to be all about the revelations. That was going to feature a lot of guitar work and be very wild. But of course, John Michael didn't live long enough to write these. I sometimes thought about writing *Gatherings*, but I never got around to it. We talked about the idea of someone coming into your life for a day who knew you so completely and loved you so unconditionally, from that, what would you become? We turned our clowns into the essence of ourselves. And I remember thinking, if someone like that walked into my life I would want to crawl up into his lap like a little girl. So I wanted my clown to be the closest to a child that I could make her. Sonja, was a wild girl at that time, so her essence was really sexy and she would have tried to have seduced this kind stranger. And Peggy was the earth mother, she was always going around going "om," she would have become the Mary image, a very down to earth girl, so not so high end clown. My clown became based on a child. In the movie they tried to match us up with one another, but on stage I was always very close to David. He and I used to hang out outside of the show. Susan Tsu, the costume designer, really got it. She watched all the rehearsals and really got it and really saw that connection we all had to our clowns. She created that moppet kind of look for me. I think my intro was OK, I couldn't have thought of another way to do it. I didn't mind that. We obviously all had to have some kind of connection to New York City, all some kind of frustration and need to find one another. I thought the audition scene was kind of cute. The mayor of New York at the time loved the show so he was the one who was very instrumental in preparing the city for the shoot. He even invited just the cast to Gracie Mansion for dinner, we had a great time! He was very instrumental in getting the city empty and that was something that was not at all easy! I thought the baptism in the fountain was a great idea, it was well conceived. It was a fun day playing the fountain. It was a long shoot. We had two costumes if we had to reshoot it. We had to go in dry into the fountain of course. We leave and then we throw out clothes away and then we're clowns. We weren't completely masked. My make-up was an extension of my smile and a little X on my forehead. We didn't have much time on stage, we had to paint up our faces very quickly. Steve Nathan would come in with his makeup already on, the heard on his brow. And we would say "Oh look! Steve has a "heart-on"!" The red make-up had penetrated his skin, so he would walk around with a heart-on all the time! As far as New York looking so clean in the film, I don't remember any cleaning crews going about. But we did shoot very early in the morning which helped. That long shot of us running through the field was very early in the morning and the police barricaded a block or two for us to skip through. And that very last shot of us going around the corner with all those people coming toward us was also done very early in the morning, the police had held them back and then they all come around the corner. It was incredible. The last supper and the crucifixion sequence was shot on a very long night. And it was strange, because once we put him up on that fence to be crucified, and those police cars lights are flashing, there was this incredible wind that just blew everything in its path. Those streamers hanging from Victor's wrists representing the blood just flew in mid-air. This wind was so strong. It was so cool. You know if you watch the film carefully you can see that some of us gain like ten pounds by the end of the movie. We would eat all the bagels and what not from the Honey Wagon, and even though the movie was meant to all occur on the one day, we were working for weeks so we had all this time to gain a bit of weight! The shoot was probably about a month or two long. It was not an easy film to make, just because of the city. We had to be sure there were no planes and nothing floating around in the background. I was sick the day of the Prodigal Son parable. I thought they would pull me back and cut me into it later but they didn't and I thought that was so wrong. You know when we're doing the Pharisee monster scene down on the docks, I was still sick, so when you see "me" at the end being stripped of the monster trash, that was a double. You see her from the back, but yes that was a double. I really, really hated my Abraham. I just thought that was so poorly done. I really hated the way it was directed. It was shot so far away—it didn't become "me learning something" about that story, it just became a stupid theatrical moment. There was nothing developed. I was suddenly just there doing this bit. This was not the case of the show. In the show I get to develop the character of Abraham and you see me prepare. Here I was just there saying lines in that Indian headdress. Just in terms from stage to film I didn't think *Godspell* was successful. The film rushed through all of the lessons, it became more about skipping and mugging and not about the intimate lessons that each of these clowns learn. As much as I had admired some of David Greene's films, I didn't think he was the right director for *Godspell*. First of all he was British, and this musical was at heart a homage to American street theatre, so I don't think he really got it. David was not an easy man to work with. He was completely out of his element. You would sometimes catch him scrambling about, desperately trying to search for something and fumbling throughout the shoot. I think he was lost. I just thought he was a poor choice and he was not at all nurturing to any of the cast. The film became more about the musical numbers and setting up a good look for the numbers, but as far as the connection it was completely missing from the film. But it doesn't matter really, John

Michael wanted *Godspell* to be kind of a seed that was planted and generation upon generation could reinterpret it and find that seed and allow it to grow. Having my song "Learn Your Lessons Well" cut from the movie didn't piss me off per say but it did lend itself to the film missing the through line. And it's an important moment for my clown. David and I didn't get along very well. He loved Lynne, Lynne could do no wrong in the eyes of David. The choreographer Sammy Bayes really saved our asses. He really did. He was the one in the absence of David. You know, when you do a film you don't know what it's looking like. But Sammy was the guy that came in and helped direct the film in terms of the emotional connection. Sammy was the one that helped explain everything to us, where David just couldn't. He was always angry and cold and just not connected to us at all. I loved the World Trade Centre. It was scary as hell, but it was just beautifully shot. I remember being so frightened because we had our cameraman was literally hanging out of that helicopter, I mean most of his body was hanging out there and I was terrified not only for myself but for him! He went to desperate measures where he could have fallen to his death to get that final shot of us dancing on the top of the World Trade Centre. That floor we were on was the one that was hit by that plane on September 11.

Fellow actress Robin Lamont adds to these recollections:

I was in the original production of *Godspell* back when it started in Carnegie University in Pittsburgh, Pennsylvania. I was in junior college at the time and I was cast with a bunch of my friends to do the original production. There was totally different music, it was not yet Stephen Schwartz's score. It was much more raw and kind of unprofessional in a way but nevertheless it brought the spirit of the show alive. We moved it to Café La Mama off-off Broadway house in New York and then it opened on May 21st 1971 at the

184

Cherry Lane theatre. I did the show then and as an original company member and sang the iconic song "Day By Day," it was a wonderful experience to do that. The song went on to become a top ten hit on the billboard charts. When I was doing the film, we would have very early calls, so I would set my clock radio and I would say at least two times a week I would wake up hearing myself singing "Day By Day" which was a strange experience! It was shot in New York City in a way where there were no people seen. It was David Greene's concept and it was to have the clowns experience their own growth and their own reactions to what the gospel was saying without anyone else around to distract them. There were some challenges to shoot the film in a way so that we were the only people in frame. We would shoot in relatively secluded places where there wasn't much foot traffic. Grant's Tomb was one location and Lincoln Centre was one as well. In many cases we would have the help from the New York City police who would block off areas with barricades. I think for the cinematographer it was much harder to capture the silence, so even if there weren't people in the shot there were always sirens and helicopters and planes and so forth making noise. However, the film was of course dubbed in a studio. One of the scenes that was most difficult for me personally was the World Trade Centre. I'm not good with heights. Of course that is gone now, and its an odd thing to see when I look back on the film, but it's a lovely thing to know that we were up there and have that treasured forever in the film.

Actor Jerry Sroka remembers director David Greene's response to the film's lacklustre performance at the box office:

It did well for the first few weeks and then it just dropped off the radar. No one was going to see it. And I remember seeing David later and he saying that he thought the film was released too late. He said, "Jerry, the whole hippie scene has died and this film just came out too late and is out of step with what is going on now. People want *The French Connection* and musicals like *Cabaret*, not this." And I think he was right in a way. And remember, I came on later, I came from a production but not from the one that conceived the production, I replaced Herb Braha who of course originated the Herb clown, but David was just amazing and he did a great job. It's also very sad to know that many of the people from the film have now passed away. Lynne is gone, David, Jeffrey. It's very sad.

One of the most moving moments in the film is also the most dramatically grim and theatrical. It appears late in the piece, where the Christ-clown instructs his disciples to remove their make-up. Firstly the John the Baptist/Judas Iscariot composite removes his blood red lightning bolt and then hands out rags and make-up remover to the other clowns as Jesus insists they take off their clown-faces. Gilmer begins the procession, and soon enough the rest follow through. After this sequence, the inevitable Last Supper occurs, and then to the sombre music of "On the Willows" (a number originally performed by the offstage band in the stage show and here sung by unseen harmonious voices) Christ embraces each disciple. The scene is extraordinarily depressing: it is a case of the clowns having to remove their pretty face paint in order to be re-introduced into the "real" world, the world of the rat race they escaped from during the last two hours or so and then having to say goodbye to their leader. When one of the clowns tries to take off Jesus's make-up he is quickly stopped. The film insists that Jesus will remain a clown until his impending death. After all, in a story like *Godspell*, there is no room for this charismatic minstrel messiah to live and function in the "real" world. The rats of the rat race would eat him up, ignore his teachings or ridicule him.

Some interesting acting choices unfold during this moment, and one of the strongest is where young Merrell Jackson looks up at Jesus with a wide vaudevillian grin and then suddenly changes his expression to one of terror. He then clings onto Jesus's legs in desperation. Another image shows Robin Lamont in a full close-up: having already said her own distinct goodbye to Christ, the camera lingers on her while Jesus bids adieu to Katie Hanley in the distance. Robin looks into the night's eye with serenity and sense of bewilderment. The clown that sung about following Christ "Day by Day" has been enlightened, but she seems conflicted by the enlightenment. All this is represented in Robin's incredible expression.

David Haskell in *Godspell* (1973)

Much of the film's magic was created behind the scenes, as well. Editor Alan Heim remembers working on the film:

> I thought it looked terrific. That was an unusual film for me. I got a call from Kenny Ott, who was a TV producer and he got me connected to Bob Fosse with *Liza with a Z* and at one point he called and asked if I wanted to meet with David Greene who was from England, he had lived in California for

Gilmer McCormick gets her face painted by the clown-Christ as played
by Victor Garber in *Godspell* (1973)

Victor Garber behind the scenes and in front of the Twin Towers
in *Godspell* (1973)

Gilmer McCormick during "Light of the World" in *Godspell* (1973)

years, but he was very, very British. He was thinking of hiring a commercial editor because he wanted very flashy editing and I said "Well if you give me flashy material I will give you flashy editing. I can't cut what's not there." So we went off at that note and ... I went off to see the musical. I had avoided seeing *Godspell* forever, it just didn't appeal to me, so I went to see it and the kids in the show were playing up to David

189

because they wanted to be cast in the movie which hadn't been cast yet. I thought it was a show that didn't sustain begging from the actors, it's very out there and they just need to do it, but these kids were paying up to David and I didn't like it. But then I was told to go and see it without David and this time it was a fun experience, before when I saw it with David it was sour, but this time I really enjoyed it. They hired a commercial cinematographer and what happened was they were shooting in very un-New York locations which were right in the middle of New York, where you just don't see traffic, I mean these days you'd take the traffic out optically. A lot of the places they chose were rather desolate, and David found these great locations which all culminates at Bethesda Fountain where they do the baptism, and the look of the film and the cinematography was just spectacular. I didn't look at the dailies every day, they would shoot every day and use all the light, so nobody was free to look at dailies until Friday, by the end of the week. A totally bizarre thing happened which is was very 1970s. We went to a screening room and it was on the third floor and everyone except for the actors showed up. The cinematographer turned up and I will never forget what he was wearing. He was wearing a brown leather vest with no shirt on underneath and brown leather pants, he was a very hip looking guy and Columbia Pictures had a lot of hope for him. We started running the film on projector number one and everyone was loving it. And then came projectors number two and everything was out of focus, and I said "Hey hang on, check your focus!" but the projectionist told me that it was in focus. I asked "Umm are you looking?" I said ok let's stop rolling and we waited around and there was a lot of film to look at. We switched it over to projector one and I buzzed the projectionist again and I said don't use projector two there is something wrong with it. But again he went onto projector two and it was still out of focus which made the cameraman go crazy, he flew out screaming and yelling and flew around to the booths and was so angry.

I calmed down the situation down and we ran the entire film on the first projector and then I tried to get Danny the projectionist fired, which I wasn't successful at. He eventually apologised to me and told me that he had eaten a bad oyster, but I know that he had drank a lot and it was clear that it was his blunder. David was one of the greatest directors I've ever worked with. He was very open and very good at what he did. He did some interesting stuff. I remember one night, at one of his parties, I was getting married at the time and he said "Don't be nervous I've been married all my life of course to five different women." I think the actors from *Godspell* having a problem with him is a very actor-ish thing to say, I mean think about the history of street theatre in England, with busking and the like. They were shooting all over the place and a lot of the places were very hard to get to and a lot of the shoots were at very early in the morning and late at night. I thought his use of the electric sign on Broadway was just inspired. And the World Trade Centre was of course just being built at the time and it was very hard to get a helicopter pilot to get that shot because no one would know what the winds would do, it was very dangerous. It took a long while to get brace enough helicopter guy to do it. I was cutting the film without David. The opening number at the Bethesda Fountain had a lot more material that was cut from the playback. But Stephen Schwartz, much against his will, wrote an orchestral bridge. I know that he and I had a bit of an argument about that. Right after *Godspell* I was working on *Lenny* and Stephen Schwartz did the music for *Pippin* and Fosse hated, I mean really hated the music for *Pippin*. Stephen was a very arrogant guy back then, and he was not at all charming. I didn't have much contact with him after *Godspell*. We had no time to float around. Everything that was shot was generally in the movie. There is the scene in the junk yard and there is a place in the sequence where someone throws a doll at someone to catch and I looked at it in the dailies and I thought that was a nice shot. David never talked to me during dailies, he gave slight clues as to what he liked, but not much talk went on there. When I showed him that part with the doll he reached over and gave me an embracing pat on the shoulder and said "Oh I'm so glad you can use that because I had no idea where to put that in the shot." With *Liza with a Z*, Bob Fosse was very much involved, whereas this was the first time I was left to my own devices.

Actor Herb Braha who was in the original production (but not cast in the film) has also shared his feelings on Greene's vision:

> I really hated it. I thought the idea of using New York City as the backdrop was just fucked. The show is intimate and all about the lessons taught, not about capturing famous and not-so-famous locations in New York. The direction was all fucking wrong and when it came to the time of the film, us original cast members were all extremely nervous about being cast in it. We all worried so much that when Paramount executives were going to be at the show, (and even when they fucking weren't!) it affected our performances very, very much. We all stressed about being too old, or at least looking too old for the movie, we all stressed that some of us original cast members would be rejected while others will be picked and we also stressed about the fact that established "movie stars" were going to be signed on instead. What happened was that some of the original cast members were taken on board and given a role for the movie. Robin, Gilmer, David and Jeffrey, while the rest of us sat it out. I thought Jerry Sroka was awful in my part. I just felt that he didn't have the same comic abilities that I bought to that role which is extremely important for that clown seeing that he's the only one that doesn't get a number. Also cutting Gilmer and Jeffrey's numbers was a stupid mistake and the casting of Victor Garber was also a mistake. Stephen Nathan will always be Jesus as far as I'm concerned. He was a naturally gifted hoofer and vaudevillian, as we all were. We all came

into that show from the essence of American street theatre and vaudeville. I loved doing *Godspell*, although of course singing something like "Day by Day" over and over and over again became fucking nauseating at times, but besides that it's a great piece.

A number that comes late in the second half of the film that lets the audience relax again into bouncy joy is a song written specifically for the movie, "Beautiful City." The song is joyous and loaded with lovely harmonies that lift the spirit and truly capture the solidarity and camaraderie of these young people, the last of the flowerchildren. It is shot with a lens that captures the setting sun as we follow the loveable clowns from the streets of Manhattan back to Bethesda Fountain: they have come back to where they began. It is this bittersweet moment with inspired lyrics such as "We see nations rise in each other's eyes" that gives *Godspell* a sense of community. This is a film about family, unity and friendship. The religious aspects of the film are ultimately just a structural background for what truly is a film about the celebration of community and the coming together outside of the mainstream.

But with all this joy and frivolity comes a price and *Godspell*—much like its relative *Jesus Christ Superstar*—comes across like an elaborate suicide. The messiahs in these films die without any resurrection, and the bleak ending of *Godspell* is not only surprising, but also unnerving and depressing. After all the joy and sentimental acknowledgment of togetherness and compassionate companionship, there is nothing left to go back to but the cold mess of normalcy and conformity. It is as if Christ's message—when told through this vaudevillian shtick—is rendered meaningless and unnecessary. As his disciples who carry his limp dead body off camera and disappear into the city, they too are rendered as unimportant and as invisible as Christ's message. Another interesting thing to note is that *Godspell* opened the same year as the smash hit *The Exorcist* did—another film about Christ and the purpose of faith. *The Exorcist*, however, remains the conservative film of the two in that Christ is presented as a saviour, used to free young Regan MacNeil (Linda Blair) from demonic possession whereas in *Godspell*, Christ is a buffoon: complicated and bizarre and also left invisible and insignificant amidst the rat's nest. *The Exorcist* is a fire and brimstone horror picture, complete with visceral monstrosities and a powerful intensity that jolts the nerves and gets under the skin, however its message is loud and clear—the protagonist, Chris MacNeil (Ellen Burstyn) is a libertine actress with no religious convictions but she is forced to seek the help of Jesuit priests to help save her daughter from the grips of Satanic forces. However, in *Godspell*, the disciples re-enter the world of the non-believers and disappear, carrying their dead messiah out with them. Both *The Exorcist* and *Godspell* are incredibly important films about the mystery of faith and speak volumes about the message of the messianic, both films come from surprisingly different attitudes however: the horror film tells us that there is good in the world and that this goodness can triumph over evil (albeit sacrifices must be made) and the musical tells us that the message of Christ can be completely insignificant, alien and turned invisible. These are two films that sit at the same moral compass of cinematic experience, co-existing within theme and context but at polar ends of the structure of climactic outcome: *Godspell* ends on a downer, *The Exorcist* however leaves it ambiguous, but all in all, God is in his heaven, and a little girl is free from malevolence. But little Regan MacNeil's older counterparts (dressed in their clown garb parading around an emptied New York City) return to the facelessness of the "real world" and quietly fade into faithless normalcy.

An off-camera still of Lynne Thigpen and Gilmer McCormick waiting to shoot the Lazarus parable in *Godspell* (1973)

194

**Lynne Thigpen and Gilmer McCormick at Cannes Film Festival
for _Godspell_ (1973)**

Stephen Schwarz and John Michael-Tebelak on location for *Godspell* (1973)

Gilmer McCormick and Jeffrey Mylett sign the cast recording for *Godspell* (1973)

CHIN UP: *Charlotte's Web*

Much like *Snoopy Come Home*, *Charlotte's Web* is a wistful and melancholy animated feature and its action runs through sombre colours. It is fuelled by a perpetually non-relenting idea of realistic outcomes. In *Charlotte's Web*, sacrifices are essential, and growing up and letting go are synonymous with each other. Longing and loneliness are palpable feelings, and death is presented with blatant honesty. Along with the sadness, however, is a sense of camaraderie among the animals who are different but who essentially have "lots in common where it really counts," as sung in one of the numbers by the versatile Sherman brothers who wrote the great songs for the film.

The story follows the life of a pig named Wilbur (voiced by Henry Gibson) who is the runt of a litter on a struggling farm. The farmer's daughter Fern (voiced by Pam Ferdin) rescues him from being put to death and raises him. The duo form a beautiful bond that matches many of the more famous friendships shared between children and animals in film history, and all seems to be pleasant and perfect until Fern is told that Wilbur (now fully grown) will have to go to another farm where he can be looked after, fed and be in the company of fellow animals. Fern is distressed, but continues to visit Wilbur, and her love and appreciation for him and the other animals grows. Fern's friendship with animals is a subplot (the core of the film is about Wilbur learning about the harsh realities of life), but it is absolutely crucial to the film and shares many similar motifs and characteristics with other movie musicals of the 1970s that deal with children. This thematic element runs throughout these musicals that depict children as distant and alienated from fellow children or adults, as also seen in films such as *Raggedy Ann and Andy: A Musical Adventure* (1977) where a loner little girl is more interested in playing with her dolls than spending time with other children (more on this film later). Other examples include *Pete's Dragon* which features an orphan boy whose best friend is a Christ-like figure dragon named Elliot, and so forth.

Fern's alienation from other children feeds her closeness to the animals, but all this changes when she develops a friendship with a neighbourhood boy. When our pig protagonist Wilbur notices that Fern is growing up and developing an interest in this boy he is told by

Charlotte, his arachnid mentor and confidant, that although Fern will always love him and treasure their past, she is also a human and there will be human needs that will always come before the needs of animals. This is something that Wilbur, in his adulthood, learns to accept. Both Wilbur and Fern have to learn life's dilemmas, its ups and downs and the notion of change. Fern's father is heard saying "Fern is learning the hard facts of farm life," and the girl is presented in a number of depressing moments, as is her pet pig.

Charlotte's Web is a film that runs through emotionally stirring moments and refuses to sugar coat the facts. There is a toughness to the material, and a brutal honesty that producers Hanna-Barbera confidently deliver with gusto. Sensitive children will find the film traumatic, as they should, and the essence of the film walks a fine line between the importance of friendship and the gradual acceptance of death. Although rebirth is promised by the end of the film as the children of the deceased heroine Charlotte spin their webs as a post-grief stricken Wilbur watches, the film leaves us with a sense of the necessity of mourning, sorrow and moroseness. But the beauty of friendship and compassion runs alongside the maudlin attributes of the film.

Charlotte the philosophical spider (voiced so beautifully by long time Hollywood legend Debbie Reynolds) is Wilbur's friend from the get-go. She helps him simply because she likes him. There is no motive on her behalf to help Wilbur avoid being turned over to the farmer to be slaughtered, and turned into bacon and ham. Charlotte's heart is so big and loving that she chooses to do selfless acts throughout the film that manifest as a kind of artistic expression. This is one of the strongest points to the film (although there are many): that wit, whimsy, intelligence, sweetness and tenderness can triumph over ritual and tradition. In *Charlotte's Web*, change is also a positive thing. It is not only the passing of a loved one that enforces a change in the way things are or have been, it also saves lives. Charlotte's "miracles" (as Wilbur calls them) is that she can spin words in her webs, and she writes words or phrases that inspire other animals, farmers and soon the entire county. These little miracles save Wilbur from being chopped up, and in turn Wilbur returns his love for Charlotte by bringing her newly orphaned babies back to the farm after winning a coveted prize at a country fair.

Charlotte's death is one of the most heartbreaking moments not only in an animated feature film, but across film history more broadly. It is so heartbreaking because it just happens. Charlotte states that she will die soon, and this destroys Wilbur and the film's audience alike. This bluntness is so cutting and sobering that it makes everything else in the film all the more bittersweet. This enchanting tale about friendship and sacrifice is more than a children's fable, it is a true testament to spiritual awakening and the birthing of a belief system. Its tenderness is so palpable that it tugs the heartstrings with all four legs. Of course, there is some room (but only some) for humour, and most of that comes from Agnes Moorehead's turn as a goose who repeats words and repeats letters when she insists certain words are spelled with multiple R's or E's. And then there is Paul Lynde's wonderful portrayal of Templeton the rat, which is refreshing in a maudlin film made from the heart and populated with sweet, caring, nurturing and understanding critters. Templeton is a ruthlessly self-involved rodent and it is terrific! He is crude, and his main love is food. His number that comes late in the piece and is most certainly the final moment of cheeriness as the film closes with sombre sequences is a joyful song as he ravages scraps from a litter-infested carnival.

Templeton the rat in *Charlotte's Web* (1973)

The songs are both pure in their joy and also in their lamentations. They are written with such a gentle understanding of the film's characters and situations that it is impossible to choose a favourite. "I Can Talk" is the Sherman brothers at their wordiest best—a semi-patter song with triple-end rhymes in the verses and a sweeping chorus that is both catchy and chipper. Once again, this number is necessary in a film obsessed with "learning the hard facts of farm life." "Chin Up" is sung by Charlotte, and is bright and energetic. Debbie Reynolds's lovely vocals are crisp and have a warmth to them that glides gracefully with her harsh truths about life. When Charlotte explains to Wilbur how she drinks the blood of flies to survive and that if she didn't eat bugs the world would be overrun by them, they are cold hard facts that Wilbur just has to deal with. She tells Wilbur this direct information about the balance of nature to which he replies "It's just so cruel." And that's what *Charlotte's Web* toys with, the cruelty of nature, and the injustices of 'live and let die'. This is summed up with the beautiful and haunting song, "Mother Earth and Father Time," sung by Reynolds in such an elegant and thought provoking manner that it elevates the film entirely. The song is graceful and sentimental, and its words and intent are so finely tuned that it does two things magnificently: it symbolizes the order of nature and reflects the human condition in relation to coping with life and death. These two factors are exactly what *Charlotte's Web* is all about.

THE THINGS I WILL NOT MISS: *Lost Horizon*

Based on James Hilton novel of the same name that was a paean to peaceful living and harmonious unity, the 1937 film adaptation of *Lost Horizon*, directed by Frank Capra, was adapted into a musical that completely lost its direction, its message, its concept and its look and feel. But it has one saving grace: the gifted Burt Bacharach. The original Capra film is a brilliant character study, deeply moving in its set up and execution with some poignant moments that are remarkably haunting. However, in this musical retelling all of those elements are lost. This was reflected at the box office: the film was made for $12 million dollars and did not even clear $3 million in its initial release. The ambitions of *Lost Horizon* were spawned from the successes of *The Sound of Music* and other musicals that made a huge splash and took millions from ticket sales. But with a screenplay by playwright Larry Kramer and produced by Ross Hunter who had a big hit with the disaster film *Airport* (1970), this version did not fare as well. Its confused direction by Charles Jarrott and bizarre choices in casting make the movie an uncomfortable watch. Something is just not quite right throughout it.

Bobby Van leads the children of Shangri-La to "Answer Me a Question" in *Lost Horizon* (1973)

Although Burt Bacharach's fantastic music opens the film with a title sequence that shows a helicopter shot gliding over the mountaintops of the snow-coated Himalayas, the film holds off from presenting us with any musical numbers until our heroes reach Shangri-La. This is not a bad choice as such, as the idea of music only surfacing when we reach this otherworldly utopia could play well, but there is most certainly room for a musical introduction to the film's characters that could have been negotiated. The first twenty odd minutes seem to be fixed in the world of *Airport* as we are thrust into a disaster film with our protagonists having to board a getaway plane in Tibet only to have it crash into the frosty mountains. But there is no reason as to why there couldn't have been a number before Shangri-La is introduced: a number to establish these people who we are supposed to care about would have been a good idea, considering we are going to spend the next two hours or so with them. Because this song is missing, the characters are just put on screen where we quickly have to decide who we like and who we hate, and try to figure out what on earth they're on about. Even in *The Wizard of Oz*, Dorothy sings "Somewhere over the Rainbow" in dreary Kansas before she hits the song-heavy Oz: however, in that masterpiece, there is merit and reason. The number is Dorothy's longing for something more than the mundane and humdrum, therefore it makes sense for her to sing it at the farm. Here in *Lost Horizon*, the idea that the film turns into a musical once the lead characters get to their own variant of Oz is treated as a surprise but is also grimly valid because there is nothing that these people are notably running from or wanting to escape from until we hear them whine about their problems. They are presented as five individuals simply stuck in Asia, and then casualties of a plane wreck.

Behind the scenes on *Lost Horizon* (1973)

When we finally get to Shangri-La, we hear Bacharach's lush music in all its glory and enter an entirely different film. Even though the picture at times does look like a 1950s fantasy film where a wonderful Ray

Harryhausen stop-motion creature might pop up and bite off Michael York's head or carry off Olivia Hussey, it is most certainly a product of the times. It quickly becomes clinically obsessed with the personal problems of the characters and the social ills that befall them, and tries to fix these via a hippie idealism that is hidden within the utopian philosophies of the civilians of Shangri-La.

Prepping Liv Ullman and Peter Finch on the set of *Lost Horizon* (1973)

But this utopia is problematically a contradictory place of racial harmony which the film tries to employ: the lead characters, including one of the heads of Shangri-La (played by John Gielgud) are all white, while the Asian residents of this peaceful, halcyon sanctuary away from the real world are subservient and know their place. It is a strange take on the peace and love ideals the film is supposed to be celebrating. When the concept of Shangri-La as a refuge for those who do not want to face their problems comes under scrutiny, there is the promise that the film may take a turn for the better and that a degree of intelligent complexity is on its way. But the film lets us down by having its characters sit around reading and philosophising. Even the romances that blossom seem to pop out of nowhere and remain unbelievable. When Michael York tries to romance Olivia Hussey it is forced and underwhelming, and Peter Finch's love affair with Shangri-La resident Liv Ullman is bizarre and unfeeling.

Another misstep was the idea of having the High Lama (Charles Boyer) give expositional backstory as a spoken monologue rather than a sung soliloquy. This could have been aided by some flashbacks or the type of stylized visuals that the 1970s were so good at. Following this lengthy rant about the importance of peace and love and so forth, Peter Finch belts out a number with such stiffness and uncertainty that it just adds insult to injury. Paramount's casting is questionable, as a lot of the people in the film look way out of their depth in a musical. Some are not at all singers or dancers, or even look like they really get the medium, and this shows.

Troy Garza, one of the legitimate dancers in the film, who is featured in an early number "Living Together," remembers the film:

> I was one of the loin-cloth men and only did the one number. I got the job by auditioning in the traditional way. They were seeking small ethnic-looking men but used a whole lot of the old-guard Caucasian Hollywood dancers too. I was also an acrobat and almost always 'got the job' after doing my aerial backflip. Working for Hermes Pan was a dream experience for a young dancer; can you imagine? I was just seventeen at the time. The older guys would ask me my age and roll their eyes when I told them what it was. We rehearsed on the back-lot at Warners inside a set-house with an empty interior converted to a dance room. On the first or second day of rehearsal they gathered us around the piano and taught us "Living Together" the horrible song later covered by The Fifth Dimension. The song was plodding and pedestrian. As for the rest of the songs, I don't recall any... but I thought the dance-music for our number was quite good. I had seen the original film *Lost Horizon* as a child, of which my memories are fuzzy. Also, we only worked

with Olivia, who was lovely but really nervous about being lifted in the air. As far as the sets went, like all cast members of all movies everyone oooed-and-ahhhed over the set; it's remarkable what scenic departments can do but ultimately I hated the film, it was terrible, the critics were justified.

As terrible as the film is, the songs are fantastic, and the best thing about it is the well-written score. Burt Bacharach is a master musician and his complicated melodies and rich orchestrations are delectable and stirring. Adding to their appeal is something that would normally prove detrimental to a musical, however, for some bizarre reason in *Lost Horizon* it works; the songs seem to pop out of nowhere. There is no real structure as to where these numbers should be plotted. One of the best examples of this is "Living Together" which has a multi-layered melodies and a schizophrenic skeleton that seems to work as it is tossed onto the screen. Sally Kellerman is possibly the best of the cast and here she plays a drug-addled photojournalist who at first becomes stressed by Shangri-La, but then learns to respect the virtues of contented healthy living. Her bouncy duet with Olivia Hussey "The Things I Will Not Miss" is terrific, and is a successful number in terms of the movie musical in that it is one of the only songs that organically arises from the story and from conversation. The two women—one completely downtrodden by the "real world" and longing for paradise and the other totally bored by utopia and dedicated to returning to the dramas of everyday life, agree to disagree through a charming song that shifts melodic gear with such precision that it is infectious. The film's hit song is of course "The World Is a Circle" and that is presented as a highlight of the movie. In this number the native children of Shangri-La parade around with Liv Ullman and then are joined by a third rate comedian and song and dance man played by Bobby Van who then later leads the same children into a fun number "Question Me an Answer." Both songs became staple Bacharach hits, and the simple and yet fascinating syncopation of "Reflections" (once again sung by Sally Kellerman) is astounding. If it was plotted in another movie musical, it would be a perfect example of 1970s bubble gum, but instead these terrific songs are wasted in a very average film.

MARK TWAIN GETS A MUSICAL THANKS TO *READER'S DIGEST*: *Tom Sawyer*

Tom Sawyer has warmth but lacks the lavish visual dynamics needed to boost its appeal. It is plotted rather unevenly, as the songs do not seem to be placed in dramatic subsectors of the narrative, nor do they act as the foundation of a plot point. Although the film takes its time and moves at a steady pace, it does seem rushed and the iconic moments in its young hero's life come across as drab and uninteresting. Delivered by the long standing famous literary group *Reader's Digest*, this American classic is cautiously (and for the most part, unnecessarily) turned into a musical with songs written by the Sherman brothers that have energy and elegance, but are wasted in a relatively insipid film. It is hard not to be moved by a Sherman brothers song, however in this motion picture there is no true connection made between the numbers and the story at its heart. Or, for that matter, its characters. Everybody involved seems to be working in a vacuum, painting by numbers and plodding through the piece with uncertainty.

The title song sung by Aunt Polly (Celeste Holm), Mary (Susan Joyce) and Sidney (Joshua Hill Lewis) is a bright and charming number where each character sings their views on the troublesome Tom Sawyer (Johnny Whitaker), but it is one of the rare occasions where the song marries comfortably with the characters. Aunt Polly gets the wordy patter moments which are delectable in classic Sherman brothers style and the counterparts shared between the three of them are also great. But the staging of the song is dreadfully dull: Aunt Polly setting up a dinner table while the children wash up and prepare to eat and so forth is uninteresting, and not a good setting for the terrific song.

The famous moment where Tom Sawyer has to paint his Aunt Polly's wooden fence is one of the most successful scenes in the film as the charismatic and shifty Tom Sawyer persuades his friends to do all the work. The number "Gratifaction" where the boys paint the fence is fun, but once again not highly imaginative in terms of its structure or blocking. Not only did the Sherman brothers write the songs but they also penned the screenplay, adapting Mark Twain's romance of the south and the whimsical lyricism of childhood for the screen. However, what they choose not to thoroughly explore is the political and social

Fishing for the truth in *Tom Sawyer* (1973)

Johnny Whitaker as *Tom Sawyer* (1973)

207

of Twain's classic American novel. They sidestep a lot of the themes of race and class, as well as downplay the novel's preoccupation with death. This both works for the musical and does not. If the adult themes were left in and adapted in an honest and straightforward way, it may have been a better musical: richer and more dramatic. This is not to say that the film does not have its bleak and sombre moments, such as the scene where Tom and Huckleberry Finn (Jeff East) witness a murder and hide in a dark shabby shack, the grim scene in the classroom where Tom is punished by his cold stone-faced teacher, the moments where Tom and Huckleberry exchange intense dialogue as they share secrets and make pacts, or the court case sequence which ends abruptly with Injun Joe (Kanu Hank) jumping through the window crashing to the ground and then taking off to escape the wrath of angry white civilians. But these sequences fumble, and are not thoughtfully delivered.

The film also features Jodie Foster, already a super talented child actress, who is at ease in the role of Becky Thatcher. When she and Tom become smitten with each other, it is not cringe worthy or awkward, but rather completely natural and their relationship is established with ease. Foster and her co-star Johnny Whitaker are effortless young actors in control of their craft. Director Don Taylor delivered *Escape from the Planet of the Apes* (1971) a few years earlier, and later took over directorial duties from Mike Hodges for the horror sequel *Damien: Omen 2* (1978) some years later. *Tom Sawyer* sits between these two films, and rounds out Taylor's keen interest and passion for all genres from science fiction, horror and of course (considering *Tom Sawyer*) musicals. Sadly, his take on this genre is not as focused as his take on his post-apocalyptic simians or the young Anti-Christ entering the military.

THE PHONY KING OF ENGLAND: *Robin Hood*

A minstrel rooster with a soft and gentle country twang (voiced by country singer Roger Miller) leads us into the story of Robin Hood, but in this case it is the Robin Hood of the animal kingdom. And so begins one of the most underrated and relentlessly magnetic animated features of the 1970s. There is such a genteel ease about Disney's *Robin Hood*, and the major reason it is one of the most charming movie musicals of the decade is simply because it oozes such emblematic 1970s sensibilities and styles. It breathes with a coolness and airiness that employs leftist hippie ideals and combines that with intricate and highly evolved story telling techniques. This is Disney at its most informal, much like the magnificent *Lady and the Tramp*, and like its related anthropomorphic-centric predecessor its narrative is complex and multidimensional while also being incurably romantic and swiftly told.

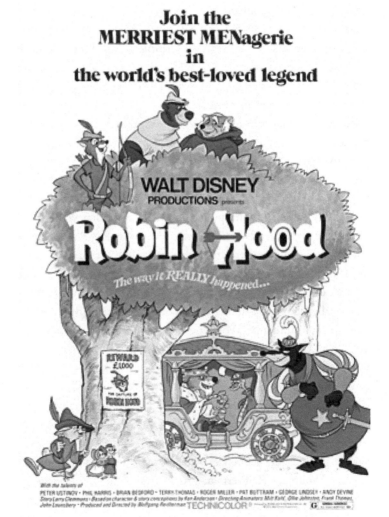

The poster art for *Robin Hood* (1973)

At the heart of the film is a story that developed outside the main run of the feature, in that its hero Robin Hood (voiced by Brian Bedford) and its heroine Maid Marian (voiced by Monica Evans) have already had their passionate romance off screen, before the core action of the film takes place. This is something that is risky in a fairy tale and especially in one from the Disney canon. Most of their films about romantic unions generally involve lovers, star crossed or otherwise, meeting *during* the picture, but here in this 1970s folk/country musical our loveable and completely adult foxes have history and rekindle this through complicated and thoughtful writing. Robin Hood is anarchic and yet totally submissive, while Maid Marian is lovely and yet aware of the fleeting nature of romance. This is a Disney animated feature at its most cynical, and also at its most self-aware.

The film is populated by all kinds of animals, from jungle dwelling beasts such as a lion Prince John (voiced by Peter Ustinov), to farm yard animals such as Marion's lady in waiting, the chicken Lady Kluck (voiced by Carole Shelley), to woodland animals such as the bear Little John (voiced by Phil Harris). Adding to its gentle anarchy, this is a film completely devoted to anthropomorphic characters that come from all sectors: some are refined British critters, others drawling Americans from the deep South, while others are mid-western leftovers from vaudeville. Some of them are caricatures and others are built from scratch and given their own unique take of the role their filling in a story much loved and generally known by audiences all over the world. But the genius of director and animator Wolfgang Reitherman (aka Woolie) is that he injects all of these characters with charming and rich writing, and from their initial conception they are easy to understand and to gravitate towards, from the mean spirited and nasty wolf Sheriff of Nottingham (voiced by Pat Buttram) through to the sweet little bunny rabbit children.

Although the film employs the "reuse" method of animation (meaning previous work from films before it is traced onto the cell animation for certain sequences), *Robin Hood* remains authentic and whimsical. Wolfgang Reitherman was instrumental in introducing the "reuse" method and this was simply because there was not enough money going into the production of his take on the inhabitants of Sherwood Forest. There are dance sequences used from Disney's first feature *Snow*

White and the Seven Dwarfs (1938) in *Robin Hood*: here Snow White is replaced by Maid Marian and the dwarfs are replaced by Marian's fellow woodland animals that she dances with. There are also scenes that repeat later in the picture, such as the little rabbit laughing herself silly (the exact same animation is used twice). But none of this matters because the film is not only fun and loaded with charm, but it also makes a fantastic addition to the cinematic interpretations and adaptations of the legend of the prince of thieves, who stole from the rich to give to the poor.

Lady Kluck and Maid Marian in *Robin Hood* (1973)

The romance of Sherwood Forest is alive and well in Disney's version, and the characters are funny as well as dramatic. Later Disney would bring forth highly dramatic turns with *Beauty and the Beast* (1991) and *The Lion King* (1994), and 1973's *Robin Hood* is a great forerunner in that sense. There are scenes where the impoverished animals of Nottingham fall under the bullying menace of the Sheriff, and a sombre sequence that involves Prince John imprisoning various animal civilians who morbidly shiver in the darkness, chained to cold stone brick walls. The sequence is made all the more depressing with the lonely lament

211

"Not in Nottingham" as sung by the rooster. This sense of real danger, real oppression and real sadness permeates the film in a skilful manner, and the delicate handling of the quieter, introspective moments stand in contrast to the bigger grandiose moments of action.

Carole Shelley played the loveable, feisty, and festively plump Lady Kluck. Shelley remembers the production:

> It wasn't until we got into the studio and started playing around that Wolfgang said he wanted as much as a character as possible because it really wasn't written in the script so he wanted to come up with a voice that would fill out a character. The script was sweet and well written but I think turning her into this little Scottish chicken. My favourite moment is when they have her racing across the football field like a half-back or whatever they call them and I love the way she elbows everybody out of the way. She was a tough chicken. Once you work doing Disney you accept that it's going to be animals. What they don't want is animal voices, they want real people voices. They didn't want me to do a chicken voice it had to be a real voice and I played with voices until Woolie said "Yep! That's the one!" I did an awful lots of radio when I was a kid and you have to have an awful lot of energy in animation in your voice because you're not being seen your only being hear and I think that experience came into my work. So really that is all you have to go on—the sound of the character and of course you introduce certain attributes to the character. When I did *Hercules* I played one of the three blind furies and I wanted to sort of find some sound that could be made visual, and I had an idea so I went into a candy shop and bought some sour balls and put one in my mouth and made myself salivate as much as possible and then read my lines spitting the whole way. I did that when I got into the studio first thing, I said "let me do something for you that I think might be fun!" and I sucked the sour ball for a few seconds and started reading the script and slurping and spitting. I then looked up and said "Well what do you think?"

and I couldn't see anybody in the sound booth because they had all fallen to the floor laughing in hysterics. They loved this because they could do an animation of drool falling out of this character's mouth. The rolling of the R's for Lady Kluck is very Scottish. I think he liked the Scottish aspect of her. Disney are wonderful to work with. It is a very exciting thing to be done. I think anyone would tell you that doing a voice for a Disney film is great fun and an important legacy. I never met anybody that played the other characters in *Robin Hood*. You very seldom do, you do it in limbo by yourself in a studio. Sometimes you night get to do a duologue but that is very, very rare also. They piece it together afterwards coz they can't get two people in the same place at the same time. I never met anybody except Monica, and I know Brian Bedford very well, but I don't think we ever met at all during *Robin Hood*. Now they get stars to do it and I haven't had a look in on a Disney film for quite a while. Monica is lovely. We hit it off very well and worked wonderfully together. I don't know where she is now, she went to England, got married, had children and I can't find her. I don't think she's in the business anymore and probably wants to be left alone. I don't remember doing any singing in "The Phoney King of England," so that must have come and went very quickly in the studio. The animators were lovely to chat to and hear about the old days as chief animators. I also met them over at Roddy McDowell's house. He used to host lovely lunches and invite incredible people. I had done a play with Roddy in New York and we had become great friends, and whenever I went out to LA he would call me and invite me to these lunches. The industry is changing and I'm changing, now I'm somebody's grandmother like it or lump it, the business has changed, Broadway has changed, it was always changing really, but yes it's a very different place now. I get grandmothers. A lot of the young actresses from that period of the 1970s are now more than middle aged, they are stars and they are happy to play something juicy rather than just being relegated to grandmother or aunt.

Peter Ustinov's Prince John is a fantastic addition to the pantheon of Disney villains, and like all male Disney villains he is foppish, effeminate and catty. He is also joined by the sycophantic Sir Hiss (voiced by Terry-Thomas) who is simply incredible as a sinister, slithering, serpentine sidekick. The duo have such fun revelling in their nastiness and the film's most fun moments come with these two terrific character actors having a ball being evil. Prince John is a wonderful predecessor to his relative, Scar, from *The Lion King*, voiced by fellow British actor Jeremy Irons. Both felines are ferocious, fey menaces, completely detached from the "circle of life" that Disney usually celebrates as something healthy, wholesome and good. *Robin Hood* presents us with a natural order, and all animals knowing their place, but the wealthy and the oppressive as represented by Prince John and the Sheriff of Nottingham are outside of this natural order. However, the "good guys"—much like many of the "good guys" as seen in the films of the 1970s—are outcasts. Misfits were slowly becoming the biggest film trend of the decade, and *Robin Hood* is littered with them.

A sketch of *Robin Hood* (1973)

IT TAKES TWO BABY: *Dr. Jekyll and Mr. Hyde*

With a musical score from Lionel Bart, who of course made magic with *Oliver!*, *Dr. Jekyll and Mr. Hyde*, a made for TV musical retelling of the Robert Louis Stevenson gothic horror classic, is a fevered effort that has to be seen to be believed. Not only does the film take drastic liberties with reshaping the classic monster story to fit the sensibilities of a 1970s audience (an audience that were starting to become interested in more grounded, "realist" horror fare) but it does it surprisingly well. The film boasts some delightfully deranged performances, headed by Kirk Douglas in the titular dual roles of Jekyll, the suave and sophisticated proper gentleman, and Hyde, the snarling, ferocious and deadly cretin. Douglas is bright, energetic and throws himself into both roles with a bravado that is completely necessary for these kinds of extremes in performance. He disallows the audience to sympathize with both personas, which gives very little room for any sense of pathos for this egotistical scientist playing with the complexities of human character. This is a fantastic thing. Because Douglas is an actor who seldom seems to evoke a sense of sentimentality, sincerity, tenderness or even genuine kindness. This is where the musical is at its strongest—it has an unadulterated mean spirit, and although it may come across as pompous, silly and even comical, underlying it's bizarre imagery and take on the gothic story of multiple personality, the film remains grim, nasty and dire.

One of the highlights of the film is its use of the sets and lighting—here, the locales are all painted up sets that cross cut over each other, embody a cartoon aspect and are highly stylized. Harkening back to German expressionism and horror masterpieces of the silent era such as *The Golem* (1920), *Nosferatu* (1922) and *The Cabinet of Dr. Caligari* (1920), overall, the production elements are grandiose and conceived with remarkable intelligence, the songs and the score are surprisingly bright for the subject matter but also dark when necessary and the performances (although most definitely not perfect) are fun to watch—of all of them, the fantastic Donald Pleasance steals the show while Douglas really has a ball tearing it up as the sinister and treacherous Mr. Hyde.

Much like the made for TV horror outings from Dan Curtis such as *Dracula* (1973) starring Jack Palance as the infamous Count and *The Picture of Dorian Gray* (1973) which is slick and a great showcase

215

of wonderful talent, *Dr. Jekyll and Mr. Hyde* reads like a filmed play, but unlike the aforementioned Curtis features, and also because it is a musical, the Kirk Douglas Jekyll/Hyde deal is other worldly and reads more cinematic. The restraints on budget don't seem to come across as obvious or blunt, instead there is enough crafty work here to disguise such detrimental elements. The aforementioned Lionel Bart was the maestro who delivered the musical magic of *Oliver!* and Irwin Kostal, whose credits include *The Sound of Music* and *Fantasia* (1940), was one of the top orchestrators. Together they concocted one of the strangest and yet most endearing made for television musicals ever put to screen. What makes this film completely bizarre is that it goes to feature some of the least likely actors to perform in a musical with Kirk Douglas, Donald Pleasance and even the shaky and unsure Susan George in the leads. But the results are incredible.

This is a made for TV event that is truly inspired, enchanting and a fantastic addition to the legacy of the oft-told story of horror's most famous mad scientist who toys with personality crisis and jumps right into the heart of the complexities of duality.

Film historian and writer Howard S. Berger shares insight:

> Boy, how I miss 1973. Still under the age of 10 by a couple of years, I recall my life was ruled by constant states of anticipation, excitement and epiphany for and by cinema. A huge part of feeding these states were horror film magazines like "Famous Monsters of Filmland," "Castle Of Frankenstein" and "The Monster Times" (which was actually the world's first horror film newspaper—a genius concept that only exacerbated the need for a kid to watch or own anything mentioned within its pages). I was always obsessed with films in general, practically since birth, but the horror genre was what hooked me in the first place. Kids back then didn't have everything they wanted at their fingertips like they do today—no 1000 channels of movies or cartoons like what they have now on cable or satellite or endless portals to music and video like YouTube, Netflix or Hulu if you can imagine it. We had 5 or 6 stations on TV and any given

movie would play once a year in our area (if we were lucky). Our phones were limited to land line and had 100ft. extension cords, dammit! We suffered for our stimulation! Because of the vast limit of entertainment, whatever we were exposed to had an exaggerated impact; and 1973, for the eager eight-year-old, provided genre sustenance like no other year—no condescension, even in juvenile mini-epics like ABC-TV's Saturday morning "movie" the animated Rankin/Bass *Mad, Mad Monsters* or Clive Donner's live-action *Vampira*—just a good old (and somewhat "new") fashioned faith in classic horror characters and tropes; innocent as much as they were potentially disturbing. It was this consistent indulgence in moral contradiction (we were introduced to an extraordinary array of "monsters" who killed with zero inhibition, yet were rendered sympathetic in back-story or exposition) that helped negotiate us light-hearted kids into a darker, harsher maturity—Dracula, the Wolfman, Frankenstein's monster, Creature From The Black Lagoon, The Ape Man, King Kong—all the poor accursed creatures envisioned by Universal Pictures, RKO and the like in the '30's and '40's and '50's who we could be, at once, terrified of and simultaneously weep for. On TV we were given a constant stream of special made-for-TV events like the myriad Dan Curtis productions like *Dark Shadows* (a daytime soap opera!), *Dracula* and *Dr. Jekyll and Mr. Hyde* with Jack Palance, *Frankenstein* with Bo Svenson, *Picture of Dorian Gray*, *The Turn of the Screw* and *The Night Stalker/Strangler*. William Castle had his *Ghost Story/Circle of Fear*. Rod Serling was showing off *The Night Gallery*. Right around Halloween there was a 2-night presentation of the lavish and strongly sentimental *Frankenstein: The True Story*. In theaters we were given (if we were lucky to have a parent brave enough to defy the R-rating and take us, like mine did) the gory, perverse and really sad *Theatre of Blood* with Vincent Price. All these shows (and more) really struck at us pre-teens with an emotional blowtorch and psychological ball-peen hammer—we were introduced (sometimes for the very first time) to graphic multiple atrocity and a killer we could care for. One of the defining moments of this magical year for me, most indelibly, was the NBC-produced, Lionel Bart-penned musical version of *Dr. Jekyll and Mr. Hyde* starring Kirk Douglas. Before re-watching the presentation recently, my memory retained several extremely bold impressions: the fog-shrouded 19th century London streets, Jekyll's basement laboratory experiments and certain extremely brutal and shocking (both psychologically and physically) sequences of cruelty and violence. What remains interesting to me, 40 plus years later, is how compulsively edible it was, not just because it was a horror film, not just because it had some (already) favorite iconic actors like Douglas, Donald Pleasance and Susan George, but because of it being a musical. The music certified the surrealism of the environment as well as tempering the horror with consoling tunes—an equation that perfectly matched the initial idea of a monster that could also charm your sympathy. Lionel Bart had previously tinkered with this mixture of music and mayhem in his international stage hit and multiple Oscar winning film adaptation of Charles Dickens' *Oliver!* that traumatized us considerably younger viewers (me, personally, at 3 ½ years old) who had to come to terms with watching Oliver's trusted friend and protector (a pub singer and, perhaps, prostitute played by Shani Wallis) beaten to death by Oliver Reed's imposing, brutish and vicious Bill Sykes. Bart had a unique formula with which to explore the societal use and abuse of good and evil that is perfected *in Dr. Jekyll and Mr. Hyde*—a formula that was commercially amenable to the broadest of audiences of that era. Immediately, with the opening songs "Something Very Good" and "This Is the Way It's Always Been," Bart deftly defines both his main character of Dr. Jekyll and the unjust world of Victorian England—impressively transforming and transcending a classic tragic piece of horror literature into a metaphor for the hardships of surviving under repression by exploiting Jekyll's eventual "chemical" separation of good and evil and equating it to the rest of society's separation of class, sex and status: wealthy/poor, male/female, sane/insane, conformist/non-conformist, the captor/the prisoner, the powerful/the weak. To me, it's fascinating seeing Jekyll as the one character who actively, heroically, battles the basic idea of oppression and repression by embracing all the negative aspects of society that he wishes to obliterate and, is, in turn, somewhat pessimistically, destroyed by them. This portrayal by Douglas (with a bare minimum of special make-up effects) of Jekyll/Hyde seems deeply, personally, invested in embracing the moral/immoral shades of grey whereas the majority of his career was spent realizing characters who either were more definitively "good" or "bad," heroic or corrupt. Like Anthony Perkins painfully confessional performance as Jekyll/Hyde in Gerard Kikoine's *Edge of Sanity* nearly 15 years later, Douglas' doctor and "friend" is far more ideologically desperate to exact immediate philanthropic societal change. Jekyll's ultimate loss of control of his own identity, his sense of pure good, is overwhelmingly tragic in that it takes down so many others (good or bad) in his wake. The main victim in the Bart version is pub singer Annie. Dialogue clears Annie of any mistaken assumption that she's a prostitute—she wants to be taken seriously as an entertainer and it's horrifically sad to see her so quickly taken advantage of by the (wealthy) Hyde. He lures her into a relationship where she is literally held prisoner in a private lodging in exchange for dancing lessons but instead mocks and tramples her ambitions and dreams, finally destroying her will for survival against a completely inhospitable class system to which she belongs to the lowest rung. This is exemplified in the surreal graveyard musical sequence where Hyde shows Annie her own gravestone and burial plot and sings (at the bench of a rotting, vine covered grand piano) the story of how he's convinced everyone she ever knew that she had died—leaving her completely alone in life, isolated from all hope of ever being freed of her imprisonment to (and sadistic torture at the hands of) Hyde. The outcome of what assuredly is the single most harrowing number in the history of musical cinema is the disintegration of Annie's mental stability and the remorseful abandonment of her in the local asylum by Jekyll (representing Jekyll's abandonment of his once progressive societal ideals). His sudden embrace of conformity is nearly as shocking as what he's become as a result of the "successful" result of his anti-conformity experiment. Jekyll has transformed, not into either good Jekyll or bad Hyde, but a new Jekyll—one who is desperate to abandon progress after discovering that everyone lives simultaneously in the shadow of or in the grip of a heart of moral complexity, self-centered arrogance and darkness. To date, Douglas' Jekyll is cinema's most intricate Jekyll—the actor's own explicit inner-dialog with his moral conscience. Perhaps this was a reaction to decades of whispered charges that he had raped Natalie Wood when she was only 15— rumors of an event distressingly similar to that depicted, not just in Jekyll/Hyde's "relationship" with the doomed existentially impaired Annie, but some 8 years earlier as well when Kirk was cast as the unlikely hero of Otto Preminger's *In Harm's Way*—as a crooked, lazy pilot whose failed seduction of his buddy's (and superior officer's) son's girlfriend leads to her rape and suicide. His character also sacrifices himself to the Japanese naval forces in order to prevent a surprise attack on American vessels. A Jekyll/Hyde character if ever there was one. Knowing how Preminger would infamously cast actors with vulnerable private lives as characters in direct provocation of their own actual "hidden secrets" (such as closeted gay actor Sal Mineo's character's homosexual rape—a source of shame and humiliation—at the hands of Nazi officers in *Exodus*), it's certainly plausible that Preminger (and Bart) was after that same open-wound performance from Douglas, whether the allegations were true or not. It certainly takes an actor with an intimate understanding of spiritual, emotional and psycho-sexual perversity, to define those dense shades of grey so that praying for the villain to fail wasn't as easy as you'd expect and admiring your hero came at a great moral price. Douglas' *Dr. Jekyll and Mr. Hyde* is a masterfully disturbing, traumatizing and impeccably etched socially conscious musical horror film that does its most productive damage to viewers at the youngest age and provides its most profound, sophisticated social satire in wounded middle-aged retrospect. 1973. It was a very good year. I miss it so.

David Bowie performs in *Ziggy Stardust and the Spiders from Mars* (1973)

ROCK 'N' ROLL SUICIDE: *Ziggy Stardust and the Spiders from Mars*

This movie would be the last time musician David Bowie would be seen in his Ziggy Stardust persona, and this confused his loyal and dedicated fans who thought this meant that he was retiring. A sudden retirement for an artist just on the brink of becoming a huge sensation and icon of the burgeoning glam-rock movement was an idea that threw his legions of fans. The glam-rock explosion began with the demise of hippiedom and the idealism of the peace/love generation and quickly exploited the newly discovered tendency towards hedonism. These excesses expressed themselves in a narcotic-fuelled drug culture, the complicated sexualities of the gender unidentified, and the "divine decadence" expressed earlier in Bob Fosse's *Cabaret*. But instead of pre-World War II Berlin, this was happening in America and the United Kingdom, embodied by artists such as Alice Cooper, New York Dolls and T-Rex. David Bowie was also instrumental to this movement.

Ziggy Stardust and the Spiders from Mars is a concert film and backstage exercise directed by D.A. Pennebaker. He recollects about the film:

RCA was developing video records that you could play and it was produced like the way DVDs are now. They wanted to have a sample to show the people who worked at RCA. So they asked me to make a film about David Bowie, and because he was contracted to them it turned out cheap to get that happening. So we flew over to England to film the concert and it turned out to be the last one he was going to do, and it turned out that no body, including a lot of the people that played in his band were not aware of this. When he announced this on stage a few people just went into shock. We got there and we were only supposed to do a half hour sample of what he did. We got there the night before the concert, and we shot a bit of the rehearsal and that was mainly to make sure we got the right light and so forth, but once we got into it I thought, this is an amazing person: we have to make a film. He is so filmic. So we decided to do it. We found someone else in London to get way on top of the theatre to get all the long shots which my team and I never really did. So we filmed the whole concert, but RCA didn't know what to do with it. So I edited it down and turned it into a feature film. In our studio back in New York on 45th Street we mixed the film and chose the tracks for it which were all RCA properties, and we had figured out how to do the tracks. In those days the way you did stereo tracks was that you made a 35mm print and then you put four tracks, two on one side and two on the other of each print that is, you couldn't make it like an optical track where you print it. You had to actually record it in each print that you were going to send out to show. It was a little bit complicated to do, but when we were finished and worked it all out, people just flocked to come and see it and see what we could do. So I knew that it could work in theatres. And eventually ABC wanted to run it on air and I just let them have it. They demanded a lot of beeps in it because there was mentions of suicide and all the swearing. But at the time was that FM radio had a system that if you gave them the track of the copy in stereo they would sync it to the original airing, so that didn't have any of those beeps. David had a listen to it and called me up and spent a month together editing and getting it released. David was a really interesting man. He's like all really good musicians, he would retreat into this part of his head and disappear. You'd see a bunch of people drinking beers and he would disappear and retreat and you could tell that he was lost in his musical depths. In comparison to someone like Stephen Sondheim, David Bowie was far more introspective and not at all as outgoing.

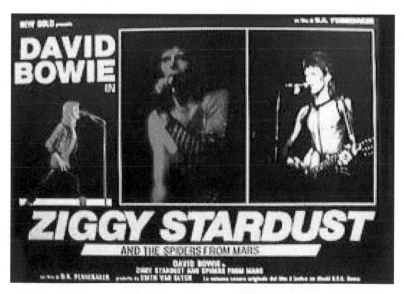

The theatrical poster for *Ziggy Stardust and the Spiders from Mars* (1973)

The film is a shining example of how the concert film can be captivating as a performance piece as well as a character study, or in this case, a persona study. Ziggy Stardust is a contradictory creation coming from a space of both paralysing insecurity and gregarious outlandishness, and the songs are vibrant and remote. There is a troubled spacey creepiness about them, and the sentiment of both David Bowie and the intention of his performance as his alter-ego sit together like estranged relatives at a family get together. Like a horrific accident and like a breathtaking landscape, it is hard not to watch and be emotionally involved. Pennebaker's film cemented the rock concert feature as a narrative and character driven entity, so that when a director such as Alan Parker delivered *Pink Floyd—The Wall* (1982) years later, there was already a standard set with grounded expectations.

Concert films receded into the background when it got to 1974, however. Instead, nostalgia ruled, existentialism turned its somewhat misguided head and carrying from where *Dr. Jekyll and Mr. Hyde* hit home, the rock musical continued to triumph taking on movie monster motifs as its primary focal point...

1974

Phantoms Haunt the Paradise (and MGM), Lucy Sings, and Dorothy Gets the Filmation Treatment

IN 1974, AMERICA WAS SWIFTLY TRANSFORMING. THE GLAM-ROCK explosion had taken off in the early 1970s across parts of North America and Europe, and the ferocity of punk rock had started to hit the mean streets of New York and other urban cities devastated by the oppressive recession of the time. The phrase "starving artist" became much-used in describing city dwelling bohemians struggling to make ends meet while they fine-tuned their particular art. In this climate, the gypsies of Broadway were given a voice in Michel Bennett's incredible musical *A Chorus Line*, which acted as a metaphor for people living on the line and in desperate need for a job.

In all its kookiness and conventionality, the movie musical tippy-toed around the fact that America was at a financial low, and with

Hollywood showcasing gritty and dark films that embraced this reality—such as the intimate *The Panic in Needle Park* (1971) and the excessive *Death Wish* (1974)—the musical expressed similar angst and nihilism with its own voice and unique flair. Instead of its traditionally frivolous, light-hearted fare, the movie musical grew darker, embracing changing trends in musical style and its audience's tastes. Rock'n'roll finally made a massive impact on the musical; it was no longer a tokenistic excursion or an edgy experiment, but rather *the* genuine article. Crowds were torn—some remained hesitant while others took to it with the same rabid fan devotion that they did for The Beatles, The Rolling Stones or Elvis Presley. Artists such as Alice Cooper and The Stooges were thriving at the musical edge, while the sheer rage and angry cry of the inner city outsider from the burgeoning punk scene lived alongside the torch song antics of phenomenal talents such as Bette Midler. Along with her piano accompanist Barry Manilow, Midler performed at the Continental Bathouse in New York City with other acts such as New York Dolls, The Pointer Sisters, Lou Reed and many more. Musicals reflected this energy and married it with high theatrics. The glam-rock scene seemed to be the most fitting in terms of narrative-driven, monstrous musical movies.

Nostalgia clawed its way up through the grungy glitter, and replaced it with some glimpses of traditional show business ethos. But both these bizarre worlds–of artists and freaks—co-existed and somehow (goodness knows how!) they complimented each other and said "We are movie musicals, we are either edgy and angry and new or traditional and classicist and rich." And for the most part, it worked…

SWAN SONG: *Phantom of the Paradise*

Brian De Palma is an auteur in the purest sense. His artistry and vision unique and memorable, and during the 1970s he was one of the most influential and interesting directors working in the industry. Although he makes no secret of his direct influences (the much discussed Hitchcock legacy, plus his keen interest in *Giallo* and the films of Italian horror maestros such as Dario Argento), De Palma has his own filmic voice. He also has a complicated love of his subject matter, and his aesthetic and storytelling style is versatile and varies from film to film. His sensual, vivid, lush filmmaking practice is a celebration of garish, nightmarish imagery, and violence is expressed with the most operatic of sensibilities. There is a lurid sexiness and sadism to his motion pictures, especially those from the decade being discussed.

De Palma made a massive impact with his horror masterpiece *Carrie* (1976), based on the novel by Stephen King, which told the story of a misfit teenager with telekinetic powers who unleashes her "gift" at her high school prom, turning it into a frightening hell-on-earth. The film was a play on *Cinderella* (with Samson tearing down the temple thrown in for good measure), and it hit a nerve with moviegoing audiences. Horror had come home. But before the critical and box office success of *Carrie* that granted De Palma worldwide attention, he made equally ambitious and highly stylized features such as *Sisters* (1973), a character-driven horror film with a strong nod to Hitchcock (including a magnificent score from Bernard Hermann), that got people talking. However, even *Sisters* would not match the magnetism and majestic anarchy of his rock musical *Phantom of the Paradise*. This energetic and frenzied Faustian tale set in the world of glam-rock embraced hedonism, and was uniquely aligned with the decadence of the 1970s. *Phantom of the Paradise* is a high-concept film, and yet the plot is simple and straightforward. But it is the vibrant and garish visuals that give this superb film a complexity that is hard to pinpoint. It screams monster movie musical, and it hits all the right notes.

The marriage between horror and the musical has a long history, but strangely enough it is seldom tackled critically. This is a bizarre oversight, seeing that both genres, by their very nature are escapist fare, and also plotted in similar ways structurally: in horror, moments of terror or moments of character-centric evil occur, while in a musical songs pepper the story. Musicals such as Andrew Lloyd Weber's *The Phantom of the Opera* got a filmic treatment much later while other stage productions such as *Jekyll and Hyde* and horror films that were adapted into musicals such as *The Evil Dead* (1981), *Re-Animator* (1985) and even *Carrie* have yet to be adapted for the screen. *Sweeney Todd: The Demon Barber of Fleet Street* would also get a motion picture adaptation with Johnny Depp in the lead, but one of the best was to come out of the 1980s. Frank Oz's magnificent movie adaptation of the Howard Ashman and Alan Menken rock musical *Little Shop of Horrors* (1986) was a massive hit and boasted some of the best stop motion and animatronic puppetry ever put to film in its monster Audrey II, the bloodthirsty plant. Much like *Phantom of the Paradise*, this Motown-flavoured nostalgia piece is a Faustian tale about a put-upon schmuck named Seymour (Rick Moranis), who "sells his soul" to an aggressively hungry plant in order to gain success. The fabulous Ellen Greene, who played Seymour's object of affection, the sweet but tragic Audrey remembers the film:

> Audrey was one of the very first characters that I put lots of myself in and luckily I had the freedom to do that working with Alan Menken and the brilliant Howard Ashman. I got the script and I fell in love with the song "Somewhere That's Green." It made me cry. Usually if something touches me emotionally like that I know it will touch the audience; I'm a very open and instinctual performer and I can tell if something is extremely important and has lots of heart because it instantly moves me. Creating Audrey was so much fun. I went in to audition for Alan and Howard and Howard and I got each other in an instant! Audrey's voice just came out organically and I offered Howard who was also directing me suggestions on how the character should look and be played. I decided to make her blonde, I suggested she be dressed in tight outfits that she had to continually adjust and that her heels were so tall that she teetered around like a fresh peach which was just ripe for the picking! I offered alternatives to some of the lines and gags Howard had written; for instance, in the scene preceding the beautiful duet. "Suddenly Seymour," Audrey mentions the Gutter, a seedy nightclub she and the demented dentist met at, and I said to Howard, the word "nightclub" isn't funny, so I suggested I say "nightspot" instead and he loved it straight away and changed it! It didn't matter that I was only making $50 a week playing Audrey, I had an absolute blast! I love *Little Shop of Horrors* so much. A lot of my own personality is in Audrey and I just adore her sweetness and the ability she has to see the beauty in everyone and everything. Of course

on the flipside of that I had to channel a character who doesn't quite see the harsh realities of life for what they are; you see, for Audrey life could be or should be the way she envisions it in the number "Somewhere That's Green." She's such a sweet character and I love her so much. Firstly John Landis was going to direct it and then Martin Scorsese was next in line as a potential director after Landis was dropped from the project. But things weren't working out for him either. One day I was with hanging out my boyfriend at the time, Marty Robinson, who was part of the wonderful Muppet crew and he was working on *Follow That Bird!* puppeteering the beautiful Snuffleupagus. I met up with Frank Oz and said to him "Frank, you should totally direct *Little Shop of Horrors* the movie version!" The reason I told him this is because I was in love with his Muppet Grover from *Sesame Street*. I said to Frank, "Grover is so sweet and has a heart of gold but he also lives in such a fantasy world where he can't decipher what is real and what is make believe and that is perfect for *Little Shop of Horrors*." A few meetings later, the amazingly talented Frank Oz was on board to direct the film and the rest, as we say, is history! When I was told I got the part I nearly upchucked my lunch at the Russian Tea Room in New York! I had heard that everyone from Cyndi Lauper to Barbra Streisand was in the running to get the role. It's funny, most people who do the original stage production of a musical don't usually get the film role as well. I was lucky and extremely grateful.

It is also interesting to note that a lot of horror movies and musicals have been maligned (mostly unfairly) because audiences are completely thrown by their sheer concept. It is very common to hear non-cinema fans quickly remark "Oh I don't like horror movies" or "Oh I don't like musicals" and sometimes in the same sentence. These people are clearly denying themselves cinematic brilliance from both genres, and in the case of something as spectacular as *Phantom of the Paradise*, they are missing out on both.

Jessica Harper is beautifully suited to the role of Phoenix, a young girl singer who is effectively the Christine figure from *The Phantom of the Opera*. Harper's vocals are extraordinarily haunting, and possess a deep soulfulness akin to the heartbreaking talents of Karen Carpenter. Harper's performance of "Special to Me"—her audition piece for Swan (Paul Williams)—is a terrific example of her versatility as an artist. Here she bounces along to the rock-pop of Williams's wonderful music, and it is pure 1970s bliss. Harper throws her body around from one side of the stage to the other, and then jettisons off and calmly walking back in with confident elegance. This is what Harper exudes in this film: a quiet confidence that is just enchanting. Her vulnerability is palpable, and excels when she sings one of the greatest songs in the film, "Old Souls." She is a perfect counterpart to Winslow (William Finley), a tragic figure who is much like his ancestor Eric the Phantom of the Opera (and there have been more than few incarnations of this dark horror icon): he is a man who has been done wrong by and completely tortured by loneliness.

Behind the scenes on *Phantom of the Paradise* (1974)

The film opens with the image of a dead canary spinning around, an incredible image that is emblematic of a company morbidly titled Death Records, a rock'n'roll label that is in servitude to a personal Xanadu, a Shangri-la known as The Paradise. A voice-over explains that Swan, a megalomaniacal musical maestro who creates and destroys bands and artists with ease, needs to find the "new sound" for his beloved Paradise. His current band The Juicy Fruits is a nostalgia act who have served him well for the 1950s nostalgia trip the young are seemingly interested in. But as musical tastes change, "the next big thing" needs to be exploited. De Palma's film notes the obsession the 1970s had with American 1950s culture—the "hub," the greasers, the poodle skirts, the cars and of course its energetic and melodic rock'n'roll. This is established in the opening number, "Goodbye Eddie Goodbye" a 1950s pastiche executed with great exuberance.

Actor Archie Hahn recalls this nostalgia trip and his work on the film:

> You look at the lyrics of the songs and the kind of groups they were and that would pretty much dictate the style in which you would sing it and each of us would choose the number that we wanted to sing. Paul never appointed the lead vocal for any of us, he just let us choose and we did it. We met him at a studio and he played the music and he had done all the temp tracks so he had sung everything in our introductory to the music and then each of us individually said which song we'd like to do and I put my hand up for the 1950s rock'n'roll song. Paul said "OK." He was very agreeable throughout the whole process, I mean we had questions and he would answer them, but it all ran smoothly and we understood all of it, and especially after we sang it was clear that we had picked the right songs for each other. I grew up in the 1950s so I was exposed to all of those bands and loved rock'n'roll and loved to dance and I was a big fan of Bandstand, so I just fed off from all that impact those bands and artists made on me and sang the song the way I would have sung it if I fronted a rock'n'roll group back in the day.

231

I wasn't conscious of ever copying anyone, I just wanted to capture that look and that style with the DA and the clothes. Back in the 1950s that's how I dressed anyways, every boy back then wanted to look like Elvis Presley or a rock'n'roller. This was my first film and also my first time in a recording studio so it was all very new to me and in terms of movies that I had seen around that time I don't recall there being a 1950s nostalgia kick happening. At the time I saw it as a film about a rock'n'roll group. Brian De Palma guided us but really didn't have much to say as far as his direction went. He seemed pretty happy with what we were doing. I have to say that I used to refer to him as Mr. De Pismo and Mr. De Plasma and I was always intentionally screwing up his name and he would look at me and think "What kind of creature is this? This silly fop!" But he liked our energy and I don't think he really had a sense of what to do with us except putting us in our place. I really don't recall him giving us any direct or specific direction other than moving through a scene and positioning us physically, but in terms of performance I don't recall any complaints or any suggestions either. The art direction was all in keeping with the story and as a beginner you're kind of in awe. So you're just thrilled to be there and watching the collaboration of so many artists was a great introduction to working in the movies. As far as the art direction went it was just perfect, Jack Fisk was a terrific guy and Sissy Spacek was just a sweetheart. Each of us was most comfortable in the song we were singing. But I loved playing those other characters too. The Beach Bums was just silly fun to spoof that style in that blonde wig and the glam rock thing was great too. I think it was Peter Elbling who came up with the idea of doing a stark black and white make-up for the glam rock band The Undeads. At that point I had never experienced KISS, and there was always some issue as to who started it first, but I think KISS had performed prior to the release of the movie and it was just a complete coincidence that we did the black and white make-up, because Peter, Jeffrey Comanor and I had never seen them. We gathered around the costume designer Rosanna Norton like moths to a flame, and it was a total collaboration. I love every song on that album I think that album is sensation. My favourite song is probably "Old Souls," it's the emotion and the intellect behind it, and its great lyric writing, its poetry and the music is just perfect for the lyrics. I appreciate it on the most fundamental primal level, I appreciate it on the most visceral and personal level. My first reaction was seeing myself on the screen right at the beginning of the film, I had no idea it was the opening, we had never seen a cut of it or anything, so that was a big surprise! I remember when we were shooting in Dallas in a real theatre, and on a real stage for The Beach Bums number; we had a moment in that scene where there is an explosion when the little car blows up. Well a ball of flame went up into the ceiling and lit the fly system up on fire. I also remember that the girls in the shoot were all in bikinis and bathing suits and I thought, OK, well, when something blows up there is almost always going to be embers scattered around as the fire settles. So I grabbed a bunch of gaffa tape and cut out these little soles for these girls' feet so they could pity-pat over the floor and not burn themselves. They were all very grateful for that. Jessica Harper was the sweetest and loveliest person ever, and she had the most beautiful voice. I remember sitting there watching her rehearse and no one else being around, and I was just mesmerized by her voice. William Finley and I didn't have many scenes together and he always kept to himself working on his character, so there wasn't any opportunity to socialize with him, but he was very nice and gentle. Then after the film, on later occasions at gatherings celebrating the film like in Winnipeg I got to know him a little better socially, so he was funny and witty and charming and a very nice guy.

Winslow is told by the talent scout that his sound could be "really big," but as a dedicated musician, he explains that his music is not just "songs": he is writing an opera of sorts about Faust, a rock opera about the legend of the soul-marketplace. "I am the only one who can sing Faust!" he insists. His aggression comes from out of nowhere, but then of course this is a horror movie and violence can erupt wherever it wants—just in the same way that a song (even in a diegetic context as it is here in *Phantom of the Paradise*) can suddenly appear out of nowhere in a musical.

Classic horror movie motifs in *Phantom of the Paradise* (1974)

Winslow's first attempt to get into Death Records finds him ushered out by security, so he innovatively makes his way to Swan's manor instead. An off-screen Greek chorus of sorts explains that he is about to "meet the devil." Inside, he comes across a group of young girls auditioning, and among them is Phoenix, a beautiful young brunette with a lovely tone (as opposed to the shrill and out-of-tune other girls). She sings his own song and this enchants him, much like Eric various incarnations of *The Phantom of the Opera* being seduced by Christine's talents as a youthful soprano. Winslow discovers out that Swan is reopening The Paradise with his cantata and this sets the movie into motion, along with some visually provocative images: the character of Philbin (George Memmoli) making use of the casting couch, young groupies (much like the Brides of Dracula) carousing on Swan's bed eagerly awaiting their master to serve and so forth. When Swan rejects Winslow, the turning point is imminent. Bloodied and beaten, Winslow is framed for drug possession and arrested. He is taken to Sing, a volunteer program funded by the Swan Foundation where his teeth are removed and he is tortured. He escapes, and heads back to Swan's estate demanding respect.

Winslow's anger leads him to the record pressing room, and in a horrific accident he is caught in the pressing machine where his face is severely burned. Finley plays out the high-energy physical horror of the piece to perfection. He squirms with half his face burnt off, and it's a wonderful sight to behold; a well-articulated tribute to the ghoulish lumber of a movie monster from the golden age of horror. In the classic horror movie tradition, Winslow is also believed to be dead, but of course isn't: when he returns, De Palma uses a shaky POV shot to reintroduce our newly disfigured musical genius staggering around The Paradise. With his heavy breathing and scaring the likes of passers-by, this moment is a perfect tribute to the history of the movie monster.

On top of De Palma's visceral brilliance (manifesting of course in his signature split screen), are the impressive story elements and the phenomenal music written by the talented Paul Williams. His divine melodies fuel the movie's rock'n'roll bliss, and breathe a new voice into this Faustian retelling of Gaston Leroux's classic horror story. Winslow, now the embodiment of the Phantom of the Opera, gives Phoenix an opportunity to sing, and what Williams writes for her is beautiful. "Old Souls" is a triumph of song writing, with lyrics that delicately glide over lovelorn sentiments: "our paths are crossed and parted this love affair was started long ago, this love survives the ages in its story lies the pages fill them up theirs turn slow."

Phoenix's addiction to stardom and to the adoration of her audience adds to the lonely deformed Winslow's trauma as he watches Phoenix and Swan in a loving embrace. Set to the sound of the falling rain, the droplets act as his tears as "Old Souls" is reprised. More Faustian elements unfold as Winslow finding a tape of Swan selling his soul to the devil to retain his youth—the devil being in fact the very image of himself—and this exemplifies Paul Williams' commanding presence. When lit so dramatically, he conveys a towering air of menace. The deconstruction of the movie monster is imprinted within the subtext of the film with the real evil being within Swan himself. The film also shrewdly comments on its heroine, a dedicated artist who starts off claiming "I'm not a screamer, I'm a singer," and continues to stay true to that ethos. This is a testament to Phoenix's integrity: when she does fall in love with the limelight, it is both forgivable and meaningful. Swan, however, remains a mystery, and much like Ursula to Ariel in *The Little Mermaid*, he requests Phoenix's voice: a sacrificial devotion to the world of music and the gift of music. A Faustian deal is made in the diegetic rock opera written by Winslow.

Another important addition is the art direction from Jack Fisk, with help from his wife, actress Sissy Spacek (who would later wow audiences and critics alike with her performance in De Palma's *Carrie*). Fisk remembers the shoot:

> I met Ed Pressman working on *Badlands* in Colorado and after that film he asked me if I would work with Brian De Palma on *Phantom of the Paradise*. I was excited but I don't know if Brian was so excited. He has a quiet cynical way about him that can intimidate people, and when I showed up to work I remember him asking in a non-impressed way; "So what have you done?" *Phantom of the Paradise* was one of the most difficult film's I've worked on. We built tons of sets in three cities with little money. I fired my art director the day before we began shooting and Sissy started helping me get the sets ready. So many stories getting that film done, but I remember a scene where the Phantom is busting through a brick wall and I was laying the brick during lunch on the day we were going to shoot it. The company came back from lunch and I had not completed it. The grips were complaining on how ill prepared I was—I was so tired and felt bad that they had to wait for me to finish (20 minutes) but I heard Brian tell them to shut up; "Jack's making this

film look great." That was the first positive comment I had heard from Brian and he announced it to the entire crew. I was so excited that he liked what I was doing that nothing else mattered. By the time *Carrie* came around we were old friends and I knew Brian trusted me.

Sissy Spacek adds:

I had done *Badlands* and then I had to audition for *Carrie*. Brian held several weeks of readings with a lot of the young actors, most of them ending up in the film, and during the readings he would have us change roles; so one day I'd be reading for *Carrie* and then another day I'd be reading for someone else; but when it came time to do the test, I was only testing for *Carrie* and a lot of the other actresses were testing for more than one role and it just so happened that I had gotten a major commercial on the same day. Now I knew Brian before all this because I had worked for him as a set decorator on a previous film *Phantom of the Paradise* with my husband, production designer Jack Fisk. Brian had fired his previous crew on *Phantom of the Paradise* because a set wasn't built in time so I had just come to Dallas, I had a cousin there, and that's where they shooting it and so Jack and I got pulled in by Brian as emergency set designers and decorators just because we were available. When I first met Brian he thought I was a very bad set decorator because one day Jack left the set and he left my cousin Sam and I in charge and he told us that nothing out of the ordinary will happen, the set is ready, it dressed, all you have to do is sit here and if they need anything help out and this was of course before cell phones so I had no way of contacting Jack and as soon as the cast and crew turned up they went into rehearsing the planned scene but then Brian turned up and said "We're not rehearsing that scene! We'll be doing another scene!" and this other scene was on the same set, but the set had to be redressed and repainted; and here we were repainting the set and it became magenta because we weren't aware that we had to paint the set white before anything else and it turned out to be a nightmare because there was Brian, sitting watching not happy at all. So from the get go Brian didn't think of me as an actress, he thought of me as a very awful set decorator! And going back to after the tests for *Carrie*, once I had gotten that big national commercial I called him and told him and he said "Do the commercial" which made me so mad that I thought, "No way! I'm gonna get the role of Carrie and blow everybody away!"

Another highlight is Swan's latest discovery, his "next big thing." Beef is a lisping, flamboyant and bratty rock star played delightfully and with prissy perfection by Gerrit Graham. He steals the show as the enigmatic diva, and captures the spirit of Carlotta from *The Phantom of the Opera* with zest. He becomes the sacrificial prima donna, and the *Psycho*-with-a-plunger moment is wonderful as Beef is threatened to never sing Winslow's music because it is strictly meant for Phoenix only. Of course, Beef is forced to perform and dire results unfold.

1950s nostalgia in *Phantom of the Paradise* (1974)

Phantom of the Paradise is a wild, rollicking rock musical that captures the decade with both vibrancy and depravity. It highlights the talents of the man central to 1970s musicals—Paul Williams. The versatile song writer went on to write songs for *Bugsy Malone*, *A Star is Born* (1976) and *The Muppet Movie* (1979)—all of which will be explored further late in this book. Chris Alexander, the editor of Fangoria magazine, had the pleasure of interviewing Williams, where he said the following:

> Brian wrote the original script *Phantom of the Philmore*. He went to A&M Records film department to discuss the music for the film. An executive there suggested me as a songwriter for the project. I met Brian and we hit it off. He very quickly suggested that I play the Phantom/ Winslow. He saw him as this creepy little creature living in the rafters of the theatre. Sort of a Peter Lorre-come-Golem type I think. I thought I was too small to be threatening. Also, I didn't want to play someone whose music was stolen. Didn't want people to think I had a case against the music biz. Swan was more my speed. The more he thought about it the more he liked it. We worked closely on the project. A major change occurring where we decided to kill Beef on stage instead of in the shower: "an assassination, live on coast to coast television....That's entertainment!" is my favorite line in the film. Brian originally wanted Sha Na Na for the film. I wanted a group that could evolve through all the different styles of music I intended to satirize. I had everyone at the NY audition, including Jessica, sing Leon Russell's "Superstar." Jessica was singing it quietly to herself as she waited her turn. I stood behind her and listened. Beautiful. When she sang for Brian and I she sang out like a Broadway actress reaching the back of the house. I told her to sing softly. It was magical. She killed it. I also knew Swan had two or three personas. The pre-deal with the devil bathtub puny whiner, the disturbed slave we witness watching the horror footage every day. Seeing how horrible he's actually become. And then my favorite. The charmer. Never rattled. Walter Huston's Devil in *The Devil and Daniel Webster* meets a casket salesman. I never knew anyone exactly like him and I'm told some see a Phil Spector energy there but I never was

consciously attempting that. I tried to create what Brian gave me and his vision was spot on.

Williams quotes his own wonderful lyrics:

"To work it out I let them in

All the good guys and the bad guys that I've been
All the devils that disturb me
And the angels that defeated them somehow.
Come together in me now ...."

I didn't realize it when I wrote it ... But, it's a prayer. A prayer that assumes goodness will win out in the final mix. The title song I wrote for "Still Alive" has a *Phantom of the Paradise* reference:

"And someone asked me once
Where do we go when we arrive
If you're lucky
When it's done
The dreamers still alive
A blessed mystery
For sweeter souls did not survive
But if you're lucky
When it's over
The dreamer's still alive"

I walk in gratitude for the life I have today.

FRIENDS OF LIZA: *Journey Back to Oz*

As the farm girl who wished to leave the drab Kansas and go over the rainbow, Judy Garland would forever be linked to the classic musical fantasy *The Wizard of Oz* (1939). So when her daughter Liza Minnelli was asked to take on the role of Dorothy Gale for a full-length feature sequel, she was inspired and felt that it was time to continue this legacy. The film was an animated theatrical release from the animation studio Filmation, headed by inventive and passionate entrepreneur Lou Scheimer. Filmation was devoted to modestly budgeted Saturday morning television cartoons that acted as a core rival to the popular shows from Hanna-Barbera whose most successful exports such as *Tom and Jerry* (1940-1958), *The Huckleberry Hound Show* (1958-1961), *The Flintstones* (1960-1966) and *The Jetsons* (1962-1963) were now re-run staples. During the 1970s, *Scooby-Doo Where Are You?* (1969-1970) was a success for Hanna-Barbera, and feature films such as the lovely *Charlotte's Web* were critically and financially successful, providing current, healthy competition for Filmation. Scheimer's company had moderate hits such as *Sabrina* (1970), *Groovie Ghoulies* (1970), *Archie's Funhouse* (1971), *Star Trek: The Animated Series* (1973-1974) and *Fat Albert and the Cosby Kids* (1972), but they needed to prove themselves a worthy competitor to Hanna-Barbera, delivering something as enchanting and as tender as their friendly rival's movie about that the previously discussed pig who learnt the harsh realities of life through a spider named Charlotte.

Journey Back to Oz was Filmation's brave venture into feature film, and Liza Minnelli's tribute to her mother is made all the more special when you hear her incredible singing: she sounds like Judy, and it is lovely. But for an artist making her own work and leaving her own imprint on theatre, film, television and music, Minnelli still had her own individual artistic signature, delivered always with flare and warmth: Garland was a phenomenon, and Minnelli is as well. While distinct artists, in *Journey Back to Oz*, Minnelli channels her mother's performance from the 1939 masterpiece beautifully. In this unofficial sequel, Minnelli is joined by legendary stars such as Ethel Merman (who belts out everything like a huge trumpet), Paul Lynde (who favours a weak and cowardly persona as opposed to his usual lascivious sensibilities), Milton Berle (who croaks through his lines with an agitation that is comical), Risë Stevens (offering some grandiose semi-operatics), as well as Garland's leading man back in the 1940s, Mickey Rooney, who lends his voice to the Scarecrow. Original *The Wizard of Oz* star Margaret Hamilton (who played the Wicked Witch of the West) lends her voice here to the small role of Auntie Em. Minnelli is in incredible company, and the film is all the more enjoyable with these gifted artists behind its brightly colored but rather cynical 'toons. The characters that populate this animated Oz are depressives, tortured by their failure as functional citizens. This is what makes the movie distinctly 1970s in tone.

The movie musical of this decade was obsessed with social misfits and outcasts, consistently presenting us with characters that cannot live up to expectations. This is found as much in movie musicals geared towards children, such as *Raggedy Ann and Andy: A Musical Adventure* (1977), *Jack Frost, Rudolph and Frosty's Christmas in July* (1979). *Journey Back to Oz* is no exception. In this film, much like the original classic, Dorothy collects friends who are incomplete, haunted by their differences, and unhappy with them. She also revisits her old friends the Scarecrow, the Tinman (Danny Thomas) and the Lion (Milton Berle) and they are perplexed by their newfound power and positions as authority figures in Oz. Thankfully, these maudlin male characters come into contact with the strong-willed Dorothy, who enlightens them and teaches them to "believe in themselves." This is something she learns from the matriarch of Oz, Glinda the Good Witch (Risë Stevens).

Continuing the original film's central theme of finding home and having faith, *Journey Back to Oz* travels through the same concept: again, it says that if you believe in yourself, you can accomplish anything. This gets picked up again—albeit with a very political bent—in 1978's *The Wiz*, which we will get to later.

Unlike the empowering *The Wizard of Oz* where even the most heartbreaking moments lift the spirit, *Journey Back to Oz* settles with a foundational sorrow. There are some bizarre lines that celebrate the maudlin: for example, at one point Dorothy says "I love sad stories, they're the best kind," and when she mentions that she has a strange feeling, her Auntie Em insists that she is sick. This moroseness continues throughout the film and climaxes with Dorothy leading into a song with "There's a sad little feeling you feel when you hear a train..." This number is a list of her "sad little feelings," which all lead to her longing to get back to Kansas. Weirdly enough, Dorothy is seen as a lazy nuisance in the eyes of her Uncle Henry (Paul Ford), so the idea of missing the place seems somewhat illogical. But we are so familiar with the Joseph Campbell's infamous "hero's journey" and its famous manifestation within *The Wizard of Oz*, so we know our pintsized rural heroine must return home to find herself and complete her quest.

Film poster for *Journey Back to Oz* (1974)

Journey Back to Oz also side-peddles the gay subtext that has become synonymous with the legend; during a period the Stonewall Riots and a new gay liberation movement had surfaced. The original film hit a nerve with pre-gay liberation "queer" analysis because it tackled notions of sissyhood as it deconstructed masculinity. A major theme here is the inability to run with the pack, and the anguish caused by difference. This is a perpetual narrative device where the off-horse is not able to fit in or live up to straight expectations. In *The Wizard of Oz* , this manifests in Dorothy meeting three characters who each represent aspects of pre-liberation gay men. They are all missing something, and troubled by not feeling quite right: the Scarecrow cannot live up to the expectations placed on him (he fails at frightening the crows), therefore he is unable to be who he feels he is supposed to be. The Tinman is without a heart, and therefore denied the permission to love. The Lion, a cowardly sissy, sings to Dorothy, "It's sad you see dear Missy, when you're born to be a sissy, without the vim and verve." He then becomes the influence for one of Hanna-Barbera's most treasured inventions: the campy, sissy pink mountain lion Snagglepuss.

Dorothy's friends reflect the struggles of gay men during an era where the closet was the most comfortable place to live. Sadly, Filmation did not want to delve into this notion in their sequel, although at the time, homosexual readings of *The Wizard of Oz* flourished, and both Judy Garland (then eventually Liza Minnelli) were gay icons. These elements do remain to some degree in the film's subtext, however: Dorothy has returned to her gay friends, and they are jaded and disenfranchised. She needs to provide a passion for these characters, who ultimately need another struggle to feel alive again. Later, in *Return to Oz's* (1985) nightmarish, dystopian vision of Oz during the AIDS crisis, these gay readings become diluted but still permeate the text as Dorothy (Fairuza Balk) discovers more characters living under an oppressive figure who denies them a decent quality of life. While often maligned, this film therefore offers an intriguing critique on Reagan-era America and his horrendous denial of the AIDS epidemic.

Gay celebrity Paul Lynde built a second career during the 1970s voicing animated characters in films such as the Oz sequel and *Charlotte's Web*, as well as Saturday morning cartoons such as the Hanna-Barbera series *The Perils of Penelope Pitstop* (1969-1970). This wonderful showman with his acerbic tongue and campy antics found a home masked behind the world of cartoon characters. There is a remarkable parallel here: the ground breaking gay-themed film *The Killing of Sister George* (1968), where Beryl Reid's unapologetically butch dyke actress character is turned "invisible" by only being cast as a cartoon cow!

Filmation would eventually become hugely successful in the toy-centric 1980s with the advent of animated television series such as the popular *He-Man and the Masters of the Universe* (1983-1985). But *Journey Back to Oz* didn't hit the mark with audiences until some years later when the film was screened on television and then subsequently released on VHS. In the television cut of the film, Bill Cosby (who was the moral human link to Filmation's successful *Fat Albert and the Cosby Kids*) pops up as the Wizard of Oz himself, which neither adds nor detracts to the film. Unlike the clean cut crisp coolness of say Gene Kelly dancing with Jerry the mouse in *Anchors Aweigh* (1945) or Julie Andrews being wooed by Dick Van Dyke and a crew of dancing penguins in *Mary Poppins*, the marriage of Filmation animation and real live stars is clunky and uneven.

WHO ELSE BUT A BOSSOM BUDDY?: *Mame*

The unfair criticism dished out to *Mame* was unwarranted in 1974 during its initial release, and most targeted at its star, comedy legend Lucille Ball. There was also unnecessary comparisons drawn between Ball's take on the iconic roaring 1920s heroine and Rosalind Russell's acerbic brilliance in the original, non-musical version of the same story, *Auntie Mame* (1958). This no doubt contributed to the musical being considered "old hat." However, here is a film trying to deliver a good old-fashioned musical romp, loaded with intelligent comedy and social satire. It is strengthened by an exciting and frisky jazz age score by legendary composer Jerry Herman. *Mame* deserves to be respected, and there are many reasons as to why.

This is a "whistling in the dark" musical that works without pretentiousness or the hiccups that marred *Man of La Mancha* two years prior. The idea of celebrating life during the darkest of times is a core theme in this fun and frivolous film. At one of her lavish and decedent parties (soon to be the last, as the story unfolds) one of Mame

Dennis's (Lucile Ball) guests cries out "Mame! What the hell are we celebrating?" Mame's reply establishes her character in five seconds: here is a woman that makes her own rules, doesn't need a cause for celebrating life and embraces hedonism with big broad open arms. Mame is a good time girl, and her famous quip "Life is a banquet and too many sons of bitches are starving to death" is the thematic skeleton for this charming musical that celebrates life, even when life runs you to the ground. It is also a crowning achievement in nostalgic sentiment and a sophisticated rehashing of golden age farcical musical comedy. Besides the hurried staging of the number "Loving You" sung by the robust Robert Preston as Mame's wealthy beau, Beauregard Jackson Pickett Burnside—with its clumsy zoom ins and outs and reeking of 1970s sensibilities—the film is an authentic piece in that it looks as though it could have come from the 1950s.

Lucille Ball in the title role of *Mame* (1974)

Director Gene Saks has a natural eye for classic Hollywood visual flair. The sets look like the kind of manors and estates that would feature in a screwball musical from the 1930s and 1940s, and Onna

White's choreography is classicist and a tribute to the ragtime period. The cinematography also gives the film a much needed air of glamour in an era so dedicated to bleak and stark imagery. The look of the film is what caused the main backlash from critics and audiences alike in 1974, and they scoffed at the way Lucille Ball was shot. The idea of this aging superstar filmed in soft focus caused laughter and grief, but this is Saks's and Ball's homage to golden age Hollywood, where every leading lady was shot in soft focus and given that supernatural element of high glamour. *Mame* celebrates this glamour, and it is no reason to shun it.

Lucille Ball gives a passionate and honest performance, and she throws all of her energy into this fun literary creation. Her performance is nuanced, and her character develops convincingly. In the beginning, she is presented as a good time gal, and although she is seemingly out of touch with the needs of the small child she is forced to become "mother" to, she is the best friend and mentor that young Patrick (Kirby Furlong) could ever wish for. Mame's politics are leftist and liberal, and this is how the film can be located as a product of its era of production. Her sensibilities reflect the youth culture of the time: she is repulsed by racism and prejudice, she is a feminist and pioneer for the rights of single mothers, and is a patron of the arts. Her connection to the arts is presented in her best friend Vera Charles, the "first lady of the American stage." This grand dame of hyper-theatrics is played by director Saks's wife at the time, Bea Arthur, who is brilliant. Next to Doris Day, Arthur is the reigning queen of the double take and her comic timing is incredible. Every time Arthur is on screen, the results end in hysterics.

But at the core of the film is Mame's relationship with her nephew, Patrick. When Mame's outlandish ways catch up to her early in the piece and Patrick is taken away, we feel for this self-proclaimed free thinker. On top of this, the stock market crash renders Mame penniless. But materialism is not a concern for the newly maternal Mame, as she declares "I don't give a damn about money, I lost my child." Here is a perfect example of how well this character develops: this more enlightened Mame instantly becomes more loveable because she is not afraid of compassion and tenderness. Gene Saks plays his role throughout the film as Mame goes from warm strength to warm strength, without ever losing her kookiness and proud individuality. Saks reveals Mame's compassion for the people she surrounds herself with in the climactic moments of the film where she is seen embracing the principal players—all of them touched by the wacky sweetness of this glamorous biddy.

After the fox hunt, the title song is staged in *Mame* (1974)

"You're my best girl and nothing you do is wrong, I'm proud you belong to me," Patrick sings to his Auntie Mame, and this song establishes a relationship that will soon face strain when Patrick grows up.

The adult Patrick is played by Bruce Davison, who recalls his work on the film:

> I met Rosalind Russell one night. Allan Carr introduced me, the night of the Golden Globes or the Academy Awards, I'm not sure which night it was, it was many years ago. She was unable to speak because of her cancer, I just stood there and we just smiled and nodded at each other, he told her I was the Patrick, the adult Patrick in the new version. It was kind of a poignant moment. When I first came to town I was befriend by two guys, I moved into this apartment, they were little houses, sorted like under the Yum Yum tree places, right in Beverley Hills. I was renting a single apartment and across the street were girls I knew, they took me and

introduced me to the Hollywood scene at the time, and there was a place called the Bumbles and another place called the Daisies, and they had two friends that were Hollywood royalty, named Dean Martin and Desi Arnaz. I went to dinner and I was with them for a while and we would hang out together. Dean Martin would be telling me "Don't let this town get to you kid," I was like early 20s at the time. I got up to go to the bathroom and this guy moved his chair out of the way, and he said "can I get you kids anything? Do you need anything are you taken care of?" and I said, "No Mr. Sinatra everything is fine." So that was my first introduction, then I became friends with Deano and Desi. So when the time came, I was starring in a number of movies at that time, and Lucy basically said, "My son says you're a great actor, so you got the job." Robert Fryer was a friend and he was producing, and he had a young Patrick that had red hair. I never got to meet Patrick Denis, never did. I worked with Jerry Herman a bit before, I didn't really have much of a range at that time. My voice was small, I wasn't a trained singer. I had done a few musicals. I had done *Oh! What a Lovely War* and stuff. I hadn't really sung, as far as "You're My Best Girl," and all of that. I don't think Jerry was real happy with my casting. He was very gracious once I was cast but he didn't think I had the voice and the range to cover it to well, so it was a struggle for me. Well, as far as the music went he was very deeply involved. Gene was great, he was a very easy going director; he was herding cats with both hands at the time so things were a bit strange. I can tell you the story of my first day on the set: I walked on the set, this after they had been shooting for months and months and then it was delayed and delayed and finally it was my first day to shoot and it was a scene where I come up the steps and see Auntie Mame for the first time since Beau has died—Robert Preston's character. I walk up to her and hug her and say "I love you Auntie Mame." As I did it, as I hugged and kissed her, I walked out and the director Gene said "OK that's cut, that's a print," and Lucy said "I didn't believe it" and I thought, "Oh shit. I'm in for trouble now. So I'm back down in this?" Again, I'm humiliated and embarrassed and beyond myself this first shot of the picture you know, it obvious who is running the show here, so I came out with whole other attitude, so many mixtures of feelings, went up to her and grabbed her by the shoulders and said "I love you Auntie Mame" and kissed her with I don't know what. Walked out of the shot and thought "OK how's that?," and I hear her, she was wearing gloves at the time, and I heard her gloved hand starting to applaud. And she said "See? I knew you had it in you." That was my introduction to Lucy. She challenged me to come up to my best game. I did in that film, at least she challenged me to move into a position in which I really had to come up to her game. She wouldn't settle for anything less. And she never did, she was used to running a studio, I remember the first time I ever saw her she was barrelling out of Paramount with a cigarette in a holder in her mouth in a Bentley going full boar coming out of there going 80 miles per hour out of the gate onto Wilshire Blvd. I had a wonderful opportunity to observe her, and I found her to be as tough as nails and as fragile as a five-year girl. All in the same person. She came in tears one day, I remember in the make-up room, where a lot would happen, and I looked over and said ok to her make-up artist after she left and he just looked up at me and said "Don't ever get married kid." She was during this period of time because she was getting up there, a lot of the shots were showing her age. Well that was it, everything was "Vaselined" on the lens, I think, it's hard to say what vulnerabilities people have, but Lucy coming from that old school, you got to remember back in those early 1970s it was still a time in which you were, when you reached a certain age in America you were done, finished. So she was still fighting the image of who she was. From *I Love Lucy* and what that meant and instead of a dignified withdrawal, as they say. I have a very interesting perspective now because I just finished a play which was successful years ago but shortly after that into the 70's it was buried as an old drawing room comedy, in the old British tradition, that was obliterated by Joe Orton and Robert Osborne and *Look Back in Anger*, there was this trend of "let's get rid of this sort of old thing." And it was diminished, and was really pushed aside, and it's been sort of under a rock for over twenty years. Now suddenly this play has come out again and it's timely. Suddenly people can look at it and say "Oh that was a period of time that was denigrated by the movement that followed it." But now we look back on it from another time and see its worth. I feel the same is true for *Mame*. *Mame* has been around for a long time, there's the old Hollywood tradition of growing old gracefully and all of those things. At the same time there was value that was denigrated. My greatest memory is Mame's message: "Life's a banquet and most sons of bitches are starving to death." I know Pauline Kael liked me, and I ran in to her at a restaurant years later and she said "I was afraid you were going to hit me' and I asked why and she said "People like George C. Scott and such, well, they hate me because I pan them, but I gave you some great reviews in *Short Eyes*, but I thought you were pretty crappie in *Mame*, especially wearing that dumb hat!" Pauline Kael had her own sensibilities at the time too. And she was great at throwing hand-grenades and blowing up the old order. And *Mame* was certainly the old order. Plus, they didn't forgive Lucy for fighting her vulnerability of aging in it, which I think, is the main reason for it being so ill-received. Even Peter O'Toole in *Goodbye Mr Chips* wasn't a great singer and they really came down on that film, people didn't suffer aging or stars that were vulnerable to it and frightened of it, very well at the time. Or older tradition was being obliterated. As Bob Dylan said, "Brothers and sisters get off the new world, if you can't lend your hand." Bea Arthur was a sweetheart. You know originally Madeline Kahn was supposed to play Bea's part. I don't know what happened it all disintegrated before I got there but I feel that Lucy was a bit threatened by Madeline. I don't know I wasn't there. I really can't comment on what he situation was. I was there for the first reading but after that I don't know what happened, it could be a number of things. It might be worth looking into. I love Bea and Bea called it as she saw it forever. I remember riding to premiere, which was at the Cinerama Dome at the time. I remember coming there with Bea and her husband and director Gene and Merv Griffin was greeting everyone at the door and all of that, and she came in and turned to Gene and said "Alright we came here Gene, we did the ride in the 1920 Duesenberg, we did the Merv Griffin show, now can we go home?" And he just shook his head and looked up at the stars. And I said "Aren't you going to stay for the movie?" and Bea replied, "I've seen it. It's a bus baby." I remember every time I would see Bea on the set, she would just look up and say "ill fated" she was always quoting that line over a lot. I loved Bea, I thought she was great and she was always calling things as they are. I saw her years later when I was doing *Longtime Companion* and she just went out of her way to be gracious to me and compliment me on my work. And I think she and Gene divorced shortly after that. I was in love Doria Cook who played my fiancéeGloria, I found her just a delight, great sense of humour and fantastic. Nothing delivers what it's supposed to deliver; in my opinion things always fall short. I have a very difficult time watching myself on film because I never achieve what I had indented. Only in accident does that happen, so very rarely do I enjoy watching what I do. I don't know whether it achieved what intended to do. I think it was a movie, a group of people that got together to try and make something. And time tells how that holds up over the years. The reaction at the time was a pan but I don't know what people will think of it years from now. It was fun to do and I'm glad I had the experience and I'm glad I got to know Lucy. I went to her house and spent time at her home. Every time I drive by where her home used to be, I have a fond memory. What you see is what you get with Lucy she ran the show everywhere she went, and she ran the show well. She knew everybody. She was the woman who created Hollywood and television! If she wasn't a woman she would have been one of the great studio executives that created Hollywood. I don't know if she ever allowed herself that emotion. I don't think she felt cheated. The only way she felt cheated was in her love life. But she was a powerful woman, who had her vulnerabilities. I really don't know how she felt about things. She was always giving out great advice, not only about acting but also about surviving life. I remember one time she was talking about Max Jacobson the doctor feel good. We all had to get physicals at the same time she says "Well you know how these guys are, they come in now, they say are you breathing, then sign here." She said that Jacobson was like that, and he had them all on amphetamine to keep us all going, the early days. I also have a picture on my wall from 1973 by Theodora Van Runkle of one of her costumes that she gave me.

Bea Arthur and director and husband Gene Saks on the set of *Mame* (1974)

Joyce Van Patten in *Mame* (1974)

Joyce Van Patten is fantastic in *Mame* as a snooty Southern snob who acts as a minor rival to Mame during the Georgia visit that closes the first act of the film. Van Patten has such fun with her smarmy, well-bred character, and she remembers the shoot:

> I saw the stage production starring Angela Lansbury and I also saw the version of *Mame* without the music starring Rosalind Russell. I was working with the producer of that at the time, Bobby Fryer was the producer, he was the producer of both the stage and the film version. And I remember watching the Rosalind Russell version and saying to myself, "You know, this would be great with music..." I never said that to anyone else though! And then there it was! I always loved the movie with Rosalind, and then when finally they

254

created the musical a few years later they were going to turn the musical version into a movie and at the time Gene Saks the director and Bobby Fryer both wanted me to play this part and they were very, very, very nervous about Lucille Ball. They arranged for me to go to Warner Bros. to meet Lucy and she was rehearsing some dances. Now these guys, Gene and Bobby were super nervous about Lucy, so they made sure that when I met her I was in the make-up room and all done up and they went over the scene with me a couple of times and there was a lot of anxiety. And so I went in and met her, and of course she was an amazing creature, it was a great moment in my life to meet the great Lucy. And she was sitting down having a hamburger and she said "Hi" to me and the boys said "Oh we have Joyce here and we want her for this part" and Lucy said "Oh sure! Does she want to do it? That's fine with me!" and they asked her "Would you like her to read with you?" and Lucy replied "Nah she doesn't have to read for me!" They were as shocked as I was, so that was lovely. When we shot it was up at Disney Ranch and most of the scenes of course were shot outside and they were having a lot of very bad weather. So they would drive us up to Disney Ranch in the mornings and then by ten o'clock they would send us home and head back to the studios to work on a dance number. So I was making a pile of money which was just wonderful. I mean I should have been on it for ten days but I was there for a month or something, so it was wonderful, I got to make more money than I expecting as they had to pay me for every day I was on location. It was a flop. And they were very hard on Lucy. I don't really ever read reviews, but I had a sense of it being a bomb in a way. They were angry because Lucy had a soft screen over her face to make her look younger and they picked on her for that, and that really upset me. The thing is Lucy was incredibly insecure. She was lovely to me always. Whenever we were working together she was very chatty, she talked constantly about Desi Arnaz—their first house and places they had lived and so forth, and she kept in touch with me afterwards. And I got the sense that she was very lonely; I mean that's only my sense and only what I think, but I do, I truly thought that she felt extremely lonely. She was married to Gary Morton and he was great, a very social guy and he would have all these drinks nights and dinners and he was very good at hosting and introducing people to each other, and I went to many of these events but it wasn't Lucy. You know she was an extremely busy actress, even before *I Love Lucy*, she was working a lot and then suddenly she wasn't working constantly and she was getting older. But time passed and I got married and our lives went on and I couldn't keep going to their house and we stopped seeing each other. And I felt that after that, after parting ways, she had gotten upset with me. I felt like I had disappointed her in a way. I don't think it was her singing voice that made the producer and studio nervous. I don't know what it was that made them nervous. Lucy just seemed very insecure. Gene Saks was a director that I have worked with many times and I'm not sure if he made her insecure, because he wasn't the kind of director that hugged you and pampered you, and I feel that in a way Lucy needed that. *Mame* was a step outside for her. This is all what I observed on set. Robert Preston was a prince. He couldn't have been nicer. It was a lovely job. I never met Patrick Dennis. He was never around when I was around. It's pretty clearly written how she was to be performed. She was competitive and snooty and I knew a lot of southern women who were a lot like that. I had a good vision of it, she's a fun character. All the characters in   are real fun! It was definitely a flop. They all said Lucy was wrong for it. The critics said she wasn't elegant enough for the role. But I don't agree. Rosalind Russell and Angela Lansbury had the elegance for it and so did Lucy. They can all act goofy but they have this inate elegance. I thought their criticism was mean. Onna White was great. I was so lucky to get into the

movies just near the end of the studio system. I had moved
from New York to LA to work in films and it was just at
the tail end of the great Hollywood we all knew. You had
the master costume designers, the master hairdressers, the
master make-up people and you got the best clothes and
these seamstresses would make the clothes on you. That's all
gone now. They had to teach me the horse riding. Al Yank
was the teacher. I had ridden when I was a kid, but it was
English saddle and I was pretty nervous. I had to meet up
with Al for a couple of weeks out at Griffith Park and he got
me on the horse and he said to me, "Every bruise that you
get and every injury you get, remember that a horse did it to
you. That this is how important this animal is." And I'll never
forget that. And by some miraculous thing he told me that I
sat a horse well. I had no idea why, but he told me I looked
good on a horse. I mostly treasure my friendship made with
Lucy. But ultimately I was disappointed in Mame. When
you make a film you want to be in a hit, and it had all the
elements that could have made it just that. But it wasn't. So
I felt disappointed. They all raved about me so much on set
and they all liked me a lot, but I felt, "so what?" because the
film was a flop. Everyone wants to be in a hit movie. I grew
up in New York in the theatre and I never thought I would
be making movies. You know I was a kid actress on stage and
then all of us went over to Los Angeles and I found myself
working a lot on TV and then was excited to work in movies,
I thought it would be amazing. I never thought of any of
that. New York in those days was such a theatre orientated
place and it was my home and the state of theatre back then
was just incredible, it's not like that now. Now it's made for
the tourist market and you have big corporations producing
things with no substance. I had known Bea Arthur for years.
She was married to Gene Saks and I knew them as a couple.
It is my opinion that there was and is no one with greater
timing than Bea. She is perfection when it comes to that.

Lucille Balle and Kirby Furlong behind the scenes on *Mame* (1974)

Actress and dancer Sandahl Bergman was among the many dancers in *Mame*, she remembers:

> I loved working on *Mame*. The movie was at Warner Bros. The choreographer Onna White, at that point in time, auditioned all of us and it was one of those auditions like the opening in *All That Jazz*, where there is like eight hundred people auditioning for six positions. A huge cattle call. I auditioned for that at Warner Bros. and got the job. They needed six and six—six boys and six girls. We were hired as what you would call a skeleton crew. So we did all of the preliminary choreography. So, that shoot for me was, probably about a three to four month job, because I got hired as skeleton crew person. We worked on all the choreography, so Onna could get it together, and actually put it together when they hired all the other dancers to come in. Lucy used to come in and work with us a lot. At that point in time, as I

remember, she had had that very bad skiing accident, I think. Where her leg was really crumby, and what I remember about her that made us all laugh is, she goes, "Dancers, I know you guys pull muscles! I got the greatest thing for it! Its horse absorbine!" She would rub that on her leg! Which is what race horses use! They use it on race horses to heal their injuries. So, she would talk about that. Onna White later hired me to do *Gigi* on Broadway. She hired me from that job to open on Broadway. It lasted not even six months. I got hired to play stepping out of the chorus, which was great. So, from Onna White, doing *Mame*, she hired me for that. We got to New York, and that is where I stayed, and that is where my career took off. I stayed in New York ten years almost. I never came back to LA. I stayed in New York, and one thing lead to another. And one of those things was my eventual meeting with Bob Fosse. That was amazing! So, that is sort of what happened to me and a lot of it had to do with being in *Mame*.

The very adult and risqué jokes come as quick punches in the film, for example where Mame asks where Beauregard is from and he replies "Peckerwood": Ball's expression is priceless. Mame is a character that cannot pass for normal: she is perpetually and incurably unique, marching to the beat of her own drum. This isn't the sole thing that makes the character appealing, however—she is also incredibly righteous and warm, but also fragile and flighty. The character is perfectly complex and propels this celebration of old-fashioned farce and musical comedy. And the film pokes fun at itself: there is a great moment where Mame complains that Vera's musicals are far too old-fashioned, to which Vera protests that her latest production about a lady astronomer is "very modern."

If you don't smile with a tear in your eye when Bruce Davison says "She hasn't changed. She's the Pied Piper," then something is wrong with you. The film is a charming and entertaining look at unconventional love and the solidarity between those affected by social and personal tragedy. Its comedy is bright and never jarring, and the musical numbers are directed with love and care. The number "Open A New Window" is

Bruce Davison in *Mame* (1974)

presented as a movie montage where Auntie Mame takes young Patrick to a boozy speakeasy, his New Age school where children run amok covered in paint, and even the top of the Statue of Liberty. This is the kind of zaniness that opens this musical up to pure escapist entertainment, and as the next film considered claimed in its tagline, "Boy do we need it now!"

MGM AIN'T WHAT IT USED TO BE: *That's Entertainment*

When MGM closed their studio and sold off their wares, it marked the end of an era for the motion picture industry and the termination of pure escapist enchantment. Movie musicals created that studio, and it was a symbolic moment when the entire company folded and tore down the majestic sets and sold off their glamorous costumes. This was the death of movie romance. Escapist genre cinema was gradually becoming considered passé, and this was a tragedy for contract players, contract crafts folk and numerous other artists wishing to continue to uphold a legacy that celebrated fantasy and that great maker of myths: Hollywood. But as Liza Minnelli says in *That's Entertainment*, "Thank God for film, it can capture a performance and hold it forever!" She's not wrong.

That's Entertainment was made in the wake of the Watergate scandal and during a time where the US government was not the most popular rulership known to man, so just as the tagline promised, entertainment—pure, simple and without pretension—was completely necessary for an audience in need for a nostalgia fix. The montage movie event of 1974 is a spectacular monument to a time when movie musicals were the most popular form of entertainment, and as the prologue unfolds with a brief dissection of "Singin' in the Rain" and clips from various films featuring this Tin Pan Alley number, we are thrust back into a time that was fuelled by passion for music and dance, driven by some incredible talents. When the "Singin' in the Rain" montage closes, we are greeted by the phenomenally gifted Gene Kelly, Debbie Reynolds and Donald O'Connor marching toward us in their galoshes and raincoats, sporting oversized umbrellas: from here on, we are in for a fun trip down memory lane. Stanley Donen's *Singin' in the Rain*—which as the first narrator Frank Sinatra explains might just be the best ever movie musical ever made—heralds the beginning of *That's Entertainment,* one of the most unique and innovative documentaries ever made, and certainly one of the most influential. It even arguably spawned its own genre of documentary filmmaking, the art of *docutainment*!

At the press junket. Fred Astaire, Liza Minnelli and Gene Kelly remember "the good ole days" in *That's Entertainment* (1974)

The film is strung together by clips from incredible—and not so incredible—movie musicals from the MGM canon, but even the clips from average motion pictures are given a brand new lease on life here. They become exciting, fresh and engaging because out of context, even the most mediocre examples become celebrations of something bigger. The numbers from the more impressive movies are made even more vibrant because these clips highlight how lovely these films are. *That's Entertainment* inspires audiences to seek out these movies, and to revel in a studio that was founded upon them.

The image of Elizabeth Taylor descending down the stairs in her 1970s cocktail gown is a show unto itself, and her warm recollections about working as a young child actress at MGM are a dream for any cinephile. The aspects of self-depreciation in the film are great as well, as Taylor explains that she was never a threat to Jane Powell or Judy Garland (two amazing singing talents), as she shows us a clip of her wobbly singing in the musical *Cynthia* (1947).

That's Entertainment does much more than showcase a studio that once boasted it had more stars then there were in heaven. It brings sentimental depth and loving affection to the past itself. There is a sense of family here, so when we see images of Clark Gable, Angela Lansbury, Jean Harlow, James Stewart, Esther Williams, Jimmy Durante, and so forth, we feel a cosy, familiar feeling for these megastars that created an empire of magic. The thought of these idols up on the silver screen, singing and dancing and acting their hearts out, is enough to make you weep with joy: *That's Entertainment* captures this with tremendous heart. There is nothing insincere or cynical about this film, everything is whimsical, moving and respectful, and rightfully so. These are the artists from behind and in front of the cameras that deserve to be cherished, and—yes—even worshipped.

Where young filmmakers in 1974 were trying to create new works, *That's Entertainment* was celebrating old ones. Yet the young auteurs coming out of the 1970s were massive fans of these films: the nostalgia kick was blossoming, and a film like *That's Entertainment* would have certainly set the scene for cherishing old Hollywood. Musicals such as "everybody's favourite college musical" *Good News* (1947); the romantic and fun *Two Weeks With Love* (1950) (with Carleton Carpenter and

Debbie Reynolds monkeying around with "Aba Daba Honeymoon");
the spectacle of *Million Dollar Mermaid* (1952) with Esther Williams
completely at home in her Technicolor swimming pool, the elegance
and athleticism of Gene Kelly in *An American in Paris* (1951), *The Pirate*
(1948) and *On The Town* (1949); the class and sophisticated suavity
of Fred Astaire and Ginger Rogers; the rich tapestry that is the still
controversial *Show Boat* (1951) starring Howard Keel and Kathryn
Grayson and, so forth are all exalted in *That's Entertainment.* The eclectic
beauty, the relevance and the fundamental importance (both artistically
and culturally) of the movie musical as a whole grounds this film and
make a magpie's nest of glamour, history and art. Even the blackface
minstrel shows—now maligned and hated—are included, not for their
dubious racial politics, but for their inclusion of Busby Berkley routines,
such as the Garland/Rooney fare *Babes on Broadway* (1941).

There is not one unnecessary moment in this documentary, and
not one iota of cynicism. Even when James Stewart explains that all the
contract actors had to do at least one musical for MGM and a lot of these
people (including himself) never felt comfortable singing or dancing,
his tone is sly and tongue-in-cheek, and these stories are funny. Other
stories about the studio and working hard to not only make movies, but
to simply survive (eat, pay rent, etc.) pieces the film together, and there
are a lot of devoted artists interviewed including Peter Lawford, Mickey
Rooney, Debbie Reynolds, as well as Liza Minnelli reminiscing about
her first film where she played her mother's daughter in *In the Good Old
Summertime* (1949) alongside Van Johnson. They all reminisce lovingly,
and paint a picture of what went on behind the scenes of these much
loved films. The scenes where Lawford and Rooney walk through the
now ghost towns of the studios that once were jumping hot spots are
remarkably melancholy. These beautiful sets now turn to dust as the aged
stars of the golden age of the Hollywood musical recall magical memories
from the past in the hope that someone out there is listening. Luckily,
we were, but there is an overwhelming sadness in the documentary in
a film all about a lost past, about the ghosts of yesteryear. When Peter
Lawford walks through the run down set talking about how musicals
were "a special kind of escape," it is heartbreaking. A made for TV horror
movie *The Phantom of Hollywood* (1974) explored the idea of the change

in movie making from the golden era to New Hollywood. It does it with such sentimental intelligence that it almost feels like it was made because of *That's Entertainment*—after all, it was made right after it in the same year.

Many movie musicals that made a massive impact sit beside more low-key musicals that churned out by MGM throughout the early years are put on pedestals equally. *Seven Brides for Seven Brothers* (1954), *Girl Crazy* (1943), *A Date with Judy* (1948), *Gigi* (1958), *Meet Me in St. Louis* (1944), and *Idiot's Delight* (1939) are just some of the films given the *docutainment* treatment, and there is wonderful archival material that may surprise even the most well versed movie fan. For example: Joan Crawford sings up a storm by a baby grand piano long before she became the working class heroine of the films of the 1940s (and decades before she became the monstrous gorgon in fabulous horror films such as 1962's *What Ever Happened to Baby Jane?*). Intriguing facts are sprinkled throughout the film, such as the first ever song written/modified for a contract player is to be found in the film *The Broadway Melody of 1938* (1937). A very young Judy Garland sings the Al Jolson hit written by James V. Monaco and James McCarthy to a picture to Clark Gable, and she begins: "Dear Mr. Gable I am writing this to you…": this was the first time a popular song from the Hit Parade was edited for a movie star, that star being the man who breathed life into Rhett Butler from *Gone With The Wind* (1939). Surprises come in neat and sweet packages in *That's Entertainment*, and this nostalgia trip is so perfectly realized that it is as re-watchable as the movie musicals it champions. Every movie lover should be forever grateful that it exists.

GENE WILDER IS A FOX, TWAIN'S DIGEST, JAPAN'S BEANSTALK AND HARRY NILSSON VANTS TO SUCK YOUR BLOOD: *The Little Prince, Huckleberry Finn, Jack and the Beanstalk and Son of Dracula*

The Little Prince is a strange, existential piece that contemplates life philosophies such as personal commitment, mental health and wellbeing (especially the experiences of dismay and distress), the importance of self-discovery, and the moral vacuum of social conditioning. What it is fundamentally mostly about however, is death: as a concept, as a reality, as transcendence, and as an inescapable fortress. The film refuses to celebrate experience, and the story is secondary to these thematic elements that string together this odd and unnerving allegorical film. Its depressing notion that life is meaningless without tangible achievements hangs over it like the Sword of Damocles.

Gene Wilder as The Fox adds an element of creepiness to the maudlin
The Little Prince **(1974)**

The Pilot (Richard Kiley) is a spiritually lost egotist haunted by a childhood memory of where his drawing of a boa constrictor is misinterpreted as a hat by a number of adults. This man-child is stunted, and escapes in his airplane like a child with a toy, claiming he "needs air." He is a totally disinterested in connecting to others, lost in his own perpetually airy spiritual vacuum. When he crashes back to earth, he ends up in a vast desolate desert, and here is met by the cherubic Steven Warner who plays the title character. This Little Prince himself is a reflection of the man-child Pilot protagonist, but is far wiser and more self-reflective. In fact, the Pilot does not really let himself learn much from him, instead the Little Prince is forced to comprehend the emotional turmoil and personal struggles *for* the Pilot: the child lives for the man, and by the end of the film, dies for him as well.

The Little Prince continually asks the Pilot to draw a sheep in their first interaction (automatically a symbolic gesture), and from here out we are in for a creepy ride. It is an unsettling and eerily remote movie musical that quietly pricks you with its needle, drawing blood delicately as it slowly drains you to the point of near-death. It is a silent snake in the grass—epitomized by the slinky Bob Fosse who pops up later in the film—and director Stanley Donen (who pioneered the movie musical and delivered a cavalcade of brilliant classical films) seems slightly out of his element here. Much like the ill-fated *Lost Horizon*, *The Little Prince* is a slightly off-balanced film, where its timelessness and airiness evokes not much in the way of substance. Its deep philosophies get muddled, the aggressively allegorical vignettes are tepid and unclear, and the unrelenting weepiness of the film is pointlessly depressing.

The creepiness of the film is also palpable and vivid, and these elements are the best part of the journey. Gene Wilder's wistful Fox is eerie and bizarre, who stalks the Little Prince, greets him with terrifying poetry, and looks at him with sadness and woe. Wilder lets his quirk shine in Donen's film: tragic and mesmerizing, elegant but sinister. The fact that each character that the Little Prince comes into contact with is for the sake of the Pilot's spiritual salvation and his true awakening is hard to swallow. Donna McKechnie's spoiled and self-involved Rose is not as dynamic as Bob Fosse's predatory and hyper-sexualised snake, who is fuelled by the sinister and the seductive. Fosse conveys a genuine threat, and when he kills the Little Prince it is a shocking moment. The death of a child in film is always taboo and depressing, however it shouldn't solely be avoided just for taste concerns. Children are vulnerable, and *The Little Prince* never shies away from this concept. The problem is the reasoning behind it is not clearly defined: if the Little Prince dies, does that mean the self-absorbed Pilot is spiritually redeemed? This is never made clear. The Pilot *does* emotionally invest in the child (and at points there is even a subtle, uncomfortable pederast element to their relationship), but when the little angelic precocious tyke dies, is the Pilot mourning the loss of a genuine friend and teacher, or is he mourning the passing of his reflected self? In this sense, the Little Prince's passing is the death of ego and the death of self for the Pilot: he is forced to be something that he has avoided all his frivolous life, a human being. His negative experience as a child with the drawing of the boa constrictor is dwarfed in importance by the end of the film, but the poetry of this musical is neither alluring nor entertaining. What it is, however, is eerie and disturbing.

Maudlin and morose, grander philosophies are far more important than plot and character development in Donen's film, a vast jump from his usual musicals that rely heavily on character and whose themes never jeopardising the artistic merits or entertainment value of the film as a whole. Donen does experiment with certain film techniques here, something that he may have felt justified in doing in by the 1970s and outside of the studio system (although the film being a product of Paramount): some lengthy sequences are shot through a fishbowl lens, a large number of the film's opticals feature a floating Little Prince in space and circling the earth, and there are jump cuts galore.

The Little Prince is an unnerving exploration into the destructive nature of self-discovery, the depressing realisation that death is imminent, and that experience can be meaningless. Donen's film teaches these lessons in a bleak and unflattering manner, and there is no escape from the oppressive melancholy of this grim, allegorical musical. But it is *different*, and assertively disinterested in golden age, whimsically romantic musical movies of the type that Donen once delivered so brilliantly and effortlessly. Sometimes embracing difference and entering dangerous territory is essential, although this was clearly not the case for the next film.

When Roberta Flack sings "Freedom" in *Huckleberry Finn*, it indicates a passionate dedication to classical, old-style movie musicals, becoming rarer amongst the creeping success of bleak, angry and metaphoric musicals such as *Phantom of the Paradise* and *The Little Prince*. In many ways, Flack's powerful performance upholds the musicals of yesteryear. But the problem is that the film's subject matter is not innovative enough to uphold a traditional book musical format, or even a traditional feel-good anecdote. The idea of adapting Mark Twain's great American novel does not inspire classic hummable show tunes that can be welcomed on the silver screen. Perhaps if something lesser known was translated from page to libretto, then the power of the old-style movie musical would have resonated more. Audiences might have paid more attention is something less obvious was adapted in such an uninspiring way.

Tom Sawyer spawned this film, and was a great success. Cynically, the only thing a production company can do with a success like that is to follow it up with a film that promises to be even more grandiose and visually stunning. Unfortunately, *Huckleberry Finn* is neither. The set pieces are not exciting and the film plods along without any of the romantic idealism necessary to a story of liberation, be it social or spiritual. The Sherman brothers not only wrote the songs, some of which (especially the classic "Freedom") are terrific, but also wrote the screenplay as they did for *Tom Sawyer*. These master musicians and legendary songwriters finely tuned their screenwriting talents. The script is tight, but possibly too tight as it does not allow itself room to breathe, or to do anything surprising or interesting. Unfortunately, the film goes through the motions and spends most of its time wandering down a dusty track where the trees all look the same. The two leads are adequate, and devoted to their performances, but only to a certain point. Sadly, there is a restrictive cage in which these characters live that does not allow Huck or his oppressed friend Jim to run with nuance or to make complex acting choices. The stagnant nature of the piece denies any potential from the wiry and wily Jeff East as the titular character and the normally brilliant Paul Winfield as the slave Jim. Luckily, most musicals from the 1970s rattled cages and delivered movies that were both erratic and engaging. Unfortunately, *Huckleberry Finn* does not accomplish this.

Another film not exactly frightening the horses or rattling cages, but doing a lot more interesting things than *Huckleberry Finn*, was the Japanese produced *Jack and the Beanstalk*. Outside of the traditional Anime that companies such as Group TAC were so accustomed to producing during the mid-1970s, this film directed by Gisaburo Sugii is surprising because it tries to employ as much western influence as possible. The character designs are more reflective of such works churned out by studios such as Filmation more than what Sugii was solely known for— namely traditional, very Eastern stylized Anime. Here in this retelling of the classic fairy tale, the mood, the direction, the music, the narrative construction is all extremely western in its influence and in its execution. The film itself is not better or worse for this fact and it is a relatively safe ride, staying well clear of subversive themes, intellectual underlying motifs or ideas and introducing fun but not incredibly interesting story elements to the story about a poor boy who comes into contact with giants in the sky. 1974 was a strange year for the animated movie musical, and in Japan the safe, muted tones of *Jack and the Beanstalk* failed to do anything crazy or outlandish, when really there was much room for it.

The British rock'n'roll horror extravaganza that is *Son of Dracula* came from Apple Films, a subdivision of Apple Corps., which was responsible for The Beatles movies *Let It Be* (1970) and *The Yellow Submarine* (1968). *Son of Dracula* is certainly neither of those musically inclined films, it is its own strange monster and it comes from the brain and dedicated enthusiasm of actress/screenwriter Jennifer Jayne and Hammer and Amicus horror director Freddie Francis—with the music of Paul Buckmaster weaving it's strange, and incredibly alluring magic within.

Poster art for *Son of Dracula* (1974)

Starring songwriter Harry Nilsson and Ringo Starr from The Beatles, the musical tells the story of Count Downe who avenges the death of his father the legendary Count Dracula. Thrown into the mix are staple Draculean characters such as Van Helsing and fellow literary figures from gothic horror such as Baron Frankenstein, as well as Merlin who acts as advisor and confidant to the central undead Count Downe. Set to a raucous and rollicking musical score, the film is highly entertaining, completely dedicated to its tongue in cheek attitude towards both rock music as well as horror films from Britannia and yet utterly focused, strong, dynamic and charming. The film does not at all look down at the popularity of musicals, rock'n'roll, horror movies or the Theatre of the Absurd, instead it champions all of these things and brings them all together in successful and harmonious unison. The film comes across as satisfactorily grisly, which is a remarkably handled effort from the well-learned hand of Freddie Francis, and on top of this informed direction is a complicated and sophisticated approach to the subject of vengeance and solitude. Count Downe is just as feral as the best incarnations of Dracula throughout the years, and Nilsson gives his vampire a saucy repugnancy which is tricky to pull off, but this musician turned actor does it very well. As fun and as electric the film can be and manages to be, it doesn't truly succeed in generating a shattering explosion in a keen interest in what was happening at the time—and it most definitely could have. *Son of Dracula* may have not rattled cages, but it had the potential to introduce a generation of longhairs to the world of glam rock and the burgeoning heavy metal scene.

But cages were aggressively rattled by early 1975, when two raucous rock musicals hit motion picture houses. *Tommy* was a psychedelic extension of what Norman Jewison accomplished with *Jesus Christ Superstar* in the exhilarating and exhaustively entertaining rock opera about the hypocrisy and terrifying reality of organised religion. The other movie was a celebration of sexual ambiguity, sexual liberation and sexual diversity colliding with 1950s nostalgia, horror movie tropes and B-science fiction fare, all in the subversive and saucy *The Rocky Horror Picture Show*, which would eventually become one of the most successful midnight movies ever to hit cult cinema circles.

1975

"Today It Rained Champagne"

Pinball Wizards, Sweet Transvestites and Altman Country (and Western)

BY 1975, THE ROCK MUSICAL WAS ALIVE AND THRIVING. IT WAS THE KIND of experience that attracted the youth market, and the more outlandish they were, the better. This new form of musical motion picture excited experienced filmmakers that decade, as it gave them space to make liberal and often extreme choices. The energy of the era was chaotic, vibrant and anarchic, but it also came from a place with historic reference and relevance. The reckless rock musical was neither messy nor careless. These innovative new musicals were drawn from a sensibility that was fresh and brutally extravagant, but also from a space of intelligence and incredible heart. Sex and violence ruled the cinematic set during the decade, and this kind of movie musical fit right in.

If the 1970s were about changing the face of genre, then musicals were the most cosmetically altered. *The Exorcist* (1973) and *The Texas Chain Saw Massacre* (1974) set new standards for the horror genre, while themes and motifs common to the western started to form the action genre, manifesting in films such as *Dirty Harry* (1971) and other films that began both replacing and adding to the works of auteurs such as Sam Peckinpah. Movies like *Rocky* (1976) and *Network* (1976) broke new ground, both simultaneously examining and satirizing the human condition, leaving the tamer ventures from the 1960s and earlier far behind.

The movie musical felt the same transitional pull. The violence and devastation of *West Side Story* was now turned up to full throttle in musicals that gravitated towards the exploitation cinema circuit. The sexual liberation of 1960s culture that was seen in musicals such as *The Umbrellas of Cherbourg* (1964) and *Sweet Charity* (1969) now screamed even louder with orgasmic glee. This was a period where musicals could be as violent and as sexually free as they wanted. For example, new equivalents of the gang rape in *West Side Story* or the suggestive child molestation in *Finian's Rainbow* (1968) were even more explicit in pieces like *Oh! Calcutta!* (1972) or *Tommy* (1975), and the overt sexuality of characters like Billy Bigelow in *Carousel* (1956) or the concept of prostitution as seen in *Gigi* (1958) could be even more graphic in sex-centric musicals that went from borderline sexploitation to full-blown pornography.

The times were changing, and so were the movie musicals. In 1975, the birth of the cult musical surfaced with *The Rocky Horror Picture Show*, generating a legion of devoted fans—who called themselves Transylvanians—who would congregate at special midnight screenings, dressed as their favourite characters. They created "call back" culture, where the audience would scream back lines at the characters in the film and have a shout out set to each line or lyric. It was a phenomenon that inspired other fan communities of movies like *The Blues Brothers* (1980), a film we will discuss later.

Besides *The Rocky Horror Picture Show* and its cultist leanings, 1975 was the year directors Robert Altman and Peter Bogdanovich delivered diegetic musicals that were a hit in the case of the former, but a miss in the case of the latter. As well as these newcomers to the movie musical was old hand Ken Russell, who translated The Who's 1969 concept album "Tommy" into one of the most visually exciting and marvellously performed musical fantasies ever made...

DO YOU THINK IT'S ALRIGHT?: *Tommy* and *Listzomania*

Bombastic and brilliant, Ken Russell's *Tommy* is the definition of a blockbuster cinematic rock opera. Everything about the film is perfectly realized and it is a strong example of how the sung-through musical can be at its best translated on celluloid. Opening with a wonderfully directed musical prologue introducing two devoted lovers (Ann-Margret as Nora and Robert Powell as Captain Walker) in the throes of World War II while The Who's cataclysmic music crashes through with complexity and a vibrant feverish energy, *Tommy* is visceral, wild chaos that at the same time critiques multiple social issues. And if that is not enough, the film is also a thorough and thoughtful character study.

The image of a sole, silhouetted figure backlit by a burning sun— an image that bookends the film—is the thing we see, and Russell's assault of confronting and magnetic images does not stop, accompanied by complicated and sometimes terrifying scenarios, and an onslaught of thunderous and roaring songs. These combine seamlessly to produce an energetic and frenzied rock opera. The film is loaded with foreshadowing and reflective imagery, such as when Nora is working with fellow Rosie the Riveters making bombs. Loading them with what looks like pinballs from a pinball machine, this point of reference will become a major element later in the film. Russell repeats imagery like this throughout the film to make his lasting point that everything is both meaningful and connected. The very things that Nora fuels the missiles with will ultimately later inadvertently free her from her working class confinements, and this is just one simple example of the mirroring that intelligently permeates the film. The art direction plays the key role in this aspect of the film, and it is out of this world! Take for instance the wallpaper in Nora's working class suburban house, that emphasises again the notion of mirrors: once she is wealthy (thanks to the success of her son Tommy, played by Roger Daltrey) and dripping in champagne and jewels, she is still surrounded by far more real mirrors, which she eventually uses to end Tommy's torment. The design is so lucid, well-constructed and highly articulate that it becomes another character in the film.

The first lyrics sung are off screen by a Greek chorus: "Captain Walker didn't come home; his unborn child will never know him." Of course, Captain Walker didn't exactly perish in the war (he comes back later to "haunt" the already moved-on Nora) but this opening lyric perfectly opens the film in that it alludes both to plot (Captain Walker is missing in action or presumed dead), while commenting on character (the unborn child never connecting to his father). This is the genius of The Who and the way their lyrics and corresponding eclectic music is presented on screen by a master director. Russell also pieces together one of the most phenomenal casts ever put to screen, and all of these people—mostly rock musicians—are led by two legends of the silver screen, Ann-Margret and Oliver Reed.

Ann-Margret, Roger Daltrey and Oliver Reed in Ken Russell's
Tommy **(1975)**

Ann-Margret is in total service to her character and the film as a whole: she is quite simply magnificent, and steals the show. She delves into the complexity of a character that is so perfectly conceived and nuanced, becoming the epitome of the rock'n'roll diva—a figure who will gradually populate rock musicals throughout the following years. Nora is one of the most perplexing and complicated characters ever written for a screen musical this decade, and what makes her so captivating and intriguing is that she begins as a starry-eyed lover, consistently remains a devoted mother, but also becomes a hapless victim of the essential need to be desired and needed by a man. This casualty of complacency is then tormented by loss and guilt, and then finally becomes a soulless vamp who is eventually reborn: baptised in the ocean to become an enlightened leader as a burgeoning religion takes form. Ann-Margret sings and acts her heart out, and some of the film's best scenes involve her (including the infamous baked bean sequence!)

Ann-Margret asks "Tommy can you hear me?" to the deaf, dumb and blind Roger Daltrey in *Tommy* (1975)

Ken Russell's collaborator and long-time friend Oliver Reed grimaces and mugs at the camera as Tommy's stepfather Uncle Frank, harassing fellow characters with the crass bloated egotism and opportunism that reeks of a master actor at the top of his game. He and Ann-Margret's emotionally damaged but soon-to-be "happy again" Nora meet at the "Bernie's Holiday Camp" sequence in neat perfection. This scene is set at a health spa, featuring a group of people in need of escape as they exercise and compete in a "Lovely Legs" competition. Here as Nora and Frank, Ann-Margret is an actress who can sing while Oliver Reed is an actor who can bluff his way through, and it works brilliantly. This energy

275

reappears when the two sing alongside Jack Nicholson's The Specialist, as they try yet another attempt to resurrect Tommy's now-lost senses.

Roger Daltrey takes heed of director Ken Russell on location for the closing moments of *Tommy* (1975)

Tommy is a critique on organised religion and faith, and tells the story of a young boy who is shocked into deafness, blindness and muteness. He is thrown into this catatonic state by his guilty mother and stepfather after he witnesses his real father (who had survived the supposed plane crash in World War II and returned home) killed by his wife's new lover in a violent rage. Nora and Frank insist that the scared young tyke "didn't hear it, didn't see it" and that he "won't say nothing to no one, never tell a soul, what he knows is the truth!" After this trauma, Tommy's childhood is spent in a void. These lyrics are from the song "What About The Boy?," one of the most horrifying moments in film history: the violent outburst, Nora and Frank's sweaty rage, and the terrified little boy lost in the traumatising image of what he has just seen catapults the film into full throttle. The return of the scarred Captain Walker is a confronting moment for Tommy, with his own mother screaming at him to not tell a soul. This sends him into a catatonic state. Following this powerful number is "Amazing Journey," and its montage of fantastic imagery depicts young Tommy (played by Barry Winch) lost in his sensory deprivation. But somewhere within his trauma is a little boy bouncing around, smiling, kicking, and thumping. Internally he lives the life of a healthy, happy child, but he is ultimately trapped within the labyrinth of oppressive mirrors of his own mind.

Russell's innovative direction elevates The Who's concept album to a new level, and he delivers a mesmerising and nightmarish vision of the corruption of youth, the allegorical terror of religious fanaticism, and hero worship. The child in Tommy is a seer; he knows the truth, but is too afraid to speak it until his own mother forces him to smash through the catatonia. "Do you hear or fear or do I smash the mirror?" she screams, before setting him 'free'.

Barry Winch as the young *Tommy* (1975)

Barry Winch who played young Tommy recalls the shoot:

> I never went for the audition. What happened was I went along to keep my brother company, as my mum couldn't get a babysitter, and my brother actually went for the part. It got down to about the last two or three people, and Ken Russell came out to take a break, saw me and said "That's it, everyone go home. Thanks for coming." Yeah. I had never done anything before. Ken told me to do something and I did it. He just said "I can't believe you have never acted

277

before." I had started at the age of ten basically. So that was all there really was. We went from there and as the film went on, the more I got used to the way he was. I started learning it from then. All the music was live. Especially the Christmas scene. I mean, they were literally blowing trumpets in my ear, and it went on for most of the day. I did try doing the singing, but they didn't think my voice was good enough. So they had a girl named Alison Dowling—she sang some of my words. She went on to become a great actress. I wasn't very quick at reading when I was a child –especially at six. My mum come up with a technique, because I was really into comics and stuff. When I was reading my comics or watching TV, my mum used to play a tape. She would say all the lyrics, or say the words I had to say, or anything like that and put it on tape. That would be in the background when I was doing something. It just come natural to me. When they started speaking or I had to sing, I just knew exactly what to say. Alison basically copied me for the lip-synching part. I just thought it was all fun. I was a bit of a wild kid as they called it and I would just disappear forever. They had to send search parties looking for me because it was a bit like a bombsite as well. I was in my element as a kid. The one scene I remember the most, is skipping down and getting onto the bus. Oliver Reed picking me up and taking me onto the back of the bus. And endless driving in the bus and coming in. We did that for about three or four days. Ann-Margret was very protective of me. She often had a go at Oliver Reed, for being too rough with me. All we were doing was running around the hotel playing hide and seek—things like that. We got Daltrey and a couple of others, and they were trying to find me, playing hide and seek. I don't actually remember that, but that is what mum told me. Ann-Margret and my mum spoke quite a lot because Ann-Margret wanted to know what I was like, what I did. Was I a quiet child? Was I a loud child? When my mum told her exactly how I was, she said "Jesus Christ!" It was quite a funny story. I am a bit wild I must admit. I didn't really get to meet the man that played my father that much. Because obviously you see me looking scared stiff, but I never actually saw that. That was all done when I wasn't there. My mum insisted on that. Ken Russell just said to me, 'When you walk up and you get to the door. I want you to look as terrified as you can." I vaguely remember thinking to myself, when my dog got run over, and how scared I felt, worried and what not. That's how I imagined it. Ann-Margret was very nurturing during the scene where they're screaming at me. She said "We will be shouting a bit. We aren't angry at you. It is all part of the process while we are making this film.' My mum said the same thing. It was the spitting in the bucket that got me on the first day from Oliver Reed! Obviously they poured water on him for the sweat, and it was still dripping down and he was spraying water in my face. I think in a way that helped a bit relax me, and I think we did another two or three takes. Ken was always right and he was conscientious about how everything affected me. At some stage, Oliver was supposed to hit me real hard. But he said "No, because that wouldn't have happened. I'm not doing it. I'm not hitting the boy. I'm a huge man, and he's like two feet tall." He was kind of caring in that way. There was a few times like the one in the arcade where we were shooting planes down in the machine. He stunk of booze. You could smell it on him. That was seven o'clock in the morning when we first got there. It was quite weird. I had only ever smelt it on my dad Saturday afternoon when he went down the pub to have his Sunday roast. To be on someone that close who was a stranger was a weird feeling. It did actually remind me of my dad coming home from the pub. There wasn't a problem with the smell, it was just weird, being that close to another man and getting that smell. Oliver was a heavy drinker as we all know. Ann-Margret and Oliver were very close as actors. They were very professional at what they did. I didn't really get to see anything outside the film. I could only work a certain amount of hours and then there was school tuition. So I was quite busy after shooting. By the time when I did get to sit around, have dinner and then I was off to bed. It was easier to do the deaf part because I always had problems with my ears when I was a child. I went deaf when I was about three, for about a week. Basically, my ears were just so clogged up, because I was always getting into trouble, I had to have an operation. So, I had experienced what it was like to be deaf, if you know what I mean. You could only hear people like mumbling and not clearly. So the deaf side wasn't a problem. I would get lost in my own world when I was a kid, like reading or watching TV. My mum could be talking to me and I would be completely blank. You could have to push me or nudge me to bring me round. So Ken Russell said to me, "See that red dot on that camera man's head," and I went "Yes." He said, "I want you to look at that. Don't blink. And just stare at it. He is going to stare back. You are going to have a competition and see who blinks first." That is what we did, and I won every time. Ken obviously knew I came from an acting family. He knew that I kind of understood the process, because my brother had been in a couple of films before that. And I went along because mum couldn't get a babysitter. I had seen the process, but he knew I hadn't done acting. So he was quite patient. He said, "I had never met someone so young that could act so well." My mum was very proud of that comment. One thing that I had trouble with apparently was the box on my head during the "Amazing Journey" sequence. I use to have nightmares after that for a long time. It was like claustrophobia. I would be screaming in my bed sometimes. My mum would come in and explain what it was like to sleepwalk and sleep talk. I never really thought that when I was awake, but apparently my mum said every night for about three or four weeks afterwards I did those things. But, yeah, she puts it down to the box on my head. She said, "Yeah, that's enough. No more." That was probably the third take when she said it. Just three takes for that on the beach.

He took about twenty minutes, and my mum said "No, that is enough." The second take was the one he chose. The whole thing was shot in south beach, near Portsmouth. And they hired this fair. The local fair. It was it here or was it on the beach? I can't remember. They hired the whole thing. No one else was there, except for the actors and some crew. Everything that was shot in there—the funny mirror sequence—that was where most of it was shot, you know with the effects on the faces and all that sort of thing. He liked the area of that, and he could use the mirrors. During the Christmas scene, I had a big crush on the girl with the pig tails. She is now in a big thing in America. *Real Housewives* or something like that. Yeah, she moved up to America with her husband. She is *in Beverly Hills Housewives*. I've tried to speak to her here on Facebook, but she doesn't actually get on Facebook, someone does it for her. Yeah, she was the tall girl with pigtails. I had the biggest crush on her in the world. That was my first let's say. I met all the musicians from the film like Tina Turner afterwards at the premiere. A lot of the time if I wasn't working, I was running around with Ken Russell's daughter, Victoria. We were quite close. I very much appreciate the fact that they gave me the car from the Christmas scene to keep! In the Christmas scene, the nativity set, I got given that as well. Roger Daltrey took me out a few times when he was going out. He went clubbing one night, and I got taken along with my mum. Basically, they hired the whole club out. The Who, all the film crew, the cast and what not. We all went. About half an hour later, I was fast asleep. Yeah, he used to pick me up sometimes, I'd fall asleep, take me up to my room or whatever. He was like a big brother. Oh, the premiere was fantastic because they were not going to let me in because I was underage but Roger Daltrey turned around and said "We ain't coming to the cinema, if he ain't coming!" I only really saw my part because of the time of the film and everything. I watched my part and then Roger came on, and my mum said apparently after about ten minutes I got bored, and fell asleep. I didn't understand the second half of it. But then we went to the after show, and I got to meet my hero which was Bobby Charlton and I sat talking football with him all night. I don't really remember much what I talked about. It's like you meet your childhood hero. I was right into football when I was about ten. I was a Manchester United fan and he was there and basically just turned up in his jacket. He'd look around, smile at me and say "Are okay, Barry?" I'd just smile and run off again. I was just fascinated by the man. I don't know why. One story I remember while shooting the film was when Keith Moon came bursting into the swimming pool at the hotel. He drove a Rolls Royce through a fence into the swimming pool. Smashed out of his head on drugs apparently. I don't remember it much. I remember him coming towards me when I was sitting at the channel. He was a very funny man. He was like a big child. He and I got along quite well. He was out on the piss every night, getting drunk and whatnot. They were literally like twin brothers. They did it all together. They were both of the same mindset. They loved to party, drink, and do all of that together.

Sally Simpson (Victoria Russell) is the other child in the movie as the ultimate groupie who becomes a dissatisfied wife, quickly capturing the essence of pure love devolving into something mundane and suburban—again, the film's mirroring process continues in this caricature of Nora. Other children are seen during the Christmas sequence where the ghoulish youngsters taunt poor Tommy, who later suffers from varying extremes of physical abuse and violence bought on by Cousin Kevin (Paul Nicholas), followed by horrific paedophilic sexual abuse from Uncle Ernie (a scene-stealing Keith Moon revelling in playing this perverse cretin). When Tommy grows into a young adult—still in a state of catatonia—he is played by The Who's cherubic lead singer Roger Daltrey, who looks innocent and like a lost babe in the woods, while also completely angelic and messianic.

"Tommy...can you hear me?" is a recurring mantra heard throughout

282

the film, and Nora's desperate need to have her son regain his senses fuels a majority of the film's action. The first attempt to cure the boy is by The Preacher (Eric Clapton) who fronts a cult that worships the deity of Marilyn Monroe. Here the repetitive guitar riff, the image of people with Cerebral Palsy touching the statue of Monroe and the vision of the crashing Monroe when Tommy touches her epitomizes the film's view of religion as a frenzied, rabid money-making institution that exploits blind faith in all its terrifying forms. This makes *Tommy* an incredibly cynical musical, perfectly suited to its time. The garish horror and psychedelic monstrosity of its imagery is attained with such gusto that the film moves from strength to strength. Tina Turner is a knockout as the Acid Queen, a prostitute who peddles mind-altering drugs. Her facial expressions are remarkable: an animalistic woman in all her hedonistic glory singing up a storm as she bargains "I'm the gypsy, the Acid Queen, pay me before I start!" The graphic religious imagery of Tommy in the Acid Queen's iron maiden covered in poppies and bleeding from the crown (much like Christ) is a sadistic and nihilistic twist on Christian symbolism; that has now become a meaningless commodity. Later in the film, fans of Tommy and devotees of his "religion" blindly buy merchandise peddled by the pederast Uncle Ernie and opportunistic Uncle Frank.

Beyond its religious critique, Ken Russell's genius also lies in how he presents the rock'n'roll aspects of the film. When Ann-Margret applies lipstick and asks "Do you think it's alright?," he turns the staccato-esque simple lyric into something muffled and unclear, while Cousin Kevin belts out his number with all the bravado of a bratty punk sporting swastikas on his cut-off denim jacket. Keith Moon is appropriately repulsive in the role of the pederast Uncle—excitedly going through Tommy's belongings, pulling down the bed sheets and lifting up Tommy's nightshirt only to tamper with the poor boy—who sings in a blurted spew, vomiting lyrics like a guttural nuisance.

When Tommy realizes he has a knack for playing pinball and throws the Pinball Champion (Elton John), the film moves into its next act and the musicality of the film—soon to be now dominated by Roger Daltrey—changes. The pinball sequence soulfully captures youthful exuberance. It symbolically announces that the young now own the movie musical: it is no longer for their parents—this is a reality that will dominate the genre as films such as *The Rocky Horror Picture Show*, *Hair*, *The Blues Brothers*, *Fame* and *The Apple* (the latter three all from 1980) will later demonstrate. Illuminated by the brightly lit anarchy of the pinball game, Russell dresses Nora completely in white in contrast with her lush surroundings. She looks divine, but as she celebrates her newfound wealth and decadence she also laments her son's inability to connect or to see, hear or say anything. Angry and dismayed, she smashes the television playing commercials—because she is now so wealthy (thanks to her son prodigy) commercials have become meaningless and inane. The soullessness of wealth and decadence crash into Nora's world, and she is soiled by the mundane: the soap, the baked beans, and the chocolate. The image of the unsoiled white flowers that she grabs hold of and sobs into pulsates with symbolism questioning if this film has one moment of narrative laziness. Which it doesn't.

By the end of the film, Tommy's devotees and disciples angrily turn on him and chant: "We're not gonna take it, never did and never will!," increasing in their threats to declaring "Gonna rape you! Let's forget it better still!" During this violent protest against Tommy and his religious order, Frank and Nora are killed and a distraught—and once again isolated—Tommy races off a pier, fleeing a burning Holiday Camp and ending at the very point where Captain Walker began. The film reaches a full circle, and in doing so it cemented the movie rock opera as a legitimate type of film musical. *Tommy* makes you wish more rock operas made it to the silver screen beyond the 1970s. Bigger, later hits like *Evita* (1994) would hit the big screen and *Les Misérables* (2013), but pale in comparison to *Tommy* and its equally raucous and angry cousin *Jesus Christ Superstar* which are marvels of filmmaking. They are cinematic triumphs that surpass their original concept albums.

Director Jeff Liberman designed the promotional poster for *Tommy*, and recalls:

> The assignment wasn't to merely design a poster, it was to come up with an overall concept on how to advertise the movie. The entailed an entire ad campaign including T.V. and radio and yes, print where an image would usually be employed that would also be used on a poster. Robert

Stigwood, the producer of the movie, chose a big advertising agency for the job and the creative head of the agency called me in along with many other creative types to work up concepts for the ad campaign. I was only around twenty four years old at the time but a short film I had made called *The Ringer* caught his attention and, even though I had no experience in advertising at the time, he thought I'd be well suited creatively off that. By the way those other creative types counted Andy Warhol among them. I liked the whole concept of it, the deaf dumb and blind kid who becomes some messianic figure based on his uncanny ability to play a Zen like game of pin-ball. It was very in keeping with the times, a 'far out' idea. Nothing religious about it. We were all shown the rough cut of the movie, then went home to work on concepts. When I thought of the movie I'd seen, one image stood out from all the rest, and that was Roger Daltrey with the blacked out eyes and black cork in his mouth, dumb and blind. Nothing about a church, all about the pin-ball machine. The image was my idea, but *flipping* that image and making it look like a sort of Rorschach test done was by a staff art director at the agency and I thought it was brilliant. Yes I do. Me. I came up with all the copy, every word of it, starting with "Tommy. The Movie. Your senses will never be the same." Then the lines for the characters; "Tina Turner is the Acid Queen," etc.—always followed by that "Tommy. The Movie. line." So with all the other people working on it, my stuff wound up being the entire ad campaign; print, TV, radio, posters, even lunch boxes and tee shirts. I must admit it was very cool hearing Scott Muny, a famous WNEW rock disc-jockey croaking out those words "Tommy... the movie... your senses will never be the same!" I like it for what it was but I was never into "trippy" imagery so I found all that razzle-dazzle a bit off putting. But I loved the use of such a wide variety of talent for the cast. Since it's my one and only attempt at advertising, it's kind of cool that my work on it has become synonymous with such an iconic movie of the 1970s.

Daltrey and Ken Russell collaborated this same year on *Lisztomania*, a decedent, perverse and rollicking biopic about composer Franz Liszt. This film is no way near as successful as *Tommy* in its narrative, use of imagery or its broader psychotic ecstasy. It seems muddled and confused, and looks rushed without much thought. The concept is simple: Liszt (Roger Daltrey) is a highly desired, over-sexed rock star who balances sexual conquests with musical creativity. The result is a silly mess that features an indolent performance from Daltrey, who shined so brilliantly in *Tommy*. Here, the rock-star-turned-sometimes-actor looks weary and bored, while his co-star—the charismatic Paul Nicholas—steals the show with his exuberance and a demonic trickster energy as Wagner (as he also does in his small role as the abusive Cousin Kevin in *Tommy*). Nicholas' tortured librettist is a great counterpart to Daltrey's flamboyant show pony, but in all honesty—who cares? The film makes no real statement about their relationship nor does it attempt to dissect their opposing artistic interests. For instance, the scene where Liszt is playing the opera that Nicholas' character has written to an auditorium filled with devoted "Lisztomaniacs" who scream for him to play "Chopsticks" on the piano (which he does, shifting in between his friend's opera and the ludicrous "Chopsticks"), Wagner's tension, frustration and anger is lost. The film goes into overdrive with a woman who claims to be the mother of one of Liszt's bastard children, as she circles him and his piano with her pram. This film is a perfect example of how a reckless rock musical can simply not work. It is frantic for the sake of chaos, rather than driven into a frenzy by the emotional extremities that drove *Tommy* thematically, stylistically and narratively. Its nonsense is not planned, and if it is, then it does it wrong.

The best thing about the film is that it is having fun and enjoying its crass nature. There is plenty of filth to hold the attention of shock cinema fans, and its luridness is appealing to a certain degree. But for the most part, it is cold and dumb. The opening shot depicts Liszt kissing a lover's bare breasts in time with a metronome, interrupted by a jealous, fey and foppish Count who challenges Liszt to a sword fight. And so begins a crazy but frustratingly muddled musical. *The Music Lovers* and *Tommy* it most definitely is not.

Writer and filmmaker Staci Layne Wilson discusses the film:

Before Beatlemania, there was Lisztomania. The phrase was coined in the 19th century as a result of feverish fan frenzy during composer Franz Liszt's passionate piano performances. Director Ken Russell's venal 1975 film *Lisztomania* has little to do with the life and music of the venerable Miszter Liszt. It is based, in part, on a kiss-and-tell book, Nélida, by Marie d'Agoult, about the couple's affair— but mostly, it's a delirious dissertation on rock-stardom, excess, and its pitfalls. Following hot on the heels of the success of *Tommy, Lisztomania* also stars The Who's Roger Daltrey in the title role. While the action defies description, this psychedelic panorama of cinematic splooge basically follows Franz Liszt in a series of vignettes which explore his sexual and political exploits through musical farce. It's an incomprehensible mess. But it is an endearing, and visually stunning incomprehensible mess. From narcissistic Nazis, to Freud and Frankenstein—all are thrown into a jam-session of wet-dreams, and comedy so kooky it makes The Three Stooges look like Shakespeare. Perhaps the best-remembered and more revered segment is the one in which Liszt's magnificent member grows to glorious proportions and leads him through a whacky world that begins with groupies and ends with a guillotine. In case you are wondering whatever happened to Lisztomania's infamous penis prop of prodigious proportions, it wound up living in Daltrey's backyard. According to the June 2, 1977 issue of Rolling Stone, "When he recently erected the eight-foot cock on the grounds of his 200-acre farm in Sussex, complaints from outraged neighbors led to a visit from high-ranking police officers who requested that the offending organ be removed. "It could only happen in England," sighs Daltrey. "There were probably banks being robbed and people being

287

murdered, and the police force were concentrating their efforts on my eight-foot penis." Unbowed, the singer simply planted another next to it. Apparently, two heads <u>are</u> better than one! The musical numbers are just as out-there as the visuals. Rick Wakeman, from the British prog-rock band Yes, did the soundtrack, which includes original compositions and synthesized arrangements of works by Liszt. Daltrey and Russell wrote the lyrics, and Daltrey provided his own vocals. Wakeman also appears in the film as the Nordic god of thunder, Thor. Regardless of its barely-there cult status, *Lisztomania* is still extremely entertaining and it's clear it's not to be taken too seriously.

ALL-STAR OLE GRAND OPRY: *Nashville*

With its inventive opening title sequence where an excitable announcer shouts out the impressive line-up of cast members that we will soon be lucky enough to meet, Robert Altman's *Nashville* is an instant classic. It is unique, perpetually seductive and an endearing look at a culture that should be cherished and celebrated: the Country and Western music scene of Nashville, Tennessee. The characters that populate the film are an eclectic mix of musicians, fans, producers, sound engineers, journalists and passers-by who all make up the dynamic fabric that is *Nashville*. The film is a multi-layered slice of life that brilliantly dances the fine line between social satire and musical showcase, delivering both with a laid back diligence. There is an obvious intelligence to the film, but it is also an expressionist's dream. The concept is bizarre, but the outcome is nothing short of genius. On an artistic level, the film pushes boundaries and establishes set pieces and characters without overtly worrying about cohesion. The overlapping story arcs play out flawlessly and are successful without drawing too much attention to the necessity of steady plot. This slice of Americana is a cinematic tapestry of all-encompassing sweetness, sadness and awakening.

The film takes place over the five days leading up to a political shift in Nashville where an off-screen Replacement Party candidate is up for election. During these five hot days in the home of Country and Western, twenty four people go through the motions of chasing fame and political ambitions, relationships are deconstructed and soul searching and artistic enterprise are put under the analytical microscope. Each snapshot pieces together a larger situation and comments on the interpersonal connections between the twenty-four central figures. The film is effortless and airy as it moves forward (and backwards) both delicately and intimately, sometimes painted in big broad strokes that confuse and dilute as well as provide constructive clarity. This is an ambitious task that is managed splendidly.

Keith Carradine in *Nashville* (1975)

Critically praised and listed as one of the 1970s most important films, *Nashville* micro-manages a lot in the character study department. It often introduces you to someone, lets you decide if you like them or not, then shakes them up and gives them a place to sit within the film's broader satirical context that adds new dimensions. Each of the twenty four major players has a flaw, a strength and is moved by the humdrum. In Altman's film, the subtle changes of gear, the mundane mediocrity of the "real world" and the non-eventful shift like the ups and downs of life across the course of its five-day timeframe, are made all the more meaningful through this featherweight poetry.

The cast take on their roles with an appreciation of subtle nuance that comes across as effortless. Each performer uses their character as an extension of themselves: they don't inhabit a caricature that whines and wails "for the sake of the children," but rather use their vulnerabilities, their strengths, their self-absorption or their selflessness to feed these people and to bring screenwriter Joan Tewkesbury's script to authentic life.

Ronee Blakely is a knock out as Barbara Jean, the highly successful and much lauded country star who has returned to her home town. Blakely injects this fragile, delicate beauty as Nashville's sweetheart with such honesty and warmth that it's hard not to feel sorry for her. She is a woman caught up in success and not really sure what to do with it. Karen Black plays Connie White, a glamorous and overly confident Country singer who isn't a hit with the hardened fans that frequent the Grand Ole Opry. Black's Connie is set up as the rival of Blakely's Barbara Jean, and it's a great feud. This battle of the divas relies heavily on the love and admiration of their fans and those that surround them, and is one of the strongest parts of the film. This is in large part because Barbara Jean first feels this threat from afar when she initially sees Connie perform on television and internalizes it, with an overpowering fear of inadequacy plaguing her. But her anger fuels her and helps her spacey and demented performance later in the film where she starts and stops in a lengthy, show-stopping performance.

Shelley Duvall is a stand out as Martha, who has since changed her name to L.A. Joan. Duvall has such a distinct and beautiful look with her long, gangly body and stunning expressive wide eyes that adds to this free-loving and free-thinking character who cruises men who are strapped to a guitar. Among those is Tom Frank (Keith Carradine), a member of a folk trio. He is good looking, lean and a great lover, but also self-involved, rude and piggish. Geraldine Chaplin as Opal the British journalist who acts as the glue to keeping the film together and introduces a lot of the characters into Altman's tapestry. Chaplin does a great job as the annoying groupie posing as a journalist, and oozes nuisance. When Chaplin is on, it's like you have been sprinkled with fleas! Opal is grating and obnoxious and doesn't shut up, while her male counterpart (a silent motorcycle riding Jeff) strings together scenes with an entrance and exit that is comparatively quick and painless.

Lily Tomlin in *Nashville* (1975)

Nashville copped criticism later down the track from film essayists who detailed the apparent sexism that peppered Altman's world, and one of the major contributions of this supposed sexism was the Chaplin character being the most wordy of the female roles and yet the most used by the men she encounters. The less chatty Duvall appears more in charge and far more in control of the men she encounters. This has been interpreted that supposed worldly-wise, professional women (although Chaplin's Opal seems completely out of her element and a phony at that) are disposable, while the restrained (or supposedly restrained) women are represented more attractively. This is a misreading, however: the film is about character, and about *all sorts of people* be they personable, trusting, naive, egotistical, fragile or emotionally stable or unstable. That Chaplin's Opal is a mess and Duvall's L.A. Joan is seemingly self-possessed is a testament to Altman's control and interest in character, both male *and* female: they have the right to be complicated, diverse and to have flaws.

Among the other characters sprinkled throughout the film are Sueleen Gay (Gwen Welles) a talentless waitress oblivious to her awful voice. Her aspirations and almost self-enforced denial of her lack of talent contribute to her downfall. Haven Hamilton (Henry Gibson) is an aging star of the Grand Ole Opry with political ambitions that are made all the more interesting when placed in comparison to Sueleen's musical ambitions. This is what Altman does so beautifully: he weaves together a complicated tapestry that juxtaposes character arcs and allows them to intersect.

But even in this massive ensemble, *Nashville* is Ronee Blakley's film. Her performance as Barbara Jean is an outstanding portrayal of a flighty, neurotic, multi-layered and complex Country and Western star perplexed by the trappings of fame. When she hits the stage and sings, then falls into conversation which ultimately acts more like a soliloquy recited for the benefit of herself, the film takes on a documentary vibe (recalling in a way the then-very new rockumentary film). But this intimacy also bleeds into the film beyond its musical numbers. When Lily Tomlin as white gospel singer Linnea Reese listens to her deaf son talk about his swimming classes, it is pure fly-on-the-wall tenderness. Her bright smile and the love and warmth in her eyes is intoxicating, as is Ronee Blakley's quiet suffering as she sits in a hospital bed, abandoned quickly by her supposed adoring fans.

The film is an incredible musical accomplishment. There are some fantastic songs that are given depth and integrity simply because a lot of the performers wrote them themselves. Ronee Blakley wrote the "Bluebird" which is performed so beautifully by Timothy Brown (who plays Tommy Brown, the only black artist in what is otherwise the white country and western culture). She also wrote "Dues" and "My Idaho Home," the latter one of the greatest songs in the film. It is a perfectly concocted classic country story-tellin' song, documenting memories of her mother, father and childhood. After finishing the song, she is shot down by assassin Kenny Fraiser (a Howdy Doody looking David Hayward). Bleeding to death and unconscious, Barbara Jean is rushed off stage while Haven insists that "this is Nashville, not Dallas, let's show them how strong we are here in Nashville." Referencing the gunning down of President John F. Kennedy, the comparison is clear: politics and art are intertwined and reflect upon each other. This may only be the case in Altman's film, but it most certainly is more than enough. By the end of the film, Winifred (Barbara Harris) takes to the stage after the shock of the assassination attempt dies down. She gets the audience's attention and asks them to sing along, "It don't worry me." Here is a woman who starts the journey as an aspiring singer who has left her husband to start a brand new life as a Country and Western star. Although disappearing for a while, she is the one that ultimately finds her voice through tragedy, giving voice to the concerns of others while also giving strength to an audience stunned into life.

Altman has painted a picture so clear and true to the American experience, and knowingly dismisses the counterculture revolution going on around the United States at the time. Right at the beginning, Haven scolds a longhaired hippy honkytonk piano player and says "Get a haircut, you don't belong in Nashville!" This is a place in America untouched by the contemporary. Country and Western exists on its own plane, as it should: much like vaudeville and musical theatre, it is a distinctly American institution and the film celebrates the idea of it being unblemished by the outside, and the order and disorder of popular culture. Altman expresses this through this and other elaborate films that celebrate and dissect the arts such as *The Player* (1992) which ruthlessly toys with the film industry during the 1990s and in his more intimate films such as *Come Back to the 5 and Dime Jimmy Dean, Jimmy Dean* (1982) which dances with the cult of celebrity and gives it a black comic injection. *Nashville* is a masterpiece, and much like *Fiddler on the Roof* and *Cabaret* before it, is an exceptional example of the movie musical and what the movie musical can say, do and sing about.

HOMAGE, SEQUEL AND HIPPO:
At Long Last Love, Funny Lady **and** *Hugo the Hippo*

Burt Reynolds, Cybil Shepherd, Madeline Kahn and Eileen Brennan are a few of the great talents in *At Long Last Love*, an ordinary musical directed by Hollywood's prince of 1970s nu-cinema, Peter Bogdanovich. *At Long Last Love* is a bumbling mess, but still has some innovative ideas. Its initial concept was sparked by a genuine romance with 1930s movie musicals. Originally, Bogdanovich wanted his film to be shot in black and white, but then decided against it seeing that his previous film—the phenomenal *The Last Picture Show* (1972) (one of the most important films of the decade)—was also painted in stark black and white. Instead, he decided to set the art direction in black and white but to film in color, a strange decision, but one that worked extremely well. It is possibly the best thing about the film and most certainly its most successful element. The glamorous sets, the rich costuming and the transition from realistic or semi-realistic scenery to full-blown sound stage Berkley-esque bliss are all respectfully depicted though the decisions governing color and its lack of color throughout the film. In Bogdanovich's tribute to the golden age of the movie musical, the art director is the true star. Everything else—including the terrific songs by Cole Porter—sinks.

As impeccable as the look of the film is, its core is limp, disoriented and useless. Nothing gives us a sense as to why this homage is being paid beyond nostalgia's sake. But if this is the case, the film doesn't truly pay much attention to the charm of the bygone era, and instead it privileges the farcical and throws out the sophistication of the movies populated by the likes of Fred Astaire and Ginger Rogers. Reynolds and Shepherd are competent actors, and together have been in some incredibly important and beautifully made films. But in a musical comedy that is light, silly and fraught with anxiety, they are not comfortable or even at peace with the medium.

The cast of the ill-fated Peter Bogdanovich musical At Long Last Love *(1975)*

Just as flawed and misdirected is the sequel to the brilliant *Funny Girl*, *Funny Lady*. Barbra Streisand returns as an older Fanny Brice, the legendary vaudevillian performer, who is now in a romantic partnership with songwriter and impresario Billy Rose (James Caan). The problem with the film is exactly this: to have Fanny in this passionless romance (a relationship uninspired and not at all convincing) is not a smart move, especially when in *Funny Girl* the character was a fully developed artist who grows, shrinks, learns, looses, wins, loves and prospers. In the 1968 smash hit that delivered an Academy Award to Streisand, Fanny Brice is a multi-dimensional, flawed, fabulous, silly and sentimental creature who catches your heart and holds on for dear life. Here, Fanny is uninteresting and relentlessly limp, saddled with a yawn-inducing affair. Instead of the revolutionary performance that she delivered in *Funny Girl* (a beautiful example where she hits the stage with a swollen belly, instantly offending "good taste" audience members who were shocked at the thought of a woman pregnant outside of wedlock), Streisand turns Fanny into a woman consumed by the promise of domesticity. This could be dignified and interesting if it was handled appropriately, but instead she is subject to some kind of bizarre dedication to Billy Rose, making the film not only relatively anti-feminist, but also making this bland sequel all the more boring.

Streisand reprises Fanny Brice in *Funny Lady* (1975)

Something not at all boring is the psychedelic, almost hypnotic animated oddity that is *Hugo the Hippo*. This Hungarian/American co-production (partially funded by the perfume company of Faberge) tells the story of the Sultan of Zanzibar having to import hippos to keep sharks at bay in order to continue his work as a tradesman. This insane concept for an animated musical is beautifully complimented by its equally zany look, feel and vibe. This is a quintessential 1970s manic musical and something that does a fine dance between drug induced/ influenced rock'n'roll kook-show and high brown intellectual fodder for savvy kids. Featuring the vocal talents of the Osmonds, Burl Ives and Paul Lynde, *Hugo the Hippo* is a bright, energetic and symphonic ride into the world of spaced out animation that looks and feels distinctly 1970s in all its wonderful uncompromised artistic scream.

Director Bill Feigenbaum remembers the film:

> The film took around four years to complete. Robert Halmi, a producer of nature and travel shows whom I had done some title design work that he liked, asked me if I would be interested in directing an animated movie based on an African legend about a smart little hippo that liked kids. I said sure, never believing it would happen. He gave me some seed money to have a story outline and partial script done and do some presentation art. He said that if he got the financing based on my work I would get to direct the film. I said, "Sure Bob," but put it in writing, which he did. I hired Tom Baum, who I had worked with at NBC to work with me on the story and script. For the art, I wanted something very special and unusual. The so called psychedelic look, a la Yellow Submarine was popular then. I wanted something in that vein, but unique. I found what I was looking for in Graham Percy, a fantastically talented children's book illustrator, a New Zealander now living in London. Much to my surprise Halmi got the funding from the Faberge cosmetics company's new film division Brut Productions. The next step was to find an animation facility large enough and talented enough and to do the complicated production within our budget. At the time there were no large studios in New York and very few in LA. Halmi, a Hungarian ex patriot, recommended the Pannonia Film Studio in Hungary. Halmi had been a freedom fighter, working for the CIA helping smuggle out Hungarians at the time of the 1956 revolution. He was on a most wanted list. Even though the Russians suppressed the uprising, the revised Communist government

was more open, especially to doing more business with the West. Soon I was off on the Faberjet corporate plane to go to Budapest and check out the Pannonia studio. Halmi didn't come along saying that he had enemies there who wanted to kill him. I loved the studios work. They liked the challenge of working in Graham's style. I also loved the food in Budapest and the lovely girls. Once we made the deal the communists gave Halmi an official pardon. Halmi hired an excellent voice cast. The only big names at first were Paul Lynde and Burl Ives. Robert Morley and the Osmonds were added during the post production in LA. Paul Lynde was fantastic. He memorized the entire script and never had to do more than one take, unless he was dissatisfied. He made the other actors better. During the production I had more than 200 animation people working for me. Separate teams of animators would work on the elaborate musical numbers which took around five or six months each. Other teams were assigned specific characters and special effects. Naturally everything was hand drawn, inked and painted. Even though after Hugo the Hippo I became a kind of pioneer in CGI, I still prefer the old hand drawn cartoons. Pure art. My only problem with the people at Pannonia was that some of them were constantly asking me to help them escape. I fantasized being like Claude Rains in Casablanca getting pretty girls letters of transit. Some of my experiences there were very James Bond like. In my spare time I'm writing a book about my HTH experiences. One of my fondest memories was getting to know Cary Grant, who was on the Faberge board of directors. He gave me some terrific advice about comic timing. He stressed not over doing good things. Always have the audience wanting more. Nobody takes that kind of advice these days in the age of excess. I was very influenced by Stanley Kubrick. Instead of wild distracting camera moves I chose to me more methodical, long slow pans, very deliberate moves. Wild camera moves only when necessary. When the animation was completed, Faberge liked it so much they decided to give Hugo the Hippo the first class post production in Hollywood at the Burbank studio. The Jacksons wanted to re do the soundtrack with their own music and little Michael doing Jorma. Everyone loved the songs and music to much to do that. I had as my editor, Bob Lawrence who had edited Spartacus. He would have weekly phone conversations with Stanley talking mostly about chess. Hugo the Hippo has grown in popularity over the years, now something of a cult favorite, especially in the UK. I constantly get e mails from all over the world many of them telling me how much *Hugo the Hippo* has affected their lives. A Mexican playwright said that watching the movie saved him from suicide.

WE NEED HIM: *It's a Bird...It's a Plane...It's Superman*

There is no denying that the 1970s was *the* decade of the variety show: *The Sonny and Cher Comedy Hour*, *The Muppet Show*, *The Johnny Cash Show* and so forth, so when a Broadway or Off-Broadway musical made the transition from stage to the small screen (much like the aforementioned *Applause!*, 1970), it oozed variety hour and squealed with a song-and-dance sensibility. When composer Charles Strouse's comic book musical adaptation *It's a Bird...It's a Plane...It's Superman* found its way to television, it got a zany, irreverent, "stay tuned for another exciting episode" treatment. And in a bizarre way, it works!

The idea of turning comic strips and comic books into musicals is terrific: after all, both have the distinction of being specifically American art forms, and both are escapist fare. However, adaptations could only work if the source material was easy to adapt, and the tone of the musical was in service to this original material. Some have been inspired, such as *Lil' Abner* which got a lavish movie made in 1959 starring Peter Palmer as the muscle-bound hero and featuring the stunning Julie Newmar as Stupefying Jones. Just over thirty years later, Chester Gould's tough as nails detective *Dick Tracy* (1990) got a filmic adaptation that boasted some beautifully conceived songs by Stephen Sondheim and performed by pop sensation Madonna who played gangster moll and songstress Breathless Mahoney (with Broadway superstar Mandy Patinkin on piano playing

299

criminal 88 Keys). Some, however, have not been so great: one that will be in discussion later is Robert Altman's confused and misguided *Popeye* (1980), and some may argue that the next musical in discussion is more the same. But they'd be wrong: *It's a Bird...It's a Plane...It's Superman* is clever, fun and captures the essence of the 1970s television variety show, all the while paying loving tribute to serial-era superhero fare.

**Lesley Ann Warren as Lois Lane gets carried away in *It's a Bird...
It's a Plane...It's Superman* (1975)**

This musical is a bright and energetic take on DC Comics' most famous superhero, the Man of Steel himself and his mild mannered alias, Clark Kent. It is told in episodic snippets, much like a comic strip (the original New York conception of the musical was staged in comic strip panels). This inventive art direction doesn't make its way onto the small screen, but its high camp silliness and kookiness does. It doesn't take itself seriously and successfully takes the idea of an alter-ego and heroic activity in a big city (and a small town) and throws it all together with a mixed bag of vaudevillian shtick, explosive pop culture wackiness and sweet natured romance that counteracts the campy dramatics and over the top fight sequences. To fault this seldom seen television gem would be missing the point, and the point is *fun*.

Sets are hand painted cardboard cut outs and flats that are designed to look like the rough etchings from early period comic strips and the numbers are staged with heart and endearing camp.

Composer Charles Strouse remembers the conception of the musical and its transition to television:

> The co-writers of *Superman* David Newman and Robert Benton, who also wrote *Bonnie and Clyde*, were very good friends of mine and one day David said to me "You know Charles, my son said it would be a great idea to write a musical based on the comics of Superman." And I thought that was a great idea. I just loved it! It's one of my favourite shows, we had so much fun writing it. There was no scrapping at all. In the theatre its very commonplace to have arguments with everyone, or not see eye to eye, but this was not the case with Superman, everybody got along, everybody had the same vision and it was the most pleasant experience I had working on a musical. At the time however it was very unusual. New York just didn't know what to make of it. One critic said it was one of the most innovative interesting shows of the season and another said that they didn't know what to make of it. Today it is looked at as "camp" but that term was not in the vocabulary back then plus I think that term gets thrown around far too often these days. The

words were comic book words and Lee Adams and I gave the choreographer and director a clear idea of how to use these characters by designing the set to look like panels in a comic strip. So one scene would be acted out in one box and then answered in another box. When I was nine years old I loved Superman and I wanted to bring that charm and fun to the stage! There is nothing wrong with Superman being a fun experience. When it was turned into a TV special I thought it lost all its original charm. I love what Hal Prince did with the original run and that wasn't translated well at all on TV. Frankly, I got a big crush on Lesley Ann Warren, but the fact of it being adapted and shown on TV and in that framework of the TV screen took away the quality that I enjoyed, and one of the main things I love about Superman on stage is that this one dimensional man through stage craft which the audience completely buys and accepts can say "Up, up and away!" and fly and it's charming. Hal Prince did a magnificence job on the original stage production. We never did the production as "camp," we did it straight. We had wanted to make some changes and Warner Bros. advised us that the contract we had signed gave us the rights to do that on stage, but unusually it did not give us the rights to make changes to our own piece. There was an arbitration and they won. And to be honest, I think that's good, that's a good thing. There is no need for any changes in that show.

The gifted and lovely Lesley Ann Warren shines as the comic book world's number one girl reporter Lois Lane, who steals both the show and Superman's heart. The moments featuring Lois and her tumultuous relationship with both Superman and Clark Kent are enchanting and funny, and the chemistry between Warren and her Man of Steel actor David Wilson is palpable. Warren recalls:

> Honestly I didn't know much about *It's a Bird...It's a Plane...It's Superman*, but when I was first approached to do it I was very excited because I thought it could be

tremendous fun and of course I loved musicals, I mean that is where I come from, that's my background and great love. Musicals were my first foray into this business. So, I was excited to do *Superman* and flattered. I had already been studying ballet since I was six, and when I was fourteen, a lot of my friends from dance class were in the musical, *Bye Bye Birdie* on Broadway so without my parents' knowledge I went to audition for the national company and I made up a name, I picked Lisa Robbins. I picked Lisa because she was a ballet dancer that I aspired to be, she was in the professional class, I was in the children's class, and I picked Robbins because of Jerome Robbins who was my all-time favourite choreographer at that time. And I got the job! My parents wouldn't let me go because they wanted me to finish high school, and I thought that was going to be the end of my career, but it was my first introduction to Charles Strouse and I was such a big fan of that musical. I started on Broadway when I was seventeen, and I did my first Broadway show straight out of high school. It was called *110 In the Shade*, which was the musical based on *The Rainmaker*. It was a tremendous opportunity for me and I won the Most Promising Newcomer Award that year. Then I went right into *Cinderella* which was a television musical written specifically for television by Richard Rodgers and Oscar Hammerstein. From that, I went into my first Disney musical, which was *The Happiest Millionaire*. I was then put under contract to Walt Disney, which then led me to my next musical, *The One and Only, Genuine, Original Family Band*. Following that I went into dramatic television, but my real upbringing and my first love was musicals so when *Superman* came along, I was completely thrilled. I was incredibly young and very grateful that I got the role so all of my energy and focus went into creating that role. I understood the tone and the feel of what they wanted. I just needed to figure out who she was and to get the style right, which was clearly high camp. I came from the Actors Studio so I had all that training behind me and I approached the character of Lois Lane the same way I would approach a character for a straight dramatic piece, which is to create the character, create her history, understand her relationship with the people around her, what motivates her, what is her intention in each moment, and then to adapt to the style of the piece that you're in. That's a really important part that sometimes actors forget about. Sometimes, actors can almost appear to be in another movie, they're playing something totally different in their head, but this had a very particular style and during the rehearsals, that style became a lot more clear. It was completely comedic but also heartfelt and it was in the rehearsal period that it began to gel for me. I watched the George Reeves *Superman* show on television. That was the *Superman* I was most familiar with. Kenneth Mars was hysterical. Absolutely hysterical. And in a way, his sort of extenuated characterisation kind of set the tone for how far this production might go and David and I were, I think the heart of the piece. He was so lovely. He was all the things you would want in both Superman and Clark Kent. He was strong and empathetic, sweet but powerful, you know, he had everything, all the qualities you would want for that character and he was a joy to work with. And Loretta Swit was absolutely wonderful, it was certainly the first time I had ever met her and worked with her and she was generous and funny and acerbic when she needed to be, so she was perfect. It was a very congenial shoot, that's how I recall it, maybe other people have different opinions but that was my experience. I don't believe it was a one-day shoot. I remember we rehearsed a lot; we rehearsed for a couple of weeks. When we did *Cinderella* we rehearsed for two to three weeks, and I remember shooting that in ten days. I believe it was a lengthy shoot; there was a lot to take on. I don't know if there was any connection between me doing the musical and doing screen tests for the film. I remember I was off doing a play in Chicago, and I got this call to come to London to test. All these wonderful women were testing,

Stockard Channing and Anne Archer, but whether or not my involvement with the musical influenced me getting that screen test, had any connective tissue, I'm not sure. I guess it didn't hurt that I had already played Lois Lane. But that still didn't get me the part! All the roles I've played are all so different and that's one of those things I love about acting, you get to live in another world and invent another character, whether it's a comedy or a drama or a stylized musical like *Superman*, so you get to inhabit someone else's skin and then you go off to live another life. And that's a great thing. But you know I don't think there is a correlation between the different roles I've performed. Each character is individuated and fleshed out on their own.

The first number is "We Need Him," which not only sets up the story but it also comments on the time this musical was adapted for television. The lyrics sing, "In this time of moral decay we need him!," a perfect assessment of the necessity of fun and frivolous musicals at the time when musicals were angry, filled with despair, and sexually provocative. Strouse's take on Superman elevates the musical comedy, marries it with high camp and pop culture sincerity and brings to it a Saturday morning cartoon mentality. The change in musicals and then tone of genre was prevalent during 1975, and this crazy adaption of a moderately successful musical worked beautifully in the middle of an era populated with musicals about Nazis and nudists. Lesley Ann Warren felt the change:

> Oh I definitely felt the shift in musicals, especially because I came out to Los Angeles when I was eighteen, and I got signed with Disney and then I was also under contract with Paramount and I was supposed to do *Goodbye Columbus*, which I couldn't do because I became pregnant, but when I did the second musical with Disney I felt a change. Even though there was a lot of money spent on the production, it had a fabulous cast, and it was received really well, you could feel that people's taste and styles were changing, and that was

the late 1960s. By the time it got to the 1970s, people were no longer wanting that particular kind of escapism, that light musical comedy; they wanted something more gritty, more real and more edgy. And I think then there was a real void for musicals for a really long time. I think Rob Marshall with *Chicago* put them back on the map. Which was very exciting. I went to everything. I grew up on *An American in Paris* and *Lili* and all of those musicals, but then when I got older I was really interested in where musical theatre was going, and it was going to places I never dreamed it would go. So come the 1970s and seeing films like *Cabaret* and *All That Jazz* it was thrilling, musicals started to grow with the times.

It wasn't like *It's a Bird...It's a Plane...It's Superman* didn't have its own essence of sophistication. The song "You've Got Possibilities"—sung by the vampy and sexy Loretta Swit as another employee of the famous *Daily Planet*—reeks of sexual proactivity as she lists Clark Kent's flaws (bad haircut, square tie and suit, etc.), but then undresses him and sings about the merits about what is "underneath." This pops up again in the sexually charged *The Rocky Horror Picture Show* (our next film in discussion), where the transsexual alien Dr. Frank N. Furter unleashes the "possibilities" in the film's hero, Brad. However, in this sexually free rock'n'roll musical, Brad embraces his feminine side and he comes out dressed in garters and fishnets, while Clark Kent comes out of his experience with Loretta Swit's saucy vixen a little bit more in charge of the guise of his human persona (as opposed to his true Kryptonian self).

This in turn gives resonance to Lois Lane's much used mantra of "Oh Clark! Have you been there all along?" Finally, she realizes that he has been: not just some social awkward misfit, but someone as appealing and as attractive as Superman. Lois's complicated duality is just as enlightening as Clark Kent/Superman's: when she daydreams, she sings about wanting to be a suburban housewife, cooking and cleaning and being loved by a simple man like Clark. It's a far cry from the bulldog reporter that she is. This doesn't make the musical anti-careerist, but rather makes it interesting and gives a character associated with the quintessential "working woman" layers ultimately a degree of sensitivity.

This sequence also briefly showcases Lesley Ann Warren as a dancer, something that she showcased more so in *The Muppet Show* shot some years later. She remembers:

> The producers of *The Muppet Show* called my agent or my manager at the time, and asked if I would be interested in doing it and of course, I was. So I went over to London and we rehearsed the musical numbers and that went on for about three or four days before we shot and it was so much fun. It was like living out *Lili* and it was like I got to do my very own version of *Lili*, so it was like coming full circle for me, it was one of those movies I loved and cherished and grew up on, so I finally got to be that girl dancing with these puppets! And falling in love with those puppets! It was fun with Miss Piggy! She was very competitive! It was hysterical. Jim Henson and the others were so brilliant at what they did and so supportive and embracing of the actors and the celebrities who were coming over to work with their puppets. And they were real to them; they were characters that they had created and built, so they were very protective and had a strong sense of love for their puppets. And because of my own enamoured appreciation of *Lili*, it was very easy for me to only see the puppet and not see the puppeteer. The reason why variety shows became so popular in the 1970s was possibly because the appreciation of that kind of fantasy musical had gone out of style but the desire for musical entertainment had not. So with the advent of television becoming so popular, those stars that were musically inclined as well as being great actors, like Judy Garland and Barbra Streisand, could also incorporate incredible singing voices in a new context. There was probably a hunger to continue to enjoy music but not necessarily have it presented in a fantasy situation like in the 1940s and 1950s. You know, I did *The Jackie Gleeson Show* and *The Carol Burnett Show* where I sang and danced. I did a lot of those variety shows that allowed that transition out of that 1950s musical style to a newer

fresher style but still at the same time keeping the musical alive. But then sadly the musical variety show soon fell by the wasteland as well.

Lesley Ann Warren and Link Hogthrob on *The Muppet Show*

Lesley Ann Warren sings "Just the Way You Are" to Rowlf on *The Muppet Show*

Sadly, when *It's a Bird...It's a Plane...It's Superman* aired on television, it was the only time it hit the small screen so for years it was lost in obscurity. But this made it all the more valuable, and once released on film but it generated new interest for avid collectors. However, for the most part, audiences found the TV special too silly for the time it was released. William Dozier's fantastic *Batman* TV series (1966-68) did everything it could for camp culture, with its overt theatrics painted in swinging 1960s colors, so by the time it got to Strouse's 1960s musical being given the self-contained episodic showbiz treatment on television it was too late. Besides the great gags and bizarrely surprisingly poignant moments (one for instance is where Superman laments "Why does the strongest man in the world have to be the saddest man in the world?"), the special didn't appeal to a cynical audience who were interested in something with more bite.

Lesley Ann Warren adds:

> I think a lot of the cynicism that comes from people who don't understand or appreciate musicals comes from them not buying into the unrealistic nature of the medium; they can't comprehend the notion of characters breaking into song, and I think it's really interesting when *Chicago* blew that away. So many people who had that perspective all of a sudden felt very differently. I think that musicals will always have that contingency of people who look down their noses at them because they're not of that naturalistic realism which is also very powerful in film. But honestly, there will always be some part of our culture that doesn't want to buy into that so I think musicals are here to stay. My taste is pretty broad; I like everything from tremendously real and gritty to *Brigadoon*, a fantasy world I can enter into. Just because I love one doesn't mean I love the other one less. Some musicals have at times embraced the dark side. Even in *An American in Paris* there is alcoholism and a theme involving a young man kept by an older woman, the benefactor of the arts. I think people need to broaden their perspectives, and not be limited by their possibly antiquated notions.

Strouse's music isn't exactly presented at its finest in this TV special, but the essence of fun is there in full swing. Strouse's articulate and spirited musical talents would eventually be heard in full orchestral glory come the early 1980s with the film adaptation of *Annie* (1983) hitting the big screen, with John Huston directing and boasting an all-star cast including Carol Burnett, Bernadette Peters, Tim Curry, Albert Finney, Ann Reinking and Geoffrey Holder. Another musical based on a popular Depression-era comic strip, *Annie* was a hit and most certainly one of the best musicals of the 1980s, a decade that presented some great works such as dark and brilliant entries like *Pennies from Heaven* (1981) and silly but enjoyable romps like *Grease 2* (1982). But Strouse loved an incarnation of Lil' Orphan Annie from the 1970s called *The Annie Christmas Show* from 1977. He states:

> I love *The Annie Christmas Show*! It's my favourite version of my Annie, or at least my favourite adaptation of the show. It was directed by a very talented man who just did wonderful things with it. It's the one where the original Annie, Andrea McArdle comes out in a big theatrical version of a show that she and Daddy Warbucks have just gone and seen.

Comic books would be just one of the ingredients added to the melting pot that birthed one of the most popular and important rock musicals of the decade, if not of all time.

I'LL GET YOU A SATANIC MECHANIC:
The Rocky Horror Picture Show

The Rocky Horror Picture Show is a melting pot of everything distinctly American such as horror movies, science fiction serials, romance comics and rock'n'roll. But it is seen through an Englishman's eye and injected with British sensibilities, most notably in its take on the sex comedy and its construction of a sexpot Mary Shelley. And thanks to director Jim Sharman, it also has an Australian anarchic, punk spirit. *The Rocky Horror Picture Show* is a delight from start to finish and is funny, fevered, fresh and moving all at the same time. It is a sermon for the eternal misfit, a mantra for the alienated and a religion for those who cannot be anything but different. The ethos "Don't dream it, be it" rings true to both the characters and the audience watching, where girls are allowed to be "dirty" and boys are allowed to dress as Fay Wray in *King Kong* (1933). This is a musical that is not only socially important, but also politically and culturally. *The Rocky Horror Picture Show* celebrates the necessity and also the dangers of the sexual revolution, while at the same time it dissects and trivializes the not-so-sacred institutions of matrimony, monogamy and domesticity.

Tim Curry, Barry Bostwick and Susan Sarandon take a break on the set of horror musical *The Rocky Horror Picture Show* (1975)

311

Brad Majors (Barry Bostwick) and Janet Weiss (Susan Sarandon) are the quintessential EC comics couple, complete with the drive into the woods in a heavy storm where their car breaks down and they are forced to seek help. After leaving their friends' wedding and being inspired to elope, our heroic Brad and his sweet fiancée Janet head out to meet the man who inadvertently introduced the couple, their high school science teacher Dr. Scott (Jonathan Adams). Already the film is keenly interested in science coupling up the young as later, another very different doctor will *create* his own lover. But with Brad and Janet, the heterosexual pairing is initially straight out of classic American soap opera, with the duo singing out their virginal devotion to one another in "Dammit Janet." En route to Dr. Scott, they notice a group of bikers heading in the opposite direction to which Janet says something about them taking their lives in their own hands being on such dangerous machines and out in the middle of a storm. "Yes Janet, life's pretty cheap to that type!" remarks Brad. He completely sums up the notion that those out in the storm and on dangerous machines and going in the opposite direction are the people playing with life and death, but also at the same time the idea of class resentment is bought up in a rock musical obsessed with sexual awakening. Later, when their car gets bogged, Janet insists she and Brad go to a castle they have passed to which he replies "There's no sense of both of us getting wet," highlighting a direct commentary on sexual discovery: a blatant and graphic comment, implying what is to come.

The next song, "Over at the Frankenstein Place," is one of those great musical numbers that suggests monster movie mayhem and character struggle. "The guiding star" that Janet sings about and ultimately understands through sex is something distant for the time being, just out of reach. The light at the Frankenstein place is salvation for two young people literally and metaphorically stuck, the latter in their in perpetual virginity (virginity being both literal and also socially symbolic). The horror movie motifs used throughout the film ground Brad and Janet's liberation and awakening, through the bestial howling of wolves, the thunderous crackling of a storm and the meeting with the ghoulish butler Riff Raff (Richard O'Brien) and maid Magenta (Patricia Quinn). Through these elements, Brad and Janet become subject to monstrous

Tim Curry gets his hair tended to on the set of *The Rocky Horror Picture Show* (1975)

seduction. It escalates as they witness "The Time Warp" a celebratory dance that embraces sexual freedom and recklessness. Live-in resident and fellow denizen of depravity Columbia (Little Nell) tap dances her way through the number, harkening back to a classical era of the movie musical but lit up and painted up as a kooky punk rock glamour ghoul singing about the excitement of meeting a guy in a pickup truck.

Columbia's outburst is a whirlwind, raucous throwback to the movie musical. If the film is a horror movie, a sci-fi romp, a sex comedy and a comic book trashfest, it is also important to note that all of this is done in the guise of a loud, rollicking musical. Columbia's tap dance routine therefore escalates the tribute with much higher stakes. The musical reigns supreme over fellow genre trappings, but it is always in the service of what the film is about, and not so much about what happens. *The Rocky Horror Picture Show* is made for analysis because the plot is straight forward and stark. By the middle of the second act, and as it bleeds into the third, the film becomes a tribute show to the diegetic musical that was a central core of many of the backstage and backyard musicals of the 1930s and 1940s. What *The Rocky Horror Picture Show* says and sings is far more important than what it does narratively. Its importance is in its message and its intelligence.

Tim Curry and Patricia Quinn eagerly await the waking of the monster Rocky Horror as played by Peter Hinwood in *The Rocky Horror Picture Show* (1975)

Right after the iconic "The Time Warp," Brad, Janet and the audience are introduced to the other doctor of the piece outside of Dr. Scott, and the star of the film: the transsexual Dr. Frank N. Furter played with delicious vibrancy by the talented Tim Curry. Curry's Frank is not only the personification of the now overused "genderfuck" trope, he is iconic: a character that will become as culturally significant as James Bond and Count Dracula. The image of him descending in his elevator—thumping his sequenced platform shoes a la Paul Stanley from KISS, swooping his cape like David Bowie and strutting like Mae West—is electric. His delivery and humour is one of a kind, and so distinctly Tim Curry's own invention that the character is a monstrous recollection of everything the young British actor/musician has done previously. *The Rocky Horror Picture Show* is a magpie's nest of all the best things! When Brad and Janet "experience" Frank, their worlds change: their sexual awakening propels the film into hyper-drive with a blood drenched massacre, a variation of a wedding that mirrors the opening heterosexual union of Brad and Janet's friends, cannibalism and even alien activity (quite literal activity that gives voice to its socially alienated audience).

This misfit element cannot be understated, and each character represents different facets of the eternal outcast. Riff Raff and Magenta are straight out of Gothic horror, depraved domestics personifying the ghoulish and outlandishly creepy with a glam-rock injection. They are siblings, and dedicated to each other in an unhealthily incestuous way. Eddie (played by rock musician Meatloaf, who made a career out of recording concept albums and mini-rock operas) represents traditional fun and frivolity. Although he is reckless and rebellious in his rock'n'roll celebration, he is a threat to Frank, because he upholds a bygone era, a time that Frank has no interest in. Frank is progressive, but Eddie (and to a certain point Columbia) is a creature of nostalgia, something that has no room in Frank's new world of liberation and progressive pansexuality. The monsters in this piece are literally aliens from another world, but they are attractive to humans such as the show business obsessed groupie Columbia, and eventually even to the puritanical Brad and Janet. Dr. Scott enters to bring order to the madness, there not because of Brad and Janet, but because of his nephew Eddie, who has been slaughtered by Frank and served up for dinner. The clever addition of Frank serving up Eddie's chopped-up body is terrific, and what it says is profound: the new wave, this new order of leather clad, suspender wearing aliens devouring the epitome of rock'n'roll in Eddie. In turn, the congregation are eating the real essence of rock music, and as they all learn about Eddie being a "no good kid" it is set to bouncy classic rock'n'roll which comes to a crashing halt with thunderous guitar slamming down on the visual of the organs and bloodied corpse. Life and death are intertwined in this superb musical, and sex and rock'n'roll are the puppets that dance around a stage set in tribute to horror, musicals and other escapist fare.

The creation of Rocky Horror the "creature" (Peter Hinwood) is more Theatre of the Absurd than Mary Shelley, and when the monster emerges from a rainbow colored tank the film briefly turns into a beach blanket movie where the bronzed muscular hunk parades around showcasing his chiselled physique. The film outs the subversive homosexual subtext of the gladiator and Hercules motion pictures of the 1950s (starring bodybuilder/actors such as Steve Reeves, Mickey Hargitay and Reg Park). When Frank sings about Rocky's body and the particular muscles that turn him on, it is a musical muscle worship session that brings all those wonderful B-grade sword and sandal pictures out of the closet and into the realm of the sexual freedoms of 1970s America. Gay liberation was happening during the time *The Rocky Horror Show* was on stage, and by 1975, gay rights and gay visibility was on the political and social agenda. However, it was fraught by attacks and objections. In relation to this muscular male aesthetic, the growing visibility of gay liberation is what underscores Frank asking Brad and Janet what they think of his creation. Janet replies "I don't like men with too many muscles" which causes Frank to react violently. He responds aggressively, stating "I didn't make him for you!" This is a perfect summary of the gay agenda and a celebratory articulation of the gay male gaze, as opposed to the dominant assumed heteronormativity that has otherwise governed mainstream cinema. Frank snaps at straight-laced Janet that his creation is not for her (and her "kind"), that this muscle bound bodybuilder represents homosexual pin-up culture. The film celebrates what artists such as Bob Mizer with his 1950s physique pictorial magazines such as the Athletics Models Guild quietly stated: that the semi-closeted sexual titillation of scantily clad muscle men was now out and ready for a gay male gaze.

Eventually, Janet understands. At one point, she cries "I'm a muscle fan," filling in the gap for Frank. Her own sexuality is birthing and she is also becoming a younger, fresher and distinctively more feminised threat to Frank. She also embraces the "sins of the flesh" that Frank will mention near the end of the film. However, what liberates Brad and Janet also destroys them and leaves them lost in ruins, crawling and trying to desperately clasp onto something. Even Frank's statement "It's not easy having a good time, even smiling makes my face ache" suggests that fun—sexual freedom, promiscuity and frivolity—comes at a price. This is profound, considering especially the AIDS crisis that would rear its ugly head some five years after the film's release. The cult of *The Rocky Horror Picture Show*, with its midnight screenings across America, would pop up in Alan Parker's incredible *Fame* (1980) (a film we will delve into later) which hits right at the starting point of the AIDS epidemic, acting as a catapult for one of the character's blossoming into womanhood.

Eating Meatloaf! Richard O'Brien, Tim Curry and Patricia Quinn in *The Rocky Horror Picture Show* (1975)

You fall in love with everyone in *The Rocky Horror Picture Show*. Susan Sarandon as Janet is sweet and spirited, the all-American good girl who blossoms into a sexually aware young woman, empowered and doing things on her own terms. Barry Bostwick as the straight laced Brad is a delight in both his anally retentive virginal form, then as the newly liberated homosexual. His love for Janet never falters, he holds onto her during the horrific climax of the "floor show," so there is an understanding that their love is real and not just a cartoon. Columbia's good-time girl is a party unto itself, and when she confesses her love for Frank it is a moment of sincerity and longing for something deeper than just the knowing of the "sins of the flesh." She suggests something meaningful outside of sexual experimentation. It grounds the film and turns these bizarre freaks into well-developed, interesting characters with their own personal struggles to scrutinize and deal with.

The finale reveals the truth about these characters, and ironically it is within the context of a show within a show that it comes to the fore, sticking out like a sore thumb in a musical that is outrageous but also surprisingly linear in structural terms. When it gets to the "floor show" that Frank has arranged, it then becomes anarchic: there are no rules, but during these final moments, we find all the answers. Opening with the presidium of an attractive old fashioned theatrical stage complete with lavish lavender layered curtains hanging and lit with lush floods, the finale crashes in with riveting rock'n'roll. The four featured chorus kids come to life, decked out in sexy lingerie and singing out a summary of who they are, what they've achieved and what they long for. Columbia and Rocky explain that seeing life through a rose tint helps them deal with their personal pain. Brad is perplexed by his newfound sexual confusion, and Janet revels in what Frank has opened her mind (and heart) to. In orgasmic bliss she announces that "reality is here," one she has been introduced to via a sexual awakening bought on by Frank's lifestyle which proves to be "too extreme" in the eyes of his "faithful handyman" Riff Raff. In a great take on the "butler always does it," Riff Raff kills Frank with his sister Magenta by his side, and the duo take off to Planet Transsexual, leaving Brad and Janet destroyed by their own sexual liberation.

Before he is killed, Frank sings a torch song where he accepts the fact that earth is not ready for his sexual politics. He acknowledges his loneliness and that his ideas are isolating. In a cruel twist of fate, instead of regrouping with his domestics, he is killed by them—betrayed by Riff Raff ,who never felt loved the same way Columbia or Rocky did. The Criminologist (Charles Gray), a narrator who chronicles the story (and at one point teaches us the steps to "The Time Warp") concludes the film by stating that "Crawling on the planet's face are insects called the human race, lost is time and lost in space and meaning..." It is a profound coda to such a depressing ending. The rock'n'roll monster show has come to a close, and the final number—a reprise of the opening number "Science Fiction"—sadly laments the loss of innocents and the loss of control: "Frank has built and lost his creature" and "darkness has conquered Brad and Janet." This final number is a perfect mirror to the opening number that celebrates B-movies, horror and science fiction by listing everything from *Flash Gordon* to wonderful classic monster fare as *The Day of the Triffids* (1951).

The Rocky Horror Picture Show is a love letter to American popular culture painted within the realm of the sexual liberation movement, where feminism, gay liberation, civil rights, cross dressing, art, silliness, politics and show business all dance up a storm, and dive into an orgy of reckless fun while aware of the consequences. This is what makes this moving musical all the more profound: it became a phenomenon for a reason. It teaches us that there is a space for freedom, but that the trappings of responsibility will come crashing down leaving us "crawling on the planet's face."

Rock musicals became a staple of the style of integrated musicals during the mid-1970s, and this continued into the later years of the decade. But two other musical styles started to influence musicals and did so with great energy: gritty, angry, loud, and sometimes-dumb-but-sometimes-smart punk rock, and the vivacious and flamboyant disco craze. By 1976, in the United States, New York City became the hub of the punk explosion with bands such as Blondie, The Patti Smith Group and Television making waves in the underground while mainstream rock acts like the ghoulish glamour hounds KISS showcased their showmanship on television musical specials. In the traditional sense of the movie musical, influential and prolific contemporary composers and songwriters like Paul Williams dived into diverse projects, delivering unique works. In Williams' case, 1976 proved to be fruitful with one of his projects being a high concept child-centric dark fantasy in *Bugsy Malone*. His other teamed him with megastar Barbra Streisand for a third round remake of the classic story of an artist on the rise to stardom and an established star with nowhere to go but downhill in *A Star Is Born*. But these are but only two of the movie musicals that came out of 1976, which proved to be a very busy year...

319

1976

"You Give A Little Love and It All Comes Back to You"

Pint Sized Gangsters, Dancing Dildos, and a Return to MGM

1976 PROVED TO BE A SIGNIFICANT AND DIVERSE YEAR IN THE HISTORY of the movie musical. It was the year that delivered the genius of songwriter Paul Williams twice, with the prohibition-era all-child star musical *Bugsy Malone* and the Streisand vehicle *A Star Is Born*, both showcasing his talent as a musician as well as collaborator. With a number of hits for artists such as The Carpenters, Three Dog Night and Helen Reddy and the incredible score and songs for the magnificent *Phantom of the Paradise* already under his belt, the decade was shaping up to be *the* era of Paul Williams—and rightfully so. His musicality is intricate and intimate, yet completely accessible. His bouncy melodies are an upbeat road show that cleverly meet with sombre heartstring-pullers to make us ponder and cry. His inspired lyrics are intelligent, thoughtful, nourishing

321

and always dedicated to character, making Williams the epitome of the musical film songwriter: there is no doubt about that at all.

Beyond films featuring the magic of Paul Williams, 1976 also saw the rise of pornography and the grindhouse experience started to merge with the movie musical through the sexploitation musical craze that started to gather some not-so-shy interest. Mainstream cinema started to embrace sexually risqué films and openheartedly welcomed porno-chic with sexual-charged musicals like *Oh! Calcutta!* and *Hair* already having caused a stir on the Broadway stage. Movie musicals like the sexually free *The Rocky Horror Picture Show* began collecting a devoted cult reputation amongst horny teenagers and drag queens, and the straight-up sexpot musical popped up everywhere, giving the term "dirty play" a brand new meaning. These musicals also made their way on the big screen: pornographic show tune riddled movies that attracted musical enthusiasts and peepshow devotees alike.

During the mid-70s, the recession had a massive impact on film and theatre in terms of how it was shaping culture more broadly. The excesses of glam-rock and its "divine decadence" slowly became incidental to what was really happening during this turbulent time. Punk was an angry animal ready to bear its fangs to the mainstream. New York City was the Mecca of the punk rock revolution in the United States, and just as much as it was the "syncopated city" that Gershwin wrote about during the formation of the musical theatre revolution, punk was a monster from within the city that never sleeps. As much as the Jazz Age ushered in youthful rebellion and the 1950s sparked the idea of the teenager, the 1970s was where it got really messy. Angst-ridden punk began to get coverage and independent filmmakers Ivan Kral and Amos Poe documented influential bands such as Blondie and future icons like Iggy Pop in DIY-style grit and grime. Their film *The Blank Generation* was instrumental in the world understanding this new wave of rock'n'roll that was angry, apathetic and that celebrated the alienated.

Alongside this youth-orientated punk revolution, suburban families got both tricked and treated with made for television musical specials. One of the most bizarre and entertaining ones starred charismatic showbiz legend Paul Lynde, who won the hearts of sit-com lovers as Uncle Arthur in the much loved *Bewitched* (1964-1972). *The Paul Lynde*

322

Halloween Special was a landmark in one-off TV musical variety shows. Another legend that would grow into superstardom came from punk arena rather the traditional television city, Los Angeles. Bette Midler had sung her heart out and told dirty jokes at the gay bathhouse The Continental in New York, and got her first television special in 1976. People were wowed with her natural ability to make them laugh, cry and think, all while delivering some of the most heart wrenching and powerful singing ever put to the small screen.

But before Lynde and Midler, we should look at some of the most talented kiddies who ever donned the attire of adults from a bygone era...

HE'S A MAN, A MOUNTAIN, HE'S A ROLLING STONE:
Bugsy Malone

The idea of a musical completely cast with children is one thing, but putting these children in a gangster film with all the trimmings—the corruption, the crime, the violence and the grim nihilism of a desolate and downtrodden city, right at the cusp of the fall of the stock market—then you have a bizarre and captivating movie musical besieged by an alluring darkness. In *Bugsy Malone*, director Alan Parker creates a dystopian view of a world without adults, and much like the more "serious-in-tone" child-centric films such as *The Lord of the Flies* (1963) and confronting horror masterpieces such as *Who Can Kill a Child?* (1976), he *gives* a discerning look at an anarchic world controlled and governed by children. These pint-sized gangsters and gangster molls have made up their own rules within the context of an urban crime thriller, and with a healthy dose of self-deprecation and wry humour, *Bugsy Malone* is a perfect American self-referential tribute. At the same time, it is also a cluey and insightful look at children as both spectators and the focal point of entertainment.

The cast is beyond talented: not only can they perform these roles to a tea, but they also seem to 'get it'. They are all in on the joke, and have a reasonable amount of understanding of what Parker is parodying. Some audiences might perhaps find some elements of the film questionable: dancing chorus girls in skimpy outfits, the suggestive and provocative nature of Tallulah's (Jodie Foster) number, and the very adult ways some of the characters interact (for example Scott Baio's Bugsy and Florrie Dugger's Blousey's stressed romance and the strangely abusive relationship between John Cassisi's Fat Sam and Tallulah). But the film requires all these elements to give this devoted homage authenticity.

The gangster film and film noir presented in a child-centric musical in *Bugsy Malone* (1976)

The songs are incredible pieces of Americana, highly aware of the era to which they pay tribute. These masterfully written songs are a 1920s pastiche, but bought to life with a distinct 1970s sensibility. Musician and songwriter Paul Williams has injected these smart and catchy numbers with a modern "wink and nudge," as well as a sophistication that helps build the film into what is effectively a bizarre happening. When these children sing about speakeasies and criminal activity, their delivery is frightfully relatable because their innocence taps into a belief system that shatters the structured fabric of its subject matter.

Author and film academic Alexandra Heller-Nicholas reminisces about her personal experiences with the musical, offering enlightened insight into the film:

I was very small—too small—when I first saw *Bugsy*

324

Malone, and it was the first movie I remember seeing at the cinema. A well-meaning uncle with no idea of age appropriate viewing for toddlers thought it would be a nice day out, which to this day I still recall it was. As an adult, I am surprised by how much I remember of that original viewing: perhaps because it was my first cinema experience it burned itself into my memory with more than usual intensity. While this may in part be true, I suspect it also has to do with the fact that *Bugsy Malone* is also a remarkable film: sure it left an imprint on me at 3 years old, but I suspect it would have done the same at thirteen or forty-three. Most immediate of the reasons for this is simply that it's a hugely engaging film. Along with other great films in the genre, *Bugsy Malone*'s power as a musical lies in its ability to fluidly shift the boundaries between audience and performance, granting even its most conservative efforts an element of subversiveness. In *Bugsy Malone*, these lines are established and collapsed with what even for a musical is impressive frequency: a classic example of this is the scene where Blousey nervously auditions as Bugsy—besotted, supportive and smiling goofily—sits in the film's internal, diegetic theatre and watches her perform. In film, traditionally the space between the audience and the filmic action is relatively distinct. In the musical, however, the proscenium is not only granted a much higher degree of elasticity, it also can multiply at will: in this example Bugsy is both performer and audience, creating three spaces, not the usual two. Blousey is performer-performer, Bugsy is audience-performer, and we (of course) are audience-audience. Even more immediately, of course, is the fact that *Bugsy Malone* was cast solely with children and young teens. When I first saw it, this fact held little interest—anyone older than me was 'grown up', so whether they were 14 or 24, it seemed neither here nor there to me that the cast was so young. I had no dominant traditions to refer to as my point of comparison, and in retrospect this is a curious point: why *was* it seen as so novel to cast a film with

325

young people? Certainly their performances were not any less solid or compelling than the usual adult-centred musical, and more importantly, it refused to reduce children to the usual clichéd ciphers. In *Bugsy Malone*, children are not used to fetishize adult obsessions with innocence and naivety. They are granted a space to perform the range of emotions and experiences that they of course have in real life, but that are rarely permitted to express in mainstream cinema: joy, terror, fear, insecurity, doubt, love, passion, anger—perhaps most challengingly for contemporary audiences today in particular—desire and violence. What I also didn't know then that I know now is that *Bugsy Malone* was a parody. I'd never heard of—let alone seen—a gangster film, and iconic figures like Edward G. Robinson and James Cagney were a long way for becoming readily identifiable pop cultural points of reference. It seemed perfectly logical to my tiny, developing mind that this mystical place called 1920's New York would be inhabited only by young people who would seek to eradicate rival gangs through the deployment of semi-automatic cream pies. For adults, this is a clever, hilarious spoof on the traditional gangster genre, but watching the film today—decades after my first magical encounter with it—I can't help but envy my earlier assumption that the most evil thing in the world one could encounter was a delicious dessert, and that as kids, we could've be anything that we wanted to be.

As songstress Tallulah, Jodie Foster is a marvel. Among other children, she seems comfortable and blends in beautifully rather than sticking out like a seasoned sore thumb. Foster was performing for years before *Bugsy Malone*, and the film she made before this Prohibition-Era musical was *Taxi Driver* (1976) where she played a child prostitute destined to be "rescued" by Robert De Niro's avenging angel. But it is Florrie Dugger's Blousey who is the most well-developed of the characters, and the most complicated: she is a singer, but she is also an anchor for the chaos that erupts around her. She is a dedicated and more than competent artist, but one continually crushed by the messy crime wave and the selfishness that is paraded around her at every given moment. The concept of pies replacing gunfire is a sophisticated way tackling the overt violence of the piece. The push-pedal cars are more of the same. This is a world for children who are more sophisticated than adults seem to ever give them credit for.

Jodie Foster as Tallulah, the quintessential gangster's moll
in *Bugsy Malone* (1976)

Scott Baio's performance in the titular role oozes with child star confidence and solid professionalism: he is at one with the character, and never winces or bumbles through a difficult role. He is, after all, the centre of the piece, an ego when everyone around him seems to be fulfilling a feature on an archetypal totem pole (pintsized, perhaps, but a pillar of character prototypes nonetheless). A Greek Chorus-style narrator sings that Bugsy is a "man, a mountain, he's a rolling stone," a larger than life character who sits at the comfortable side of the table of running along with cat-like agility. He is not to be messed with, but ultimately he does not want to get messy. Much like Tony in *West Side Story*, Bugsy is trying to leave his shady past behind but is called upon by fate to bring forth justice to a city besieged by corruption, alienation and fury.

The most surprising aspect of the film is that it is a dark child fantasy. Where *Willy Wonka and the Chocolate Factory* explored the consequences of disobedience, *Bugsy Malone* is set among the corrupt world of children, a left-over world ruined by adults that now remains for their young to struggle within. In this sense, the film could be read as a "sins of the parents" trope, and in many ways it is. The adult aspects of the film linger like a pendulous cloud, forever haunting the lexicon of these grimy, showbiz- and crime-obsessed kiddies. A perfect example of this is the comical and yet stupendously grown-up moment where Fat Sam bemoans, "You spend more time putting yourself up than there is time in the day!," to which Tallulah confidently responds, "Listen honey, if I didn't look this good you wouldn't give me the time of day." It is this kind of slick and sophisticated writing and delivery from these very grown-up kids that gives the film its edge. The movie does not dumb itself down for the "kiddy crowd," but plays it with dedicated straightness. Even in the comedic moments—particularly the witticisms in the dialogue—there is a sense of necessary cynicism. This is a masterpiece, a movie oddity that is so much more than a "playgroup for children who are playing "dress up"." It is a serious and gloomy movie, and all the more brilliant for it.

These same traits would mark director Alan Parker's next movie musical when he would later go on to direct one of the most bleak and brutal musicals ever made three years later with *Fame* (1980), a film which embodied the youth angst of teen-centric cinema that would flourish come the early 1980s (more on *Fame* later). But Parker's Prohibition-Era Paul Williams musical with children as gangsters and gangsters' molls proves it's distinguished. Both films set up worlds encompassed by grief;

in the playful *Bugsy Malone* each character is swamped by disappointment (Blousey's struggle to be respected as a performer, Tallulah's desperate longing to be loved, and so forth), and in *Fame* this is exactly the same: the students at the High School of Performing Arts are plagued by insecurity, depression, drug abuse issues, etc. Both films—one a fun and frivolous high concept semi-integrated musical pastiche and the other a grim, highly dramatic and hyper-realist movie musical—are testaments to the director's talents at tapping into the human condition, whether he be dressing it up in a period piece like *Bugsy Malone*, or down with the decrepit music halls and dance studios that feature as the oppressive backdrops to the passionate but emotionally fragile arts students in *Fame*.

Actor and singer Archie Hahn had worked with Paul Williams before on the magnificent *Phantom of the Paradise*, and was asked to lend his vocal abilities for *Bugsy Malone*. Hahn gave voice to a number of the youngsters, and granted a distinguished edge to each of his characters. Hahn remembers:

> Paul called me and said he was working on a film called *Bugsy Malone* which was to be a movie about kids with splurge guns being hoodlums. And I thought wow this sounds great, what a great idea. And Paul asked me if I knew anyone who could sing in kids' voices. And I said yes, because I had a lot of friends doing voice over work and I remember calling Julie McWhirter and Liberty Williams and then I did voices too. We went to the studio and we sang. I ended up doing three or four voices. I did Cagey Joe who was the fight manager and so I sang "So You Want to Be a Boxer" and then there was the little janitor, the little black boy who sings "Tomorrow." There were two other background characters that I did harmonies for, one was the little Italian don for Bugsy's side of the family then there was one of the guys carting off a rug or something. We didn't know who was going to play what parts at the time, so it was a guess as to what they were going to sound like and we pretty much hit everybody on the head except for Scott Baio because his voice was way high and then when he gets

to the song "Down and Out" I had his voice drop, I missed the mark on that because I didn't know who was going to be playing the part, so it didn't fit. The artistry of Paul Williams is outstanding. And it's a perfect marriage of style, music, character and lyrics. I would expect no less from Paul, he had a great track record to begin with before he got involved with *Bugsy Malone*.

The way an artist can channel a character and find their voice is epitomized in the following anecdote from Hahn, who remembers the way he fuelled the vocal performance of the Albin "Humpty" Jenkins as Fizzy, the janitor who dreams of becoming a tap dancer. The song "Tomorrow" (lamenting a world without any tomorrows—once again, speaking of a nihilistic and sorrowful world typical of *Bugsy Malone*) is a testament to Paul Williams as a writer. What Hahn tapped into through this small African American performer links to broader issues about the subjective experience of racial discrimination:

> I was a very young boy when I discovered what segregation was and I was appalled. I could not believe what they called back then colored people have their own fountains, own waiting areas, it hurt, I just couldn't understand that. So when I saw this little character, I just felt a well spring of sorrow about how these people were treated and it definitely finds its way in that song and it's exactly what I put into that song.

Hahn also used personal history to help materialize his characterization of other characters:

> My father had been a boxer in college and I think he was a bantam weight and he had a lot of speed. He was fast! So I had some background in boxing simply having watched it when my father had matches and that character had a lot of energy so that little character dictated how I sang that song, so in turn when he heard how the song was sung for the first

330

Guns that shoot cream pies in *Bugsy Malone* (1976)

time he may have fed his character from the singing. I never met Alan Parker. Paul directed us. Most of the stuff was done state side. I was always a little embarrassed in my skills as a singer. I was never trained I don't sight read and pretty much what I do is by ear so when I'm in a studio with people who can sight read like backup singers I am blown away they're so incredible, so for me to get a lot of attention for what I did it seems inappropriate to me. But I don't want to take away any of the gifts I have, but I didn't feel comfortable by taking those experience by projecting them out into the community and saying something like I wanted to do more musicals, I've always been very difficult for agents. I'm not difficult in nature I'm just very withdrawn and shy and introverted which makes it hard for agents to put me out there. *Phantom of the Paradise* and *Bugsy Malone* are the only two experiences I had singing—and I've been asked to do more but I have declined because I was never trained and felt I could not do more. Paul is great at mining the area for talent—he gets an

331

idea in his head and sometimes he sees someone and that sparks an idea. He gets the best out of people without having to say anything half the time!

Phantom of the Paradise, A Star is Born and *Bugsy Malone* would boast some of the greatest songs from a movie musical of the decade, and Paul Williams would go on to write more throughout the years for television and films including a brilliant song performed by John Travolta for the made for TV "disease of the week" classic *The Boy in the Plastic Bubble* (1976). But it would be his work in 1979 for *The Muppet Movie* that would have audiences everywhere wiping tears from their eyes and filling their hearts with "The Rainbow Connection." *Bugsy Malone* in some ways was great practice for director Alan Parker to move onto the superior *Fame*, but it was also phenomenal practice for *The Muppet Movie* which would harken back to movies like *The Wizard of Oz*. In Parker's stylish gangster-kid fest, a semi-meta climax is almost as poignant and as magical as the soon-to-be released Jim Henson extravaganza. In the closing moments of *Bugsy Malone*, the entire cast of children, covered in cream pies and caked-in ice-cream (the actual metaphoric bullets for their metaphoric guns but here obviously unaffected–it's all part of the fourth wall diminished-ending) sing and dance together and state that "they could have been anything that they wanted to be." A beautiful poignant message: these kids that can build and destroy worlds with ease can be whoever they want to be. In *Bugsy Malone*, this manifests in a Warner Bros. gangster flick complete with their own hidden agendas, conflicting politics and shady dealings. But the film ends happily: solidarity between children flourishes and is nourished, and being covered in ice-cream and creamy pies renders them are all the same. White, black, tall, thin, fat, short, male, female—it doesn't matter. They are all children, escapees from a world of adults and paving their own way through the compounds of genre cinema.

The push-pedal cars, the cream-pie shooting tommy guns, and the miniature sets made just the right height for its pint-sized cast are all now the stuff of an iconic legend. A poignant tribute to the gangster films of the 1930s and 1940s, *Bugsy Malone* is an inventive and yet bizarre musical that empowers children. It never dumbs itself down, it never sells itself short, and most importantly, it never fails to deliver a genuinely endearing generosity of spirit.

TITS AND ASS: *The First Nudie Musical* and *Alice in Wonderland: An X-Rated Musical Fantasy*

Pornography was and always will be an incredibly lucrative film market. Sex and sensuality on the screen is a necessity and an essential addition to certain kinds of cinema. But the adult film industry itself is a very different animal, solely devoted to serving up titillating and sexual excesses. The 1970s proved to be the decade of porno-chic, which marked the victory of tits-and-ass-centric cinema into the mainstream. Long gone were the days of stag films secretly being carted off to speakeasies back in the age of Prohibition, and distant were the red faces and sticky fingers of cagey teenage boys of the 1950s hiding behind magazines and pulp novels featuring busty girls tying each other up. The sexual revolution of the 1960s heralded by hippiedom now looked *passé* in retrospect when compared to the pseudo-glamour of the 1970s' glittery pornographic subculture. The decade introduced pornography as a legitimate industry, and a fiery entry in the world of the new-wave of Hollywood cinema. During the 1970s, pornographic films stepped out of the grindhouse theatres and made a brief appearance at semi-mainstream cinemas with films such as *Behind the Green Door* (1972) starring adult film star Marilyn Chambers, *The Devil in Miss Jones* (1973) which married pornography with outlandish melodrama, and the film that punched the face of the mainstream *Deep Throat* (1972) which singlehandedly got people interested in adult film. These movies all attracted a broad audience beyond the "trench coat" crowd, who incidentally were also frequenting the rock musical *Hair* across the country for a glimpse of full frontal nudity. Movies like *Deep Throat* were also attracting society people and the middle classes.

A cinematic musical delivered more in the way of sexual extremities than the revolutionary *Hair*. Produced by Paramount, *The First Nudie Musical* is a surprising and bright satire on pornography and the people behind it. It poses the question: "What can we do that is *different* for the pornographic film?" The answer: "Let's make it a musical!" There is a lot of heart in this movie and a definite love and respect for genre films, most notably of course the Hollywood musical. It seems to pay direct homage to the golden age of the movie musical, but paints it with freshly liberated 1970s, sex-crazed frivolity. It is also funny and fabulously offensive: thank God for the film's dirtiness, smut, goofiness and sheer fun!

The First Nudie Musical (1976)

The First Nudie Musical (1976)

Co-director, writer and actor Bruce Kimmel remembers the origins of the film:

Back in 1969, I was living in New York, trying to make it as an actor (I was born and raised in Los Angeles, and it was my first time living elsewhere)—I didn't have much success, and at some point I was working at a telephone survey place with some other wacky out-of-work actors and we all loved going to see what at that time were called "nudie" movies (this was pre-mainstream hardcore). We saw things like *The Lustful Turk* and *She Came on the Bus* and we'd just howl at their ineptitude. I suggested that we should do a musical "nudie" and I wrote some songs as a joke—in that initial batch were "Orgasm," "Lesbian, Butch, Dyke," "I'll Kick You with Boots," and "Ménage à Trois," and maybe "Let 'em Eat Cake." All of them ended up in the film except "Ménage à Trois," which was lame, and, of course, we ended up cutting "I'll Kick You with Boots," even though you see some of it in the time passage montage. But at that point, that was all there was—we were going to call our movie, *Come, Come Now*—but back then it wasn't a movie-within-a-movie thing, it was just the movie. When I told Cindy Williams about it (we'd gone to college together) she loved it and from that point on I started thinking of the movie-within-the movie concept and paying homage to the classic backstage musicals, specifically *Footlight Parade*.

The First Nudie Musical (1976)

The film is also a celebration of exploitation cinema and pornography, and Kimmel shares his love for all cinema:

I was a fan of anything that played in a movie theatre

from the time I was five. I went two or three times a week and saw everything—big, small, whatever was playing I'd see it. In the 1960s, of course I discovered the real sexploitation films—discovered Russ Meyer via *Mudhoney* and *Faster Pussycat, Kill, Kill.* Prior to that, I'd been intrigued as a new teen by the titillating ads for Meyer's *The Immoral Mr. Teas* but I couldn't get in to see it, much as I would have liked to. I did see a couple of "nudie" films in LA—I think Cindy might have even come with us to one of them.

The First Nudie Musical (1976)

For Paramount to make the film was bizarre, and to think about it in today's context is insane. But as Kimmel recalls, it seemed to be all systems go for extremities in sexual content at that time. But a lot changed when star Cindy Williams was about to grace the family television set with the hit sitcom and spin-off of the hugely successful *Happy Days* (1974-1984), *Laverne and Shirley* (1976-1983):

> Paramount was in a weird place back then. The studio was being run by Dick Sylbert, who was one of the greatest art directors ever, but who was a little out of his league as a person running a huge studio. An executive from the studio came to one of our sneak previews—in Westwood, where we

were previewing with Woody Allen's *Love and Death*—we got more laughs—I'll never forget that night. They loved the film and bought it immediately. At the time they bought it, not only were they not concerned about the content, they felt there were six or seven minutes in the middle of the film where it lagged a little—so they gave me half of what the film cost to go shoot one additional sequence, the only requirement being that it was funny. That new sequence became "Dancing Dildos." Once Cindy's TV show got green-lit and she began shooting *Laverne and Shirley*. But then the content became sketchy for them, because suddenly Cindy was starring in a huge hit family-hour TV show. And from then on, much drama ensued.

The film unfolds with terrific energy, as Harry Schechter (Stephen Nathan), an heir to a Hollywood studio, is cornered into making a new kind of musical to save the company from impending bankruptcy. With the help of his intelligent and resourceful secretary Rosie, Harry is advised to hire John Smithee (played by Bruce Kimmel himself) to direct the film. The problem is Smithee is a virgin, and completely out of his depths directing this sex-infested nudist musical. Throughout the course of the film, this musical within a musical introduces us to a cavalcade of characters including Joy Full (Susan Stewart) who auditions in the nude and presents the casting panel with orgasms. When she is asked to sing a musical scale, she literally sings the word "scale"!

Alexandra Morgan as Miss Mary La Rue is another knockout, bringing both the power as well as the insecurity of a performer into this hysterical and satirical musical. Kimmel remembers Alexandra Morgan:

> Alexandra (we called her Sandy) was, and I'm sure till is, a terrific actress. She loved her role and just dove into it. I remember her doing her lines at the end of the Dancing Dildos scene—you know, where she says, "I will not do this number until these damn dildos know their steps. I am actress, I've studied with Strasberg and I don't need this shit!" She said it so angrily and dramatically in the first take, and

337

after, I went up to her and asked her to do one more, just not quite so seriously. When I saw the dailies of the two takes the clear winner was her original take—it was hilarious because she WAS so serious. Lesson learned.

Another empowering element to the film is its uncompromising comedy: there are jokes that reference rape, sodomy, and masturbation, and the sexual liberties of each character is elemental and part of their everyday experience as employees of the adult entertainment industry. Combined with their simultaneous roles in musical theatre and film, both forms rely heavily on notions of repetition, practice and perpetual motion. These parallels between sex and art are palpable in this film, and the filth and silliness that straddle this comparison make it an endlessly fun and hilarious expression of anarchic sexual freedom.

The First Nudie Musical **(1976)**

The songs are nicely conceived and peppered throughout the film as both integrated to diegetic numbers. Those that move plot and give an insight into character are the strongest, while the numbers used within the musical aspect are sharp, short, crude and delightful. Bruce Kimmel remembers:

Some of the film-within-a film songs came first. Once I

The First Nudie Musical (1976)

was ready to write the actual script, I wrote all the additional
songs first, then the script. The most enjoyable in terms of
the craft was "The Lights and the Smiles," just because it's
a real musical theatre song. There weren't any what I would
call songs that were difficult to write. I write very fast and
if something is difficult I throw it in the trash, as I know it
won't be good. Neither *Hair* and *Oh! Calcutta!* made it easier
to get the film made, because they were stage and we were
film. And we really pushed the envelope further than it had
been pushed back then by a film being released by a major
studio. The ratings board wanted to give us an X originally—
but not because of the nudity—isn't that funny? It was too
many F words (we ended up cutting one totally and removed
the sound on one other) and one tiny shot of the stunt cock
and Mary going at it—really minor stuff and we had our R
rating. But believe me when I tell you, that the film shocked
a lot of people—straight-laced people, yes, but boy did some
folks get on their high horses about it. Younger audiences
ate it up.

For the most part, the supporting cast are naked, dancing around
clever sets and tap dancing with breasts bouncing and penises jumping.

339

Bruce Kimmel remembers this was not a concern for these trained dancers:

> Interestingly, all the gals in the chorus had no problem with the nudity—they all understood what we were doing and that it was all in good fun—and several of them had careers going. The guys would not do it at all—only two men are seen full-frontal in the film—Alan Abelew, who plays George Brenner, and Artie Shafer who is in the nude buck-and-wing number in the audition sequence and later in a small scene where he quits the film-within-a-film because of Mary's mistreatment of him. Today, the men would probably do it faster than the women.

In a very small role, *Happy Days*'s Ron Howard plays an audition hopeful who has a brief scene with the talented Cindy Williams going over the concept of the nudie musical. Kimmel recalls:

> I think deep down he liked it. We've actually never talked about it. I'd already done two episodes of *Happy Days* as an actor and we got along really well and he wanted to be a director and he came over and did the little cameo as a favour to Cindy and me. I've worked with Cindy for a long time, starting way back in 1965 when we were in college together. We did lots of shows back then. For me, she is just a stellar actor—brilliantly creative and instinctive, with great comedy and dramatic chops. She made *The First Nudie Musical*—her performance is the heart of the film and the film wouldn't work at all without it. She brings such warmth and heart and reality to it, but she's also really funny. We love working together because we know each other so well and I have her back and she has mine. I've been madly in love with her as a person since the day we met. Stephen Nathan wasn't our first choice. Our first choice was someone named Henry Winkler, who Cindy was dating at the time. He loved it, but smartly knew it was not the kind of thing he should do at

that point, given his Fonzie was the biggest thing since white bread. Our next choice was an actor named Archie Hahn, who Cindy and I both knew—I love Archie, but am eternally grateful he said no, as he just would not have been the right person. So, we then heard about Stephen and he read it and loved it and said yes immediately and as fate would have it, he was the perfect choice for the same reasons as Cindy—because he grounds the film in reality and is likeable and you root for him.

Outside Cindy Williams, Stephen Nathan and Ron Howard, the film's art direction is so excellent it should be considered a starring role in itself. It complements the staging of the musical numbers, highlighting the nudity in an organic way that makes it at one with the background. There is one moment where chorus girls dance in top hats and tails with their breasts and genitals exposed, and because of the spectacle it takes a second look. This is a demented, sleazy revision of Busby Berkley, but with Berkley asleep at the wheel: it is as if he has forgotten to get his costumer to fully clothe these dirty grandchildren of the Ziegfeld Follies.

Kimmel says:

It was just another luck-out. We'd just moved into our offices at Producer's Studio and we met Tom Rasmussen, who was working on the lot regularly. He had a wicked sense of humour and agreed do everything—sets AND costumes for a shockingly low amount of money. And he was brilliant every step of the way. Boy, did we get our money's worth with him. There are some things, like Harry's office, where people thought we shot in a real office—but everything in the film is a set—the only time it isn't is the location stuff like The Lights and the Smiles and the handful of exterior shots. Even the whorehouse was a set and a pretty amazing one given our budget. Then again, he came up with the idea of doing all of the casting sequence and the rehearsal sequence in front of the blue and yellow backdrops—it made those sequences so easy to do. And, of course, he will live in infamy

341

for his design of the Dancing Dildos. Tom's actually in the film—in the "Perversion" number, he's the Bishop.

Kimmel is excellent as the naïve and nervous virgin Smithee, who has no idea how to direct a film let alone a pornographic musical. Kimmel explains:

> Knowing I was going to co-direct, I just wrote a part for myself that I knew I could play in my sleep. I wanted something that would show off my comedic strengths as well as let me be endearing—I just instinctively knew that if the audience loved the three of us (Stephen, Cindy and me) that we could get away with just about anything, and that proved to be true. A lot of people's favourite bits of mine were actually created in rehearsal or at the time of filming. All of the mispronouncing Schechter happened in rehearsal. And the pulling the chair up bit happened when I saw that set for the first time and where the seat was placed. I was about to tell them to move it closer to the desk when I thought, "No, let him tell me to pull up a chair." I love when that stuff happens and if you're smart, you're always open to those little gifts that come out of nowhere. One wishes it had been the hit it should have been, but it was ahead of its time by a few years. As it was, it was very influential on other films that followed. But I'm happy to have made something that people love and that they find funny—and that's really lasted for what will be forty years come 2015. Can you believe it? I can't. I don't know where its place is in the history of American musical film—it's not really thought of all that much by the wags who wax on about that stuff— the film just isn't on their radar. All the smart people know about it, though, he said laughing. We weren't really trying to "comment" on anything—we were just trying to make a funny movie, one with lots of laughs and a few musical numbers, and we were trying to have some fun at the expense of the porno world, and, of course, we all loved the classic film

musicals of old, and I think that comes through a lot of the film. Every day was a funny story and they're all in my book, "There's Mel, There's Woody, and There's You—My Life in the Slow Lane." I spend over one hundred pages on *The First Nudie Musical* alone—it's really more than anyone would ever want to know. But here's one that I don't think is in the book: When we were shooting the "Perversion" number, we ordered Arby's for a meal for the cast (all we could afford). It was the worst food ever, and if you remember the number there's a German shepherd in it and the German shepherd wouldn't even eat the Arby's.

The comedy is simple and biting, such as when Smithee instructs the chorus kids to "dance" the way he does (of course, just like everything else, dancing is not one of his specialties) so when they resort to doing their original steps, Smithee feels like he has made an impression. There is also some confronting language in the film, but it is there beyond shock value; the inclusion of the healthy amount of "cunt" and "cock" talk adds to the film's authenticity and the realization of its central, thematic sleaze. Kimmel continues:

> The "dance" scene is one line in the script. No one, not even me, knew exactly what I was going to do—and I just did it when the camera rolled, with no rehearsal, and what you see is the one and only take. I'd told everyone that no matter what I did they were just to go back to the original steps they were doing. In regard to writing comedy—I don't think in terms of punch lines or jokes, even though I suppose if you analyse my writing over the years it probably does fall into that kind of thing. And I never think in terms of shock. I just write what makes me laugh and hope that it will make others laugh.

The First Nudie Musical is an explosion of ideas that works well. The performances, numbers and throwaway gags come fast and furious (the piano player comes to mind as he struggles with rhymes and tiny little musical moments) and are combined to great effect, and the film entertains while both saying something about the industry and titillating at the same time. And aside from anything else, a musical featuring dancing dildos just has to be seen to be believed! Kimmel concludes:

> Tom Rasmussen, our set designer designed the Dancing Dildos. He designed them and built them and then the poor fellows who did the number had to wear them and they were not so comfortable or fun for them. They were made out of wood and were really heavy and awkward. I think one guy passed out when he got knocked over.

In contrast, rather than being a film *about* pornographic musicals, *Alice in Wonderland: An X-Rated Musical Fantasy* is a straight up porno musical. Porno-chic was essentially a 1970s institution by this stage, and when films like *Deep Throat* made such a great social impact and attracted mass audiences who lined around the block to the old grindhouse theatres, it was only natural that genre films would seek to themselves exploit the popularity of blue movies. *The First Nudie Musical* featured pornography at its core theme and employed a movie within a movie structure, and earlier musicals such as *Oh! Calcutta!* dissected sexual practices. *Alice in Wonderland: An X-Rated Musical Fantasy* joins this subgeneric category as a surprisingly poignant pornographic excursion into sexual awakening.

In this film, a virginal Alice grows into a sexually ambitious and sexually free young woman. The film opens with a delivery man (a porn film staple) approaching frigid Alice (Kristen DeBell). He asks her out but she rejects him. He tells her "Your body is all grown up, but your mind is still a little girl's" as Alice, a librarian, goes back to her work. She comes across a copy of Lewis Carroll's "Alice in Wonderland," a book she never read as she laments that she was "too busy growing up." She does not mean sexual development, however, rather more about entering the world of "adult drag": a world of denial where she misses out on experience. After her opening number, Alice is greeted by a sleazy little rabbit-man who leads her down the "rabbit hole" where she enters an X-Rated Wonderland. After falling into a river—a metaphoric baptism—she is greeted by a group of over-sexed woodland animals.

"If it feels good it is good," explains one who, along with other bizarre chorus kids dressed as furry beasts, lick Alice clean, exploring her body. The film continually reminds our heroine to let go and enjoy whatever it is that brings her pleasure. The film also focuses on refusing to grow up and to hang onto childlike wonderment, somewhat bizarre themes in a sexploitation film—the concept might be innocently concocted by the writers (the notion that losing your inner-child might cause emptiness in the future) but it is a bit alarming when the entire film sets up Alice in sexual scenarios with a range of characters from woodland animals to talking eggs.

The awe that the animals talk about is ultimately imagination, and it is this that they persuade Alice to use to enter the world of sexual pleasure. The scene with the licking woodland animals gets even more perverse when one of the creatures asks Alice what her breasts are for and she explains that when she falls pregnant she will use them to feed her baby. The critter responds "When you do have a baby, can I have some milk too? I like milk." This is a perversion of maternal intimacy, and while motherhood is something that Alice is aware of however, she is still blind to everything else (hence why she believes breasts are only for weening babies). More strange moments follow and there are such ridiculous scenarios that it's easy to fall in love with this film. For example, when Alice sits down, a large talking rock beings to instruct her and inspire her to take off her dress and fondle her breasts. The rock gets increasingly frisky and guides her through her the steps of masturbation. The rock insists that she is "all alone just with her imagination" and Alice proceeds to masturbate.

A highlight is the iconic Mad Hatter's tea party, and here there are some inspired lines. Alice asks the Hatter if the number on the tag of his hat is the size of his hat, to which he quickly responds, "Oh no, that's the size of my ding-a-ling!" and shows her his penis. She covers her eyes in shock and the White Rabbit explains to the Hatter that she is a virgin. The Hatter is repulsed, and screams "I've never heard of such a thing!" to which Alice explains that she is "trying to learn, but I can't have things just shoved down my throat." The Hatter asks "Why not?" and persuades young Alice to fellate him.

345

The poster art for the pornographic musical *Alice in Wonderland* (1976)

Later, Alice cures Humpty Dumpty's impotence. He says "I used to be big you know?" and the tender and sweet Alice goes down on him also, helping him rediscover his erection. Two naked nubile nurses, the Hatter and the White Rabbit all rejoice by singing "We got his ding-a-ling up!" Tweedledee and Tweedledum are lovers who look very similar—instead of being two overweight, odd-looking men, they are a straight couple who look very similar, like brother and sister—in fact, they *are* brother and sister! They sing a song that eventually ends up being a backing track for their "performance" for Alice. The sequence is a highly stylized slow motion sex scene with garish sun-kissed colors and dissolves that captures two people enjoying sexual interplay. Alice watches with delight (clasping onto a Raggedy-Ann doll of all things), and the thrill of voyeurism is serviced. In the final sequences of the film, Alice successfully seduces the King, with the Queen (a bratty woman dressed only in a headpiece and a garter with stockings) demanding that she service her as well. Alice is not too keen on "serving the Queen" and requests a fair trial and a court case ensues. This is where the film makes its biggest statement, as the musical number that follows presents us with the notion that you "treasure each and every moment of the day." The movie informs us that we can have fun, but the fun is to be treasured: pleasure is fleeting and not guaranteed. As soon as this sentiment is made explicit, we are bombarded with multiple snippets of various characters having sex and fondling themselves and each other. The sexual liberation of the 1960s has now morphed into the gender politics of *Alice in Wonderland: An X-Rated Musical Fantasy* where characters are given sexual opportunities galore but ultimately come out of them unchanged.

The film is a well-made pornographic feature but the songs give it an added sense of craziness. They are equally surprisingly good. Bucky Searls is a talented songwriter and his numbers work throughout the film: not one sounds like a tacked on tune for the sake of having a number in that particular moment. Searls delivers a fully functioning, integrated musical where the songs extend both the story and the character of Alice's sexual awakening. All in all, it is a well-structured musical film that channels 1970s fetishism and its broader cultural climate of sexual explicitness.

THE DIVINE MISS M, THE DIVINE MISTER LYNDE AND MGM REVISITED: *The Bette Midler Show, Paul Lynde's Halloween Special* and *That's Entertainment Part 2*

Into a dark, steamy room filled with near naked young men cruising one another comes a loud, brassy diminutive Jewish girl who takes her boys on a journey from madcap filthy humour to heartbreaking torture: the Mae West of the 1970s and the torch song gypsy girl of the Continental Bathhouse in New York, Bette Midler. If Judy Garland was the voice for the invisible generation, than the Divine Miss M was the voice for the "not so quiet generation," a powerhouse of energy and a formidable songstress who demanded attention. When Midler got her first television special, it blew fellow musicians, audiences and critics away.

The Bette Midler Show was a filmed for HBO and was attributed to the artist's "Depression Tour," shot at the Cleveland Music Hall at the end of Winter 1976. In this performance, Midler shows off her remarkable talents as a storyteller, as a comedienne, as a theatrical performer, and most importantly as a singer. Midler's vocal capabilities have the power to make spirits soar, bringing them home to a place you either never knew existed (or perhaps wished you didn't!). She is fundamentally punk in her rawness of expression, and purely rock'n'roll in her versatility as she goes from war-time girl group ("The Boogie Woogie Bugle Boy") through to champion of the underdog in the anthemic "Friends," then to anguished torch singer with "Hello In There" as she examines the loneliness that comes with old age.

Spontaneous and fun, Midler gives her audience a hilarious good time, but has a natural ability to bring the metaphoric lights down to bring on the waterworks. Midler is one of a kind, and understands the delicate balance between high drama and hijinks. In 1980, Midler would get another television special with *Divine Madness* which delivers more of her fabulous wit, spectacular singing and dramatic skills *par excellence*.

Similarly fuelled by sly innuendo and dirty jokes was Paul Lynde, who sadly never got a chance to serve his serious or his more romantic side (admittedly, he probably never really wanted to, seeing that he lived such a secret life). Lynde was an acerbic genius with a forked tongue and a sophisticated, sardonic sense of humour that ran through his body of work from television sit-coms to game shows. In 1976, Lynde hosted

Bette Midler in *Divine Madness* (1980)

Midler's comic and musical brilliance in *Divine Madness* (1980)

349

his very own Halloween special *The Paul Lynde Halloween Special*, one of the wackiest and most endearing celebrations of the 1970s variety show format ever put to the small screen: to its credit, it epitomizes the entire decade in only one hour! There is nothing uninteresting, uninspired or negative about this special that screams 1970s good times bliss.

Paul Lynde in a publicity still for *The Paul Lynde Halloween Special* (1976)

Lynde is matched with the likes of Billie Hayes as Witchypoo from *H.R. Pufnstuf* and Margaret Hamilton as the Wicked Witch of the West from *The Wizard of Oz*, first introduced reading first editions of *The Exorcist* and *Rosemary's Baby* (books they call "light entertainment"). Dwarf superstar Billy Barty joins Lynde, and Florence Henderson does a sizzling disco rendition of "That Old Black Magic." Lynde complains about the "kids today" while Donny and Marie Osmond bounce about around him wearing matching jumpsuits: yep, *this* is entertainment, folks! The highlight of course is when KISS hit the stage and perform, but what is even more intriguing is that the band interact with both Lynde himself and Margaret Hamilton. It's astonishing to see the members of this hugely successful rock band (one that terrified parents everywhere) given lines to say and talking with lounge lizard Lynde. The 1970s gave us a glut of outlandish concepts for television specials such as *The Benji TV Specials* (1972-1976), *The Brady Variety Hour*, *Halloween with the Addams Family* (1977) and so forth, but *The Paul Lynde Halloween Special* is one of the most insane and twisted. For this alone, it should be treasured and immortalized in every 1970s enthusiasts personal collections.

MGM compiled more incredible clips from their vaults as a follow up to the successful *That's Entertainment* with *That's Entertainment Part 2*, a collaboration between producer Daniel Melnick and musical producer and director Saul Chaplin. These two enthusiastic cinephiles gathered clips from various MGM movies and shuffled them about in a visual stream of consciousness hosted by Fred Astaire and Gene Kelly. These two great names from the Golden Age of Hollywood narrated their way through a seemingly endless array of marvellous movie moments from the 1930s, 1940s and 1950s.

This would also mark the first time Astaire and Kelly worked together in the thirty years since they co-starred in *Ziegfeld Follies* (1946), and it seems to be a dream come true for Kelly as he states in the first *That's Entertainment* that he would love to have the opportunity to dance with Fred Astaire once again. And here, he gets his wish. Fred Astaire was seventy six years old at the times and Gene Kelly was sixty three, but they don't seem to have aged a day when you see these two icons dance with such grace and ease. It is as if they are in their prime, these timeless hoofers with their masterful control of every part of their bodies (not just their remarkable feet) as they trot, skip, bounce, and pirouette around a soundstage set up for this equally impressive and equally fun docutainment feature, just as engaging as its predecessor.

The set-up for *That's Entertainment 2* is similar to a 1970s television variety show. Unlike the previous film with the stars/hosts walking through a crumbled MGM lot, Astaire and Kelly introduce various clips and sing and dance through them in a stylized sound stage, with large flats featuring stars of the golden age of the MGM musical. They sing outros to clips including legends like Judy Garland, Jimmy Durante, Ethel Waters, Eleanor Powell, Mickey Rooney, Ann Miller, Lena Horne, Cyd Charisse, and the king and queen of the cinematic operetta, Nelson Eddy and Jeanette MacDonald. Unlike the first film, the sequel doesn't just showcase MGM musicals. It also includes non-musicals from the studio such as the films of the Marx Brothers and the screwball comedies of Spencer Tracy and Katherine Hepburn. It also uncovers some obscure musicals that weren't featured in the previous film, as well as mini-features that preceded many of the golden age musicals of the day (one including Jack Benny when he was already building his shtick which would become hugely popular with television audiences in the years to come).

Gene Kelly reminisces about his first film, *For Me And My Gal* (1942) in which he starred alongside Judy Garland, while Fred Astaire gets starry eyed about his turn in musicals like *Easter Parade* (1948). There is a showcase of Frank Sinatra's crooning that made bobby soxers go crazy, and stars not normally associated with musicals such as Robert Taylor and Greta Garbo shown doing their bit for the genre. Bob Fosse dances with Carol Haney in *Kiss Me Kate* (1953), while Ann Miller leaps and tap dances about in exuberant excellence. Gene Kelly explains that one of his happiest discoveries was that of the beautiful Leslie Caron, with whom he starred in *An American in Paris* and who went onto sing with wonderfully designed puppets in the haunting *Lili*. Kelly introduces himself and Judy Garland dancing about as clowns in *The Pirate* (1948), introducing an entertaining montage of famous comic geniuses from W.C. Fields through to Ed Wynn. Laurel and Hardy and Abbott and Costello are paid tribute, and Fred Astaire sings about the Marx Brothers as we are graced with some of their mischievous antics in movies such as *A Night at the Opera* (1935). More stand out moments include the glorious Kathryn Grayson singing "Smoke Gets In Your Eyes" from *Lovely To Look At* and oddities like Fred Astaire dolled up as a baby in *The Band Wagon* (1953). The sweet sentiment sprinkled throughout the film is not only there to highlight the tenderness shared amidst the Hollywood community back in the day, but also historically correct, for example, composer Irving Berlin being described as "*The* American musical."

When Gene Kelly sings about the wonders of black and white entertainment, the 1970s pays homage to a bygone era of classic cinema that people such as Kelly urge modern day cinema lovers not to forget. *That's Entertainment Part 2* celebrates and validates great film from the past. These musicals and comedies of the 1930s, 1940s and 1950s are not to be forgotten and should be revered. The importance of a film like this is invaluable and completely necessary. When the original *The Great Waltz* (1938) is examined (albeit only one scene, but it is remarkable), it is done with the hope that audiences will hunt it down and watch it, rather than being subjected to its 1970s remake which is below mediocre. In *That's Entertainment Part 2*, the original *The Great Waltz* is given respect. Clip presentations are at their best when they leave an audience wanting more, and this film does this successfully and with heartfelt compassion. Along with its predecessor, it is an integral document for film criticism, film culture and film preservation. Thank God for the *That's Entertainment* movies! As if this is all not enough, this film also boasts one of the greatest title sequences ever put to screen: to see names like Doris Day, Elizabeth Taylor and even Lassie presented in such a grandiose manner is a testament to the genius design work of the legendary Saul Bass, who provides this tribute to the credit sequences from classic MGM musicals.

BABS AND LIZA DO IT AGAIN:
A Star is Born and *A Matter of Time*

Barbra Streisand's brilliant turn in *On a Clear Day You Can See Forever* was re-sparked in a very different musical which thankfully eclipsed the uninspired *Funny Lady*. *A Star Is Born* is a remake of a remake, and a continuation of a narrative trope of the rise and making of a brand new star as an established figure goes down. It is, for the most part, a fast paced and sizzling rock'n'roll extravaganza, co-starring the enigmatic Kris Kristofferson who oozes sex appeal (women all across America

353

responded to him in masses). Streisand plays a sexually hungry and sexually charged character with multiple dimensions, and above all else an intelligence and complete dedication to her craft. She and Kristofferson have an alluring chemistry, and when locked together in their artistic passions they write songs that support one another (albeit Kristofferson being incredibly pessimistic about his own). The results are intoxicating. These moments in the film are far more interesting and genuine than the endless sequences involving the two superstars embracing in a tub, driving across dusty plains and building their home away from home. Those sequences (usually presented as montages) bog the film down and are unnecessary, and most offensively they take a harmful detour from an otherwise perfect movie about artists falling in love, becoming addicted to each other and career success.

Barbra Streisand watches the action take shape in *A Star Is Born* **(1976)**

Streisand gets a taste behind the camera on the set of *A Star Is Born* (1976). Later she would go on to direct a number of films

The original 1937 *A Star Is Born* starred Janet Gaynor as Esther, a small town farm girl who dreams of becoming a movie star. She travels to Hollywood with no money but a heart full of dreams, and meets Fredric March who plays an actor she greatly admires but whose life is ravaged by alcoholism. In 1954, Judy Garland took on the role as the star on the rise and her relationship with an alcoholic James Mason. In this version, directed by George Cukor, this movie musical took a major step forward for the entire genre: it generated a legion of musicals that looked, felt and sounded just like this incredible, ground breaking film. The 1970s brought to the story the excesses so prevalent in the decade's rock arena spectacle, and the result is, for the most part, great. It is not, however, anywhere near as rich in character, plot, style and broader importance to the genre as a whole as the previous Garland/Mason/Cukor masterpiece.

There are some inspired moments in the 1976 version, such as when Kristofferson first meets Streisand. In this wonderfully directed and performed sequence, drunk and eager to drink more after pissing off his audience and then redeeming himself at a packed out concert, Kristofferson goes to a seedy bar where Streisand performs with her band The Oreos. "You're blowing my act," Streisand says to him, encapsulating how utterly devoted she is to her work, and how unimpressed she is with the loutish, drunken tomfoolery of a reckless rock star. It foreshadows what is to come: Kristofferson will nurture and support Streisand, and she will desperately try and involve him as best she can. From the moment Streisand sings out "I Want to Learn What Life Is For," Kristofferson is hooked and watches her with joy in his eyes. He sees an artist unaffected by excess, the dark side of show business and the monotony of being a rock star in high demand. Throughout the scene, Kristofferson is interrupted by fans that want a piece of him, but all he wants to do is drink and watch Streisand. In a small role, future horror movie icon Robert "Freddy Kreuger" Englund makes a great impression as an aggressive Kristofferson fan who ends up in a fight with him. It leads to Kristofferson being chased out with Streisand racing after him, excited by his hyper-masculinity. In his limousine, Kristofferson continually compliments her: "You're one hell of a singer," "You've got incredible eyes" and so forth, while Streisand rattles on (as she tells him, she talks a lot when she's nervous). So begins a tumultuous relationship cemented in drama as it swims through the darkness of alcoholism and self-destructiveness.

One of Streisand's previous non-musical films *The Way We Were* (1973) allowed her room to showcase her dramatic talents, and her complex take on that material granted her performance nuances that seemed impressively natural and organic. Here, however, there is a certain element of strain in Streisand's performance: she looks out of her depths at times, and the film screams a little too overtly with "I want to connect with the rock'n'roll audience and make a mark in the youth culture." Her acting is stifled and awkward in places, but Streisand's voice is still a marvel, and her connection with Kristofferson is electric. Although critics panned Streisand and Kristofferson's on-screen romance, she cannot be flawed vocally with her moving, booming and iconic voice. Her voice has a smoothness and soulful energy that brings numbers like "The Woman in the Moon" (written by the legendary undisputed king of the 1970s movie musical Paul Williams) to a level of brilliance, a song where it is impossible not to get chills. Streisand is a siren with a rich desperation, and her voice is the true star in this film about doomed lovers and artists.

Streisand's personal background seeps through into this film, even more so than it did in *Funny Girl*. Here, she is thrust into the world of 1970s rock'n'roll from her humble origins as a nightclub singer. This makes the transition more believable, but outside her singing, it causes some tensions within her performance. Thankfully, her majestic voice counters this. The rock festival circuit is a different forum for someone like Barbra Streisand, but she makes it her own. Something excites her about it, and this comes across in the moment where Kristofferson refuses to play at Native American benefit concert, instead bringing her onstage where she embodies the tension between an artist both unprepared yet totally ready to win over a mass audience.

Streisand originally wanted Elvis Presley to perform the role of the superstar rock'n'roll legend besieged by alcoholism, but the King of Rock'n'Roll succumbed to his own real-life tragedy when he died the summer of 1977. Kris Kristofferson fares remarkably well in his place. His reckless behaviour is supposedly for the audience, yet it seems to bore, concern and ultimately mock them. He is self-destructive because he is a depressive alcoholic, but he wishes to give Streisand an opportunity because he strongly believes in her, despite being so troublesome to those around him. He also bears witness to the sexism in the industry and the disposability of popular music. Kristofferson wants Streisand to not only become a star, but to take over from where he leaves off. He is obsessed with involving her in his life and having her be a part of his world, but at the same time his world is crashing down around him. This is most visible in the scene where he is lying in a large Hollywood swimming pool surrounded by sycophantic assistants with who he is out of synch and disinterested. He throws himself into the water, submerged into the depths to escape the high demands placed on him, all the while thinking of this curly haired Jewish girl who sings her heart out in a bar full of loaded people who don't *hear* her. It's up to him to get people to listen, and he does.

"Are You Watching Me Now?" is a terrific song, but used at *ad nauseam* to highlight Kristofferson's disinterest in continually playing it. It's one of those numbers that annoys artists because it seems to be the only song that audiences can't get enough of. Right at the start of the film he performs it and stops mid-way, claiming the audience has heard it hundreds of times. He puts on a monster mask (his band do too) and performs another song that the audience eventually warms to. The masks are grotesque, reflecting how success can shape (or misshape) performers: while Streisand blossoms, Kristofferson sinks into ugliness with his continuing hard drinking and drug abuse. At the end of the film when Kristofferson's path of self-destruction has taken its toll and he is killed in an alcohol-fuelled car crash Streisand belts out "Are You Watching Me Now?" (since recorded by many artists, including Tina Turner on *The Sonny and Cher Comedy Hour*) with seductive nymphet-like softness as a passionate tribute to her departed lover, it is magical and delivered with demented genius. In this moment, a star is truly born.

Kris Kristofferson and Barbra Streisand in *A Star Is Born* (1976)

Streisand watches direction and focus on location for *A Star Is Born* (1976)

Kristofferson walks through his drunken stupor with ease, and his self-loathing is palpable. He is over life, but shares his final moments with someone he believes in more than loves. His performance seems effortless and he looks at ease when he scorns his adoring fans and refuses to perform: it's as if Kristofferson himself enjoys the idea of this "fuck you" behaviour almost too much. His animalistic, drugged, panther-like performance is enigmatic, but the actor will soon sink his teeth into a far more intense and sombre role in the complex and moody Yukio Mishima adaptation, *The Sailor Who Fell from Grace with the Sea* (1976), released around the same time. In a terrific supporting role in *A Star Is Born*, Gary Busey plays Kristofferson's manager, always on-hand a narcotic to pick up the booze-riddled musician. Two years later, Busey would take centre stage in one of the greatest rock biopic performances ever to hit the silver screen in his masterful creation as the title role in *The Buddy Holly Story* which we will get to soon.

Another *A Star is Born* co-star is the gifted Sally Kirkland, who remembers the film well:

> Marion Dougherty cast *The Way We Were* for Barbra and she brought me in and I got the part of Pony Dunbar immediately. Unfortunately the scene that they hired me to do with me and Barbra never made it in the film; the scene had the two of us walking down the street on the west side of New York, and she was deaf in one ear and I was deaf in one ear and we were crashing into each other laughing and then finally the director Sydney Pollack called out "Cut!" and Barbra turned to me and she said "I like you, you're a klutz like me!" That's a direct quote from Barbra. And so that lead to Barbra wanting me to be in *A Star Is Born* and again the scene that I was supposed to be in was cut. Originally, I had a lot more to do in the film than what you see in the final cut. I was the Rolling Stone reporter, doing my job to get her on the cover. In both situations Barbra was lovely to work with, I had heard rumours that she was very difficult to work with but I didn't find that at all as far as I could see. She was a sweetheart. It was a blast working with her and working on those movies lead to me playing the Nurse to her Juliet in a production of *Romeo and Juliet* at the Actors Studio where I studied. It wasn't a whole production of the play but it was all the scenes between the Nurse and Juliet. She was so excited because she had never been to the Actors Studio and we both approached Lee Strasberg and I said "Would it be OK if Barbra could do a scene with me?" and Lee said "Sure, but Sally don't worry about the age, just play the character, play

this nurse to this kid." So Barbra and I both just played the essence of the characters rather than their ages. So, I went to Barbra's house in Bel Air and she had a big pool and we rehearsed and improvised what it would be like if I were a nurse and she were a bratty kid. And at one point she tried to get me into the big pool while I had all my clothes on and then we did something called emotional recall on what it was like for her when her father died when she was six years old and after a while I put the script in front of her so that when she was talking about Romeo to me she started crying and was really thinking about her father. So she said in her Playboy interview that doing *Romeo and Juliet* at the Actors Studio with me was one of the highest points of her life so that made me feel great. I saw her at the Hollywood Bowl concert backstage in 2013 and when she saw me she called out "Romeo and Juliet!" straight away so clearly there's a little chapter of her life right there and I am indebted to her because she was the first person to hire me to go out to Hollywood. When Barbra did *Yentl* in the 1980s and there is that great scene where she is singing "Papa Can You Hear Me?" and she's crying, well, all that she learned from me in that I taught her how to feel comfortable crying on cue. I remember we spent a lot of time doing exercises involving her father. Once she took me to a deli in West Hollywood and she bought me all these different kinds of cheeses; she loved to go to Jewish delis and we got to know each other well during those times. I remember I had gotten to know Kris Kristofferson through Bob Dylan who was a friend and it was fun seeing him again. A lot happened in 1976, Bob was around Kris quite a bit and Kris was around Barbra a lot and I remember we shot the scene where I'm taking her photos in a huge house. Both Kris and Barbra are such great actors and method acting means a lot of truth and they played off each other just great. I met Paul Williams back when I did *Cinderella Liberty*. I used to host these big parties and he was a guest. That movie was another example of my scene being cut, I guess they felt that my part was just far too S&M. I was a hooker and Mark Rydell told me to go down to the docks and buy all these S&M things and then I had this scene with James Caan which was an incredibly sexy scene, but I think it was cut because it would have gotten in the way with the relationship stuff that goes on between James Caan and Marsha Mason. I had a whole strong of those movies where you just see me for a second. I played the cashier lady in *Blazing Saddles* and I said to Mel Brooks "Maybe I should do this uncredited" which was very silly, but I was very lucky to be in all these great movies. The 1970s was such a great time. It seems as though I went from one great big movie to the other until I went into independent film. I am a workaholic and have to keep working so when work wasn't coming my way I would jump on board with someone like Roger Corman and get involved in the independent film scene. I just wanted to keep working. And then *Anna* happened and that changed my life. Roger taught me a lot. He had me cast for him and then he trained me to be a director. He wanted me to direct *In the Heat of Passion 2* but the dates for that shoot conflicted with the dates I had to get my breast implants removed. But he had taught me all about producing and I went on to produce six films. Roger has been a complete mentor for me and I am also the godmother of his eldest daughter Catherine. Being a method actress helped a lot when I worked on a Roger Corman film. These movies are shot in very short periods of time so with all that method training I was able to get to those emotional points in time to play out the scene, without the training it would have come across as fake.

As much as "Rain on My Parade" from *Funny Girl* is an incredible example of Streisand as a musical diva, her beautiful tone and sharp ear in the creation and delivery of "Evergreen" (which she co-wrote with Paul Williams) is sheer magic: a melodic, airy and melancholy song that can be performed with playful whimsy as depicted in the film with

Kristofferson, or played as a straight solo and fuelled with quiet, sad tenderness.

As good as the film is; there is so much room for it to be better. In *A Star Is Born*, Streisand shines only when she sings: her character is an ill-fit, even though in a film like Vincente Minnelli's *On a Clear Day You Can See Forever* she is an unstoppable force and a powerhouse of talent. Perhaps Minnelli was so brilliant a director that he could provoke that range from Streisand for his film, but in his follow-up (and last motion picture) *A Matter of Time*, his delicate genius got muddled, and there is an overwhelming sense that this master had lost his sense of artistic and cultural beauty. He had one more opportunity to tell a story in the classic Minnelli way, but the film seems tired and painted by numbers.

A Matter of Time is an awkward film, with little of interest other than the novelty of it being a collaboration between father and daughter Vincente and Liza Minnelli. It is a tragedy that the only film that he directed his daughter in was this one, a staggering, uneventful and wafer thin piece, a disconnected celebration of the Golden Age of Hollywood which was well and truly over by 1976. He attempts this through flashbacks, flash forwards and everything in between, but the end result is shambolic.

With the MGM of yore effectively a closed-up shop, Minnelli approached associates of MGM's distribution line American International Pictures, who were incredibly successful for mostly low-budget horror and science fiction films. AIP's golden years were during the 1950s under the rule of the flamboyant and enigmatic Samuel Z. Arkoff, but were still going strong during the early 1970s with drive-in hits as *The Abominable Dr. Phibes* (1971), *Blacula* and *Frogs* (both 1972) being box office smashes. To work for a Hollywood legend like Minnelli appealed to Arkoff and his company, but creative differences between them caused great stress, and the film went from a smooth ride to a bumpy road. Minnelli eventually finished the film, but refused to see the final cut as he knew he would not be happy with it.

Liza Minnelli was by this time a massive superstar, and is let down in this production, but not by her father. When she pours out her heart on screen in *A Matter of Time* it is all pure, and when she screams and wails it sends cold shivers down your spine: there is nothing half-assed about her performance in this otherwise ill-conceived movie. We are left with fragments of a performance from an actress who was spectacular as a disfigured mental patient in Otto Preminger's *Tell Me That You Love Me, Junie Moon* (1970) and of course *Cabaret*. Long-time devotee of Vincente Minnelli's work Martin Scorsese would pay tribute to the golden age of movie musicals with his extremely dark and confronting *New York, New York* (a film we will get into soon) which starred Liza, knocking the socks off her "Papa."

Sally Kirkland tells a lovely anecdote about Liza Minnelli:

> I got to know Liza quite well, I had met her in the 1960s. When I was nominated for Best Actress for *Anna,* I was being interviewed by an incredibly cruel woman who grilled me and tried to make me look stupid, and Liza sympathized with me and tracked me down and gave me a beautiful pin that had belonged to Judy Garland and she said, "You wear this to the Oscars." From then on we became buddies and she would invite me to wherever she was going and then she wanted me to coach her because she was doing this trilogy on television and really wanted to learn how to cry on cue. And we worked on her father and memories of her father Vincente Minnelli, and when she did her big Vegas show she would show clips of her father on a big screen and she would cry as she performed. And at one of those shows she said to the audience "My acting coach is here tonight." That made me very happy and very proud.

INNER CITY PUNK AND OUTBACK BAUM:
The Blank Generation and *Oz*

The heart of the American punk rock revolution beat in New York City, and venues like Max's Kansas City and CBGBs played host to eclectic bands that screamed and shouted the war cries of alienated, angry youth. Bands such as the dynamic, ferocious The Stooges, the hyper-energetic Blondie and the big loud fun of The Ramones contributed to a scene that was dirty, urban and rejected the structures that governed how American rock'n'roll was popularly conceived. Media blackouts and the refusal to compromise and enter the mainstream was standard practice amongst the punks of the early to mid-70s, and the bands that came to give voice to these inner city working class kids. These were not the same the slum kids that populated *West Side Story* or who would soon turn up in *Grease*, for they were "real" (in all senses of the word). These gutter-dwelling punks rejected acceptance and consumerism, and were instead passionate about creating art through a spirit of destruction. Punk wanted to rattle cages, express anger and cause riots through its own unique mode of artistic expression.

Punk was a burgeoning scene in inner city New York, but it manifested globally, from Europe to Australia. Fanzines, screen printing, sculpture, theatre, music and filmmaking were employed as artistic practices by indie punk artists who wanted to give a face to their own experience. Andy Warhol and his Factory were integral in the formation of the punk movement in America, and his troupe embraced artistic expression and street culture. Muscular and handsome hustler turned epitome of the male aesthetic Joe Dallasandro made a huge impression in underground arts circles, and along with debutante drop-outs such as Edie Sedgwick and Andrea Feldman and cardboard box dwelling culture vulture creators such as Holly Woodlawn, Candy Darling and Ultra Violet, the origins of the punk movement had a cinematic quality and a language all its own. Warhol peers such as John Waters with his Dreamlanders (consisting of artists and performers like Mary Vivian Pearce, Edith Massey, Cookie Mueller, Mink Stole and the drag superstar Divine) created their own punk cinema—a celebration of trash and trash culture, a new kind of "divine decadence" colored in bright cartoony broad strokes and littered with dog shit and pink flamingos. Alongside Warhol and Waters were punk filmmakers Amos Poe and Ivan Kral who pioneered not only the indie punk film, but indie film scene in general. Poe, a native to New York, was inspired by an underground scene in the slums and backstreets of New York while the last of the hippies were still hoping for world peace and slowly becoming relics in their own political and social identities. Poe emerged into a world of seedy bars, dimly lit tiny venues with low ceilings covered in grit, grime, dried vomit and the eternal stench of beer. Joined by European filmmaker Kral who fell in love with the nihilistic zeal of bands such as Television and Talking Heads, Poe began to shoot what would eventually be *The Blank Generation*: a DIY punk rock document about a number of bands that came from art punk, NYC hardcore, American nu-vogue and the filthy underground obsessed with popular culture, apathy and anarchic angst.

The film is shot out of synch, and jolts from image to image and scene to scene without any kind of structure. Some of the footage is barely watchable, the sound falters and fades on occasion, and the editing is messy and nonsensical. But all of these are strengths, not weaknesses: *The Blank Generation* is a marvel. An exercise in pure punk rock perfection: there is nothing phony, contrived, ill-conceived or patronizing about the film. It is made with a genuine acute interest in the essence of punk, its sensibilities and its revolutionaries.

The Patti Smith Group whine and wail as Smith herself thrusts about like a sea-witch washed up to shore and covered in seaweed. Blondie front woman Deborah Harry epitomizes punk, and adds a sense of pornographic glamour. Harry is an astounding talent and beauty, and her pitch marries perfectly to the trebly guitars of Chris Stein and the primitive complexities of Clem Burke's drumming—all these musicians mastering their instruments effortlessly and intelligently. The New York Dolls bring 1970s va voom to 1950s rock and doo-wop with their agitated "up yours" sensibility, while The Shirts front woman Annie Golden (who would later go on to star in the film adaptation of *Hair*) bounces like an excitable puppy looking for a playmate and a glimpse of a leash that will guide her outdoors. Violent energy is bought to leather jacket-clad life with The Ramones who are captured beautifully, as is the artsy intellectualism of acts such as Talking Heads who introduce a science fiction element (not to mention a bizarre creepiness) to the film. Johnny Thunders, Jerry Nolan, Iggy Pop and the others who made the New York punk scene what it was appear in Poe and Kral's film as the new poets of a drug-fuelled city underground, driven by an anger that comes across as a spewing hate. *The Blank Generation* is essential viewing for counter culture enthusiasts and music lovers alike, and a document of one of the most important youth (anti-) movements that ever culminated. The way the filmmakers present this scene is perfect DIY ruthlessness and the result of pure, haphazard genius. This is far more than a rockumentary: it is a piece of history that never experienced any of the spotlight that films like *Woodstock* did.

On the other side of the planet, Australian punk rock was itself a force to be reckoned with. It was dangerous, aggressive and fundamentally pub-centric, a vibrant and brutal menace. A film that somehow channelled this into a workable plot is the rough and tumble *Oz*, a take on "The Wizard of Oz" set in the world of Aussie pub rock. *Oz* is a noteworthy achievement in Australian cinema and yet a continually overlooked. It blends a distinctly Australian brand rock'n'roll with the road movie, and cements it within the confines of the 1939 *The Wizard of Oz*. Directed, written by and co-produced by Chris Lovfen, the film tells the story of a sixteen year old rock 'n' roll groupie who hits her head in a touring van and falls deep into an unconscious state. When she wakes up she is in a fantasy world that is gritty and mean, while still similar to the world she is used to. This is a clever play by Lovfen, who tricks his audience into believing that his heroine is not in a fantastical Oz that his audience would expect. Rather, he gives her a landscape as barren and as dusty as the outback she is accustomed to. When combined with the fantasy elements, these realistic surroundings heighten the bizarre turn of events that will soon unfold.

Australian rock'n'roll meets The Wizard of Oz in *Oz* (1976)

Joy Dunstan plays groupie Dorothy with a vivid sensuality and an honest, working class earthiness. When she awakens from her accident and realizes that she has accidentally killed a thuggish hoon, she is torn between pensive reflection and a restrained, nervous strain. It is a subtle and nuanced performance and one that Australian film goers (and the rest of the world) really should champion. The thug's violent brother wishes to avenge his death and follows Dorothy through the film. He becomes increasingly sadistic and even tries to rape her on a number of occasions, granting the film a malicious edge. But this is necessary for such a dirty pub rock musical/pseudo-fantasy tribute. Dorothy's plight is strange: she wishes to see the elusive and enigmatic Wizard (Graham Matters), an androgynous glam rock superstar. It appears pub rock is becoming stale for groupie Dorothy, who wishes to branch out and experience something new. The glam rock fad had of course hit Australia, and Melbourne (the locale of *Oz*) was strongly affected. But it was a grittier scene; dirty and undignified, unpolished and still pertaining to a pub rock sticky carpet sensibility. There is an acute authenticity here, and Dorothy's quest is a significantly cultural one.

Newly visible Australian gay culture is also represented in *Oz* when Dorothy meets the ultra-camp clothier Glin the Good Fairy (Robin Ramsay) who gives her a pair of ruby red slippers that will assist in her journey to the Wizard. At the time, gay sensibilities in Australian art circles were as traditional as meat pies and football. Television was riddled with gay in-jokes and theatre was loaded with drag and "poofter" gags: Glin the Good Fairy is an extension of all of this. He is a commodity, a left-over sissy helper to the heterosexual heroine. He is joined by fellow queens who "Oohh" and "Ahhh" with permanently limp wrists and swivelling hips: later mainstream Australian cinema would become even more increasingly obsessed with gay lives with films such as *The Sum of Us* (1994), *Priscilla Queen of the Desert* (1994) and *Head On* (1998) gaining success at the box office and international praise.

Oz takes place in a world of stereotypes and side show freaks, and Dorothy's Scarecrow, Tin-Man and Lion take the form of a brainless surfer dude, a heartless mechanic and a cowardly biker. With music by Ross Wilson (from popular bands like Daddy Cool and Mondo Rock), *Oz* is a captivating and carefully constructed ride that while not as revered as a film like *Mad Max* (1979), it deserves a place in both Australian film history and in the broader cannon of Oz-inspired movies. Two years later, *The Wizard of Oz* would be re-imagined on the big screen again but with a completely different take: instead of Ozploitation, it will be told through the eyes of Motown and urban Harlem in *The Wiz*, a film we will get to shortly.

CINDERELLA LIBERTIES AND OTHER OUTINGS:
The Slipper and the Rose, Sparkle and *Rock'n'Roll Wolf aka Mama*

The Slipper and the Rose is a sophisticated and appealing musical retelling of the Cinderella story, notable for being requested as the Royal Command Performance for 1976 (a big deal seeing the film was relatively low-budget and hurried, and far from a hit at the box office). What it delivers, however, is a beautiful score and some of the most underrated songs ever written by the imitable Sherman brothers. The lyrics are urbane and cheeky, and this modern twist on the classic French fairy tale is made all the more alluring and sexy for it. Songs like "What Has Love Got to Do with Being Married?" and "Suddenly It Happens" are perfect examples of a style of wit from a bygone era: not from the 1970s as such, but rather inspired by the likes of the Great American Songbook. This is a movie musical that owes more to Gershwin and Cole Porter than to rock'n'roll or whistling-in-the-dark melodramatics.

Musically, it is a triumph for the Sherman brothers who deliver one of their finest works. There is something so organic about the narrative progression and the way the story is structured: it travels along a pulsating rhythm while maintaining a delicate balancing act between songs that successfully move the story forward with attractive synergy. The plot complicates the Cinderella story by adding characters with their own motives and dilemmas around our put-upon heroine, but the familiar elements are captivating enough to feed into this dual narrative structure. Over-simplifying this aspect would hinder this new take on the much-loved and continually told (and remodelled) fairy tale, and its complexities give the film a more meaningful, stronger edge. The romance in *The Slipper and the Rose* seems to be born from the Sondheim musical: in his works, people are disenchanted, lost, anxious and alien as they long for acceptance and security. The Cinderella fable lends itself to this kind of thinking as characters lose things, forget their importance, deny who they are, pretend to be happy and comfortable, don't live up to expectations while at the same time desperately wanting to. The bleak world of the devastated and loveless infiltrates this musical that tries desperately to remain light and bright, but thankfully even with its grandiose exuberance and joyous glamour, this Sherman brothers musical is a descendent of the sombre operettas from the turn of the century. That being said, there are many moments throughout where the mature content recedes behind saccharine silliness that lives outside the songs and tampers with the book elements of the film. When characters stop singing, the magic dies: this is a magic that is not always escapist and fun, but it is a magic conceived by an overwhelming sense of loss and despair.

The cast for the most part do their job with style and seeming ease. Richard Chamberlain may seem to be too old to play the dashing Prince, but he exudes warmth and a charismatic command so his less-than-youthful appearance can be excused. Gemma Craven as Cinderella prefers to play up a serene demonstrative princess-to-be rather than a whimsical hopeful. Although the film's focus is her plight, struggles, hard work and her rise above adversity, Craven downplays the heroine as a survivor and favors a more airy approach. Her Cinderella is wistful and lonely, and this carries through the numbers even outside of the songs that do not focus her isolation such as "Once I Was Loved."

Despite a few moments so sweet they can send you into diabetic shock, *The Slipper and the Rose* is lavishly designed and engaging, and a perfectly realized adaptation. It is also masterfully in charge of how it plots the songs, which are the definite highlight of the film. The Sherman brothers tap into the realm of adult-themed children's entertainment that they were already well accustomed with having written mature material in the guise of family fare such as *Mary Poppins* and *Bedknobs and Broomsticks*. Some years later, Sondheim himself (along with talented playwright James Lapine) play with the world of fairy tales and add a degree of psychoanalysis into the mix with their clever and equally dark musical *Into the Woods*, which would get a Disney filmic interpretation in 2014.

At odds with the graceful but at times overly sugary take on one of the world's most favourite fairy tales in *The Slipper and the Rose* is a film that still employs the Cinderella legacy. It is all about dreamers who struggle, work hard and who ultimately get their wishes fulfilled. But these dreamers end up suffering the fate of many shining stars who fade out all too quickly.

One of Hollywood's greatest film editors Sam O'Steen directed *Sparkle*, and he had worked on masterpieces such as *Who's Afraid of Virginia Woolf?* (1966), *The Graduate* (1967) and *Rosemary's Baby* (1968). His directorial effort is loosely based on the rise and fall of the Motown R&B singing sensations The Supremes. *Sparkle* certainly adheres to the Blaxploitation category that sought out urban black audiences (as well as curious and culture-vulture whites) during the decade, and is as gritty and as visceral as its non-musical counterparts. O'Steen's direction is pensive and reflective as he navigates a fine line between harrowing and joyous, and his take on the musical biopic is never compromised. There is an eagerness to tell his story, an almost overzealous energy that wants to prove artistic integrity and gain respect. As an editor, O'Steen had an innate understanding of what was necessary in a film, but there are points in *Sparkle* that hit a brick wall. Things get stuck and when they finally peel themselves off, the injuries are far too noticeable. Sadly, a lot of the excess that should have been omitted creeps in and becomes a distraction, a shame because it jeopardizes the comparative earthiness that levels out the story of four sisters running after a dream.

The rags-to-riches motif deserves careful handling, and for the most part there is a necessity to like characters that go from poverty to eventually hitting the road to stardom. If we don't care about these people whose ambitions can be quite easily perceived as selfish and self-serving, then we don't have a winner. O'Steen channels some terrific performances, most notably from Irene Cara (who later went on to blow critics and audiences away with her turn as Coco the *triple-threat* in Alan Parker's *Fame*) who throws herself into the role of the titular Sparkle Williams. She sings up a storm and goes through hell and back while wowing audiences alongside her talented sisters. Some of the greatest moments in the film deal with its most depressing material: drug addiction, domestic violence and racism. These themes in this performance-heavy film bring the story home: when the movie becomes preoccupied with these social ills and its

371

effects on these artists on the road to success, it is where O'Steen's handle on his material is the strongest.

Musically, the film is a triumph. The singing is electric and the orchestrations are stunning. Motown is alive and well in *Sparkle,* and the enthusiasm of 1970s-era R&B is captured perfectly in this low-key and sadly ignored motion picture musical. But there is something lacking in the way the film unfolds and presents itself and there is an uncertainty in its efforts and an overwhelming sense of "I have to do justice to this story if it kills me" hanging like a cloud over its director. *Dreamgirls,* a musical that hit the Broadway stage in the 1980s with an eventual film adaptation in 2010, is clearly inspired by *Sparkle* and is a sanitized variation of the story, yet it still manages to be better even in its shiny, polished drag. The fairy tale elements of *Sparkle*—a Blaxploitation take on the Cinderella mythology told in Harlem—should have been developed with more confidence, but with all its ill-conceived portions outweighing its more successful sequences and set pieces (such as when Lonette McKee is spotted with bruises on her arms by her sisters in a scene that plays out naturally yet melodramatically), it falls flat far too often to stand proudly in its glass slippers.

Other fairy tales would get the musical treatment, but far from Harlem and America. The Russian musical *Mama* (sometimes known as *Rock'n'Roll Wolf)* is the epitome of bizarre: and this is a good thing, because if was a straightforward child-friendly fable then it would lose its creepy appeal. Loosely based on a Brothers Grimm fairy tale about a wolf who tries to mimic the voice of a goat to seduce her kids so he can kill them and eat them, *Rock'n'Roll Wolf* is an endearing and lavish production that champions anthropomorphic animals in a very literal sense, years before Andrew Lloyd Webber did a bunch of chorus kids up as alley cats in his musical adaptation of T.S. Elliot's poems. This story is dark and complex, yet at the same time supposedly geared towards children which—much like *Bugsy Malone*—can sometimes seem misguided. This is a world of very adult themes, and the story should not to be taken lightly: it is about the seduction of innocence and a play on Saturn in retrograde with the elders eating their young. While in America audiences were celebrating the dawning of the Age of Aquarius, in this Russian/Romanian/French co-production, Saturn is in full force: youthful vibrancy and energy is seen as a threat, and it must be controlled, destroyed and devoured by those living in a perpetual fear of change.

Folkloric rock opera in *Rock'n'Roll Wolf* **(1976)**

The film's opening credit sequence showcases the talented acrobats, singers, dancers and ballerinas we will soon meet, donning their animal attire and painting on their bestial faces. Already the film elevates itself above the usual anthropomorphic excursion into the woods, as here the children in the audience have had the magic removed from the outset and are forced to witness performers becoming animals. There are sheep, birds, and woodland critters such as reindeer and so forth. The main players—the animals that have solos and provide structure and have well developed character traits—include a much lauded travelling parrot, a sympathetic but ultimately mean donkey, and Titi Suru, a wolf played by enigmatic Russian superstar Mikhail Boyarski, who is obsessed with devouring the children of goat Rada (played by the lovely Lyudmila

Gurchenko). On top of this is a strange sexual attraction between the wolf and the matriarchal goat, a wacky sexual "dance" that plays out through the musical with rhythmic nuance and borderline sadomasochistic exuberance.

In the early moments of the film, the duo flirt and discuss their concerns about the goat children disturbing the wolf in a playful manner. This soon changes as the movie employs very adult and dark themes like loneliness. One of the children asks his mother if it's bad to be lonely, to which his mother replies, "It's not bad, it just doesn't make you feel good." Some scenes later she sings to them the famous number from the film, "Mom is Home" which is reprised multiple times throughout the movie and enforces the notion of safety and tenderness bought on by togetherness. In this musical, the idea of loneliness and isolation leads to the desire to kill, while closeness and a sense of family helps build communities. When the wolf sings it to the children, pretending to be their mother and tricking them to open the door so he can slaughter them, it is a perversion of the bond shared between mother and child. In doing this, the musical examines the disturbing notion that the interruption of parental importance can easily occur and disturb familial unity for good.

Politically, the film is a commentary on the naiveté of newfound establishments and movements being tricked and diminished in importance by a roguish old force and a set standard that dismisses and wishes to destroy the equilibrium that these baby goats champion. In the nursery rhyme styled "Equilibrium," Rada's young celebrate their youth, and yet seem to not have any control over the lyrics: it is as if they have no real concept of what they are singing about. They have a simplistic notion of free thought that will eventually put them in jeopardy. Their youthful counterpart, the wolf's nephew, is an outsider, but unlike his aggressively violent and hungry uncle, he is eager to share the equilibrium and become part of the fabric of a community that needs to co-exist in order to thrive.

There are some terrific set pieces within the film, such as where the wolf and his misfit band of predators chase after one of Rada's children and race through the picturesque settings. There is a real sense of danger here, as the wolf in all his malice desperately wishes himself to tear the goat apart. This scene is complicated further because of the sexual nature underlying it all: throughout the film, the wolf and Rada are intrinsically linked in this way, as if the predator and the prey need each other in order to sustain a healthy eco-system. But in this musical, sexual deviance is also at work. This adds to the menace of the wolf to her children, and there is a weird sense that if Rada is not interested in succumbing to the wolf's seductive "dance," then the children will suffer the fate of being metaphorically and literally being devoured. Rada's denial may have dire results for her precocious and precious young. Another interesting element to the film is the role of the parrot who continually announces to a calypso beat, "Tickets! Tickets!"; selling various lifestyles and therefore selling a diverse range of fateful events to his animal associates. He is a guest of the village and represents structural change: he is another threat to the stoic and stubborn Titi Suru and his friends.

Complementing the darkness of this strange film is the music itself. Some is incredibly catchy with its unusual rock and pop kookiness and a schizophrenic nature: the diversity in its musical stylings is outstanding. The songs range from straightforward 1970s punk, whimsical lullabies, stadium rock, folk and country. For another musical this could be a disaster, but for *Rock'n'Roll Wolf*—with its bright colors, grandiose sets and assortment of critter-folk—it works a treat.

1976 was an eclectic bag of mixed of tricks, some that revolutionized filmmaking in general, others that introduced new styles and approaches and others that were underrated benchmarks in the history of the genre. The musical was becoming as diverse and as versatile a genre as horror, which still boasts an array of subgenres (the eco-horror film, the slasher film, and so forth). Musicals were becoming just as multifaceted, however many critics and audiences alike were oblivious to this: it was if the word "musical" was bad language, a term people associated with nostalgia that provoked disinterest and unwarranted and incorrect assumptions of irrelevance. Would this attitude change in 1977? Two major movie musicals opened that year which would cause quite a stir: one both celebrated and exposed a dark side to the big band era, while the other ushered in the disco inferno but buried within it the devastating emptiness of youthful disillusionment, embedded in its working-class trappings...

1977

"Send in the Clowns"

Swedish Sensations, Sondheim's Swedish Farce, Friendly Dragons and Mice on a Mission

1977 WAS A LANDMARK YEAR FOR MOVIE MUSICALS. DISNEY RELEASED two moving and yet remarkably subdued films with *Pete's Dragon* and *The Rescuers*, director John Badham delivered a gritty and blunt urban drama around a new craze in the world of disco in *Saturday Night Fever*, Martin Scorsese revisited the big band era and injected it with cynicism, nastiness and brilliance in *New York, New York,* and while not as epic perhaps, Stephen Sondheim has another musical adapted into a film directed by long-time collaborator Hal Prince with *A Little Night Music*. Although all these films would be eclipsed by George Lucas's space opera/Western hybrid *Star Wars*, they were all diverse in tone and texture. A melting pot of musical drama and satire was emerging, and new stars were on the rise.

John Travolta would inspire masses of urban youth to hit the streets in polyester and to throw themselves into emerging disco culture, while Scorsese would impress audiences with an electric disdain for the human experience with his increasingly interesting and complex filmography. Taboo subject matter was slowly becoming the norm, as concerns with sex and violence became part of the everyday lexicon of cinema during the 1970s, especially in films set in big North American cities. A nastiness and brutality permeated the mean streets of places such as New York—the birthplace of the American musical—and this was reflected on the screen.

Beyond the harsh realities of the adult world that were translated into a musical context were films geared more towards children, such as *Pete's Dragon* and *The Rescuers*—both moody and melancholy pieces in their own right. Disney weren't the only studio jumping on board this sudden trend towards maudlin child entertainment: Joe Raposo (head songwriter on the Jim Henson produced *Sesame Street*) wrote the songs for *Raggedy Ann and Andy: A Musical Adventure*, which made a note of the new breed of "latchkey" kids that was part of the 1970s cultural mindset. *Emmett Otter's Jug-Band Christmas* by Jim Henson and his team soulfully explored economic struggle at a time of recession and uncertainty. Divorce rates skyrocketed during this period, absentee fathers made their mark, and the apathetic cry of the alienated teen culminated in a split between punk rock and disco. The rock'n'roll musical flourished on stage as an antithesis to middle class theatre, with shows like *Grease*, *Pippin* and *Evita* both dividing and unsettling audiences, and stretching the theatrical form boundaries even further.

These three Broadway musicals each in their own way tapped into the broken family. In *Grease*, parents are absent and therefore clearly dysfunctional: it is a stage whose characters are rebellious rock'n'roll kids who are out of control, sex-crazed lost causes. In *Pippin*, the hero's relationship with his father is plagued by failure and disappointment, and when he is forced to marry the lovely but ordinary Catherine and to father her son, he becomes lost and is nearly talked into committing suicide. *Evita* is a musical biography of the Perons' rise to power in 1940s Argentina, and there is an overwhelming implication that the titular protagonist Eva Peron becomes the "mother of the Argentine," a role she is committed to, but ultimately betrays through corruption and an increasing turn to fascism. Audiences were shaken by no-hope teens, and dismayed at motherhood's turn towards monstrous egocentricity.

It was on the silver screen during this period that musicals more directly addressed families—especially the rising number of families that were shaping outside of the nuclear model—who lived beyond the city that never sleeps. Audiences of these movies were from the suburbs, often young mothers left to fend for themselves and their children post-divorce. During the late 1970s and early 1980s, these single mothers were affected by emotional and financial worries, and had to work hard to keep their families happy and healthy. It was in these films that their children (and themselves) could find a place of refuge for their children for a short moment. Cinema was an escape, and in the dark they could watch dragons and mice make dreams come true and who could take care of the problems their little ones faced, at least for a little while…

IT'S NOT EASY TO FIND SOMEONE WHO CARES:
Pete's Dragon and The Rescuers

Two Disney features were released in 1977 and did great business, one a gently told story about two mice who become unlikely heroes in America's south, and the other a Christ-like tale celebrating friendship between a boy and his dragon. Both films differed in narrative construction and delivery, but both were remarkably similar in tone, meaning and their shared sense of tenderness.

Pete's Dragon opens with a beautiful instrumental medley of the songs that we will soon come to know as the camera steadily drifts across an oil painting of a town called Passamaquoddy. This film is far from the golden age of Disney, but it is still as charming, tender and as captivating as earlier live-action/animation hybrids such as *Mary Poppins*. It borrows from *Mary Poppins* in that it tells the tale of a messiah-figure and his soon-to-be enlightened, and this incurably romantic film does so with such majesty and beauty that it is a joy to watch. *Pete's Dragon* is a sweet parable about friendship and the importance of family. Despite some minor narrative hiccups, it is a thorough delight.

The idea of animated characters and humans sharing screen time was not new (remember *Bedknobs and Broomsticks* hosted some of the greatest examples of that ever put to screen). By the late 1970s, this was a skill Disney had developed to perfection: Elliot the dragon is such a wonderful creation that at times you forget that he is only a number of animation cells interacting with the gifted Sean Marshall, who plays Pete. Elliot feels like a living, breathing dragon, and with his unintelligible mutterings and cute, expressive face, he is the epitome of a lonely child's best friend. Animator Don Bluth was in charge of the team who would create Elliot, and Bluth's tender touch and flair for elegance fuels this beautiful character with such precision that we are left to wish the loveable creature had even more screen time. Bluth would leave Disney after the completion of *Pete's Dragon*, taking a team of animators with him to create his own company that would later do odd jobs for filmmakers: this included delivering animated sequences for films such as *Xanadu* (1980), and rich, full length features like the fantastic *Anastasia* (1997). *Pete's Dragon* was a perfect launch pad for Bluth to pave his own way beyond Disney.

The opening number is "The Happiest Home in These Hills," a delightfully demented piece of song writing by the talented Al Kasher. Both the melody and the internal rhymes are intoxicating. The fabulous Shelley Winters leads a crew of hick mountain people who are after Pete, and are presented as gleefully grotesque. When they end up in the mud, it adds to their ghoulishness—these people are subhuman! There is nothing glossed over or overtly sugary or nice and safe in *Pete's Dragon*: thankfully, children's films in the 1970s at least did not pander to over-sensitive, highly strung parents wanting to protect their offspring from what they deemed "unsuitable." In this decade, in terms of screen culture, children were allowed to be threatened, and not kept out of danger's way. Winters and her family of crooks are scary, descendants in a way of The Child Catcher from *Chitty Chitty Bang Bang*. They are unrelenting, without pathos and hell bent on capturing innocent children for their own benefit. A few years later, children are mercilessly chased and tormented by adults in other musicals such as *Ginger Meggs* and *Annie* (both from 1982).

The second song in *Pete's Dragon* is "Bop Bop Bop Bop Bop (I Love You Too)," a whimsical and charming number with a strong pop sensibility. Elliot is a beautiful companion for young Pete, but he is more than that: he is the embodiment of Pete's confidence, and representative of how Pete can relate to the outside world. Pete insists on Elliot's invisibility not only out of fear of what the townsfolk of Passamaquoddy would think, but in response to his own insecurity as a child lost without parent figures.

Helen Reddy on location for *Pete's Dragon* (1977)

The loneliness of childhood and the longing for family and self-empowerment is examined in *Pete's Dragon*, at the cusp of a number of other films that would be released about little boys with absentee fathers (*E.T. The Extra-Terrestrial* being one of the most successful). But the 1970s featured a number of movie musicals that focused on isolated and lonely children who learn to love. These young people discover how to be true to themselves through a magical force, often embodied by loving guardian angels or other best friends that vary in shape and form. In *Charlotte's Web* for example, the sensitive Fern finds solace in her pet pig Wilbur. In *Raggedy Ann and Andy: A Musical Adventure* the little girl is lost without her enchanted toys, a theme that recurs again in *The Many Adventures of Winnie the Pooh* (1977), where Christopher Robin is alienated from child peers but finds companionship with his loving stuffed toy animals. Sean Marshall in *Pete's Dragon* embodies this lonely and imaginative child figure, a staple character in 1970s cinema (especially in movie musicals). Pete is delicate, sensitive and aware of his surroundings. He longs for warmth and acceptance, which he finds in Elliot the dragon but soon discovers it in the very real loving embrace of warm but lonely Nora (Helen Reddy) and her loveable alcoholic father Lampie (Mickey Rooney).

The film constantly reminds us that Elliot is possibly not real, and rather an extension of Pete's alienation and determination to find a home. When Elliot finally appears before the other characters, it is the film's way of telling us that Pete is an honest little boy, and that his dragon can enlighten and touch the lives of everyone as long as you have faith. This notion of believing in yourself and in the importance of magic slowly resurfaces as the years go by in musicals and non-musicals, rendering the "age of not believing" that Angela Lansbury lamented in *Bedknobs and Broomsticks* as distinctly past tense. Cynical musicals started to take the backseat, with whimsical, character driven narratives on the rise (especially in the realm of child-centric cinema).

Performance wise, *Pete's Dragon* showcases some great work both on and off screen, but the screenplay sometimes gets bogged down with repetition. This impedes character development to some degree, in what is otherwise almost a perfect little film. Mickey Rooney's Lampie is a delight, and his youthful exuberance is fun to watch: this diminutive

Shelley Winters gets lit in *Pete's Dragon* (1977)

show business icon with gigantic talent is as dynamic as he ever was in the Arthur Freed musicals of the 1940s. Onna White's choreography is charged with excitement and finesse, and while nowhere near as elegant or dynamic as her magnificent work in *Oliver!*, big stagy numbers like "I Saw A Dragon" are a highlight, taking place in a tavern filled with booze-downing Seabees, climaxing with exploding beer kegs. Helen Reddy as the haunted Nora is as earthy and as lovely as Sherry Miles was as Nancy in *Oliver!* but unfortunately the writing leaves her little room for nuance. Nora is a lonely woman who mans the lighthouse with her dotty father—she is a nurturing, diligent woman. But her character is not allowed to blossom into something vibrant, a problem with the writing and not in Reddy's otherwise excellent performance. Although a singer, Reddy is a more than competent actress, and her vocal work in the film is outstanding, so it is sad that this potentially excellent character is given the short end of the stick in terms of her growth and the dynamics of her story arc. This is even more unfortunate because Nora ultimately runs the show, but instead of being a multi-dimensioned protagonist, she is saddled as the pragmatic workhorse. Homeliness is a tricky characteristic to satisfactorily capture in Disney features, but even the maids in *Mary Poppins* had a kind of pizazz and brightness to them. Sadly for Reddy and her soothing, warm voice, she is given a very ordinary role.

The sombre tone of the situation Nora finds herself in still compliments the moroseness of the part, however, and her longing to be loved is beautifully paralleled with Pete's. This is apparent with the song "It's Not Easy," a masterfully handled number that is staged so simply, yet provides tender insight into both Nora and Pete. Here are two people who have found each other, and here in the lighthouse—a building used to lead ships to shore, reuniting the sea bound with the land—these two isolated characters come to understand that life and love are most certainly "not easy." When Pete describes what his dragon Elliot looks like ("He has the head of a camel, the neck of a crocodile"), Nora takes it with playful acceptance, as she recognises the child's friendship with the mythical beast because of her own desire to hold onto something out of reach and as intangible. The lyrics are charming and work on a number of levels, as Nora sings "Now that you have him, hold him, treasure him from day to day." While singing about this supposedly fabricated dragon, she is also lamenting her own personal angel, her absentee lover, a sailor believed to be missing at sea. Later in the film, Lampie scolds Nora for not "being realistic" about her dreams of reuniting with her lost man, reminding us of the film's determination to examine the blurring of reality and fantasy. Although Elliot does materialise for Nora and Lampie to physically see, the idea of these two jaded adults coming to accept Elliot is about a lot more than their discovery that Pete was telling the truth all along. Instead, Nora and Lampie now have the things *they've* been longing for, companionship and clarity: through Pete, Nora has her seafaring beau and Lampie has stopped drinking. Elliot represents these things and is the catalyst to the beginning of believing.

Along with Shelley Winters and her family of cretins who want to use Pete as a slave, the secondary villains of the film are the showbiz charlatans who peddle phony remedies. These two are straight from vaudeville, human realizations of Pinocchio's bestial theatrical villains Honest John the Fox and Gideon the Cat in that they play out a dominant and submissive role through camp slapstick. These characters are a major problem in the film, as two sets of villains is completely unnecessary, especially when Shelley Winters and her crew are so delectably evil in the opening number. These secondary villains (secondary only in order of appearance and not in screen time as they come to dominate the film) mean Winters and her crew recede off-screen- until late in the picture, leaving the screen time for villains who are not nearly as interesting or as horrific. Jim Dale and Red Buttons play these crooks who peddle phony elixirs and the like with energy and exuberance, and once they hear talk of a dragon they wish to capture and use his body parts to capitalize on. Their performance is humorous and busy, but ultimately uncalled for. Although they get terrific songs like "Every Little Piece" (highlighting what dragon ears, eyes and so forth can do for humans with perpetual ailments) and "Passamaquoddy" (showcasing their knowledge of fictional and not-so-fictional towns), they are a distraction and a lazy attempt at unnecessary comic relief. As great as Dale and Buttons are, their characters are not as creepy or as menacing as Shelley Winters and company. Although the Winters role is small, her presence is overwhelming as she wickedly grins with a repugnant set of rotten teeth and soiled, round cheeks.

Actress Sally Kirkland remembers Shelley Winters and recalls working with her on *Pete's Dragon*:

> Shelley Winters was sort of like a godmother to me. She had introduced me to Roger Corman and I had introduced her to Robert De Niro. There was one night where Shelley, Roger, Bobby and I went to go and see a movie I made called *Coming Apart* with Rip Torn and Viveca Lindfors and then *Bloody Mama* came out from that evening. Shelley was amazing, she taught me how to be strong and how to survive without a man, how to mix drama and comedy at the same so when the audience thought they were going to laugh they would cry and when they thought they were going to cry they would laugh, and she taught me to be much more politically aware. She introduced me to Martin Luther King and she was working with Bobby Kennedy and got me involved and always said that all actors should understand what's going

on with the world and be politically active. She took me in when I was about eighteen and I was her assistant, teaching her lines from around 1962 while she introduced me to all of Hollywood. I became her caretaker years later when she was dying, and I was there for her up until the moment she died. I taught Shelley Winters her lines during *Pete's Dragon* and this is where she introduced me to Jeff Conaway who of course went on to do *Grease*. He and I dated. There were a couple of people I dated thanks to Shelley.

Comedy is muted in *Pete's Dragon*, and is not specific to the mugging madness of Winters and company. However, the film's quiet, solemn moments are mostly its strength. The sombre conversation about "being realistic" between Rooney and Reddy culminates in the elegant (but far from perfect) song "Candle on the Water," performed with tenderness and heart and became a hit song in its own right. Sadly, the flat direction of the number undervalues its message so it feels like an uninspired music video, unfortunate when so many possibilities remained unexplored. Much like "Cheer up Charlie" (the forever—and unfairly—bemoaned song from *Willy Wonka and the Chocolate Factory*), a different take on "Candle on the Water" could have proved beneficial. Perhaps instead of the stable shot of Nora standing at the lighthouse rafter, she could have been filmed climbing the tower and reaching the top, looking out to the sea—this surely could have provided a more thematically appropriate and far more uplifting and momentous ending. Nora gets most of the songs and one of the best is "There's Room for Everyone," which comes right after the fishermen declare that Pete is a jinx and bad luck. This upsets the maternal and nurturing Nora, and she sings that "there's room for everyone in this world" (even dragons). This is indicative of the 1970s sensibility regarding inclusion. What Nora is really saying is that there is room for everyone: blacks, Caucasians, Asians, African Americans, Hispanics, gays, straights, the poor, the wealthy, etc. *Pete's Dragon* is the most socially aware Disney film of the 1970s as it talks about acceptance and family-building. It also embraces the simple things in life, celebrated in the spirited, beautifully shot number "Brazzle Dazzle Day." Reddy, Rooney and Marshall clean the lighthouse and parade around cheerily, singing about simple joys like running through a meadow barefoot and so forth. The number is significantly the first song that is not antagonistic, does not serve the plot explicitly, is happy and not maudlin and—most importantly—it doesn't mention Elliot the dragon. Here, young Pete has found a home—a real mother and a real grandfather, and as the film moves forward, he will soon also find a father in Paul (Carl Bartlett) who is rescued by Elliot and reunited with his beloved Nora.

The most moving moment in the film is where Elliot has to say goodbye to Pete. This scene saw children and adults alike wiping their teary eyes with sweet surrender. As a Christ-figure, Elliott has to metaphorically die (which he does when he is symbolically captured and made redundant) and then resurrect (when he returns as a hero to save the entire town). He also has to move on and enlighten future generations, and in this film's case those generations are the child audiences that will follow. When Elliot farewells Pete, he is continuing his beautiful and important work that assists children in growing up into happy souls, free from unease and potential abuse, free from isolation and most importantly, free of the threat of growing up too fast. Elliot celebrates the importance of being a child, and this is the film's most powerful and poignant element. These thematic concerns will be revived again in *E. T. The Extra-Terrestrial* where little Henry Thomas as Elliot says "Ouch," touches his heart and then bids farewell to his alien messiah who ascends to the heavens leaving his new disciple empowered and enlightened.

Of all the elements that link the film to the specific experience of childhood, it is Pete's insistence that Elliot remain invisible. He says this at the start of the film when the duo are trying to hide from Shelley Winters, and again at the end when Elliot flies off to help another child. This is an important, subversive message, underscoring the fact that childhood wonderment, innocence and "pure imagination" is personal and comes from within. It is a sanctum of secrecy and wishes, a place only little kids can see, hear and feel. Just as Elliot in *E. T. The Extra-Terrestrial* explains to his younger sister Gertie (Drew Barrymore) in reference to their new alien friend who hides in their closet surrounded by their stuffed toys: "Only little kids can see him." *Pete's Dragon* lets us know that the most important magic is that which is unseen and unfelt by the jaded and morally bankrupt adult world, and only grown-ups kind hearted enough to let child-like bewilderment and beauty in will be allowed to "see" and experience this magic: these include Dee Wallace's Mary in *E. T. The Extra-Terrestrial* and Nora and co. in *Pete's Dragon*.

Pete (Sean Marshall) and his dragon in *Pete's Dragon* (1977)

Pete's Dragon is a beautifully made and cleverly told allegory of the story of Jesus Christ, and although while weaker in some ways than *Mary Poppins*, it ultimately knocks it out of the ball park with its sweet sensitivity and quiet hope. The final moments of *Pete's Dragon* see Pete and his new family racing across the hillside, echoing the sentiment of "Brazzle Dazzle Day"—waving goodbye to Elliot who flies through the sky ready to rescue another child at risk of losing their innocence. This same kind of magic will permeate movie musicals to come in the latter period of the decade: angst ridden downbeat endings will start to fade, and bittersweet melancholia with cheery and teary-eyed rapture will begin to dominate the movie musical.

Although this cynicism was starting to lose momentum by 1977, *The Rescuers* somehow still incorporated a degree of it into its otherwise optimistic adventure tale. Once again, it is a film about a lonely isolated child lost spiritually and emotionally, and it is also another Disney film (although this time a traditional, fully animated feature). *The Rescuers* is sombre and has a maudlin dynamism that permeates it unapologetically, but there is also a breezy richness to it. This is Disney at its most clearly unaffected: there is a steady disinterest in what audiences or critics and even children want to see, or what they might think or say. It is painted in honest colors with ruthless individualism, and it is a spellbinding beautiful film that also did exceptionally well at the box office. With its adult themes, its dramatic dark energy and its sophistication, the movie won the hearts and minds of its audience without the studio or the artists involved pandering to the overtly saccharine. *The Rescuers* makes its point with a firmly outstretched arm, and never shies away from subtlety with its muted designs, story and characterizations.

Penny (voiced by Michelle Stacy) is a little girl who is kidnapped, and the film does not withhold the perils she is about to face. It remains the job for a secret collective known as The Rescue Aid Society to help the orphan girl, and they must do it fast! The twist is that The Rescue Aid Society is made up of mice from around the world: Hungary, Africa, India, and so forth. Among these brave little critters who risk their very own lives to protect and defend innocent children is Miss Bianca (elegantly voiced by Eva Gabor), a glamorous. adventure-loving rodent who chooses as her partner Bernard (Bob Newhart), a stammering and nervous janitor mouse. Together they set out to rescue Penny in the dark recesses of the Bayou where our human heroine is held captive by the menacing and maniacal Madame Medusa (feverishly brought to life by the voice of the fantastic Geraldine Page).

When the old cat Rufus who is a friend to the kidnapped Penny says "faith is a bluebird that you see from afar," it makes an explicit sense of vague hope that permeates the film. Goodness and hope are just out of reach, and that we have to suffer and be held prisoner before we are granted any semblance of a happy ending. The movie presents some muted comical moments, such as when the mice clamber about a large briefcase, running through dark corridors where they are dwarfed by even a box of matches. Ultimately, however, the film pushes us into corners where we are forced to face up to the fact that we need to suffer before we can learn or truly believe in anything. Jonah and the Whale is a strong influence on this Disney mice-to-the-rescue motion picture, and the grim realities of human selfishness, self-involvement and bullying are made all too real. This is why *The Rescuers* is so brilliant.

Artistically, the film takes surprising risks. The color palette is overblown and dense, there is a thickness to the detailing, and Milt Kahl's work is lyrical yet leaves a nice sense of unease. The animation genuinely makes you feel slightly off-centre, a difficult feat to accomplish but that works tenfold here. The movie avoids feeling unfinished or lacking finesse, and instead reeks of a conscious strain, the fruition of a kind of realized rawness. The backgrounds are unique, more stunning for their very unconventionality. They are for the most part painted in lush pastels with a grainy creaminess that resembles an aged oil painting.

The film was the first of Disney's animated features to spawn a theatrically-released sequel with *The Rescuers Down Under* (1990) which boasted some lavish imagery and scenes that were the polar opposite to the moodiness of the original. There is even a much-lauded sequence with an eagle soaring through the outback, hovering and swooping over and under caverns and cliffs that reflected Disney's changing focus at the beginning of the 1990s, where big spectacle and highly dramatic set pieces became their primary focus. In the original *The Rescuers*, however, this is not a concern: story and intimacy dominate, but do so quietly.

Madame Medusa is a fantastic villain, and she is animated with such splendid outrageousness as she mopes about and throws tantrums. The scene where she removes her make-up, gleefully peeling off her fake lashes with an almost masochistic flair, is inspired animation. Geraldine Page's vocal talents are fabulous, yet this character is never hyper-real. There is a subdued rage within her and a simmering violence that never gets out of control. There is a consistently nuanced sliminess to her wretched villainy.

Musically, *The Rescuers* has the distinction of being the first Disney animated feature since *Bambi* (1942) to have the most important songs performed outside the main action: in other words, these songs aren't sung by characters populating the film's central storyline, but are sung by an off-screen voice (reminiscent of a Greek chorus), much like the choir singing about the changing seasons in *Bambi*. The songs themselves are not a highlight of *The Rescuers*, and in fact the film could quite successfully be songless. It is a rare occasion in a Disney film where the story is

Splash sheet for Medusa from *The Rescuers* (1977)

so strong on its own that it could survive without the aid of musical accompaniment. This does not mean that there are not successful songs in the film: "Tomorrow is Another Day" is a delicate song that recalls Joni Mitchell with its whimsical folk vivacity, and marries well with the dramatic imagery that accompanies it such as the dark and foreboding sky that Orville the seagull glides through, carrying our rodent heroes. Orville is a great addition to the film, but it didn't need designated comic relief—the film could have been even more risky if it decided to leave out such a character (Medusa's fat associate Snoops seems to fit this buffoon role already). The darkness of *The Rescuers* is penetrative and real: when Medusa leads her pet alligators to capture young Penny there is a genuine sense of danger. This darkness would continue to inject itself into later Disney fare with *The Black Cauldron* (1985) which possibly went too far, seeing that it flopped at the box office and scared children away from animated features (at least for a little while).In the end, *The Rescuers* asks what can two little mice do? And the answer is: plenty.

LONELY CHILDREN AND THEIR TOYS:
Raggedy Ann and Andy: A Musical Adventure
and *The Many Adventures of Winnie the Pooh*

With its surprising psychedelic energy and its equally surprising unsettling visuals, *Raggedy Ann and Andy: A Musical Adventure* is an extraordinary little film from the Bobbs-Merrill Company, a publishing firm based in Indianapolis who were integral in releasing the works of authors such as Ayn Rand. This bizarre fact aligns neatly with this surreal and subversive animated musical which features unapologetically oddball elements across its story, animation style and songs.

Opening with a live action sequence that features a little girl Marcella (Claire Williams) running out of her school bus and hurrying home with her rag doll Raggedy Ann, the movie is permeated with a dreamlike eeriness. The live action scenes in the film (which are minimal) are 1970s bliss: the sun-kissed autumn leaves, the bright yellow school bus roaring off, and little Marcella racing to her bedroom, her secret haven, complete with a sign that reads: "Marcella's room, members only." Aesthetically, these celebrate an era addicted to made-for-television dramas, ABC and CBS specials of the week and the midday matinee that dealt head on with issues such as divorce, shoplifting, child kidnapping, drugs and so forth. What also makes the film similar to many of the other child-centric musicals of the 1970s, however, is that Marcella herself is a lonely child, isolated from her peers and her parents. Although we hear her mother (or who we assume to be her mother) call out for her to "get ready for her party," we never see her or the supposed friends that will attend this celebration. Instead, we are presented with a solitary girl with a highly developed imagination and sense of self-reliance. She epitomises the second wave of "latchkey" children, and although we don't get any real insight into Marcella, we gather that she is a child well aware of the double edged sword that comes with early independence. In her sweet, touching performance there is a sense of weighty responsibility and overwhelming loneliness. Marcella is never seen with other children and her mother exists off screen, and although she is supposedly having a birthday party to celebrate turning seven (something that sits in the background of the course of action involving Raggedy Ann and her friends) she is never around other human beings. Instead, she prefers to surround herself with her dolls.

Marcella's dolls are a collection of misfits, all dedicated to their child-mistress's happiness. Leading the group is Raggedy Ann (voiced with warmth and sincerity by Didi Conn), an eternal optimist. When she sings about the things that she has seen in the outside world, she is rapturous as she explains that everything is lovely and exciting. The other toys sit around doe-eyed listening to her. Raggedy Ann is a heroine caught in a decade of cynicism and disbelief, and even though films such as *Pete's Dragon* encourage audiences to give themselves over to childlike wonderment, Raggedy Ann is continually tested by the nihilism that surrounds her. Even her brother Raggedy Andy (voiced by Mark Baker) is cynical and jaded, constantly bemoaning anything that he doesn't see fit to be worthwhile. He is the perfect counterpart to Raggedy Ann's outlook of eternal sunshine. Raggedy Ann epitomizes Nellie Forbush's song "Cockeyed Optimist" from *South Pacific* (1958), but unlike the Rodgers and Hammerstein wartime heroine, she is not given a near-the-end-of-act-one character attribute that makes her unlikeable (in Forbush's case it was racism). Instead, Raggedy Ann remains loveable and kind throughout. Some may argue this could be problematic for a character who is supposed to run the show and to develop, grow and learn, but not here. Raggedy Ann is the tale's anchor, and she is strong *precisely* because she goes from strength to strength. She begins bright and nurturing and ends up heroic and enlightened. Her love for her fellow toys, her brother and Marcella is palpable and honest, and plays out with respect and elegance. She is pragmatic, dutiful, kind hearted, intelligent, resourceful, and sympathetic, and a great believer in solidarity.

Raggedy Andy is also a terrific character and also rather complex, but deviates substantially from the simplicity and warmth of his ragdoll sister. Andy is driven by a preoccupation with gender difference: in a nutshell, he is determined not to be a "girl's toy," and he is continually defending his masculinity throughout the film. This zealous upholding of his rough and tumble masculinity is an important element of the film, and Andy insists that he is not interested in playing with Marcella. He is frustrated at being swamped by so many "girly" toys. Andy comes from a backlash against feminism that was beginning at this time, and Andy's bizarrely acceptable misogyny is at the very least a backlash against the fear of femininity and a female-dominance that ultimately emasculates boys and men.

Raggedy Ann and Andy: A Musical Adventure was released during a period where divorce rates were climbing and single mothers were doing what they could to raise sons on their own. If *Bambi* (1942) dissected the loss of innocence where mothers can die and fathers can be distant and scary figures, then this film explores a vision of boyhood housed-in, feeling misunderstood, underdeveloped and fearful of the feminine. This animated musical examines the defensive nature of boys and the nurturing kindness of girls, and although it is told as a female-centric story, it spends a lot of its time devoted to male characters. These male characters are not standards from the "Raggedy Ann and Andy" legacy, but instead they need our heroine's help in order to re-enter a loving, caring and equal world. Raggedy Ann's job is to make everyone around her happy—she is the eternally sacrificing, selfless angel that empowers characters who are devastated by depression and unable to believe in themselves.

There is an obsession across 1970s characters in animated features and other children's entertainment of being "different" or "not-quite-right," and *Raggedy Ann and Andy: A Musical Adventure* is no exception. The curse and gift of being a misfit pops up consistently in kid-friendly fare, and it's always up to our beloved hero or heroine to make sure that those feeling unlike the others believe that they are special just the way they are. Lyrics such as "as different as we can be" as sung by Raggedy Ann, suggest the importance of individuality and celebrates diversity. With children's TV shows like the remarkably successful *Sesame Street* making powerful statements worldwide about all kinds of children, it makes sense that feature films would employ the same loving notion of togetherness and unity.

This obsession with curing the despair in the different is however a slight narrative hindrance in *Raggedy Ann and Andy: A Musical Adventure*. One major issue with the film is the fact that Raggedy Ann and Andy are more reactionary than active. They seem to exist in a perpetual state of response rather than proactivity: in other words, it's up to the other characters that they encounter such as the Camel (Fred Stuthman) and the Greedy (Joe Silver) to move the story along, while our heroine and hero listen and watch. When they offer solutions that will allow the community to feel happy, accepted and meaningful (so much of this film takes on the friends of Dorothy motif used in *The Wizard of Oz*) it is quick and we move on to meet more characters. The film assumes that we already know all there is to know about Raggedy Ann and Andy, and this is unfortunate, because these two would have been even more loveable had we known more about them.

But ultimately, none of this matters when we get a film that looks and sounds like this one. Visually, it is quietly revolutionary. Although the film was considered unfinished as it was subject to budgetary restrictions as money ran out during production, the look of the final product is enthralling and has something to offer audiences with a taste for 1970s psychedelia. It makes sense that the film left a massive impression on children of the late 1970s and 1980s who grew up with it, who now in their adult years reminisce about it and recall how hazy and how "drug-influenced" the film looks. The music is complimentary to the direction and the design; the songs by the very gifted Joe Raposo (who made a career out of writing for *Sesame Street* and *The Electric Company*) are quirky, curiously constructed numbers that both move the story along and delve into character and themes about difference. "Candy Hearts and Paper Flowers" is 1977's answer to "For Me and My Gal" in a way, a song that celebrates unity, togetherness generating safety, giving and loyalty. The lyrics express a liberating knowledge of whimsy within the dark elements of loss, and this kind of "whistling in the dark" is soulfully plotted into the film, and a perfect example of the 1970s movie musical at its best.

Although the plot moves slowly for a film supposedly for children (and is rather long), none of this matters because the charm and slight creepiness make it a must-see. This is a dark fantasy, and it makes no apologies for it. The story is simple but is generated with intelligent and crafty complexity as it follows the arrival of Babette, a new doll from France, who has moved into Marcella's bedroom. During this period, France was the ultimate symbol of romance—you would find many film and TV shows featuring young girls going to France, meeting a French boy, falling in love with the idea of France and so forth. Babette is presented as a delicate beauty. Initially, "Poor Babette" is a melodramatic operatic number as the doll laments while Captain Contagious breaks free from his snow globe and kidnaps her, prompting Raggedy Ann and Andy to rescue her. Other characters include twin dolls who are bizarre and freaky. There is also a pincushion Jewish Yente-type, a southern grandpa puppet and a neurotic and fretful jester marionette. Originally some of the characters that feature in the film were considered far too disturbing for children, and critics claimed that the film became distracting because of their design elements. For example, the Greedy is an insane invention and shows the film at its full blown psychedelic best as it morphs into numerous shapes and consumes everything. LSD-fuelled, he is a creepy and monstrous entity, and his lasting impact is palpable and grossly weird. There is also a great sequence that reads like an old Max Fleischer cartoon where Raggedy Ann and Andy descend into a pit and enter a black and white silent movie where frantic ragtime piano dominates, and no singing or talking is allowed. When they re-enter the world of 1970s psychedelia, they meet King Koo Koo the king of the loonies—yet another incomplete character—and it's from here that the plot picks up and the frenzied animation begins to serve the story.

Structurally, the film has some wonderfully engaging and inspired elements such as certain characters being presented as villain or victim and then having it turned around that they are in fact the opposite. They surprise us once again by turning them inside out and forcing them to redeem themselves. Babette turns out to be a double-crossing power hungry meanie, but of course thanks to the forever-moral Raggedy Ann, Babette comes to learn from the mistakes she makes and redeems herself. Captain Contagious has far too little screen time to be a properly developed villain but when he needs to be evil, he does so with gusto. But we are turned on our heads again when his lustful leanings towards Babette—he is smitten with her and there is a shockingly sexual nature to his attitude to her—turn into gentle romantic courting. In fact, after Contagious and Babette redeem themselves, the duo become lovers— live-in lovers no less!

The final moments of the film are its most disturbing in a cool and calculated way, placing again an emphasis upon Marcella's loneliness. She finds her dolls in the pond and collects them all, but forgets to pick up the Camel, who she doesn't know yet. This is a character who sings a number while a bizarre hallucination unfolds, harkening back to the "Pink Elephants on Parade" sequence in the exquisite *Dumbo* (1941). The mirage is unsettling but doesn't faze Raggedy Ann who welcomes the Camel into Marcella's bedroom and insists that her human friend will love him just as much as the rest of her toys. "We like him just the way he is" she tells the other toys who eagerly come to stitch the Camel up and "fix him." The film's central message lies in the importance of togetherness, but it never really offers unity for Marcella—the toys are unified and learn that loneliness can be cured. And even though Marcella seems to be a happy and healthy functional child, she is ultimately on her own and making her way in the world with the unseen help of her toy friends. The film is even stranger when you consider the background of the characters: Raggedy Ann and Andy's history is a rather sombre one. Artist Johnny Gruelle created Raggedy Ann in honor of his daughter Marcella (her namesake the name of the little girl in the film) who passed away at aged thirteen of diphtheria. This macabre background aside, the film is a fantastic example of freaky 1970s fun.

Actress Didi Conn did a beautiful job as the sweet and life affirming Raggedy Ann remembers the film:

> Oh, I loved the director Richard Williams In fact, he didn't eat, he was so frustrated, because he was such a perfectionist, and it was going on too long. I don't think he got to finish it the way he wanted to, because he was a revolutionary in what he was doing, you know with the colors and everything. And all that detail. I just loved him. I would say, that was one of my top three favourite jobs because Joe Raposo's music was so wonderful. And I didn't know that I was auditioning for an animated movie. It was one of the first real animated musicals—modern animated musicals. Of course later, we have so many after that, the Disney ones and whatnot. I thought I was going up for a Raggedy Ann commercial actually. They said 'Well, where's your music?' and I said "Oooh, sorry, but I can sing something if you'd like?" I think I sang "Where Is Love?" from Oliver! I was

in this little booth, and they said "Can you sing that again here with a little gravel in your voice? You know, have it a little more gravelly.' I said "Sure!" So I sang "Where Is Love?" and I turned around, because I was facing away from all the people in the booth—my microphone was facing the other way. I turned around, and literally everyone is jumping up and down in the booth with such joy and excitement! So that was great! And the way Richard conducted Mark Baker who played Andy and I was that he would come on over and hold our hands. We would be facing our music stands but he stood in between us and held our hands, and conducted us that way. It was just wonderful. I think I was a dancer in another life because I really respond to music. I move when I read or sing. My body just starts to move and I feel very, very connected, especially with good music. I have always been musical, even in school. So doing this was just something very natural for me. For the film *You Light up My Life*, I didn't know they weren't using my voice until I went to see the movie and it was a pretty traumatic experience and it stopped me from singing for a very long time. So I did do *Grease* and then I did the movie version of *The Magic Show* with Doug Henning, but it was tough and it kind of was heartbreaking when you lose the connection made between your head and your heart that comes our through your singing. The director of *You Light up My Life*, Joseph Brooks killed himself. He committed suicide and for some reason, all of a sudden I could breathe again, this just happened a few years ago. So now I'm singing again. It sounds bizarre, but it's just something that happened and has somehow restored my faith in my singing. In regard to *Raggedy Ann and Andy: A Musical Adventure*, everybody enjoyed the script, the music and the drawings that we were seeing. It was my first experience to have animators actually watching us while we recorded. You know, we see all the time now but Tissi David was the lead animator for Raggedy Ann and what I did with my hands is all in that animation. If I was scared,

I'd put my hands in my hair, or things I did with my facial expressions. She got it in and she developed this character. It was wonderful to see. She really captured the fact that Raggedy Ann was such a mother figure to Marcella. She was in charge of the nursery. But it was so wonderful. There was no jealousy, it was all out of love and protection that she goes on that journey. It's interesting to think about the children in these kind of movies. I have a son who is autistic, so I live with someone with a disability and someone who's behaviour is quote, unquote "different." My husband, David Shire, the composer and I have created an animated series, and every episode is a mini musical, so we created this show, and part of one of these characters actually is a non-verbal autistic boy. We put a child who is different, but who also is very much a part of the community. But with this film, there is a little sadness in my heart. Richard Williams wasn't able to finish it the way he wanted to. I haven't been in touch with him in all these years. I have no idea how he feels, but I think I might be feeling a little bit of regret that he had, but because I think it is so beautiful and he is a perfectionist. And I hope that he got his recognition, I think he has in animation world for being an innovator and a genius.

Another animated film that dealt with pensive daydreaming children and their toys was Disney's *The Many Adventures of Winnie the Pooh*, built around three stories that were originally bought to the silver screen earlier. It also featured a fourth instalment that had human child hero Christopher Robin having to leave his toy friends to start school. Once again, here is a 1970s animated musical that is sombre in tone and all about letting go, coping with separation and quiet sorrow. This final vignette is rich in tone and theme, but it is also the most morose. Even though Pooh promises to always be there for Christopher Robin whenever he needs him, we know that this period for this loveable bear is going to be one of the last. Winnie the Pooh and his friends will slowly recede in popularity, and whenever they'd be resurrected and bought back to life, artistic attention would be not as slick nor as charming, and certainly not as engaging or entertaining as it was during this golden age of Pooh adaptations.

The songs from the Sherman brothers are wonderful, and they piece together the vignette driven story with bright and cheery ease. Even the melancholy songs are still light hearted enough to have an airiness to them. The major flaw with the film is how the songs are treated: they aren't given a proper moment, and it is as if they're staged for the sake of a sequence transition or a shift in mood. As good as these numbers are, they are in service of the script and they don't save it. What results is an unremarkable film; labored and empty, flat and uneventful. This is the exact opposite of what you would want from a film about one of the most philosophical characters in literary history.

WHEN THE RIVER MEETS THE SEA: *Emmett Otter's Jug-Band Christmas, Wombling Free* and *Dot and the Kangaroo*

Right from the beginning, *Emmett Otter's Jug-Band Christmas* blesses us with soulful Americana through Paul Williams's song writing. Williams gave voice to the most diverse and excitingly fresh musicals of the decade with intelligence and heart, with classic songs written with seemingly effortless perfection. *Bugsy Malone, Phantom of the Paradise* and *A Star Is Born* are strengthened by Williams's music—whether a kiddy gangster film, a Faustian horror show or and second-wave retelling of an artist's rise and fall, these films all illustrate how a great song can truly illuminate the already sturdy base. When Williams brings his genius to woodland dwelling otters, badgers, foxes and gophers, it is again just as enthralling, mesmerising and unique. Williams never repeats himself, never compromises his craft and always delivers strong, whimsical, and powerful songs that urge us to surrender to a sentimental journey. When teamed with Jim Henson—the softly spoken, gentle genius and innovator of one of the oldest crafts in history—the results are spellbinding. *Emmett Otter's Jug-Band Christmas* is a marriage made in heaven, and the musician and master puppeteer show their devotion to the project by generating an energy, warmth and sophistication, creating a final product that is endearing and endlessly enchanting.

As is usual for the work of Jim Henson and his team of talented artists, the puppetry is truly beautiful. Although *The Muppet Show* (which was in its second successful year at the time) featured some imaginative and complicated work, this film exists beyond the vaudeville/variety structure and instead has a world formed by its own structural logic. If Kermit, Missy Piggy, Fozzie Bear and the other Muppets exist in a world pertaining to the stage, the presidium, the audience, the dressing rooms and backstage (and sometimes, rarely, even outside the theatre), then Emmett Otter and friends had an entire village to inhabit. This makes the film unique, because this isolated world is complex in design and it is refreshingly liberating both in terms of its filmic qualities and its grandiose scope. Henson would become increasingly attracted to challenging himself, expanding his horizons and branching out to never before seen new worlds throughout his career, be they fabricated mini-sets or on location. Here in this Christmas Muppet musical with characters that were someone else's creation, the sets and models are still amazing inventions, all beautifully conceived and never over stated. The naturalistic settings give the characters a gravitational centre, as they are allowed to exist without seeming displaced, out of the ordinary or there only for show.

Emmett Otter (voiced and puppeteered by Jerry Nelson) is a sweet-natured and resourceful boy, and his relationship with his mother is tender. It is a beautiful connection and based in and around their natural ability to create great music together. The duo sing terrific songs and their harmonies are inspired, the result of Paul Williams as a great song writer, but also as a fantastic storyteller. Jim Henson understands the nature of relationships like no one else, and with Williams by his side, he articulates a loving relationship cemented in the passion mother and son have for all things musical.

This relationship is a key ingredient in this fifty odd minute long feature primarily concerned with poverty and financial stress. Alice Otter (voiced by Marilyn Sokol and puppeteered by Frank Oz) is a selfless, loving single otter-mother. She is haunted by her late husband's foolish but well-meaning mistakes that left her and Emmett penniless. Alice cleans and mends clothes for little amounts of money, while Emmett helps out as well. For Christmas, Alice is inspired to buy Emmett a guitar, while he wishes to get his mother a piano, an instrument she used to love playing. These impoverished critters are given a chance to win the money they need at a local talent contest, which becomes the focal point of the film's second half. There is a great sequence that crosscuts between Alice and her friend, a muskrat named Hetty (puppeteered and voiced by Eren Ozker), and Emmett and his friends talking about the impending contest, and we get an insight into the loving relationship shared between mother and son beyond time they share on screen. For the most part of the film, these two are shown together, but when away from each other here they are still dedicated to each other's happiness, emphasising their loving connection. This fuels the story, and Henson and fellow puppeteers such as Jerry Nelson and Eren Ozker understand this and nourish it. Henson is devoted to constructing real emotions in his characters: he gives them pathos, respect, honesty, strength and compassion. But he never strays away from negative aspects like selfishness, bad attitude or disdain. This is epitomised in the film's featured villains, and these punk critters are fantastic: consisting of a bear, a rattlesnake, an iguana, a weasel and a fish of some kind who is ingeniously plopped in an extension of the hooligans' getaway car which is a tank of water. These angry and edgy menaces are from the wrong side of the tracks—a town called Riverbottom—and by the time of the talent contest, these disenfranchised beasties take to the stage with one of the best songs of the year. "Riverbottom Nightmare Band" is a celebration of angst, disrespect and violent disinterest in anything respectful or sweet. This is where the film finds its narrative centre, as the darkness that Jim Henson had already alluded to manifests with such energy and exuberance that it contrasts perfectly with the genteel tenderness delivered in the bulk of the film. To do this in one number is quite an accomplishment.

When these crass cretins win the competition, it obviously disappoints Alice and Emmett, but it inspires something that is even more meaningful—the kind of magic that can only really exist during the Yuletide season. Christmas as a musical festive time is a source of inspiration for dozens upon dozens of specials and seasonal films and television shows, and the 1970s were enthralled with it. During the decade, many Christmas specials and features popped up in theatres as well as on television, and this Henson-produced venture was just one of them. It also inspired new Christmas songs that would become part of the lexicon and fabric of seasonal festivities. Along with "Silent Night, Holy Night," many churches, schools and other institutions incorporated songs such as "When the River Meets the Sea," a number sung by Alice that appears in the middle of the film. We learn that it was her late husband's favourite, making the scene even more emotionally stirring. Emmett sings backup and helps build the song into something elegant and sentimental. It is sung with such graceful gentility and features subtle, spiritual undertones that give it an ethereal edge. This song becomes the thematic backbone of the story, and the plot device of material gifts—even when thoughtful, and reflective of the passion and love between Alice and Emmett—are rendered meaningless in comparison to the gift of song.

The film is a celebration of lower class unity, a kind of compassion birthed from poverty that finds itself in numerous films during the 1970s, most notably ones geared towards families and children. Rankin/Bass will employ this also, and animal-centric movies such as the following year's *The Magic of Lassie* and future Henson features all share this notion of good and honest poor people coming together to learn the true meaning of both Christmas and life in general through simple joys like music, love and understanding. Much like the rest of Henson's other work, the sentimentality comes thick and fast, but there is such sweetness, tenderness and warmth that it is impossible to not be charmed by the film.

Fox emcee Harrison Fox and his vixen wife, the glamorous Gretchen, are also terrific characters. For Muppet fans, it is also lovely to hear beloved Muppet performers lend their vocal talents to new characters, and Henson himself voices some characters here as does Gonzo's Dave Goelz. George and Melissa Rabbit are also fabulous: without dialogue , as they compete in the talent quest they are reminiscent of a young Judy Garland and Mickey Rooney knocking about and dancing to good time swing back in the days of the Arthur Freed musicals. This tribute is perfectly realized by Henson and Oz, furthered by Paul Williams's astute understanding and love for the golden age of the movie musical.

The film also featured two technical elements that distinguish it from *The Muppet Show*. Using marionettes was something that Henson seldom did on his TV show, but in *Emmett Otter's Jug-Band Christmas* there are many sequences involving characters strolling about as marionettes. The film was also one of the first to introduce remote control mouths, where a puppeteer would wear a mitten with ratio gears that would manoeuvre the facial expressions and lips of the character. Two years later, Jim Henson and his troupe of artists would go on to somehow re-create the magic of *The Wizard of Oz* in his magnificent *The Muppet Movie* (1979). Emmett Otter, his loving mother and their woodland critter pals helped that magic come to fruition as an experimental space for Henson's enchanting and enigmatic practice.

Wombling Free is based on the highly successful BBC television series *The Wombles* (1973-1975) which featured furry, loveable critters who looked like a bear/possum hybrid, who were obsessed with cleanliness and rallied against littering. This film adaptation doesn't add or detract from the charming series, and does little remarkable or different. Except, of course, for one major factor: here, the Wombles are no longer presented through stop motion animation (which in the television serious was both gorgeous and impressive), but are instead actors in costume parading around Black Park in Wexham with child entertainer Bonnie Langford who made a career out of TV specials and shows in England.

The film boasts a large number of songs, and in many ways, it might have been more interesting if it was written as a rock opera. If England was the birthplace of the legitimate and most successful rock operas with *Tommy* and *Jesus Christ Superstar* taking audiences and critics by storm, then a child-friendly and "nice" rock opera should have made sense: *Wombling Free* could have been the perfect choice. The songs are fun, but not necessarily memorable. They are sung with sincere enthusiasm, but tend to skim around a purpose and fall flat on their musical faces as the plot sleepily carries on around (rather than through) them. It is charming to hear Terry-Thomas singing, but because he is off-screen, it's difficult to completely feel his presence. Unlike the way he leant his voice to Sir Hiss in Disney's *Robin Hood* a few years earlier, here Terry-Thomas isn't given meaty material, and there is no delectable, devilish elegance in his Womble.

The Australian-made *Dot and the Kangaroo* is just as dull its British ancestor, *Wombling Free,* and its only charm lies in its innovative blending of live action and animated characters. This kind of filmmaking was popular during the 1970s, but here it is approached differently: the backgrounds are real, while the characters are animated. The backgrounds are the sometimes lush and sometimes dry and barren outback of the Australian bush, shot with a stark realism that gives the film a strange otherworldly feel when combined with the animated animals and the central figure of little girl Dot. Adding to the under-developed and mediocre plot is the fact that the songs are lacklustre, the humour is listless and the mood is unrefined and poorly conceived. *Dot and the Kangaroo* has a degree of charm, but little of anything else.

MORE CINDERELLA LIBERTIES (X-RATED STYLE):
Cinderella

Pornographic musicals continued to flourish in 1977, and yet another fairy tale was given the tits'n'ass treatment: this time, the legend of Cinderella. Here, the story of this much put-upon girl saddled with an oppressive step-mother and nasty step-sisters who dreamed of bigger and better things is granted a musical pornographic retelling, Cinderella (Cheryl Smith) is helped and guided by her fairy godmother (Sy Richardson) to perfect a laundry list of sex-acts in order to stand out in an annual orgy set up by a dweeb Prince Charming (Brett Smildy). After the orgy, the blindfolded Prince wishes to find out who this young damsel was that sexually impressed him, so he sets out to find the girl who fits the acts performed. This basic set up is simple and silly, and the film is both hilarious and nasty, typifying campiness and the theatre of the absurd. From this perspective, it fulfils its promise as an erotic journey, rather than a straight down the line porno.

Produced by Charles Band who made a career out of straight-to-video horror movies with the *Puppet Master* films being the most successful and well received, *Cinderella* is a lavish production boasting some of the most inspired comical and camp dialogue put to screen in this kind of film. Every element is (perhaps surprisingly) perfectly constructed, and much of the film's structure stems from a shock theatre perspective that made its mark in the seedy bars, nightspots and underground theatres in cities like New York and Los Angeles during the 1960s and 1970s. Shock theatre and its marriage to musical theatre is something that American anti-movement enthusiasts revelled in, as it delivered everything they wanted: it had all the traditional trappings (the book musical format, the songs, the dance sequences, the characters, the plot), but brought to it a

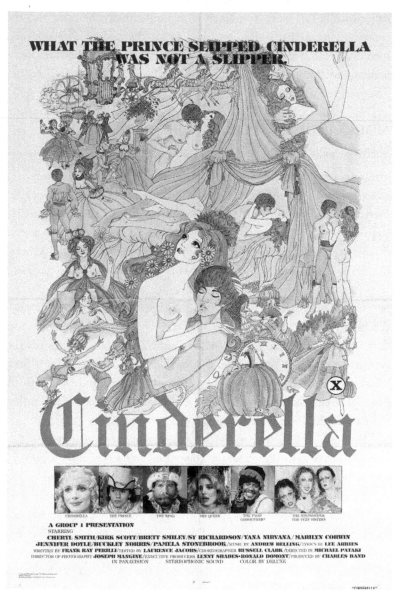

The poster art for the porno musical *Cinderella* (1977)

fresh, punk rock spirit that attracted interest from artists who would later evolve into shock theatre groups such as The Cockettes, Andy Warhol's The Factory and the Strewsberry Players as well as prolific and well respected writers such as Peter Weiss, Edward Albee and Harold Pinter. Shock theatre, punk theatre, Theatre of the Absurd and Dada enthusiasts would churn out works all over the globe, and this also spread to cinema. *Cinderella* is a perfect example, and as a highly stylized Grand Guignol musical porno, it is even arguably more bizarre than your standard shock theatre romp.

The art direction in the film is impressive, and garish lighting elements are used and mis-used, sets are painted with psychotic exuberance, flats and building platforms that one would see in a high school play and soundstages are used with all the intention of turning over a good product. Beyond the design aspect, performances are spirited, passionate and finely tuned. These pornographic performers know how to deliver camp and shock, and have a firm grasp on language, necessary because it is loaded with terrific dialogue that goes way beyond a standard blue movie. The power of the words is the most important focus in this musical—the sex scenes and the songs are nicely staged and enticing, but it is the book element of the film and its script that ultimately makes this film a cut above the rest.

DISCO INFERNO: *Saturday Night Fever* and *ABBA: The Movie*

In John Badham's bleak, down-and-dirty *Saturday Night Fever*, the enigmatic John Travolta glides across the screen like a strutting peacock on the grubby streets of New York, lighting up with raw energy and talent as he wields his tail feathers dancing at inner-city discotheques. Trapped in an oppressive, dead-end day job, Travolta's Tony Manero is a cynical and angry young man, undervalued and disposable, but when he hits the nightclubs to show off his incredible moves, this hardware salesclerk becomes a night time hero, a prince of the polyester crowd. When he says "Fuck the future," he is coming to terms with his social and cultural cage: Tony is swamped by mediocrity, and only allowed out of this metaphorical prison when he dons his silky shirt, tight, flared trousers, and his high-heeled boots.

407

Tony is an anti-hero who exists without any clear or distinct character attributes that push him to strive, to better himself or to even relate to the other characters that populate the film. This is where the film's strength lies: Badham and Travolta have created an egotistical and empty protagonist who is an antagonist from the first frame right through to the sombre and perhaps surprisingly quiet last. The film is stripped of sentimentality and warmth, and New York is depicted in all its grit, painted in crisp colors and with a sharp and stark honesty by cinematographer Ralph D. Bode. This depiction of the city swiftly and intelligently compliments the dense and lonely apathy of the ghetto kids going through the motions of youth before they are saddled with marriage and children while working in even more depressing dead-end jobs. This is a part of the Big Apple that shows children of working class immigrants as aimless, angry, easily agitated and complacent. It is an ugly world, but one that needs a voice. Badham's film does this skilfully and without missing a beat.

In his loud and consistently agro household, Tony Manero is a spindly self-assured inner city Adonis who spends hours tending his precious hair. He practices karate moves in front of his bedroom mirror and admires his good looks and fancy clothes, swamped by iconic 1970s imagery surrounding him in the form of posters hanging on his grubby walls. These legends of 1970s pop culture—from the warm, sun-kissed smile of Farrah Fawcett to the attentive lean muscularity of Bruce Lee—are his cultural references. He is a young man consumed by an artifice that is successful and alluring, and with his good looks and (more importantly) incredible dance moves, he could be an addition to that magpie's nest of cultural significance. But instead, when he leaves his den, he is thrust into the world of working class responsibility and Italian ghetto mentality: there is no escape. Even his own vanity has no real place at the dinner table, when his father slaps him across the head, oblivious to his son's perfectly sculpted hair.

This dinner sequence comes early in the piece and shows Tony draped in a table cloth to protect his clean silk shirt, like an ancient Roman,; a leftover of Italian royalty slumped into New York City in the peak of recession and stuck in a rut living with his defeatist family. The film garnered some negative criticism regarding the depiction of Italians, making note of numerous Italian stereotypes such as the aggressive mamma and papa, but Badham handles them too with tenderness and understanding. He is not creating cartoons, but rather concocting an acute dramatic portrayal of the distress that underlies percolating domestic violence. Just as the scene where Tony's father smacks him is played for laughs, there is a subversive message here: this reincarnation of an Italian godlike superstar who struts his stuff on the nightclub circuit is not welcome in modern day Little Italy. There is such a palpable anti-intellectualism in this film that can be felt even over the pulsating rhythms of disco which had made its mark in the underground, that soon (partially thanks to the massive success of this film) will attract legions of fans who would come to worship untrained dancers hitting the floor, much like Tony Manero. When Tony enters the discos he frequents in and around Brooklyn, he becomes a god: he is in charge, carefree, highly sexual and the object of everyone's admiration and affection.

John Travolta owns the dance floor in *Saturday Night Fever* (1977)

409

One of the most carefully constructed sub-plots in the film is the treatment of Tony's brother Frank (Martin Shakar) and his relationship with his family. Although Frank's picture sits on the mantle in his family home (a constant reminder to Tony of his brother's status as a moral compass), it is at the frenzied and busy discotheques that Tony himself comes alive and is honored by his peers—this is something that his brother may never know. Frank remains an absent character throughout most of the film, but when he does return it sends the story into an even more desolate direction. Frank is a handsome priest and a model for Tony in the eyes of his mother, but on returning home he has informed his family that he has lost his faith and left the church. His brother leaving the priesthood is something that at first shakes Tony, and he is perplexed by this decision because Frank was the one person Tony was supposed to look up to. Now dissatisfied with religion and impressed by Tony's lothario ways and hypersexual energy at the discotheques, Frank has fallen even deeper than his brother, becoming even more of a let down to their parents. Tony becomes increasingly excited that his brother has left the church, because he now has an excuse to be the biggest "fuck up" he can be. It also boosts his confidence, and he even talks to the beautiful dancer Stephanie (Karen Lynn Gorney) who previously shunned him.

Stephanie is a terrifically conceived character. She has had a taste of another life outside of Brooklyn, but like Tony seems stuck inside working class trappings. She is a secretary for a bunch of Upper East Side New Yorkers and sees these people experience highbrow cultural phenomena such as Franco Zefferelli films or Cat Stevens concerts, and through them she vicariously experiences these things too. When she talks about artistic happenings and movements to Tony, he is confused (he has no idea who Lawrence Olivier is). But through Stephanie's passion for art and what art can do we discover that these comfortable wealthy people that she works for have a flippant regard for it all, with no intention of admiring or acknowledging the creative process that goes along with the work. But for someone like Stephanie, a working class girl who is hungry for experience and art, culture is important and feeds her passion for dancing.

And dancing is what *Saturday Night Fever* is ultimately about. It uses dance as a tool: for Stephanie it is a craft that she wishes to tune more finely, while for Tony it is a means of survival. Dance as a means to thrive and live will pop up in many films in the wake of *Saturday Night Fever*, the birth of the "dance film" will suddenly sprout out in droves with films such as *Footloose* (1984), *Girls Just Want to Have Fun* (1985), *Breakin' 2: Electric Boogaloo* (1984), *Flashdance* (1983) and many more bursting from an era devoted to alienated and angst-ridden young people with no direction, and lots of working/middle-class rage to set free in the form of high jumps, pirouettes, acrobatic leaps and jazz ballet.

Travolta argues with his family in *Saturday Night Fever* (1977)

Most of these films held class and issues born from social structures at their core, and Badham's film is no exception. The film consistently reminds us of the lower working class backgrounds of Tony and his friends, but instead of championing them as heroes (which is what cinema often does) it paints them as deadbeats looking for another fight. Much like the youths in *West Side Story*, these inner city kids are angry and violent, but instead of giving us a romantic centrepiece (albeit a tragic one) as seen in *West Side Story* with Tony and Maria's doomed love affair, *Saturday Night Fever* delivers its plagued young with isolation and problems stemming from overwhelming apathy. Added to that is the devastating effect of drugs and booze and the racism that permeates the film's community. In the Italian-centric *Saturday Night Fever*, our central figures refer to "spics" and "niggers," and are constantly ready to fight. Not to mention their rampant homophobia where they pick on a gay couple on a basketball court. Later in the film, a young girl explains her devotion to David Bowie to which her boyfriend remarks "You like that fag?" to which she replies "He's bisexual, so he's only half fag." This racism and homophobia contradicts the chosen pastime of our central Italian disco-hopping teens, oblivious to the fact that the disco movement was of course born from black and gay/drag culture but quickly appealed to second generation immigrants in America's cities plagued by the recession. Much like the movie musicals of the 1930s that appealed in particular to Depression-era poverty stricken Jews, Irish and Italians, disco hit a nerve with next generation of Europeans because these brightly lit parlours of play and polyester provided a moment of escape from the grim realities of working class oppression.

One of the highlights of the film is Travolta's dancing. He is phenomenal as he moves around the dance floor with confidence and bravado. When Fran Drescher wishes to dance with this Romeo of the disco world, she is quickly pushed aside as Travolta takes over on his own, clearing the floor and showcasing some inspired dance moves. This is *his* world, and *his* domain. And just like every tragedy, this world will soon prove to be dishonest, chaotic and violent. Later in the film, Tony and his friends are beaten to a pulp by disgruntled peers, and when Tony discovers that the dance competition he and Stephanie win has been rigged by the Italian owners, he is disillusioned and pissed off. He realizes that this world is a deceitful and corrupt one, and hands over his prize to the Hispanic couple who came second, walking out of the disco aggressively stating that "there is always someone else ready to hang you." In Badham's film, Italians hate Latinos, Latinos hate Italians, children resent their parents, parents are continually disappointed in their offspring, and so forth.

This despair and hopelessness is epitomized not in Travolta's Tony, but in the remarkable performance by the very talented Barry Miller. Miller's performance is heartbreaking and he will go onto to similar (and far superior) territory as the tortured clown-crying-on-the-inside Ralph Garcia in the harrowing *Fame* (which we shall get to later). *Saturday Night Fever* gave him practice for this role in the figure of the suicidal and depressive Bobby C. He is a neurotic compulsive liar and a deeply troubled young boy who is desperate for attention and affection from Tony (some similarities may be drawn between Sal Mineo's admiration for James Dean in *Rebel Without a Cause*, 1955). Bobby C. is ignored by his peers and not respected like an adult. He is obsessed with impressing Tony and lies about a fabricated girlfriend that he has "gotten pregnant" to get attention. This tragic figure meets his final blow when the self-obsessed and self-absorbed Tony forgets to call him to discuss "what to do with the unwanted baby" that Bobby C. is supposedly "responsible for." Scene after scene where Bobby C. desperately reaches out to Tony and also other characters including Stephanie and Frank, we get a sense of dread. He provokes many questions –who is this guy? What does he want? Is he mentally ill? Is he in love with Tony?—but none of these things are explored because Bobby C. kills himself before we have a chance to find out.

Every teen-centric film about self-discovery and coming of age needs a locale that is reflective of the turbulent times of its production, and in *Saturday Night Fever* it's the Brooklyn Bridge. Here the characters parade around on the beams and toy with the large boom lights. Tony gracefully dances across the platforms as others clown around. But when Barry Miller's Bobby C. finally works up the nerve to cross the bridge, it eats him alive. Bobby C.'s suicide is hugely important in teen-centric cinema because it sparked a keen interest in teenage suicide in films from the late 1970s through into the 1980s. The idea of the mentally ill teenage boy, deformed by inner-turmoil also permeated a lot of movies of the time in films. Films like *Endless Love* (1981), *The Warriors* (1979), *Ordinary People* (1980), *Christine* (1983), *A Nightmare on Elm Street 2: Freddy's Revenge* (1985), *The Outsiders* (1983), *Eddie and the Cruisers* (1983), *The Wanderers* (1979), *The Boys Next Door* (1985), *Amityville 2: The Possession* (1982) and the aforementioned *Fame* all dealt with teen boys who were either working class greasy haired tough guys, Ivy League sons of wealthy parents, boys born into single parent households or boys born into post-hippie ideals who all suffering from personality disorders that eventually culminate in tragedy. This may have been a backlash against feminism (mothers who lost touch with their sons and families in favour of fighting for a cause or working outside of the home), a fad determined to appeal to disenfranchised teen boys (a generation of self-involved

413

brats who are angry for the sake of being angry) or simply a demented, direct rejection of the bearded gentle giants that Kris Kristofferson, James Brolin and a host of other male stars of the time epitomized as attractive and functional new-wave 'real men'.

John Travolta himself would go on to be a star, and in the following year would shed his disco attire and go onto serving the gods of rock'n'roll in his next movie, the incredibly successful *Grease*. This would become the highest grossing film of the year, even knocking *Superman: The Movie* from the number one spot.

The characters that populate *Saturday Night Fever* are not unlike the teens in Peter Bogdanovich's *The Last Picture Show*: they are just as disenfranchised, disillusioned and haunted by the inadequacies of their parents. The ultimate difference is time, locale and—most significantly— music. In Bogdanovich's film, country and western permeates the air, however in *Saturday Night Fever* disco is an active distraction, a musical background to alienated inner city kids of Italian immigrants. The songs used throughout the film give thematic voice to the situations at hand. For example, the Bee Gees's "You Should Be Dancing" comes along right after a moment of distress for Tony: here the high-pitched vocals insist that the anti-hero forget his woes and instead impress clubbing Brooklynites with his top-notch moves. Even more subversive is "More Than a Woman" which comments on the machismo that fuels Tony and his friends.

Saturday Night Fever responds to feminism with a fervent outrage. Not only do the boys see women as objects, but they have a disdain for them as well (even the seemingly sensitive Bobby C. calls a girl a "stupid bitch"). The film implies this misogyny is culturally ingrained: there is a quiet moment where Tony's father stops him from clearing dishes from the table and explains that that is a job for girls and women. When Frank tells his family that he has left the priesthood, Tony screams at his mother: "You got nothin' but three shit children now! Good!" Referring to both himself and his now non-priestly brother, the reasons as to why his younger sister is "shit" is left unclear. Perhaps it's because she is a girl which renders her meaningless and unworthy in this aggressively macho Italian ghetto (and in the eyes of her mother)? But because Tony can dance—something that requires compassion, concentration and elegance—he has an untapped potential to be a "better man" and this is glimpsed at (only ever briefly) when he is in contact with Stephanie. Tony complains that his father has never told him that he was ever good at anything and this generates his motivation. He finds an inner-heroism at the discos, where he is worshipped, admired and adored. He is a prince of the dance floor, but during the day he is a dysfunctional shmuck whose assertive machismo is executed to his detriment. Tony is of a breed of urban young people that will forever be stuck in the bleak existence of lower income. By the end of the film, Stephanie herself has told Tony: "You're a no body, heading nowhere," and he finds himself with nowhere to turn. Having the girl he admires tell him this is a shocking truth that makes Tony defensive and angry, but it's what he has to hear. The closing scene depicts a beaten and spiritually dead Tony crawling into Stephanie's arms as the sun rises over a soot-swept Brooklyn.

The film creates its own iconographic language for disco culture and started the cinematic craze for the subculture. This is the world of disco dancing amidst drugs, racism, machismo and working class people trying to make ends meet. The tough talking immigrant boys and girls of *Saturday Night Fever* are a significant part of the success of disco culture—beyond the black community and gay world—as it is here that the heterosexual Italians of Brooklyn created their own distinct world, dolled up in paisley shirts, taffeta dresses and skin tight polyester, with the Bee Gees and fellow disco acts sending these youngsters into a dancing frenzy.

The film may be a reminder of class resentment, a lyrical sonnet to the downtrodden and generations to follow who don't want to better themselves. It is an acutely articulate reminder of the social breakdown of a city plagued by traditions long lost. As depressing and downbeat the film is, it is necessary. The sorrowful, quiet moments are remarkable, and the intense violent outbreaks are shattering. The reflective and pensive moments where Tony comes to accept his rut are heartbreaking. Badham's *Saturday Night Fever* is a tremendous accomplishment, and one of the most important films of the late 1970s.

Less culturally important or concerned with social critique was a concert movie that made note of a Swedish sensation that took audiences by storm—and primarily audiences many miles away from their homeland: Australia! In *ABBA: The Movie*, Agnetha, Bjorn, Benny and Frieda travel to the land down under to perform a packed out concert tour delivering some of their classic hits, while a wafer thin plot involving an opportunistic journalist played by now convicted pedophile Robert Hughes circles the energetic showcase of this quartet of European talent. The film does not need this superficial storyline to aid the musicality of the concert, and suffers for it. *ABBA: The Movie* is truly only going to find its audience in ABBA fans, and unlike the far more interesting and fun *KISS Meets the Phantom of the Park* (1978) this film offers nothing but a great performance from one of the most significant pop sensations of the 1970s. It doesn't deliver in regard to its "the movie" subtitle, because there is no movie to speak of. What audiences need to take out of this live footage is that ABBA always churned out brilliantly conceived songs that a lot of people even today fail to appreciate.

Journalist and ABBA fan Adam Devlin shares his insight into the film:

> Released in 1977, following their ridiculously successful Australian tour, *ABBA: The Movie* was an attempt to tap into the global phenomenon that came to be known as ABBAMANIA. In 1977 ABBA was one of the biggest pop/rock bands on the globe—and they were no bigger than here in Australia where their 1975 compilation "The Best of ABBA" went platinum 22 times and their single Fernando held the #1 spot on the pop charts for over 3 months and is still one of the most successful single releases in Australian history. The film followed the release the year prior of their album "Arrival," which went platinum 18 times over in Australia, selling around 1million copies. But enough of the background—onto the movie. *ABBA: The Movie* contains 19 songs filmed live from their various concerts around Australia in March 1977 and many scenes of backstage footage of ABBA preparing for the concerts etc. All of this footage is amazing. It really gives us the viewer a glimpse into one of the world's most popular bands on tour. We get to see them arriving in Australia at the beginning

of the tour, we get to see the girls backstage warming up with vocal exercises before hitting the stage. We see Frida doing aerobics with her buff bodyguard. We see their press conference in Sydney (or part of it at least). We get to see them bring the Melbourne CBD to a standstill with an appearance at the Town Hall. And we see ABBA live on stage, performing their biggest and best hits. All amazing stuff. And if it were left as that—a rockumentary of sorts—it would stand as one of the best examples of that genre. Sadly, that is not the case. Apparently *ABBA: The Movie* started out with ABBA deciding to document their Australia tour on 16mm film as a record of the tour. Lasse Hallstrom, who had directed most of their video clips, was to film it for them. The Australian entertainment entrepreneur Reg Grundy, whose production company was co-producing the film, talked them into upgrading the film—at Grundy's expense—to 35 mm Panavision and to make it a cinematic release and to intertwine a storyline—a sub-plot—into the film. Lasse Hallstrom wrote the "screenplay" on the flight from Sweden to Sydney. The storyline of hapless reporter Ashley Wallace (Robert Hughes) was hatched. Basically, said hapless reporter is sent by his Radio Station Manager (Bruce Barry) to get an "in-depth" interview with ABBA while they are in the country on tour. Of course said hapless reporter sets out without a press card to get the interview with ABBA—and ABBA's burly bodyguard (Tom Oliver) thwarts his every attempt to speak with the band. He ends up following ABBA around Australia, trying to get into every press conference and hotel room, etc., without success. Along the way he conducts a series of "Vox Pops" with Aussie fans to use in his interview. As ABBA are about to leave the country and hapless reporter has given up on getting his interview, as he is leaving their last press conference, he gets in an elevator only to find himself alone with ABBA. You probably didn't see this coming but he ends up getting the interview and it airs on time! This whole sub-plot is rather silly and the film would have been a very different and much better film if it had not been included. The footage of ABBA off-stage—at various hotels, airports, functions, etc.—is all compelling viewing for any serious ABBA fan. You get to see a glimpse into their private world (on tour at least). You get to see how they interact with each other—and I must say they appear to be really "nice/normal" people. The inclusion of "I'm A Marionette" in full—with video footage inserted of ABBA dealing with the media and fans along with an amazing live performance from Agnetha and Anni-Frid (topped with blond wig) from their "mini-musical" "The Girl With Golden Hair" hints at a change in direction for ABBA that was realized post-ABBA with Benny and Bjorn teaming up with Tim Rice to write the Musical "Chess" in 1984. "ABBA: The Movie" is a brilliant glimpse into ABBA's 1977 Australian Tour. It is a great insight into one of the craziest times in Australian pop culture—a time when Australia was obsessed with ABBA. The footage of Australia and Australians in 1977 is brilliantly twee—the "Vox Pops" with ABBA fans of all ages are very amusing and lovely watch some 30+ years later. If the rather silly reporter sub-plot had of not been added this could have been seen as a masterclass on the rock/pop tour doco. Sadly that inclusion weakens the impact of this great film somewhat. But it is still well worth seeing. It is a captivating snapshot of an Australia long gone. And we see one of the world's best pop bands performing some amazing live versions of their hits and some more obscure material as well while at their peak. If you look past the reporter story line, you will have a great time watching "ABBA: The Movie." As an historical snapshot of Australia in 1977 in the grasp of ABBAMANIA—"ABBA: The Movie" is fascinating viewing.

DON'T BOTHER, THEY'RE HERE: *A Little Night Music*

Stephen Sondheim: the name alone suggests the saving of musical theatre and the reshaping of the musical in both style and theme. Sondheim's musicals are dark, gripping, character-centric, intelligent and moving, and are integral in the historical development of languages marriage to music. He is both a wordsmith and dramatist who understands the human condition almost too well. He seems to have an inbuilt actor within him that effortlessly emerges to give voice to characters that are complicated, messy, driven, angry, anguished, frightened, passionate and multi-dimensional. Studying under Oscar Hammerstein, Sondheim gradually became the most respected and admired musical theatre composer and lyricist ever to write for the stage. With his dedication and respect for playwrights, he has also collaborated with many remarkable writers such as Hugh Wheeler and James Lapine whose works are perfectly balanced with the magnificent music and lyrical wizardry of this magician of the musical theatre.

Interestingly Sondheim's musicals are rarely adapted to the screen, as many of them are not streamlined narrative pieces but rather written for the stage and would take a considerable amount of reworking to translate successfully. But by the late 1970s and with the help of long-time collaborator producer/director Hal Prince, his musical based on Ingmar Bergman's farcical romantic melodrama *Smiles Of A Summer Night* (1955), *A Little Night Music* got a cinematic deal. But the results no way reflect the passion and intricate beauty of Sondheim's original musical: it is flat and dull, except for the musical orchestrations of Sondhiem's work, the finely tuned adaptation of the Hugh Wheeler book into a screenplay and the terrific performances by a star-studded cast. The film is otherwise insipid, but the story, cast and most notably Sondheim's beautiful and captivating music and lyrics are of course perfect. The musical is set to three quarter time (a waltz) and chronicles the sexual entanglement and romantic crossovers of a group of people apparently influenced by the "smiling moon." The marvellous Hermoine Gingold as matriarch Madame Armfeldt explains to her young granddaughter Fredericka (Chloe Franks) that the moon "smiles for the young who know nothing, for the fools like Ferdericka's mother Desiree who know too little and for the old who know too much." The script is brimming with intelligence and humor, and its sardonic cynicism hits hard and fast, however the film lets all of these great moments down with a broader absence of oomph.

419

Sondheim wrote new lyrics for the "Night Waltz" theme that originally opened the musical, and for the movie (where the characters that will eventually play out a straight forward book musical format are presented first off on stage dancing to the choreography of Patricia Birch) the music is accompanied by "Love Takes Time," which sets up the linguistic wit of the piece. However his greatest achievement is the dark and sexually driven number "The Miller's Wife," which was ultimately was cut from the final film. "The Glamorous Life" (a song that Fredericka sings about her mother) bursts with an enthusiasm that is a testament to Sondheim's musicality. His music and his remarkable words are robust and whimsical and with a fiendish cleverness, and the little girl's song about her actress mother is a perfect example of this. The montage that corresponds with "The Glamorous Life" is nicely plotted: Desiree (Elizabeth Taylor) overacts in her plays, nibbles at her sandwiches and glares at lascivious men on a travelling train and so forth. But the production values just let this incredible song down, sung with delicate sweetness by Chloe Franks.

Elizabeth Taylor in a publicity still for *A Little Night Music* (1977)

Taylor as Desiree Armfeldt is more than competent and a delight to watch. The mean spiritedness of reviews that viciously attacked Taylor were crude and unnecessary and—much like Lucille Ball in *Mame*—problematically scrutinized the way Taylor looked. Although she at times looks uncomfortable in the role, it is only for fleeting moments, and she delivers some high-energy comic moments of nuanced, serene sobriety. Taylor is a phenomenal actress, but the production elements in this film don't do her any justice. When the film gets to the climactic moments where she gets the man of her dreams and a family that is already half baked (she already has her semi-estranged daughter) she is shot in overpowering darkness, as if the movie itself is being filmed in an inkblot. It is lazy and ill-conceived. Elizabeth Taylor is acting and singing her heart out, but barely visible. The sets, the muted color palette, the clumsy cinematography and the rushed job on the overall look of the film (including the bargain basement costumes) don't matter when you take into account the sheer brilliance of the score and song, the script and the performances. Everybody involved is on the mark and remarkably slick, but the film has some of the weakest visual components ever put to screen.

The interweaving characters and their farcical romances make up for the below average production values. Erich's (Christopher Guard) seriousness is made all the more palpable by the fact that he plays the cello, that most mournful of instruments, which he violently with angst and frustration. Originally, Sondheim wanted each of the characters to play an instrument that would reflect their personalities, which would have been interesting, but alas, only little Fredericka (who tinkers with the piano) and Erich play an instrument. When the sexually free maid torments Erich, it is right out of the sex comedies from the turn of the century. As Anne Egerman, Lesley Ann Down is a knockout as the gorgeous and virginal wife of Len Cariou's stoic, but secretly passionate lover of Frederick. "Now, Soon, Later" is a magnificent three-way shared soliloquy sung by Erich, Anne and Frederick, with the latter expresses his sexual frustration and contemplates the manners in which to seduce Anne. The entire musical is presented in three quarter time, making it fraught with anxiety and an overbearing nervousness. The musical is a farcical composite of longing and sexual knowledge. Parlour comedy is a difficult kind of humour to pull off, but Hugh Wheeler's script—adapted from his book from the original stage musical—is a stunning loaded gun that fires in perfect rhythm. There is nothing forced, tedious or highbrow, and his writing is simultaneously funny and moving.

Desiree Armfeldt is a great creation, who has a romantic outlook on certain aspects of life balanced with some completely out of touch moments where she is lost like a bewildered young ewe in the meadowland. Her estrangement from both her mother and daughter is a focal point of the musical, along with the tense romance she rekindles with Frederick. When Frederick explains to Desiree that "You Must Me Wife" we get a sense of his phoniness, and Desiree sees right through it, singing the counterpart to the number by showing a disdain for this girl she truly never wishes to meet. And when Desiree finds out that Anne is a virgin, she is repulsed.

Diana Rigg's comic abilities shine with vigour and precision: she is hilarious as the neurotic and highly-strung Charlotte Mittleheim. Her duet with Lesley Anne Down is fabulous as they sing about the woes and worries of love in "Every Day A Little Death." But the comedy is also beautifully counterbalanced by the drama of the piece. When Len Cariou confesses his love for Taylor, it's genuinely beautiful—their love is honest and rich. The song "Send in the Clowns"—a magnificent piece of writing and truly the only hit from Sondheim who made it known early in his career that he would not write the hummable show tune—is sung with tenderness. Actress Glynis Johns originally sang the number for the original production of *A Little night Music* and Sondheim wrote it for her silvery wispy voice. It is structured through short phrases, and allows space to breathe: a rarity in Sondheimian musicals. Taylor handles the song beautifully, and when it is reprised in the closing moments of the film, Cariou and Taylor complement each other with sweet surrender. This magical and devastating song has been recorded by the likes of Judy Collins, Bernadette Peters, Barbra Streisand, Judi Dench and even KISS's drummer Peter Criss. It is a show tune that doesn't scream "show tune," but instead it lets us understand what the musical in all its diverse forms can do; it can make you think, weep, become uneasy, bemuse and make you feel alienated. Sondheim's musicals are the best at this.

Playwright Hugh Wheeler would go on to write the horror musical masterpiece *Sweeney Todd: The Demon Barber of Fleet Street* which would later be filmed for television with such gusto starring George Hearn as the titular bloodthirsty barber and Angela Lansbury as the immoral cannibal-enabling Mrs Lovett. But in this adaptation of the Ingmar Bergman film his writing is just as lean and just as sharp. There are some great moments specifically designed for film adaptation, such as Erich's suicide attempt ending when the branch of the tree he wraps his rope around to hang himself comes crashing down and dropping him onto the ground in front of Anne (who he secretly has a crush on). The Russian Roulette game between rivals Magnus (Laurence Guittard) and Cariou's Frederick that begins stressful and bleak ends with breezy humor.

While the film is not at all perfect, it does have a gentle charm and a soothing quality to it. The performances are so rich in energy, and the orchestrations of Sondheim's score are unsurpassed. When "Send in the Clowns" swells in the closing moments of the film, you forget the inadequacies of the production as this master musical genius takes you down a path you might not necessarily want to go down.

Lesley Anne Down remembers making *A Little Night Music*:

> Oh well I have to be brutally honest. I knew nothing of Stephen Sondheim back then. Of course I knew *West Side Story* and of course I knew *Gypsy*. And of course I knew his work but if somebody had said to me "Who composed any of the music for *Gypsy*?" I would have said "Well shoot me now. I'm not winning this one." And now I know he didn't write the music for *Gypsy*, he wrote the lyrics. I didn't know names though but of course I knew his work. I loved his work, and *A Little Night Music* I thought was brilliant. The first theatrical thing I ever saw on the planet was the ballet of *Sleeping Beauty*. I believe I was nine. And then I saw Juliet Prowse in *Sweet Charity*. And those were the two things that I saw before I grew up, in the theatre in London. I didn't come from a theatrical family so I didn't realise who was who for the most part. I didn't realise the importance of the people I was working with, except of course for Elizabeth Taylor. On the other side of the camera and their genius, I did not.

The person I was closest to on the film was Hugh Wheeler. Hugh and I got on famously and we truly did love each other very much and he was just lovely and kind and we were very comfortable together. Hal Prince and I were also very comfortable together. Stephen and I really didn't have anything to do with each other because I can't sing. And so the only stuff that I did on that movie as far as the music was concerned was a lot of the talky stuff. It's very difficult not to do your own talky stuff in the songs because your voice changes. So I did a lot of that but I didn't do any of the singing, so obviously that eliminated my time with Sondheim. But never the less we did go to Vienna. We did work for I think two or three weeks every day, a bit like doing a play where we'd all turn up to the hall and Sondheim and everybody were there and we would all rehearse songs! Ha! Rehearsing songs! Well, what they said was "We need somebody to sing for this woman!" But it was kind of fun. Elizabeth would be saying "Oh, would you like some orange juice?" and you'd say "Sure, I'd love some orange juice!" You'd take a sip at ten in the morning and it would be virtually straight vodka. So, Elizabeth and I got really close, very quickly and we really liked each other. Oh and Diana Rigg! Diana and I were very, very close. We had enormous fun together. We walked together to the hotel and went straight to the bar and we had these great drinks. I can't remember what they were called, but it was a glass of champagne with a sugar cube in it and I think a tad of brandy. I want to say a champagne cocktail but I'm not sure what it is! It is something else. But that is what we use to have. So we had fun! Hugh Wheeler and I loved each other very, very much. And then Bruce, my boyfriend at the time came out to the shoot and because he was also a writer, he and Hugh got on very well together. Bruce was a crazy hypochondriac and a very strange person. Loveable but strange. I remember one day, Bruce taking the car that would get me to the locations and he would take it back into town, back to the hotel and then back again because he would be having one of his super anxiety attacks! Hugh would drive off and find him and pull up on the side of the road and call out "You're alright! You are not having a heart attack!" Bruce was always thinking he was having a fucking heart attack or that he had polio or that he was going blind. It was constant with Bruce. But it was very funny. And Hugh helped a tremendous amount with him! Elizabeth Taylor wouldn't have shown her nerves. She is Elizabeth. She wouldn't have shown her nerves, and if she did have nerves, she kept them to herself. And if she did have nerves, she certainly calmed them with vodka. I do know that she was having a tough time. She had a tough time on that film. She had fallen off her boyfriend's motorcycle and she had hurt her leg so it was kind of bruised, so she was in bed and we would all have to go to her bed to rehearse, she couldn't get to rehearsal. And then Richard Burton married Suzy "racing car driver" Hunt, and that kind of set her back. She had a real hard time and she and her best friend Norma Heyman who I knew very well back then, became even closer after that. Norma was lovely. She was so kind to me in many ways, as was Elizabeth. So Norma had to come out from London to be with her when Richard married Suzy. That was very bad for her. You know, when you have a love of your life…doesn't matter what they do, or if they do something, it affects you. But with all that going on, Elizabeth was funny. What can I say? It was not her thinnest period and she loved ice-cream and she was in all those corsets so she would have a board that she would put her arms on and she would kind of lean back to take the pressure off the corset so that she could be fed a little bit of ice-cream. It was very important to her; ice-cream. She was going through a hard time. She was a bit miserable, so she liked vodka. She didn't have anyone to marry. She was going out with John Warner, and she was going out with some Persian guy. I have no idea. We never met him. I would go to her dressing room and she would say "Lesley darling, which one of these men should I marry?"

425

She was hilarious! The fucking casting process was so absolutely typical for the time. Back then I didn't go to interviews. My agent called me on a hot summer day, and I was on my way with Bruce, going down to his mum and dad's house. My agent Steve Kelly called and told me that I need to go for an interview. I was a bit hesitant. But he said "Can you just do this for me?" I said "Oh God, what is it?!" He said "It's the lead in a new musical," to which I replied "I can't sing!" He said "Just go, will you!" So I do it. I get out the shower, my hair is fucking wet, I put on the crappy clothes that I am going down to the country in and I'm in no make-up. Bruce says "Right. I'll stay here at my folks, but be as quick as you can." I zoom up there. I knock on the door. There is this huge suite room and there is Elliot Kastner the producer. 'Hello. Hello darling." And I sit down and the chair I'm in seems miles away from this man. I don't know why. It seems like one of these dreams where that camera angle is pulled in and out at the same time. I just sat there. Not caring, not being interested. Thinking "Shit, I got the fucking train all the way here and how am I getting back?" And this is what I said quite frankly, during the meeting. I said "Oh, I have a train to catch. Okay, thank you! Goodbye!" Two days later, I start rehearsals for *Hamlet* that I am doing with my darling friend, and this was during the hottest summer in British history. The hottest fucking summer. We were doing matinees and people would be taken out on stretchers. It was so fucking hot! I have this long, stupid blond wig on to add to this! At one matinee I couldn't stand it anymore, I said to this guy who had shaved heads who was very cute, and had done his own hair "Just cut my fucking hair off!" Good old Shakespeare doesn't have Ophelia on stage for two hours, so I had two hours. I ripped the fucking wig off and I said "Cut my fucking hair off! I can't stand it, I am so hot!" All the white make-up I had would run. It was the worse Ophelia performance you had ever seen! So this cute boy cut my hair off. My hair is now like a quarter of an inch all over badly cut. I just remember we were staying in this pub, which was so hot, it was unbelievable! I wet all of my bed before I got in it at night. By twelve o'clock it would be dry and I would wet it again. Anyway, I was in the bar drinking away, and somebody comes in and says "Lesley-Anne?" and tell them I'm coming and it turns out it's a phone call. The voice on the other end says "I'm calling you about your costume fitting." I asked "What for?" And they reply "Well, for the film." And I'm like "What film?! I'm doing *Hamlet!*" The voice on the other end then says, "Um, *A Little Night Music.*" I said "What's that?!" I didn't even remember! And that was how I got the job. So the first thing I thought of was my hair! And that wig I am wearing in the film is a really bad wig. I finished *Hamlet* and the next day I was on a plane to Austria. The wigs in Austria back then were not very good, and exceptionally archaic and communist. They sort of dug out this thing that looked like a piece of straw and the hairdresser combed it through, washed it and did her thing with it and that was my wig, but if you look closely it is really bad fucking wig! Oh but once I realised what I was doing, I was enthralled. I can sing a little, but honestly and truly, if you kind of think about all the girl songs in that film, well, Anne's songs are the hardest and quite operatic. I'd sometimes sing in the car depending on my mood. And now these days, I look around at what's going on at home and if my cat is about to go and kill my bird, I'll start singing "Soon I promise, soon I won't shy away." I loved all the dancing and the movement and it was exceptionally rewarding and wonderful and marvellous and easy! I have to say easy and pleasurable and gave me a joy I have never had to be able to act in all of those musical numbers. It was lovely. I honestly think that if you look at the movie, you do not think for one second that I was dubbed. I had such a joy singing and doing everything that I had to do. It was wonderful because, you know, I am an old-fashioned person. I was bought up on strangely enough on *Gypsy,* and then eventually got to work with Stephen Sondheim himself! And what is so interesting is the fact that for *A Little Night Music* was based on the Ingmar Bergman movie. At the time when I worked with Liv Ullmann, she was married to Ingmar Bergman. So, I got to meet and know Ingmar, her husband, their child and it was all very round-robin. However, I think it was probably a film that shouldn't have been made. I think it is one of those things that really shouldn't have made it on the page. I mean, *Gypsy* has such filmic qualities to it. *A Little Night Music* really doesn't. Honestly, truly, it doesn't. You need oomph! There was no oomph! It was a Swedish farce and they are very marvellous on the stage; we would all probably go to see a bit of Chekhov if somebody is in it we like, and that is what *A Little Night Music* is, a Chekhov of the musical world.

START SPREADING THE NEWS: *New York, New York*

Director Martin Scorsese loves cinema, and one of his favourite kinds of movies are musicals. He has cited amongst his most beloved films from the Busby Berkley canon as well as outstanding achievements such as the much championed *The Red Shoes* (1948). Scorsese also has an affinity for the big band era, and this is what he pays tribute to in his gritty—and at times psychotic—homage to the Big Apple at the end of World War II, *New York, New York*. What makes this a masterpiece is that it is a magpie's nest of extraordinary talent both in front of and behind the camera, as well as its total dedication to a bygone era and style of film fuelled by a 1970s, street-smart violent edge. The nastiness of the film is an extension of the darkness delivered in *42nd Street* (1933) from Busby Berkley and co-director Lloyd Bacon, a movie which truly captures the grim reality of show business as well as presenting the mean streets of New York on its stage in its diegetic staged climax. However, instead of a young starlet's rise to supposed stardom and the megalomaniac antics of a producer driven by corruption, misanthropy and stomach ulcers, Scorsese's focus is on two artists who have one of the most electrically turbulent affairs ever put to screen.

Robert De Niro and Liza Minnelli on the set of *New York, New York* (1977)

New York, New York is fundamentally about artists—one a charlatan but gutsy, and the other ambitious but delicate. Both are incredibly talented, and so the film is also about how artists connect to one another. Part of the relationship is driven by competition, while the other half is founded on support and collaboration. Unlike *A Star Is Born*—where one artist is ready to give it all up and does everything he can to make a fellow artist succeed and take his place—in *New York, New York* the two star crossed lover-artists are on the same path, but their intentions are different. Their goals are contradictory and their passions are jeopardized by the other.

Opening with a fantastic sequence highlighting the end of the war and the frivolity and jitterbug energy of the big band era, *New York, New York* plants us inside a world that 1970s audiences had only known through movies from the 1930s and early 1940s. Swing bands and Glen Miller were part of a lexicon of the post-jazz age explosion where artists such as Bing Crosby and Judy Garland belted out dance numbers to celebrate to. Celebration is supposedly at the centre of Scorsese's film, but it comes with violent inoculations and a temperamental menace. It is a superb and highly articulate summary of the formation of a new, post-war social fabric where on the surface peace and a spirit of victory prevails, but underlying this halcyon promise is ugliness and domestic unrest. Scorsese paints a picture that is unsentimental and fraught with hidden agendas, personal anguish and frenzied, schizophrenic passions. This is a film that delivers the marrow before it even pretends to show you the bone, a gut wrenching excursion into the world of two people locked together in love, hate and everything in between, and set to the wild, stylish symphonic sounds of big band which provides the film's backbone.

At the heart of the piece are its two stars, Robert De Niro and Liza Minnelli. Both have a fevered presence: they are irresistible to the eye and ear, and their chemistry burns with sex appeal, vicious back-and-forths and exhausting ups-and-downs. De Niro plays Jimmy Doyle, a self-involved and easily agitated saxophone player who meets a small time nightclub singer named Francine Evans, played by Minnelli. From their first interaction there is a sense of urgency—he insists he get her phone number and she gradually becomes increasingly nervous in his company. Eventually they are forced to share a taxi and we share their ride from here onwards: a beautifully conceived plot device that leads them to the same audition. At the audition, the nightclub owner (played with such down to earth breeziness by the fantastic Dick Miller) is impressed by the two as a duo, and wishes to hire them as a boy-girl act, rather than individually. Francine and Jimmy are thrust into each other's lives, forced into an artistic union and through this sense of overwhelming urgency and uncertainty they are also forced into a romantic coupling and eventual marriage. But the romance is destined for doom as Jimmy's violent temper and incessant need to get into fights with everyone around him (including Francine) escalates, despite having a child together.

De Niro is a time bomb in the film, there is no doubt about that. His performance is saddled with an energy that is terrifying and chaotic. When he looks as though he's in a relatively serene mood, it is guaranteed he will snap into a vicious outburst, and this happens often on-screen. He is magnetic, monstrous, violent and exciting. There is a reality grounding his and Minnelli's onscreen romance, and in *New York, New York* we feel like a part of their stressful union, while understanding why they are addicted to each other. It might not be the healthiest of relationships, but it most certainly is a passionate one. The anger and the miscommunication and the dangerous ground covered by these magnificent performers is where the film's shredding sophistication is housed. When Minnelli and De Niro scream at each other in the car, it is a thing of nightmares. There is such a terrifying element to the scene and it is so confronting that you are left feeling uncomfortable and distressed, as if bearing witness to your own parents having a horrendous fight right in front of you. And this is what Scorsese does so well with his characters: he gives them a scary edge. When performers as emotionally wound up as Robert De Niro and as emotionally fragile as Liza Minnelli come together on screen under a master's direction and inside a world that can be as ugly as it is pretty, the results are phenomenal.

In all its ferocity and anger, the quiet moments are the most telling. For example, when Minnelli's Francine wakes up to find De Niro's Jimmy tickling the ivories and playing fragments of what will become the title song, there is a quiet tenderness which ends with Minnelli asking about the theory of relativity. This captures the couple's strained connection: a

431

stunned romance as they are trapped in a grubby apartment with a piano as their window out. Another touching scene involves the duo in hospital looking upon their child with both warmth and heaviness, weighed down by uncertainty and guilt.

Their performances are complimented by art direction that goes from theatrical and stylized to gritty and dirty. The film boasts some lavish sets that highlight the artificial elegance of Hollywood and Broadway during the 1930s and 1940s: Minnelli and De Niro stroll through a winter set piece complete with cardboard cut out trees that frame them, and the club that De Niro ends up owning is framed by bright bulbs and a flashy flamboyance. Later he is beaten and thrown down a hallway and this scene is made all the more intense with the glamorous backdrop.

Martin Scorsesse and Liza Minnelli at the premiere of *New York, New York*
(1977)

Jimmy and Francine—as well as the man and woman playing them—are artists, and these people are complicated. The songs are therefore just as multifaceted and as busy. John Kander and Fred Ebb delivered outstanding songs for *Cabaret* that gave their dear friend and artistic associate Liza Minnelli some of the greatest numbers ever put to film, and when they return to their beloved siren, the outcome is just as breathtaking. Minnelli herself would go on to say that "But The World Goes 'Round" would be her all-time favourite song to sing, and when she lets those incredibly soaring and vibrant lyrics out it is magic. A dark magic, yes, but a magic for the fretful as well as the hopeful. The title song (made famous by Frank Sinatra) is Minnelli's in this film, and it is her song, her city and her anthem. Martin Scorsese, Kander and Ebb together give this moment to Minnelli, and her take on the music, words, emotions, turbulence and scary elements of falling in and out of love is nothing short of brilliant.

Unfortunately, audiences didn't flock to the cinemas to see the film as much as Martin Scorsese had hoped, and the lack of box office takings sent the talented director into a drug addled depression where his cocaine addiction became a real problem. Some critics felt his loose direction on *New York, New York* that let De Niro and Minnelli (but mostly De Niro) go on ad-libbing tangents was detrimental to the movie's success. There seemed to be an idea floating around that there was no reign put on the horses, and that this style of direction did not serve the plot. But 1977 was the year of *Star Wars*, and a feel-bad big band musical was always going to be a hard sell. *Taxi Driver* (1976) was another masterpiece, but it got audiences in droves because it was a new kind of avenging angel film. *New York, New York* was a musical that wasn't a rock musical and it wasn't a musical that had been on stage with an already built-in crowd, but in retrospect it didn't matter. Either way, the film is a masterpiece and one of Scorsese's most personal films.

Its darkness and violent energy makes *New York, New York* a perfect example of 1970s musical excess, and it is also representative of Scorsese's broader work, which is almost always stitched together with an oppressive machismo that is volcanic and mean. But what gives this film another angle is its treatment of Liza Minnelli's character and its ability to let her shine. As fantastic as De Niro is, Minnelli is at the top of her game.

When she performs the numbers in the films that made her a hit with audiences, she embodies the world of Busby Berkley and Arthur Freed, channelling her late mother's essence as she carries herself with grace and flair down spiralling staircases, tap dancing across grandiose sound stage set ups and singing her heart out in optical labyrinths designed with geometric ingenuity. In comparison to a film like *Saturday Night Fever* and Bob Fosse's bleak and uncompromising *All That Jazz* (1979) (the latter a film we shall go into later), *New York, New York* is a glitzy cynic with its aged brutality, It is the great grandchild of the swing era, but painted in such raucous and murky colors that Scorsese does something near impossible: he delivers one of the most visceral tributes to the golden age of the movie musical while at the same time weaving together a story that is distinctly 1970s, distinctly his own and—most importantly—a sharp critique of an America that champions show business but chews up and spits out its artists.

By the end of 1977, the movie musical was alive and well, and the following three years would play host to an explosion of musicals that were diverse in story, theme and style. Provocative works started to sprout out and highly stylized and subversively political musicals also generated some attention: mostly negative, but attention nonetheless. A sudden interest in musical biopics began in 1978 with a focus on artists such as Buddy Holly and fellow rock stars from the 1950s becoming a focal point for gripping and powerful movies, boasting inspired performances from young actors who were not only devoted fans of the musicians they were playing, but who channelled their essence and delivered something unique and truthful, well beyond the realms of a simplistic homage. 1950s nostalgia also existed outside of the biographies that championed and highlighted gifted rock'n'rollers, and one of the most successful movie musicals of all time opened to mass hysteria and huge box office takings: hopelessly devoted to rock'n'roll, drag races, high school dances, it made a loud bold statement that *Grease* was the word…

434

1978

"When I Think of Home"

Harlem's Yellow Brick Roads,
Summer Lovin', Mae West's Lovers,
and Buddy Holly's Dilemma

By 1978, MOVIE MUSICALS WERE RESURFACING WITH AN ASSURED confidence, and coming out in a steady stride. Brilliant and bleak films such as *Saturday Night Fever* and *New York, New York* made audiences realize what the movie musical could do and how song could contribute to character and establishing dramatic scenarios. Innovative works like *Pete's Dragon* and *Raggedy Ann and Andy: A Musical Adventure* injected the already complex world of child's entertainment with informal adult qualities, and proudly cemented the notion that even family-centric cinema was permeated with a complicated melancholy in a way unique to the musical genre.

From 1978 to 1980, over thirty movie musicals hit the silver screen. They varied in content, theme and mood. Some were bright and cheery, some were dark and gritty and others were high concept, genuinely superlative misconceived and misdirected messes (be they loveable and not). Television was also delivering the goods in musical entertainment with variety shows taking suburban audiences by storm. When else but in the 1970s would you find a television show featuring the likes of The Osmonds, KISS, Benji, the cast of *Happy Days* and *Laverne and Shirley*, Sonny and Cher, the Muppets and a cavalcade of other superstars? This was the decade on a television spectacular, and it was about irreverence, fun, and warm-hearted silliness. It showcased dedicated talent and show business itself, and wrapped it all up in brightly lit specials just loaded with heart.

The diversity of musical styles also dictated the varying styles of movie musical: the soulful ingenuity of Motown flooded motion picture houses with what would be one of the very last official Blaxploitation movies ever made, *The Wiz*. Folk music hit centre stage—possibly ten years too late—with Bob Dylan and Joan Baez delving into the language of film in *Renaldo and Clara*. Fresh from their success on the soundtrack for *Saturday Night Fever*, disco kings the Bee Gees sang through The Beatles' "Sgt. Pepper's Lonely Hearts Club Band" album in a bizarre rock opera based on the groundbreaking album. Jukebox musicals also started to surface, giving legendary stars in their twilight years something to sing about, with Mae West strutting her stuff in the camp cult favourite *Sextette*.

But 1978 was a year for rock'n'roll in its varied incarnations— primitive, derivative, genuine, manufactured, and almost always true to the 1950s (although genetically modified for a 1970s sensibility). Rock legend Buddy Holly got his own biopic in *The Buddy Holly Story* which earned Gary Busey an Academy Award nomination. The legendary disc jockey who coined the term rock'n'roll Alan Freed (aka Moondog) was the subject of a film boasting a cavalcade of enigmatic rock stars such as Screamin' Jay Hawkins, Chuck Berry and Jerry Lee Lewis in *American Hot Wax*. And come 1978, one of the biggest movie musical hits—and greatest blockbusters of all time—hit the silver screen and sparked a keen interest in 1950s nostalgia.

Grease would become one of the most successful films ever made, and with its high energy, teen-centric sophistication and its preoccupation with sex interwoven with a warm and subtle sentimentality, the film got audiences excited about movie musicals again. The soundtrack for *Grease* would go on to be one of the highest selling records in history, and the eventual 1980s VHS rentals would rank alongside *Jaws*, *The Exorcist* and *Star Wars*. *Grease* fandom would lead "sing-a-long" screenings for retrospective movie-going audiences from the 1990s onward. The film would also do something that most movie musicals never did: it influenced eventual mountings of an original stage production. There would be a number of versions of *Grease* ranging from the original down and dirty production, a kid-friendly variant, and one that was a combo of both. But it was the film adaptation of *Grease* that had its own language, its own look and its own voice—something that appealed to the masses and rejuvenated the keen interest and love for the movie musical (at least for three more years)...

YOUR BANGS ARE CURLED, YOUR LASHES TWIRLED. BUT STILL THE WORLD IS CRUEL: *Grease*

There is no denying the fun, frivolity and energy that permeates *Grease*. It is a legitimate good-time masterpiece and pure escapist joy. A jaded cynic can decry the warmth of this triumph of the American musical, but even the elements that cop eternal criticism (such as the age of the actors, the flying car, etc.) still do not exclude the movie from a permanent place in pop cultural history. It is an institution, a legacy, a tribute, and a formative rite of passage. Most of all, it is perpetually magical. *Grease*, quite simply, is *the word*.

Grease opens with the distinctly 1970s animated stylings of John David Wilson (who would also work on *The Sonny and Cher Comedy Hour* and *The Carol Burnett Show*) to a song by 1970s disco sweethearts the Bee Gees. This title track was, written specifically for the film and became an international hit, later to be integrated into consequential stage mountings. The film is the epitome of the nostalgia kick of the late 1970s, and the lyric from this song "this is a life of illusion..." is exactly what *Grease* delivers: it is an illusion of a bygone era, a stylized tipping-of-the-hat to that most valued and popular of American musical forms—rock'n'roll. It is a fabricated ode to a supposedly simpler and halcyon time, laced with an overwhelming preoccupation with sexual knowledge, awareness and awakening.

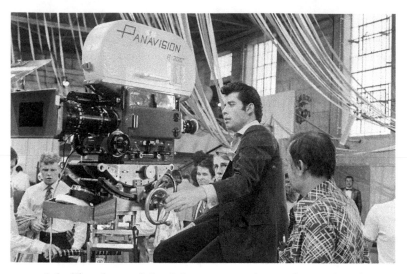

John Travolta gets behind the camera on the set of *Grease* (1978)

Grease is a pastiche on 1950s sentiment for a 1970s audience, and this is set up even before the opening titles. The self-aware and subtly satirical pre-credit sequence with Danny (John Travolta) and Sandy (Olivia Newton-John) on the beach is a tribute to 1950s cinema. It is a tribute that only 1970s culture vultures would get, a homage to romance films such as *From Here to Eternity* (1953) and teen melodramas dished out by the likes of American International Pictures. This subtle spoof sets the mood as we are introduced to the virginal Sandy and the image-conscious, self-defined lothario Danny. Along with these two leads are Frenchy (Didi Conn) the "fairy godmother" to Sandy, who also needs her own personal teen angel, Kinecki (Jeff Conaway) who is the second in command to Travolta's Danny and is equally sexually confident oozing (a sometimes phony) bravado, and Rizzo (Stockard Channing) who is the most complicated of the film's characters. Superficially, she is presented as the whore with the (eventual) heart of gold, but subversively she is concocted as the most liberated but also most fragile of the group. Rounding up the troupe are Marty (Dinah Manoff) who has urban pretensions and carries a façade of sophistication, overeater Jan (Jamie Donnelly) and sex-crazed hooligans Sonny (Michael Tucci), Doody (Barry Pearl) and Putzie (Kelly Ward). But with all their flaws, insecurities and masks, these kids are all loveable and incredibly charming. They form a mini-community within Rydell High School (the atypical American high school for working class kids) and they truly care about each other.

Behind the scenes on *Grease* (1978)

By experiencing the journey of these young people—the working class children of immigrants—we find our own place. The sadness that permeates the closing moments of the film stems from the question: where do these dead-end kids go from here? Is high school the be all and end all for them? There is a sense that there is nothing for them beyond the safe and character defining confines of the all-American high school. The car that takes Danny and Sandy away ends up flying into the heavens becomes an expression of ascension, higher learning, venturing into the full blown realm of fantasy which the film seems to be embody. Life here is an illusion as described in the film's very first song. Even though *Grease* is earthly and semi-realist in its delivery and its subject, it is also a teenage fantasy—the two fantasy sequences of "Greased Lightning" and "Beauty School Drop Out" are testaments to this, but the final moment where the car suddenly turns into Chitty-Chitty Bang-Bang is an extension of this fantastical element. From this perspective, that actors such as Stockard Channing seem too old to play high school kids doesn't matter. By the end of the film, we accept the fantasy, grounded in the reality of teen drama or not.

And besides, Channing is incredible in this film. Her song "There Are Worse Things I Could Do" is one of the rare moments in the film that genuinely strives to be serious in tone, and because of this it becomes an even more bleak and sombre sequence. It is incredibly jarring just considering that the rest of the movie is fun, bright and funny. Rizzo begins the song as the tough-as-nails good time gal, claiming that she can "flirt with all the guys" and "press against them when we dance." But by the end of the number, we find a softer, vulnerable little-girl-lost as she laments, "I don't steal and I don't lie, but I can feel and I can cry," a fact that she has never let on in the entire musical. By the end of the number we discover something new about the streetwise, sexually free Rizzo, as we experience a girl growing and coming to terms with her personal insecurities. There is an arc developed throughout this short rock'n'roll torch song. The number is certainly not as complex and rich as something like "Soliloquy" in *Carousel* (where Billy Bigelow goes through a gamut of emotions when he finds out that his wife whom he has been rough on is now with child), but the character transition in Rizzo's song is palpable and informs the viewer of her teenage angst beyond simply about getting laid (which for the most part the film remains preoccupied with). This song is about the repercussions of sexual indiscretion, and is necessary.

The movie focuses on these kinds of character transitions, as well as the sexual curiosity and determination to be desired. Transitions close the film, as straight-laced Sandy blossoms into a sexualised young bombshell. At the end of the film (and with the off screen help of Frenchie) Sandy becomes a sexually aggressive vixen who vamps her way through the add-on hit number "You're The One That I Want" where she expresses her sexual needs, desires and demands with graphic condition listing. Danny attempts a transition when he takes on various sports to impress Sandy. Changing for the sake of a relationship acts as a narrative anchor in *Grease*, and the two characters that undergo this are our protagonists.

But ultimately, it is their supporting cast that remain surprisingly more interesting. The culture of the Pink Ladies and the T-Birds (the female and the male groups that the central kids belong to) is born from legend and sprouts from historical events such as the 1950s urban

A publicity still for *Grease* (1978)

turf gang warfare, white subcultures that broke away from immigrant parents/traditions, the creation of distinct and personal lexicons and the new (sometimes violent) traditions and the formation of the "teenager" that happened within the 1950s. The Pink Ladies and the T-Birds are hedonists: they are on the fringe, they are outsiders, they are far more sexually knowing (at least they think they are), they are apathetic and they are also completely of the "slacker" ilk (with the exception of the ambitious Frenchie). Parents are absent in *Grease*, replaced by Eve Arden as the principal, Sid Caeser as the gym teacher and a host of others cast members reminiscent of 1950s cinema.

The fish-out-of-water in *Grease* is the Australian character Sandy. Olivia Newton-John was on the rise of becoming a major star by 1978, so producer Robert Stigwood cast her and kept her Down Under accent and attitude that was a major departure from the original musical where Sandy was Polish. Sandy is said to be "too pure to be Pink," therefore not easily accepted into the clique of sassy, sexy girls headed by Rizzo. Sandy is virginal and naïve—she believes in true love, romance and tenderness, which the other girls (once again with the exception of the sweet Frenchie, who possesses a little bit of hope) don't buy. Sex is sex in the eyes of Rizzo, while for Sandy it is something foreign and to be made special. Danny is all about sexual conquest, and throughout the film we get a sense of the amount of girls he has successfully seduced. But with Sandy it is different—there is something more here, a deeper, more meaningful connection.

"Summer Nights" is one of the best songs in the film. A beautifully written number about hearsay and a wonderful call back number that builds from its foundational contradiction. Sandy explains that "He got friendly holding my hand," to which Danny responds with "She got friendly down in the sand." Here we get a clear idea of how Danny and Sandy view their encounter: Sandy sees the summer fling as romantic and special, and also innocent, Danny however makes clear suggestions of oral sex ("she was good you know what I mean?" he sings out: cockily bragging about his sexual escapades). Throughout the song we get a sense that Sandy is telling the truth, while Danny is modifying it for his sex-crazed audience (the boys). The final moments of the song isolate the two star crossed lovers and this is where the honesty pours out. Danny wonders "what she's doin' know..." in a moment of genuine affection. This typifies what *Grease* is about: the breakdown of fabricated personae and the social stigma of shedding these illusions. *Grease* wants us to embrace truth: that Danny genuinely loves Sandy, that Sandy will grow into a self-possessed woman, and that the world doesn't have to be so complicated.

Behind the scenes on the "Greased Lightning" number in *Grease* (1978)

The cynical Rizzo and her disbelief in the existence of romance ("True love and he didn't lay a hand on ya? Sounds like a creep to me") is the most honest of the characters, and she sparks the feud between Danny and Sandy at the pep-rally where we discover the cultural separation gap. Here, our glimpse of the charming and sensitive Danny quickly dissolves into the egotistical and arrogant greaser that he pretends to be. There is also a wonderfully sharp commentary on class in *Grease*; here we have working class children of immigrants trying to make their way in the world. Beyond their crew exists characters that embody different spectrums of the high school experience: typical nerd Eugene (Eddie Deezen), over-achiever Patty Simcox (Susan Buckner), the jock as played by Lorenzo Lamas, and so forth. These kids are never accepted or allowed into the two groups that we follow because they may have goals or a place in functional society, but the T-Birds and the Pink Ladies don't. Well, beyond cars at least: for the boys, outside the obsession of girls and getting laid is the love and attention given to cars. In *Grease*, cars are just as important—even more important- than girls, a theme that will pop up again in another rock'n'roll obsessed teen film, John Carpenter's adaptation of Stephen King's *Christine* (1983). "Greased Lightning" is a celebration of male sexuality: the car as phallus, the conquests are young unsuspecting girls, the lyrics that ooze with predatory sexuality such as "a real pussy wagon" and "the chicks'll cream." The song is loaded with sexually charged lyrics that are authentic and honest about the reasons why these boys drive: cars are freedom and a place for sex.

Significantly, Frenchie is the only character with obvious ambitions. She wants to be a beautician and sees a life planned out for herself beyond high school. This is lacking in the other teens that strut through the film apathetically (although they are charming and funny). In the slumber party sequence where the girls try to introduce Sandy to the world of rebellion, Frenchie also tries to pierce her ears. When Sandy bleeds it's a graphic symbolic of Sandy's delayed entry into womanhood. The mockery that follows as Rizzo points out with "Look at me I'm Sandra Dee, lousy with virginity..." alienates Sandy, and a decision has to be made. Olivia Newton John's performance and treatment of this transition and development is as organic and as natural as the writing. She is spot on, and her tender performance of yet another add-on song "Hopelessly

Devoted to You" is a thing of pop beauty. This is the one moment of the film that exists outside of the preoccupation with sex because it is about devotion and honest love. The sexual expression in *Grease* ultimately lies within the film's language: there are constant references to genitalia and various sex acts. Gang bangs, flogging the log, sloppy seconds and so forth are part of *Grease*'s colourful lexicon and this is one element of the film's brilliance. It uses language to showcase the layers of persona and the dilution of illusion.

There is an informal law in theatre that it is easier to accept an older actor playing a younger character than it is a young actor playing someone old. This is a combination of things but mainly because older performers have a broader and more learned sense of self and the world around them, therefore can paint up a youthful variant of themselves in a cleaner and swifter way. In *Grease*, this is part of the musical fantasy and it works fine. The musical is light and escapist, which helps: unlike the devastating *West Side Story* where being a teenager means playing with life or death, the youngsters from *Grease* are not faced with any mortal danger, prejudice or horrific attacks. Instead, their problems are born from sexual liberties and inhibitions. In *Grease*, innocence is a nuisance and a hindrance, and sexual knowing and freedom (to a certain extent) are welcomed and accepted.

In place of the violence that fuels *West Side Story*, *Grease* focuses on personal social sacrifices (Danny attempts to change, Sandy goes through a major transition, Rizzo becomes aware of her vulnerability and so forth). When Danny tries out various sports in order to impress Sandy it is discovered that he is not at all a team player, and the track field is the only real place for him. This is representative of his lone-wolf characteristic. Although Danny leads the T-Birds and creates his own congregation, he is ultimately a rogue loner, completely isolated by a societal fabric that will only ever oppress him. Sandy is different from the others not only culturally and sexually, but she is also from a middle class background while the other girls and Danny are working class. But it is the energy of these children of immigrants that have made America their playground that attracts Sandy, and her superficial relationship with the jock character is indicative of her interest in socially acceptable boys. But it isn't genuine—much like Danny's egotistical bravado, it is a facade.

She wants the dangerous leather-clad lothario, and she will do what she can to get him. As stated in "You're The One That I Want," she will have him with clear conditions and on her terms.

The romantic union of Sandy and Danny sits in the centre of the film however the other unions: Kineckie and Rizzo, Doody and Frenchie and so forth are partnerships drawn from necessity. They act not only in simple service of the story, but give these young people external connections outside of their own selfish desires. The film is about transcendence, and by the end of the film we love these kids, warts and all. The camaraderie between them is palpable and sweet, and there is an endearing and enchanting togetherness that is hard to deny. Even if the entire movie is about a fabricated illusion, the solidarity that culminates by the end of the film is very real. It is also a necessary escape, as summed up in "Beauty School Drop Out" (another perfectly written song mixing comedy with sweet sincerity) where the teen angel to Frenchie (1950s superstar Frankie Avalon) sings "Your bangs are curled, your lashes twirled, but still the world is cruel." Even with all the pretty trimmings and innocent loveliness, there is a dark and mean world out there. And although *Grease* is in no way a whistling in the dark musical, it most certainly knows that the coldness of humanity exists, just around the corner.

The major set pieces—the dance sequence and the car race—are pivotal moments that encompass the teen spirit. The dance is perfectly executed and beautifully handled by director Randall Kleiser. Here we get a lot of character insight and motivation: Marty's keen interest in the older host for the evening Vince Fontaine (Edd Byrnes), a whimsical moment where Frenchie tells Doody that "Blondes do have more fun" with the terrific music by the fictional band Johnny Casino and the Gamblers (as played by Sha-Na-Na) swelling, the introduction of Cha Cha (Annette Charles), another lady from Danny's past, and the magical moment where Sandy and Danny emerge from the crowd dancing with the strings soaring high and lifting us into the magic of the movie musical.

From "Born to Hand-Jive" through to "Sandy," *Grease* is musically strong. And that is something that cynics really cannot argue. Patricia Birch's choreography and then direction of the sequel with the same set up (straight laced kid meets hyper-sexual rogue) is frenzied at times, but it works. The art direction is sparkling and crisp. Paramount Studios have never looked so bright and sun kissed. *Grease* is a film that is all about being sparkling, it is about fun and wackiness, irreverence and togetherness. The dramatic moments in *Grease* do exist of course, but they come in, do their thing, and then disappear (Rizzo's solo being the only true sombre moment of the film). Perhaps it was because at this point in time audiences and filmmakers alike thought that musicals should become joyous again. The dark and bleak *Fiddler on the Roof*, *Man of La Mancha*, *Jesus Christ Superstar* and *Cabaret* had their time, but now there was some room for light, frilly fun. *Grease* heralded this change. Of course, happiness and joy met head on with anger, despair and grit in the last few years of the 1970s with dark musicals such as *The Rose*, *All That Jazz* and *Fame* taking audiences and critics by storm.

Grease was a major success, but it the only hit that was bright, cheery and optimistic. It is not that Grease is without bittersweet tones, which come at the end of the film with "We Go Together." Here, the number sums up the feelings everyone has at the end of high school—part celebration and part yearning. The song is most certainly a whistling in the dark number much like "Singing in the Rain" as it makes light of what is truly happening: these kids are leaving each other, but insist that they'll "always be together." There is a melancholy energy here, and it marks the end of an era and the kind of experiences the film has just so lovingly documented. *Grease* says that if our hearts are open and our spirits are high, then we all have the ability to go together like a-wop-ba-ba-boo-lop and wop-bam-boo. And there is nothing remotely wrong with that.

Actor Didi Conn who played Frenchie shares her *Grease* stories:

> I had to go pick up the script at Paramount Studios, and when I got it all it was just one page in a Manilla envelope and it was right at the little guard's gate stand. I said "Seriously, this is just one page…isn't there a whole script?" I pulled my car over and went into this little booth and I actually sat under his desk and he gave me the whole script to read, and I thought that Rizzo was a better part! And it was very helpful because the page was just a little scene but

then when I got to read the whole thing I got to see more of who she was. I had my hair done. Actually, for the audition I went in with my new doo and that was for the producer, the director, the choreographer. They had call backs after call backs and it went on and on and on, where they would keep eliminating people. Until one day there was about three of us for each role and they had us do some improvisation to find the perfect T-Birds and the perfect Pink Ladies, and it was fun. It was shaking down to what you see. I never was offered any other role, just Frenchy. Patricia Birch, the choreographer told me that when they all saw me they said I had the part, so that was pretty cool. They said, "Was there anything else I wanted to do?" and I said "Yeah, read for Rizzo!" and they laughed and that was it. I know that they wanted Lucie Arnaz to play Rizzo actually. Her mother, Lucille Ball, didn't want her to audition. They wanted her to do a screen test, and she just wanted Lucie to be offered the role and not have to audition. They didn't want to do that; they wanted her to audition to see her; not for her skill as an actress, but to see her with Travolta and Jeff Conaway. And she wouldn't do it, so they didn't hire her. So, that is how I won, really. Oh, it was fun! During that scene where we perform "Summer Nights," we were actually at a real high school and outdoors on those tables and it was just fun! What was really great was that all of us were older than the characters we were playing, so when we would come into work in the morning we would get into make-up and costume and call each other by our character's name. So we were in a constant improvisation all day long. That gave us the license to be as silly, childish and play it so was freeing and whatever. So we just had a lot of fun every day. Actually, I think we were all hired because we were so youthful and had a child spirit living in all of us. Even now, thirty-five years later, everybody I know who was in that movie still has that same energy—an innocent kid and wild side. So, it was easy just to tap into that and have fun. Also what was interesting about the movie is that a lot of people who were hired to be in it, had either been in the Broadway Show or in one of the national companies, so they had performed these songs, these dances and they had found wonderful characters. They would have these traits all sorted out by doing the show so many times. Allan Carr was brilliant in getting the stars of the 1950s like Eve Arden and Sid Caesar and Frankie Avalon—it added to it, just the idea of getting these stars of that time. So that was appealing to the parents of the kids going to see the movie, and I think that is why the film has lasted so long with so many generations, that it is appreciate for different periods that it represented. They were wonderful! They loved every minute of it. It was a wonderful experience. I absolutely loved working on *Grease* from top to bottom. In fact, while we were making the movie, there was already talk of making the sequel, and in the last scene, the scene in the carnival; the boys are throwing pies at Sid Caesar, at the coach, and Eugene throws a pie and hits him right in the face and he says "Hey, who are you? I hope to see you in summer school!" And that was going to be the sequel—Summer School. But Paramount had no idea that this film was going to be such a big success, but when it made so much money they were keen to get set on Summer School. We all had such a good time and wanted to do the sequel, so they proposed it to the powers that be, and guess what? They passed. And after it came out, when it was such a big success, of course they said "Let's do it!" but John and Olivia didn't want to do it anymore, and that is how *Grease 2* was born. Working on *Grease 2* was great! I was doing the series *Benson* at the time so they had to kind of fit in my schedule, I think I filmed everything in like two days or something and it was great. I loved it, and I loved meeting Michelle Pfeiffer—she was so beautiful and you knew she was going to be a big star. So I was happy to be a part of it. Also, back to the original *Grease*, I have to admit that there was no acting going on when I shared the scene with Frankie Avalon. He was gorgeous! I just had to look at him and I was drooling! And it was so wonderful to have my own set for two days. I had worked on that scene, two days prior to that with my acting coach, and when they put that pink wig on me and my whole costume it was just great. That morning, to do that scene there was a lot of setting up of the shot; we didn't get any filming done before lunch. And you're not supposed to go out on the Paramount lot at lunch with the costume on, but I snuck off to go to my acting coach, and as soon as he saw me, he said, "Don't do anything! You look outrageous! Don't do anything, but just listen." And that was great advice because it was pretty wild having that pink hair so that was good advice. And it was great! I had a wonderful time. The boys who were the angels, had to hang up there all day long and they were very uncomfortable up there. Their family jewels were getting kind of numb, and that is where the expression "numb nuts" come from. Well that's what they told me! But it was wonderful. Also, Frankie Avalon has told me that of all the hits that he had in the 1950s, the most requested song when he performs is "Beauty School Drop Out." Olivia had made one other movie before called *Toomorrow*. Her first scene was with me and she was nervous. She told me she was nervous. And I just said to her, "Hey, you know, Sandy…" and I just starting speaking to her as though she were truly Sandy, and I just started improvising with her, and she looked at me kind of quizzically and she said, "Oh, okay," and then she kind of played with me, improvising like we were walking to school and asking her about her high school in Australia, and she started telling me that she had to wear white gloves, and before we knew it, the camera was rolling and we went right into our dialogue and afterwards she just thanked me so much. It made it fun and she just played. She is a wonderful, wonderful person. We're very good friends until this day. She's got a huge imagination. She loved playing the hot Sandy. She loved breaking out of that role, and she is just a terrific person! I think it was the original make-over show and Frenchie wanted to help her be the best she could be. So it was really to show that side of herself because she wanted to show it: she did it for Danny the same way he became a jock for her—it was just another aspect of themselves which is broadening who they are. I did go to a beauty school to do some research and found out there was a lot more to know than just hair. You really learn all about etiquette and manners and chemistry which is what Frenchie failed at. Every scene I had, because I worked out with my hairdresser on set, had something in my hair that was representative of the scene—like in the car chase, I had a little car in my hair. These are things you don't see but I thought it was something she would have adorned herself with; something that was kind of thematic to what the scenes were. For the scene in the bedroom, for the sleepover we were actually on a sound stage at Paramount, and we were so into this scene; the girls were making a lot of noise. At one point, I jump up and close my bedroom door. That wasn't in the script but I thought "Oh, my mother's going to hear!" I was so into it. And it was great! Stockard was great! We were into our characters and she was our leader. She was tough and someone to admire, and we were all a little afraid of her. It was good.

Actor Barry Pearl who played Doody remembers the original production of *Grease,* as well as the filmic adaptation:

I had been cast in the stage play in the second national tour in 1972. And the story goes that in the summer of 1972 I was working with the Chicago Street Theatre. It was the summer before my senior year of college at Carnegie Mellon University, and in that production what had happened was I was working with the Chicago Street Theatre, I had befriended a fellow by the name of John Lansing, who went on to write and produce *Walker: Texas Ranger* starring Chuck Norris. When we were doing Street Theatre, it was January of 1973 and I went back to finish my

451

last semester of college. John went on to understudy in the first national tour of the stage play of *Grease*. It starred at the time, Jeff Conaway, may he rest in peace, playing Zuko, Mary-Lou Henner playing Marti and John Travolta playing Doody. Barry Bostwick who originated the role of Danny Zuko on Broadway came out to do the show when it came out to Los Angeles. Jerry Zaks, the very successful Broadway director was playing the role of Kineckie. It was star studded or it became so in retrospect. So John went on to do this show and I went back to college. During my college years, I had friends of mine who were transfer students from colleges out here in Los Angeles, who kept telling me how much I am remind them of their friend Michael Lembeck. We were doing the same roles, the same plays and so forth and well *Grease* comes through Pittsburgh, and my friend John calls and says "Hey, you gotta come down and see this play. There are roles that you are right for in this." I had never even heard of *Grease*. So I went down and I saw the show, and sure enough this Michael Lembeck fella was in the show and playing the role of Sonny. He comes walking out on stage, and the dynamics of this are interesting. If you can picture this, he enters the stage from up centre stage and he is walking backwards. You don't see his face. He turns around, it was like looking at myself. I was blown away by the show. The very next day I got on the phone with my New York agent. I said "You got to get me an audition for this." Sure enough by the following week, I was in New York at a general audition for the play. There will be replacements, there will be other companies etc., etc. So I got this audition for the very next weekly. I got a telephone call from my agent saying "Michael Lembeck has broken his ankle in "We Go Together," which in the movie it is the last song, but in the play it isn't so they said "They want to see you again to replace Michael for the time he is going to be out." So I flew back into New York and I got the job. They wanted me to come immediately to Toronto, I guess it was. I had two weeks of school of finish. They let me finish school while they put their understudy on. I was flown up to Detroit for the remaining three weeks that Michael was going to be out. I understudied the understudy basically. So I was there for three weeks working my bottom off, and I go to Jerry Zaks who was playing Kenickie and say "Hey, can you fake an illness on this one particular day so I can at least get some fruits for my labors, only if the management says that it is okay?" He said "Alright, if that is how you want to play it," okay, I knew that they weren't going to. Sure enough they didn't. That particular Saturday morning I get a telephone call from the stage manager saying "Jerry Zaks is sick. He isn't going on as Sonny." He may have had that planned. Who the heck knows? It was May 19 of 1973, I stepped foot onstage in the role of Sonny in the play. A couple of days later, Michael Lembeck had come out, and I was laid off. They didn't need me anymore. But I had made an impression because at the end of that summer of 1973, they called me. The show was out in California. Michael Lembeck had lived down here and wanted to leave the show, so they called me to replace him, and I did the last ten months of the show which were in Chicago and Toronto. So I had my experience with the stage play before auditioning for the movie. That was 1973. So we fade out and fade in, and I had moved down here in 1976. I came out on speculation, which I had always contended that one should never do, come out here with a job because it is brutal out here. In a week and a half I gotten a television series called *CPO Sharkey* with Don Rickles. I was on top of the world, I had gotten a television series. Well by the time we had finished shooting that thirteen weeks later, I had become rather despondent because they weren't really writing for me. I had actually replaced another actor who was playing an Italian fellow, and if you know Don Rickles and if you have ever seen this show, it was basically like Sergeant Bilko on the high sea. Phil Silvers who had played Bilko back in the day would kind of berate and kid the guys, well Rickles would kid us about our ethnicity. So he would insult the Polish guy, the Swedish guy, the Italian guy, it was hard for him to insult the Italian guy, so they were finding it hard to write for the Italian guy. They replaced one actor who was the Italian and instead of making me somebody else, they wound up letting me go. Not picking up my contract. They then with my character wrote for a Greek guy. The series lasted for another year and then it was gone, but the point of this whole thing was I was despondent and really despondent after I found out they weren't going to pick me up for the second season. If that had not happened, I never would have gotten *Grease*. Getting *Grease*, we were told that nobody who had done the stage play was really going to have a shot at the movie. But I got an audition, somehow my agent got me in there. I wound up getting the job as Doody, in the movie four years to the day after I stepped on stage for the first time as Sonny in the stage play. This was May 19 of 1976. Four years from 1973. So that is how I got involved, doing the paces just like everybody else. What I do in the movie, I am basically playing the role of Sonny, but the name is Doody. The fellow who plays Sonny in the film, Michael Tucci, was one of the understudies in the first national tour of *Grease*. He didn't understudy me. He was cast as Sonny but he was basically playing the role of Roger, a character dropped from the film. The fellow playing Putzie was really playing Doody. They changed the names around basically. That's how that rolled out. So there is that story. I think first of all the music of this particular movie was very 1970s. The Gibb Brothers or Barry Gibb himself wrote the title track. There is some real 1970s disco feel to it, though they certainly captured the flavour of the 1950s, now that being said of course, much of the film contained the stage music, though there was much of that music that was not contained, and that music was more 1950s than "Grease is the Word" and "You're the One That I Want," but those songs that I just mentioned are spectacular songs and fit into

454

that particular construct. It was a time where, first of all, the 1950s we attribute with that era as the beginning of rock'n'roll, making that music popular so they were born in that age, so therefore we are constantly paying homage to that. The Beatles did the same thing in the 60's. They were hugely influenced by Elvis Presley and Buddy Holly and the like. So the twist I think that this particular film that *Grease* puts on it for the ears of the folks of the 1970s helps with the appeal. I think that the 1950s music still stood alone and was still listened to and still is listened to because it just holds. It's anchored in our psyches somehow, in our musical psyches. I don't know what it was about the 1970s were there this collective decision to pay homage to the 1950s unless *Grease* set that in motion possibly because I guess it was the first, if not the first to do that. I think *The Buddy Holly Story* came after that. I remember being in Chicago doing *Grease* at Blackstone Theatre if I am not mistaken and being told there was this new television show that was going to be paying homage to the 1950s called *Happy Days*. And of course that came out of *American Graffiti*. It really took place in the 1960s if I'm not mistaken, or was that also an homage to the 1950s? And actually it was *Love American Style* in which there was an episode that introduced the Cunninghams I believe. And that is where *Happy Days* sprung. I think that to the fact to that *Grease* continues to have its appeal is because of the story of boy meets girl, loses girl, finds girl, the coming of age and this music, this choreography and Olivia and John, you can just not take your eyes off them, and the rather talented supporting cast. Well let's forget that there is money to be made which is why we make movies. You need to melt down the edges to be able to have a wide appeal as it has, and if you listen to the words of "Grease Lightning," they didn't get changed for the film. I'm a purist. I have directed two productions now of the stage play and each time they use the clean version. There are several versions of the play. The first one is the quote unquote raunchiest. I think the very first time we hear it is Sonny in the stage play, they are referring to a girl and what sexual acts they got up to last summer, and Sonny says "Does she have big knockers" and Zuko says "Is that all you ever think about Son?" and Sonny looks around and says "Fucking A." Well in the 70's when this play first hit the board, it was sensational and funny. It opened the envelope, it bent the rules and it landed. You do that today and because the pendulum has swung more to the conservative side and in politics. I am using that as a broad term for how we're all living today under that particular conservative umbrella. It has swung to the right. Hopefully it is swinging back a little bit now. Today you cannot do that particular version of it. You can't do it. It will not land. You'll lose audience. There is the version that is on the complete opposite side of that, there is a high school version where Sonny says "Friggin A." Or not even that, so there is that version. Then there is the version that kind of fits in between. That's the version that I have been using but I tweak when I am allowed to. I run it past my producers and I say "Can we say 'shit'?" Every little while we can say "shit." Also in that same version where Sonny says "Friggin A," Marti says about dropping her rhinestone from her brand new glasses into the macaroni salad, she says "Son of a bitch." There is this nice talk about all of that, she says I have just dropped a diamond into my macaroni and then there is a blackout before "Summer Nights." So that is allowed into this but elsewhere Sonny has to say "Son of a B" so it's not consistent. There is another version that Jim Jacobs has been working on for the last several years and it had a great response in Chicago a couple of summers ago, and that is a thing he called the original *Grease*, which is the very original play that was done in Chicago in Kingston Mines before it even hit New York, coupled with the version that was done on Broadway in 1972, and then the version that it finally became, where Kenickie is a supporting character and the role of Miller is what the Kenickie character was. It is really raunchy apparently. They are using songs that they had cut originally. There is that version that is going to be out. There's more money to be made. Shows like *Hair* and *The Rocky Horror Picture Show* could not be transformed in that fashion. Choreographer Pat Birch really had autonomy there and has always been known, she has always been under the choreographer that works so well with non-dancers or movers if you will. She can make a non-dancer look like a dancer, that is what she did with most of us. You will actually see in the stage play, the character of Sonny doesn't dance much or nor he have a song, that is because Jim who created Sonny was not a dancer, he could not dance at all, so he gets drunk during the dance contest and he and Maria Small who played Frenchie in the stage play, they don't have songs either, they weren't as strong a singers as the others were, so that was in the stage version. In the movie none of us have any individual songs really when you look at it. "Grease Lightning" is now Zuko's song when in the play it was Kenickie's song. "Freddy My Love" was a song that Marti sang during the pyjama party and that was gone. Doody sings "Those Magic Changes" and that was gone, however those songs are in the background in the dance contest. Roger which is no longer a character who is basically the Sonny character would sing "Mooning" and when you cut to the dance contest you can hear that playing in the background. As far as how it was shot we spent at least a week, possibly two or maybe a week and a half doing "Summer Nights." It was fabulous. I think it was the first big number that we did and shooting it on the bleachers, and the girls parts shot were underneath that by the outdoor cafeteria. It was wonderfully imagined and pretty much stuck close to what we had done on stage. She did the best she could and better at bringing it on to the bleachers. I mean, quite a feat if you ask me. It was a joy to shoot and it was working under that hot sun take after take and yet we all rallied. I would say again that it was probably a week or two when we began to work because we actually rehearsed in the studios and basically put together a play at Paramount. And they actually had us perform it for all the execs and for all the people that were shooting on the lot back in that day. Jack Nicholson came to watch, the late Michael Landon came to watch, there were many others there that I don't fully remember. Jack Nicholson was shooting *Goin' South*, and I think Michael London was doing *Little House on the Prairie* at that time, may he rest in peace. We rehearsed it like a stage play and then brought it before the cameras. So we had it all worked out before we got it to principle photography. As far as the dance goes Pat put it together like she would have on the stage. And every single bar, every measure of that song, something was happening. Because you will notice, Vince Fontaine is tapping people out. You know so she stages it that way. They break it down into sequences, into shots and then it is up to Randal Kleiser to storyboard that and shoot it in the sequence that he shot it in. It was originally done in Toronto. Like the stage play. I believe it took us at least a week or possibly two in this un-air conditioned gymnasium next to I think it was Marshall High next to a pork plant, and it was very hot. People were keeling over in the heat. Michael Tucci I think had to be taken out on a stretcher, so it was very uncomfortable at the time shooting that dance sequence. If you notice in one of the shots, Didi Conn and I, there is a group shot, a master shot of everybody doing a sort of a side step to one side and then coming back. Well Didi and I screwed up and we went the opposite direction, and your eye goes right to us at that point because we're the only ones not doing it correctly. They kept it in. I had known Sid, I had directed Sid in a production of *Olivier!* in Vegas back in 1970. I was a mere twenty years old so I had worked with Sid before and got to know him and then I had actually done a television show that we both were co-stars in so we didn't work together. I don't know if I remember him on the set in a thing called *The Munster's Revenge*. These were all the originals—Fred Gwynne, Yvonne De Carlo and Al Lewis. They were all doing this thing. Butch Patrick of course had grown up. I played one of Marilyn's boyfriends when she brings him home but I was just talking about this the other day how I didn't spend as much time with Sid on the set as much as I would have liked to. He was a little reclusive. Eve Arden was delightful, Dody was fabulous, Alice Ghostly... every single one of them. As any of the cast members we are all still in touch. A big family. I see Frankie every once in a while. He came to see the production of *Grease* that I directed out here in music theatre, so we bump into each other quite often. We had done a pilot together called *The Romeos* for CBS years ago which I play one of his back-up singers and his poker buddy. It was going to go to air but they changed regime and that whole idea went down the toilet, which happens when regimes change, they don't want to have an ego about it...they don't want to use anything that the previous president had on board. In any event so he looks great, he sounds great. Of course Dody is gone, Eve is gone, Sid is unfortunately now gone...Alice, I don't remember if she is gone or is up there in years, she may be gone too actually. Joan Blondell, too. It was fabulous to work with the icons. It was a wonderfully loving set. Allan Carr really had it together when he decided to incorporate those both absolutely. It was because we were working down in the L.A River bed and the water, there is a screw of water that kind of goes through a gully...a gutter..it's not a gutter, it is some kind of indentation. In the middle of that cement construct there and there was all this tainted water and the very first thing shot there, our director, Randal Kleiser, it was the dead of summer. He was wearing shorts. He had a terrible cut on his calf, well he walked through that water. The following day, the entire production was shut down because he had come down with an infection and a terrible fever. He had got infected by that water. So at the very end of the race when Danny has won the race and we all race over to the car, and we're running through that water. They had actually put some planks over that water but some of us are running through it. We had to put cellophane around out feet, and then our soaks over that and then put the shoes on in order to run over so we wouldn't get infected. It was tough. It was a hard sequence to cement. It was the dead of summer, it was very hot and it needed all to be choreographed within an inch of its life…the race certainly, so it was a hard sequence to shoot. Especially again with that water was very scary. It cost them thousands of dollars to shut production down for that one day that Randal could not shoot. It was dangerous. Well gosh. It's hard to say. I suppose Michael…well Didi actually. I would say Didi and then Michael because we had a history with the show. We loved to hang out, and Jeff Conaway, we were kid actors together. And in my life he was Zuko, he was the Zuko in my life, so it is hard to distinguish people out because we all hung out together. We'd go out. There was the time John picked us all up in a limo and we went out to dinner, we went to a strip club and hung out. We all got close. I think Didi and I because we worked so close together and we became real tight and still are to this day. Kelly was my choreographer in the *Grease* that I directed out here last year. It is the core of both the film and the stage play. And there is a reason why it is at the end of the movie. It happened at the end of the first act in the stage play. The whole piece is about camaraderie. Besides about the coming of age that it is, of boy meets girl story. It's really about these lovable, you know being a member of a gang does not mean what it means today, this is extended family as they claim it is today but in a much more degraded way. It is a hugely dysfunctional family but it was a club, it was a Mickey Mouse club, and that is even referred to in the stage play. I can't remember if it is in the movie. They talk about going over to watch the Mickey Mouse club because Annette is starting to grow boobs, which happens at the end of the play. It is the core and I think that it was a manifestation of how all us actors felt about each other that lived through that song that you see up on that screen. It is very honest. It probably lends to the success of this too, in a very subtle yet very powerful way. I would like to believe it has to be part of the movies success because we all cared a great deal for one another. There were no divas on the set, everybody just got along. You know, I have done so many interviews where people looking for some sordid stories. Tell us some details. There were no sordid details. Every once and a while Jeff Conaway's Honey Wagon, his portable dressing room would be rocking back and forth a little. It gives joy to people that are seeing these films are from those cultures and it speaks to them, it doesn't speak down to them. I think it elevates people of different colours, races and ideologies, and heads again, part of its huge success from generation to generation. You know, we didn't see much of Robert. He was around certainly but he was very much in the background. Allan was more of a presence. Allan was just Allan...hugely flamboyant, lovely and loving...and Mr Hollywood. The biggest thing I ever did was a thing called *Bye Bye Birdie*. *Bye Bye Birdie* is the first rock musical. When you think about it, it is the first rock n roll musical. We can't bookend my life yet, we can't bookend my career yet because it is not over. It's funny because consider this as well. *Bye Bye Birdie* was the first job I ever did, my first rock musical. So the 50's keep pulling me back. So how important it is in my career...it is huge to be part of that phenomenon. I am blessed and I think about it every day. I don't take it for granted. It is what I call in many other interviews, is my wonderful haunting. This is what haunts me as it has been and what could continue for the rest of my life...that I have made of this life, something to have been worth living. The mark has been made. If what we ultimately want to do as artists is to leave the mark...I have done that, I have been part of a larger mark that has been left by being an integral part of that larger hole, so it is very rewarding.

Actor Eddie Deezen who played high school nerd Eugene remembers the shoot:

> My old agent, Regina Penner, found out and told me about it. I had never seen or heard of "Grease," so I went to see the show, it was actually playing at the Hollywood Pantages theatre, by coincidence. I went in, it was a huge cattle call. A bunch of guys dressed like Fonzie and tons of girl's in poodle skirts and saddle shoes. I was the only guy there who looked like a nerd. I put greasy stuff in my hair that morning, I remember. Why? I don't know. Nerds don't grease their hair, do they? But that's what I did. I read and was interviewed as Eugene. Joel Thurm was there, he had cast *Taxi*, and Randall Kleiser, the director, and Allan Carr, the producer were all there. As I read the script, I could see them smiling and nudging each other, nodding. So I knew I was doing well. They all looked happy with me. The nerd character Eugene is a very sad character, in actuality. He can't fit in with the real world, so he holes up and dives into his own world. And that is where he lives. You can see this in all nerds. They live in their own universe. The character has more to do in the stage musical. I was sad so much of my stuff was cut. I was really hurt when I saw my scenes cut at the premiere. There was a lot more stuff. All cut out. But they did leave in the scene where I get hit in the face with a pie at the carnival. So I am happy at least that is still intact. They cut a scene of me writing loudly at the chalkboard as the teacher is talking, Right before Olivia enters the classroom they cut a scene of me as the waterboy and they cut scenes of me at the dance. Pat Birch was a marvellous choreographer. The dance scenes were fun, but it was super-hot in the auditorium. It was like 116 degrees there. They couldn't open the windows to ventilate the place because planes kept flying over and making too much noise. A few of the extras actually passed out from the heat. It was a blast! I loved it. Oh, just basic nostalgia, you know, the grass always seems greener in

previous generations, doesn't it? I saw the stage show a year or two ago and it was very crass and raunchy. The film avoids most of the real crude stuff, I think, and I'm glad it did. The dirty song lyrics cannot really be discerned easily. When I went to the *Grease* sing-a-long, I read the actual lyrics. Pretty gnarly stuff!!! Holy cow!!! I was closest to the dancers. They were all so nice and friendly. All the cast was very nice. I remember John Travolta was such a wonderful guy. He'd call me "buddy," "Hey buddy, are you okay?" He'd always come over and make sure I was alright. The scene where I get roughed up on the stairs, John said, "Are you okay, buddy?" I only spoke to Olivia once. Four of us hijacked a convertible on the Paramount Studio lot and drove it around. Olivia turned and looked at me sitting in the backseat and said, "You're funny." I said, "Thanks." Jeff Conaway tried to get me laid with a hooker (no kidding!!!) but it never happened. Jeff was the only scary cast member, the only one who wasn't real warm. But later, Jeff and I did many signing shows together and he became like a brother to me. I loved the guy very much. I am very happy and proud to have been a small part of what is now regarded as a "Classic." It is the most popular musical of all-time. I think only *The Wizard of Oz* perhaps, is a most widely loved film than *Grease*—especially with girls and women. I have grown to love the film. It is a joy to watch. Also working with those seasoned pros. Eve Arden was a doll. She told me about her film *At the Circus* with the Marx Brothers. I loved eve very much. Dody Goodman was a very nice lady too. I never met Frankie filming *Grease*, but we did a signing show together two or three years ago. He and I got to sit and chat for 15 or 20 minutes. He is a very nice, wonderful guy. I had said hi to him and he kind of brushed me off earlier in the day, I was very sad and disappointed. But then he called me over and wanted to talk to me. I will never forget how kind he was to talk with me that day, to take the time to make me feel welcome. Although I have done around 30 films, *Grease* is, by far, the most beloved, the most popular. I get called to go, "Hey Eugene!" all the time. I have gotten fan mail from all over the world. I am so happy to have been a part of this lightning in a bottle film. It was like a two-month party. It was one of the greatest experiences of my life.

Sha-Na-Na member and co-writer of the song "Sandy" Scott Simon has also offered some anecdotes about *Grease*:

> We were on the set of our Television series *Sha Na Na* when Louis St. Louis and Pat Birch came in during a break to ask us if we would please portray Johnny Casino and the Gamblers in the movie. They said we were the best band in the world to do the music for their National Bandstand Dance off scene. They needed a song in 6/8 to stroll to (we suggested "Tears on My Pillow"), they needed a warm up bop song ("Rock'n'Roll Is Here to Stay," sung by yours truly, but my face never appeared on camera during the entire vocal; they were too busy shooting the dancers, another bopper "Hound Dog," and two songs from the stage musical ("Born to Hand Jive" and "Those Magic Changes"). And of course "Blue Moon" done ballad style, so they could have the T-Birds moon the camera. We had been contacted early in the workshopping of the *Grease* Off-Broadway musical eight years previous by the authors/composers/producers but we were Woodstock rock stars at the time playing the Fillmore and had zero interest in taking the BMT subway down to the West Village to workshop a musical featuring faux sound-alikes of 1950s music. We were covering the real songs. Pat Birch was a genius at choreographing her dancers. She had the movie principles the T-Birds, the Pink Ladies, sixteen principle dancers (you can see the women featured in "Beauty School Dropout" and the men are featured at the end of the movie strutting in "We Go Together"). My sense was that Pat was the engine that drove the dance sequences, and her collaboration with the director was pointing him in the right direction. I think she "set up" the shots and he captured

them. Kleiser was a great director in that regard. We had been representing the 50's for about ten frigging years before shooting the movie in 1977. We were at Woodstock in 1969. We were the originators of looking back into the one-hit wonders of the rock'n'roll era. The *Grease* musical was pastiche musically. The *Grease* movie allowed for actual 50's-60's songs performed by us to enter the soundtrack, as well as fantastic original songs not in the original musical by John Farrar ("You're the One That I Want," "Hopelessly Devoted to You"), Barry Gibb (the title song, sung by Frankie Valli) and "Sandy" composed by Louis St. Louis and myself that John Travolta sang at the Drive-in. The prom sequence is brilliant. Credit Pat Birch and her collaboration with Louis St. Louis for that sequence. She did the Choreography, he was the in-studio musical liaison during our recording process making sure that the exact number of measures/musical bars were recorded to accommodate her intricate choreography. My collaboration with Louis St. Louis was in the studio and in his hotel suite at the Sunset Marquis where we composed "Sandy." On set, I got nearest to Sid Caesar and even got him to play a few notes on the prop tenor saxophone. And of course John Travolta, who had approved "Sandy" as his solo number (the song in the book show musical was one played for humor called "I'm Alone at the Drive-In" which had zero gravitas.) John was quite grateful to have a song tailored to his vocal range (credit Louis St. Louis) and good words to sing (my doing.) I guess it's what I've felt about show business/rock business since the band played at Woodstock in its 6th professional gig. My motto is: Get luck, stay lucky and in between the luck there's a shit load of very, very hard work. Robert Stigwood got Barry Gibb to write the title song. Allan Carr was the hands-on producer, and Louis St. Louis and Bronte Woodward who co-wrote the script with Carr were his collaborators. Let's say it was a fortuitous accident waiting to happen. Really after Louis and I wrote the song, Louis shepherded it through the maze of approvals necessary to get it into the film, Kleiser, Carr, Travolta all loved it. John thanked me personally in his trailer on the set, and since then over the years we have crossed his path at a health spa in L.A. which we both frequent and he has always been cordial and expressed (again) thanks at being handed a tailor-made song for his big solo in the film. I saw a touring company which included it and the other original songs. The singer absolutely butchered the ending. There's just no respect for the song on the page once you put it into the hands of actors (who know better!) on the stage. Having said that, overall one word comes to mind. Gratitude! Robert Stigwood owned RSO records which released and promoted the soundtrack. "Thriller" by Michael Jackson has sold 66 million units worldwide. Second place: *Grease* soundtrack at 40 million. Stigwood was the label head of RSO which stands for ROBERT STIGWOOD ORGANIZATION.

I'M THE GIRL THAT WORKS AT PARAMOUNT ALL DAY, AND FOX ALL NIGHT: *Sextette*

Mae West: the very name evokes the marrow and the intangible spirit of innuendo and assertive female sexuality. These elements were the foundations of her play from the 1930s—a sex comedy that was banned and caused quite a stir—that the 1970s musical *Sextette* is based on. *Sextette* is the epitome of everything West stood for: unadulterated sexual prowess, self-aware self-commodification, and an intelligent warmth and strange sophistication born out of the golden age of Hollywood. The film opens with famed TV newscaster Regis Philbin announcing the latest marriage of Marlow Manners (Mae West), and amidst a sea of adoring fans and devotees of this seasoned vamp, Philbin ushers us into a frenzied, bizarre and ultimately silly excursion into the camp and at times jaw-dropping mess that is *Sextette*. With all its ludicrous faults and its mishandled take on West, it is a charming idiotic creation with some fantastic performances from the likes of Dom DeLuise and Timothy Dalton. DeLuise camps it up as the statesman who fusses over Marlow, a throwback to the "helper sissy" characters of the 1930s who looked after Ginger Rogers and Fred Astaire in films such as *Top Hat* (1935). Here

DeLuise's bright and energetic performance does a fine balancing act, countering the aging West with vitality and good humour. As the film progresses, its learned that DeLuise's statesman introduced Marlow to VIPs and politicians to broaden her horizons and make a better name for herself. This is a nice little commentary on celebrity: that living legends such as Mae West who created her own lexicon and mythology (nobody really knows a lot about this elusive figure) would go about "bettering" themselves by adapting to new ideas and new waves of artistry. In *Myra Breckinridge*, West reinvented her already steady and stoic image by bringing it to the foreground in a motion picture about a Hollywood obsessed transsexual, while in *Sextette* she surrounds herself with young stars of the 1970s such as Alice Cooper, George Hamilton and the man playing her husband Michael, soon-to-be James Bond Timothy Dalton. Dalton does a great job hamming it up and feeling right at home with the broad and silly comedy, such as the running joke about his sexuality which clearly a not-so-subtle extension of the film's obsession with gay in-jokes and innuendo (including the parade of muscle men that flew and strut about and the prancing bellboys who cruise each other while pirouetting up and down stairwells). When Timothy Dalton sings Captain and Tenille's "Love Will Keep Us Together" with Mae West it is a complete cinematic oddity and has to be seen to be believed.

Mae West and Timothy Dalton do a bit of The Captain and Tennile in *Sextette* (1978)

Dalton fumbles about with the lyrics and melody while West purrs them out at her own speed and by her own terms. West famously had an "eye" for talent (the legendary story regarding Cary Grant comes to mind) and Dalton follows in the grand tradition of this established vixen giving a platform for a new handsome dark haired leading man. Every one of Mae West's lines are loaded with innuendo and it is seriously hard not to grimace at their audacious efforts, when she says things such as "I'm the girl who works at Paramount all day, and fox all night" and "Everything goes up for Marlow!" These are made all the more shocking because its presented in the film in such an overt light—the imagery that plays off these sex-charged one liners not only compliments the wordsmith that is West, but exaggerates the explicitness. Because of this, the film succeeds. In films such as *I'm No Angel* (1933) and *My Little Chickadee* (1940) (two of West's most famous films for Paramount), the sexual innuendo was there but muted by the classy stylings typical of the era. Here in a warts and all 1970s sex comedy, West's phrases are provocative and displayed with an aggressive thrust. However, the film does not look good: it is visually banal experience, and the hotel in which the film is primarily set is decked out in bland colors. As great as West's costumes are, they don't hold up to the glamorous outfits she paraded around in in the earlier (and much better) *Myra Breckinridge*.

Musically, the film is also inferior. Much like the terrible *Sgt. Pepper's Lonely Hearts Club Band* (which we will look at in a moment), *Sextette* is a jukebox musical for the most part including standards from the golden age of Hollywood such as the anthem of "Hooray For Hollywood" through to public domain hits such as "Happy Birthday Twenty One" and songs popular at the time of production such as the Captain and Tennille example. This is a magpie's nest of nonsense, but it is fun and ridiculous. Mae West is a force to be reckoned with—an artist who risked her personal freedoms in order to unleash her art and here in her last film she continues to defy critics and the "good taste brigade." And good on her! Timothy Dalton carries himself with confidence in the awkward comedy, but for some strange reason he is actually perfect and does the stiff, uptight Brit caught up in a mumbled sex comedy to perfection. Tony Curtis also does a great job as a sleazy prince. But the film is a Dom DeLuise vehicle: he is as great as he always was, and part of filmmaker and writer Mel Brooks's alumni, it is second nature to be the song and dance man that he truly is. Mel Brooks is a musical theatre obsessive—he would continually inject musical numbers into his comedies such as *Young Frankenstein* (1974) and *Blazing Saddles* (1974)—would later create *The Producers* (1968) with Gene Wilder and Zero Mostel following an attempt to create the worst musical ever (about Hitler, at that!). This would be translated into massively successful Broadway show and then back into a film, and Brooks's is an important reference here because his comic stylings are not a far stretch from Mae Wests's. Both are acutely interested in social stigma and like to push boundaries, and *Sextette* has a lot more in comparison to something like *The Producers* than many critics would like to admit. They are both about monstrosity: the over-the-top, the loud, the brash, the opportunistic, the old estate, the dysfunctional, the messy and the alien. They both also celebrate nonsense and present situations that while anachronistic, still serve a comedic function.

The ex-husbands—a prince, a film director and so forth—are toys for Mae West's Marlowe, and her interest and interaction with the bodybuilders is both a feminist strong point in the picture as well as a nice homage to her nightclub act back in the 1950s where she had the likes of Mickey Hargitary and Ed Fury working with when she was past her box office appeal. West is a one-woman show, but Rona Barrett who also makes an appearance as a woman of a certain age who is a commanding and great presence on screen. When she interviews Timothy Dalton's sexually misread Michael, she controls the madness with ease. *Myra Breckinridge* gave West an opportunity to make an impression, and her plays such as *Catherine Was Great* truly encapsulate what a smart person she was. Marlow Manners is a perfect creation for West; not far from her own persona, and like West, a personality more than an actress. West was a terrific writer and someone who should be given a lot more respect. Her underrated comedy is a thing of genius—slick and dirty.

The notion that West is genuinely attracted, interested and invested in Timothy Dalton never really comes across on the screen, but it doesn't matter. After all, he's just another toy. The jokes come fast and heavy—there is no subtlety here, and there is no room for it either. As dreadful as the film gets, West's sexual aggressiveness and assertiveness is intoxicating. The homosexual gags are necessary in a film all about the "queen of camp" and the gay appeal is palpable and dense. The muscle worship sequence where West acts for all people interested in the male aesthetic counters musicals such as *The First Nudie Musical* and *Cinderella* which played for a heterosexual male gaze. Here in *Sextette* there is a selfless welcoming to a closeted variant of gay charade with the hyperfeminine West as an extension of gay male experience.

Mae West and "all this meat and no potatoes" in *Sextette* (1978)

The film is not amazing, and it does not really showcase its cast's best assets even though some of them are terrific. But what it does is provide an insight into the insanity that brewed in the late 1970s, and the risks filmmakers were prepared to take. It is fun, and that's what it wants to be. Dalton proving his masculinity (read: heterosexuality) is ludicrous and also weirdly humorous. Tony Curtis does a pantomime Russian Tsar who West has also been married to, and they play off each other with a joyful silliness. Curtis has a good handle on comedy, but it would have been nice for him to have sung a number with Wes. In fact, that's the main problem with the film: there isn't nearly enough song and dance, and even though every single song has nothing to offer the already watery script, it would have been a good idea to embrace the frivolous vaudeville spirit more.

West's original play was risqué to say the least for an audience of the 1930s swamped by the Depression, but in the late 1970s it comes across flimsy. Fun sometimes isn't enough. The bodybuilders, the bellboys, the endless references to "getting it up," "pole vaulting" and "being hard" are all part of the fabric, and when Mae West announces "All this meat and no potatoes" when surrounded by a bevy of beefcake, it's as deep as this romp will get. Ringo Starr and Keith Moon round up the cast: West was surprisingly interested in rock stars of the era, and her friendship with Alice Cooper is a thing of legend. There are moments where West looks like she's having a great time and other times where she looks tired and in need of some serious R & R. This is what makes the film even more bizarre, and important in the history of "last-evers": when West sings "After I'm Gone" it is hilarious simply because she is having so much fun singing it (West was a recording artist as well as an actress, writer and icon).

Mae West does what she can to make the film work. Her writing is manufactured in a way to string together some unnecessary nonsense, in fact the film may have worked better as a faster and more condensed play on innuendo as a form of comedy. The musical numbers should have been fresh and written for the film adaptation of the play and slotted in there at moments where the dialogue runs out of things to do and express. There may have also been room for some high-end slapstick, for example De Luise ends up being hung out over the ledge of the hotel, and adding insult to injury pigeons come and nest upon his shoulders. Dalton proves to be quite the athlete as he is given the opportunity to jump around, throw punches, leaps across ledges and dart and dash around a building loaded with narrow hallways and sidewinding corridors. In a strange way, it is a nice preparation for James Bond.

An actual genuine athlete also co-starred in the film, a former Mr. America bodybuilder Ric Drasin. He shares some stories regarding the shoot:

> The 1970's were the most popular times of bodybuilding known now as the Golden Era of Bodybuilding. It was a

471

time where we all grouped together as a family in Venice, training and eating together and week end parties. It will never be duplicated again and now is only a memory. The producers called Gold's Gym on our wall phone looking for bodybuilders for the movie. Many of us went down and we were all hired. It was supposed to be a week's work but ended up 6 weeks as Mae couldn't show up all the time. Was fun and the money with overtime was great.

Film historian Michael Gregg Michaud offers some insight into the production of *Sextette*:

> *Sextette*, released by Crown International in 1978, was Mae West's final film—and first certifiable box office flop. The movie was based on her self-penned play, *Sextet*, in which she toured during the summer of 1961. The aged sex symbol drew enthusiastic standing-room-only crowds, but critics savagely panned the play. Nevertheless, West felt that the play was a "star vehicle," and she tried to get the property produced as a film for the next fifteen years. A 1972 MGM Studio production deal fell through, but did provide her with a recording contract. West covered a few classic and contemporary Rock 'n' Roll hits in her 1972 record album "Great Balls of Fire" (MGM Records SE-4869). In 1977, *Sextette* finally went before the cameras, shooting at the Goldwyn Studios and on a rented stage at Paramount. West excitedly told the press her film would include several songs. With the exception of her first motion picture, *Night After Night* (1932), all her films had included "lavish" musical production numbers. Experienced musician Artie Butler composed music for *Sextette*, and provided musical direction. Like all creative aspects of her films, the actress had song approval as well. Ever the shrewd marketer, she included "Happy Birthday Twenty-One," a reworking with special lyrics by Ian Whitcomb of the Neil Sedaka/ Howard Greenfield 1961 hit "Happy Birthday, Sweet

Sixteen," which was included in her "Great Balls of Fire" album. The other songs in the film included an old standard "After You've Gone" (1918, Layton/Creamer) popularized in 1927 by another "Red Hot Mama," Sophie Tucker, and the Sedaka/Greenfield composition "Love Will Keep Us Together"(1975)—which West sang to 33-year-old British actor Timothy Dalton, who was playing the role of her seventh husband. The Captain & Tennille recorded "Love Will Keep Us Together" and had won the Grammy Award for Record of the Year in February, 1976. West balked when she was presented with an original ballad that had her tearfully pining over a man who had left her. "Mae West," she pronounced, "would never cry over a man." Fresh after his Grammy Award winning #1 Disco hit, "The Hustle," musician/song writer/arranger/producer Van McCoy, was brought in to write "Next Next," an upbeat song, which was acceptable to West. In the film, she performed the number with rock star Alice Cooper. McCoy also wrote "Marlow's Theme." What once worked for the star seemed awkward and dated. Her considerable fan base was delighted with *Sextette*, but the film was a dismal failure.

RABBITS, DOGS AND WOOKIES: *The Easter Bunny is Coming to Town, The Magic of Lassie* and *The Star Wars Holiday Special*

Rankin/Bass once again hit all the right notes in an Easter film special, taking a detour from their normally Christmas-themed stop motion musicals such as the tender and sweet *The Little Drummer Boy* (1968) and *Rudolph the Red Nosed Reindeer* (1964). *The Easter Bunny is Coming to Town* is a bright and loving look at one of folklore's most respected and honored lepines. In the role of a neighbourly postman, Fred Astaire lends his voice to a character that would become synonymous with the look, feel and style of Rankin/Bass male heroic leads—impish, lanky and almost ethereal. This look will embody the new-age male that will be increasingly visible during the late 1970s, but suddenly disappear come the 1980s in favour of more aggressively macho male protagonists in both animation and live action cinema.

473

In this piece, the small town deliveryman narrates an enchanting story about Kidville, a halcyon little hamlet run by and governed by children. Heading these children is a seven-year-old king who befriends a baby rabbit that introduces the town to the wonders of Easter celebrations. The number one threat to this almost picture perfect scenario (and the representative of the much needed conflict) is the king's spinster aunt who detests joy and fun, putting a ban on Easter and being numero uno enemy to our cotton-tailed hero.

Much like previous Rankin/Bass motion pictures, characters who are cantankerous and mean spirited either lose the narrative battle or submit to the beauty of life and the sweetness of it all. In this film the crabby aunt does the latter—she sees the Easter lily and is touched by the importance of friendship, rebirth and change. In *The Little Drummer Boy*, misanthropy rules the pint sized protagonist and he grows into someone who can finally trust fellow humans when he comes into contact with baby Jesus, and in *The Easter Bunny is Coming to Town*, the jaded and spiritually dead aunt softens and has a re-birthing, a Jonah-and-the-Whale moment where she welcomes the idea loving humanity once she accepts the power of Easter and the importance of the Easter Bunny's message. This is what Rankin/Bass do so well: they provide good guys and bad guys incredible arcs and complex motivations and needs.

Actress and singer Laura Dean leant her voice to one of the children from Kidville in the film, and remembers the making of this seasonal classic:

> I've always loved the Rankin-Bass shows and specials and was thrilled to have gotten a chance to work on one. I don't remember meeting Mr. Rankin or Mr. Bass. They probably were not at the sessions we did in NYC. I was 13 years old then, working all the time while juggling being a full time student, so I can't really remember a whole lot about each gig I had. I'm certain I auditioned for it, but details are fuzzy. In animation, actors are often recorded separately, and don't even cross paths. Fred Astaire, most likely, recorded his part in L. A. I do remember recording with most of the ensemble together in a studio in NYC. And

that Skip Hinnant (who was one of the cast members of *The Electric Company*) played the Easter bunny, but, honestly, I don't really remember much more. Again, in animation, sometimes the actors record the script before things are filmed. Sometimes, as in *The Adventures of the Galaxy Rangers* (a series I was a regular on in the late '80s) the animation was produced in Asia before the voice production, and the actors record separately from each other, literally dubbing our lines over the existing animation. On *The Easter Bunny Is Coming to Town* we never saw actual puppets or animation. We were shown story boards and drawings of our characters. I can't remember whether I met Alan Swift or if we recorded at the same time.

The Magic of Lassie is the first Lassie film in almost three decades. Although it doesn't have the tenderness, charm and elegance of the original masterpiece *Lassie Come Home* (1943) or later fare such as *The Courage of Lassie* (1946) and *Hills of Home* (1948) it does deliver a Lassie for the 1970s. Here is a pooch that teaches us that greed corrupts people, and that materialism is unimportant. She reminds us that companionship, friendship, unconditional love and unity are the things that matter. This is of course not entirely an exclusive 1970s filmic ethos, as movies such as *National Velvet* (1944), *Old Yeller* (1957) and *Fearless Fagan* (1952) have taught us that the devotion and love shared between a human being and an animal is the most nourishing and fulfilling, and can happily exist outside of a desire to selfishly succeed or make a fortune. *The Magic of Lassie* harkens back to those times, with stories delivered the likes of Elizabeth Taylor and her beloved thoroughbred, the loyal golden retriever who unfortunately contracted rabies and the full grown lion who joins Carleton Carpenter on his induction into the US Army. The opening number is a testament to this. It suggests that "we need that ole home town feelin' again"—and this is what the musical tries to do. It attempts to bring back family entertainment untainted by cynicism and grit.

This was a tricky task in 1978. The film was of course released at a time where musicals were angry, rebellious, outrageous, and often dark

475

The poster art for *The Magic of Lassie* (1978)

and edgy. This attempts to deliver a serene, peaceful and joyous musical, paying tribute to simpler times. But this does not mean that the film is without its underlying melancholy and deep sorrowful undertones. After all, it *is* a Lassie picture, and these films were capable of being both maudlin and emotionally stirring. And bleak *The Magic of Lassie* most certainly is. There are moments in the film that are painted with such dense sombre tones that at times you really wish it lived up to its original promise delivered in its opening number: you are invited to this nostalgic, sweet movie musical that is cherry and bright and you wish it would stay that way. When the film kicks into gear when Lassie has to leave her happy life at a vineyard to be taken in by a materialistic property investor (the bad guy), the plot becomes quietly morose. Being greeted by Hollywood's legendary gravelly voiced man-for-all-seasons James Stewart—who sings this promise of good old fashioned entertainment early on—still doesn't help.

Stewart was an MGM contract player back in the day where the studio made their major contribution to the realm of cinema with their lavish (and low-key) musicals. He was assigned to do *Born to Dance* in 1936, which marked the first and last time he ever sung on screen until *The Magic of Lassie* (the only other time he ever did it). Stewart looks tired in this film, and there are moments where the he looks as though he is just going through the motions. However, there are scenes that truly give him the opportunity to perform. One such case is where he asserts his devotion to Lassie and becomes emotionally distressed at the thought of this beloved pooch having to go along with the likes of the investor who wishes to also purchase his family estate. Sadly, when the film opened to terrible box office, James Stewart went into semi-retirement, disheartened by the lack of interest in his Lassie vehicle.

Although Lassie and her cinematic adventures were a product of the 1940s, the 1970s and early 1980s were obsessed with dog movies: the dogsploitation craze was alive and well. Dozens of films featuring canine stars popped out of nowhere: some horror films, some crime-centric cinema and some family adventure movies. Some of these films were either overtly saccharine or genuinely moving, while others were completely bizarre or wacky high concept outings. *Benji* (1974), which featured a lovely song by Charlie Rich called "I Feel Love," was a massive success. The whole world fell in love with the terrier with the heart of gold and that sweet little face that could melt even the toughest of audiences. Benji (as played by the terrier cross Mr. Higgins and later his daughter Benjean in later movies) was *the* dog for 1970s audiences, and sadly *The*

Magic of Lassie just didn't have the same appeal as the other dog movies to come out of the period. *Mooch Goes to Hollywood* (1971) (an extremely entertaining oddity starring the likes of Vincent Price and narrated by Zsa Zsa Gabor), horror films such as *Dogs* (1976), *The Pack* (1977) and *Cujo* (1983) which were incredible achievements and exceptionally successful, the Hanna-Barbera produced *C.H.O.M.P.S* (1979), Michael Winner's star-studded tip-of-the-hat to the golden age of cinema *Won Ton Ton: The Dog That Saved Hollywood* (1976) were much loved cult favorites, while Benji (and some other woofers) reigned supreme in both film and television, leaving the once world famous Lassie lagging behind.

But *The Magic of Lassie* does have some things going for it. Within the fabric of its depressing fatigue, the film has some touching moments and pits megalomaniac industrial investors against the sweet connection shared between Lassie and her family headed by James Stewart with nuance and poignancy. Written by the fabulous Sherman brothers who made a massive contribution to 1970s movie musicals (starting with Disney's terrific *Bedknobs and Broomsticks* in 1971 and the surprisingly flat and uninspired *The Aristocats* in 1970 and then ending the decade with *The Magic of Lassie*), the film has a musicality to its plotting and its pace, but only when Lassie herself is on screen.

Screenwriter Jean Hollaway fine tunes the piece and helps in moving it steadily, but unfortunately the film never does anything to involve us in the drama. Nor is the script strong enough to build a concrete tension, and in all honesty there is a lot of room for this underdeveloped conflict. The movie crawls rather than sprints, and when the stakes are high they come far too late for us to care. Because this is a Lassie movie, we want her to reunite with her rightful family, but it's only when the dog is on that our attention pricks up: for some bizarre reason, however, she doesn't feature in the film nearly enough. This is a problem, especially when there are some inspired lines that help in establishing this Lassie. Herastute perception is demonstrated early on—she is weary of strangers crossing through her garden and when an undesirable comes through the plains only to have Lassie growl at him, her master, little Christopher (Michael Sharrett) asks his grandfather (James Stewart) "Why doesn't Lassie like him?." Stewart responds "Well he's not very likeable." In this film, good people are associated with loveable critters like Lassie, and this is a plot device that could have been developed further and injected throughout the script to give us a sense of what makes a good person a good person. This is, after all, what Lassie does for her audience: she helps us understand honesty and compassion.

The film also uses the very 1970s narrative trappings of commerce over domestic comfort, and it employs rather dark sensibilities most notably in the monologue delivered by Stewart who tells the story of Lassie's birth. He explains that she came to him and his family when his son and his wife were killed in an accident: "It was like life in the midst of death." The film also sprinkles some holy intervention as Stewart goes on to say: "She came from God. She needed us and we needed her." This could be laughable, but when Stewart desperately pleads to the investor to not take Lassie, we feel his anguish and his deep sorrow and believe every word. The Lassie of the 1970s could also be as much of a Christ figure as her counterparts in the dragon in *Pete's Dragon* and Angela Lansbury in *Bedknobs and Broomsticks*. She is a dog who reminds us that superficial wants are completely unimportant, and that love and understanding is what truly matters. This of course comes up in earlier incarnations of the Lassie franchise as well as the television series, but here it is most palpable because the film is so out of its element in a decade marked by the excesses of glam-rock, the apathy of punk and the chaos of disco.

The film is frustrated by its sometimes soaring music and sometimes inspired performances that are always let down by the subdued and pasty cinematography and direction. When little Christopher cries "If Lassie isn't going to be in this family, then I don't want to either!" and races off with Lassie by his side, the camera clumsily cuts away and doesn't give us time to take in the emotional declaration. Some of the songs boast lyrics that are clever and whimsical, while others plod along and don't serve plot or character whatsoever. Most of the songs act as commentary over montages involving Lassie playing with her human friends, helping out or running. Disney's *Bambi* (1942) was one of the first films to employ this technique—the unseen Greek chorus that sings about the changing of seasons and so forth—and here in *The Magic of Lassie* it is used as well, but obviously without much inspiration or creativity. The main reason behind why Walt Disney and associates thought it was a good idea to fuel *Bambi* with these songs was because the feature itself only consisted of about one thousand words of spoken dialogue and they felt that audiences would get restless if there were long stretches of film without any talking. The songs serve the film narratively (the changing of seasons and in turn the growing knowledge of the Prince of the Forest) as well as commercially (audiences getting a sense of a far more wordy, therefore easier to swallow, motion picture). In *The Magic of Lassie*, the songs are more of a soundtrack than a full-blown libretto serving plot, character and structure.

This doesn't mean that some of the songs aren't good, it's just that a lot of them do nothing to enhance the film. "Nobody's Property" is great 1970s pop that sounds like the Sherman brothers are channelling Burt Bacharach, whereas "There'll Be Other Friday Nights" is a strange ballad that pops out of nowhere and bogs the film down with a thud. It is unnecessary as it comments on the blossoming romance between a young lawyer and James Stewart's granddaughter, played by Stephanie Zimbalist who looks remotely bored in this picture.

The most appealing thing about this film is its intentions of being a good old-fashioned adventure movie. However, it is so laden with misery and is so lacklustre that it doesn't keep up with this promise. Another film to suffer in the wake of the incredible success of *Star Wars*, *The Magic of Lassie* was classed as "out of touch" and "not hip," and therefore flopped at the box office. But Stewart was not alone in MGM stars popping up in this mess of a movie: Alice Faye makes an appearance as a waitress singing along to Pat Boone who croons "A Rose Is Not a Rose." Instead of being charming, it is a little bit cringe worthy—after all, here is an actress from such marvellous movies such as *Sing Baby Sing* (1936), *The Rose of Washington Square* (1939) and *The Gang's All Here* (1941) wasted in a bit role in this out of step not-so-thrilling adventure flick. One of Faye's contemporaries from the golden age of the Hollywood movie musical June Allyson would take on a remarkably different role than what she was known for in another dog-centric 1977 film with *They Only Kill Their Masters*. Along for the ride with Stewart and Faye is the mugging and maniacal Mickey Rooney who reunites with his old MGM alumni in the form of a collie named Lassie.

The film's young cast was headed by Michael Sharrett as Christopher. Once again, the 1970s "latchkey" kid is embodied in this little boy who becomes a runaway, in search of Lassie. The sequence where he tries to find a truck heading to Colorado where Lassie has supposedly been taken is played out in menacingly at first, evolving into an ill-staged chase sequence where a truck driver races after him, who clasps onto a sandwich made for him from Alice Faye. As shown here, the film is uneventful and tedious when Lassie is not on-screen: we want Lassie back, because after all, the actors who aren't James Stewart, Alice Faye or Mickey Rooney aren't that interesting! The film is also let down by the fact that Lassie herself doesn't get enough to do. There isn't enough adventure in the film involving her. When she meets The Mike Curb Congregation (a bunch of banjo playing minstrels) in the park there is a sense of something fun and entertaining about to happen, but instead the film cuts to these hyper-happy left-over vaudevillians performing on stage at some country county fare. This is where the film then introduces opportunist characters who want to kidnap Lassie to make big bucks from her from a reward they found. A fire starts and it's up to Lassie to put it out. She even rescues a kitten from the inferno! All these incredible feats happen far too late in the movie. By this time it has been so slow and weighed down by mundane happenings that it doesn't really matter that Lassie is performing these incredible stunts.

To make matters worse, the director doesn't even focus on Lassie and her heroic efforts, but instead cuts to Stewart and company preparing for a Thanksgiving dinner. But it is at least here that we get the moment that we've all been waiting for and the moment that makes the entire film worth sitting through. As James Stewart leads his family in prayer, saying thanks for all the good gifts they have been blessed with, we hear a distant barking. As the barking gets closer, James Stewart lifts his head and all seems right in the world. Along comes the lovely Lassie racing over the hillside, while a rapturous little Christopher runs towards her. Boy and dog are reunited and *this* is that magic of Lassie. The union of child and beast, the innocence and simple joy shared between two loving friends is what makes *The Magic of Lassie* worthwhile. The gentle vocal stylings of Debby Boone singing the Academy Award nominated number "When You're Loved" forgives all the misdirected and mishandled previous scenes. James Stewart, with tears in his eyes, watching his grandson and Lassie embrace and play in the middle of a lush green field, sums up the essence of the lasting legacy of dog-centric movies: unconditional love reigns supreme, goodness triumphs over greed, tenderness hits home and the power of the pooch is what makes all the day's woes worthwhile.

This is crucially something that filmmaker George Lucas (who of course redefined cinema with his landmark *Star Wars* from the year earlier) famously forgot to   in his *The Star Wars Holiday Special*. Opening with Han Solo (Harrison Ford) and his co-pilot Chewbacca (Peter Mayhew) flying through the galaxy in their trusty Millennium Falcon eager to get to Chewbacca's family home to celebrate the holidays, this bizarre TV special is as much hated as it is weirdly loved by fans of *Star Wars,* But it is mostly hated! *The Star Wars Holiday Special* is not only over ninety minutes long and unrelated to George Lucas's plans for a franchise, it is also tremendously kooky, off the wall and uncompromisingly ruthless in its silliness, nonsense and frenzied, wacked out creepiness. Regardless, it is stillridiculously engaging and a beautiful testament to 1970s weirdoville! "What were they thinking?" is something that you can hear being chimed out as you sit back and let this mess unfold, but a truthful answer is "who cares?." The results are insane fun.

Beyond the *Star Wars* mainstays and cast members from the original film (along with Ford, Mark Hamil returns as farm boy turned intergalactic hero Luke Skywalker and Carrie Fisher reprises Princess Leia), the special features guest stars including Bea Arthur, Art Carney, Diahann Carroll, The Jefferson Starship and Harvey Korman. Some of these additions compliment the superficial "plot" such as Art Carney who plays out his scenes rather straight and with a determined dedication to his portrayal of someone who genuinely cares about the Wookies, which is the special's primary focus. The show has silly moments, but there is a steady string of seriousness which adds to its strangeness. Of course there are snippets from the 1977 film with inserts of dialogue looped in to feed the wafer thin plot that carries the special, but for the most part the feature is made up of brand new live action sequences, cartoon segments, musical performances and a tip of the hat to vaudeville.

At the core of the film is Malla's love and devotion for her Wookie husband Chewbacca, as she patiently waits for him to return home to celebrate Life Day (a holiday that honors family, friendship and being alive). *Star Wars* had a sentimental foundation with the concept of the

Force, the idea of believing in yourself, the growth and development of an unlikely hero and so forth. This TV special tries to carry those elements on its wonky shoulders, but doesn't really accomplish it successfully because it is so disorientated and runs away into the deep dark recesses of distraction. This is a vaudeville show of sorts (albeit one with a minimal plot about a Wookie family reuniting) and so therefore aids the entertainment value. The comedy and musical sequences are helpful in breaking up the monotony of its watery storyline. The scene where Malla gets some cooking advice from Harvey Korman in drag is weird, and yet works fine. The use of Korman again giving instructions to Chewbacca's son Lumpy as to how to fix circuits or something along those lines is just plain crazy.

It is difficult to understand that the massive *Star Wars* hit sparked this subdued and messy holiday special, but it did something that fans of the franchise respected: it introduced audiences to bounty hunter Boba Fett in an animated segment. This is the one thing that has garnered some love and appreciation from hardcore *Star Wars* devotees. Boba Fett would eventually become one of the most important figures in the George Lucas's universe, later to be a fully fleshed out (as much as he could be in his small screen time) in the first *Star Wars* sequel *The Empire Strikes Back* (1980), a darker and more complex follow up to the original movie.

What is most incredible (and somewhat brave) about the television special is that the first few minutes or so is told without any dialogue whatsoever. Instead, it features Chewbacca's family worrying about his safe return to them. However, even the Wookies can't compete with the true star of the special. The stand out performance in this wacky show is Bea Arthur's turn as a Tattooine bar tender. She delivers the slight gags with droll elegance and quick wit, and as the reigning queen of the double takes, she lets herself get lost in the silly situation that she has fallen into. She compliments the strange aliens that she tends to and her musical number has to be seen to be believed. This is Bea Arthur post-*Mame* and pre-*The Golden Girls*. Her bizarre in the *Star Wars* universe was unlikely, but she handles it with grace, flair and fun.

Star Wars celebrated old fashioned swashbuckling and was a magpie's nest of *The Wizard of Oz*, the Hollywood western, Japanese folklore and opera. It blended these together to make one of the most widely consumed manifestations of Joseph Campbell "Hero's Journey" for a mass audience. *The Star Wars Holiday Special* championed the odd and distinctly 1970s phenomena of the variety show. And in a strange and alluring way, it works. The 1970s was a place for larger than life fads and pop-religions—the worship of bands such as KISS and the awe-inspiring magic of *Star Wars* have become a major part of contemporary popular culture. Back then, the cult of the variety show was just as celebrated, just as worshipped and just as loved.

Writer, director and film historian Mick Garris operated R2-D2 for the special. He remembers the shoot:

> I knew it was a network TV special, which was weird in itself, and was going to have lots of TV stars of the era in it, which was incredibly bizarre. Bea Arthur? Art Carney? It seemed a far cry from the galaxy far, far away that I had been working on. Television was an alternative to the cinema from its very beginning, and it was always far removed from feature films by budget and immediacy. Musicals were the norm then; I think that because they could appeal to the broadest possible audience, and because people had few choices of channels in those days, the "spectaculars," which later became "specials," were a genre that came into their own on television exclusively. They could mix comedians, singers, a dance troupe, all of those variety elements to try to pull the whole family in after dinner. And the 1970s were the graduating class of this era. Today, the television series have all the production values of feature films. They compete with feature films. There are dozens of channels and networks, so they don't have to appeal to all people at all times. In those days, there were three networks in the USA, and they did not want segmented audiences. They wanted everybody. And even the musical shows had a mix of celebrities and entertainers to bring in the whole family. The master of this was Ed Sullivan, who started on radio with his show "Talk of the Town," and later owned Sunday nights

and introduced The Beatles to America, on shows with a little Italian puppet mouse named Topo Gigio, broadway entertainer Tessie O'Shea, singer Jack Jones, circus acts, the whole damned thing. I was working in record stores, playing in a band, and very, very interested in movies, especially genre movies. A journalist friend named Carl Macek told me that the Star Wars Corporation was looking for somebody—I had no idea what the job was, but that was good enough for me—and set up a meeting with a fellow named Charley Lippincott, who, it turned out, was the marketing genius who specialized in selling science fiction films to the fans. He started with *Star Wars*, and went to places like San Diego Comic Con, when it really was a comic book convention, and World Science Fiction Convention, with slide shows and actors from the film. No one had ever done this before. (I later did this for Charley on *Alien*). Anyway, they hired me to answer phones. I was the receptionist at this little former doctor's office a half-mile from Universal Studios for the princely sum of $150 a week. They arranged personal appearances for Darth Vader and R2, and Miki Herman was in charge of that stuff. I was a fan, and understood the other fans, and they entrusted me with operating the R2-D2 robot. And a fellow named Kermit Eller was the guy in the Vader suit in personal appearances. It was amazing, and a total blast. What was namely involved in operating R2-D2? It was run with a Futaba remote control unit, the kind they flew model planes with. There were forward and backward controls, turning, and then switches that would activate a little cassette recorder inside the robot head so that I could make him "talk." It was very simple, technically. I think they thought that it didn't matter who was in the suit. Most of the time it was a remote control robot, which was different from the suit robot. I believe the little person inside the suit for this show was Felix Silla, who has done tons and tons of creature work. One of the things that I worked on was when they were shooting the scenes on the Wookiee planet in the treehouse, which was something to behold. I have no idea who did the suits for the show, but it seemed they probably just cloned Stuart Freeborn's designs. I met Harrison Ford once, who was very, very quiet and removed from everyone else, but it was just for a moment. Never met Carrie Fisher, but I did get to know Mark Hamil, who was a nice guy and lots of fun. Later he worked with me in the opening of *Sleepwalkers*. A big genre fan. I was pretty much a puppeteer, and knew to keep out of the way—and out of their eye line. I was low man on the totem pole; I was not about to approach these celebrities... but even then it was weird having them in the world of *Star Wars*. The musical special is so far removed from the world he created. George Lucas didn't write it, it was filled with songs that were a far cry from a world he spent meticulously crafting for years, and it really did cheapen his vision. He had made it a movie, and CBS turned it into a TV special, completely ignoring everything that made it the most successful film of all time. He kept it from being released on video for years, far longer than any other film at that moment. He was—rightly—very protective of his baby, and I would guess that he saw this as a network cashing in and throwing something together for the "family" to get ratings. He cared about his movie, and it almost killed him to make it, and now it was dancing jawas and Bea Arthur singing songs sandwiched in between commercials for diapers and beer. I don't blame him a bit.

IN YOUR OWN WAY, BE A LION: *The Wiz*

The original stage musical of *The Wiz* was a massive success. Here was an all-black version of an updated *The Wizard of Oz* where Kansas became Harlem and Oz was a variant of a black-centric New York City. But when the musical was adapted into a film, it sadly failed. Box office turn-ins were at a low and audiences seemed to be disinterested. Critics such as Victor Crowley made harsh statements: "*The Wiz*: If it only had a brain," and Pauline Kael found the film grotesque and unappealing. But the film adaptation, with all its many flaws, does something that only a socially conscious director such as Sidney Lumet can do—it says something profound about the African-American experience and the complexities of racial politics. Crowley is wrong: *The Wiz* most certainly has a brain. And a heart. And plenty of courage.

The most distinct difference between the stage musical and the film adaptation of *The Wiz* is the treatment of Dorothy. No longer is she a young girl, but instead a grown woman. Screenwriter Joel Schumacher introduces EST and other pop-psychology of the time to *The Wiz,* loading the film with multiple experiences for Dorothy (Diana Ross) to endure and learn from. In his adaptation of the musical, Dorothy is a neurotic, perpetually terrified and depressed young kindergarten teacher who has never left Harlem, as opposed to a young girl born into a low-income black ghetto looking for experience as originated by talented Broadway youngster Stephanie Mills.

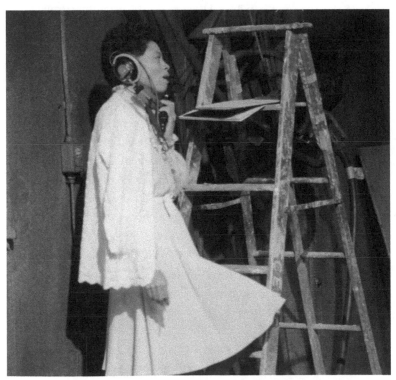

Diana Ross goes over the songs on the set of *The Wiz* (1978)

Sidney Lumet directs Mabel King on the set of *The Wiz* (1978)

The story of how Diana Ross talked her way into getting the role of Dorothy by having meetings with the executives at Universal and assertively insisting that she do the film instead of the originally proposed Mills is a thing of 1970s film legend. Schumacher had to quickly turn it into an adult woman's story. In doing so, he peppered the film with a deep psychological edge and an intense interest in the touch-me therapy fad that was becoming increasingly well documented and popular in the mainstream. Dorothy in the film version of *The Wiz* is changed by each and every decision she makes, she is forced to learn to ask questions and also to nurture and become a true "teacher" as well. She sets out on her journey horrified and puzzled and instead of becoming centred and whole. She is emotionally drained, continually distressed but ultimately changed. This film does not shy away from the "woman in the storm" narrative motif, nor does it step away from being a film about female neurosis. It embraces these complex concepts by giving heroine an ongoing and steady nervous breakdown: throughout the film Dorothy is screaming and whimpering, cowering and fretfully shaking, but all the while she is also learning, understanding and becoming aware.

In simple terms, Dorothy comprehends her existence, something she would never have been allowed to had she not experienced the urban nightmarish Oz that Lumet delivers. When her extended family sings about that "feelin' that we had," she replies in one of her many soliloquys "I don't even know the first thing of what they're feeling." Dorothy is so out of touch with humanity that she cannot let herself "feel." This emotional retardation continues to be explored, but at the same time the film speaks volumes about black history, the representation of black characters and the idea of black culture being jeopardised, homogenised and trivialised. *The Wiz* is just as important as *Cabin in the Sky* (1940) and other musicals that brought black experience to the foreground.

The Wiz is that it quietly dissects the social struggles, courage and survival strategies embedded within the black experience in America. Dorothy has never been out of Harlem, she is dwarfed in importance and swamped by an oppressive fear that dominates her very existence. Auntie Em insists that she gets out there in the real world and experience life, she tells her niece that she understands that things can get scary but that it is important for her development to leave her comfortable (and yet oppressive) situation and fend for herself in the world beyond Harlem. The opening sequence with Harlem residents gathering to celebrate what seems to be Thanksgiving or Christmas lunch is subdued and unremarkable, but that's the point—it is the humdrum which will be contrasted by the frenetic dizziness of the fantastical elements that will soon unfold. But the opening establishes character and is an articulate insight into Dorothy. When Auntie Em's daughter arrives with her husband and baby (a woman "complete") she is the polar opposite to the frightened and jittery Dorothy. Here, the film is letting us know that Auntie Em's daughter is someone who has experienced love and experienced life, whereas Dorothy is stuck in a rut. Her eventual conversation with Auntie Em lets us know that Dorothy is scared of change, scared of personal growth and finds nervous comfort in the confines of her bedroom and the trappings of Harlem. She isn't interested in taking a new job with high school students because it means relating to people closer to her own age—something she just cannot bring herself to do, let alone taking on the young suitor that Auntie Em has set her up with at dinner.

Dorothy's appearance is also worthy of note. Diana Ross looks surprisingly haggard, tired and not at all attractive throughout the film, but her vocal abilities and soaring soulful singing is nothing short of magnificent. In a sense, it is a very brave choice for Ross, as she is frumpy but her beauty shines through her incredible singing. Dorothy's bipolar energy is a thing that has to be seen to be believed and the very talented Ross plays the role with a frazzled fragility that is demented and also somehow completely inspired. She owns the film, and she owns the bizarre incarnation of the role.

Sidney Lumet's direction seems a little distracted at times and he has no concept as to how to stage a musical number (he continually bombards us with long wide shots which strain to Dede Allen's editing style). This does not at all mean he is the wrong director for the job. Yes, it is true that Lumet doesn't know how to properly block the songs, nor does he know how to present a song that doesn't require grandiose direction and major chorography, but what he does know exceptionally well is how to make a highly political and socially aware film. *The Wiz* is no exception. The spirit of African-American struggle is unpacked in *The Wiz*, and this is what Lumet is interested in. He ingeniously disguises the anger, despair, history and defiance within the context of a musical fantasy so well, that there is nothing overt about any of it—to a white audience, at least. But for an African-American audience, this concealment may not be so elusive.

Perhaps critics were not looking for politics, interested more in ensuring the terrific Motown inspired score was given a spectacular cinematic treatment, and that the overwhelming grandiosity of the piece was magnetic and charged enough. The overall gist of an urban Oz is palpable and interesting, and as a director uniformly interested in political and social message movies (see *Network*, 1976, *Serpico*, 1973, and *Dog Day Afternoon*, 1975), *The Wiz* provided Lumet with fertile territory, even if it went broadly unidentified upon its release.

Tony Walton's designs compliment this grittiness and are terrifying. There is something so creepy and bizarre about the costuming and the look of the film that it reads like a night-terror, a dreamscape of horrors and monstrosities. Legendary make-up artist Stan Winston designed the look for each character and they are distinct and oddball. Winston's

490

stroke of genius is in the details—notice the popcorn bag hat that the Scarecrow (Michael Jackson) wears as well as his Reese's Pieces chocolate wrapping nose, the real frayed collar on the Lion (Ted Ross) and the boils on Evillene's (Mabel King) face caused by incessant sweat. Winston's Tinman (Nipsey Russell) is a marvellous creation, a metallic jawline, bolted on plates, chrome toned skin. All of this adds to the horrific unnerving eeriness of the film. Much like fellow-rock musical *Godspell*, *The Wiz* has an airy, haunting feel to it. The jive talking characters and the ghetto stylings of each set piece contradict the menacing look and feel, and on top of this is the lively, fantastic score.

The Wiz might all over the shop, but it works. The weirdness of the movie hits us as soon as Dorothy is whisked away by an inner city snowstorm. Her first encounter is with The Munchkins who are spray painted graffiti caricatures that come to life as soon as Dorothy crashes into the Harlem-inspired Oz. Into a graffiti riddled playground Dorothy comes into contact with these spindly street urchins who were kept as artifice by an oppressive witch who Dorothy accidentally kills. The world of the urban is what grounds *The Wiz*—bag ladies, street kids, derelict amusement parks, bums and drug pushers decorate the yellow brick road and are presented as abstract minstrel show freaks that parade around, make nuisances of themselves or hinder/help Dorothy on her journey. Sometimes the film falls into a homage to the so-called "coon" shows of the turn of the century that continued through to the early 1940s with the African American musical experience as its primary focus, In *The Wiz* there is the soft shoe, the tap dancing, the shuffling and the celebration of the "new black experience" with the distinctly urban Motown score.

Megastar producer and musical genius Quincy Jones adds to the original piece and his treatment of Charlie Small's original numbers is fantastic. The music is brimming with exuberance and energy and is fuelled with vibrancy. Although at times the numbers seem to go on far too long (the film is also over two hours, which is unnecessary), the electricity of the music is heart stopping and you cannot help tapping your feet. But the length of the film is an issue. Some songs, most notably "He's The Wiz," "The Emerald City Sequence" and "Brand New Day" seem to go on forever and once they make their point and/or further the

Filming "Brand New Day" in *The Wiz* (1978)

story they continue to repeat the message and become tedious. But this is a minor complaint in the film as an overall experience.

There are some fabulous strokes of genius in the film such as the yellow taxi cabs that drive on down the iconic yellow brick road which continually drives away from Dorothy and her friends who venture towards the Emerald City. But then there are some strange elements that act as red herrings, such as this freaky addition: a street peddler follows Dorothy throughout the film and it seems to not really make any sense. Why is he following her? Who is he? Why does he set those oddball balloon-men to attack Dorothy and her friends in the subway? It's all very strange. The sequence in the subway is a horrific and insane. Garbage bins come to life and gnaw at the Scarecrow, electrical fuses burrow themselves into the Tinman and most weird of all is the fact that pillars within the subway come to life and surround Dorothy eager to crush her. It is a strange world this Oz, but it is unique, out there and scary.

But it's not all Kookville: there are some heartfelt moving moments in the picture. Most of them come from the soulful singing of Diana Ross. Dorothy's final number "When I Think Of Home" is a testament to the Afro-American experience as well as a beautiful expression of female empowerment, growth and transition. When Ross sings her heart out, you feel her journey, you experience her anguish, her frustration, her depth, her loneliness and the triumph of her will. And it is magical. Michael Jackson's performance as the Scarecrow is tender, moving and sensitive. The man can act, and his portrayal of the tormented philosophy quoting straw man is deep. There is a beautiful chemistry between Jackson and Ross, and it comes across so powerfully on screen. Not only do we feel Dorothy's anguish, but we also get a total understanding of the Scarecrow's dilemma, as well as the soon to be introduced Tinman and Lion.

In *The Wiz*, each of Dorothy's friends are products of oppression, loss and failure. The Scarecrow is "a product of negative thinking" and the crows hold him as a prisoner forcing him to sing an anthem (a fantastic add-on song that replaced another number from the original stage musical) called "You Can't Win (You Can't Break Even)") which Jackson sings with passion. Nipsey Russell as the Tinman is the

Michael Jackson hangs around on the set of *The Wiz* (1978)

consummate showbiz song and dance man—oppressed by Teeny Weeny (a fat animatronic mammie) who he is supposedly married to—"the tragic point" is that the Tinman can't "feel" (something that connects him directly to Dorothy). Here the film examines the numbing of black culture and the danger of white washing the art of the urban black ghetto.

494

The first moment of "light" comes with the "Slide Some Oil" song where the Tinman is liberated from Teeny Weeny (a throwback to the mean sassy mammie characters of yesteryear who were forever nasty to their Uncle Tom counterparts) and comes alive again. "I'm A Mean Ole Lion" is a great Motown number that the Lion sings right after breaking out of his proverbial closet in the form of a State Library statue lion. Here the song showcases the bravado of the black buck character archetype that peacocks around, looking proud and sexy. The Lion in reality is not this, and quickly falls to the ground terrified of living (another distinct similarity to our heroine Dorothy). When she tunefully soothes him with "Thought there may be times, when you wish you wasn't born..." he literally leaps up into a community—a new formed community of lost, lonely and desperate fragments of urban black culture—and the four launch into "Ease On Down The Road" which marks a very distinguished urban synergy. This is where we get a sense of where the white dominant culture in the original *The Wizard of Oz* is reinterpreted from a black perspective. "Don't you carry nuthin' that might be a load..." is one of the lyrics in the number and that is a perfectly condensed summary of the burden of struggle—the "load" is oppression and to "ease on down the road" is to not have to be saddled with that turmoil—personal, local and global.

The inventive interpretation of the poppy field that renders Dorothy and friends asleep in the original film is smart inspired in *The Wiz*. Here, bumping and grinding prostitutes peddle opium and cause the susceptible- those that aren't made of straw or tin—to nod off into a drug-induced slumber. This consideration of drug culture infiltrating the black culture is made with a subtle, sly wink and ultimately sends the Lion into a suicidal state. It's as if Sidney Lumet is saying that the negatives of ghetto living (addiction and susceptibility to the dark side) impede the progress of and cause pain and despair those who are otherwise capable of surviving and thriving. This is the moment where Dorothy comes to the rescue. She comforts the Lion and sings one of the most important numbers in the film, both musically and politically. "Be A Lion" is a masterpiece, as Dorothy sings "there is a place we'll go where there is mostly quiet." The imagery it evokes is superb, and the complexity of the lyrics is divine. Is Dorothy discussing heaven or a utopia for the eternally subservient blacks, or are they the same thing? She insists the Lion be a lion in his own way—a beautiful play on bravery, and that you can be a hero in your own way. This is something that black activism has long embodied. The song ends with the four heroes announcing that in their own way they're each a lion—a testament to their strength, courage and determination to find the Wiz to be granted their freedom. This is what the film does so well: it is a powerful expression of black power. Its flaws are rendered meaningless in this sense. From the sublime to the ludicrous, The Wiz's Emerald City sequence is a glitzy fashion conscious orgy of superficiality—there is nothing honest or captivating about it. The flashiness and extreme egocentric nature of Emerald City is reflective of black tokenism as a product of opportunist whites. The number that accompanies this sequence is also distinctly disco—for a moment, The Wiz leaves R&B and the soulful purity of the Motown sound in favour of the new trend of disco (a culture invented by progressiveblacks and the so-called "gay mafia"). The sleazy disco compliments the phoniness of the sequence, but it is far too long and distracts from the brilliant messages that Lumet and his talented cast delivered until this point.

The film's villain is Evilene, who runs a sweatshop. This is a very obvious but smart symbol for the oppression of black people. She is the ultimate angry mammy character and wears it proudly. In The Wiz, stereotypes exist and they are both liberating (given depth and complexity) and damaging (still pertaining to discriminatory clichés) and here, the mammy is a menace. Glinda the Good (Lena Horne) is the epitome of the classical trope of the supposed "magical Negro" who comes in and teaches the protagonist to believe in herself. The Wiz himself is played by a tottery Richard Pryor, and he is is a mess. Much like his white predecessor from 1939, the Wiz is a charlatan, but unlike his golden age Hollywood ancestor Richard Pryor's Wiz offers no compassion or wisdom, and isn't capable of even suggesting that "what these characters thought they were missing were always a part of them." Pryor's Wiz is a politician—greedy and corrupt—he lives like a drug addict in a desolate wasteland that possesses a very stagey look to it, adding to its bleakness. And The Wiz is bleak. But hope arises through the anxious Dorothy, who ends up becoming a far more important teacher in this world than she ever was at a Harlem kindergarten.

The idea of 'home' is treated in a fresh manner in *The Wiz*. Instead of Judy Garland's heartfelt understanding that love will help her overcome defeat, in this update, Dorothy's "home" is her place beyond a life lived in fear. Dorothy's reluctant quest for happiness and the experience that will fuel her inspiration lie at the heart of the film. She becomes more than a teacher to her friends and the Wiz himself, she becomes their liberator and their emancipator. After Evilene sings "Don't Nobody Bring Me No Bad News" (a bright gospel number) she is melted just like Margaret Hamilton, allowing her trapped, enslaved sweat shop workers to peel off their grotesque skins and emerge as healthy, young and attractive people, free from oppression. Dorothy has freed them and they announce that it is a "Brand New Day" which is an exciting and exhilarating (albeit too long) song and a celebration of freedom and the end of their slavery. *The Wiz* was incredibly important for young urban black kids during the time who only knew the white Garland and company playing out their journey to Oz on their TV sets every Thanksgiving.

The Blaxploitation musical helped pave the way for Afro-American artists and audiences to have a face and voice, but it was coming to an end by the time of *The Wiz*. One of the most interesting films in this subgenre was *Don't Play Us Cheap* (1972), directed by the energetic and provocative director Melvin Van Peebles. This was a musical that was rich and profound, painted with street-wise complexity. *Carwash* (1976) used music to frame its structure and subversively commented on the situations that its characters faced. And films such as *Shaft* (1971) took the power of song and turned it into a focal story element. Beyond white country and western, the black urban experience became the staple soundtrack of the grindhouse. Blaxploitation brought the soundtrack to a heightened place in narrative, and turned what auteur Kenneth Anger originally did in his gay cinema classic *Scorpio Rising* (1964) into not only an important factor contributing to story, but to the idea that film can influence song and make money from official soundtrack releasing. Soundtrack sales for *The Wiz* were higher that tickets at the Box Office.

Lena Horne had wowed audiences in important works as *Stormy Weather* (1943), and as Glinda the Good she sings all about believing in oneself. She embodies a healthy attitude of self-awareness but not self-involvement. Added to this is the fact that Dorothy sings out "it taught

497 .

me to love, so it's real…" Dorothy's Oz is a place of truth and knowledge, but most importantly experience. Horne's Glinda teaches Dorothy the importance of self-esteem, and explains that "home" comes from within. It is more than just a physical place where one eats and sleeps. These are messages left over from the original Oz from 1939, but what makes this even more poignant is that the lessons learned are universal. They are not only for white farm girls from Kansas or black kindergarten teachers from Harlem, but they are lessons for everyone. Home is a universal terrain for the spirit to blossom, and that's what *The Wiz* teaches us. But it also insists that the world can be scary, unforgiving, dark and best to be explored and experienced with brains, heart and courage.

Michael Jackson as the Scarecrow is prepped for *The Wiz* (1978)

THAT'LL BE THE DAY THAT I DIE: *The Buddy Holly Story*

The Buddy Holly Story centres on Holly's artistic integrity and musical taste. Instead of other music biopics such as *Coal Miner's Daughter* (and many to follow like *Sweet Dreams, La Bamba* and *Great Balls of Fire*), this tale lacks the usual tale of struggle because—quite possibly—Holly faced very few. Race comes into the picture, but it really doesn't make a massive impact: it steps in and shakes up the mood for a moment and then runs back into the background. Rather, the film privileges Buddy Holly the musician, the business man and as an instrumental force in the introduction of rock'n'roll to a mass audience. Whereas a film such as *The Rose* starring the spellbinding Bette Midler is confronting and harrowing, *The Buddy Holly Story* is safe, almost as clean cut as Holly's own image.

Gary Busey as rock legend Buddy Holly in **The Buddy Holly Story (1978)**

But this does not necessarily make it a dull film, it's a quiet and thoughtful one. The gifted Gary Busey does wonders as Buddy Holly, and his methods are careful. This is a biographical portrayal delicately woven together through thorough observation and meticulous meditation. There is a power to his softness and a gentle handling of a young man dedicated to his music. But on the flipside of this, when Busey is the "performing" Holly, he is driven by a fiery possession. Where Midler's take on a tortured rock star is like an emotional exorcism, Busey as Holly does a fine balancing act between insular introspective off-stage Holly and the onstage riotous preacher casting out demons. Ultimately, this is

Gary Busey's film, and it is a film about performanceL nuanced, subtle, strangely subdued and incredibly enigmatic.

The film opens at a roller skating rink with Holly playing "Mockingbird Hill," a hillbilly standard. Clearly he is frustrated by the laidback mood of the number and the entire rink is disinterested (with the exception of some older ladies). He grabs hold of his Fender Strat and we get to hear the Buddy Holly we all know and love. Electricity in the air is sparked and the "boppers" get up and dance the night away. Buddy Holly is a hit and Busey's performance here, even so early in the piece, is fuelled with the same kind of electricity that "be-bop" rock 'n' roll evokes. This promises to be an energetic and ferociously rebellious movie and Holly, an unlikely hero for the wild with his spectacles and clean-cut look, looks to be a character that will deliver. Busey does this, and the music is as captivating and brilliant as he is, making it the other star of the piece. In a film that often feels like a made for TV movie with its flat direction and underwhelming visuals, the thunderous music (authentic in both its orchestrations and loyal to the era it is presenting) is fantastic and jolts into your system, just as it should. You get a sense of the mess halls populated by rock'n'rollers back in the 1950s and it is a wonderful place to be.

Following the charged roller skating rink scene, the film cuts to a local Texan church where Buddy Holly is seen with his parents listening the sermon of about the evils of "jungle music." Here we get the feeling that the film is going to be all about cultural difference and it's take on the notion of "colored" music within the confides of a very white America. And in a way, it is. But as previously mentioned, this is a subtle hum that sits in the dark recesses of the social disorder that creeps around this picture, and unlike something like *La Bamba* (which presents Latino culture in a very complicated and fractured manner), *The Buddy Holly Story* gives us a hero who is enlightened by all forms of musical expression, but most notably black inspired rhythm and blues.

There is an early dispute between Holly and his parents which addresses this concern, although it turns very quickly into the usual "You have to start thinking about your future" deal. Even questions here about "bettering oneself and direction" recede in importance as Holly's ambitions take centre stage, with his growing success becoming the main focus. All of these assets serve what fundamentally a performance piece: Busey is outstanding as Holly. He does not simply mimicking the rock'n'roll legend, he injects the character with his own unique talents. Busey is an intense actor, distinct and always interesting to watch, and in this film he is defiantly on top of his game.

A memorable moment is when Holly and his band mates are driving and flesh out the mechanics of whatwould later become the big hit, "Peggy Sue." It is an inspired and captures the essence of song writing genius, showcasing musicians at their most resourceful and on-the-spot-creative. The recording of "That'll Be The Day" is another highlight. Holly's disdain for hillbilly and the trappings of that style of music that led to his growing interest in rock'n'roll, and this is handled with prowess. The anger of Holly and his explosive attitude towards the racism that permeates the recording industry are wonderful additions to a sequence early in the piece, which dissects the artistic differences and the transformative experience of "shoop" music into full blown rock music that he will face throughout the film. This is film's most successful narrative tool: it sets up the challenges of Buddy Holly the artist, and shows reacting to and working around them. This establishes his faith in his own music. "I feel a lot better when I have it on!" chimes out Holly when he is told by a recording producer to take his guitar off while in the sound booth. The film runs with this spirit of resistance and creativity through to the final moments.

The Buddy Holly Story (1978)

501

The idea of rock'n'roll being a threat to the fabric of a conservative white America has been the foundation of dozens upon dozens of teensploitation films of the 1950s such as *Rock Baby Rock It* (1957) and many more. *The Buddy Holly Story* touches on this, but only slightly. It's instead preoccupied with Holly himself: the man and the bizarre mystery surrounding him. The film also sidesteps the notion of class: the lower and working class backgrounds of the rock'n'roll stars in comparison to some of their middle class fans. Here, small town Texas is in an effective vacuum, a dustbowl suburban tract nightmare town that has newly been introduced to rock'n'roll. This leaves room to explore concerns about class and class resentment, but once again, its not what director Steve Rash is interested in. Instead, he presents small-town America (the kind of place that would send a genius like Buddy Holly insane) as an emotional and creative trap. Rash introduces us to the little world that Buddy Holly has sprouted from, but quickly and suddenly gets him to leave his high school sweetheart and pursue his career. When Holly's demo is mistaken as a master and pressed by a successful record producer, everything takes off and the superficial notion of exploring class in a southern hickville town is thrown out the window. But there are elements that grant the film a warmth that can from a Norman Rockwell sensibility: for example, when Holly and his band mates attempt to record a demo, they hear the chirping of crickets, and these pesky insects interrupt their playing. This is of course how the band got their name, Buddy Holly and the Crickets.

The idea of a guitar, drums and bass making up a band shook the music world, and there are endless moments in the film where well-meaning producers and recording directors remain quizzical at the very concept of a simple three piece band. It is also haunted by comparisons to Elvis Presley and his determination to be unique is something that Rash scrutinizes. Holly was adamant about being his own producer, and Busey's believability in the scenes where he is told he can't be are magic. When a recording session in Nashville leaves a bad taste in his mouth, Holly turns into a business savvy artis and it takes a lot of convincing for him to use a producer in New York at RCA Records. He eventually gives a reluctant yes, so his character shown to have a degree of flexibility despite remaining headstrong.

The notion of Buddy Holly and the Crickets being black is a

running gag in a section of the film, culminating when they play an all-Africa-n-American show at the Apollo Theatre to a surprised all-black audience who warm to them instantly. The reverse racism that is explored in the film is refreshing, albeit kept rather light as opposed to the fervent aggressive racism that permeates musical biopics like *Lady Sings the Blues*. The prejudices that come up in *The Buddy Holly Story* are treated lightly and without deep insight, but this doesn't matter when a massive black audience leaps up in glee dancing to the loud thunderous rock'n'roll of corn-fed white boy Buddy Holly. It is a moment of joy and overwhelming beauty: rock'n'roll sees no color.

On top of all this is the depiction of Buddy Holly's love interest. She is the niece of the head of the Latino music department and secretary to the producer that signs Buddy Holly. Maria Elena (Maria Richwine) is a sensitive and beautiful soul who is drawn to Holly and his creative impulses and energy. Racism also stems from characters that exist outside and in between the white Holly and the Latino Elena, but ultimately, this beautiful romance comes to represent the diversity that colors the rock'n'roll world. The music may not "see" color but it painted up by whites, blacks and Latinos. Buddy Holly as an innovator and revolutionary is one of the many artists to lead the way in the melting pot mentality and the integration of race within the fun and rebellious frivolity of rock'n'roll. Buddy Holly's hatred of racism comes on strong, most notably when he punches his drummer (Don Stroud) in the face after a crack about Maria Elena. The scene where Holly meets Elena's aunt, Mrs. Santiago is memorable: he visits the Latino music director and wins her heart, charming her and showing her all the respect possible in order for her to understand that her niece is in good hands.

Holly is never egotistical in the film, unlike other musicians presented in biopics who become violent and aggressive (such as Dale Midkiff's portrayal of Elvis Presley in the TV movie *Elvis and Me* (1988) and self-involved and pathetic addicts such as Jeff Bridges as the non-specific country star on the downfall in *Crazy Heart* (2009). But the star power of Buddy Holly causes some grief for his band mates: dramatic tensions do surface, but late in the film and not with any real depth. When fellow rock star Eddie Cochran reintroduces Buddy Holly to the stage (the audience chanting "We want Buddy" repeatedly) it is the turning point in the mandatory "the front man is bigger than the rest of the band" deal (as Don Stroud's expression suggests). But this is fleeting and disposable. By the end of the piece, Stroud returns to Holly's life and meets up with a very pregnant Maria Elena to surprise Holly on tour. The rise of the business minded savvy Holly fuels most of the latter half of the film, and Busey plays that out as strong as the struggling artist. There is something electrically charged in seeing 1970s actors (children during the 1950s) taking on the decade that introduced rock'n'roll to the world. They have a sense of respect, genuine love and dedication to these rock stars that they grew up loving. Busey's most intimate moment on screen is the most telling, where he plays guitar to two neighbouring children. It's a touching moment, brief and not at all overly sentimental.

Even Holly's ill-fated tour and his accidental death is presented beyond the realm of sentiment. And sadly, this in a way is a detriment of the film. In *The Buddy Holly Story*, Holly is adamant that he does not want to go on the fateful tour that will eventually kill him because it would be the first time he would be on tour without The Crickets. This is despite even his own pregnant wife explaining that he is the music with or without the band. The scene where he says farewell to her, leaving her on the bus heading out into a storm is moving and sombre, because we know what is to eventuate. The final moments of the film are a lengthy presentation of the tour. "True Love Ways" has such a romance to it—the cool, soothing vocal talents of Busey here are remarkable. This is where we understand the Academy honoring the score with an Oscar.

Those beautiful strings breathe such elegance into what ultimately is a doo-wop song, is completely changed and turned into something unique and different. This was something that Buddy Holly himself was integral in the formation of, just as Wanda Jackson introduced hillbilly to rock'n'roll, Holly and a host of others including acts such as The Everly Brothers and Ike and Tina Turner would marry the coolness of the big band era and orchestrated swing to the heart of rock music. "Not Fade Away" is rock'n'roll bliss, and when the Big Bopper sings "Chantilly Lace" it is fun, perfumed by bourbon, cherry cola and varnish.

The film reads like a telemovie in many ways, and there really isn't much in the way for it that screams "cinematic." But it celebrates an artist who was faithful to his craft and his innovative energy. Busey plays each dramatic scene with a subtle passion, engaging in his understated quiet perfection. When he hits the stage as performer, we are treated to an authentic rock performance. Here, a wild animal emerges, a bizarre contradiction of animalism with his bottle-rimmed glasses, neat suits and polished shoes. Holly's look was such an incredible anomaly and this is something that is simply taken at face value and never at all delved into. There is a moment where he dons his famous specs but it is once again treated as throwaway. Character depth is not the film's strongest point, but it is all about performance. This is a strange contradiction that stitches together this unremarkable but still very good biopic. *La Bamba* certainly does so much more in the way of character development and relationships: if much is embellished, it doesn't matter. It is a far more interesting and captivating film that *The Buddy Holly Story*, and the almost supernatural elements included (the endless dream sequences that depict Valens's fear of flying) is commendable and interesting.

The scoring of the end title credits in *The Buddy Holly Story* are beautiful as we are told about Holly's death via a title card on a frozen image of Busey mid-flight in performance. The music is recorded in an authentic manner; the trebly guitars are raucous, the drums tinny and lose and the bass fat and warm, The instruments (most notably Holly's Fenders) are technically the wrong models, but this kind of thing would only upset Holly purists (as it should) but it doesn't get in the way of the fantastic music. Buddy Holly was a song-writing magician, and this unlikely rock star would go on to be one of the most revered icons of the 1950s, his untimely death also contributing to his legacy. Gary Busey's phenomenal performance is inspired, sharp, careful and nuanced. Not receiving the coveted Academy Award for Best Actor that year was a travesty, although later more actors and actresses playing musicians would become candidates for Oscar nominations with stars such as Sissy Spacek taking home the glory as Country and Western legend Loretta Lynne in *Coal Miner's Daughter* (1980)—a film that we will discuss very soon.

SHOUT IT OUT LOUD: *KISS Meets the Phantom of the Park*

The incredible popularity of rock phenomenon KISS during the 1970s lead to a cavalcade of merchandising and a permanent place in the world of popular culture. On top of that came a made for TV movie thanks to Saturday morning cartoon tycoons Hanna-Barbera. Produced by Joseph Barbera, *KISS Meets the Phantom of the Park* (1978) (sometimes known as *Attack of the Phantoms*) was aired on NBC and became a nationwide hit when it first screened. But rabid KISS fans and KISS members themselves generally despised it. In fact, there were even reports suggesting no one was allowed to mention the telemovie in the company of Paul Stanley, Ace Frehley, Peter Criss or Gene Simmons during their late 1970s and early 1980s tours.

A young KISS fan in **KISS Meets The Phantom of the Park (1978)**

Although inspired by the likes of The New York Dolls and Alice Cooper, KISS were the masters of grandiose theatrics. A KISS movie made sensee. Enter British horror movie director Gordon Hessler (*Scream and Scream Again, The Cry of the Banshee*, 1970) to take the reins on this vehicle for one of America's most enigmatic and iconic bands. Hessler's direction is simple and straightforward. There is nothing flash going on here, but he captures all the bright energetic imagery of the time. This is best during daylight, where he lets his camera cruise the amusement park. Hessler delivers all those lovely bright 1970s colors with ease and it's sugar to watch. In fact, this is the kind of musical— much like the TV adaptation of *Applause!*—that is so addictive and easy to swallow that it may not be good for you. Still, you have one hell of a good time taking it all in!

The plot reads much like an episode of *Scooby-Doo Where Are You?* (an

506

extremely successful product from Hanna-Barbera) and borrows from horror film masterpiece *House of Wax* (1953). KISS have superpowers and take on an evil scientist Abner Devereaux (Anthony Zerbe) who is hell bent on destruction. Zerbe has fun playing Devereaux, the amusement park engineer responsible for the many animatronic figures that populate the park (one is a gorilla, and is referred to as Magilla Gorilla, another wonderful cartoon creation from Hanna-Barbera).

KISS Meets the Phantom of the Park (1978)

The opening title sequence is wonderful in the sense that it really does excite fans not only about KISS but about 1970s popular culture in general: made for TV movies, the magic of the not-quite-perfect green screen and the fun and frivolity of the party atmosphere. And that's what this film is: a party. It's not perfect, but who cares? What it represent is a musical phenomenon. Just as as powerful as The Beatles at the advent of heavy metal, KISS were an institution and this film celebrates that. It also incorporates the doppelganger plot device (Gene Simmons has a robot alter-ego terrorize the onsite police), superhero tropes (KISS's distinct powers have to be seen to be believed) and the fun of cybernetic monsters! With all of this and some terrific footage of KISS in their prime, what's not to love? Hessler's film could also be responsible for a short-lived robot and statue-come-to-life invasion trend that hit small screens in the late 1970s and early 1980s. This can be seen in *The Munster's Revenge*

(1981), an ill-fated follow up to the glamorous, brilliant Technicolor *Munster Go Home!* (1966), which also relied on the "robot doppelganger" motif. In some instance, many of Abner Deveruex's mechanical monsters from *KISS Meets the Phantom of the Park* look like they pop up in the inferior Munsters full length TV feature from 1981.

One of the highlights of the film is seeing genuine late 1970s KISS fans gearing up for an electric show. Suburban teenagers were given free tickets from local radio stations to come along to the car park at Magic Mountain on May 19th 1978 for a full throttle KISS concert, some portions which would be captured on film for this NBC movie of the week. The kids are excited and decked out in their KISS make-up; the image of these youngsters painted up as the Space Man, the Demon, the Cat Man and the Star Child is seductive in a strange 1970s chic kind of way. An image of a young girl painted up as Peter Criss's feline counterpart bouncing through the crowds is intoxicating and a young man peddling KISS balloons and painted as Paul Stanley is a sight to behold, especially when he stares t into the lens and looks at us. Something about that image—a mere mortal nobody donning the mask of his rock 'n' roll hero looking into camera and staring at us—is not only unnerving but also enchanting.

Paul Stanley in **KISS Meets the Phantom of the Park (1978)**

This is what makes this feature appealing: it's not about the production values or the performances, but it's all about the mystique and allure of this band that has become a cult, a phenomenon and a religion. KISS fans of the time bemoaned the film, but since then it is not surprising that they have grown to love it, as it is part of their KISStory. Admittedly, it does take a good half an hour for KISS to arrive on scene and become integrated into the plot. Ace points his fingers into space and through pure white lasers he produces Peter, readily equipped with his drumsticks at hand. Paul appears striking a series of poses and then magically creates a stairwell leading him to stage while Gene spreads open his cape, lets loose his trademark tongue and blows fire. The foursome descend onto stage and perform "Shout It Out Loud" in front of a roaring, ecstatic crowd. The film cuts away from KISS—possibly a mistake—and goes back to the plot where stock actors perform as robots (and semi-robots). The film could showcase KISS's incredible talents more as showbiz icons, not only the masters of great rock 'n' roll, but also maestros of macabre showmanship. The make-up, the flamboyant outfits, the pyro explosives, all this is what fans want to see. At one point in the film Paul Stanley remarks "You're looking for someone, but it's not KISS." This statement is unintentionally comedic in that the only reason most audiences would ever want to see this film is to see KISS and to see KISS perform.

When the songs are performed off stage, there is a clumsiness to it. When Peter Criss, accompanied by his band mates, sings "Beth" to the lonely and desperate Melissa (Deborah Ryan), it is strange and awkward. The attempt to place a song within the narrative just doesn't work. In what is ultimately a jukebox musical (most certainly one of the first of its kind that isn't a rock biopic) there is really no need to structure the songs around the wafer thin plot. They could have easily had Criss sing his signature ballad on stage where he and his band are far more comfortable, or the song have played over a montage of the pining Melissa hunting around the park for her missing beau. And pine, mope and worry is all young Deborah Ryan spends the entire movie doing. Her continual moaning about her missing boyfriend is tiresome, and although she is gorgeous and has a perfect "KISS babe" look to her, her character is uninteresting and not allowed to be sexual, which is ultimately what you would want in a film about a band celebrating the seduction of the innocent. KISS are sexual, but the film is far from it. Of course, if it wasn't a Hanna-Barbera production there could have been more possibilities. The film also sometimes has moments where it could have been developed as a full-fledged integrated book musical, but it doesn't seem it wants to.

KISS Meets the Phantom of the Park (1978)

The film somehow revels in its inconsistencies, and there are some numbers that are used extremely well. For example, when Devereaux is relieved from his duties at the park by his boss (Carmine Caridi) he walks off to the melodic "Mr. Make Believe." The song's melancholic nature adds to the scene, injecting it with sympathy for this lonely loathsome inventor. Devereaux himself becomes this Mr. Make Believe that KISS are singing about. This simple decision makes the film work on at least one level.

But the brilliance of all the levels in this TV gem is that it is completely and unapologetically bizarre. Much like the strangeness of the ragamuffin clowns in *Godspell* occupying an empty New York City, when KISS stroll around the Californian amusement park it's an odd visual. Stanley pouts and loves the camera while Criss hides from it and trots behind the hazy Frehley. And the heavy-footed Simmons dominates each scene with a powerful presence that is reminiscent of a classic movie monster from the days of Universal. When KISS appear on screen, you pay attention.

It's like seeing a walrus ride a bicycle—it's not something you'd see every day and quite possibly a clumsy visual, however it is something you just cannot take your eyes off. KISS is that kind of band.

For an interesting plot, good performances and inspired filmmaking, audiences would want to look elsewhere. This is fundamentally a cult film for KISS fans and fans of TV movies of the 1970s that aren't social issue focused. However, Hanna-Barbera's attempts at live action films have not always been so clumsy. Some have proved to be engaging, such as the charming *C.H.O.M.P.S.* (1979) which cashed in on the dog movie fad that was taking off thanks to the popularity of the *Benji* films and TV specials. The KISS movie is purely about this enigmatic band and the impression they are on pop culture. KISS are an institution and this film is part of that fabric. There is nothing wrong with it besides the fact that it is solely about a band's impact on a generation of rock 'n' roll loving kids. This is something to celebrate not something to dismiss. Much as *Fiddler on the Roof* celebrated change and *The Rocky Horror Picture Show* celebrated sexual ambiguity, *KISS Meets the Phantom of the Park* is a celebration of one of the greatest rock 'n' roll bands of all time.

Author, journalist and critic John Harrison shares his personal insight in regard to *KISS Meets the Phantom of the Park*:

> To this young teenager growing-up in the Australian suburbia of 1979/80, *Attack of the Phantoms* was just another cog in the mighty KISS merchandise machine that rolled over this country during those two great years. I collected and traded the bubble-gum cards, bought the KISS showbag from the Royal Melbourne Show, hung the TV Week posters on my bedroom walls, played the grease-spattered KISS pinball machine while waiting for my fish & chips to be ready, and wore the t-shirts, badges and even KISS underwear with pride and enthusiasm. Hell, I even listened to their music! So I was naturally excited to hear that KISS were to appear in their very own feature film, which was being touted (rather optimistically, it would turn out) as "*A Hard Day's Night* meets *Star Wars*." Though it first aired on American television in October of 1978, it wasn't until

1979 that the Australian KISS Army got to see *Attack of the Phantoms*, after Avco-Embassy picked-up the film for theatrical distribution outside the US. Retitled *Kiss Meets the Phantom of the Park* (or, in some countries like Italy, simply as Kiss Phantoms), the telemovie was significantly re-cut for its theatrical release, and had music from the recently released KISS solo albums inserted in place of Hoyt Curtain's original score. In some countries, including Australia, audiences were also treated to the music videos for *I Was Made for Lovin' You* and *Sure Know Something*—the two big hits from the band's 1979 Dynasty album—which were screened prior to the film. I can still recall a cinema full of teenaged girls squealing with delight whenever Paul Stanley's cherubic face and red lips occupied the whole screen during these clips, while the guys cheered Gene Simmons and Ace Frehley as they strutted and stalked the stage, posing and plucking on their respective Kramer axe bass and flashing Gibson Les Paul guitar. The extra joy in watching the movie for me was the fact that the bulk of it was filmed at the Magic Mountain amusement park in Valencia, California, which I had recently visited on my first ever vacation to the US (it was also the location where the climax to one of my favourite 1970's disaster/thrillers—*Rollercoaster*—was set). I probably sat through *Attack of the Phantoms* a good ten or so times at various Melbourne cinemas and suburban drive-ins. My friends and I bought Icee smoothies so we could collect the two-for-one vouchers they were giving away to see the movie, and we sat in the cinema lobbies between screenings listening to our cassettes of "Double Platinum" and "KISS Alive II" on a tinny portable tape player, the songs often slowing to a crawl as the four C batteries wore down from continual overuse. After the movie, full of energy and teenage bravado, and usually adorned in KISS t-shirt and make-up (straight from the KISS Your Face make-up kit), we would invade the record bar of the Bourke Street Coles, looking through all the KISS albums we hadn't yet added to our collections. A couple of times we would hang out at the City Square on the corner of Swanston and Collins Streets, playing out the Good KISS versus Bad KISS moments from the movie, much to the bemusement of shoppers and passers-by. It was a great time to be young, silly and a fully-fledged member of the KISS Army. Little did we know how quickly the local ranks would dwindle after the band finished their first ever tour of our shores in November of 1980. I've always been someone who finds an artist's failures to be amongst their most interesting work, and *Attack of the Phantoms* is no exception. While it is not as eclectic or accomplished as "Music from The Elder," the band's ill-fated concept album which was met with universal scorn and dismal sales when it was released in October of 1981, *Attack of the Phantoms* is a great souvenir of a band who were at the height of their mainstream success but on the verge of disintegrating and losing it altogether. It is also a hell of a lot of fun, and a must-see for anyone who loves American telemovies from the 1970s. It's a pity that the members of KISS, Gene and Paul in particular, are so vehement in their dismissal of it. After years of being available primarily on grainy bootleg videos traded amongst fans, the foreign theatrical cut of *Attack of the Phantoms* finally received a legitimate DVD release in 2007 on "KISSology Volume II: 1978—1991." Rip, Rip, Rip & Destroy!

Fangoria writer Justin Beahm had the pleasure of interviewing director Gordon Hessler in regard to the film. This is what Hessler had to say:

> Since Hanna-Barnera were an animation studio, I knew nothing about them, and they knew nothing about me. It was a former producer, Deke Heyward, who worked for AIP. In the AIP days he moved to London and produced most of the films there. When he left AIP and came back, he asked me to do this film. He was working for Hanna Barbera at the

time, and this just came out of the blue. It wasn't really what I'd call a regular film. It was more of a longer television show. There was a script done by a couple of very young writers. They were somewhat inexperienced, but it was a film that could be easily made today, but was incredibly difficult to do on a television budget, because of the special effects. It inhibited the script that they wrote because I could only do what was technically feasible. All the television people didn't really know about blue screen, and how easy it is to work with. I tried to convince them to use blue screen, but it was out of their understanding, so we went the old optical way of doing things, but I think the film lost something because of that. It was a bad decision. I am sure the writers were disappointed because we couldn't execute everything they wanted. We had to amend the script, because we couldn't do certain things they had written. It was a story about KISS with special powers that improved their stature. I was not familiar with KISS, it was not my kind of music. Music is very much a part of me, from classical to jazz, but I was not into the genre. The genre they were in at the time was really talking to kids to say they are important people and can deal with the problems they have. That was the message they were giving. KISS were all extremely cooperative. There were no problems at all. They had unlimited money for anything. Gene Simmons seemed to be the brains of the outfit, and was very well educated. I think all the ideas came from him. He was the leader of the group and the one I communicated with the most. He was highly intelligent and very much into horror films. Paul Stanley was very impressive, but I didn't get to know him that well. As a director you are so busy, you really don't spend that much time with the people because you are setting up, doing a quick rehearsal, and then you shoot. I enjoyed all of them quite a bit. The general discussion was to get to know one another in those first meetings. We had a meeting at Hanna Barbera, and they came with all their entourage. It was quite devastating to see. I enjoyed working with them very much, but they are very bizarre, and lived in a world of their own that I had never seen before. I got to know them pretty well, and enjoyed them very much. Anthony was a wonderful actor, and was able to put more into the character than was intended. He was marvelous. When you get a wonderful actor who knows his job, the best thing a director can do is leave them alone. He got it instinctively, and I had to say very little to the man, because he knew what he was doing. Six Flags was close to town, and very easy to get to with the crew. It is in an area where people could easily get to it. I remember watching Six Flags being built. I actually had some shares in that area, of that land, and it was nice to eventually work on that property. People had been given free tickets to induce them to come. Being on a film set was all new to them, being so new to the film process. The director isn't usually aware of these things because you are so busy with so many things. Terry Morse was incredibly efficient and took care of any of those sorts of problems before they got to me, which is the producer's job anyway. I think the most interesting story is of these four characters working in the film industry for the first time. They really seemed to enjoy it. These four guys had an incredible manager, and you have to realize the wealth they had. They had a whole floor of an office building in both New York and in Los Angeles. He was their agent and manager, and he could, and would, get anything they wanted. They were earning such extraordinary money. It was another world, and whatever they wanted, they got. At that time everybody was slightly high, and it is very hard to know if that was an inhibitor, but I don't remember having any problems with lines. I have had bigger problems with much bigger actors, where they couldn't remember lines. I don't remember any problems. I don't remember Peter being dubbed. I might have not been present at that dubbing, because when you are a freelancer, you are usually off to do another show, and someone else would supervise something like that. That post-Beatle period was particularly strange. To come out with the theater they invented, was quite extraordinary. And the music was really about the sexuality of girls. Gene invited me to a party for his girlfriend Cher after the film was over. What lengths he went to to impress the girl. He had a skywriter writing her name in the sky, it was unbelievable. He was a great showman. She liked Dr. Pepper, so he had a tank come in, down Sunset Blvd, and he had these men come out of it, delivering her Dr. Pepper. A military tank. It was so bizarre, you couldn't believe it. It was spectacular. He should really be a director. You wouldn't think he would be in the entertainment business. You think of him as the school teacher with all this knowledge, and he was the one with fire coming out of his mouth and that tongue.

FOLK, PUNK, ROCK'N'ROLL, DISCO AND CHER:
Renaldo and Clara, The Punk Rock Movie, American Hot Wax,
The Last Waltz, Thank God It's Friday **and** *Cher...Special*

For many musicians, there is an egotistical element to what they do, regardless of how good they are and regardless of how much they love and respect their audience. They are not serving a story or a collective consciousness, but are dishing out an extension of themselves on a personal (sometimes synthetic, inauthentic) level. Bob Dylan and Joan Baez were two of America's leading figures in folk music and to argue that would be imprudent. These two musicians and songwriters bought the American folk song to the foreground during an age of rock'n'roll, giving protest music a soothing melancholia that was just as angry and as wistful as their louder contemporaries. In *Renaldo and Clara*, this is the basis of the plot and structure of the film. Using Dylan's lyrics as short vignettes of dramatic sub-pieces, the rest of the film incorporates backstage style footage and concert footage of artists such as Joni Mitchell and Ronee Blakley with some inspired appearances by T Bone Burnett, Allan Ginsberg and Harry Dean Stanton.

Co-written by Dylan and Sam Shepherd and directed by Dylan, it is is a melting pot of dreams and logic. It plots together a tapestry of musical excellence (especially from the female musicians) and interweaves them with a minimal narrative, egotistically stitched together from Dylan's own songbook. And egotistical the film is. Unlike *New York, New York* which takes on artists thrown together out of necessity and turbulent romance, *Renaldo and Clara* moves its characters (supposedly fictional but obviously a result of Dylan's own sense of self-importance) through the motions and never really gives them anything to do or to fight against. There is lethargic slow-po movement in the storytelling and the character development, so the music is the only thing keeping you waching. This is not a bad thing, but whiny folk musicians talking about themselves for nearly two hours in a pseudo-docudrama is frustrating. The music is the only thing that keeps your attention.

Far more exciting and riveting is *The Punk Rock Movie* and although, , it is in service of musicians executing their irreverent anger through trebly guitars and jarring drumbeats, the film is an expression of one of the most vital anti-movements ever to grace the streets of London, New York and Los Angeles (with other cities to follow). The X-Ray Specks' front woman Polly Styrene belts out "Oh Bondage Up Yours!" to a pit of alienated and angry teens is a sight to behold, and the obnoxious ravings of The Sex Pistols work up into a frothy frenzy. The reggae stop-starts of The Slits, the high voltage energy of Slaughter and the Dogs, the gothic death-stare Siouxsie and her Banshees, and the powerhouse prowess of Johnny Thunders interweave and interlock in this film shot on Super 8.

The origins of the film are just as punk as the acts depicted. Disc jockey Don Letts was given a camera by fashion Caroline Baker as a gift and the inspired soon-to-be filmmaker went along to the famous Roxy Club in London to film the burgeoning punk scene that was seething in the backstreets of Britannia. Letts had shot a number of acts but ran out of film midway, forcing him to sell most of his possessions to complete this project that he was now invested in. The results are terrific. Not only does the *cinema verite* style work for a musical, it works as a documentary, and would go on to influence the likes of more films that would capture a city that was defined by a youth culture explosion such as *Hype!* (1996), which explored punk's grandchild grunge and its marriage to the Pacific Northwest (especially Seattle).

Another film that celebrated a distinct musical style and sound from an earlier period, is *American Hot Wax*. Part biopic and part rock show, it featured performances from artists who were in their prime during the 1950s. *American Hot Wax* tookits lead from the successful George Lucas film *American Graffiti* (1973) which chronicled the lives of dead-end teens who cruised the streets looking for a good time with rock'n'roll as their soundtrack under the watchful eye of world renowned disc jockey Wolfman Jack. It tells the story of the Cleveland man who coined the term rock'n'roll, Alan Freed. And along with performances by Screamin' Jay Hawkins, Chuck Berry, Frankie Ford and Jerry Lee Lewis, the film is an exhilarating experience that remains far more engaging than Lucas's coming of age romp.

Tim McIntire plays Allen Freed, the legendary music enthusiast. McIntire plays it with a cautious and keen interest in authenticity, and marks the role with distinct characteristics and moody dynamism. McIntire injects the famed DJ with sensitivity and quiet determination. The character is so gracefully realized that the film is carried on his shoulders with a loving warmth. When McIntire plays off Fran Drescher as his feisty secretary, or Melanie Chartoff as an aspiring song writer he throws himself into the nuanced differences in their characters. He is a perfect chameleon, an informed magician who understands the unique nature of Freed, a man who knew how to play different people and different situations. As a sleazy record promoter, Jeff Altman does a terrific job providing the much a needed adversary to McIntire's Freed, and their confrontations are fun to watch.

The film is interested in Freed as a passionate artist, not just a living turntable. He is sincerely addicted and supportive of this new breed of music that is taking the world by storm. His love for country, rhythm and blues, and honkytonk heightens because he has now discovered that these musicals forms have evolved into something new: this evolutionary take on shoop-shoop and do-wop, the monster he christenss rock'n'roll. As the film moves from strength to strength, it looks at family groups not wanting their young to enjoy such "distasteful" music and issues concerning race. The film tackles these well, but in regard to both its plotting and politics, it is made all the more incredible because artists from the early years of rock'n'roll—pioneers of a new world that was geared towards the newly-marketed teenager—perform with gusto and exuberance.

1959. New York City.
The battleground was
Rock and Roll.
It was the beginning
of an era.

You shoulda been there.

American Hot Wax

'AMERICAN HOT WAX'
Starring TIM McINTIRE • LARAINE NEWMAN
JOHN LEHNE • JAY LENO
CHUCK BERRY • JERRY LEE LEWIS
Screenplay by JOHN KAYE
Story by JOHN KAYE and ART LINSON

R   OMMENDED
AS
ADULT E TERTAINMENT

Poster art for *American Hot Wax* (1978)

Jerry Lee Lewis is a man possessed, while Chuck Berry sweats gallons and delivers a sermon for rock. Even more incredible is the unique Screamin' Jay Hawkins, an artist who made a career out of scaring teeny boppers with his love for the macabre and grotesque. This rock'n'roll monster emerges from a coffin, covered in bones and frightening make-up. His spindly body is draped in velveteen and he moves about the stage like a voodoo witchdoctor, ready to turn his adoring fans (and terrified audience members) into frogs, weasels and pigs. Spookiness lives in his veins and his electric voice catapults and plummets like no other.

Much like Alan Freed, Screamin' Jay Hawkins was a Cleveland native so this film meant a lot to him. This granddaddy of "shock rock" with his leopard prints and his declaration that he shall surely "put a spell on you" is a stand out. His kooky operatics round the film out, because when Hawkins comes on we get the sense that rock'n'roll can do more than one or two things. It has its own lexicon, it is its own cultural expression, celebrating diversity and revolution. *American Hot*

Wax expresses these attributes, and does it without pretentious self-indulgence or sentimentality.

It isn't simply a "tell it how it is" saga: it jas a strong and dynamic narrative and a poetic edge. If *American Graffiti* was too poetic in its delivery and its subtext, *American Hot Wax* is steadily paced and a methodical exploration into the diversity and cultural significance of the new form taking shape. Before Alan Freed consolidated the phenomenon under the label 'rock'n'roll', musicians knew they were doing something new. The effortless connection between artists and music is something that Alan Freed understood, which is why his label was embraced. *American Hot Wax* says that the father of the term of rock'n'roll reflected the music itself, with all its anger, fun, silliness, and sexiness.

1950s rock'n'roll took a backseat in Martin Scorsese's rockumentary *The Last Waltz* which honored the last ever performance from seminal Canadian/American roots/rhythm and blues rock band The Band. The Band were active for over a decade by the time Scorsese signed up for the project, and here in this film they are joined by the likes of artists such as Joni Mitchell, Bob Dylan, Muddy Waters, Neil Young, and Emmylou Harris who deliver the goods in a rich and emotional film that never shies away from sentiment. Scorsese creates a unique film, and thanks to his previous work on *Woodstock*, he understands the "fly on the wall" documentary approach can be a subtle, and clever way to serve up a music documentary. Scorsese's insight and outsight doesn't stop there, because he also makes this film somewhat story-centric. This is a perfect example of how what essentially is a concert film can make a transformative leap into narrative.

A film that is supposed to be linear in its multi-layered text and also supposedly story-heavy is the disco feature *Thank God It's Friday*. It never gets going in the plot department, but for some strange reason it remains all the more better for it. In many ways, it borrows from Robert Altman's masterpiece *Nashville* with its interloping subplots and its multiple characters with individual agendas and attitudes. Taking off from where the brilliant *Saturday Night Fever* left audiences feeling devastated by the gritty realism that disco narrated (the Italian ghettos and the street violence and so forth), *Thank God It's Friday* reminds that disco can also be the soundtrack to what it was supposedly created for:

fun and liberation (this is made with a lot more insight in 1980's *Can't Stop the Music*).

Poster art for disco burp *Thank God It's Friday* (1978)

The film follows the lives and dreams of a number of patrons of a fictional discotheque called The Zoo in Los Angeles at the height of the disco craze. Although the film is produced by Motown Records (a company solely dedicated to R&B and rock) and as Casablanca Records (an incredibly successful company responsible for some of the biggest albums produced during the 1970s), it is determined to bring disco to the foreground and give it an accessible and friendly voice. Headed by the likes of the swinging sultry Donna Summer, it also stars Jeff Goldblum, Debra Winger and a number of other talents. *Thank God It's Friday* is a surprisingly good hot mess that doesn't necessarily any tangible strong points, but casually is still executed with ease. This is a light romp: it is not *Saturday Night Fever* or even the surprisingly dramatic *Roller Boogie* (1979), but it requires a degree of gravity to give this assortment of characters some depth (much like the sea of people that populate Altman's Country and Western gem). *Thank God It's Friday* remains brightly entertaining and is a great example of the almost psychotic energy of disco. Donna Summer (who later would become a controversial figure when she declared that AIDS was "God's gift to homosexuals") performing her hit "Last Dance" is the key scene that would symbolize not only this film but of the disco scene as a whole. Musicians everywhere would experiment with disco, including the aforementioned KISS as well as artists as diverse as Blondie, John Lennon and Yoko Ono, and Cher.

Cher would feature in a TV special born out of *The Sonny and Cher Comedy Hour* called *Cher...Special*. In this fantastic example of the variety show format, Cher sings a medley made up of songs from *West Side Story* where she plays both the female roles (Maria and Anita) and male roles (Bernardo and Tony). This has to be seen to be believed, as Cher the actress shines—she delicately handles the lovely Maria, fuels Anita with a sexual assertiveness and then moves on to the boy parts with ease. Cher struts around with her fists wedged into her jean pockets and sports the ducktail with confidence. Outside of this incredible medley, Cher is joined by the equally fantastic Dolly Parton who knocks out "Two Doors Down" with passion. This legend of the Country and Western circuit and one of the most important and prolific song-writers of the decade and beyond, Parton had her own television series *The Dolly Parton Show* (1976) and joining forces with Cher on this gives her room to play with various styles of comedy and music. Rod Stewart also appears on the special, but this is an event dominated by the ladies. Cher's talents are on show for all to see. She would go on to become a bankable movie star, but more importantly phenomenal dramatic actress, shown in Robert Altman's *Come Back to the 5 and Dime Jimmy Dean, Jimmy Dean*, and *Mask* (1985) and the Oscar winning *Moonstruck* (1987).

MEAN MR. MUSTARD MAKES A MISTAKE:
Sgt. Pepper's Lonely Hearts Club Band

The high concept yet inherently stupid *Sgt. Pepper's Lonely Hearts Club Band* is a mess. It could have been an interesting experiment—a landmark record turned into a musical where the songs could be structured in a way that would carry out a successful narrative—however it results in simply being a motion picture nightmare. As rock opera, the film was correct in believing that dialogue would have been a mistake, as it would no doubt make it longer and more of an ordeal to comprehend. It does feature some talented artists but they are thrown in this messy excuse for a film just to sell records. The film plods along with a grotesque unease and everybody involved seems to be fishes out of water, most notably George Burns who acts as the film's narrator of sorts, tying together the bumbling plot in the moments where the songs can't. These moments come thick and heavy. There are easy routes the film takes adopting diegetic elements where the Bee Gees as the Sgt. Pepper's Lonely Hearts Club Band perform the songs as numbers to entertain townsfolk that congregate at the centre street down at Universal Studios, but when the film strays from this and tries to integrate Beatles numbers into a narrative, it is an atrocity.

Sgt. Pepper's Lonely Hearts Club Band (1978)

The Bee Gees are so uncomfortable on screen, they reek of insecurity and seem bewildered about what the film is supposed to be about .Paul Nicholas is wasted here, despite being stunning films such as *Tommy* even the ordinary *Listzomania*. He is still is one of the only good things about this movie as he grimaces and mugs the camera with demonic glee. But he is seldom on screen. The music is watery, the idea of having the Bee Gees perform Beatles classics is strange to begin with. As capable as they are to pull it off, there is an overwhelming question demanding to

523

be asked throughout the film: why? Unfairly critics at the time compared the film to the original album, which is laughable—the record is a major entry in the history of rock'n'roll, and the film is a weird, cynical commodity to cash in on its success. The plot that unravels is supposedly an allegorical take on the pressures and seductive nature of the record industry and the alluring temptations that come with having the world as one's oyster. Aesthetically the film is garish and uneven: the colors come are jarring rather than complimentary and the art direction is sloppy and uninteresting.

Something has to be said however about the stand alone set pieces that serve the darker moments of the film. Here the motion picture succeeds because the visual extravagance and decadence is determinedly excessive. These scenes—such as the sequence involving Aerosmith—are relatively entertaining, but they disappear fast and serve as a predecessor to the soon-to-rise MTV phenomenon and the culture of the music video. More entertaining moments include cameos by Alice Cooper, who is terrific in his one scene, and Steve Martin getting some training in musical feature film before his fantastic turn as the demented dentist in *Little Shop of Horrors*. Martin—much like co-star George Burns—is a song and dance man as well as comedian, and his work on *The Sonny and Cher Comedy Hour* and his lovely duet with Bernadette Peters in the wonderful *The Jerk* is great. There is no real reason for him being wasted in this cold and awful film. The brilliant Donald Pleasance also turns up wearing a truly terrible hair piece, and why he is in here is beyond me. This was the same year where he was shooting in and around Pasadena with filmmakers John Carpenter and Debra Hill in the horror classic *Halloween*: to think that this esteemed star of the silver screen would go from a landmark genre hit such as *Halloween* to Universal Studios and Culver City to shoot one or two scenes in a bad wig in this woeful musical is unfathomable!

This is also one of the first ever jukebox musicals, which is arguably the worst thing about the film. Jukebox musicals are a those where the songs are already written and pre-recorded by a particular artist and then maneuverer in such a way that they serve a story. These are usually awful. Adding insult to injury is getting bands such as Earth, Wind and Fire to dish out some tunes, and even though they add their personal touch on a Beatles doozy they are still misguided and misdirected. It sounds terrible.

This film has minimal plot. There are moments in the feature that could have worked, as The Beatles write image-rich lyrics. Yet the film serves up nothing. The villain Mustard is assisted by two robots, and when he sings out "When I'm Sixty Four" it is cringe worthy and walk-out material. The death of female protagonist Strawberry Fields comes suddenly and surprisingly, and gives the film a moment of sadness. But again, the song of choice here is awful and tasteless. Once again, there is nothing genuine or moving in this film. There is no anger, no statement, just meaningless set pieces and tokenistic imagery.

As a jukebox musical, the film in many ways foreshadows those that have been made into movies such as the bloated and ugly *Moulin Rogue* (2001) which used a bunch of pop songs to make a dreary and stupid movie. *Mamma Mia* (2008) used the songs of ABBA to weave together an equally insipid plot featuring a screeching Meryl Streep in faded denim overalls. Others have not yet had a filmic adaptation, such as the dreadful *We Will Rock You* which trivializes the importance of a band like Queen. If *Sgt. Pepper's Lonely Hearts Club Band* ushered in the dawning of the age of the "jukebox musical" (although this branch of musical did flourish many years later and became a plague on Broadway and eventually Hollywood in the 2000s) then it needs to be scolded for that reason and that reason alone. "Jukebox musicals" are the laziest form of musical writing and the most insincere, and that is exactly what this Bee Gees/Beatles mash-up is—lazy and insincere.

DOUBLE TROUBLE: *Movie, Movie*

Stanley Donen was instrumental in movie musicals and is a vital figure in the history of the genre. *Movie, Movie* is a homage to two kinds of motion picture—the sport-centric rise of the underdog and underclass and the backstage movie musical. Again George Burns introduces us to a world of a bygone time where audiences would be treated to two motion pictures for the price of one—the immortal double feature—and promises us that this venture will be just that complete with all the trimmings. Harry Hamlin does a great job at playing a poor boy who dreams of becoming a lawyer. When he learns that his sister is losing her eyesight and his family don't have the money to treat her, he is forced to resort to being a boxer, something that pops up unexpectedly and by accident when he delivers bread to a boxing ring and punches a thug.

The film is a tribute to two forms of movie that flourished in the 1930s—the boxing movie and the backstage musical. Similar in their formula and their structure, Donen captures this in the film, explores and mirrors it. Both tropes have similar story set-ups: the young male protagonist who is seduced by an industry and a woman while trying to stay true to a just cause. In some releases of the film the boxing film called "Dynamite Hands" was shot in black and white while the musical "Baxter's Beauties of 1932" (a nice play on films such as *The Broadway Melody of 1932* etc) was in color.

The homages are not silly and do not making light of these two subgenres. *Movie, Movie* is a triumph and one of the biggest assets to the film is its art direction. Jack Fisk had just come off working on films such as *Carrie* and *Badlands* (1973) as well as the rock musical *Phantom of the Paradise*, and does a tremendous job at capturing the essence of two styles of film and the era itself. Ann Reinking is a knock-out as a cabaret performer in *Dynamite Hands*, and she represents a world that Hamlin has never known. George C. Scott and Art Carney embody their characters. Blessed with a strong body and a handsome face, Hamlin would go on to play Perseus in the last of animator Ray Harryhausen's works *Clash of the Titans,* then onto Arthur Hiller's yawn-inducing "liberal" gay themed film *Making Love* before becoming a TV star on *LA Law* (1986-1994). In this film, he does his best at playing a 1930s ghetto kid trying to better himself. He is a stand out in the film along with his counterpart in the musical part of the film Barry Bostwick.

The comedy is bright and swift, but it isn't as punchy or satirical as it could be. Gags may have come thick and fast much like the ones that propel a film parody such as *Flying High* (1980), which suggests what *Movie, Movie* could have been. The second half of the film—the backstage musical component—is the strongest. Barry Bostwick is brilliant as the enthusiastic and overly zealous songwriter and composer who is hired by George C. Scott to write twelve numbers overnight. Donen knows this kind of cinema all too well: *Singing' in the Rain* of course it is not, but that masterpiece is the backbone of the second story. It's great to have all the staple archetypal characters peppered throughout the film—the sweet, out of towner ingénue, the enthusiastic starving artist, the megalomaniac producer, the hardened chorus girl and the demanding diva. The backstage musical aspect is wonderfully mounted and mirrors the boxing film as the boxer and the songwriter lead the same life, but in different genres. They are both tempted by fate and by a woman: giving the film a film noir aspect. Bostwick is never disillusioned by the allure of Broadway and carries the latter half of the film beautifully.

Bostwick's performance as Brad Majors in *The Rocky Horror Picture Show* is fantastic, , counterbalancing talent with outlandish characters such as Tim Curry's Frank 'N' Furter. Here Bostwick is allowed even more space to expand his talents and he goes through some nice emotional ups and downs while staying true to his vibrant character's true self. There are some lovely moments for musicals fans such as a nice tribute to *42nd Street*, playing on the great moment where Peggy is told that she is going on stage a nobody and coming back a star. The musical within the musical is great, if somewhat brief and choppy. The song "Gee Whiz" is reprised many times, but never gets old. It seems to exist in varying terms as delivered by Bostwick and then by chorus girls and so forth. The sentimentality of the film is light, but present, centering around what George Burns invites us to in the beginning of the film: a nostalgic trip to genre cinema. The film says sport movies and backstage musicals are important contributors to the world of entertainment: high and lowbrow and everything in between. When George C. Scott's character dies dies, it's moving: "One minute you're standing in the wings and the next minute you're wearing them."

Movie, Movie is a stylish and thoughtful film. It is not as extreme a parody as *Flying High*, but it accomplishes three core things. It is a genuine love letter to motion pictures and the culture of the double feature, it celebrates sport movies and backstage musicals with loads of heart and sleek intelligence, and it also steadily brings the era of these two subgenres back to a non-cynical foreground. The latter of these is the most important. In a decade that wanted to dissect and deliver the darkness, *Movie, Movie* wanted to paint these grim realities up in a 1930s sensibility, where subtle and lightly nuanced dramatics dominated.

As busy and as diverse 1978 would be in regard to musical motion pictures, it was nothing compared to the unique tapestry that would unravel come 1979. Rock biopics were still the rage in the wake of the success of *The Buddy Holly Story*, and although deterring from being a biopic about Janis Joplin, the gripping and grim *The Rose* hit all the right notes, catapulting Bette Midler from torch song singer to superstar actress. A rock musical from the late 1960s that transformed the way musical theatre was looked at and imagined was transformed into a liner-centric and narrative-heavy film with Czech born auteur Milos Forman at the controls of *Hair*, taking this tribal, edgy and yet cynical vaudeville show into the story-by-numbers arena, creating something nearly as vivid and as powerful. Disco movies continued to flourish with the surprisingly complex *Roller Boogie*. Punk was now in the mainstream's eye and given the fabulous Roger Corman treatment with *Rock'n'Roll High School* starring the likes of New York's most influential bands The Ramones. And two major artistic forces Bob Fosse and Jim Henson would deliver two of the most powerful motion pictures to ever hit the big screen— different in tone and subject matter, and they would both move audiences for two very dissimilar reasons. One would be a gruelling, dripping-in-sweat, bleak vision of the world of dance while the other would introduce us to the humble beginnings of the world's most famous frog dreamer.

1979

"life's like a Movie. Write Your Own Ending... Keep Believing, Keep Pretending"

flower Children, Rock Divas, Speed Addicts and the lovers, the Dreamers and Me

BOB FOSSE WAS A GENIUS WHO REVELLED IN THE DARK SIDE AND danced in the shadows of the bleak. *All That Jazz* defines this aspect of his work, a unique kind of divine decadence he established and brought to the fore in his 1972 masterpiece, *Cabaret*. But here, something more personal was brewing, dripping with sweat, anger, rage, passion, power and absolute vulnerability. *All That Jazz* became one of the most vivid and dark excursions into what it meant to be a dancer on the Broadway stage, and to be a creative force who pounded at death's door haunted by a powerful ambition and struggling against the odds. Here, the movie musical became devastatingly personal, an emotional exorcism. *All That Jazz* was Fosse's mirror on himself and the world he was a part of (a world he partially shaped and created), and his vision was both unnerving

529

and unsettling. Along with films such as *The Rose*, movie musicals in 1979 continued to push the envelope and dared not smile. This was not the high school musical with chorus kids high-kicking, but rather a nightmarish world of drug abuse, war and personal demons.

But not everything was so grim. Roger Corman—another undeniable genius—grabbed ahold of punk and waved his magical wand, injecting it with a tremendous amount of fun and frivolous anarchy, while masterfully creating a film that would both sing out to the alienated and also to the kids who just wanted to have good time. Corman's new wave of movie mavericks such as Joe Dante and Allan Arkush opened the doors to *Rock'n'Roll High School* and it made a splash, proving that the rock musicals of the 1950s could be translated into something contemporary with a 1970s sensibility. Spunky actress P.J. Soles leads the way as seminal punk rock act The Ramones smash out anthems and chanting "Hey ho! Let's go!," shaping what would become the voice of the blank generation heading into uncertainty as the 1980s approached.

John Carpenter was another auteur who would also deliver the musical goods in 1979, on the back of the previous year's horror opus *Halloween* (a film that generated a slew of slasher films, rendering it one of the most successful and prolific of horror sub-genres of the early 1980s). At the end of the 1970s, however, Carpenter dished out a fantastic television miniseries based on the life of the recently deceased king of rock'n'roll, Elvis Presley. And of course, there was one more maestro of the motion picture industry who made an impact. Unlike these previous directors, he didn't originally hail from America, but he turned his attention to the Age of Aquarius and adapted an iconic musical of the late 1960s into a calculated and crisp film, besieged by the unfair dismissal of it being made and released almost too late. That man was Miloš Forman.

MY BODY IS WALKING IN SPACE: *Hair*

Hair was undeniably one of the most important American stage musicals of all time. It opened at the very moment that Broadway was transforming, on the cusp of the anti-war, hippy movement that provided its core scenario. With its raw, tribal and often-angry anti-linear construction, it was fuelled with a youthful vigour. It shocked audiences with its nudity, sexuality, drug use and profanity, and most confronting was its anti-

American sentiment and its rejection of the establishment (represented by the church and state). When Czech-born director Miloš Forman first saw the musical he was hooked. Born into a Communist dictatorship in a country torn apart by the after-effects of war, *Hair* resonated and spoke directly to him both politically and spiritually. So when the opportunity presented itself to adapt a film version for this "American tribal love rock musical," he jumped at the chance. Having recently won the Academy Award for Best Director for his incredible *One Flew Over the Cuckoo's Nest* (1975) –another film exploring anti-establishment sentiment and the adversarial confrontations between authority (as represented by the frigid Nurse Ratched) and the oppressed rabble (the inmates of the asylum or "cuckoo's nest"), Forman was a significant choice for the job.

The extended tribe in *Hair* (1979)

Hair finally got its film adaptation in 1979, over ten years after it hit the New York City stage in 1968. As many critics and audience members alike noted, for many it was felt to be far too late in capturing that essence of the flower power period. Many film critics observed how the film looked out of step with what was going on in the late 1970s as opposed to the late 1960s, but the motion picture which reimagined the stage show and granted it a straightforward narrative (care of its screenwriter Michael Weller), still did well in many circles, and what it says a lot about youth culture and the idea of conflict were still poignant (particularly with the horrors of the Vietnam War in its unseen background so fresh in the popular memory). Ultimately, the film version of *Hair* is a rollicking, intelligent piece that, for the most part, transforms an important piece of working theatre into an engaging movie musical. It contains enough of the original's anger, tenderness, passion, apathy, and recklessness, and is a yet another variation of the traditions established by the original source material.

The internal tribe in *Hair* (1979)

The film opens in silence in Oklahoma, with left-over cowboy Claude (John Savage) saying farewell to his father near their farm ranch as he waits for a bus to take him to New York to be inducted into the US Army. Forman's direction is crisp and understated, but at the same time both dynamic and nuanced. Forman injects the film with a dry sense of humour and cleverness that never skips a beat. Even the concept of opening in Oklahoma is a sly and ever-so-subtle wink to the musical theatre history buff, who can conceive this to be a commentary on the transitional element of the American musical: here in Forman's film, we are leaving the world of *Oklahoma!* (one of the earliest traditional book musicals) and entering the world of *Hair* (one of, if not the first, rock musicals without a sturdy backbone of plot). But in the film version of *Hair*, plot is heavy, but the songs are for the most part expressions of American tribal angst, celebration, romance, violent reaction or protest. Unlike *Oklahoma!* where the songs move the story forward, the songs in the film of *Hair* are like numbers slotted into a variety show. This was similar to the stage musical: it had a wafer thin plot, and effectively worked as a gritty, hippy, youth-centric vaudeville show.

Beverly D'Angelo and John Savage in the acid trip sequence in *Hair* (1979)

When we board the bus heading to New York City with Claude, the exhilarating rock music punches in, and we are in for a shaky—but ultimately memorable and mesmerising -ride. The "Aquarius" number invites us into the world of these Central Park dwelling flower children.

After we meet the tribe consisting of airy but sweet pregnant Jeannie (Annie Golden), militant and stoic Hud (Dorsey Wright), the sexually free and wispy Woof (Don Darcus) and their tribal leader, the enigmatic and Pan-like Berger (Treat Williams), we are greeted by a beautiful couple—a white girl and black boy—locked in an embrace that becomes symbolic in the sexual freedoms and hedonism that we will soon be inducted into. "Aquarius" is a phenomenal song with its complicated rhythms and inspired lyrics, and soloist Renn Woods sings the hell out of it. Her vocal abilities are complimented with quite possibly the best thing about the film—choreography by legendary Twyla Tharp. Here, lithe and athletic hippies throw themselves around the green utopia that is Central Park. They lift their bodies high (almost reminiscent of Butoh-type performance in places), and then leap into flight, piling onto the ground then carrying each other off to another section of the park. Tharp's choreography is a sight to behold, and her most inspired moments include having the hippies being so in tune with nature that they have police horses mimic their movements and having girls thrusting upon boys and then moving on to the next lot of boys to embody the free-love aspect of the culture. And the gymnastic mastery of a spindly chap doing backflips as others race toward a park bench to collectively flop upon it like living, breathing ragdolls.

Aside from Tharp's astounding choreography, the work of Oscar winning costume designer Ann Roth is worth noting. Her fabulous designs for these kids find them decked out in street gear, but at the same time the costumes are remarkably mythic. Dressed in their filthy rags, aged vests and hand painted skirts, the hippies that populate the film (the extended tribe of the principals) all look individual and yet uniform. They all physically seem at one with their surroundings—be it the streets of New York or the lush greenery of Central Park. Both the dance element and costuming capture the beauty of *Hair* as well as the image-shattering truth that underscores it: *Hair* doesn't paint a picture of peace and love, but instead it highlights the apathetic, providing us with both the pretty and the ugly sides of the flower power generation. It delivers something cynical and nihilistic, which is also embodied by the essential (but sometimes detrimental) hedonism. *Hair* is subliminally excited by the adversary, and is underscored by a sense of Satanic panic.

When the fire that Berger throws his draft card into dissolves to the image of the mixed-race couple in a sexual (almost hypnotic, possibly drug influenced) embrace, we enter an era of fervent anti-Christian behaviour. In *Hair*, God is dead and the Satanic doctrine of woodland creatures (these oversexed, hedonistic and high youths in Central Park) are ushering in a world proudly celebrated by the father of the Church of Satan, Anton LaVey.

Treat Williams as the Pan-like Berger dances on a table top during "I Got Life" in *Hair* (1979)

When the plot cuts away from the dancing, it does feel like a bit of a nuisance: yes, it is necessary, but it could have been made clear after Tharps's phenomenal troupe do their thing. For example, the exciting contemporary dance that Tharp infuses into the film is interrupted by Claude noticing a beautiful young woman on horseback: Sheila (Beverly D'Angelo), the wealthy debutante who turns back and looks at this innocent who has stumbled into New York, and who will soon be introduced to the world of Berger and his tribe. Class distinctions are a major theme in the film—wealthy New Yorkers, country hicks and street kids who live off nothing make up its fabric.

Producer Lester Perksy and choreographer Twyla Tharp on location in Central Park for *Hair* (1979)

Director Milos Forman has words with "3-5-0-0" soloist Melba Moore on location for *Hair* (1979)

Annie Golden and Milos Forman behind the scenes in Central Park for *Hair* (1979)

Premiere at the Cannes Film Festival for *Hair* (1979)

In its journey from stage to screen, the treatment of Sheila and Claude differs substantially from the original source material. In the original stage musical, both characters are already members of the hippy tribe: Claude is about to be shipped off to Vietnam and is terrified and angry about it, while Sheila is a student protestor. In the film, Claude is a patriotic soldier-to-be, while Sheila is oppressed by her wealthy background and breaks out of it, rejecting it for the impoverished, but liberating hippy lifestyle. When Claude comes into contact with Berger and company, Jeannie's very clever statement "Listen man, I know how it feels, I used to come from Kansas myself" is a wonderful hat-tip to the tradition of an outsider in a foreign world: a nice reference to *The Wizard of Oz* underscores our understanding of the cultural difference between the cynical, worldly, streetwise hippies and fresh faced, green innocence of rural America, embodied by Claude. This sits at the centre of what Forman and screenwriter Michael Weller showcase. Highlights span from hiring the horse for Woof who sings a list of sexual practices in "Sodomy"; Sheila's stuffy sorority, getting Claude stoned for the first time as an unseen chorus sings a list of drugs in "Hashish"; the anger and agitated revolt of the internal black tribe headed by Hud in "Color Spade" where a laundry list of black stereotypes are dished out; another equally inspired list of have-nots in the brilliant treatment of stand-out number "Ain't Got No"—these are all memorable moments in musical film history, and work splendidly.

But, as fantastic and as sharp the songs are, they don't serve the newly constructed plot in a traditional sense. Instead they appear out of nowhere and come across as acts in the hands of street tricksters. For example, when Claude retrieves and masters Woof's horse and shows off for Sheila, Berger hits us with "Donna," an anti-religious song mocking the Madonna and her virtue. For a cynic, this may not make any sense, but it is conceivable that the number is about two virginal characters (Claude and Sheila—virginal as in pure and untempted by the ways of Berger and his tribe who experience an even heightened "enlightenment" though sex and drugs) coming together to show each other that "life on Earth can be sweet." Some songs serve plot, while others most certainly don't, and for the most part simply showcase an element of hippiedom: but all this works for a film pre-occupied with the magus and the Satanic minstrel trickster that appears and disappears at the drop of a hat. The animalism of the hippies is aligned very clearly with Satanism: the idea of the hedonistic as opposed to the idealistic runs throughout. New York City itself looks crisp and lush at one point and then filthy and grubby the next, and itself feels like a forever-transforming trickster character, as well as a playground for these drop-outs. The takes a literal detour as the main cast drive out west to the deserts of Nevada, and for a moment recalls the road movie. But for the most part—the most effective and memorable part—it is the early moments in the film from "Aquarius" through to the final moments of "Ain't Got No" where the film is at its strongest, reminiscent of the devilish trickery that it seeks to embody.

Weller's screenplay sets up some terrific set pieces, such as Berger and company crashing Sheila's parents' formal ball. This is a great new take on the common folktale motif where the gypsies of Europa turn up to events in which they are not invited. Eight years after he wowed savvy audiences with his troubled pre-teen in *Bless the Beasts and Children* (1971), Miles Chapin is great as Sheila's straight-laced brother, a perfect polar opposite to the freedom (or perceived freedoms) established by Berger and his friends. Sheila is attracted to the vibrancy and free thinking of Berger, and the film sets up her rebelliousness beautifully as she goes from someone born to privilege to somebody deeply concerned with the horrors of war and passionate about the hedonism that Berger represents. As noted previously, in the original musical Sheila is a working class student protestor type, but here she is of a wealthy background and eager to rebel. She is seduced by the freethinking attitudes of Berger and company, and when Berger proudly sings "I Got Life," it resonates with her. He ends the number standing before her, presenting himself to her—animalistic, sexual and anarchic.

The scene that precedes this is uncomfortable to watch, and Berger and Sheila's father and uncle's confrontation is lengthy and unnerving. However, when it ends with Berger calling her uncle a "penguin" (referring to his tuxedo), we are allowed a much-needed laugh. Later in the film, Berger confronts a soldier manning the gates on an army barracks and the argument is relentless and aggressive, and before that he confronts his own parents in a shouting match. The film continually sets up Berger and his friends in these kinds of confrontations because the movie is obsessed with the relationship between the adversary and the free thinker. And this is part of the film's genius. As much as the Vietnam War sits at the centre of the film, the urban landscape of conflict—the police against hippies, the wealthy against hippies, the army against hippies—is where it marches forward with the greatest confidence. The comic entries that ease the tension and almost suffocating dramatics are necessary, and also part of that trickster element that the film plays with. Berger's declaration "I Got Life" evokes class resentment and is a great parallel to "Ain't Got No" (famed singer songwriter Nina Simone would merge these two numbers and make it a hit).

The music in *Hair* is stellar. In fact, the orchestrations for "Ain't Got No" are spellbinding, and once again Tharp's choreography is at an all-time career high. But not every number from the original stage musical made the film. Songs cut from the film such as "I Believe in Love," "Frank Mills" and "The Air" make a big difference, especially in terms of the reduced number of female voices in the motion picture, and this is the film's biggest tragedy. Perhaps the movie would have ran for an extra twenty minutes or so, but to keep those deleted numbers would have added so much more: every single song in *Hair* is fantastic. "Going Down" even opens with Berger singing "Me and Lucifer, Lucifer and me..." making explicit the relationship between these hippy girls and boys and Satan himself.

Performance wise, the film is brilliant. Forman understands actors, and sees the American context from an outsider's perspective—he is a foreigner with a European eye, looking in and seeing such suffering and anger. *Hair* is an angry piece, but it also a funny piece, a tender piece, and—most vividly—a moving piece of artistic expression. The film has its faults, but it is a successful translation of what is essentially a vaudevillian masterpiece, working a tribal element into this traditional theatrical style. Berger is met with numerous oppositions (from Sheila's father and brother, Claude, his own parents, officials and more), and he is the woodland Satanic trickster who remains an adversarial figure throughout the film. If Satanism represents the adversarial spirit and the opposite of an ordained order, than Hair is a perfect expression of this sentiment. *Hair* is both a celebration and manifestation of Satanic panic. Remember, the musical opened the same year as *Rosemary's Baby*, evidence that Christianity was starting to be scrutinized and undervalued by the young.

The title song is performed in a prison in the film, a choice made by Forman that highlights freedom of expression. The song articulates the fact that long hair on men represents rebelliousness and a disregard for authority, while in jail (and in the military) short hair and crew cuts are mandatory, evidence of submission to dominant paradigm. The Be-In at Central Park is a beautiful piece, with the number "Initials" showcasing its dancers all in white and singing about the wonders of L.S.D. The taking of acid is treated as if a Holy Communion, with Claude being 'blessed'. The Be-In sequence excuses numbers such as "Electric Blues" because they are treated as performances (like a diegetic musical), but for the most part all of the musical numbers in the film are red herrings in that they don't move the story forward (perhaps except for the reflective "Where Do I Go?," staged effectively in the busy streets of Manhattan).

Following the serious tone of that number—Claude's "Gethsemane" moment from *Jesus Christ Superstar* where he questions his chosen path—comes a playful number that is both sexually charged and politically bent. The song is a celebration of miscegenation and mixed relations, where young spritely white girls sing about their love and desires for 'black boys', while sassy soulful black girls let us know about the beauty of 'white boys'. It is not only remarkably feminist in its depiction of women as sexually assertive, but it is also deeply political in its positive spin on integration.

Editor Alan Heim remembers working on this sequence:

> I did one scene on *Hair*. I did very little. I got a call from Lynzee Klingman who asked me to re-edit one of the scenes from the film which was the draft call scene which intercut with the "Black Boys/White Boys" number. So I said that I'd take a look and I came in and I saw the scene and thought "OK they've missed the point here!" I had seen Hair on stage in Yugoslavia, it was the only time I had seen it, and I really enjoyed it even though I didn't understand a word they were saying or singing, but I did know that the "Black Boys/White Boys" song was much like a standard big show

stopping number, and because the film was being done by
Milos who has a very interesting take on American life and
American morays, they just kind of missed the point with
the number by not understanding that this number should
be as gaudy and flashy as possible, and that whatever message
came out of it would come out organically without being
forced. I remember when I saw the film and that moment
was just not enjoyable when it should have been. I spoke to
the producers and told them that this would take me about
a month and they agreed and Milos was always down for
reworking material. I showed up on a Monday morning and
I asked them to break the sequences down and go throughout
the dailies with me. Now when I turned up, sitting there on
the table was a very expensive, very nice bottle of wine, and
that surprised me. However, I found out that it turns out
that Milos would do mean things to people; to one person in
particular, you see, he would make you work overtime when
it wasn't necessary, he would be rude and scream and yell
and then finally he would apologise and give you a bottle
of wine to say sorry. Well, let me just say I ended up with
about three or four bottles of wine after working with him!
Although I didn't do anything to deserve them, but oh well!
When I started work on *Hair*, Milos had left American to
go off to Mexico to judge the Miss World beauty contest
which was like putting the fox out to guard the chickens, so
I was left alone. I recut the number and I really liked what
I did and Milos came back about two weeks later with gifts
from Mexico, a belt buckle which I still have and a money
clip for the producer which was very symbolic. So he saw my
cut of the number and liked it and then I bid him farewell
but he stopped me and said "No, no, no why don't you stay
on the rest of the movie. Go through the whole picture
and see what you think could work better." Now I was very
good friends with Lynzee and she agreed for me to have a
look through the film, I mean basically it all comes down to
what the director wants and says anyways. I went through

and watched the scene where Treat Williams is dancing on the large dining table and swinging on the chandelier and I remember that cut going back to what it was originally edited down to. I had also done some work on the opening number "Aquarius" and Twyla Tharp didn't like what I did, it wasn't her style. She really liked and really wanted fragmentary unfinished motion, she wanted the cuts to come while her dancers moved and that's what's left in the final product, I was just trying to make it flow smoother. It's a great opening where you are introduced to all these people and you don't really know who these people are and in a way it's similar to *All That Jazz*'s opening but I do remember feeling that it was a little bit overworked, I think Twyla put in too many cuts in it. The way Milos works is that he likes to have a couple of editors and he would sit down with one of us and make some suggestions and go through it and then work with the other one, so in this case he had worked with Lynzee and with Stan and then he did his own version and that didn't work either, so people had been through the sequence, and for me it just struck me that they all had missed the point of what that scene was supposed to do. I've always felt that you can take material and the message would come through without being stressed. When the film was made the idea of interracial relations was very advanced stuff! I was invited to the premiere at the Ziegfeld Theatre in New York which was a gigantic movie house with great sound, and all of us who worked on the film and our families were all given the first two rows of this enormous theatre. And we were so close to the screen that it was impossible to watch the film, it was doubly worse than sitting in a multiplex these days in the front row. The screen was fifty feet tall and it was so hard to take in and plus we could see what turned out to be the heatwaves that came from the light source which were travelling downwards because they were reflected in the mirrors of the lenses, which was very distracting. And the sound level was deafening! And the reason we had gotten the seats so close is because Milos had treated the screening as a fundraiser for a local college, so that the best seats were given to donors. We then went off to the after party which was wonderful, they had set up the venue as an indoor Central Park which was just wonderful. The material clearly wanted to go back and forth from the girls to the soldiers, I'm not sure if there was ever an idea to keep it all girls at one point and then all boys at another point.

This number is also significant for including male soldiers in charge of the draft induction praising both black and white boys, as white soldiers ogle the muscular black inductee and black soldiers become googly-eyed watching the white military man-to-be stripped down to nothing. This latent homosexuality of the military in *Hair* could be deemed as homophobic, however, simply because the entire film is so anti-army. It considers war is the truest evil, therefore those in charge of enlisting young men to die in the jungles of Vietnam being presented as lascivious "faggots" left over from an era of evil "queer" characters that populated the likes of many movies is rather undesirable in retrospect.

One of the girls in the "Black Boys/White Boys" number is musician and actress Ellen Foley, who remembers her experience in *Hair*:

> Well, at the time I was playing Sheila on Broadway. I was working closely with Rado and Ragni. I auditioned for the part of Sheila, which I did not get. But they did cast me for this part. And Milos Foreman did definitely not know about the Meat Loaf record! That would not be in his sphere. I think it was fabulous. They took the source material, and created a real fleshed out story, and the characters were fleshed out. You saw where they came from. The whole thing with Claude, we absolutely empathized and related to that character because people in my era—I knew people who went to Vietnam, and the terrible waste of people my age who were there. I think it was great because the show is pretty loose in terms of story. The songs told the story and the songs told who the characters were. But Michael Weller

544

really took it to the next level, and made it into a movie. I mean the movie and the Broadway show are definitely two completely different animals. The fact that they did see Milos and Michael Weller's, they saw a movie in there, was great because I think it was a great movie. I think it was underrated. I think maybe people are discovering it. I hope they are, because I just think for me, It was so emotional, that movie. And not even because I was a part of it. I'm sure that was it, because being in that movie was really a prime experience for me in my life! It was vaudeville, and the vaudeville meant, kind of it was a little episodic, and there were skits. I think since they were trying were creating worlds for these characters. The fact that they didn't do "Air" would have definitely fit into any plot from that time, because it is sort of when, you know, post-nuclear terror in America, and a time when people were starting to look at the environment and how the environment had been affected. So, yeah, that is definitely a song that could have fit. But yeah. I don't know. I don't know. It always happens when one medium is changed to the other and you know, people are always going to be mad and disappointed. I mean one of the songs cut is my favourite. That is "Frank Mills." That is my number one favourite song from the show! Oh, my god. I don't even know why they would have cut that? I said that is my favourite, but "What a Piece of Work is Man" really is. Unbelievable! So, maybe it was the movie that is more of a film with new plot development rather than quote, unquote a "musical." It was a movie with songs and not all the songs from the show fit their plan. But it is too bad. There were definitely some songs that were missing. But, how long can a movie be? You have to think about the length of a movie. The economy of it, you know, that people don't want to make a three hour movie. I mean Milos Foreman, my husband and I have been watching movies, and we just watched, *The Fireman's Ball*—the Milos movie, and that movie was like eighty minutes long! It was so short and so compact and it did everything that it needed to—so I think that is his philosophy; not to flog a dead horse, you know. But in regard to my work in Milos's film of *Hair*, mainly it was a show stopper with the "White Boys" segment because they always had these amazing black chicks singing that song, but in the movie, because of the staging and Twyla's choreography, I think that the "Black Boys" segment had a much stronger effect than it did in the play. I didn't sing it in the play but the black girls really just killed, you know, and though the white girls were kinda there. But in the movie, I think it was just so much fun, just the staging, so I think it came out in the movie an equal partner. It was shot on one day. It was an amazing day. I will never forget, it was like a fall day; incredibly beautiful, in Central Park. And, you know, it took a full day, and when you are young and having so much fun, it didn't feel like, "Oh my god! Here we are sitting around!" Because also it was dead outside, so there wasn't the question of sitting around while they lit it and stuff like that. It felt like a real performance, and we were just having a blast! And those gorgeous black guys were playing basketball all around us. Milos was really fun, and Twyla just became my absolute hero! I'm actually reading a book of hers right now because she has written a couple of books about, you know, sort of how to work; it's about collaboration and you know, almost a how to life your life as a creative person. It was a peak experiences, seriously, of my career, of my life I've had. Twla brought me back to dance with her dancers because she thought I was funny and liked the way I did her stuff, even though I am not a dancer. So, I ended up hanging around with her dancers, and it was like during the acid trip, I did some stuff with them. She brought me back, so not only did I do "Black Boys/White Boys," I spent time and rehearsed with them. What was really fun was I got to be friends with them and we would go out to Studio 54 and go dancing. You could imagine what it was like being in a club dancing with those guys, but you know, I held my own. I definitely had my own thing going on, you know, in terms of that dance. I think when I perform, you know, my kind of movement, I really think after all this time, part of it is informed by Twyla. I really do because I tend to do that herky, jerky, you know, semi goofy stuff. I think it is still in there. Still in my body. Other people in the film that spark memory is someone like Cheryl Barnes who was such an enigma! You know, she kind of just disappeared after that. I heard that she joined some religious cult or something. When the play first came out obviously it was really controversial. It's funny because when that play was first done in '68, I was still back in St Louis, in High School. I listened to the album all the time. One day, I was in there and I was listening to the song, "Sodomy." My father came in and said, "What is this goddamn shit?!" He took it off and broke it over his knee. So, it definitely stirred up a lot of emotion, believe me. But of course, my scene in *Hair*, because it was shot outside, I don't remember it being like one of those gruelling "I'm bored sitting around!" shoots. It might have been, but my recollection of it was that none of it felt like a job. It was so much fun. But of course, saying that, when you are doing choreography on film, naturally it takes longer because Twyla took a lot of time in terms of marks and camera, because when you are doing all that movement, you can't get carried away and flail around because you are going to be out of the shot. You know, obviously it takes a lot more time to make a musical than it does a straight movie. I thought having the army inducters being gay and singing the praises of white boys or black boys along with the gils was just so funny, and that how they snuck in, right, the guys were there at the induction getting their medical. Once again, that talks about gayness is probably everywhere; you know, they are talking about gay military, you know. So I imagine there are a few people who are pissed off by that too that couldn't possibly be true! So, obviously there is a lot of iconoclastic stuff going on. Black and white romance, gay black and white romance and real thrown in the face. In regard to my costumes—those were my clothes! Everybody wore their own clothes. I mean, Ann Roth had tried some stuff on, and then she said, "Bring some stuff in." And she liked. I can't remember if the other girls that were there, if it was their cloths or not. I think so. She liked what I had, more than what she had. She is one of the great costumers! The fact that she is not married to any one idea, that with their ego, if it is not something she designed or came up with, she is not going to use it. She looks around for all sources to make it work. I kind of knew Laurie Beechman because she had been around Broadway, and you know, Cabaret, and everybody knew that she was a great singer. I knew her but I did not know Debi Dye before the filming. She was married to an actor that was kind of around that scene at that time, but I did not know her. But we had fun! It was a very positive experience. I had known Nell Carter because we had done like a staged reading of something at the public theatre, so I had known her from there and became friendly. She was a trip—she was great! She was larger than life—her personality I mean, not her physical qualities, yeah. She was a blast. So, it was kind of cool because, you know, it was kind of this community of Broadway flash, movie actor people. I mean, Treat Williams, Annie Golden, Beverly D'Angelo, all these people, we all knew each other from Broadway work. So that made it so much more organic. You know, that all these people came together for this movie from a Broadway show, a lot of people came from Broadway. I really felt the difference because I came from a rock n' roll background, and when I first came to New York I went to see some musicals and thought, "Oh, my god, this is not of this time!" They had been doing the same thing, the same characters, the old fashion. So when I first came here, the first shows I saw were *Pippin* and the excitement of seeing that choreography of Bob Fosse was amazing. Then I saw *A Chorus Line* and having these people play themselves and breaking down the fourth wall and sort of that feel, and then being able to be in *Hair*. I mean, some of the old stuff I love. I adore *Guys and Dolls* and I always will, and I love Sondheim. I always will. It is two different animals. Some in each school is better than others. But, yeah, I understood the difference and it was exciting. I would said, to me the 1970s, for me, I came of age in that time. The 1970s were probably the most exciting decade for me, period. Because not only was I sort of new to New York, being very quickly thrust into doing a lot of great things, but being a part of an amazing energy that was going on.

Rendering internal political commentary meaningless in the film, is Twyla Tharp's choreography which is an authorship more than just dance. She brings a very unique "rag doll" balletic energy to the piece that is strangely alluring. Her dancers go from classical dance to late 1970s interpretive to outright running to slowing right down to clowning and gymnastics and back to classical dance again. It's an incredible achievement. Also, another stroke of genius is that you never clearly see the faces of her dancers; they are usually shot either in unison and bunched up together forming interesting shapes or in clean distances, rarely getting even a mid-shot. The most engaging moments come in and around Central Park, where these talented performers look ridiculously at home and at ease within their surroundings— like organic street urchins costumed by the instinctive Ann Roth, giving them an authentic urban filthiness that totally compliments Tharp's disciplined work.

Ann Roth also recalls working on *Hair*:

First of all, Milos is a very strong guy and I suspect that the producer Lester Persky turned him onto Twyla Tharp. Milos was someone that had no idea about choreography and for that matter probably didn't really want to know anything about choreography, but Lester told him that a choreographer was essential. Twyla's so strong, very, very strong and Milos is very strong and I suspect that in the beginning it was going to be "Who's going to actually be directing this movie?" But they got along very well and I loved working with her. It's a lifetime when you're working with her, you can't do anything else while you're working with her—her work is extremely innovative and it takes up all your being. I got a vision of what I wanted and I would do a sample and then we would make changes. The way you'd do in ballet. During the L.S.D. number ("Initials") in Central Park I had dressed the dancers in white. These clothes were vintage clothes and I said to Twyla that I was not going to remake these, that they would be used for this sequence and that is all. Of course her dancers are worked to the bone and extremely rough on the outfits and these pure white costumes became soiled with grass stains and dirt, but it worked for the piece. Twyla's dancers have a very, very tough life! A long time ago, a dancer told me that they would wear broken glass if they were told to wear broken glass. They just do what they're told. I remember I wanted Renn Woods who was on a camera crane to have little white flowers in her hair during the opening. But of course there were no little white flowers around so I went over to the honeywagon that was near by and asked them for some white paper and I got some toilet paper and tissue paper and stuck it in her hair because I wanted it to look like little white flowers. Also two of the skirts worn by the girls in "Aquarius" were completely hand painted and almost everything worn by the dancers were made. I thought Hair was a very good movie and it looked great. Stuart's work is divine in it. We worked very much in the city, but I mean we were mainly in Central Park a lot, we had some street stuff but most of the time we were using Central Park. Cheryl Barnes was one of the most incredible singers. I remember that scene well, we had shot that twice; the first time was shot out in front of a movie theatre on Waverly Place in Manhattan but then they changed it. And this was to pay tribute to the song "Frank Mills" which was cut from the film, because there's that line that refers to The Waverly in that song. I was very good friend of Twyla's. We did a lot together. In fact we did a Broadway show right after Hair. I loved working with her. I remember the kids coming down the steps in the park during "Ain't Got No" and I remember five seconds into it I would say something like "I don't like those shoes" and we changed them. We were very young and very irresponsible! I would quickly send for another pair of shoes, we did that a lot. Shortly after Hair a lot of the original drawings of the costumes were sold at charities. I know that Nell Carter had a scene during the acid trip, during that psychedelic scene, which I am sure that they cut. Nell's "White Boys" costume was not the one that I designed for her, I think perhaps Milos changed it. It was not my intended costume, I lost there. I had Treat Williams's vest for many years. You see, we have a barn where we keep our favourite things, out favourite costumes, and yes a lot of them were sold off at auctions but I do remember seeing that vest in the last five years, so if I rummaged through the place I could probably find it. I like that vest a lot. It was hand painted and antiquated and tortured and burned, I mean we did what we had to do to make it look aged and dirty and very "street." Certain painters and artists of that time were a source of inspiration for that vest, you see, I went to school with Andy Warhol, he was four or five years older than I, but he was still hanging around, and he was a bit of an influence on me. I had worked on *Midnight Cowboy* and a lot of his friends were in a party sequence in that and I took a lot of that look for Treat and designed his style based on that kind of artistic bohemian street kid. In regard to aging and making the costumes look dirty and "street," the costume houses in New York at that time were not prepared to do that work, I mean in the 1960s they were still being used to work on Broadway musicals eight shows a week, so they were made to last on Broadway; these were costumes that would stand many nights of wear and tear and still look great. However, for Hair, I wanted to tear these things up and age them and destroy them, and I did this in front of these costume house workers' eyes which made them quite ill! They were absolutely shocked! And I had a whole room where I had painters and scrapers and agers working for me. I had wonderful dyers as well. We had a great time. There was an awful lot to do, it was a much bigger show than I expected. Sheila did not have the dramatic change in the clothes that I thought she should have. I guess it was really justified, but she did not pick up any amusing clothes on her journey from society debutante to hippy. It was what she left in which was slightly New Jersey conventional. I mean her hair had fell and her make-up had fell and she became loose and sexy. But she did not get into cheesecloth or anything. John Savage had done The Onion Fields before Hair and he was a very serious actor and I never knew that he had that voice, he had a wonderful singing voice. Milos Forman did a great job and it was a very, very tiring long shoot, I mean there were times where we'd stop shooting and thought it was over but then months later we would start all over again. Milos would try very hard to run off to a quiet room and have a lie down and get some moments rest, but he would be interrupted and away we'd go again. Milos was exhausted by this film. I was very young and very ambitious in those days so when it came to dressing the massive crowd scenes I had two kids with me with walkie talkies and phones and I would say to them, "If they have any old work out jeans tell them to wear them, if they have any macramé have them bring that, if they can dance in bare feet, please let us have that." I would make a list and then the first fifty would come and we would go through them and we would have things to do, and things to put on them. I had the hairdresser standing by all the time, so we would add the feathers and the beads and at times I'd do a make-up and then other times I would say to some of the girls, "Take off your bra" and the girl would faint, but it was those tiny things worked and made the film look as though it was the late

1960s. I also needed to have a patently wash. I do think that the colours in that opening for "Aquarius" are very good and much planned. I remember having to re-dress the dancers with different clothes when it came to the night time sequence in Central Park. It was one of those nights which really represented the time and really showed us how unconventional this movie was. We were in the realm of the auteur and children of the experimental. I mean we did stuff that you wouldn't normally do under the supervision of a major studio, I mean people like Stuart Wurtzel was pretty straight down the line, but we were drunk with power and freedom. Look at Twyla Tharp! She is the quintessential experimental free thinker and it worked so beautifully for the film, and it worked for Milos as well. Although, Milos was very much a super macho man. And I was never interested enough if he was getting enough of what he wanted from Twyla. Of course we used an army and the clothes were the real deal, they were authentic United States military uniforms. I do remember that all the boots for a hundred and fifty or so men were at one point soaking wet and covered with mud and we had to use them the next morning, so I had a wardrobe team wash them, put newspapers in them and go off to a laundrette that was miles away and get them cleaned up. I worked very hard during the shoot around the army camp. It was difficult probably because I was always very nervous around the military and what the military represented. Everybody in the movie business with either their husband or wife was at that table in the party scene! It was payback time! All of those debutante dresses were all handmade by myself and I had made them hoping that they would be properly seen in the film. They were all made to look like cookie cutter dresses, so they would all look the same; these girls who fit into a particular mould. They were very conventional and without individual excitement as opposed to the hippies that crashed the party. But I felt that they were not depicted properly. There's no way to suggest to

Milos anything. He had strangely enough asked me to do his first film in New York which I couldn't do, but he is "the man" and comes from the world of a non-collaborative effort at all. It's funny, Milos's films that he did had a certain manner, for instance if Milos's mother was going to be in the movie and she was to play the cook and she said "I'm going to wear my orange sweater" she damn well would wear her orange sweater. There was no collaboration with any other artist. Milos really wanted to do Hair, more than anything. I don't remember any other directors attached before him. I got a phone call one day from him asking me to work on it and I thought if you searched the world for somebody to design the costumes for Hair, the last person in the world would be me! I never dreamed I'd be asked to do such a film. I remember the streets of New York back in the 1960s were filled with hippies but I was a conventional designer, I don't know how it happened. But it was a wonderful experience, but it still confuses me and I haven't worked like that since. Twyla is so unique and so physical. And quite honestly her people could not dance in clothes that would not allow them to do such violently physical activity that you see in Hair. That's Twyla's choreography in that film—it is violently physical. Shelly Washington and one of the very tall girls who's name I can't remember were incredible acrobats and very beautiful, and the movement is very beautiful and very rough and aggressive and almost creepy and unique. A lot of the psychedelic trip was cut. There were some Indian dancers who did some work for the piece and they were cut. I remember seeing that scene in full at the premiere, but it must have been cut. They were extraordinary. Stuart's work is beautiful in that piece. And it was the American Ballet Theatre used in that sequence, those girls were great.

Claude's acid trip is an inspired piece of psychedelia. We are transported back to the little weatherboard church in Oklahoma that we first caught a glimpse of at the beginning of the film, where Claude

Ann Roth costume design for *Hair* (1979)

is dressed in his finest ranch gear. He enters with the beautiful Sheila, decked out in a pure white wedding dress, complete with veil. Claude's trip is pure wish fulfilment, and reveals he is a romantic at heart (in a very traditional way at that—"an old fashioned melody"). The revelation of his trip is his desire to marry Sheila, but because of his involvement with New York hippies, this fantasy is constructed through a distinctly anti-conformist (and anti-religious) manner. Forman reintroduces scenarios previously seen in the film, but alters them in keeping with the context of a hallucination. It's a masterful turn in that everything is so perfectly recreated and staged, and another prime example of Tharp's highly inventive choreography. The hippies from Central Park stumble onto a park bench like limp clowns, and the hippies from the "Ain't Got No" number also appear but now showered in gold dust (some taking on monstrous forms, reminiscent of non-Christian—therefore supposedly non-conformist—Hindi deities). Sheila's debutant party is in full swing (again) with Berger up on the dining table (again) dodging a swinging chandelier, and the horse comes back to add to the madness of L.S.D. usage Claude's drug experience is based on what he has recently experienced in his short time in New York City, and the only reminder of Oklahoma is the small church where his trip takes place. Claude's experience is dominated by recent activity, Forman suggesting that New York its flower children will ultimately shape Claude from here on out. This is his Jonah and the Whale moment; through drugs, he is reborn. This is something that the more worldly Berger has experienced already, as noted in the song "Donna"—"I'm evolving, I'm evolving through the drugs....."In this hallucination sequence, Berger is presented as the Pan-like monster he truly is. Berger dances around provocatively and in turn represents everything that Claude is not. Berger is sexually powerful, potent and exists outside the norm. Berger is a demonic force who celebrates the flesh and lives for experience. Claude, even under the influence of LSD, is traditional and out of step with the freethinking and free-loving his new friends are drawn to. This difference will soon come to a more dramatic head when Claude and Berger have a standoff in Central Park by the lake.

Art director Stuart Wurtzel shares his stories about working on *Hair*:

> Here is the thing. I started in theatre. I went to school for stage design so my history up until that point had been mostly theatre and a couple of films that I had done that I had worked on earlier. I was very familiar with the stage production. I was in San Francisco when the touring company came in, that was late 1960s. We took our daughter to see the stage production and you know at the end of the first act those kids were out there with everything hanging out. She had never seen...it was a real eye opener, and actually at the end they got the whole audience up onto the stage to dance and I took her down and we got on stage and we danced with everybody else there. It was a great time, not only a great show but for us living is San Francisco at that

time, it was like the epitome of being at the right place at the right time. It all came together then of course a couple of years ago they restaged it for the public theatre Shakespeare in the park here in Central Park was another big success. It was great to see it all over again. It is a piece that is full of joy and sadness and great music. I was not involved originally in the production, I mean I sort of threw myself into it when I had heard that Milos had seen several designers in New York. I was not on that list of the original people that he was seeing. I was relatively new. I think I had done I don't know.. three or four films. Hester Street was the first film I did, then I did a couple of others in between those. I worked for a great designer friend of ours. Producer Bobby Greenhut, who was for a very long time Woody Allen's producer and had done all of his, I would say, ground breaking films. I had covered for about three weeks of additional still photography on *Broadway Danny Rose*. The designer who was a friend of mine who was not available and he said "Why don't you take this on?" so I met Bobby on that, during that time. So I had a bit of a relationship with him and then when I had heard that they hadn't settled yet on a designer, I saw Bobby and said "Listen Bobby, for whatever it's worth, I would like to throw my hat into the ring." Just because my background is theatre. I love working on anything that has killer theatrical relationship, you know, something that started on stage. I just find working in film now, I have had to divorce myself from working in the theatre simultaneously. I mean, I did that a couple of times, ready to check myself into the looney bin. It's one thing. Working in theatre you can do a lot of stuff in advance and you are only needed full time for the last couple of weeks you are putting into the show, that checking in and everything. Working on a film, you are there every single day, and the days are long, and I have a hard time divorcing myself from that. I remember hearing "Well, why don't you go in and meet Milos?" I went in and met Milos and we had a good talk, and he said "Well how would we

solve this? And how do you think we would do this?" Not
having read the script or anything I was sort of tap dancing
blind. I thought I had gave him a few ideas to mull over. So
I met the producer. The next thing I knew, I had the job. I
wasn't privy to the script. There was a script. I just didn't have
it before I saw Milos and sort of talked about it. I didn't have
a chance to read it before I went in. I think we talked about
the reality of being in New York. The fact that it was a street
movie. The fact that it wasn't the stage show, you know there
was some linear story in the film. We talked somewhat about
the fantasy sequence. How I thought we might handle that.
You know I sort of threw out a few ideas there and we sort of
left it on good terms like that but there were no yes or no or
anything at that meeting. It was just the fact that it was
probably going to be pretty much all location work. I mean
Milos had a personal relationship with the piece. That is
pretty much when he left Czechoslovakia and came to the
states, and he knows that time intimately. He had been in
Central Park. I often find many times that Directors or
people who are not from the country they work in, can bring
something to a piece because they have a more objective
attitude towards it, so I think in that sense he really had a
great affinity for not only the time, therefore that project. The
thing is, the play is more of a celebration of life and music
and it is more about character and not so much about story.
I mean there is a little bit of story there but it is more about
a life turned stark, and there are individual characters in the
piece, but it is not so much a beginning, middle and end. You
could almost take any number out of any piece and play it at
any other time and it would work. I think what Michael
Weller and Milos tried to do by giving it a more linear story,
it is something you can understand and relate to more
personally to the characters because you can follow their line
of reasoning and their transition. Certainly in the very last
scene when they are at the cemetery, and you see the group
of people, I mean just by seeing them and looking what Ann

has put on them, you know that their character has changed, and their life has changed because of this whole experience. And you see a growth in the character in which I don't think you necessarily saw in the stage production. We had many friends who worked on the production, and one of our dear friends to this day was one of the road stage manager that lived with the show while they were performing in Las Vegas if you could imagine. I mean *Hair* in Las Vegas, you try and get the actors back on stage for a performance. I have other friends who worked on props for the show. I mean we really had a real sort of personal attachment. In regard to the film, I guess the general consensus was why are we making this movie, at this time? Why it couldn't be made earlier? I don't know the reason about the rights, the coming together or not the right people. All I know is that ten years after it opened, we were making a movie and everyone said, "Well you know this movie is not current enough to ride on the coat tails of the success of the original show. I mean it wasn't done within the first couple of years of the show so it had that momentum, and it is not long enough to be nostalgia. Maybe in another ten years then we can look back on this period. In fact I have a feeling..I know when we finally saw a preview, and there were people sort of attached to it. New people who knew people so they were invited, and every person loved it but said they didn't know what they were going to do with this movie? And in fact, if you see the original poster, you know, these dancers in a line, multicolours or something. I mean talk about a poster that did nothing. As far as I was concerned it was sort of a miss design for a movie that was full of life and real. I mean actually Mary Ellen Mark, who is a really fine photographer, made a photograph of the dancers in the park from the very first number, that has all the life and would have been perfect, and was given basically as a gift to some of the crew members, and I am happy to have been one of the recipients. That at least, if you look at it now, you know exactly what that film says, and the film poster says nothing.

In a sense I think that they didn't know what to do with it, how to sell it. Tywla's work is amazing. It was so unusual, and it still is unusual. I mean if you had never seen Twyla's work before hand, now you see it, it is idiosyncratic, and it is sort of funky, there is some wonderful movements to it but it is sort of eratic, and to see some of her pieces on stage. The piece that was incredibly moving was the piece that we did down in Washington, in front of a reflecting pool ("3-5-0-0"). It's an anti-war film…when you saw the whole piece together..in the film it is sort of cut, you sort of see bits and pieces, there is some wonderfully erratic movement, but as a whole piece from beginning to end, I mean it was incredibly moving to watch them rehearse that. I think she tried to do it once, I saw In one of her seasons on stage, and it did not work as well. I loved it. I think the critics were a little less enamoured. I think it might have been the fact that originally it was outside, and you had that sense with the soldiers and death and the whole sense of the world around you, as opposed being encompassed by a theatrical setting being on stage, it had more power, especially being in that location. It was quite amazing. I have to say that, that film probably could not be made in Central Park again. I know that whenever you have to deal with anything in the park there is a hierarchy you have to go through, you can't touch this, you can't do that, you can't build. What we were filming, it was sort of a downturn, economically in the park. The park was actually not in the best shape possible. The upkeep was more about keeping more of the roads and the bridges going, so we were allowed…not that we did anything that was damaging but the fact that we were dancing on grass, that you can't do now. In some sequences, we painted the leaves on the trees because we did the opening number with the horses in the fall, and we didn't have John Savage. It happened the Saturday after we had the wrap party. We went back and we used a water based paint that was all approved and everything like that, but there were areas of trees that were painted fall leaves, that we could match the other part of the pieces that were already filled in the fall. We did that with permission, but I am not sure permission would be given now. Now you can't even tie anything on a tree. Renn Woods who sings "Aquarius" is on a crane, it is a plate form that is turning. It's her spinning around the city. I'm not sure, I think it wasn't that long, I mean with her singing, it wasn't that long. The dancing was probably a couple of days. It was a couple of cameras but I think the dancers did it a lot. They were incredibly strong. I can't give you all the particulars because I would be there as long as I could, then I had to sort of move on. I do like to be around as much as possible because my philosophy is of course, the DP is lighting every set up, and I'm adjusting everything. You know, you shove the chair three inches, you know it is all about the framing. So I do like to be around when the decisions are being made because I feel it is my responsibility. There are times when you just can't so. I don't think that number was more than a couple of days. It's organic. He said "I've got something for you and you are the next thing." We have them smoking and do this whole mind trip, all of a sudden people start arriving, you know we are singing about the baby possibly being a black, beautiful, chocolate baby. It keeps building and building and building and it's just them and then the next group comes in, and then another group comes in and then they are outside, and they are dancing in puddles and then they all just sort of take off and disappear into the park. It is one long sequence. It's funning because I have to say that when I first read it, you know this whole thing about let's keep moving around, you know you don't want to be too long in one place, but because it evolved, you were in the tunnel, and then they were sort of outside the tunnel, and then they were up and down the stairs. Then we went up to the upper level. So it kept moving, so it wasn't a static piece, it wasn't trying to cover the same thing all in one place. The plan of the park, there is an upper level road way, and if you are standing on that roadway and say you look straight ahead..if you are on the road and look to your right, you will look into this plaza, and in the plaza is that wonderful fountain. There are two grand stair cases that lead from that upper level down to that plaza wall, one of each side, and behind the fountain is what's called the lake, which is sort of a boating lake. People can take boats out. It's all man made. The whole park is man made. One of the great parks in the world. Under that road way that you are standing on is a tunnel. S there is this tunnel that looks at the Bethesda Fountain, the tunnel goes under the roadway and then at the end of the tunnel are stairs that go up to the other side of the roadway, which is on the same level as the roadway itself. Our biggest concern was, in the time of the story which was 1968, there was no graffiti before, by the time we were shooting it. I'm not saying there was no graffiti, there was here and there, it hadn't taken over to the point where, if you had seen those subway cars, where you feel like you are riding inside of the graffiti. The entire inside of the car is covered in graffiti. That was another time, that was the late 1970s, and that was something that we really had to fightactually because there was in fact a little bit of graffiti on some of the columns down at the bottom of the stairs that I wanted to eradicate, and we had to show the park people what we wanted to do with this water based paint so that we could basically blend it in and cover it over. It just meant that we were then making the movie in '78 instead of '68 where it took place. Although the city is gritty, and it is and it is a much different city then it is now. The construction boom is incredible, there was a wholeabout, I'm sure you have heard stories, you know on 42nd street. That's what the city looked like, and it was a great. There was a certain reality. I think that is why the picture is so successful. I was working I think in Austria, working on a television film, and *Hair* was playing in some little theatre somewhere, and the art director I use to work with had never seen it, and the location manager. There were about three or four people, I said "We gotta go, we gotta go, I really would love you to see it." I hadn't seen it in such a long time, I don't know how many years..about ten years since it had been made, and we went. There were not a lot of people in the theatre. There were a group of young people who I would say were in their late teens, about seventeen, nineteen. There was about six or eight of them, and when the movie was over, I tell you, they were in tears. See the thing is, I feel that, it is a film in a way somehow the songs take on more weight because they were picked very specifically for how they moved the story along and the characters who are singing them, because I think some of the songs in the film are sung by other than the people who sung them in the stage production, but if you follow the songs, I mean they take you to that place. When Claude is going through basic training and then you see the picture of the face of the little Vietnam girl. It is incredibly moving. That's what I mean by juxtaposing it to some other visuals, it takes on a different meaning and more weight, I think, and that is why I think it has a lingering effect. I don't think it is a dated film. I think anyone who sees it at any time, even though it was of that time, and now a days it is sort of fashionable to poo poo the anti-war and all the demonstrations, was it that charming, was it that sweet because literally everyone is just trying to make a living so they can get through day to day. I resent a little bit that attitude because it wasn't all fun and games at that time, I mean it was a very real situation, and I think the film makes it palpable. It is fun and games at the beginning, you know with kids hanging out, it's a whole different world. For Claude, he doesn't know quite how to deal with it, and then he is off to the real world. for him, and the responsibility which is the war, I got to do this for my country.. I love my country and then unfortunately Berger gets caught up and it's his death. Creating that whole twist, taking his place and then getting caught up in the movement and not being able to get out. Claude realising what had happened which helps turn him into a protester. So is so much in such a short time.

All that happens in the last, I don't know, twenty minutes of the film. The reality of the world situation is what it is all about, and of course when it all becomes personal, then it really hits home.

The acid trip sequence as designed by Stuart Wurtzel for *Hair* (1979)

Hair's hippies seeth with anti-religious and anti-traditional values and are creatures of adversary and opposition. Berger's rape of Donna and the Madonna, and his dismissal of her in the acid trip sequence spinning choreographer Twyla Tharp (dolled up in heavenly blue holy garb) into the recesses of darkness inside the church is provocative, as Eastern mysticism takes the place of Christian ideology. The acid trip ends and Hare Krishnas parade about with white kids embracing their ethos. But in essence, it is less a melting pot than a spiritual void. The nihilism of Satanism runs rampant in the very fabric of *Hair,* teaching us to dishonor thy father and thy mother, and to do what you want without worrying about the repercussions. Curiously, the character of Berger ultimately becomes a Christ-figure: he becomes the sacrificial good friend to the innocent Claude. The solidarity of this tribe (Berger, Sheila, Jeannie, Hud, Woof, and eventually Hud's fiancée and her child), leads them to being determined to rescue Claude from entering the war. Friendship is now meaningful and sacrificing, and therefore the hedonistic are revealed to allow a place for love and compassion in the lived experience of these hippies.

"Good Morning Starshine" and its glorious melody lines as sung by Sheila, Jeannie and Hud's fiancée (and then doubled up with the boys), is a beautiful sequence and the last moment of surrender and bliss in the film. After that, it takes a dark turn, and death is more imminent than ever. Reality seeps in as war takes hold of not only narrative but in the film's themes: this previously joyful take on hedonism takes a dramatic transition. When Claude and Sheila enter the black and filthy water earlier in the film, it recalls a witch's brew of disorder. As Claude says to Berger "I happen to think you're ridiculous," it is revealed the Christian hanging onto his belief in God and all that is supposedly good and American is no longer as seduced by the hippie's lifestyle. Here rivalry—in all its forms—maps out the internal dynamics that make up the tribe, and those that exist outside beyond their troupe. *Hair* is ultimately besieged by confrontation. The songs also reflect this: some are dirty, saucy and expressive of youth culture, while others are life affirming, truthful and enraged. The staging of "Where Do I Go?" recalls David Greene's take on an emptied New York City in *Godspell*, where Claude walks against the mob, while Treat Williams's performance of "I Got Life" is a remarkable centrepiece for the film. Here he shines: Williams is outstanding as the hedonistic Berger and the chemistry between him and John Savage is powerful and loving. He is like a barbarian, an elfin trickster. Savage is one of those actors who just makes all the right choices, and there is something enigmatic and intense about his performance. Coming off *The Deer Hunter* (1979)—another movie dealing with the Vietnam War—Savage is even more dynamic and complex in his performance in *Hair*. Bevery D'Angelo is a wonderful comic and while she has moments to let this quality shine here, the film hits heavy and hard with its dramatics so she gets the opportunity to throw herself into that arena as well.

The film works best as a dramatic piece with great songs and a terrific score. The arrangements for "Ain't Got No" are so strong, even though the song had been re-written for the film version. The third soloist ends his section and we go back into the original verse, therefore the music is altered. Originally "I Believe in Love" (one of the omissions from the film) follows after the third soloist, a song originally sung by Sheila (the hippie student protestor Sheila, not the Sheila we get in Forman's film) which concludes with a procession of a protest march chanting "What do we want?" "Peace" "And when do we want it?" "Now!" Right after that, it returns to "Ain't Got No" in full force. The film does something special with the final chorus of "Ain't Got No," as it builds it to a chill-inducing climax where the score lifts, changes key and brings it home with gusto. Tharp's street urchin dancers race towards us, their fit and lean bodies coming for us as the charged music swells and builds into a frenzy. These athletic children of the street throw themselves around and it is quite simply magical. Finally, at the climax of the number two of the extended tribe fall into each other's arms and embrace (recalling the opening of "Aquarius").

Cheryl Barnes as Hud's fiancée does an impressive job at belting out "Easy to Be Hard," a song (again) originally sung by Sheila in the stage musical. This is the one moment that exposes the ugliness of the peace and love generation, and the misogyny that permeates the Peter Pan-syndrome of the male longing to remain free from responsibility. The scene sneaks up and rattles the narrative cage—we understand Jeannie is pregnant (and now as the film has moved through a course of time we can physically see how pregnant she is) and that she doesn't know if Hud or Woof is the father. Hud's fiancée has here been left behind, and we are given more insight into complexity and selfishness of the responsibility-fearing hippies. In the original stage production, Sheila gives Berger a new shirt which he aggressively tears to shreds refusing to take it (and what the shirt represents) leading to "Easy To Be Hard." Here, however, Hud aggressively screams at his fiancée and leaves her crying "Do you only care about the bleeding crowd, how about a needing friend?" Eventually she is welcomed into the tribe and there is a terrific conversation between her and Jeannie which mirrors Claude and Berger's friendship. Jeanne says "We're all crazy / let's shake on it," and Hud's fiancée responds, "Let's not."

The most distinct protest song of the film "3-5-0-0" is set up as a clever sabotaging of the PA system at the army barracks where wailing guitars and feedback crash in on the military induction ceremony. The concept of authority explored in *One Flew Over the Cuckoo's Nest* and the maniacal expression of artistic genius delivered by Forman's other masterpiece *Amadeus* (1984), are both themes that manifest in *Hair*. As the singers and dancers sing "Prisoners in nigger town / it's a dirty little war," we understand that the savagery of the lyric and the anger of its intentions are both politically captivating and artistically edgy. *Hair* is both these things.

Head editor Lynzee Klingman remembers her time working on *Hair*:

> We were shooting it in New York, in the autumn. And it could not have been more beautiful! We were all in Central Park, for you know, the outside stuff. So that was really fun. They would play the music in the playbacks, and there were people singing and dancing there. It was just fun to see. It was fun to be a part of. It was so beautiful and there was a lot of footage because Milos Foreman likes to edit. He shoots in a way that to edit, to give him options. So, he does a lot of coverage. You know, it great to work on musicals. I've done it before, and it is just fun! Although it was hard because you had to stay in synch. It was harder. These days it's not. We didn't have the score of course but we did have that wonderful music. And Galt MacDermot who did the

music initially, did all the arrangements. I think he did all the incidental musical too, but that came later. You know, editing isn't evolution, it is a process. So, you don't go in there saying, 'I am going to cut here and there' I mean, you cut where the film tells you to cut. But then you recut and you recut. And especially with Milos who never stopped recutting. So, we tried everything. You know, every frame and every frame at some point. And "Aquarius," we had a lot of options. We could put the dancers anywhere. You know we wanted the police with that couple. And I want to say also, in Aquarius, there are no opticals in this movie. There is no tricks. Everything is a straight cut. Everything is as shot. Every day I would get the dailies we shot the day before and if you just mention a number to any of the songs, I could talk about the coverage. "Aquarius" was shot over a long period of time. Obviously, because there was a lot of set-ups in it. I love the music, I just love it. I mean, I was always happy working on that film. Always happy. I want to tell you, I was a little disappointed in the choreography. I love the fact, the rag doll stuff…some of the choreography later in the movie was so fabulous, particularly in Washington for "3-5-0-0." I love that number that ties in there. They were some of the most beautiful things I had ever seen! And we had to cut them way down. And that was a killer and this was before you could save things for the DVDs! So we lost scenes and people tried to find them. The guy whose name was Sollomita, write this in your book, was trying to save the company money and he destroyed all the outtakes and all the trims. He destroyed them to save some storage money. We could have had all those incredible numbers. We could have had that to see. Within a couple of years there was this project to project *Hair* in the park and to reconstitute all those missing numbers, and there was no film! Of course. I remember everything. Every shot we cut, yeah. Maybe not every shot. Oh, it was a pity. It was a pity…time. We were way over time. And we cut a lot of stuff down and a lot of stuff out. We took out another incredible number called 'My Conviction'. And that was sung by Charlotte Rae, and under it there is a note that she holds for a minute. And the New York City Ballet Company do a little dance, a little ballet, under that note. It was so fabulous! There was a lot of stuff that got cut and just broke my heart. She got cut at the last minute. There was a three hour cut of the movie where we all thought it was perfect. Milos had to do that. That shot where Treat Williams goes into the plane. That shot was a continuous shot (then she says she was wrong). It's a very exciting sequence, isn't it? That's how we cut ordinarily, I mean, the easiest way to cut always. Is a movement. Twyla when she like to cut, she had been a cheerleader in high school. So when she liked a cut she would go. She was really fun! She was very cute. I just wish the choreography in the number had more. I just think at the time she didn't know how to use the camera; how to choreograph with the camera. Some stuff was so good. But I was saying that last shot was a continuous shot of treat walking into the plane. And there is a cut in it now. It kills me some of the stuff we cut. It just killed me. "Frank Mills" was shot and it wasn't anyone in the film. It was just a girl at the Waverly Theatre. And it was a great number but it just didn't belong in the movie. That was the first thing to go. The freedom I have to edit, is the coverage. If the cameraman doesn't shoot it, then there is nothing to play with. On this show there was always a lot of cameras going. And there were a lot of takes. So, when we came into the play room, we had a close-up, we had a wide-shot, we had over the shoulder, and a two-shot. So then, we had the whole scenes, say, in a dialog scene; like when they go to see the parents, we had the mother, we had the father. We had coverage, so we could try different things. You see? Yeah. It was great to have it (the crowd shots). The life of it was so lively. So rich, that it contributed to the film. And we have a lot of coverage. Everything in the film was a choice. And everything not in the film was a choice. That wasn't, then we didn't have it. Well, there were a couple of things we didn't have, that were meant to be shot. One was the anti-war movement disconnecting the sound at the end. Where it interrupts the base and then it is playing in the army camps. The anti-war movement. The idea was that big, disruptive sound and that is why it was so crazy. And they hooked it up in the base. That was never shot. So, the crowd at Washington at the end, it was a huge crowd. And when they ask them to march, they ran —so it didn't look like a peace march.

When Berger finally gets his haircut, it is not about submission, it is about sacrifice: he starts the film burning his draft card and ends it cutting his hair. Imagery such as this is essential in a film that relies on character development and tribal experience over narrative. When Sheila successfully persuades an army officer to drive with her, allowing her to steal his clothes in order to help free Claude, she becomes the trickster that Berger was. This spirit wakes in Sheila as she becomes a princess of seduction—stripping the soldier of his wares and assisting Berger who gives up everything (including his life) in order for Claude to be with her. These tragic turn of events are all the more depressing when we hear the sorrowful conversation between Claude and Berger at the barracks, a farewell and testimony of their friendship. Identity is examined as Berger becomes Claude, effectively merging them into one and the same. The final moments of the film show Berger's grave being overlooked by the remaining tribe members, including new members such as Hud's fiancée (whose clothes suggest she has now inducted herself into the tribe), with Sheila and Claude huddled up while Jeannie nurses a baby with Woof by her side. "Flesh Failures/Let the Sunshine In" is an outstanding number, and the key change on the lyrics "facing a dying nation" from a minor to a major is masterful as masses of people race to the White House singing "Let the sunshine in." This is a massive, moving feat—a slice of history reimagined. As much as critics panned the film for being out of date and ten years too late in the making, it still resonates and the message is loud and clear.

Film academic Craig Martin shares his insight into the film in relation to the western genre:

My father has often told me a story set back in 1971 when I was not yet three years old. *Hair* was about to open at the Metro Theatre in Melbourne (Australia) and at that time my parents were members of a fundamentalist Pentecostal church. It was the type of place that believed in faith healing and demon possession and insisted that if you didn't speak in tongues, you were not one of God's elect. When *Hair* was preparing to open in June after a successful two year run in Sydney, it was decreed from the pulpit that Satan himself had inspired the musical and the congregation was strictly forbidden to attend. That didn't stop a group of curious young girls who had to see what all the hype was about. Like Eve eating the apple, they gave into temptation, bought tickets in secret and went along to the show. Unfortunately they were spotted out the front of the Metro and that Sunday they were brought up before the congregation and excommunicated from the church, doomed to spend eternity burning in hell. That story is my first experience of *Hair* and so, like those young rebels, I grew up with an abiding fascination with the musical. What could possibly be so evil in a stage show? It was not until 1995 that I eventually saw *Hair* but not on stage. It was Milos Forman's adaptation, playing at the grand old Astor Theatre in St Kilda on a double bill with *Abba: The Movie*. What a double! *Hair* was the second feature and I sat up the back of the packed cinema marvelling at song after catchy song while feeling a burning melancholy as I found myself becoming nostalgic for an era I was too young to even remember. When the film finished and the crowd made their way out, I sat in my chair stunned, enraged, saddened, elated, overjoyed, troubled. I hadn't felt such a whirlwind of conflicting emotions since seeing *A Clockwork Orange* for the first time. Of course, *Hair* instantly became my all-time favourite musical. Thinking about Forman's film afterwards, I was struck by the force of its images. The opening sequence in Oklahoma, when Claude farewell's his father, is performed mostly in silence. Watching this estranged father and son awkwardly negotiate what is ostensibly a final farewell is hard to watch. John Savage's awkward, embarrassed half-embrace of his father is equal parts uncomfortable and deeply moving. I like to think there is a nod here to Schlesinger's *Midnight Cowboy* as Claude abandons rural life and heads to New York City, only to be constantly overwhelmed and out of his depth. Speaking of cowboys, Forman plays with motifs from the classical Western genre, although his interest is in subverting its stereotypes. Claude, who is gung-ho to serve his country, considers himself a cowboy. After all, he comes from rural Oklahoma and shows he is at home on the back of a horse. Yet it is Berger who sleeps under the stars and has no taste for civilised society. It is Berger who gets his gang out of prison and gets the girl, but not for himself. It is Berger who leads his band of fellow travellers out west to sit around a campfire and finally, it is Berger who sacrifices his own life to save his friend. A sequence that I find fascinating is the prison riot that accompanies the eponymous song, "Hair." The sequence involves a series of crosscuts showing Hud, Woof and Claude waiting in jail while Berger is walking to his parents' home to borrow some cash to bail out his friends. During the song, a stylised riot breaks out in the prison with choreographed punches and kicks delivered in time to the music. It is an odd sequence that seems somehow out of place and yet, when considered allegorically, the riot expresses Berger's inner turmoil at having to return to his parents to plead for money. For Berger, who values his freedom above all else, going back home is like returning to prison. This metaphor is made all the more compelling when Woof is threatened with a haircut in jail and protests so adamantly that he gets his way. Likewise at Berger's parents, his father stipulates that he will only give him money if he cuts his hair, leading to yelling match. Both Woof and Berger's reactions may seem excessive, but they are reacting to threats against their liberty. Their outcries are not about their hair. They are about their freedom. Berger proves this when he switches places with Claude at the army barracks in Nevada. He doesn't have a problem with cutting his hair because *he* has chosen to do it. It is an expression of choice, which is a symbol of his freedom. Berger's entry and exit in the film is pure genius. His voice is heard before he is seen, reading the fine print on his conscription card that his friends, Hud and Woof will burn. Surrounded by the darkness of a Central Park underpass, Berger uses the burning card to light a barrel fire. At that moment, a pair of mounted police ride their horses into the underpass, prompting Berger and company to flee. As they exit the darkness, a shot from inside the tunnel shows them running into the daylight. In the same shot, flames from the barrel fire flick up from the bottom of the frame as though they are pursuing Berger as he attempts to escape his destiny. The image operates as a portent that is duplicated at the end of the film. Forced into combat gear, Berger marches into a waiting military aircraft, singing the terrified strains of "Manchester England." As with the film's introduction of Berger, where we hear him before we see him, in his final shot he boards the plane and disappears into the darkness while his anguished cries, "That's me" fade away.

I WANT YOU AROUND: *Rock'n'Roll High School* and *Roller Boogie*

The Ramones merged 1970s punk rock with their skewed take on 1950s-style fun, youthful energy and nonchalant ruthlessness, leading the way with their simplicity and the understated genius hidden beneath their loud raucousness. *Rock'n'Roll High School* most certainly compliments this aspect of their sound, but it also celebrates fun and anarchy more generally with a chaotic punk rock edge. *Rock'n'Roll High School* is the punk rock movie to end all punk rock movies, and it's relentless "up yours" permeates its very fabric, making it both endearing and endlessly engaging. While films such as *The Blank Generation* and *The Punk Rock Movie* documented what was going on with an earnest anti-movement sentiment that seeped throughout the punk scene of various cities throughout the 1970s, *Rock'n'Roll High School* delivers a plot that generated a legion of imitators as well as genuinely unique expressions of punk-centric cinema that became popular throughout the 1980s and through to the early 1990s. Produced by Roger Corman, *Rock'n'Roll High School*'s bright and psychotic wildness render it the quintessential punk rock movie.

Roger Corman is a pioneer of low budget motion pictures, and is as savvy a business man as he is a storyteller. There was a long line of rock-centric movies that Corman churned out during the golden age of teen cinema, and in the late 1970s he followed them up with this film. With punk becoming a major part of the pop cultural landscape, a film set in a bureaucratic and oppressive institution called Vince Lombardi High School headed by the stiff and stern Principal Togar (Mary Woronov)—in many ways representative of Margaret Thatcher and her dictatorship (Thatcher would incidentally be the politician who will later introduce the whole concept of "the video nasty" during the 1980s)—was too good an opportunity to let slide. This tension between the old guard and youthful rebellion is a staple film type and one that has consistently worked for Corman.

P.J. Soles dotes over The Ramones in *Rock'n'Roll High School* (1979)

Mary Woronov is outstanding as the puritanical principal with her hall monitor henchmen ready to take orders, and stands in opposition is the fantastic P.J. Soles as the relentless punk rock enthusiast Riff Randall. Soles remembers working on *Rock'n'Roll High School:*

> After I was cast Allan Arkush told me a story, he said that it was originally going to being called *Girls Gym* featuring disco music, and that was the movie that Roger Corman thought he was going to make. It was going to feature scantily clad girls doing gymnastics to disco! Might have been interesting, but probably not a cult film! The Ramones were very shy and quiet. Nobody wants to hear that, but seriously, they were completely out of their element. Here they were in sunny, warm Los Angeles not cloudy, cold NYC, and they were staying in a motel on Santa Monica Boulevard, with the only way to get around by car, not subway or walking, and they had to be on set early in the morning, and they had never made a movie before. We welcomed them with open arms, but they even resisted getting in the lunch line or sitting on the couches in our shared communal trailer. Instead, they would say they weren't hungry and sit on the floor in a corner. It was hard to talk with them, especially Dee Dee and Marky. Johnny was the most conversant. Johnny loved Roger Corman films, so he thought being in one was pretty cool. Also, there really wasn't a whole lot of time for chatting. We had a brutal timetable and schedule to keep to, so conversation was at a minimal. Also, I was in pretty much every scene, but whenever I could, I tried to engage with them and make them feel welcome. I had started my career in NYC and had lived there five years, so I felt I knew where they were coming from. They were awesome to me, especially Johnny. Maybe he had seen *Halloween*, not sure, but he was the most interested to participate. Within the first few days, Allan Arkush realized they weren't going to get through their speaking lines easily, so we had to pull out a few pages of dialogue, but their

genuine essence still came through loud and clear. Without Roger Corman there would be no wonderful and unique B movies. He invented the mould, and he enabled extremely talented writers, directors and actors to get their start and their first shot at film making. He is as important to Hollywood as Louis B. Mayer, period. I was so excited when I first read the script, because I knew this was my role! I knew who Riff was, and I knew how I wanted her to be on screen. The wonderful part of this for me was getting to play (again, after *Carrie* and *Halloween*) an American teenager, something I never was having grown up in various countries around the world. I was getting to be "my fantasy"! Living in Morocco, Venezuela & Belgium, I went to schools with American girls whose fathers were either in the embassies or the military or who worked for big American companies like Caterpillar, Union Carbide, and American oil companies. They had spent a fair amount of time growing up in DC or Texas or Illinois, before moving to these foreign posts, so they knew what the United States was like! I fashioned my Riff Randall after them, especially my best friend Cindy Clark in high school at the International School of Brussels. She was fearless, so that trait became Riff's. I knew Riff had to be kinetic, never stopping, always moving, so I knew I wanted to be high energy. Also, I planned for her wardrobe to be as colorful as the rainbow and really different from any fashion most commonly seen in schools at the time. It was a personal goal to get a lead part, especially since I knew I wasn't going to play a teenager much longer, nor did I want to! It was super exciting to get top billing. More exciting was getting to work every day and be in so many scenes. Much better than sitting around all day waiting to get called to the set for a quick, short scene. There was a $100 wardrobe budget for Riff. That was not going to work. I pulled apart my script and studied it for how many outfits I had and then went shopping. I spent (in advance) almost all of my weekly earnings for the film on my wardrobe, but it was so important to me. The striped stockings, the shorts, the musical notes jacket ($300!) and the hi tops with the tiny pocket for a tiny comb, it was all so necessary to create Riff! I had so much fun putting together her look. Now I will admit I had never heard of The Ramones, but really they weren't well known in LA yet. And punk was not really on the radio yet. When Allan Arkush gave me a cassette and said to study this album and know every song because you are their number one fan, I was horrified. I couldn't hear it as music; I didn't know what it was. But it didn't matter. Riff was their number one fan, not P.J.. Once we were filming the concert scenes and I saw them performing live, I really started to appreciate their talents. I love anything original, and I thought their style of playing insanely fast and going from one song to the next without a breath was just amazing. On stage and in person they had such a unique vibe. I grew to really love their songs, truly, but honestly it took a few years! Surprisingly, the "I Want You Around" scene was day one of filming, and the first scene of the shoot. What a day! "I'd like you to meet The Ramones and now start taking off your clothes"! Um, what can I say? It was very weird having Joey climb over me on the bed and sing to me, but I wanted it to be sweet, and Riff had to enjoy her fantasy moment. The "joint" was rosemary or something, but it was not fun to smoke. There was a bit of conversation between Allan Arkush and I, because I really wanted to stress that Riff was a songwriter, not a groupie, and even though Joey was her favorite, I didn't think Riff was "in love" with him or "wanted" him. Riff wanted them to play her songs! She had ambition, not physical motives. But we worked it out. I think that scene is one of my favorites now though, because The Ramones were so endearing in the scene; I love Johnny's brief, shy smile when Joey's singing to me on the bed, and I love when Dee Dee's playing in the shower. It's just such a fantasy to have a rock band playing in your bedroom, so fantastic! Nowadays Mary Woronov and I talk a lot when we are doing a convention together, but on set, since she was Riff's enemy, I distanced myself from her intentionally. We did speak, but there really was not a lot of time to hang out. She is really a fascinating woman, and she was the perfect mean principal. I adore her. I feel super charged when I am acting. I feel alive and immortal, like I am in a vacuum where time is suspended and captured; it's amazing to me. It's so important to me to make sure I am as real as possible in my scenes; that I am really living those moments that I am bringing to life. That's what appeals to me, the "how can I make this real?" And I love getting to play someone that I'm not; surprising I know, but I'm really kind of shy and a loner, seriously! I think creative people tend to have many outlets to express themselves. I have always considered myself primarily as a poet, so being a lyricist is right in line with that. I am so proud that I have co-written songs with my boyfriend Robert Best and my now son-in-law John Corlis for their band Cheap Rodeo. It's such a dream come true for me to have songs actually on a CD! I think most fans really love people whose work they admire because a part of them wants to do what they are doing and they probably can! It's an issue of putting actors or whoever on these silly pedestals when most fans have just as much talent in whatever area of expertise is their specialty. Riff started out loving the music that The Ramones created and performed, and that inspired her to write a song for them. She thought it was possible! I rest my case! I really love every moment of Rock'n'Roll High School. It was just such a joyride making the movie and, of course, I am so proud and thrilled to have been a part of it, especially as I get older. It amazes me that every year, more and more fans, new generations, young and old are embracing this film. So many people have told me stories of how much this movie has meant to them from teenage girls and boys to men and women older than me! I have no diamonds or pearls to leave to my son and daughter or my grandchildren, but they will always have *Rock'n'Roll High School* and that is a priceless gem.

Adding to this array of wonderful performers is the terrific Paul Bartel who shines as the music teacher trying to teach the teens about Beethoven, but eventually becomes a disciple of punk rock as the film moves forward.

Soles's Riff Randall kicks off the film by announcing "Hey everybody I'm Riff Randall and this is Rock'n'Roll High School!" From here on in, the anarchy is palpable and inspiring. In a sense, the film becomes much more than a homage to the rock-centric films about teen rebellion from the 1950s, and instead is more a revolution, a testament to youthful independence and the efforts of young people with nothing truly menacing or life threatening to fight against. A film like *Rock'n'Roll High School* fuelled the energy and was instrumental in the slew of future teen angst pictures that later surfaced throughout the 1980s where young people—with no war, no civil unrest and no global crisis to fight against—will rise up and break free from the oppressive situations their comfortable lives entail: parents, social demands, and responsibilities. As witnessed in this anarchic Corman produced film, high school and the totalitarianism of the education system also proved an enduring central theme.

The song "Sheena is a Punk Rocker" launches the film into a frenzy and from here it is all uphill—both narratively as well as thematically. Tom (Vincent Van Patten) the clean cut jock, fronts the film with his trouble with girls and of course he has a keen interest in the gorgeous Randall. Naturally, Riff is not at all interested: being a punk rocker and devotee of The Ramones, an athletic Ken Doll doesn't appeal to her—instead, she is hopelessly devoted to front man Joey. Tom's romantic dilemma acts as a secondary plot device and when we hear "Smoking in the Boys Room" (one of the songs used in the film that was not by The Ramones), we enter a world of parody, self-reflexive ingenuity and the origins of a kind of teenage satire that will come into fruition during the next decade. The school counsellor cements this hilarity and zaniness as the film becomes half teen sex comedy and half rock'n'roll blitz. Many of the basic elements of 1970s and 1980s tits'n'ass movies that would flourish with films such as *Screwballs* (1983), *Losin' It* (1983), *Porky's* (1982) and many more, appear in *Rock'n'Roll High School*, but they were also inspired as much by its specific kind of humour. But the jokes aren't all smutty; in fact, most of the film's fun comes from P.J. Soles, who shines with a bright cheery delight as the eternally loyal Ramones fan Riff Randall. She and the equally funny Mary Woronov carry the film, and The Ramones themselves are a cinematic treat—in a strange and oddball way, the camera loves them. When the film turns into a mini-Ramones concert it blossoms into an otherworldly experience. It transitions the film from a teen-centric rebellion romp that morphs into the excitement of warts and all punk rock anarchy.

With a story by Joe Dante and Allan Arkush (the latter who would also direct the film), this wacky piece is bubbly and smart, as well as consistently dedicated to paving a way to showcase the excellence of The Ramones. The film is also feminist in the sense that the leads are all women and they are given the majority of the screen time. They are painted with complex passions and flaws, moments of outrageous silliness and outrageous selfishness and it is all absolutely fun to watch. Riff Randall is a songwriter, and uncompromising when it comes to her craft. She is also a born leader. When she takes over the gym class and leads the girls into singing and dancing to the title song, we are in the realm of the rock musical and it is exciting, energetic, and blissfully untraditional. This is a musical for the youngsters of the late 1970s who responded to The Ramones as opposed to Rodgers and Hammerstein: everything is relative, and here punk rock delivers a new *Oklahoma!*

The film features some inspired set pieces that have since become iconic, such as Togar's animal experiments leading to the famous "exploding white mice" scene. Here Toga demonstrates the dangers of rock'n'roll where mice are forced to listen to the work of The Ramones, while Randall sings "I don't care about history, that's not where I wanna be!" as young fit teenage girls show off their various talents in the school gymnasium. This brilliant juxtaposition is a narrative godsend that it captures how healthy and invigorating rock music is. Helping all this move along is the music, giving the film its heartbeat. The Ramones songs are contagious and fun, and the idea of rock'n'roll being dangerous and something that needs to be eliminated is addressed by the song and the film itself directly. The Ramones are anarchic fun, and Togar is about order and discipline: these polar opposites are made so clear and rendered in such rich colors that the film can be considered a musical comedy variant of *Stand and Deliver* (1988) or *The Breakfast Club* (1985). With Riff leading youth culture like a dog with a bone, punk rock's entry into the mainstream launched unity as an important part of the teenage experience: Riff comes to represent the disenfranchised and the kids who just want to get loaded, laid and have a great time.

Her leadership also helps in the blossoming of supporting characters, such as her best friend Kate (Dey Young), the bookish introvert (along with the rebellious rock'n'roller Riff and jock Tom, she is another archetypal stock character typical to the teen-centric cinema). Although it is an unlikely pairing, Kate is attracted to Tom, while Tom pines for Riff who of course is helplessly in love with Joey Ramone. All this adds to the film's commentary on fandom, teen sexuality and the idea of restrained romance beyond of the urgency and complexity of emotions that lead to teen sex. When the school counsellor talks through the rules of a first date to the virginal Tom and Kate (including how to remove a bra, etc.), the film's subplot moves with a nice steady pace, as Riff and The Ramones (with Togar in direct opposition) are in the foreground. Tom and Kate's romance is never a nuisance, but instead an extension of youthful rebellion in its celebration of discovery and personal development. After all, not everybody is as revolutionary, self-aware or as self-possessed as Riff Randall and her favourite punk rock band, The Ramones. As important as Riff Randall is, Principal Togar is an incredible creation: a giant of a woman who struts around with tongue-in-cheek bitterness. Mary Woronov never misses a beat and her disdain for The Ramones is hysterical. It is as fully realized as Riff's love for Joey Ramone: over the top, loud and relentless.

Fandom is a gearstick *in Rock'n'Roll High School*, and this is summed up nicely when Riff camps out for Ramones tickets. But the montage does something else: it delivers a multi-faceted groupie. It doesn't dismiss her, but rather she is a resourceful heroine reading the punk zines of Los Angeles of the period while scoffing down pizza and writing song lyrics for a band she loves. As the scene progresses (and it is peppered with fun gags like an Native American 'chief' harassing Ramones fans before someone bemoans "Scalper"), Angel Dust—a self-proclaimed number one fan—gets into a fight with Riff, and tensions between fan and creator comes into play. Angel Dust is a groupie in the classical sense, whereas Riff uses her inspiration bought on by The Ramones as a way to create something for them. In her case, art inspires her creativity.

Make-up artist Gigi Williams remembers the film:

> I knew that a Ramones movie was being made so I called the director from New York which is where I lived and he said "OK, send me your make-up book!" so I sent him my book and he went through it and he called me back and said "Well, you're over qualified and we have no money and we can't bring you here." And I said "I will bring myself, I have a place to live and it doesn't matter." So I did it for two hundred dollars a week. I did all the hair and make-up myself, I had no help whatsoever. And then two weeks into it the director had heart attack and I got pneumonia so I had to finish the movie in my house, so I had the actors come into my house and finish them up in the morning and then send them off to the set. If I look back at my career, and I have seen the movie a thousand times, I sit back and think my god that is the best movie I have ever done. It was a different hairdo and different make-up for every scene and I did it completely by myself, I had no team at all. I was very young and just learning and doing all this work all by myself. And it was great! I learned a lot from Alan Arkush and we just went for it! On Mary Woronov there were so many crazy hairdos and Mary was a friend of mine. I was a punk, I was heavily into the punk scene and we just went to it. And with the Ramones, well, I just loved them. I stayed friends with The Ramones for years. I would go to every Ramones show in New York and I went with The Ramones. They were amazing. They were a lot of fun. There was a rumour that the make-up artist on the film was supplying drugs for The Ramones and when I heard this from a writer who was working on a book about them I said "Nope. Not at all." And I would admit that

if that were true, but it wasn't and it needed to be cleared up, but they were always high and using drugs. I mean Didi, he was crazy. One night we had to go and bail him out of jail! They were so high all the time. Joey never washed his hair and so I had to have just one brush that was Joey's brush and if the other boys would act up I would threaten them and say "Now if you don't behave I will use Joey's brush on you!" Joey also always spat when he talked, he had no control on his saliva there! But he was so cute, they all were.

When The Ramones finally hit the screen it is momentous. "Tonight" is an anthem of simple and pure rock'n'roll, The Ramones manifest youthful expression at its purest here. Joey Ramone's presence is incredible—this spindly creature donning his leather jacket and shredded filthy Levis, sporting a Prince Valiant haircut as he struts along leading his band mates down the street with an air of punk bravado, peacockery, unbridled sex appeal and arrogance. Joey is the epitome of the unashamed teen delinquent, and it's this rebelliousness that inspires the other characters that populate the film. "I'm a teenage lobotomy" protests Riff while Kate cries "I don't wanna have fun, I wanna be with Tom!" The diversity of youth culture—the authentic punks like Joey and Riff and the kids who use punk to hone in on their self-awareness like Kate and Tom—are all given a platform in *Rock'n'Roll High School*.

"I Want You Around" is one of the film's finest moments, with Riff imaging The Ramones performing in her bedroom. It is a sweet moment and a precursor to the rock video that will take the world by storm with the rise of MTV. It also capitalizes on the cartoony colors of the film and the otherworldliness that the picture embraces. If everything is over the top and painted in big, brash, broad colors, then this scene is the culmination of all these things. Fantasy rules in the Corman universe, and even in something as grounded as a teen flick with a band crashing a high school there is room for the bizarre and hyperreal.

P.J. Soles made a career out of playing precocious teenagers. She had worked with Brian De Palma playing one of tormentors in the horror opus *Carrie*, as well as working with John Carpenter as a sexually charged Mid-Western teen in the equally brilliant *Halloween* (1978). Here Soles gets to sink her teeth in yet another vibrant and showy teen role, but this time as a central protagonist. When she leads The Ramones and her fellow students down the halls of the high school with "Do You Wanna Dance?," it is bliss , and exactly the kind of finale that you want from a juke box rock musical: bright and electric. Bette Midler's superb variant of the song is desperate and sexually charged with a melancholic longing, whereas The Ramones' take on the number embodies high energy youth excitement and a celebration of the punk misfit. Both versions on the song are important and their respective takes on the sum up what the 1970s musical can be: tender, whimsical, anguished and mournful, as well as rough and ready, sexy, angry and a call out to the eternal outsider.

Australian musician Kat Spazzy of Melbourne punk outfit The Spazzys reflects on the film:

> Smoking in the boys room. Unreal. It seems so much cooler now than it did back when I first saw this film. Shit. 2014! Nobody smokes anymore. How delightfully old-school! As far as my favourite characters…those asshole hall monitors take the cake. Tubby little creeps running around in short pants and feeling up girls. Drunk with power. I love it. Those guys would have grown up to be cops for sure. But The Ramones are adorable. When they first appear in the movie my heart stops! They roll in in the coolest car I have ever seen, with Joey ripping into a chicken drumstick. They are so young and cute and weird. Their lines are just ridiculous. They didn't have much to say at all. I think Dee Dee's lines were limited to "Hey Pizza. It's great. Let's dig in!" But judging by their unconvincing performance with the very few lines that they did have, perhaps it's no wonder they weren't given more to say. But their terrible acting was part of what made them so wonderful. This film really does capture them and embrace them as freaks. My favourite line is when the chief of police (Dick Miller) screws up his face at the end and says they are "ugly, ugly people." I laughed out loud! I thought

that was beautiful. This film harnessed the unique personality of the Ramones, rather than trying to make them perfect and beautiful to fit the rock star mould. I did hear that they had originally asked Cheap Trick to star in this film, and when they declined they asked Todd Rundgren. Ramones were their third Choice. But it is so hard to imagine this movie with anybody else. If it wasn't for them this film it would be a completely different creature.

With punk in one corner of the movie musical market, the disco craze was still pumping in another. *Roller Boogie* capitalized on the roller skating craze that was taking off on the west coast, but it scooted on in and fell flat on its derriere. But this is not to say that the film is not enjoyable, surprisingly smart and even revolutionary for its time. Critics may have panned it and it may have lost money at the box office, but *Roller Boogie* does something that not many films can claim: it foreshadowed an entire generation of movies dealing with teens wanting to rebel from their messed up parents. In *Roller Boogie*, parenthood is something that is monstrous and oppressive and the act of roller-skating will somehow become a war cry for the comfortable but alien teen of middle class suburbia. This is a film about rich kids and rich kids with problems. Most of their issues stem from the nature of their relationship with their parents, and their parents confusion at being authority figures themselves.

Linda Blair was still a bankable name ever since she wowed audiences and critics with her performance of a possessed pre-teen in William Friedkin's masterpiece *The Exorcist*. As the lead in *Roller Boogie*, the film focuses on the fun that comes with the idea of a young girl finding herself through roller-skating and roller arena competition. But the film also shifts its attention to a drug addled mother and the conflicts that arise from this tumultuous connection. Blair's performance is also nuanced, and she has an opportunity to have fun as she takes on divisive nature of the compassion and disdain she shares with her distant mother. The film is loaded with bright and dazzling imagery: director Mark L. Lester really knows how to capture this scene in Los Angeles that was taking off. He plays this off a very intimate and sincerely directed relationship that is doomed, between a troubled daughter and her even more troubled mother.

Another roller skating semi-musical that hit theatres the same year was *Skatetown, U.S.A* that also suffered the same blow as *Roller Boogie* in regard to not hitting the mark with critics and audiences. The film would notoriously be remembered as one of the biggest cocaine induced efforts in the history of late 1970s cinema, with actress Maureen McCormack (Marcia from *The Brady Bunch*) developing a serious drug addiction during the shoot, while Scott Baio also went on the record as to saying that he had personally blocked out the film. By 1980, the roller skating fad continued however, with pop sensation Olivia Newton-John and young actor Michael Beck (who was starring in 1979's brilliant urban street gang film *The Warriors*) leading the way, joined by musical film legend Gene Kelly in something far more endearing than the aforementioned two roller skating outings. We will come to this film in the next chapter.

WHERE'S EVERYBODY GOING?:
The Rose, Elvis, Birth of the Beatles and *The Kids Are Alright*

As mentioned earlier, Bob Fosse was an indisputable genius. However, sharing that coveted title is the star of the next film, the remarkably talented Bette Midler. Midler does something in *The Rose* that actors rarely ever achieve: they bring down the house with an honesty that is both engaging and terrifying. Midler's performance in this powerhouse of a movie is a force of nature: uncompromising, unrelenting, unadulterated and unbelievably good. She captures the essence of a character living on the edge and her downward spiral with rapid speed, but loads her with insecurities, vulnerabilities, heartache and loneliness. There is nothing selfish about this woman. She is a victim of art and of life, and in *The Rose*, these things go hand in hand, living simultaneously in one dangerous joyride.

From the opening moments, we get a sense of ambivalence and uncertainty that will underpin the entire film. The movie is brilliant, touching and relentlessly excessive as it follows a tortured artist fully aware of her self-destructive nature and yet not concerned about it. Loneliness lies at its core, and the rawness and mutilated spirit of this rock'n'roll superstar is up there for all to see. We understand tragedy will unfold simply from hearing her wispy stammer in oppressive darkness, and when we move into the light and find people entering a garage in the suburbs of Middle America somewhere, we also get a sense of loss. This could be anywhere, and any young girl's den at her folks' place with her walls plastered with images of legends of music, film and art. This cave of creativity and quiet torment is a broken collage of a human being, the alien and fragile genius known as Rose.

We cut to a private jet arriving in yet another city, and after a cavalcade of rock'n'rollers comes the incredibly gifted Bette Midler who flawlessly captures a musician in all her tragic exhaustion and heartbreaking glory. When we see her take to the stage, we acknowledge that this is where she is truly alive—this ferocious, ghoulish little woman with sublime talent and a witchy monstrousness that exudes absolute authority, angst and violence, all married with a frail, fragile beauty.

The songs in the film are terrific: high energy, vibrant and all at the service of Midler's phenomenal talent. Her gravelly voice belts out exhilarating rock anthems, and is met with her uncanny ability to match this power with subdued sincerity and serenity. This is a performance to be studied and valued, and one to hold up as a perfect example of a woman completely consumed by isolation, fear and overwhelming loneliness. Rose's drug addiction, alcoholism, promiscuity and ferocity is a patchwork stitched together by a manic sadness, and Midler brings this home with energy and zeal.

Constantly at her heels is Alan Bates as her manager who drives through the film as both an anchor and an antagonist to Midler's wild beast. The first confrontation between Bates and Midler is about her wanting to rest and take a break for a while: she is lonely, desperate and afraid, and most of all, she is a victim of her own excesses. The drinking, drugs and heroin addiction that haunts her (and that will eventually be too strong to ignore by the end of the picture) prop this magnetic sassy rock star up, and Bates's manager is always ready to exploit it and to tailor it to his own needs. Exhaustion and indifference circle the artist and her opportunist manager, and when she continually asks for time off to recoup and gather some grain of self-worth, he shrugs it off with talk of more money to make and more cities to conquer.

The film is loosely based on the life and death of rock legend Janis Joplin, fitting if only because during her life Joplin championed Bette Midler, who she called a "new star" on *The Dick Cavett Show*. But turning Joplin's life into a straight out biopic proved difficult for the filmmakers, as screenwriter Bill Kerby recalls:

> There were always problems with making it a film about Janis Joplin because I had started conceiving the idea around the 1971 mark and the Joplin family were still tender with grief, seeing that Janis had just passed only a couple of years earlier. So they were still heartbroken by it. And coping. I always saw this not so much as a film about Janis Joplin, but a film about any of the rockers of the time. This film was ultimately about excess. So it could have been Jim Morrison or it could have been Brian Jones or it could have been about Neil Young who actually survived the excess or David Crosby who also survived and flourished, but it was also about the power that a manager has over his charge, or his artist. And where that was concerned, Bette Midler and Aaron Russo who was a producer on the film and also Midler's manager who was a ridiculously powerful figure in her life, they also had a relationship, and I found that to be the most interesting thing—the dynamic of the two. So it became less about Joplin and became more about the rock'n'roll superstar. There were definitely Joplin-esque feelings to the film. I was always interested in the fact that Joplin saw herself as an ugly duckling, that this wild talent was tormented by her looks. I was very lucky to be at the Monterey Pop Festival and got to see her perform! And she was absolutely stunning. And

it was a daytime performance, so she wasn't on at night, she didn't have that night time drunk and cranked up thing going for her, she was on during the day on a Sunday afternoon. It was staggering. I was down in the front row! So I was always amazed at her sexuality and her power and her skillset, but she always thought of herself as this ugly duckling and at that time other great female rock singers like Grace Slick were traditionally beautiful, so this fuelled the story, you see, the thing is with drama is that you have to have conflict and internal conflict is just as interesting as external conflict.

Publicity still from *The Rose* (1979)

From a feminist perspective, Rose is the only woman in her band and the film dances with the idea of a sole female musician dealing with men who are primarily little boys all grown up. When she crashes into her dressing room or backstage, she is amidst the world of boys and their toys, but she pushes on through with determination and fierceness. When the audience go into a frenzy chanting "Rose" repeatedly, she knows that it is *she* who is in demand. Rose's warm up with her booze and primal screaming as she works herself into a state is ritualistic: this kind of preparation would become a staple of rock stars presented in the movies, and so would the free spiritedness and the denial to play nice or by the rules. When Rose is told by her manager "Don't say motherfucker!" she hits the stage with a great big "Hiya motherfuckers!"—this is a woman who will not take orders and will not be patronised.

US lobby card from *The Rose* (1979)

One of the best things about the film is that it takes its time with the songs. Much like *The Buddy Holly Story*, Rose's performances are too electric to cut away from and they move the story forward. Her alcoholism and drug dependency is highlighted while she performs, plus her disdain for humanity and yet her same desperation for acceptance and love comes across in bold broad strokes while she blasts through each number. Midler's voice is a marvel, and has a storytelling aspect in its own right.

Kerby continues:

I wish I had a better idea for a story. I had written a middle, another middle, some more middle and even more middle and then end where we had this woman be utterly consumed by excess. I wish I had given her more of a solid background so we'd understand why she drove herself to this point—but thankfully the film had the great Bette Midler to carry all of us on her shoulders. She just took that character and gave it her all and I will love her forever for that. There were a lot of people who went to work on it after I finished my first two drafts and I don't know what each one of them did. Bo Goldman, a wonderful writer, worked on it and gets credited on it, but I have no idea what he actually did. I didn't do the garage with all the Lenny Bruce and James Dean posters and what not covering all the walls, that could have been Bo Goldman or the director Mark Rydell, but it wasn't me. I mean it could have been the designer for all I know but it's really powerful. When I was writing it Bette Midler was just starting to perform at the baths in New York City, so I didn't really know about her, I think I had read something about her in Rolling Stone or something, embarrassingly enough I was writing it with a legitimate actress in mind. Marsha Mason had just done *Cinderella Liberty* with James Caan through Fox and I thought she'd be fabulous in the role, and I didn't know if the studio would do an ole Marnie Nixon job and get a real rock'n'roller to sing the numbers and dub them in, because I had no idea if Marsha Mason could sing. But while I was writing, I wasn't imagining Bette Midler at all. So writing it for me was the most fun and one of the great things about writing is that you work alone. So I just imagined all these things and put down on paper all these ideas and thoughts and things I'd like to say that I kept pocketed for all these years and started to work on this story. All of those ideas about a music career was dumped into this thing. But in 1971 I didn't really know much about writing screenplays. I didn't know about construction, I didn't know about beginning, middle and the end, I didn't know about these things, I didn't learn about all this stuff until later. So *The Rose* was a learn on the job kind of deal for me.

Rose's declaration preceding "When a Man Loves a Woman" provides a platform for women in the audience, where the assumption that rock music is a man's arena is destroyed by this diminutive wild warrior who will not be messed with. The tragedy is that she is so broken, and it sadly reveals that she most certainly *can* be messed with, the cruelest irony being that it is at her own hand. She is her own worst enemy and ultimately, her own assassin. Haunted and broken songstresses such as Judy Garland, Karen Carpenter, Billie Holiday and Janis Joplin herself, are all recalled here as Rose goes down this self-destructive path. And yet, survivors such as Midler herself and contemporaries like Cher, Tina Turner and Liza Minnelli carried the torch song ethos and wore their hardships on their sleeves, but in a defiant and proud manner.

Midler performing live and in sweaty real living color is breathtaking, simultaneously artistic expression and a personal exorcism. The inner turmoil surfaces because Midler the actress is so brilliant at what she does, allowing the musicality of the piece a multi-dimensionality. It is sad, explosive, captivating and visceral—it is a hybrid monster show and a torch song cabaret performance, as well as a grungy rock act. Every break in her voice, every demanding cry, every plea to the gods and to her adoring fans is so beautifully delivered and drawn, and because director Rydell lets Midler do her thing, the results are triumphant. Midler the comedienne is also given an opportunity to shine, as she mouths off and swears like a sailor while being irreverent and witty. But her comic stylings are dwarfed by her heartbreaking sombre moments and her violently angry outbursts. Midler's confrontation with Harry Dean Stanton as a blues artist she covers is an intimate scene where someone she admires pans her work. Midler's aggression here is fantastic, straddling the ruthless and comical. As dark and as bleak as the film gets, there are moments of frenzied humor, but it is all cemented in overwhelming sorrow.

Bill Kerby continues:

> I had a lot of trouble getting along with the producer Marvin Worth and he had equal trouble with me. I got

Bette Midler and Alan Bates as musician and manager in *The Rose* (1979)

The self-destrucive rock star as performed by Bette Midler in *The Rose* (1979)

assigned the project because I was kind of the live-in hippy there for a while, I was the guy with the tie-dyed shirt and the American flag headband over my head and I'd been to Monterey and I was seen in the documentary and I was featured in the hippy issue of *Time* magazine and I was just "blue skying it," just making it up as I went along and luckily I got to work alone. I always have enjoyed working alone. Then I would submit my script and didn't hear much feedback, then other people were meant to be working on it, then they sent my draft to Frank Pearson the Academy Award winning screenwriter, and he sent it back to them and said "Don't change a word! Are you serious? Just shoot it like it is!" And I love that! What a compliment! They also gave it to the guy that directed *The Deer Hunter*, Michael Cimino and he worked on it for a while, then they got it to Bo Goldman and he worked on it, and I never knew any of this at the time, I was already on a number of other projects at that point. Then I get a call from my mother, my dear sainted mother, who had read in the newspaper some news about the film in a column.

She called me and said "Billy, there is someone called Bette Midler who has been hired to do a movie called *The Rose*, do you suppose that's your's hon?" And I thought "Oh my God!" So I got hold of my lawyer and we called and found out that yes it was mine. Then the credit arbitration began. I think if the studio wanted to control or limit the use of drugs and profanity they would have gone straight to the producer Marvin Worth. I wasn't ever privy to that kind of control. You know *The Panic in Needle Park* was a Fox movie and I don't think it did very well, and I think that was because it was a movie about heroin whereas *The Rose* is a movie about music with heroin in the background. Once Bette Midler came on board it became a very different kind of rocket ship and I had no idea what it was going to be like, and then I saw a preview screening of it in Dallas and that's when I got to see how incredible she was. And what a phenomenal performance she delivered. And in the beginning, when the film started, I was pissed off because when the credits came up they had spelled my name wrong—and that's the worst— but then about ten minutes into the movie and just watching her perform and just being seduced by her talents, I started to forget the fact that they had spelled my name wrong. And like everyone else, I was carried away by her. It is my feeling that we all owe a tremendous amount of gratitude to Bette Midler. We all stood on her shoulders, all of us. She carried us through that ride.

Rose's meeting with Houston (played by the brilliant Frederic Forrest) and the start of their tumultuous relationship is doomed from the beginning. In *The Rose*, art and addiction forbid normalcy. Houston is a soldier on the run, and much like Rose he is yet another terrified soul that she affectionately (and desperately) calls her "brown eyed motherfucker." The chemistry between Midler and Forrest is alluring and injected with a restless state of urgency. The generational divide seen in the truck stop diner ("We don't serve hippies" says the oafish chef, to which Rose quickly responds with "Well that's OK coz we don't eat them neither") is not only made between an older generation and a young one, it is also about culture more generally and the complicated relationships within America. Houston is a left-over cowboy, while Rose is a gypsy. However, Rose is so turned on by Houston's hyper-masculinity and his violent outbreak at the diner that it fuels her desire to keep him. The background of the Vietnam War is only really presented in the film on the radio after Houston beats the rednecks at the diner—a quiet whisper of the reality of what is going on in the bigger picture—but then later in the film David Keith pops up as a soldier and new dedicated devotee to Rose.

Kerby says:

> As far as the male characters that play off Bette, first came the manager and the core of his relationship with her character. It was a Svengali relationship, it was an old lover relationship and I planned to get around to illuminating a lot of those things in my third draft. The invention of the Freddy Forrest character was just something I thought would service well, because he is pure and not touched by the rock'n'roll world at all.

The drag bar is a wonderful moment that recalls Midler's days at The Continental Baths. In the film, she eventually goes into a men's only bathhouse in New York looking for the elusive Houston. When a drag queen offers her heroin, it is another jab at her haunted past while another drag queen (dressed as Baby Jane Hudson from the 1961 horror film *Whatever Happened to Baby Jane?*) introduces a set of fellow drag queens dolled up as Diana Ross, Barbra Streisand, Mae West and even Rose herself. It is a reckless moment, and one that is sealed with a kiss between Rose and Houston. Rose's promiscuity—her endless parade of men, one after the other, and her first sexual experience being with the entire football team while she was in high school—all come to represent the notion of the sexually free early bloomer having a rushed life, but it also masks harrowing pain. Rose's success is meaningless to her, and only an actress like Midler could comprehend the destructive excesses that come with fame.

When Rose tells Houston "I haven't been alone for three hundred years," it is a plea for help. Here is someone at her loneliest when she is surrounded by managers, fellow musicians, lovers, fans and so forth. With Houston, she feels connected. The quiet and intimate moment of Rose and Houston in bed during the secrets revealed sequence exposes her loneliness as a high school freak, and explains how she garnered acceptance through sex. When Houston tries to offer compassion and sensitivity, she recoils saying "I don't do this mushy love stuff man, wake me up when the killing starts." This is a beautiful play on spectatorship: Rose the outsider looking in at what it could be like to be genuinely loved. She tells Houston, "I got drunk once and took on the whole football team" and then "I woke up on the fifty yard line." This coy bloodletting helps set up the final moments of the film where she goes back to her old home town, wishing to return as a star and to show them all what she has become. But of course, in films like this small towns suffer from a disease where there is no room for color or importance, because everything is so set conservative and banal.

**Personal exorcism: Bette Midler's phenomenal performance
in the phone booth in *The Rose* (1979)**

The film plots itself intelligently and sets up Houston to be constantly interrupted by Rose's music. Her craft keeps her alive, and it is also what drives her to not only overdose at the end of the picture, but it drives Houston away. The romance between the two sits in the middle of the film but is secondary to Rose's inner turmoil. Houston likens her life to a grenade range, which demonstrates the inspired writing in the film. Houston is running away from a war happening in another continent, and yet he is also running away from someone who is complicated by an internal battlefield. Equating Rose's life to a grenade draws parallels to the two things Houston fears most—war and connecting with someone at war with herself.

Kirby continues:

> What the movie presented in Frederick Forrest's character leaving her because she is so hopelessly addicted to performing among other things like sex and drugs, that his rescue didn't work—that night in the hotel, wrapped up in the sheets where she tells him the pig story, that is about as how deep it will go. He's running as well, he's running from the police and over the Vietnam War. He's also worried he's going to be caught with her; this very vocal anti-war woman.

Rose's inability to connect and her strained addiction to the stage remains engaging and oddly endearing, while Houston being a fish out of water on the jet plane off to another tour ("Different strokes for different folks" when he sees two girls play with a Ouija board) is almost cute. Alan Bates, with his British accent, also seems displaced in the American rock world. He is a kind of messianic hippie in one sense, but also business minded and money driven. Ultimately, Bates's character is dead inside while Rose is struggling to stay alive. Rose's breakdown on the plane where she is drunk and drugged, and wakes up to soft strumming of guitars before crying and not knowing where she is ("All the fucking clouds are just alike...") is heartbreaking. "Where am I going?" will soon dissolve into "Where's everybody going?" and typifies the sense of loss that throws her and beats her to a pulp.

When she gets back to the stage, the film pushes itself into full throttle and from here on out the musical moments are even more, aggressive, punchy and energetic. The obvious sadness takes a back seat while Rose parades around on stage like the true rock star she is. In the moments which depict Rose in crowd scenes going through songs, singing with fellow musicians or working, we see that this is a woman who cannot stop. Houston understands her exhaustion, but everyone else around her doesn't. Alan Bates and Frederic Forrest are great at butting heads—one wants her to keep working and the other wants to stop—and these two fine actors compliment Midler's ups, downs and in-betweens.

Bill Kerby elaborates more on his involvement with the film:

> I was long gone by the time the songs were being written. Bette Midler, Aaron Russo and Paul A. Rothchild put a lot of that music together themselves. I really liked *The Buddy Holly Story*, and I really loved Gary Busey's performance in that, but it's got that built-in death at the end of it. *The Rose*, as we set it up, was not specifically about Janis Joplin, it was about a tortured artist rock'n'roll prototype who had an addictive and self-destructive personality. If we didn't have the death at the end it would have lost meaning. There was talk about saving her for a stage adaptation, which will probably never happen, but I think the death does give it power. Performance and the stage is the time and the place where she feels most alive. A lot of these rock'n'rollers just don't get "real life" and they feel the most comfortable and in control when they're on stage performing. And this is where they're happy. They surf the waves of people's admiration. The Little Richard Story was so rich that I thought we couldn't go wrong with it. It would be totally different if he wasn't gay. I was worried that he would stand in the way of our presentation of this. And all I remember in the meetings we had with him was that he had the most exquisite skin! I wrote what I wrote and everyone loved it until it got to the head of Fox and they got another writer. But a lot of my stuff was left in it. I was very happy doing it, but she dragged us along with us, she was the core reason the film worked so well. As far as the

Oscars went, and Bette not winning well, I'm an old leftie so I really loved Norman Rae and I loved what Sally Field did in that role. Bette Midler's performance in *The Rose* is overwhelming whereas Field's is just whelming, so they are very different roles but both handled so well. I just think it's about timing, if Bette was nominated any other year she would have won. I've always loved writing for women. I am far more comfortable in the presence of women and most of my friendships are with women. I grew up during World War II so a lot of the guys were off fighting against Nazis and so I was surrounded by women here, all my teachers were women and so it's just an easier life for me to write for.

Rose's "rescue" of conscripted boys by taking them on her tour gives a brief insight into her compassion, and when she slays an audience with "I Sold My Soul to Rock'n'Roll" culminating into being swamped by rabid fans, she is pure anarchic energy.

Kerby adds further:

I was long gone by the time the songs were being written. Bette Midler, Aaron Russo and Paul A. Rothchild put a lot of that music together themselves. I really liked *The Buddy Holly Story*, and I really loved Gary Busey's performance in that, but it's got that built-in death at the end of it. *The Rose*, as we set it up, was not specifically about Janis Joplin, it was about a tortured artist rock'n'roll prototype who had an addictive and self-destructive personality. If we didn't have the death at the end it would have lost meaning. There was talk about saving her for a stage adaptation, which will probably never happen, but I think the death does give it power. Performance and the stage is the time and the place where she feels most alive. A lot of these rock'n'rollers just don't get "real life" and they feel the most comfortable and in control when they're on stage performing. And this is where they're happy. They surf the waves of people's admiration. I've always loved writing for women. I am far more comfortable in the presence of women and most of my friendships are with women. I grew up during World War II so a lot of the guys were off fighting against Nazis and so I was surrounded by women here, all my teachers were women and so it's just an easier life for me to write for.

The lesbianism in the film manifests through Sarah, a character from Rose's past, which is there to make a point that Rose is someone completely open to being needed by anyone. Although Rose is a heterosexual character, her off screen romance with Sarah (which comes back to "haunt" her) reflects her ability to allow herself to be nurtured and understood by anyone who is willing. Sarah is also damaged by an experience with men, as quiet dialogue suggests this. However, the lesbianism in *The Rose* is fleeting and all about an external and almost superficial experience—it isn't meaningful nor does it service plot or character. Sarah comes across as a creepy, wishy-washy nuisance and also someone who is jealous of Rose and wants what she has. Films that featured lesbianism or pseudo-lesbianism as a sickness flourished during the period with movies such as *Windows* (1980) bringing forth a psychotic edge to women's obsession with other women. Houston's reaction to the girl-on-girl kiss is outwardly aggressive, and ends with him beating Rose (and Rose beating him). He seems to take things in his stride when Rose flirts and sleeps with other men, but lashes out when he catches her with another woman.

Bill Kerby explains:

> They cut back on the lesbian character. If they were making it now it wouldn't be stripped back. We have different views of it now, back then people were scared of bisexuality. It still is a rich relationship, her one gay relationship is just as important as her numerous heterosexual ones and every time I see that scene where she is shampooing her hair I think "Ahh good, they kept that in it at least." That one and the scene with Harry Dean Stanton. Those scenes are completely untouched. I didn't realize that there were drag queens who performed as Barbara Streisand or Diana Ross, I just had

601

written a scene with rock'n'roll drag queens who perform with Bette. They had gotten a gay gag writer to come in and give that scene a certain personal flair. He also wrote for the scene where Bette storms through the men's locker room and she says something like: "Keep waterin' honey it'll grow!" This guy had written with Bette for years. I also had written the biopic about Little Richard. And that also had a lot of concern with his homosexuality. The Little Richard Story was so rich that I thought we couldn't go wrong with it. It would be totally different if he wasn't gay. I was worried that he would stand in the way of our presentation of this. And all I remember in the meetings we had with him was that he had the most exquisite skin! I wrote what I wrote and everyone loved it until it got to the head of Fox and they got another writer. But a lot of my stuff was left in it.

Rose's downward spiral starts when she hits her home town. When she drives past her mother and father's house, she hides—the experience heightens her sense of disconnection and distance. When she stops at Leonard's grocery (a little five-and-dime store she went to as a kid), the owner recognizes her but doesn't realize that she is a star, even though he is selling her records in the store. And as the closing scenes progress, Rose's cry "Where's everybody going?" becomes a mantra in the final moments of the film. Each person close to her—her manager, Houston, her fans and family—start to disappear, as the world becomes empty and isolating, leaving no room for this fallen angel. The return to her hometown bar and performing for a bunch of drunken yokels is driven by necessity and in service to the gods of rock'n'roll. She takes some speed, drinks in excess and is greeted by old flames: men who she grew up with her and used her. These same men in her past undermined who she was as and took her as a sexual conquest. As this painful but beautiful film draws its last breathe, Rose—desperate and alone—shoots heroin and dies on stage. She is given the heroin from an old home town cretin who seems to give it to her to aid her demise—the final insult. Following this comes one of the film's most devastating moments, and the phone booth scene is one of the most brutally honest moments in the picture as Midler's own estranged relationship with her real life father seeps through the façade of cinema. Poignantly and somewhat offensively, football practice goes on behind her as she calls her folks to ultimately say "goodbye." These are the heartbreaking final moments of a woman completely at her wits end—music is her life, but it also possesses her and ruins her, leading to her downfall.

Dying on stage after wowing everyone with the ultimate swan song "Stay with Me," Midler's performance is crushing excellence and a tour de force. The film closes with the heartbreaking title song about sacrifice, juxtaposing fear, hope and destiny with choice as it whispers to us the dilemma facing "the heart afraid of breaking, that never takes the chance," and "the soul afraid of dying that never learns to live." Self-destructive rock stars would become a staple in film: excessive living, drug addled musicians that live on the edge and die way too young. But *The Rose* is most certainly one of, if not, the best of the bunch.

Bill Kerby concludes:

> My instinct was to give it a happier ending, I even entertained the idea of having her live in the end, but then I had a stunning realization that in life there are no happy endings, so I thought that this movie shouldn't have a happy ending either. "The Rose" is a fabulous song. The writer Amanda McBroom and I are still buddies. Unfortunately she had not written it for the film, it was written well before then, but Paul A. Rothchild had heard it and insisted they use it for the film, so therefore it was never allowed to be nominated for Best Song at that year's Academy Awards. If it had been nominated it most certainly would have won. It did win the Golden Globes though because there weren't so much strict guidelines. Bette Midler is so tiny, she's like 4'11" and it's just incredible the amount of power to come out of this woman! I had told her that I really loved her performance in *The Rose* at a meeting I had with her when I pitched a film idea to her. Everyone fell in love with her and rightfully so. There were two posters for the film. One had a big rose on it and had that tagline "She gave and gave and

gave until there was nothing left to give." And then there was the other poster that they tried which is her image set against the old bedroom/garage with all those posters and that one didn't work. So the one that they went with had her presented in a tiny grey image and a large rose above her, looking like it was about to eat her! That's a great poster. And the trailer was fantastic, it was screened, a whole one minute trailer, on Saturday Night Live which was huge at the time!

Film critic and journalist Amy Seidman adds:

Going by the stage name "The Rose," she is the classic showbiz case of the downward spiralling starlet breaking the world's collective heart. As the movie proceeds, we become a part of a brutal spectator sport as we watch our idol descend from a bright star to a dimly lit replica before the light is snuffed out entirely. It is a feminist tale of a woman performing within a male-centric era of entertainment where she is confined by management men who control her life and career despite her best efforts to sabotage their plans. On the outside, she is all forced smiles and excitement when called upon to promote her upcoming tour in a press scrum. However, it's live in concert when we first see her genuine pain and frustration with being undermined while singing "When a Man Loves a Woman" specifically the phrase "A change is gonna come in this man's world." She is punk rock in all its anger, volatility and tragedy. Someone who sings of love but has never seemed to find it within herself. She is the life of the party yet sees no value in her actual life at all. She emotes a feeling of self-worth onstage but when the spotlight is turned off and the curtain comes down, her stock plummets rapidly. Some of the set scenes in the film make my skin crawl in an oddly beautiful way—massive aerial shots over the final concert in her hometown, for example, or the evening one of her in a phone booth lit only by a street light. It reminded me of the struggle with meaninglessness and the passage of time you can feel in "Nighthawks," the famous 1942 painting by Edward Hopper. The final concert where she stands on rubber legs as pale as pale can be barely breathing out a few sad lyrics before collapsing is one of the most heartbreaking scenes in cinema. The collapse is followed by "The Rose," a song we will hear at karaoke bars for all eternity but the backstory is one of addiction on many platforms—fame, anger, destruction, love, men and chemical vices.. This is Bette Midler at her finest and the raw emotion she puts into this film shook me to the core. Such a stunning performance!

Artists that died in their prime would be the subject of many films, both cinematic and for television as special TV miniseries. One of the latter would be *Elvis*. Director and music lover John Carpenter, fresh from introducing the world to movie bogeyman Michael Myers in his masterpiece *Halloween* (1978), would team up with rock enthusiast and producer Dick Clark and former Disney contract player Kurt Russell to breathe life into the tribulations of the King of Rock'n'Roll, and the results were phenomenal. The intriguing connection made between Carpenter's horror film and prototype slasher hit from 1978 (which eventually became a hit thanks primarily to the *Village Voice* which championed it as an intelligent and moody independent work by a genuine auteur) and his miniseries based on the life of Elvis Presley is the stuff of legend.

Carpenter remembers when he first got the job directing *Elvis*:

> This was 1978 and I had finished *Halloween*, and I got a call from my agent and he asked me if I was interested in doing a film about Elvis, which was going to be a three hour television movie. And without reading anything I said yes! This was just because I was a big Elvis fan. Then the script came and man it was huge. It was so long and I never even got through the whole thing, it was just so big. But I thought, you know what, let's do this. I said to myself, this is a great opportunity and I would love to take it on. Apparently they had gone to director after director in Hollywood, I don't

605

know exactly who, but this is what I had heard and I knew that everyone turned it down because they were all afraid of what it was going to be or what it was going to be turned into. They had the suspicion that it mightn't be very good. You see, this was to be produced by Dick Clark and his company and this scared a lot of directors because Dick Clark wasn't really recognized for any great made for television movies or movies in general, but I was young and stupid so I said yes and off we went. I was hired because of *Halloween* and the music for *Halloween*, and the producers and the people who worked for Dick Clark thought that I would know Elvis and how to work on something about Elvis because I was a composer as well. Which is ridiculous, but I took the job!

Aesthetically, *Elvis* is a triumph. The early moments depicting his childhood are presented with such richness and honesty that it is hard to not be seduced by the film from the outset. And although his young years are fleeting, they set a mood that could be likened to the famous bronze-tinted Halloween sequence in Vincente Minnelli's *Meet Me in St. Louis*. This is simply how good a director John Carpenter is: he can capture the essence of the downtrodden and the desolate, as well as the hope, all in one take. This master of the moving image is here working as a gun for hire, but the film reveals there are much deeper, important things going on than this role would normally suggest. When Carpenter delves into Presley's childhood torment in a relatively short amount of time (most memorably when a local bully teases Elvis, scolding him by saying "Crazy ole Elvis is talkin' to himself again!" and adding the taunt of "Mamma's boy, mamma's boy") we get the loneliness, the desperation and the displacement of a child destined to be an artist. Carpenter's eye as a horror director comes across in the early gold-soaked imagery of these early years, and his presentation has a kind of windswept earthiness to it, an eerie kinetic energy brought by what feel like almost sinister breezes. In many ways, this too draws parallels with the spectacular imagery of his *Halloween*, where tranquil suburbia contorts into hellish nightmare on earth.

Kurt Russell as Elvis Presley and Season Hubley as Priscilla, tying the knot in John Carpenter's *Elvis* (1979)

Haunted by his deceased twin brother and desperately connected to his mother, Elvis's musical talents even as a child are cemented in a distorted truth. In an early scene where he sings along with his mother and father (as well some neighbourhood children), we get a sense of Elvis as being tuned into the essence of soul. This boy will grow into a man who will put soul into the heart of rock'n'roll. The warmth of these early scenes—particularly the depth and the softness in its golden colors and the intimacy shared between Elvis and his mother Gladys (Shelley Winters)—form a carefully conceived tapestry of the complexities of life in a cultural dystopia, riddled with familial oppression and the temptation to dance with demons. Even here, themes like authenticity and a kind of mournful magic permeate this remarkable film.

Carpenter recalls:

> We made it a lot more nostalgic early on, there was a real innocent look to it, everything looked a lot more golden. But then as the story progresses, and meanwhile we didn't do the entire story of Elvis's life, that we thought would be far too grim, but as the film moved on and we got to the harder parts of his life, the film itself started to look a lot cooler and the golden hue to the film early on was long gone.

The scope of the film is extraordinary. This is a miniseries that spans years and bounces from location to location without missing a beat. The film never looks or feels tired, a remarkable effort that makes this epic period piece an essential 1970s musical. Kurt Russell's energy and sincerity comes across with elegance and dedication, and in many ways he is just as mesmerizing to watch as Bette Midler in *The Rose* and Gary Busey in *The Buddy Holly Story*. Russell embodies Elvis the outsider, and he finds a voice for the alienated and artistic. This lean, flamboyant artist with his penchant for pink shirts and a well-greased ducktail is a larger than life character, and Russell brings him to life with ease and genuine love for this rock music icon. Complimenting his exceptional performance is Carpenter's direction and his visual eye: this is a director who understands his actors, and he appears to almost intuitively allow them the time and space needed for their talents to shine.

Carpenter explains:

> If you're an outsider like I was making movies about outsider characters is always appealing. Also, high school movies were very popular when I was growing up, they've

been around for a long time so I liked directing teenagers in teenage situations. I remember seeing *The Blackboard Jungle* and thinking "Wow, what a stunner of a movie!" Elvis was an outsider. Elvis was a unique character. And that was always appealing to me.

Carpenter and Russell, would go on to become friends and collaborators with follow up movies that would attain cult status: the brilliant and visceral *The Thing* (1982)—which also boasted some phenomenal special effects wizardry from Rob Bottin—would be their finest moment together, with *Big Trouble in Little China* (1986) and the apocalyptic classic *Escape From New York* (1981) also both being up there in the list of Carpenter's masterpieces. But it is this biopic about the King of Rock'n'Roll that emphasises the magic of the collaboration between Carpenter and Russsell.

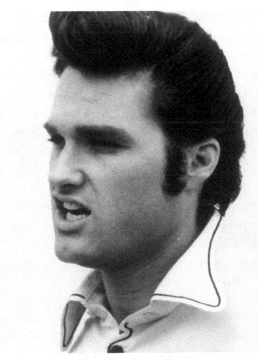

Rare scout shot for Kurt Russell in preparation for the casting of **Elvis** **(1979)**

The intimacy, moodiness, and seductive and yet somewhat strange energy in this film are contributing factors that make *Elvis* such an alluring and at points deliberately claustrophobic telemovie. This curious tension provides insight into complicated characters, and is executed so meticulously that it delivers an accessible and emotionally palpable portrait of the music icon. This is how biopics, should most certainly be made.

John Carpenter continues:

> This was a movie that had one hundred and eighty eight speaking parts and seventy odd shooting locations that were all shot in thirty days. We would do three hours a day shooting. Now that was a baptism in fire for me, directing all that. I would get up and go shoot and get home and go to bed. I was falling asleep in the dailies. The scene in the end where Kurt is singing up on stage, well I just fell asleep watching that in the dailies, I was just so exhausted. Kurt was cast as I came on board. There was another guy that was up for the role and they had showed me this guy and he was the splitting image of Elvis, like he looked exactly like him but he just could not act. So right there the decision was made to hire Kurt. Now the thing about Kurt as well as being a great actor is that he is just a terrific mimic. Kurt had Elvis down just perfectly—his voice, his moves, everything was just perfect. And as I remember, Kurt's father Bing Russell had been cast early on as Elvis's dad which was a great choice. I knew that Kurt had kicked Elvis in one scene in *It Happened at the State Fair* and Kurt had told me that even as a child he had noticed that Elvis was getting a whole lot of attention, that he was constantly surrounded by a lot of girls, he got a lot of attention from a lot of girls.

Musically, the film flourishes. Vocalist Ronnie McDowell lends his talents to the classic Presley numbers, but ultimately Kurt Russell *is* Elvis. Russell throws his body around like a man possessed and carries each musical number with pride, confidence and passion.

Kurt Russell's incredibly magnetic performance as *Elvis* (1979)

John Carpenter remembers:

> There was a big deal about Elvis's changing voice; there
> was a major difference between Elvis's voice as a young man
> to later in his career, so there was a lot of talk regarding this.
> But I was a director on hire for this project, I didn't have

much to do with all that, that was all taken care of after I finished directing.

For the first half of the film, Russell's co-star is the gifted Shelley Winters who plays his mother Gladys. Winters showers each scene with fabulous neuroses and a kind of nervous melancholy: here is an actress that lives by the moment and for the moment. Her insight into this woman—so madly in love with her son and dedicated to his success and happiness—is frightful and all too real. Winters and Russell share a chemistry that is gentle and at the same time unnerving, and their connection is so distressing because we all know that in these kind of stories, tragedy can only result. Of course, Gladys is the first to die, and the relentlessly morose energy that permeates the scenes shared between Winters and Russell leading up to this are remarkable. The relationship between mother and son is well articulated, overwhelming and over powering, driven by feelings of sadness, grief and loss. How Carpenter brings this sorrowful thunder home is mind blowing.

Carpenter remembers Shelley Winters:

> Shelley Winters was an amazing actress. She was a method actress like Brando, she was just fabulous. I had some really interesting encounters with her. We had to do an early scene where she was kicked out of her house by the landlord because of overdue rent, this was early on in Elvis's life and I found Shelley outside of set sitting down on a chair listening to some music. I asked what she was doing and she said she was using the music to get emotional, or to an emotional point. The music she was listening to was music that reminded her of one of her husbands and I was amazed at that. She could be a handful but she was a great actress. Just incredible. She knew what to do and there was a lot of things about the Gladys Presley character already. This was all public domain stuff, there wasn't really any inside stuff regarding Elvis and his life readily available, so Shelley just knew what to do. I didn't have to do much.

Rounding out the pivotal cast are Pat Hingle as Elvis's manager The Colonel, Season Hubley as his wife Priscilla Presley, and regular Carpenter alumni Charles Cyphers. These characters are pawns that come into contact with Russell's Elvis in a way that compliments his trials and tribulations. These characters react rather than act, which is shrewd. Most of the scenes involving the supporting players espouse thematic elements that grant the film a sincere realism, all the while commenting on both broader social and artistic themes. These characters are intelligently stitched together as the archetypal pillars that tower over Elvis as he dances around them, lunging onto one, rejecting another as he continues to climb. The treatment of the film's set pieces and those contained within them are perfectly composed: caricatures are not welcome here, but character tropes most certainly are. We know that The Colonel is going to be hard work, and we know that Priscilla and Elvis are going to have disagreements, but we are never swamped by rock clichés. Instead, the film is constructed primarily by smart directorial choices and insightful characterizations.

Carpenter recalls:

> I liked the Colonel a lot, he was fun. No one really knew anything about this guy, he was just an old huckster I thought, and it was more of a case of establishing a presence rather than adding anything to who they already were. Remember, we had to deal with these people when some of them were still alive. We couldn't make the Colonel evil or make him a bad guy, Pat Hingle played him very well. Because Elvis died that was the time, the right time, to do the movie. We got permission and advice from some of Elvis's mafia members, and they were helpful. Some of them acted as technical advisors. Overall, it was an incredible burn out and I had never worked so hard in my life and I never want to again. Charles Cyphers had worked with me on three movies before, he worked on Assault on Precinct 13, Halloween and Someone Is Watching Me and he played Sam Phillips really well in Elvis. We had a lot of great actors in that film. I only remember reading Season and I recall

thirty or forty NBC executives were in there listening to her read and she was really uncomfortable. Season had done some good stuff but the executives wanted to make sure she could do this, and I felt really bad for her and I took her aside and I said "Don't let them get to you, you did real good" and they hired her. And she was terrific. They're all good. Elvis was a three hour film so it had no movie pace to it, its rhythm was very different to the other bio pics around at the same time, but I do think that Kurt's performance stands up to all those other roles. Kurt knows exactly what to do and when to do it. I remember there was a scene where Elvis was hidden up in his mansion, tucked away from the world and not quite himself, and I remember saying to Kurt "You know, I think that Elvis is pretty heavy duty on drugs in this moment, how do you think you're gonna play that?" and he said "I'm just gonna play it tired." And it worked. We couldn't say that Elvis was on drugs, because we didn't have an insider for that information, so I let him play it that way, as if he were just simply tired. Kurt was just great. Kurt and Shelley were consummate actors. Both very different actors, but just consummate and brilliant. They were always so prepared and they were so great that I didn't have to do much in directing them.

Russell's range is on display in Elvis. He is given the opportunity to become moody, angry, depressed, nonchalant, plagued by insecurity, and electric as he takes to the stage to work his magic. His dynamic performance is crisp in its execution and nimble in its choices: Russell's Elvis is an impish delinquent consumed by guilt and a desperate need to be loved and admired. When he sings at his high school, he draws a crowd. When the film reaches its climactic moments as he provokes a storm with his hip-gyrating swagger and startling good looks, we witness demonic family man entertaining the masses. Delivering a sermon of rebellion and freedom, he is still conflicted by the trappings of responsibility and self-doubt.

Many sequences highlight these tensions and inner conflicts, including a scene in Germany where he meets the very young and impressionable Priscilla. The large crowd scenes dance a fine dance in their focus between a rock star in his prime and a sensitive artist having what is effectively a nervous breakdown. Carpenter brings a sense of authenticity to the film that acts as a backdrop to characters perplexed and riddled by feelings of worthlessness and emotional frailty.

In Carpenter's film, Graceland is a monstrous entity that dwarfs its occupants. When Russell's Elvis is watching James Dean perform on his projector in his den, he is a ghoulish shadowy figure, lonely and desperate, fragile and ready to explode. And yet when he is recording "Suspicious Minds" in his living room with his band, the house is by contrast suddenly alive with bouncy joy—until reality crashes in, at least.

John Carpenter elaborates on creating Graceland:

> One of my favourite scenes is in Graceland and we had this big party sequence where Season and Kurt are talking but I get a lot of the guests in the background and used a lot of dollying. I was very proud of that scene. In regard to the crowd scenes and shooting large crowds, Larry Franco who was Kurt's brother in law, was my assistant director. And he and I teamed up for a number of years. He is the best assistant director I have ever worked with and he was just great. He got those kids into that frenzied state, I didn't have to do any of that, I just got there and called the shots. We went to Graceland and looked around and it was really kitschy and real nice. It was very strange to be there. However there was no staircase and as I remember we really relied on the locations to feed the scene. I remember we went over to Long Beach and found a place that had the staircase and a big living room area that we wanted and shot there but it was nothing like the real Graceland. Sun Records was just a hovel, the place we went to was a Grand Ole Opry in Nashville was amazing. All the interiors were the real deal, no sets. I loved Elvis movies. I mean I stopped watching them at a certain point when they got pretty silly but I really loved Elvis as an

actor and I always wanted to do something with him. When you're a TV director you don't have any control over the musical score to the film. I just left after shooting and then it went into post but I do remember talking to the composer and I said "Please don't score that made for TV music that is so corny and appeals to Middle America, just do something simple." Well he scored it just the way I was afraid he would. I really had no input. That's the most important thing about *Elvis*, it started my relationship with Kurt and I think the film holds up pretty well. I haven't seen it for years, nor do I want to, I never go back and watch my movies I like to remember them how they were.

In the same year John Carpenter's *Elvis* hit small screens, Dick Clark's production company once again delivered the goods by bringing to life the early days of England's most famous export in *Birth of the Beatles*. Opening with the Fab Four on their way to take America by storm (vocalising their insecurities and fear of America spitting them up and chewing them out), the film is a steady, even ride that never favours overt sentimentality. It is a blunt and thoughtful account of the band's formative years and their ascent to stardom. Original drummer Pete Best (here played by Ryan Michael) acts as the film's technical advisor with a story by John Kurland, and between them, *Birth of the Beatles* is a driven piece that remains energetic and well plotted.

Into the slums of late 1950s Liverpool—depicted as a gritty and grimy English working class neighbourhood—we meet the enigmatic, fast talking John Lennon (Stephen MacKenna), the handsome baby-faced Paul McCartney (Rod Culberston) and the reserved, introspective George Harrison (John Altman). The boys are leather clad and sporting ducktails, and Americana is clearly imprinted into their sense of style and is a major cultural reference. They race about the streets with a recklessness evoking the punk spirit to come in decades to come: this is the very primitive punk rock years before bands like The Buzzcocks and The X-Ray Specks would dish out anger and disdain with fervent apathy during the 1970s and into Thatcher-era Britain. The struggles of the working class in *Birth of the Beatles* sits comfortably in the background, and although the film chimes in on social and personal issues (including insight into woes about what parents expect of their offspring), while not a primary concern, the film dances with these issues briefly before the film focuses on its central site of interest: the formation and evolution of one of the most important rock'n'roll bands who reinvented popular music.

Although the film employs some inspired, dark images (such as the boys slumming about a graveyard guzzling down booze and talking about ambitions and pipedreams, collectively sprawled upon a tombstone—a powerful symbol for boys living in a perpetual dead-end), the film is for the most part upbeat which makes it very different to the grim and bleak worlds of *The Rose* and *Lady Sings the Blues*. The influence of American rhythm and blues and the early days of rock'n'roll get the musical wheel turning, but this is the world of the British blue collar, There is a beer drenched pub sensibility, and the film captures the unpolished garage rock music that was emerging from the early 1960s in impoverished towns across the United Kingdom. An early showcase attracts The Silver Beatles (their name at this point) to perform for a music promoter who warns "I'm looking for musicians, not comics." When he asks why the band are called The Silver Beatles they happily explain that it is derivative of Buddy Holly and the Crickets, keeping it insect themed (another reference to their American rock predecessors). Impressing the promoter, the band are told to get a legitimate drummer and to tour Germany. An audition for a drummer, some light hearted treatment of John and Paul's alpha dog battle and a great take on John's trickster antics (his dry wit and sardonic humour are emphasised in the film, and here he tells his girlfriend "They have girls in Hamburg? No, you're thinking of Munich") move the film from set piece to set piece. The most masterfully handled element of the film is the way in which The Beatles music progresses— there is no sense of repetition in this biopic, nor is there a sense of glorifying bratty slum kids.

Into Germany, The Beatles find themselves bouncing through the unglamorous world of early gigs. There is a great sequence where the band playing a near empty pub while local roughs slog it out. It is a humorous and honest moment, but also remarkably profound. In fact, these sequences recall similar imagery from Bob Fosse's masterpiece

Cabaret where a gleefully demonic Emcee and his lecherous ghoulish chorus girls entertain drunkards while Nazi Germany unleashes unspeakable horrors unto its people. In *Birth of the Beatles*, these cocky boys from Liverpool are an extension of the Emcee and his harpies, and although the film stoically remains upbeat for the most part (as opposed to the dark *Cabaret*) the moment where The Beatles entertain an audience in a country still fresh from World War II with "Roll Over Beethoven" might be fleeting, but still subversive. Dressed in house dresses, wearing toilet seat covers over their heads and with Paul only in his underwear, this is a long cry from The Beatles audiences will come to know and love as the years go by. Here in the early days, the band is raw, gritty and unapologetically punk in their attitude and delivery. The Beatles' earliest gigs were loud, raucous and out of control. The recklessness and youthful vigour is epitomized by the endless pretty girls who throw their bodies around worshipping the distorted power chords, while male counterparts throw beer bottles at one another in a drunken frenzy. The grottiness and desolation of the early days is played out honestly, and not only does it keep the film grounded and realistic in its depiction of musicians starting out, it is also reassuringly life affirming: we understand what is to become of the band, and there is a humility to the details of these backgrounds. From the grimy and miserable seedy pubs to the international fame and fortune, *Birth of the Beatles* attempts to tell it how it is.

Manager Brian Epstein (Brian Jameson) is played like an impish sissy, effeminate and lascivious. When he first encounters The Beatles (who have just finished playing a show), he gives the partially dressed youngsters a once over, nervously leering and also set up as a polar opposite to our loveable down-to-earth Beatles. "We're happy go-lucky working class lads, that's why we play the Negro music" says John to Epstein who wishes to shape them into something different and more refined. "1962 is going to be your year," proclaims the epicene manager as the ducktails and the distinctly American greaser hairstyles on the boys make way for the soon-to-be iconic mop-tops. The unique sound and energy of The Beatles starts to develop in a hurried fashion. Harmonies replace wailing, pop sensibilities replace their crashing chord progressions, and a clean cut, bright and melodic band is born, ready to be consumed by an excitable and enthused audience. Now joined by

Ringo Starr (Ray Ashcroft) on drums, The Beatles go from one high to another, while personal dramas remain subdued in the same vein as *The Buddy Holly Story*—both these great films insist their dramatic moments remain subtle and never sensational.

Ultimately, the film tells the story of the formation of England's most beloved pop export, and it is marked with a shimmering honesty. Straight down the line and uncompromisingly direct, this rock'n'roll biopic works on every level and proves that sometimes, just telling the story—without any poetic influence—can be just as endearing, thought provoking and as entertaining as musical biopics that take more artistic liberties.

Another musical focused on a real-life band is *The Kids Are Alright*, a showcase of the talents of The Who. It is more than a standard rockumentary because it actively makes use of concert footage, promotional footage and interviews and turns these fragmented moments into a structured evolution of the band. The Who are musicians who fully understand the concept of narrative and the benefits of structure: after all, they wrote one of the most important rock operas ever to hit the screen and stage with *Tommy*, and here in this document of the band as an entity and a functioning artistic enterprise, their enthusiasm in letting filmmaker Jeff Stein know they share an interest in plotting is palpable and very earnest. The results may seem to be non-linear, but looking closely at the fabric of the vignettes that construct *The Kids Are Alright*, a savvy audience can pick up the solid foundations that emphasise the brilliance and vivacity of The Who in their rock'n'roll glory.

TAKE OFF WITH US: *All That Jazz*

1979 was a celebration of rock at its purest and most nonsensical, and also a year devoted to exposing the sadness, turmoil, silliness and frivolity all in one go. But more traditional musicals (existing outside of the context of what would be the considered "traditional" song and story piece) would do more of the same thing. Bob Fosse's semi-autobiographical *All That Jazz* is a masterpiece of 1970s cinema, a pillar of New Hollywood, and a testament to this multi-talented artist's genius. As Fosse delves into life, sex, art, death and "all that jazz," we bear witness to one of the most enigmatic but equally tortured and dedicated madmen ever presented on the silver screen. As devastating and depressing as the film is, it is also one of the most important portrayals of an artist driven and consumed by his work. Fosse's complex love letter to death is one of the most life affirming (yet still gruelling and bleak) movies to unfold, This gifted demon used his own insecurities (his short stature, his hunched back, his early balding and his pigeon toes) to create a brand new style of dance and movement, and holds up a large ballet-hall mirror to sexual promiscuity, a rejection of monogamy, the estrangement from family, addiction, personal defeats and triumphs and the overwhelming desire for perfection. The film is an exercise in brilliance and never for one moment is self-indulgent or bloated. It is a force to be reckoned with, a creepy shadowy film that dances with death only to sweep you along with its nihilism, taking delight in being sombre, depressing and downright sinister. Bob Fosse revelled in the darkness: he embodied the lecherous and lascivious, and his joy in celebrating the grit and the menace is all packed into *All That Jazz*.

Bob Fosse directs the cattle call opening for *All That Jazz* (1979)

As the film's protagonist, choreographer and director Joe Gideon (as played by the fantastic Roy Schieder) goes through dance routine after dance routine, woman after woman and addiction after addiction. He gets closer to dying, and in a sense it is only in death where he doesn't feel he has to prove himself, perfect anything or even run through a sweaty, gruelling rehearsal. Bob Fosse has created a musical about having a heart attack at surface level, but what goes and comes before it is one of the most intricate, complicated and unnerving experiences ever on film.

Alan Heim's phenomenal editing drives the picture, and his eye for detail and systematic understanding of the kinetic maneuverers the film. Plotted within the structure of the piece is a ritual as performed by Joe, where Heim's splicing highlights the vices and their results in a speedy and startling manner. Joe chain-smokes, so when he has a lit cigarette go out under the flowing water of a shower it makes sense and highlights addiction at all cost. Then we cut to speed pills being taken, drops flushing out bloodshot and overworked eyes and then finally a coughing, unwell workaholic cynically presenting jazz hands announcing "It's show time folks!" In these frenetic choppy moments we get an insight into both the character of Joe, the routine outside of the routines that take place up on stage and the nihilistic and depressing reality of the griminess (and grimness) of the industry at hand—the making of the American musical. There is no glamour here, instead it is a warts and all detailing of egos, shattered dreams, sexual flippancy and artistic difference (and indifference).

Roy Schieder preps for the opening sequence behind the scenes on *All That Jazz* (1979)

Joe is a narcissistic monster plagued with insecurities, protected by a hardened shell that has been callused throughout the years. He is addicted to nicotine, speed, sex, work, booze and himself, and through conversations with a fetishized Angel of Death (as portrayed by the very gifted Jessica Lange) we come to understand this theatrical maestro through a highly stylized confessional. At the same time, he is presented as an insincere showman, as he dolls up in clown garb and continually embellishes truths. Set up in a backstage scenario and with Lange's image of God presented as a pin up girl from Joe's youth, these fantasy sequences frame the film with a troubling dreamlike quality and act as a Greek chorus of insight into this megalomaniac who will eventually work, sleep, drug and drink his way to a heart attack and die by the end of the picture. Joe cannot connect, and that is his problem. He sleeps around because sex is something he equates to eating or drinking, he won't rest or stop because he is addicted to work and yet it is through his work where he makes artistic and sexual connections that all service his compartment-like being. Girls serve his sexual needs, his relationship with his daughter Michelle (Erzsebet Foldi) serves his emotional needs, and intellectually he is fuelled by dance—something that takes its toll on the body, but just as necessary as sex, drugs and egocentricity.

The opening sequence of the cattle call for the Broadway dancers set to George Benson's "On Broadway" is a perfect montage. The gritty reality behind the dancing and the singing is representative of the New York stage in all its grime and trauma. It is also one of the most well edited and shot opening sequences in history, capturing all there is to know about the life of a Broadway dancer. These gypsies who need a job (the core theme in the brilliant *A Chorus Line*) throw their bodies around the stage, but only some will win the affection and attention of Joe. The insatiable sexual drive and his personal conquests dictate a lot of what Joe is about, as he cruises the line and flirts with female dancers, all of them eager to get a part in a musical. Outside of working as a director/choreographer, Joe is a filmmaker, working on a feature that is a direct reference to Bob Fosse's *Lenny* (1974). The film-within-the-film "The Stand-Up" stars Cliff Gorman (who had wowed audiences as the effete Emory in *The Boys in the Band*, 1970) as a cocaine snorting, self-loathing stand-up comic. Drug addled stand-up comics would become something that cinema would soon become obsessed with during the 1980s—these clowns crying on the inside would suddenly pop up everywhere in film, and Bob Fosse seems to be attracted to that. It's familiar grounds for him: he is after all also attracted to the perplexed, anguish-laden dancer that he so often presents.

Sandahl Bergman leads the chorus dancers in the "Airotica" number in *All That Jazz* (1979)

All That Jazz is an autobiographical look at an artist who is consumed by work and his vices, his promiscuity an extension of his connection to his art and his inability to connect to one person. His ex-wife Audrey (Leland Palmer) is a polar opposite to Joe, a dancer (another conquest) but who finds herself having to remind him that he is a father and that his work matters. A complicated contradiction at its best and a perfect narrative tool to highlight Joe's split devotion to the musical he is working on and his alarmingly cynical and aware young daughter. His relationship with his daughter is distant and beset in the world of dance, but it is tender, while Ann Reinking (who plays his primary lover Katie) seems to be the closest to his daughter.

Deborah Geffner's beautiful turn as dancer Victoria (who wanted to be a movie actress when she was a kid) summarises the insecurities and vulnerabilities of the artist. When she speaks of her crooked nose, it is her desperate need to know that Gideon can tell her that she could be an actress and therefore possibly perfect. "It's a very freaky business," he tells her, then goes on to tell her that she can never be a good actress, but he can make her a good dancer. When Katie walks in on him in bed with Victoria, her expression sums it up perfectly—she expects the cheating, a manifestation of egocentric behaviour and insatiable lust. Victoria doesn't get angry when Joe tells her that she can never be great, instead she accepts it and falls for his charms. His sexual bravado is what feeds the theatrical enterprise all of these women are part of. Fosse then cuts to a flashback sequence at a burlesque bar where Keith Gordon as a young Gideon studies in a dressing room where he is interrupted by a stripper who insinuates a lesson that will be influence him later in life. As showgirls parade around him, fondling him, he ejaculates in his pants and it is all on for show as he tap dances in front of a ghoulish audience laughing in hysterics. The idea of being on stage with a semen stain comments on the relationship between sex and art: a messy situation that can be trivialized and laughed at. Exposure is what *All That Jazz* is about: it exposes truths, ruthlessness and ego.

Joe's jealousy of other men is shown where Katie calls another dancer named Michael ("straight, not gay"). Joe's insecurities about his sexual prowess are thrust under the spotlight and here is where Roy Schieder is phenomenal. As fantastic he is as the show pony perfectionist workaholic, he is mesmerizing to watch as a fumbling schoolboy, scared to lose the girls he has already had. Married to this performance is Fosse's energetic direction, peppered with overwhelming sadness. The bleak and desolate portrait of an artist trapped in self-involved ambition and desire is counterbalanced with dark comic inspired lines such as the very lyrical "I wish you weren't so generous with your cock." While Ann Reinking's Katie protests his promiscuity, God (as a voice of reason and also as the voice of what he wants to hear) explains that his sexual freedoms are a turn on. This is something that Joe has told himself many times before. In Fosse's film, even God is in the service of ego and narcissism –Joe seems to talk to the God character via mirrors, and as one of the cinema's great distancing tools, mirrors are often used for this kind of reflexivity. God is Joe's witness, not his contemporary.

Another moment showcasing the self and self-awareness is when the "Take Off With Us" presentation occurs with bubbly, flamboyant composer Paul (Anthony Holland) barking it out with exhausting exuberance. During this scene (harkening back to classic Broadway Tin Pan Alley scenario), the "catchy, bouncy" zaniness is a base line for Joe, who is set to direct and choreograph the number. His ex-wife Audrey struggles not to laugh, not only at what Joe has to salvage, but the fact that Broadway's diversity is something Joe wants channel to a new direction of semi-smut and sexual sophistication. What he does with this song is sexual pantomime and porno-chic at its best in the film's most dazzling and startling sequence, as well as one of its most tantalizing and unnerving scene, as "Take Off With Us" slowly morphs into "Airotica."

Fosse's polyamorous background (he lived with two women) also makes the song "Two Ladies" from *Cabaret* resonate, and is presented in *All That Jazz* tenderly in a scene with father and daughter dancing together. This paints a not-so-ideal portrait of what Joe Gideon considers parental obligation. "Why don't you get married again?" his daughter Michelle asks, to which her father explains that he can't marry anyone because he doesn't want to inflict pain onto anyone again. Love equals pain, and when the Angel of Death asks if he believes in love, Joe replies "I believe in telling people I love them." He also forgets sexual conquests' names, and even fails to recall if he called them "sweetheart" or "darling." He is a lothario of the darkest sense, a demonic entity that shifts from heart to heart, but only sees a body to possess. "Show time folks!" becomes a cynical mantra, and the scene where Victoria is grilled during a rehearsal exemplifies this. His statement "Stop smiling, it's not the high school play" summarises the 1970s musical—there is no room for happiness or cheer here, but there is plenty of room for nastiness, vulgarity and oppression.

Joe's argument with Audrey about the trappings of monogamy are sidestepped as older dancer Audrey breaks down when her ex-husband's genius is on show during "Take Off With Us/Airotica." He has taken something from Tin Pan Alley and made it new Broadway. And he does this even with his drug addiction—along with other things, it will eventually kill him, but speed keeps him working and makes his vision sharper and more ruthless in its execution. Joe is a ruthless revolutionary.

Jessica Lange and Roy Scheider off camera in *All That Jazz* (1979)

Bob Fosse's choreography is breathtaking. Sandahl Bergman's incredible lead in "Airotica" is outstanding as she throws and thrusts her lithe and statuesque body about like a woman possessed. This is also the case for her fellow dancers, including Deborah Geffner who launches into a frenzy that transcends and elevates the number. These two phenomenal actress/dancers recall shooting the film, and Deborah Geffner fondly remembers:

> Well, my first meeting with Bob Fosse was when I was auditioning for the chorus in *Pippin* which is one of my favourite shows. And I got quite far. If you know anything about auditioning for a Broadway Shows, there is a dance call, an equity dance call, you know, you learn the combinations then you go in fours, then you get cut down and do it again and you do another combination and then you do that in groups of four. Very, very much like the opening of *All That Jazz*. Not quite as grand maybe, but extremely like that. Sometimes women and then men. Sometimes all together. Then everyone stands and sings, just like in the opening, it is

very, very accurate. They made the decision and I got cut and I went up to Kathy Doby, who is his assistant at that time as well and said "Is there anything you can tell me to help me out?" As a dancer you just don't need stronger, sharper...you need to get stronger and sharper," and I went "That's great." I auditioned for him for *Chicago*. And he did have a habit of reusing his dancers that he knows which makes complete sense because you know the people, they know you. You know what you are getting if they are available. Of course you would use the same people and you would want to give jobs to the same people over and over. So I didn't get that. But I did get to audition for him after auditioning for him for *Chicago*, I got into *A Chorus Line*. And at that point I got an agent, and the agent set me up for a national tour of *Chicago*, for the role of Roxy. I went through the dance audition and everything and got to the point where I was working with him on Roxy Heart's monologue. That was amazing! So here I was in a studio with just me and Bob and the accompanist working on this monologue, and at that point, I just...after working with him, I didn't care if I did that show or what, I just had this physical need to work with him. To have him direct me. That is the most amazing experience I have ever had in my life. I just learned more than the last five years of acting. At that point, soon after that, he started the auditions for *All That Jazz*, and there was chorus auditions. I didn't want to do any more chorus work, even in a movie. I was like "No, I don't want to do that. I want to do roles, I want to act. I want to act and dance." A friend of mine who had left a chorus line and was out of work asked if she could use my dressing room because she was auditioning at St James, which was right across the street from the Shubert. Bob knew so many women from so many auditions. He would be lucky to remember all the women he had slept with. So I said "No. If I am right for this, he would call me for the part." And she said, "No, come on!" She said, "It is like Dustin Hoffman, you know how he auditioned for

Mike Nichols, and he said "But I don't sing." And he said "Oh, go ahead and audition for him anyway. And he did and then Mike Nichols cast him in *The Graduate* and his career took off. I said "Alright." We had the audition and of course she got cut and I got kept. I was standing there in the line and I was like "Oh my gosh, I got chosen! As a Bob Fosse dancer! This is like… this is big! This is huge for me because for Roxy Hart it wasn't a dance audition, that was like an agent submission," and you know, I danced for him but the big deal was singing and acting. I was "Aw, I'm a Fosse dancer!? I've really made it!" At that point, Vicky Stein, who had been his secretary, later told me she leaned over to him and said 'That's Deborah Geffner." He said "Who?" She said "She auditioned for Roxy for us. She's really good. You liked her." And he went, "Oh, oh." Said "You should have her come in for Victoria." And he went "Alright." He had of course seen my submission. My agent had submitted me for Victoria, for the part. He didn't call me in so I went No, no, he knows who I am. That was my reason for not going to the open call. So after that, he called me to read for Victoria, and then called me to read again, and then I found out I had a screen test. I had a scene which was not in the movie. It is on my website—the screen test that I did. And then it was postponed a week or two weeks, and I got really, really sick because of the nerves and the excitement, so I got this terrible case of bronchitis; I could barely breathe. So at that point he said screen test and I went through all this craziness trying to get the right costume because he said "I want something that shows your body" and I tried everything. I ended up wearing my dad's old flannel shirt. I did the screen test and he gave me a couple of tries. He said "That was good, just do it faster," and that was the final screen test. That was his voice on the screen test; he read with me. And he went "Good, good. That's good." And then I waited forever, and then he had me come back and dance for him again and read the actual scene that was in the movie of you know, I'm no good; I look at myself in the mirror and you know, I'm ashamed. I saw that she burst into tears, and I was like Shoot. I don't know how to burst into tears. I've never done that before. I just thought to myself, "well, what if after all this, I didn't get this part?" And that did it. I just started to cry. He read it with me and I was crying and he said "You cry really easily" Yes, yeah. And he had me dance again. It was just like a woman trying on a dress, again and again to make sure that is the one she wants, and after that I heard that I got it. But of course he had to delay because he had been working with Richard Dreyfuss, and Richard Dreyfuss quit because of creative differences, and that wasn't the story that was around but he and Richard Dreyfuss did not see eye to eye. Yeah, they totally didn't see eye to eye. Richard Dreyfuss wanted to be treated like an actor and Bob Fosse was not into working with actors. He was a choreographer and treated actors like a choreographer. You go do this, do that, feel this, cry. Good. And the reason his stuff worked was because he was such a genius and his instinct was always better than anyone else's. So it worked for him, even though it's not the way most people are used to being directed. So anyway, after that he said through my agent or after Vicky, I can't remember which, he said, "I can't offer you the part yet, but I do want you, so please be available and I can't offer you more than scale, but I am going to have you for the length of the movie which is six months, so you are going to have a weekly salary; a weekly sage scale salary for six months, so don't let your agent hold me up for money because I can't give you anymore, but I will give you the whole six months. I want you to just be available." So that was incredible. And it ended up being more because it went over time. So it ended up more than six months of sage scale salary, which was amazing. So for *A Chorus Line*, I played Christine. I couldn't sing. I could never really sing. And I understudied Sheila played by Kelly Bishop. Yeah, and the funny thing was, I was in *A Chorus Line* at the time. And I didn't want to leave because I loved that job. Well at the time, it was like being kings and queens of Broadway. You know, we got free haircuts. We'd come out of the stage door and there would be 20 people lined up for autographs for each one of us. It was the best gig in town. So, I didn't want to quit that. And I told him that, "But I want to do the show." He said, "Well I can't have you do the show and the movie at the same time." And I said, "Well, I want to take a leave of absence." And they said, "No. We have never given anyone a leave of absence. We don't do that. You know, you can quit." They didn't say anything like "You can come back." They said "No, you will have to quit. "And I told Bob I don't want to quit. He called the Shakespeare Festival and suddenly they said "Yeah, we can give you a leave of absence for 6 months. You can come back." So, the leave of absence was up and I did have to go back and do the show. But we were still doing *All That Jazz*. So I was going out to Purchase, New York. I was going up there every morning and filming, and then coming back and filming at night for weeks and weeks. So, I was getting double salary, which was really cool. It was a nice time of my life! I really, really enjoyed it. It was the hardest I had ever worked. And it was the hardest I would work for probably years and years. I kept waiting to be asked to do something that difficult again. You know, I thought, "Oh, this is what movie making is like!" It was the first movie I had ever made. But, no one had ever asked me to work that hard again. Because he would do like thirty takes. You know, twenty three takes was just warming up! He wanted everything, everything full out, all the time. It just didn't occur to him that you know, these were dancers and they were real people and...he would have done it. In fact, he never asked anyone to do anything he wouldn't do. When he wanted Sandhal to fall off the platform into the guys arms. He went up there and demonstrated it. And he went, "Okay. I am going to fall. And you guys catch me." Sandahl didn't say it was too difficult because he had just done it. Yeah, it was rested assured people will catch you but also, if an acrobat does a flip and his partner catches him, you know, that's not to say, if you do the flip and your partner catches you, you will be safe because you may not know how to hold your body but you will be safe. Broadway Arts was the rehearsal studios on Broadway that Bob had always worked in. And in fact, where we had rehearsed for the movie, we did like 3 weeks of rehearsal learning the number and then deconstructing the number. He choreographed an entire, wonderful number— "Take Off with Us" and then deconstructed it and recollaged it, and repurposed it. It looked like he was destroying it but in fact he was just cutting up bits of it and you know and making this person do this and this person do that for his own purposes for the camera. So we rehearsed that for about 3 weeks before we started filming. He had a mock-up of Broadway Arts made out in this film studio in Astoria which had been deserted, I think since Gloria Swanson's time. And this was the first thing that they had did there since then. So we walked in and it was Broadway Arts. We were all the way out in Astoria, Queens, in this huge sand studio and then suddenly it was Broadway Arts, which was really quite clever of him because it brought us back to the feeling of being in our safe place... grounded in a reality for us. Oh, this is our actual studio where we were. Oh, this is our studio again. Oh. I sit here. I hang here. It was really smart. So, when I was doing the crying scene on the bar that was the actual studio where I had auditioned for him and cried. So it was as if I was in the same place. It was really, really clever. He was really clever in that way. Anyway, we did all of those numbers. And we did, I think, I don't remember exactly the shooting schedule, but I think we even did the scenes in the apartment before we did the big...No. It was right after we did the 'Take Off With Us' numbers that we went to the Palace Theatre and did that sequence, because he wanted his dancers. You know, the dancers that he had choose to be obviously better to a knowledgeable eye. He wanted his dancers to be better than the other dancers. And the dancers who had been working with him for the last 8 weeks, you know, stressing and straining and working their butts off, would look better than the rest of the dancers he had brought in no matter how good they were. So that was his deal. That was really fun! Roy Scheider had a little ear piece in his ear and Bob would be telling him what to do. **Roy** called it rum and noodle acting. I don't know if it was rum and noodle back then. I only had rum and noodles back then. You know, instant soup acting. You know, just add water. Bob would tell him what to say. So it was very fluid. It was very improvised. But Roy wasn't doing the improvising. Bob was doing the improvising, knowing what he would do in an audition situation. He was just riffing on what he would do at an audition or what he would imagine himself doing at a huge cattle call-like audition. The beauty of Roy was, he was already a physical guy. Either he was the type of guy who would naturally, you know, take steps three at a time, run up steps, and he was the kind of guy policemen loved. Whenever we were out, you know, policemen thought he was one of them on account of *The French Connection*. So Roy was willing to work this way and willing to kind of give his will over…not will, but his artistic sensibility over to Bob's saying "This is how we are going to do it.' I think it was just incredible. So with casting, it was just like in a Bob Fosse audition. Cathy taught the number and everybody did it. There is that one scene when I am in the middle with Gary Flannery, and we were doing the extensions, we were doing the couples number, which was choreographed specifically for the *All That Jaz* audition. Bob Fosse would push himself really, really, really hard. He was always the hardest working person on set. You know, I would see him sitting quietly, but you know, it was always because he was always contemplating the next thing he had to do. He would never, never stop working. Which is way he took all the speed and drank white wine to come down and all that stuff. But he was always, always on speed. Always had a cigarette hanging out of his mouth, you know, the side of his mouth. He came up to me at one point and put his hand on my shoulder, you know, like Roy in the audition scene where he puts his hand on the guys shoulder and he shakes his head down. Well, he came up to me and put his hand on my shoulder with his cigarette in his mouth and he was like (imitates Bob coughing), and I was like, "What? what? What is it? Please. I will do anything. What do you want?" Just (cough…cough) do it better." Then he walked away! But not ironically, you know. That was all he could think of to say. Like, "You know what I mean. Do it better." That constant feeling of striving, of wanting to please him. Of wanting to get it right for him, you know. He picked incredibly dancers, like those triple pirouettes, in the audition sequence. He said, "Okay. Who can do a triple pirouette?" People raised their hands, and one after the other of people just doing a triple pirouette. It was just incredible! He was so, so competitive with Michael Bennett. He hated *A Chorus Line*. It was just a feeling of that's not what it's like. And he said, "I am going to do an audition scene to show what it is really like." You know, it is not like *A Chorus Line*. It is nothing like that of course. That never happened but maybe a work shop situation. But that is not an audition for a Broadway musical chorus line. So he said, "I am going to show what a real Broadway audition is. The real chorus line." No. That has no place. There are no therapy sessions. There's no crying in baseball! There are no therapy sessions. That's what pissed him off. You know that therapy session was considered a chorus line audition. There is a way to act without doing that but I think that is kind of the essence of acting, is taking the words and actions that you are given and bringing your own thoughts and feelings to it. I know it was not acting technique at the time, because the acting classes I had taken were mostly musical comedy, you know, how to put a song over. My acting classes were being on stage. All my life was learning how to act. I think Victoria's vulnerability is probably my vulnerability. My fragility. And I think of the three women who auditioned for that role. I think it was three, maybe four. I know two others. And the other two did not have that particular quality. I think maybe that quality in me was what Bob realised he wanted. So I have figured that is probably why I got the role. You know, 90% of directing is casting. I firmly believe that. And he was a genius about casting. Absolutely genius. I mean, I am thinking John Lithgow, Liza Minnelli, just everyone. Just genius about casting, getting the right person. So, I think he probably saw what he wanted in Victoria. As far as bringing my personal experiences, I was a gypsy. I was a dancer. I knew all that. I knew that really well. I was out to please; to be liked, like Victoria. I think that is part of being a gypsy; that kind of, "I've got to get this next job! I've got to find out what they want." I am trying to think of what else...the giggling in bed. I hadn't done any nudity before. There was a lot of back and forth about nudity. In fact, Sandhal was brought in late to do her part. I was another girl's part. And the other girl got very hoity-toity about 'I'm not here to show my boobs,' and he went, "Okay, Sandhal." I think he flew her in from the west coast. I think she was in *Dancin'* on the west coast. He just flew her back and said "You do this. I know you'll do this." So, you know, it never bothered me. I know it does bother some people. And of course, I was working with Bob, so it was like, this is going to be something good! This is not someone saying 'I want you in a vampire movie and by the way, we are going to show your boobs.' But, it was like, this is part of my vision, and I was like "Okay!" But he did in the scene going up the stairs; the scene of maybe I can become a star...so that's there...you wanna go to bed? And I walk up the stairs—that shot, Guiseppe Rotunno was his cinematographer, and he is Italian. He believes that he speaks English but in fact, doesn't. He just has this belief that what he is speaking is English. You know, and he makes himself understood largely, but as far as the focus, you know the focus was very exact in his mind, he didn't want my boobs to show on the way upstairs. He wanted that very, very, soft focus so it almost didn't show. And when he saw that in the rushes, he was so upset, that he was ready to quit, instead, the DP was fired...over my boob...over my boobs!

Sandahl Bergman discusses her experience on the film:

What happened for me was, starting out as a dancer, you were one of a lot of people and you had to look all the same. It was all about confidence, you know. *Skirts* and it was *Music Man*, all those old musicals that dancers were in costumes. What happened to me when I went to New York? I remember I bought a ticket and I saw *Pippin* for the first time, and I went "Oh, my god." You're in an ensemble, where everyone is an individual character, you know . Everybody was dressed differently. Everybody sort of played a role. It wasn't a chorus line. It wasn't a chorus group of dancers. That started to change. And then of course *A Chorus Line* with Michael Bennett which I had done a few shows with Michael Bennett before I did 'A Chorus Line' on Broadway. I had done *Follies* with Michael and I had done *Coco* with Michael. I did *Coco* with Katharine Hepburn, and that was a national company. Then I went into *Follies* I did the last eight weeks of *Follies* and went on tour with *Follies* for a little bit. I had two meetings with Michael Bennett before I ever did *A Chorus Line*. To answer your question, what did change was the dancers changed. Bob certainly brought that scope with *Pippin*, which when I saw that show, I went "Oh my god, I have to do the show." The same thing when I said *A Chorus Line*, I went "Oh my god, I have to do the show." They were two icons **to** people that were celebrated on Broadway at the same time. Sort of like, if I can make an analogy going back to Arnold Schwarzenegger and Sylvester Stallone. They were the two biggest action figures in the movie industry. They both were very different, but they were both kind of the similar, much like Arnold and Sly at that point in time

635

with the film industry that was going on. They did a bit of the same sort of work but different. It is the same with Michael Bennett and Bob Fosse. They both were just icons in the theatre. The only kind of plus that I think Bob had it on his, that I love so much about working for him, he is also a director of film. I went from the Michael Bennett show to a Bob Fosse show, back to a Michael Bennett show, to a Bob Fosse show. So, when I was doing *A Chorus Line* for Michael, Bob had this great show called *Dancin'* that he auditioned for. I went to the audition and fortunately got the job. So, it was kind of a funny situation because when we were all doing *Pippin*, for this group of working dancers, we were all doing Pippin for Bob Fosse on Broadway. We all auditioned for *A Chorus Line*, and there were probably five of us that left. So, it was always like a Michael Bennett show, and Fosse show. They both had their extreme amazing talents, and I was so grateful to work for both of them because they were the iconic choreographers/directors to work for on Broadway. When I was there in the early 1970s until nineteen eighty. You know, *A Chorus Line* was ground-breaking because it was show about dancers trying to get a job. Why it was so successful was because it crossed the line of the audience versus sitting there. Everyone has been in that position where "I need to get a job." And that was the brilliance of that show for me. Not dancers but a dancer's story. But recently, everybody I think in their lives has been on that line in an interview of "I really need this job. Will you hire me?" It was about dancers and it was a dancer's story that Michael sent everybody through, but it was really a story about every person being in that situation, "I really need this job." You know. "I gotta get this job." It was about paying bills, and about you know life in general. So that was the genius of that. You know, those are the people you want to work for, outside of not to say I worked for some amazing choreographers and directors my whole career but, in New York, those were my two favourite people. Fosse was my mentor. He sort of taught me, you know like when people said to me, that *All That Jazz* was so renowned, and I had done another television piece on Moonlighting that got nominated for an Emmy. What Bob Fosse taught me, and probably because he was a director of actors, he taught story behind the five, six, seven, eight. So it took on a little bit of a different thing. I have so many notes of doing *All That Jazz*. You know, as a director, if I was an actor, he would give me a note about what am I thinking about with doing a particular step? So for me, he was my greatest teacher because he took me already as a good dancer, which I was, don't get me wrong, because I was technically trained, but he took what I did to a little bit of a different place. I think that is why it got recognised, especially in the movie *All That Jazz*. So for me, he was my mentor, because as I said, I got to do two Broadway shows with him and then I got to do the film *All That Jazz*. I got to work with him three times in a very intimate. I say intimate because it was a show that he directed and choreographed. I got so much information from him as to sort of how to dance. So he probably was my best teacher, you know. The one thing I always get from Bob, which I always loved, was the comment "Less is more." I sort of learnt that in life. Even with fashion. Some have the earrings on and the necklace, and that thing and that other thing. You know, keep things simple and less is more. Wear a great pair of earrings but don't wear a necklace, or wear a necklace and a small pair of earrings. It has sort of taken me into how I sort of live my life a little bit. I always go back to "Less is more," and he was a great teacher of that because his work was so specific and actually why I loved it so much. The less you did, the harder it was. People look and go "Oh, this is so simple" and I go "No, but if you really do it, do it right." It is much more intricate than doing two turns then a jump then hit the floor, then bring your leg up, go down, then up. You know, that is executed technically. But with Bob it was so intricately specific that it made it so difficult, and then on the flip side of that, Michael Bennett was a genius at moving bodies in and out. Michael Bennett knew how to create pictures. And like I said, *A Chorus Line* is the greatest example of that, although we had a lot of stuff on the plate. Bob and Michael were two different sorts of geniuses, as we know about that with the death of Robin Williams, there are certain people that you come across, and unfortunately, I feel there is a bit of insanity with humans. I think even in the art world or any world you may go into, there is a little bit when somebody is so amazingly talented and a lot of people go. That person is a little bit different than normal. A little bit to the left. Everybody that I worked for, that I felt that way about; I'm pretty correct. Talent is a really amazing thing, and I think they all second guess people's sanity. I remember Michael Bennett saying after *A Chorus Line* "How do you outdo yourself?" There was an interview with Bob Fosse in Cannes saying after when he got nominated for an Oscar, "How do you outdo oneself?" I think that's the problem. I think that is where a lot of the problem lays, because how do you keep there? Life is about ups and downs. Like you do something great and then you don't do something so great. You do something great and then you don't do something so great. It never stays the same. You're never fabulous forever. It would be a very boring world if that was the case. So with those two people, I have my fondest memories as a professional working dancer in the theatre. So that was my take on that. The one thing I loved about *All That Jazz* was it was biographical. Getting Roy Scheider to play Bob Fosse was amazing, because initially on board was Richard Dreyfuss. I actually did a test with Richard Dreyfuss, to play the girl, the Deborah Geffner part. There was a huge fight that happened in my screen test and all of a sudden Richard Dreyfuss was out. Also, Bob gave me a great lesson about nudity on film. I think every actor has that story you know when you are shooting a love scene or you have to get naked. It is so not sexy. It is all about the numbers. I remember

Bob saying to me "You set the tone of the set." So if you go in and you're like "Oh god, I gotta take my clothes off now" If you set that, then everybody goes into that energy. He said, "If you go in and go; "Are we ready to go? Okay, towel off, let's shoot." Then you set the tone for the whole set as to what transpires. That was a very good lesson for me, with everything that I said. I set the tone for what happens on set. He taught me that. He said "It's what we're gonna do. I know you're going to be naked, I know you are going to be uncomfortable but you set the tone. Let's do it very professionally and boom, boom, boom." And that's how it happened. So as uncomfortable as it was…it was not uncomfortable, because it was just very professional, you know. And I mean, when Roy Scheider and Bob Fosse were on set at the same time, and Bob always dressed in black, you didn't know who was who. You know what I mean? Their body type was so similar. I'm not sure what was happening at that point in time. You know, I will say probably there were artistic problems, and like I said, if you are autobiographically playing a character and the man directing you, you pretty much need to be on the same page. You don't kind of go against that "Well I see it this way." No. You are playing me, this is how I want you to do it." And I just think there were probably problems…you know back at that point in time, I'm sure there was some sort of…maybe drug abuse happening, I don't know. I'm not privy to that at all, but I'm sure there was a lot of shit going on at that time. But like I said, what didn't happen, it probably was a plus. I never got to talk to Bob about that, like how would you feel about Richard Dreyfuss being replaced by Roy Scheider? I don't know what that was; all I know the end result was amazing! And Roy Scheider was great because you know a dancer's language is very different. , and I remember Roy Scheider because I still had to do 'Dancin'; the Broadway show at the time that I was shooting 'All That Jazz.' I sometimes would shoot the day then go back and do the Broadway show of my show. Roy Scheider I remember use to hang out backstage, and watch dancers warm up, because it is a different language talking to dancers. It is just a different language that someone from the outside wouldn't know.

The choreography is stellar and in addition to the number's motion is the overt sexuality—the dripping sensuality that is earthy and dense. The nudity and the multiple sexual practices all polarised by the straight couple, the gay couple and lesbian couple, coming together in a orgiastic explosion is an element of the sexual being that Fosse was a dancer and as a creative force. When Paul the composer whispers to the producer "I think we just lost the family audience," it is telling sentiment—Broadway has changed. *The Music Man* has packed his bags and Bob Fosse will take over from here. But sadly, not for much longer. The motto in "Airotica" is "We take you everywhere but get you nowhere" is a simple message of the "divine decadence" lasting power—the sex, the drugs, the booze and the art will be over, because formidable monstrosities are just around the corner. Fosse as one of the most integral figures that would come to introduce the dark, the decedent and the hyper-sexual to the dance world is a reflection of the man as a perfectionist: epitomized in the mini-monologue he has when he screams out "God makes a rose and it's perfect, how can I do that?"

A charming but cynical scene comes late in the piece as Katie and Michelle (Joe's steady lover and his daughter) dance for a drunken Joe in his apartment singing "everything old is new again." This brilliant coming together and awkward meshing of old Broadway with the new is presented here in a starkly lit living room with two enthusiastic chorus girls showering love onto a drunk. The respect given to the classicist American musical thrust into a new construction is so wildly handled here by Bob Fosse and crew, and dancers such as Ann Reinking are a superb tool for this commentary on the power of the musical and the angry voice it can sometimes have: a voice that comes from something proud as well as tormented and distinctly American. The Jazz age and the birth of the American musical comes crashing here into an edgy world: Fosse's background as a classical musical theatre and film magician meets up with the Fosse of the 1970s, and it is cynical, self-critical and desperate.

At the full cast reading of Joe's new musical, silence crashes in and leaves only the sounds Gideon himself makes (his tapping fingers, his scraping nails, his ashing of his cigarette). This is oppressive and unnerving, as the world goes on around him but he is consumed by his own egocentricities and personal demons. The reading is ultimately a success, but he doesn't feel it and Audrey—who knows him well—senses it. His heart condition, linked to the work he puts into his new musical, will kill him. The entire film is focused on the tension between show business itself and life and death.

His passion for the musical is more important than his own health, and death runs through the film, grimacing at Joe Gideon with barbaric glee. The artist on the verge of having a heart attack paves the way for a dark yet comedic montage in the hospital where the partying, boozing, smoking, drugs, and sex continues. The ultimate moment of whistling in the dark is where Audrey, Paul and the entire cast and crew talk about how well Joe is while deep down they know he's not going to make it: "there's no business like show business" rings its truest here. And to add insult to injury, Bob Fosse introduces a snaky character in John Lithgow who pops up as an opportunistic director, ready to step in to Joe's shoes and take over the musical.

Another important addition to the film is the talented Ben Vereen as a TV variety host and alter-ego to Joe, who becomes the emcee at death's door, ushering in Gideon to his own special that will be his farewell performance. This kind of magic throw away the fears that are articulated by Cliff Gorman's stand-up character who suggests that Joe Gideon has a deep rooted fear of being conventional and a dreadful dear of being ordinary and not special. The idea of Gideon not caring about whether he lives or dies plays beautifully against the sterility of the visuals in the hospital and the cold concrete walls, the dingy hallways, the cloudy skies and the rain-drenched, filthy streets. The use of floaty music compliments a nasty review from a critic discussing "The Stand-Up" which has its release as Joe goes into surgery. She explains that "the old razzle dazzle obliterates the drama," but here in Fosse's film, that is not the case. The model of the movie musical heightens and expresses the depressing drama all too well. The operation is depicted as a musical number- hosted by Audrey—is presented as a vaudeville show, offering something distressing and yet completely engaging.

When Katie admits that she is sleeping with someone else while Gideon lies on his death bed, it is a final act of brutality and the crushing vulnerability of the once womanizing, pill popping artist appears. Moments after this, there is a sequence that cross cuts between the troubled musical's budget breakdown while Gideon has his chest cut open. It is a gripping piece of cinema—the heartlessness of money talk in show business while we are subjected to the gory reality of open heart surgery: the blood, the raw flesh, this is what the musical says so much about the industry as its primary focus—the liability of Gideon's death causing money issues and also the notion that the show will make money without even opening, rendering Gideon's survival meaningless. "That's very theatrical, Joe," says the Angel of Death, and he is. He is now a tragic figure besieged by disappointment and cruelty. The hospital hallucination sequence becomes a lavish movie musical number: as Gideon dies, a highly stylized musical commences with the ladies in his life belting out "After You're Gone" and "There'll Be Some Changes Made" while Joe directs the musical as he lies dying in bed.

Fosse's signature choreography—the twitchiness, the cat-like gestures, the leaps and motion phrases—all add to the eeriness of the piece. The chorus girls of ex-lovers with their ghastly faces represent the grotesque element of promiscuity and a boulevard of broken vows, while Joe continues to be lothario, kissing a dying woman in her hospital bed. Joe experiences his last moments as both a sexual liberator and slave. The old Broadway "life is a bowl of cherries" mentality—when things are bad, the song can lift the spirits—punches us in the face as Joe Gideon's body bag is zipped up and Ethel Merman sings "There's no business like show business." *All That Jazz* lets us know that there's no people like show people, they smile—sometimes grotesquely—even when they are low. But sometimes they don't, they work themselves into a grave with pills, liquor and sexual conquests. And they never smile like it was the high school play.

Long-time friend and collaborator editor Alan Heim (who appears in the film as an editor working on "The Stand-Up") remembers Fosse and his masterful work:

> I did *Lenny* first which has small musical moment in it and I remember understanding that Bob was always very much attracted to working in musical numbers in a very naturalistic fashion, not the way musicals are presented in a Broadway fashion, he was interested in making the musical moments arise just as musical moments that would happen in life and that is partly how *All That Jazz* came about. He liked the cut of *Lenny* so much, and that was where he and I really collaborated, he wanted to use a technique we used where we would intercut between actors and other things. Ralph Burson used to say "when you're making a movie there is real time and flash forwards and flash backs and so forth and then there is Fosse time" and we worked in Fosse time! A lot of the structure that we developed on *Lenny* we worked into *All That Jazz*, we wished we could be more flexible but we got bitten by that. While we were making the movie he never admitted that the character of Joe was him. It made it a bit awkward, because I would refer to him as YOU and he would stop me and say no, no, it's not me its Joe or Roy, not me. But it was hard not to keep slipping and referring to the character as Bob because all of the pills had his name on them, all the addresses used were his, a lot of the people in the movie were playing themselves or versions of themselves including me, so the only fictional character was Bob. I was very moved at the memorial service for Bob, and very moved by the party afterwards. When Bob Fosse died he left a small amount of money to a group of people to host a party for him in his honor to happen right after the memorial service. So Gwen Verdon called me and asked me if I would be happy to use the money he had left me, which was about $250 to go into a fund to help put on this party. Of course I said yes and everybody else agreed and it happened at the Tavern on the Green in New York which was a magical place. It was very

theatrical and very overly done and Mervyn Leroy's son ran it and he had put in a lot of Tiffany lamps and greenhouse structures and lights on the trees outside. I went to a few parties there but this was very special. Stuart Ostrow who was a producer and a great friend of Bob's came up to me and he said to "You know, Bob always said that you were the man that edited his life." And that shocked me to say the least because all through working on *All That Jazz*, Bob never ever admitted that this character was him. Of course we all knew it that he based the character of Joe on his own life but it was one of those things that we all had to learn to ignore and just get on with our work. That was one of the few times in my life that I wanted to go to the set because they had over seven hundred dancers in this theatre. I went under the stage and to hear those footsteps was incredible. I come from a sound background and so to hear all that was amazing, so I just stood there. My first cut of the that was something like twelve minutes long, that's just the dancing without getting to the actual red nosed clown, but I remember it was a spectacular mini documentary on a phone call, but of course that's not what the film is about and I knew it before I did it and we edited it to three or four minutes and I wish I still had that other version. In those days you didn't save that. There are some beautiful moments.

There is a great moment where Roy walks over to the kid who just looks like him and I'm sure that Bob went thorough that a lot with his casting. After working with Bob twice I began to learn a lot more what he wanted. As we go along the first one is kind of funny with the cigarette in the shower and it's a little joke but later they're not jokes it gets shorted in edits and more grim, increasingly scary and at one point he looks like some weird black stork—so it got tenser and tenser in particular after he drops off his daughter and comes upstairs and he coughs and there we intercut the coughing with the wake up sequence and tie it all up together which was bobs intention to write it and tie it all up together. That is a particular chilling moment—he has to get it all in before he dies—the urgency. After about two weeks with bob in the cutting room we got to a scene that is no longer in the film where Roy comes into the editing room and he coughs and I look at him and raise an eyebrow giving him a look as if to say "God I wish he'd stop smoking." And I remember when we did *Liza with a Z* I could be a whole corridor away and I would hear Bob coughing and it was horrible—the idea was that I was going to go an eye brown raise and I have very big eyebrows! Bob never took a break after he finished shooting and this film was exhausting for everybody. First it was delayed and then they fired the lead actor who Bob had hired against everybody's wishes, then we had to wait for Roy for six months and they had to put everyone on half way to keep the company together. When we finally started there was no break until it got to Thanksgiving and that's where Bob took the dancers and choreographed the "Airotica" number but during that time our producer died. People had children on the film, people died, people had heart attacks during the shoot. It was like life that whole movie! I had a daughter during the shoot as well. There was a lot of tension in the cutting room and I tried to convince him to take a break and he never wanted to. One day he said to me "You were a better editor before you had a kid." Which I found very harsh and very upsetting and it hit me hard. So I went home that night and I told my wife, "I don't know if I want to do this movie anymore. He has never been so harsh with me before, but now, I gotta find a way to break this." Bob would say stop acting and do it smaller. When I cut the scene I had used the first take which was very short and then other ones which weren't I looked like a villain in a Chaplin film I showed Bob—Bob was so pissed off that he kicked a waste basket. He yelled "How could I let you do that!" And I said I'm not an actor—and he said "But you're a human being! How can I not get a human being to work!" And I said "that's the nicest thing you've said to me in the last two weeks' and he laughed and I laughed and it broke the tension—and it was all gorgeous from then on. Bob asked me if I would play myself—I asked if he would protect me—I got a haircut that looked like a two dollar—when they shot me bob didn't pay much attention, he was mainly concerned with Roy He was really worried about Roy. And at one time I asked to do another take—I had fallen into that acting rabbit hole! Airotica is my favourite things I've ever worked on—it covers dancing an sex and show business and all of Bob's obsessions—it's a knockout visually—there was a case in order to finish where I had to learn the edits from the musicality of that piece—Bob would hold onto things that he wanted and something—Much later he would say "you know you were right about cutting those scenes out." Would I change it now? No. I think it's wonderful. A lot of critics said that the film was self-indulgent and these people make me crazy- There's a certain point with bob and his girlfriends and his wife and Gwen Verdon was that they all cooked together and ate together I knew the girls that Bob was with—he was dating two women, Ann was one of them and I saw them later at a party and their relationships continued after—And of course Gwen was with him when he died.

CHICKEN TODAY, FEATHERS TOMORROW:
Rudolph and Frosty's Christmas in July and Jack Frost

Rudolph and Frosty's Christmas in July is a sweetly told and perfectly executed film from the much loved Rankin/Bass production team. The film is not only a successful stand-alone feature that tells the story of the world's most famous reindeer and snowman, but it is a cleverly conceived and surprisingly complex sequel (of sorts) to three of Rankin/Bass's previous films: *Santa Claus is Coming to Town, Rudolph the Red Nosed Reindeer* and *Frosty the Snowman*. The film creates a community that lives through Christmas, and concocts a world where characters that were initially invented for carols have now become functioning, fully fleshed out and dynamic. Animals, elves, snowmen and the like here now have their own personal desires, nightmares and ambitions.

When Frosty's (Jackie Vernon) children Milly and Chilly are greeted by their Uncle Rudolph (Billie Mae Richards) at the beginning of the film, we get a sense of a narrative meshing that is today now commonplace. We also are introduced to the film's first plot development: Rudolph's nose is fading, shifting the charming animated feature into an intricate and multi-layered melodrama. This is the most dramatic and complex of the Rankin/Bass films, and as much as misanthropy was examined in 1968's *The Little Drummer Boy* and pedophobia is looked into in *The Easter Bunny Is Coming to Town*, it is in *Rudolph and Frosty's Christmas in July* where emotional diversity and a number of themes are scrutinized.

Christmas specials are important when looking into 1970s musicals and musical specials on television, and Rankin/Bass are the reigning kings of Yuletide visual candy. But beneath the stop motion wonder of their Animagic characters, there is a sophisticated story as well as a tribute to old Hollywood. This film in particular boasts an all-star cast including Red Buttons, Ethel Merman, Mickey Rooney, Shelley Winters, Alan Sues, Jackie Vernon, Paul Frees and Don Messick, complete with the music of Johnny Marks and a Romeo Muller screenplay which is layered, intelligent and avoids the overly saccharine. With Santa as a narrator, the film sets up its heroes and a clear villain, unlike other Rankin/Bass villains who can be rehabilitated. In this picture, the king of the North Pole, Winterbolt (Paul Frees) is a menacing tyrant and remains sinister throughout. In direct opposition is Lady Boreal, the Queen of the Northern Lights, who has an adage that is repeated throughout the film in "Alas, nothing is forever," which plays off on the more maudlin aspects of an era obsessed with sombre children's entertainment.

The film is a perfect sequel to two previous Rankin/Bass films— *Santa Claus is Coming To Town* and *Rudolph the Red Nosed Reindeer* as it takes elements from them both and does something completely different: instead of a piece dedicated to an outcome, this film is a, a shimmering example of imagination, story innovation and character driven drama. Each character is given their own distinct motive, which is sometimes riddled with many dimensions and facets. For example, the villain Winterbolt wishes to be popular with the children—bizarre in itself, and not unlike Lex Luthor's keen interest and dedication to becoming popular with the citizens of Metropolis, wanting to be "for the people" as opposed to the genuinely saintly angel Superman, who is ultimately an alien. However, when Lady Boreal says "There is kindness and the loving warmth of the family on Christmas morn," she is summing up the magic of the season, and the importance of the holiday in relation to the gift of familial unity. This story could not exist without its Christmas context: the backstory of why Rudolph was born is a clear reference to him being a gift for Santa and therefore a gift for humanity. He is told never to use his "secret magic" for evil and much like Pinocchio, there is much pressure on goodness and taking the right path. Of course initially, Rudolph's nose causes him grief, rendering him a misfit. But in his first outing in the film he meets fellow misfits and from then on throughout the decade these movies became a celebration of not being the same—1960s and 1970s sensibilities danced around the general collective consciousness and the notion that difference makes up an interesting and rich fabric is something that audiences gravitated to as being a misfit became something that should be revered and not made fun of.

Rudolph remains an energetic and youthful presence in this film, and Rudolph and Frosty's friendship lies at the heart of the story. But it is up to the secondary turning point that really gets the film moving—Milton the flying ice-cream man (Red Buttons) comes to pick up his delivery and when greeted by Frosty, Rudolph and now joined by Frosty's wife Crystal (Shelley Winters), he explains that he is in love with Laney Lorraine (Shelby Flint) a tightrope walker of a coastal circus that is going broke. The human villain, Sam Spangles (Don Messick) (a mortal enemy and someone who is corrupt because of greed and money) wants to repossess the circus by overthrowing Laney's mother who owns it. Milton's love for Laney drives Rudolph's plight and in turn it presents an opportunity for Winterbolt.

In this film, good characters are easily persuaded into believing lies and talked into doing bad things. One example of this is where Winterbolt puts a thought into Milton's head to bring Rudolph to the coast, where his powers aren't as strong. The film blurs the lines between who is good, who is bad, who sits in between and who is easily persuaded to do the wrong thing. This complexity is exists within the narrative, and it makes use of characters that in lesser hands would not be as striking or captivating. When Frosty and Crystal decide to go along with Rudolph (they see it as a lovely opportunity for the children to see a real life circus) there are dangers involved. "We'd be real misfits," says Crystal as Frosty explains that "Being snow people has its drawbacks." This sorrowful moment is then met with Crystal singing "You Are everything I've Always Wanted" which is a beautiful little number set to a montage to the creation of Crystal by local children for companionship for Frosty. In two minutes, we understand the couple's devotion to each other and their family, and the song is reprised minutes later with Milton leading the group out to the coast. It is a testament to his love for Laney. Romance gently sits in the background of the film and colors it with a sweetness that is never overstated or dumb.

Another element that makes the film far more dense is that Winterbolt offers magic amulets to keep the snow folk frozen in July on the coast, which sets up a villain offering the film's heroes Faustian-leanings. On top of this is the fact that characters like Jack Frost (who gets his own feature film the same year, which we will discuss in a moment) also makes an appearance by the end of the film, which goes to show that the Romeo Muller is not scared of introducing new characters and situations late in the piece, as well as new themes. The film establishes rules regarding how long Frosty and his family can stay frozen, and then builds drama around it.

The aesthetics of the film are also glorious. The character designs are wonderful and iconic, and most notably the new characters—humans such as Milton, Laney, Sam Spangles and Ms Lorraine—are created with finesse and dedication. Milton has a perfectly sculpted, impish look with his spindly body and oversized head, and Laney is such a delicate beauty with her tiny waist and painted on eyes that look like those lovely kitsch paintings made famous by Margaret Keane in the 1950s and 1960s. Ms Lorraine (Ethel Merman) is such a refreshingly cynical character with some inspired lines such as "It's one thing life has told me, you can't live off banana splits." Merman is dynamite voicing Ms Lorraine and her trumpet-like voice soars and sometimes even outdoes the animation with its grandiose execution, but it is full of heart and warmth.

This is a film that sums up Christmas, and as complicated and as multi-layered as the plot is,—and as dimensional and as well-developed the characters are—the simple message of doing the right thing, being truthful and the importance of love, family and friendship permeate the very fabric of the film. It also inverts already established set pieces from previous Rankin/Bass film, such as "the island of misfit toys" which here becomes "the cage of lost rejections." Here is where we meet the reindeer Scratcher (Alan Sues)—a throwback to the lascivious sissy—who was supposed to be one of Santa's reindeer until Rudolph came along. He is a cunning and sly cretin and he will be a character type that will pop up in many later Disney films, such as Scar from *The Lion King*.

The multiple set ups in the film can seem long but the payoff is worth it and the intertwined narrative is strong. The songs are great, such as "Chicken Today and Feathers Tomorrow," a brilliant show tune that provides insight into the contradictory aspects of the film itself. This number also harkens back to Merman's take on "There's No Business Like Show Business" (which she performed on *The Muppet Show* to a melancholy Fozzie Bear) which addresses the ups and downs of life. Moralistic but never preachy, complicated and swift but without narrative glitches, entertaining and rich, *Rudolph and Frosty's Christmas in July* is an ambitious film that delivers something unique and crisp.

Another Christmas-themed feature from Rankin/Bass is *Jack Frost*. Here, Pardon-Me Pete (Buddy Hackett) is a groundhog who narrates the film, and is integral to the plot. He explains that the film is about that "one time when Jack Frost became human." The film was one of the lesser known and lesser celebrated Rankin/Bass pictures of the time, and it was released the same year as *Rudolph and Frosty's Christmas in July* which eclipses it in spectacle and its experimental approach. But January Junction and the characters that live there—such as the pumpkin peasants who are perfect representations of the put-upon earnest good folk that strive and dream—are just as charming as Frosty, Crystal and the members of Ms Lorraine's circus.

The head peasants have a daughter who is the beautiful and terminally romantic Elissa (Debra Clinger) who is "only in love with Jack Frost." Jack Frost (Robert Morse) of course is the principal lead and he dreams of becoming human so he can experience life and what it means to be in love and loved. The concept of lonely otherworldly characters wanting to experience basic human affectations is something that pops up in classic literature and film such as Quasimodo of *The Hunchback of Notre Dame* through to comic book superhero fare like Superman. "It's Lonely Being One of a Kind" is a poignant song, beautifully written and performed, and sums up Jack's overwhelming isolation. A lot of socialist ideals permeate the story elements in the film and the idea of disempowering money is something that the already relatively leftist Rankin/Bass films highlights, culturally significant by 1979 as the recession was coming to an end and the stock market boom was about to influence pop culture and politics in a major way..

In Jack Frost's life, the characters that all work together to make Winter are supportive of Jack's dilemma. However, invisibility is a factor (something already expressed in Pete's Dragon). "No one wants to meet Jack Frost" says Father Winter, and Jack replies "except for one," meaning Elissa. Jack is granted the wish to become human temporarily (a winter of humanity) and if he acquires the human essentials—a wife, house and horse—he will be human forever. At the cusp of the 1980s—the decade that pop star Madonna sung about as "living in a material world"—Jack Frost is a celebration of honesty and goodness that can only come from peasantry.

Rankin/Bass's production of Jack Frost *(1979)*

The materialistic character is of course the gluttonous villain, Kubla Kraus (Paul Frees). When the peasants use "ice money" (the idea of turning snowflakes into money) they are presented as resourceful peasants, so this is certainly a whistling in the dark musical. A song that embodies this is "It's Just What I Always Wanted," a great Broadway-style song with its beautifully prosed snippets in each verse where the characters sing about imaginary presents. There is a lesson here: children living in poverty and from broken homes can have a happy and healthy Christmas beyond the concerns of materialism. These socialist aspects coexist with both the romantic triangle involving Elissa and Jack as well as the clear villain who remains sinister and dishonest (much like Winterbolt from *Rudolph and Frosty's Christmas in July*), as well as the concept of loneliness that throws its shadow over the film. Jack Frost gives up his humanity to save his friends and Robert Morse's voice is one of those perfectly pitched voices that evokes innocence and impishness that heightens the character's sacrificial heart.

The plot isn't the film's strongest point, and for a film that sets up rules for the hero's quest this is strange, it complicates itself for no reason. *Unlike Rudolph and Frosty's Christmas in July*—complex because the themes call for it—*Jack Frost* jumps about as much as its camera work. However, it is the most adult next to *Rudolph and Frosty's Christmas in July*, and with lines such as "She's just a dreamer, but she'll always love Jack Frost," the film is in love with an idea, with a happening, with a season and lets us know that tangible humans are not the only deserving of love: skittish imps like Jack Frost can be susceptible, too. Jack sacrifices his chance at humanity when he sees Elissa marry a brave knight, who represents security and safety; much like Raul and the *Phantom of the Opera*, or Jonathan and Dracula. Here, Jack recalls the Hunchback letting go of Esmerelda: he has to let go of the idea of human companionship, a pretty heavy message in a supposedly light and cheery Christmas special. However, by sacrificing his chance to be human, he rescues the town from oppression while at the same time he realizes there is no room for him in the real world. He cannot contribute and he has to live beyond it, there to inspire winter and to capture the hearts and imaginations of people lie Elissa everywhere. These people must ultimately end up with brave knights of their own, standing for the tangible and practical.

In *Rudolph and Frosty's Christmas in July*, Big Ben the whale (a character not established in a previous Rankin/Bass film) also pops up and seems to be a god-like figure that saves the day. These characters can exist, because Rankin/Bass have created their own universe and had unspoken ownership on seasonal entertainment during this period. Of course *The Osmond Christmas Special* (1980), *Benji's Very Own Christmas Story* (1978), *The Sonny and Cher Christmas Specials* which featured the likes of Captain Kangaroo, Bernadette Peters and more were 1970s television specials that dished out the frivolous fun and warm sentiment of the season, but when it came to Christmas time (and Easter and Halloween for that matter) this kind of television extravaganza truly belonged to the legendary Rankin/Bass.

I'M GOING TO GO BACK THERE SOME DAY:
The Muppet Movie

1979 was The Year of the Child, and some kind of transcendental magic permeated creative forces at work during this period. This seeped into the hearts and minds of children everywhere who would later grow into adults at one with their inner-child, still believing in the magic they experienced as youngsters. *The Muppet Movie* is a testament to this everlasting magic. What Jim Henson and his team did for the world of children's entertainment is not only historically important, but undeniably life affirming. It is a portrait of a culturally significant belief in the fact that adults can always hang onto what The Muppets represented: fun, laughs, camaraderie, sentimentality, irreverence, warmth, sweetness, silliness and above all else, a dedication to creativity and art. When Henson and his crew wanted to take their Muppets outside of the television world—which was still serving them well—the results were enchanting. *The Muppet Movie* was *The Wizard of Oz* of the 1970s.

Opening at a private screening of what will be the film-within-the-film, *The Muppet Movie* establishes itself as an already innovative creation: part meta, part coming of age, part road movie, part backstory and all heart. Little frog Robin asks his uncle Kermit "Is this how the Muppets really got started?" to which Kermit responds with "Well it's kind of the way we got started." The backstory makes logical sense: it may not be the actual way in which this assortment of characters (a troupe of

Jim Henson and his alter-ego Kermit on the set of *The Muppet Movie* (1979)

**The Muppets settle in to watch their own origin story unfold
in *The Muppet Movie* (1979)**

misfit performers and show business critters) found each other and
gravitated towards their compassionate leader Kermit, but nonetheless,
it is an endearing Oz-like plot, with each of these beloved and complex
characters finding their own personal and communal "rainbow
connection." The wonderful gags come fast and sharp during the
prologue where the Muppets settle into the screening room ready to see

themselves on the big screen (a beautiful reflection on us the audience who has since then only been used to seeing these wonderful characters on the small screen) is a great example of Jerry Juhl's swift and versatile writing. Fozzie expresses his nervousness saying, "If I'm not funny I couldn't live with myself" to which Bunsen Honeydew replies "Well then you'll have to move into a new apartment." Animal screams his number one love "Woman! Woman!" after bassist Floyd Pepper expresses his devotion to girlfriend and fellow band mate guitarist Janice by telling her that "Nothin's too good for my woman!" Joined by Muppet regulars such as Lew Zealand, Marvin Suggs, Crazy Harry, Link Hogthrob and many more, the Swedish Chef rolls film and we enter the world of *The Muppet Movie*.

Opening amidst clouds that gently glide across a heavenly sky and then descending down into the swamplands of America, the film harkens back to the Hollywood fantasy films of the 1940s and 1950s where anything was possible. This is where we find a whimsical and sweet frog strumming his banjo, singing "The Rainbow Connection": a moving and poignant song about fulfilling dreams, written by master musical craftsmen Paul Williams and Kenny Ascher. "The Rainbow Connection" sits at the heart of the movie and its message. The song is both beautiful and uplifting but also melancholy and maudlin in its insight into endless longing and the dream for something more. It is a descendent of "Somewhere Over the Rainbow," and the opening lyric of "Why are there so many songs about rainbows..." is a verification of this. What Kermit is both lamenting and hoping for is his own personal Oz, and in doing so he can find both his place in the world as someone who can "make millions of people happy" and his own personal connection to his craft, his purpose and the universe at hand. This is something that he will discover and claim with the help of fellow "rainbow connection" chasing Muppets that he meets on his journey.

Even when the first few strings of Kermit's banjo are plucked, "The Rainbow Connection" hits the heartstrings and enlightens the audience, sending us into a dreamlike whimsy but also an unexplainable melancholy. This is what the Muppets do: they make us laugh and entertain us with their zany antics, but at the same time they melt our hearts with their tremendous tenderness and warmth. Sam the Eagle asks Kermit if the film has any social merits, and it most certainly does. The Muppets are magical creations. They are the epitome of the human condition at its most frenzied and engaging, and the elegant sweetness that permeates the film is awe inspiring. After all, the magic is expressed in the opening number itself as Kermit cries out, "all of us under its spell..."

Dom DeLuise (the first of many star cameos) is a catalyst driver: he's a Hollywood agent who introduces Kermit to the idea of becoming a star, showing him that auditions for frogs wishing to become rich and famous are happening in Los Angeles. Jerry Juhl's writing is delicately handled, and here he has given a platform for Williams/Ascher and Kermit the frog to perform one of the most tender and moving songs in the history of the movie musical. Once the number does its job, he moves straight into comedy. Juhl not only delivers the goods with the comic elements of the film—which are all fantastically bright and always hit the right spot—but he fuels the film with a finely tuned balance of the sentimental and a powerful magic.

Fozzie in his "natural habitat" in *The Muppet Movie* (1979)

Preparing "The Rainbow Connection" *for The Muppet Movie* **(1979)**

The Muppet Movie is a perfect balancing act. When Kermit understands that he can "make millions of people happy" by leaving his swamp and heading out to Hollywood, the heart of the film begins to beat as steady as Animal's drum, and the idea of "following dreams" comes into play just like the Garland and Rooney films from Arthur Freed and (of course) *The Wizard of Oz* itself. But *The Muppet Movie* is very much a creature of the 1970s, and therefore a cynical edge is necessary. There are jokes that are self-depreciating, critical and cynical, but these never overshadow the overwhelming warmth and love of the film as a whole.

The cameos that pepper the film (such as Madeline Kahn, James Coburn, Steve Martin, Carol Kane, Kojak and so forth) act as an extension to what *The Muppet Show* did: it provided a platform for artists to throw themselves into crafts in areas they were not normally associated. For example, in one episode ballet dancer Rudolph Nureyev gets to cohort in a steam room with Miss Piggy playing very broad and hilarious comedy, while Mark Hamill—who audiences only ever knew as Luke Skywalker in *Star Wars*—got to showcase his tap dancing talents. In *The Muppet Movie*, the cameos serve gags alone. This film is about the frog, the pig, the bear, the dog and the rest of the gang, the humans are there in service of the furry and felt covered puppet superstars. And superstars these characters most certainly are.

They are also facets of the human fabric and an expression of the human psyche: Miss Piggy is the superego, Animal is the id and Kermit the long suffering ego. Each Muppet reflects an aspect of the human condition and embodying the essence of a kind of person we all know— Rowlf the dog is the musical genius who just "gets by," Janice is the forever cool Valley girl who lives for rock'n'roll, Scooter is desperate to feel like he is part of something and so forth. They all make up a self-made family devoted to each other and, but not without their own distinct insecurities, flaws and dramas. At the heart of the Muppets is a definite suggestion of solidarity and a dedication to and the ability to dream.

The El Sleazo Café is a great sequence and a wonderful play on the Western, which will later resurface in the exciting climax. The film transitions from genre to genre: it soon hits the dusty highway and becomes a road movie, all the while loaded with a sophisticated and very dry, adult sense of humour. Composer Paul Williams lends his talents as the piano player at the El Sleazo as he plays against the frazzled Fozzie, whose inability to entertain an audience epitomizes his failed comedian persona: a loveable mess of a bear who wears his heart on his sleeve but just can't manage the cynics. But quick wits is what this bear is blessed with, and when he suggests that "The drinks are on the house," the drunkards literally get up onto the roof of the El Sleazo, while "Maybe you should try Hare Krishna" acts as the film's running gag. Kermit saves Fozzie from the angry audience but only for a split second as they are aggressively thrown off stage, a finely stitched commentary of the throwaway nature of show business and the cruelty of the industry.

Charles Durning is magnificent as the villain of the piece Doc Hopper, entirely devoted to money and success. The parallels to *The Wizard of Oz*—collecting an assortment of misfits and heading over to "see the Wizard" (in this case, to see Orson Welles to get a movie deal)— are also continued through to Durning's answer to Margaret Hamilton's Wicked Witch of the West, and Durning plays up the grotesque oversized Texan villain with sinister glee.

Mel Brooks and Miss Piggy behind the scenes on *The Muppet Movie* (1979)

Composer Paul Williams in his cameo role in *The Muppet Movie* (1979)

Playing Durning's wiry assistant Max is Austin Pendleton, who recalls his time on *The Muppet Movie*:

> Oh I loved the TV show, I thought Jim and the others were just great and the work was just terrific. But that was it, that's all I knew of the Muppets, of course the film hadn't been in talks then. I didn't know about the movie until they offered it to me. I think I may have heard of it in passing, but I didn't really know about it until they offered it to me. The director Jim Frawley offered me the role without having to audition. Which was very nice. That doesn't happen all the time, it's happened to me in some films later but not at that point. Jim Frawley was very exciting and very excitable. He had a whole different temperament and rhythm than the Muppet people; he was very hyperactive and broadly energetic and the Muppet people had a very calm rhythm, Jim Henson and Frank Oz and their team had a very quiet strength whereas Frawley had a temperament that was very prevailing of the time. You know the late 1970s was a very different time in Hollywood to previous years, there was a huge emphasis on high energy and high energetic directors and Henson and company were not that at all. So the balance between them was actually rather wonderful. I am not too sure if Jim Frawley learned anything about the craft of puppetry or the artistry of what Henson and his people did, and this was because I wasn't around for all that, I was namely bought on set when necessary. However, Jim Frawley had been engaged with the project for a long time before it started to shoot, so I am certain he would have had to have had meetings with the Henson group before they set out to make the film. The Muppet folk were just lovely. They were very gentle and had a healthy relationship with one another where there was a lot of respect and a lot of support given. I was just in awe of their work and how they worked together. I kept in touch with Frank Oz for years after and whenever he is in New York we would meet up. Jim Henson was an

extraordinarily magnetic man, he was just the quintessential "gentle Ben," but he was also very firm. He had a great ease about it and that pervaded the whole set. As far as I could tell the relationship between Henson and Oz, both professionally and personally, was completely harmonious, however I never really got to see them talk through scenes or what they were going to be doing or blocking the puppetry and what not, they were just there and they would in fact have all their work ready and done, so when I went into the shoot it was all smooth running. I knew Charles Durning before I did *The Muppet Movie*. I was in the original company of the musical *Fiddler on the Roof*, and he was in that on the road, but when we were on the road on the pre-Broadway route his part was cut. He had the role of a Catholic priest and that role was completely cut by the time the musical got to Broadway. That was in 1964, so that was many years before we made *The Muppet Movie*. So we had rehearsed *Fiddler on the Roof* in New York on the road for quite a while and then we took the show to Detroit and then to DC and then Charlie's part was cut maybe two thirds in the way of the run in Detroit and by the time we hit Broadway he was out, but we got to know each other very well while we worked in that. And then I was in another movie with him before *The Muppet Movie* and that was *The Front Page*. By the time we got to do *The Muppet Movie*, I was so happy that we had so much to do together, that was great! I was playing his chauffer of course and so I was in the front seat of the car and he was in back and we would go over lines and do a lot of takes. We would sit around takes of course so we got to talk and talk and caught up a lot. When I wrapped up on *The Muppet Movie*, when my scenes were all done, I was at the airport waiting for my place to take me from Los Angeles back to New York and I called up Charlie and I asked "What are you gonna do next?" and he said "I'm gonna do the new film with Alan Pakula" and he told me that there might be a part in that for me. And he told me to look into that. That movie was *Starting Over*, written by Richard Brooks and starring Burt Reynolds. So when I went to New York, I made another call to Charlie and got an audition for it and I had to read for Pakula three times because originally I wasn't the kind of guy he envisioned for that role, but gradually he liked me and I got the part. So I owe that job to Charlie and *The Muppet Movie*. When they first offered me the part, I didn't accept it. I just thought it wasn't too much of a developed role. And then finally Jim Frawley, who I didn't know at the time, called me and he went on to convince me to do it. I just said, "Oh yes, I know, I know, but it really is just the chauffer to the villain..." You see, I had a very difficult season at that time in theatre in New York, so I wanted a fleshed out good role and also, at the same time, I was being offered a part, a small part, in *All That Jazz*, the Bob Fosse film. I thought that would be fun because it was going to be shot in New York where I lived and also it was a chance to work with Bob Fosse. But then I got yet another phone call from Jim Frawley and he said "Look, I have an idea as to give this guy more depth and more of a personality. How about this character, who throughout the movie is a yes-man to the villain, finally changes by the end of the movie. He grows into his own person and stands up to the bad guy? He turns against his employer!" And then I thought that that was interesting and I decided to take the role and by the time I got to Los Angeles the character had been rewritten and became that guy who goes through the transformation. The puppeteers had it all worked out by the time I got there. There was one all night shoot on the lot, CBS in the valley and we began at eleven o'clock at night and I would drive us, Charlie and I, around on the set for hours and we would talk about our lives. I remember that night very fondly. I remember Carol Kane being on set. I already knew a lot of the actors who had cameos in the film. I mean Madeline Kahn was someone I knew, I had worked with her in a previous movie which was *What's Up Doc?* And there was Orson Welles who I did *Catch*

22 with. I don't remember meeting anyone new, I had known everyone who came in and out to do their bit. When you make a film with these kind of cameos people come and go. I spent most of the shoot with Charlie. Unless everyone is in the same scene and in most of the movie together you never get that sense of family, it was mainly just me and Charlie. The day that Mel Brooks came on set, oh my God, that was just great. He was hilarious. And I knew Mel because I had been in a play with Ann Bancroft a few years ago, so once again it was another person that I knew! And he made up all that stuff on the spot! That was all him. The Paul Williams songs were just beautiful. And Paul is a great guy. Everyone on the film was very nice to be around. The film didn't feel like a road movie to me. I mean I definitely did a lot of driving in the film, but I never felt like I was in a road movie because we didn't go to too many locations. You know in some road movies you go all across America, but it wasn't like that in The Muppet Movie, I don't think that we shot anywhere that we couldn't get back to where we staying at. It was all around the same vicinity. The Los Angeles area. I was signed on for quite a while. I went out there in August and was through by October. And at one point there were a couple of weeks off where I went back to New York. I didn't go to the premiere, but I was aware that it was a very big deal. But when it did come out I had to go back and loop a lot of my work. Because I think Jim Frawley had encouraged Charlie to be "too much" in the part, so he wanted to go back and re-record all of his parts and that meant I had to do mine all again as well. So we spent a few weeks in the recording studio looping my own voice. With Charlie they matched the rhythm of the delivery but they toned him right down. Jim had told Charlie to be over the top, but then regretted that when he saw it in context of the whole film. I didn't see that while we were shooting, but in retrospect Jim thought the tone was too much and they wanted to tone it all down. So I went back in and looped my part. I really love the scene where I get to play against the Muppets one on one, the scene were I'm dressed as a police man. They were so great to work with because they are ridiculously expressive. There is nothing too difficult when performing with them as they're created and maneuvered so wonderfully and with lots of thought and care, that it's easy. And it's also lovely that you get to play off these characters as a supportive player, it's all about them not us human cast members, and that was nice. The sentiment of the movie resonated later when I saw the film in full context. I didn't do anything out of the way in terms of characterisation. I just imagined myself in the different circumstances for the sake of the scene. Of course the shoot was completely out of order so I had to remember that I shouldn't play the transition within that, instead I was working on that particular scene we were shooting, never thinking ahead with the plot. I did four movies with Madeline Kahn. So I got to know her very well throughout those years. I haven't seen the film since it came out and at that time I saw it three or four times. I loved it. Also, I haven't seen any of the recent Muppet movies.

"Moving Right Along" is another beautiful song that encompasses the heart of the road movie aspects of *The Muppet Movie*, launching Kermit and Fozzie off across the country in a bouncing old fashioned two-hander that the Muppets celebrate so often. The Muppets come from a world of pure entertainment: the song and dance mentality, the remains of the vaudevillian era, the minstrels and comics that parade around with skittish sketches and so forth, and as much as James Frawley pieces these elements together to serve a steady and robust film, the irreverence and kookiness still hits home. And this is a terrific counter to the sturdy narrative as well as the magical visuals of the film, launching *The Muppet Show* firmly into the domain of the cinematic.

One of the strongest aspects of the film is Miss Piggy, a bona fide superstar, an icon of entertainment, a feminist role model, a style and fashion goddess and a fragile, vulnerable critter. She captures everything show business wants to hide from us: that glamour and beauty, assertiveness and confidence, defiance and elegance are all there to mask a crippling insecurity and overwhelming frailty. To present this through a "lady pig" who likes fancy gowns as well as being a master of karate is perfect. The Muppets are a complicated bunch, and characters such as Miss Piggy make this clear if you look beyond the surface. Much like the Muppets themselves, these puppets that come to life at the literal hands of artists such as Dave Goelz, Kathryn Mullen, and Richard Hunt are more than meets the eye. This is what *The Muppet Movie* is about.

The iconic Kermit and Miss Piggy in *The Muppet Movie* (1979)

Employing the structure of the road movie, under a blanket of stars our beloved Muppets question their place in the universe and the role of their dreams in one of the most romantic and emotionally crushing sequences in the film. The scene also brings forth a community that has newly taken form—a community of artists who truly love each other, and are all in pursuit of a common goal. There is something so magical about this and also mystically grounding. Gonzo sings "there's not a word yet for old friends who've just met," but that word surely is "Muppet"! When Gonzo continues singing "close to my soul and yet so far away..." we understand that dreams are just like that; they hold us together and are "the invisible strings" that Gonzo mentions. The gentle beauty of

**Jim Henson and Kathryn Mullen prepping Kermit on location
for *The Muppet Movie* (1979)**

"I'm Going to Go Back There Someday" sums up everything meaningful and precious about the Muppets, and when Gonzo explains that "I've never been there, but I know the way…" the sense of longing is at its most devastating. On a purely emotional level, when Piggy sings out a gentle harmony, soon followed by Fozzie accompanied by Rowlf on the mournful harmonica it is the stuff of magic—just try to hold back the tears!

This is what the Muppets do: they capture vulnerability, tenderness, honesty, compassion, insecurity, loneliness and togetherness, all while in service to story, entertainment and a thematic focus on unity. Gonzo continues: "We can hold on to love with invisible strings," a condensation of the magic that binds these dysfunctional characters together and paints a very real notion of family. If the Muppets are all facets of the human condition, then they are also a combined effort in focused awareness. If Kermit is the eternal ego, than he is a highly evolved intelligent and passionate frog who follows his dream taking with him a team of misfits who all embody everything else that makes up the fabric of what it means to be human (and what it means to be a Muppet).

When it takes a frog, a pig, a bear, a dog, a chicken and whatever Gonzo is to help us realize who we are as people—as a community and as lovers and dreamers—then there is something truly poignant about the 1970s movie musical. With all their craziness, sweetness and dedication to entertain, the Muppets are the most life affirming creations of the decade. In contrast to this, Doc Hopper is the enterprise man—the epitome of greed and corruption set up as a clear adversary to Kermit and his gang who wish to make millions of people happy by singing and dancing. Kermit is the movie's anchor and the level-headed, reasonable misfit among his fellow misfits. When he is perplexed by a situation you know it has to be dire.

The film is shot in beautiful sparkling colors, and when Kermit and Fozzie sing on the road we are set on a beautiful journey both thematically and visually. The idea of taking the Muppets beyond television, performing on location, greatly appealed to Jim Henson, Frank Oz and their company. Audiences were thrilled to see Kermit ride a bicycle and he and Fozzie dancing on a stage (as they should be), and Paul Williams's songs are once again perfection. Possibly Williams's best writing exists in this film (and that is saying something, especially when his work in *Phantom of the Paradise*, *A Star Is Born* and *Bugsy Malone* were so brilliant). For fans of the Muppets, Sesame Street's Big Bird gets a cameo also, and he will eventually get his own film in *Follow That Bird* (1985) which of course won't be the only Muppet follow up feature length. The first two Muppet sequels are nearly just as magical as the first outing: *The Great Muppet Caper* (1981) took the Muppets to England and threw them into a crime thriller/jewel robbery flick that boasted more great songs and gave Muppets such as Beauregard to do and then *The Muppets Take Manhattan* (1984) which was even better gave the Muppets New York City as their playground and the world of the Broadway musical to toy with. In this film Rizzo the Rat features prominently as well as a spectacular marriage sequence for Kermit and Piggy to end the film.

Human co-stars populated the film, but were always in service of the Muppets. In The Muppet Movie, Austin Pendleton is terrific as one such human, and the great wit and comic back and forth between him and Charles Durning is wonderful. As great as they are, the other cameos such as Bob Hope, Cloris Leechman and Orson Welles himself are terrific.

Costumer Sharon Day remembers working on the film:

> I really love working behind the camera. I'm very into furthering my union, working for the members and helping everyone to achieve their goals...now, after some thirty odd years of show business. First off, when The Muppets arrived, the puppets came fully loaded with their own entire...their needs were met by their own crew that had done the TV show, so they had no input at all (the American crew), when it came to their wardrobe. The puppeteering was done by the characters themselves. The show had already become a huge success here in America. The Muppets were on very Friday or Thursday night. They had huge stars as guests, and everyone was just so excited. When I had found out that I had gotten, that they were asking me to come on the show, to help do the human characters, I was just thrilled. I had not worked with Gwen Capetanos prior to that. She was someone, who was highly recommended and brought in by the director, Jim Frawley. Gwen met me for the first time on the show, when the person who was going to supervise the costume in the department, brought me in. We all got along just great. The whole idea of working on the Muppet movie, was just a dream come true. Gwen knew what she was going to do for all the characters. She created that big frock costume for Charles. So, she went to one of the costume shops, here in L.A, that specializes in big, walk around costumes. Obviously, she had designed the frock, with the director and Jim Henson's best wishes. They okayed it. They loved it. She went ahead and had it made. You know, it was hilarious. I have a story about Frank Oz that I will tell you. Then I will go on to talk about Jim Frawley and Henson. Frank and I were getting to know one another, one day, when we were doing the bar scene. There is that big and beautiful park, on the studio lot, where we dressed the extras and had that beautiful music man, kind of period look to it. I think

actually, it is a little more modern than not, because I think that was the set for *Leave It to Beaver*, that neighbourhood. We were sitting around on the lawn and we were talking. I had done a lot of work with Gwen. We had done all those characters. There was Bob Hope, the ice cream man, the guy with the balloons, Richard Pryor—he was still healthy and fun to have him that day. There were all those wonderful characters. Taking a long time to set up the shots, especially working with the puppeteers, because they work with little screens, little cameras and screens, and then they are being pushed around on little dollies, where they are laying down, doing their puppetry up in the air, and then watching through the camera to make sure they are not in the shot. It is very interesting. Frank Oz and I are talking and I asked him, "So, what is your life like now—a show that is so popular? You live in London." He said he has a flat in New York. And I said "Really, because I had lived in New York for a few years, prior to that time. I said "Where?" In New York, all New Yorkers want to know where people live. It's usually what New Yorkers care about. We were over on the west side, and I said, I use to live over there too. Oh, really? Where? 86th Street and West End Avenue. I used to live across the street from Miles Davis. Frank would ask "Do you know Jimmy, the door man?" And I said, "Yeah." We figured that out when I moved out of my apartment, with my painter roommate, he moved in. The painters would cut the light out of that window, because it was on Riverside Drive. The sun would catch the light in the apartment with paint. So, when we moved out to come back to L.A, Frank Oz and Miss Piggy were were around. I was so thrilled to know that Miss Piggy was sleeping in my bedroom! Just so coincidental. Working with Jim Henson, he was such a kind, fun loving, gentle person. He was never without the most, generous, patient, and was always thinking of something that was quirky and funny, for them to do in their shots. Of course, Jim Frawley and Jim Henson worked incredibly well together. At the end of the shoot, Amy Van Gilder, the person who created the actual puppets, created a Muppet of Jim Frawley. Oh yeah, it was wonderful. I think he even started to cry when she gave it to him. He was so touched. They were quite a tribe. They all lived together, in a beautiful old house up in the Hollywood Hills. Occasionally, when there was time off, they would have some gathering for the rest of the crew to come over. They were always very friendly. A lot of camaraderie. They were very talented. They were always making music, singing, and being a happy group. I had not expected such a gift in my life. As a matter of fact, Amy did a sketch, a little cartoon of me, because at that time, I was always wearing white. I wore white overalls, white dance shoes, white t-shirts. I was joking around saying, I was a born again virgin, which is a little risqué. She did a drawing. I have it somewhere, in a box in the garage. I should get it out and put it on Facebook. She had created this cartoon of me. It was real cute. Curly hair…younger, much younger. Calista Hendrikson was always coming up with something. They were always in their work shop doing things. They were either repairing things or coming up with something new. They also had an art director named Leigh Malone. Leigh was from the show. She was a very talented person, who worked with the art director, production designer from America in building the set, to accommodate the puppeteers, because the sets always had to have the right dimensions, in order for the puppeteers to fit and move freely a lot, so that the camera caught the action. It was scary. These people really created a remarkable environment. It was just so much fun to go on the road, and to be out there in the different locations, and one or two shots we used helicopters and cranes and when the big pie came falling out of the sky onto the car. Working with the actors, I would get all the actors ready, and then take care of them on the set. I think their might have been one or two other people that came in from time to time when we had big scenes. When we were in the

670

night club, the El Sleezo was something. That was lots of fun. There were some moments that were quite memorable for me. I had the privilege of waiting for Cloris Leachman's dress to arrive. It was late getting to me. The designer had made three identical dresses. And the dressmaker was not on the studio lot. He was down in the Wilshire district. He had made that beautiful, colour, Shamoo's dress that was draped like a dress made in the 1930s. Everything was just perfect, but the dress wasn't quite ready. So she decided that she would wait in her dressing room, in her pantyhose, nothing else and paint her nails. She wanted me to wait with her. I was a little shy. This was my first feature film. I was quite taken aback by the attention she required from me. So, you know, she was very entertaining. She is a very nice lady. She's hilarious. But she didn't want to get sweaty, she wanted to just, you know, relax, paint her nails, and as soon as the dress was ready, flip it on, have Ben and I check her makeup, and go onto the set. That's what she wanted, so that is what she got. It was just a first for me. That was one thing, and I don't know, I had a scary thing happen to me. The guy who played Lew Lorde—Orson Welles. I had gone to film school in New York, so Orson Welles. Any film student, any film enthusiast is impressed, especially in your youth, by the name Orson Welles, and some wonderful things he brought to the cinema. I mean even the camera work on *The Magnificent Ambersons* was just amazing! Especially when you are studying his work. So, I find out that Orson Welles is going to be in the movie. I am really excited. Orson Welles had gotten so humongous, that he would arrive dressed and ready and to work. He did not have fittings and it would have been difficult to fit him. So, he arrived on the set, and the first thing that we had realised was that the door to his dressing room was too narrow. So they had to take the door off. Next thing was, he needed a ramp. He wasn't going to be able to go up the steps, because he used two canes to move. They got all that ready, and then he was in his dressing room and they called for lunch. I, being an enthusiastic film student, couldn't wait to get over to his dressing room, tap on his door, and ask if there was anything I could do for him, because, you know, while I sat at his feet. I get to his door. They have arranged something for his privacy, and in his dressing room, he has his back to the door. I tap, and he turns around and he reveals a dinner plate, filled with jelly donuts, piled high, about five donuts high with powdered sugar on top. His clothing was protected by a big bath towel that had been put around his neck and tied in a knot, in the back of his neck. So he turns around and he looks at me, and I have disturbed him in an embarrassing moment. And he looks at me with a growl, and wants to know what I want. I said "Mr. Welles, I'm from the wardrobe department. Is there anything that you need prepared, anything I can do for you?" He says, "No. Now leave me alone. If I need anything, I will let you know." So, I back out. I'm stunned, and a little embarrassed. Orson Welles put me in my place. He was something, but wait, there's more. So now, in the scene when the Muppets arrive, and they go to Miss Stacey's reception, and she's trying to keep them out, then she has to let them in and the doors open, and once again, this set is filled, so the desk that he is in, is a big mighty desk. It is humungous. There are these little creatures, coming in and looking up as if he is a skyscraper. We are in there, all the muppeteers are down in like a little canyon, leading up to the desk. The Muppeteers are all on their platforms with their cameras, and their rod puppets, all up there perfect, so they don't show in the scene where bounce walking in, you know, their little muppet walk, and he's looking down at them, and the camera man stops, and he says "Sharon, come here for a minute." He makes me look in the camera lens, at Orson Welles. Now, Orson Welles is so huge that the collar on his shirt is sticking out about four inches from his neck. It looks terrible, because in order to cover his tummy, you know what I mean. We didn't tailor this shirt. He arrived ready for work. We weren't allowed to do anything as you know. The camera man says "Can you fix it?" I go, "What do you mean?," he says "Can you go over there and tuck it in, so that it looks like it fits." "Yeah, I guess I can." So now, you can imagine where the camera is. There is over beyond the puppeteers, from the canyon, where I have to traverse in order to get to the other side of the desk, to Orson Welles left side, so that I can reach over and somehow make his shirt look nice…look crisp. Like it fits. Okay, so the set photographer is watching this, and he sees Orson Welles looking like a very mad bear. His eyebrows were all scrunched up, and his lips are all bent out of shape, and I very gingerly, am making myself stretch across his desk, and like a very prissy lady with a tea cup, and my pinkie fingers sticking out. I am very gingerly, trying to make him look presentable, without telling him that he looks bad. It was the same day…I also have that photograph somewhere, of him looking like a mad bear, me stretching across the desk with my pinkie fingers. I really don't remember anymore costume malfunctions. I do remember that the suits for Charles Durning, I think we had three or four suits, I think there was a time his suit got wet. I can't remember exactly. I had to keep his stuff clean. You know, he was not a small man either. I have to say, he was a delightful person to work with. He was such a down, home wonderful guy. Nothing strange or weird. He was a true trooper. Yes, he really was. I worked on the same lot as him, when he did a show here called *Evening Shade*, and he created such an incredible character on that. He was wonderful. I am so sorry not to have him around anymore. Steve Martin was fun to be with, he really was. It's fun because, here's something. He is a very nice person, and I had double dated with a friend of his, that I was going out with, and I am telling you this because these are things that have really happened in my life. So this is true. Ben Stein and I eventually got married. We were married for ten years. When Ben did, Planes, Trains and Automobiles, Steve was the other guy, along with John Candy in the movie. Ben did a lot of work with John. We travelled with him from time to time, and if I was lucky enough to go with him and have some fun, on one of my husband's films, of course I went. Steve Martin obviously knew who Ben was, and he remembered me. He was very kind and I just wanted to say, he is a wonderful, big movie star, and he is very gifted and he is also a very nice guy. Oh, at the time Steve was not dating Bernadette Peters. He was dating Bernadette during *Pennies from Heaven*. She had such a beautiful body. You see some of these people lit up, and made up and they are so extraordinary looking. Many of the women are extremely special. I mean, she has skin like alabaster. So when they light her, she just looks magical. The light bounces off her. That beautiful, light red hair. Everything about her is just fragile. The ladies on our show were very special. Well. I remember when it opened. I remember shooting that. That was in the backlot of CBS Studios Centre, where we shot a lot of the film. The body of water was the lagoon from *Gilligan's Island*. So we used that body of water. That whole set had already been built, and was still there. The puppeteers were in wet suits. He was playing his banjo, when he is singing about rainbows. Then Dom DeLuise comes along, his Hollywood agent. So the whole atmosphere of what they created, was like a dream come true for any American frog. The whole idea of believing in something. I think the wholesomeness and also the use of some really vaudevillian, very predictable jokes. It was all just so wonderful. You know, the whole thing about The Muppets. Every week, opening up to a full audience in American television, and then probably the whole English speaking universe—Australia, London. I mean, they hit it big. It was always so wholesome and yet clever. It gave people the opportunity to bring those jokes out again. And they are funny. There is nothing mean spirited about what they did. I think it rejuvenated the audience. Gave the audience more hope. It was so wonderful that these young actors used their celebrity to get the funding to bring it back. I would love for

them to come back and do more, and even create some more
characters. I remember the last scene. They brought in a
bunch of Muppets that had not been used a lot or yet. They
had been creating more muppets for some other projects,
and also, during that period, they were working very closely
with an illustrator named Brian Froud. Brian Froud had
created a book of fairies. I remember I went to New York
after the shoot, and I went to their workshop. They were
building characters from Brian Froud's book, for *The Dark
Crystal*. Those Muppets...the magic of using materials, to
create the environment and the sets, and the clothing. Jim
Henson was a mastermind of something that opened up all
of us in this world. We were all very lucky to be alive in that
generation. It's like the tails of the roundtable, and the
characters during that period. *The Muppet Movie* gave me a
lot of courage. Not the ability, but the realisation that I was
there, I was in the room. This is part of my life. I have gone
on to do a few things. I created a little character. I had a very
successful, doggy website, called RagDog.com Very popular
in Australia and London. My doggy clothes were used for
the biggest travel agency in London...borrowed photographs
of my doggies dressed in my creations. I really believe that I
owe all of that part of my ingenuity, my creativity to The
Muppet Movie. To being part of that. To being chosen to
participate. Very lucky, I am a very lucky woman. When you
work with people like the Muppeteers. Jim Henson and
company, and you see what is possible. It really brings that
home. That if you have an idea, if you have a creative spot,
never ever think that you cannot accomplice something. You
can. We had lots of fun. We really did. Everybody on the
show. Chris Greenbury, the editor, you know, he has passed
away. Chris Greenbury went on to do so many, wonderful,
funny movies. He was a great comedic editor. He just knew
when to cut. And isn't it great that Paul Williams is back in
the saddle? I mean, that he was part of the winning team.

There was a little movie made about him, going around recently. He is still alive and he is still contributing.

Dr. Teeth and the Electric Mayhem Band are the fevered rock'n'roll group that represent the 1970s. Outside of the Broadway leanings the other Muppets tend to favour, the Electric Mayhem Band headed by the Elton John inspired Dr. Teeth are a celebration of rock in all its form up to that point: blues roots, jazz infused, psychedelic and glam. They also help the meta elements in the film where they catch up on the story by "reading the screenplay." Scooter is the road manager here in the film, later he would infamously become the Muppet theatre gopher because his uncle owns the building, so therefore going back to what Kermit tells Robin, this is a variant of the truth and this makes the film even more of a fairy tale than it already is. The band are made up of spaced out Zoot on saxophone, valley girl beauty Janice on guitar, raspy voiced frizzy-faced Floyd Pepper on bass, band leader Dr. Teeth on keys, and feisty, frenzied drummer Animal—all of them a special part of a fabric that exists within the already wild and energetic community of Muppets. The Electric Mayhem's "Can You Picture That?" is an ecstatic expression of hedonistic joy and the hippie-influenced disinterest in wealth. They also celebrate the romance of magic as Floyd and Janice sing to us directly: "Fact is there's nothing out there you can't do, even Santa Claus believes in you." Santa Claus and the Muppets share the same magic: they both exist in our imaginations and both inspire the desire and the necessity to dream.

The Muppets have dreams to pursue, however they also understand their limitations and the necessity of the dreary "day job." For example, Gonzo the great has a job as a plumber with Camilla his beloved chicken companion by his side. The duo is inseparable and as much as Gonzo is the resident weirdo, he is one with the most love, and the Muppet who is most in tune with a place outside of the norm where he belongs. For Gonzo, it is beyond human interaction, such as with the oppressive Milton Berle (the film's human menace). In fact, in *The Muppet Movie* a lot of the human cast are mean, obnoxious or uptight—the Muppets have their flaws, but they get through things together and are fundamentally good, whereas Steve Martin is hilarious but a completely jaded waiter, Cloris Leechman is also terrific but she is a stuffy secretary to the intimidating

Orson Welles and Berle's abusive nature towards Sweetums who is his personal "jack" that lifts up cars at his used car lot is plain nasty. Sweetums wishes to join the others, and throughout the film is seen following the others until he finally catches up to them crashing through the screen at the showing of the film. Sweetums drives the meta aspect of the film home, while Animal yells at us to "Go home! Go home!"

The country fair in small town America—set in a little Midwestern haven called Bogen County—is a knockout moment in the film and is where our star pig is introduced. When she locks eyes with Kermit it's a thing of magic: hilarious and sweet, a tricky combination in any film. The montage of Piggy and Kermit's blossoming relationship references many filmic romance tropes—a Euro-style romance, a romantic period piece, a film noir, and finally a wedding which will come to stunning fulfillment in *The Muppets Take Manhattan*. Back in reality however, Piggy and Kermit have a tumultuous relationship, loaded with ups and downs that will go on for decades to come. Although the relationship is rocky, it is also poignant and delicate. In a lovely cameo, famed ventriloquist Edgar Bergen (to which the film is dedicated) and his dummy Charlie McCarthy act as judges of the Miss Bogen County Beauty Pageant, while a version of "The Rainbow Connection" plays over their brief moment on film. Bergen had the dream, chased the rainbow and made millions of people happy, now it was the Muppets' turn to do the same. But what the Muppets have is so much more complex and layered than what the legendary Bergen could do with his dummies. Piggy's insecurities, Gonzo's displacement, Camilla's earthiness, Fozzie's desperation and so forth are part of the diversity of the Muppet's cultural backgrounds and methods of expression. The collection of a troupe—all of them with their personal dreams, personal quests and personal quips—existing outside of the influence of a visible human (something Edgar Bergen always was) is unique and once again, magical. When Gonzo ascends up into the sky with the balloons, the main theme of "I'm Going to Go Back There Someday" can be heard, and a different perspective—a perspective outside of social responsibility—is explored. This moment refers to the freedoms of the artist and the uplifting whimsy of the free thinker, the creative ascending from the grounded. Doc Hopper fires a gun and blasts Gonzo's balloons sending him crashing back down to earth: later, when

Gonzo sings about the "place he wants to go back to," it's all about that place away from restraints and meanies like Doc Hopper.

Piggy and Kermit's romantic dinner is hilarious and sweet, and there is a self-awareness of the restraints of puppets (such as the frog and pig stating, "we will need straws" in order to drink their champagne). Rowlf's introduction occurs just seconds after the romantic dinner for two and the way he is presented is great with his paws tickling the ivories. Here is the consummate canine musician and the greatest friendly ear known to a frog: "I finish work, I go home, have a couple of beers, take myself for a walk and go to bed" states Rowlf as he heads into the terrific number "I Hope That Something Better Comes Along" with Kermit. Both of these critters sing this clever song devoted to the blues, howling and croaking their way through men's woes about women trouble with fantastic references to dogs and frogs complete with more animalistic and pop cultural references at hand, with Kermit singing: "She made a monkey out of ole King Kong." Rowlf joins the gang right after this therapeutic musical stop over while Piggy's feminine and tough talents come to the foreground when Mel Brooks turns up as a maniacal menace tapping into Nazi gags that he's so obsessed with. When Piggy gets a genuine call from her agent (a great moment here where her sweet and demure voice turns into a hardened theatrical "Yeah Morty, whattya got?") she races off, leaving Kermit alone. Here is the snappish selfishness that the Muppets are prone to and not alien from—remember, the Muppets are complicated and multi-dimensional, they can be self-centred, self-involved and completely oblivious to their fellow Muppet's feelings and this is what makes them far more on par with the human race.

But what the Muppets do is also reflect the goodness and the wealth of tenderness that the human race is capable of. In a fond reference to Jor-El's words of wisdom to his only son Kal-El who soon will be known to the world as Superman: "They can be a good people Kal-El, they only lack the light to show them the way." The Muppets *themselves* are a magical place, much like Krypton or Smallville or Metropolis. When Piggy's dreams fail, she returns to the group: hitchhiking on a lonely freeway; the shattered dreams of the ingénue—opportunistic and also fragile—are left out on in the metaphoric storm, ready to be part of a group that will give her a much needed home and sense of belonging.

Like Superman, who as Clark Kent surrounds himself with alienated and understanding people such as Perry White, Jimmy Olsen and his beloved Lois Lane, Piggy too must share the limelight (as much as she might not like to) with fellow Muppets in order to find her place in the universe. When the car breaks down and they get stuck out in the desert here is the place of existential discovery and reflection for all of them. Kermit, Piggy, Fozzie, Gonzo, Camilla, Rowlf, Scooter and the Electric Mayhem Band make up the core Muppets of the piece and somehow they make their little community work. When the defeated and doubtful Kermit has his conversation with his alter-ego, he is told that "They believed in the dream," which is a shot in the arm. Kermit's faith is restored, and he is reborn. The beautiful speech Kermit gives to Doc Hopper about the importance of friendship and community sums up the entire film, and with Animal's gigantism (the most primal and least complicated Muppets finally setting the record straight and scaring off Doc Hopper and his associates) bringing the conflict to an end, the film is allowed to breathe and give our heroic Muppets their brain, courage and heart.

Although, of course, they had all of this from the get-go. The Orson Welles scene at the end of the film gives the genre tropes used throughout the film such as the showdown, the backyard musical, the road movie, and the western legitimacy, because the Muppets have finally reached Hollywood. When they set up their movie with their brightly colored sets and pieces that reflect their journey (an introspective account of what they have all experienced) it all comes crashing down. Dreams are shattered and the world of show business lets these hopefuls down. But the magic is still alive, and a rainbow shines through the soundstage, lighting up Kermit, Piggy and their friends. The dream is alive and well as the Muppets—now joined by hundreds of animals, what-nots, monsters and every single character that ever graced *The Muppet Show*—thank the lovers, the dreamers and you. The final number expresses all there is to say about wanting to be an entertainer, but it also says what *The Muppet Movie* sets out to let its audience know: that "somebody out there loves you."

With 1979 drawing to a close, there were a number of movie musicals ready to pounce at the tail end of the decade, made during the last few moments of the 1970s. Although not released until 1980, these are very much films that are products of the 1970s and therefore earn a place in this book. In 1980, diegetic musicals, high concept musicals and jukebox musicals ruled, and the 1970s in all its diversity, embracing all the grittiness and wackiness, the hyper-stylized and the maudlin, remained embedded in the very fabric of the films that sang out loud at the dawning of the age of the "me" generation and at the cusp of the popcorn junk pile. In 1980, brothers named Jake and Elroy dodged bullets and found themselves alongside some of soul and R&B's finest names, a comic strip devotee to spinach arrived on the shores of Malta which became his own personal Sweet Haven, the Village People and the Electric Light Orchestra provided the musical backdrop to two of the most bizarre highly watchable messes and some ghetto kids claimed that they could catch the moon in their hands (but with a dramatic price to pay). 1980 would become the culmination of everything the 1970s stood for and took us places from the mean streets of New York City to "a place that no body dared to go"...

1980

"I Sing the Body Electric"

Zeus's Muse, Comic Strip Sailors and the High School of Performing Arts

1979 SAW A GREAT DEAL OF MUSICAL FILMS OPENING IN MOTION PICTURE houses across the globe, but just as many were in production, preparing for a 1980 release. At the dawn of the decade that would introduce MTV and the birth of music video culture (a threat to the movie musical if ever there was one), a number of films were about to entertain, provoke, anger, discourage, annoy and sometimes baffle critics and audiences alike. Grit ruled, but so did silliness. Realism was a key ingredient, but so was a spirit of insanity and fabricated truths. Monstrosities were bought to life with a hardened street sensibility, often creatures born in an explosive mess.

The films made in the 1970s but released in 1980 were a mixed bag: some moving, gripping and beautifully performed, others chaotic and tragic, while some were just loveable nonsense. Cult fads sprouted in urban arenas, and along with these flamboyant fashions came a devotion and appreciation of the obscure and the manic. *Xanadu, Can't Stop the Music* and *The Apple* are three perfect examples of this wonderfully whacky year, while Robert Altman's *Popeye* for example remains ill conceived and shambolic (yet not without oddball charm). Angry musicals such as *Fame*, *Quadrophenia* and *Times Square* surfaced, and the idea of music as a feel good religion brought John Landis's *The Blues Brothers* to life. Meanwhile, Sissy Spacek blew everybody away with her refined and delicate portrayal of country star Loretta Lynne in *Coal Miner's Daughter*. 1980 was a place of decadence, diversity and demented dignity.

OUT HERE ON MY OWN: *Fame*

The musical does something that other genres cannot do: it marries music with human drama and together, song and score can conceal truth or expose it. It can give voice to a character's concerns or lie for them. This kind of psychodrama was bought to the fore in Michael Bennett's *A Chorus Line*. Some years after that Pulitzer Prize Winner took audiences by storm, director Alan Parker (who did wonders with the surprisingly dark *Bugsy Malone*) reimagined Bennett's gypsy group therapy session, and the results were astonishing. That film was *Fame*.

Opening with Montgomery (Paul McCrane) reciting a monologue from the play *The Dark at the Top of the Stairs*, *Fame* is instantly engaging, alluring and all too real. Sensitive, tortured gay student Montgomery presents this monologue with brutal truth, and is shattered when he fumbles his lines, and we cut to the drama teacher watching him audition. *Fame* is about truth: the self-made and self-constructed, and the illusion of honesty and the unashamed. The magic in Alan Parker's film lies within its grim realism and the gritty menace that permeates its situations, and its loneliness, isolation, desperation and quiet hope. The opening sequence is introduced with a title card that reads: "Auditions." The kinetic, precise editing by Gary Hambling is a crowning achievement: the Oscar nominated Hambling's handle on comic timing as well as the film's moments of desperation, frustration and anger come across with stealthy elegance. *Fame* is an excursion into the confusion, determination and crazed auditioning process for a public school dedicated to the arts. And these youngsters desperate to find a place feel familiar: some are talented, some aren't. Some have parents who push them; some are out there on their own. The grittiness of the film which Alan Parker captures so well is forever palpable—you can taste the dusty mess halls, feel the blood and sweat stains on the dance boards, and when you're outside of the High School of Performing Arts, the danger of the subway and Times Square is a harsh reality. Playing off this is the essence of what makes an artist (or someone posing as an artist) tick. *Fame* also reveals— and revels in—the insecurities and weaknesses of its youth. For example, the two music teachers understand that a young Chinese student can play the violin very well, but when they get him to sing, he can't. Dance students toss their limber, thin bodies around trying to impress the stoic and discipline-obsessed teachers, but they soon learn that they must also know how to act and play a musical instrument as well.

The talented cast of *Fame* (1980)

The eight central teens are Lisa (Laura Dean), Coco (Irene Cara), Hilary (Antonia Franceschi), Doris (Maureen Teefy), Ralph (Barry Miller), Bruno (Lee Curreri), Leroy (Gene Anthony Ray) and the aforementioned Montgomery. They all come to represent different facets of the human condition, just like the Muppets in *The Muppet Movie*. Lisa is a dancer who isn't very good, but doesn't want to hear the ugly truth. Coco is a triple threat and dedicated to her talent but ultimately a slave to opportunity. Like Coco, Hilary is also exceptionally gifted but haunted by a detachment from her family and uses sexuality to connect with others. Doris is a painfully shy drama student who blossoms into a seemingly well-adjusted young lady, but is oppressed by a domineering mother and her Jewish culture. Ralph is the tormented clown crying on the inside, while Bruno is the innovative quiet unassuming genius who has a problem with collaboration. Leroy is an angry accidental talent, and Montgomery is a lonely young man living in the shadow of his successful absentee actress mother. We follow these eight vulnerable young people as they navigate through the world and try to find their place within it—and their gruelling efforts are compelling. *Fame* is a punchy, tough movie and it works.

The music is fantastic: an exciting mix of rock, disco, blues, jazz and Broadway. It represents the dreams and passions of the youthful cast, but also scares away the ghosts that have haunted the halls of the High School of Performing Arts years before. We soon encounter the eight's adult oppressors/liberators: Bruno's father is endlessly encouraging, while Doris's mother is desperate to have her daughter remain the little girl she knows so well (or thinks she knows). Anne Meara is incredible as the home teacher and English teacher Mrs. Sherman, whose endless battle with Leroy is one of the film's most mesmerizing elements. Leroy's accidental audition—a thug from the streets who carries knives—is handled with such sincerity and bleak humor, that when he begins this antagonistic "dance" with the strict but fair Mrs. Sherman, it is engaging, dynamic and moving.

For these poverty stricken kids (Doris explains "We can't afford a professional children's school"), art is their outlet, and creativity their life source. They are stuck in permanent ruts –Doris refers to herself as a child, Leroy is plagued by ghetto life, etc.—but this allows them room to dream big and aim high. The film allows these characters room to develop—for example, Bruno comes to understand the importance of collaboration with Coco—but it also does something brave and innovative as it leaves characters to metaphorically die in obscurity. For example, although Lisa pops up in the finale opening the song with her beautiful dulcet tones, we have no idea what happened to her through the time she nearly kills herself to those closing moments. Doris is given a traditional story arc, while her male counterpart Ralph gets the most dramatic moments. Maureen Teefy and Barry Miller's magnificent performances in these roles are brilliant, and make us care about these fragile wannabes.

Alan Parker in New York City shooting *Fame* (1980)

The film is a phenomenal example of just how well cross cutting plots, narrative multiples and dramatic ups and downs can work. The comic elements peppered throughout the film are fun, but ultimately are in the service of an overwhelming melancholy and depressing realism. This is a film made for youngsters thinking that they can make it in the arts: the harsh realities and truths are expressed with a street roughness. But this doesn't mean the film is joyless, and there is light in the dark. For example, Doris's audition with the Streisand number "The Way We Were" is both funny and heartbreaking—a little girl lost, up on stage not at all understanding the lyric she sings, while her mother sobs, lost in memory of what used to be. Ralph bounces from one department to the next, lying to each faculty, before ending up settled in the drama block. There is also a determination forced into these children, Ralph is haunted by the ghost of dead comedian Freddie Prinze. The drama teacher asks Doris, "What will you do if you don't make it?" and before she can even answer, her mother steps in: "We'll make it." But the power to grow is something that the youngsters also find within one another. Bruno is the secret genius; the kid that hides away in his bedroom and composes epic scores with a keen interest in the electronic music trend that was burgeoning during the time. When Coco insists that he start a band with her, he is reluctant, but when he hears her knock out "Out Here on My Own" (a true showstopper) he is blown away and sees the merits in combining artistic talents.

All of these attributes play out on the mean streets of New York, and the grunge elements of the film are overwhelming. Parker captures the filth and the fury, the anger and alienation, the loneliness, desperation, sadness and turmoil of the story perfectly. But he also throws us on our heads: throughout the entire film we are manipulated by but also attracted to these endearing teens. We want them to succeed, but then late in the piece Parker has Mrs. Sherman scream out "Don't you kids think of anyone else but yourself?!" and this brings it all home. A film that is based on the yearnings of these youngsters is revealed as nothing more than selfishness. Parker's revelation here is a poignant and shocking one.

Inspired dialogue drives the multiple storylines, most notably through the exchanges made between black Coco and white Hilary who are fighting over Leroy's affections. It is delicious and catty, and an insight into cultural difference. Hilary is a splendid talent, slumming it to perfect her art. Her artistic life is jeopardized when she falls pregnant, and her painfully real monologue near the end of the film to a cold and unfeeling nurse as she seeks an abortion is brittle and haunting. Dreams are destroyed and trivialized in *Fame*, just as they are lauded.

The dark subject matter is biting and very real, and yet somehow disposable. Coco talks about various schools and says "You don't get raped in the hallways," giving us an idea of high school being a continual place of threat. The closing thirty minutes of the film is gruelling and uncompromising, where hardship and menace come to the fore. It is a ruthless exploration into the violent nature of art and damaged youth. The opening moments, however, come at us with lightning speed and a high energy that are both hopeful and already devastated. Leroy's audition is sexual: a talented and natural dancer, but someone completely enraged by his situation (especially his illiteracy). While the extremes in profanity, the constant "fuck you," "fuck this" and "fuck that" reflects his ghetto background, the film's different racial experiences (the white, the black, the immigrant, the Latino) are continually bought to the foreground in the film.

On location in the NYC subway for *Fame* (1980)

The film is also chilling in places. When Doris's mother answers the phone and realizes that her baby girl has been accepted into the High School of Performing Arts, the music swells and we hit the first year. It is a brilliant moment: so moving and hopeful and yet, like the rest of the film, painted with powerful bleak desperation and despair. The difference in culture is also articulated beautifully during this sequence as the naïve Doris steps out of the subway and is pushed over by an angry New Yorker. She drops her head shots and scrambles to collect them. Meanwhile, a fight breaks out in the street which doesn't phase Coco who has her head stuck in a copy of Variety, while the sheltered Montgomery is shocked by the image of a man beating a woman. Ebonics—a language that was introduced to some urban schools across America, an urban lexicon associated in the black ghettos –props up in *Fame* as Leroy refuses to learn to "speak white." This is much to the dismay of his English teacher Miss Sherman, who wants the boy to read in order to become enlightened.

Each teacher in *Fame* is both an assistant but also an antagonist. The marvellous moment as each teacher expresses their concerns to each class is perfect. Teachers in dance, drama and music all declare that they are "the most important classes," one of the finest examples of the power of adult ego and authority as the road to education within the film.

The tragic elements of the film—the drug abuse, the self-doubt, the suicide attempts, the sexual abuse—paints a world populated by people who want to catch the moon in their hand. However, these same people hear that "dance is not a way of getting through school, it's a way of life" and that most actors are waiting tables or cleaning other people's apartments. Hope and opportunity—as well as hard work and personal sacrifice—are grim realities that will drive them into a void of self-destruction or make them vulnerable to monsters. In the face of this, when we find out who Ralph's "two chicks" are, it is endearing: he is a sensitive boy after all and devoted to the health and welfare of his sisters who are both vulnerable to the "rats" that plague the city, such as rapists and junkies.

The songs (written by Michael Gore, Dean Pitchford and Lesley Gore) express character but are played diegetically. "Hot Lunch Jam" is an uplifting moment that comes in early, where the talented youngsters improvise a musical scenario: Coco takes the lead vocal and here we are introduced to Irene Cara's rich abilities as a singer. These poor working class and ghetto kids shine, culminating in the superb "I Sing the Body Electric" which acts as the film's finale. However, in these life affirming and energetic musical moments there is also a profound sadness and a desperate cry for acceptance that is both endearing and wistful. This is the genius of artists like Gore and Pitchford: they are magicians at crafting musical scenarios and painting them with simultaneous melancholy, confusion, determination, triumph and tragedy.

Dreams destroyed in Alan Parker's *Fame* (1980)

Connections between song and character are subtle but strategically constructed. This is a musical that comes from the street and lives and breathes on the asphalt stretches of New York. Coco's passionate determination to be a star is born from the streets, and the music that floats in and out of Fame is an extension, and expression, of that. Characters connect with one another, and prove their sensitivity through the numbers they get to play out. The drama kids—Doris, Montgomery and Ralph—form a lovely trio akin to Natalie Wood, Sal Mineo and James Dean from *Rebel Without a Cause*, and this connection drives their personal purpose as artists as well as friends. The characters link up emotionally and have common ground, even though they also diverge in important ways, too.

Actress Maureen Teefy recalls her experiences playing Donna:

> As far as the emotionally stirring stuff in the film it was not difficult to tap into that for me. I am a very emotionally intense person. I think Alan Parker was responsible for the chemistry between us. He cast those roles before we met each other and his intuition of how we would be together was right on. How I felt about Paul personally was very different than how I felt about Barry. Almost like it was in the film. I was like Doris in some ways. I'm not a shy person. I am a very private person. Also I did go to theater school growing up. I was a student in the Minneapolis Children's Theater from the time I was 14 on. The environment of the film was familiar to me. I did not have a stage mother. I am one of 9 children and pretty much followed my own path. My parents were too busy to pay too much attention, however they did support my acting. I never decided anything about Doris. It was all very natural. I just showed up and Alan knew what he wanted and he directed me and I did it. He told me he cast me because of my vulnerability. Alan was a bit of a tyrant. If he wanted something and he did not get it he could become a bit of a bully. Funny you should ask. I've written about that in the one woman show I am writing. That all happened by chance. I went into recording studio to record "The Way We Were" and as I was singing, Alan Parker came up to me and said, "Maureen she would never get into the school singing like that, just talk it." Originally the character of Doris was going to be like a Barbara Streisand singer but Alan hired me and just used my strengths and weaknesses. I didn't really get to know Teresa Hughes, the actress who played my mother, however we had a great chemistry working together. Everything happened very organically in the film. I think *Fame* does hold up. It's gritty and real. And it seems as though it is headed to be a classic. Probably what it's like

when you graduate from High School and you feel a sense of pride and accomplishment. I never did go to my high school graduation. Just that, lightness or something with depth. *Fame* means many things to me. On a lot of different levels. It represents a turning point in my life. Once you do something that has such a high level of exposure and touches people so deeply it changes you. I was never very comfortable with the idea of being famous and seen since I am so private. But I am comfortable with good work and the arts.

Montgomery lives in the shadow of his actress mother—a woman completely detached from her son who shares more of an affinity with his analyst who he sees to deal with his homosexuality while Lisa is constantly berated by her teacher because she is someone not committed to her craft or just not good enough. Lisa is in awe of Hilary's confidence and cultural background, while Hilary's attraction to Leroy is an insight to this sexpot's awareness of raw sensuality. Leroy's anger and frustration and his violent temper all come out care of the confronting confrontations with his teacher, but he somehow can channel it and work it into his dance. Doris feels perfectly ordinary—there is nothing flamboyant about her—and her crush on an older acting student Michael (Boyd Gaines) who sets off to LA but returns to New York waiting tables is a painful one. Ralph's growing drug dependency—anti-depressants, speed and eventually harder narcotics—destroys him, while Coco (possibly the most talented of the group in the most traditional of senses) might seem hardened and street wise on the outside, but completely under the spell of supposed fame and success. The world of the teenager come the 1980s was one represented by angry, detached, alien and usually artistically inclined youths. In musicals, they most certainly were musically inclined as music became a rebellious war cry and an extension of spirit and outrage. Bruno's conflict with his music teacher during the Sophomore Year becomes overbearing and frustrating, and this is not as examined as Doris's frustration with being trapped as a child and Ralph's harrowing distress. In fact, Ralph truly gets the most insightful heartache. Haunted by the death of comedian Freddie Prinze, Ralph shares monologues that are gut wrenching and unnerving. While Hilary's distant and cold father and stepmother becomes a commodity and Montgomery's coming out to Doris is tender and warts and all. By the end of the film, he realizes that he doesn't need to see his analyst anymore and his accepting of his sexuality is as steady as Doris becoming a pillar of strength and insight. When she cries out to Ralph "You're full of rage and pain and love, not just jokes!" we completely understand her love and more importantly her awareness of this boy who will ultimately succumb to drug abuse. Sadly, director Alan Parker gives us hopeful up moments, such as Ralph's natural high after a great stand-up gig, and her presents this with a wonderful tracking shot of Ralph and Doris running through the subway and even making light of rape in the mecca of muggings and sexual assault. Ralph jokes "Don't rape anybody!" while Doris replies "I'll rape you!" Hardened kids become immune to such horrific happenings in Alan Parker's musical.

The iconic scene where the title number is blasted through speakers on top of Bruno's dad's taxi is film legend. Irene Cara's vocals belting out "Remember my name/ Fame / I'm gonna live forever" as youngsters dance on car rooftops is one of the strongest images of 1980s cinema: a celebration of hope in a world of crushing self-doubt and despair. Bruno's father and an aggressive truck driver get into a fight as young students dance across the asphalt, a perfect condensation of the constant battle between an older generation that is completely unaware of the sincerity of youth. If they miss this pure emotionally aware mode of expression, than they must always remain detached from it. The 1980s was to be the decade of blind parents and angry, but ultimately sensitive, kids. Finding their own way is what *Fame* delivers.

Montgomery's "Never being happy isn't the same as being unhappy" in his moving monologue about understanding his homosexuality, while the *Rocky Horror Picture Show* sequence as a representation of awakening youth as Doris bursts into confidence (getting stoned helping her on her way), leading her to singing to a bunch of screaming children at a birthday party. This fuels the core of her self-realization where she says "I don't like birthday parties or pink dresses or the Silvermans or Brooklyn or even being Jewish….I mean it's not bad, but it's not all I am." Miller as Ralph gets two gripping monologues: the first is a performance in many ways, loaded with metaphor and masked with anger and bravado. The second is entirely for Doris and Montgomery (ending with Montgomery leaving his own apartment for Doris and Ralph to be alone) is very real—a desperate cry for help—about his deformed sister who was abused by his father, his mother who would jump from one abusive man to the next and the idea of laughter being something that lead to his sister being hurt is all masterfully handled in the writing, direction and performance. The clown crying on the inside is a nicely realized archetype here. And it is beautiful, right down to Barry Miller's costuming with his baggy pants and so forth, reflective of a harlequin trying to understand depression but giving people something to laugh at. Ralph's anger and rage at God and the church plus his contempt for the culture he comes from and detests is summed up when he whispers "I don't want 'em laughing...."

Lyricist Dean Pitchford, won an Oscar for the song of "Fame," and remembers the film:

> More than anything it influenced the track that Michael Gore had cut, because I think more than anything because I think the use of synthesizers as well as the use of guitars and the use of percussion—it had a very danceable feel but it did not feel synthesized in the way that a lot of the music in the early '80s did. It didn't have that kind of "bum bum bum" sound that was indicative perhaps of Donna Summer. It didn't have a disco kind of thing. It was very danceable but it also had street credibility. It got great guitar work on that song, and in terms of the lyric, I think that lyric; what was so amazing for me about writing that song at that time, is that only a few years before, I had been performing and then I had transitioned into songwriting, and one of the first assignments I get is to write songs about wanting to be a performer. And so I got to pour all the feelings that I had about being a struggling actor in New York- not like I had to do any research—I had been living it. And so I poured all of that into it. And so I think if anything the lyric to "Fame" is very hopeful, it's very aspiring and I hope inspiring, and consequently it doesn't it doesn't get down and dirty, it rises up out of that; it reaches for "catch the moon in my hand, you know." I think Irene Cara was very nervous about working with me and Michael at first because she thought we were

coming to her with a kind of Broadway sensibility, as she thought she was bringing kind of an RnB street credibility to the thing. We would give her notes in the recording sessions and she would say, "Don't you hear what I am trying to do here? Don't you see what I am trying to bring to this?!" And she was going off riffing and going off melody, and we sent her off with the first rough tracks of "Fame," and she called Michael Gore, much to her credit the next morning, and she said (because she hadn't laid down the song) it was almost as if she was doing the 30th recording of it, so she was like, Oh you know how this goes, I'm going to sing around the melody, and she called Michael Gore and to her credit she said, I really screwed this up, can I have another chance at it? And we booked another session, and we went in and she came in and she stuck to what we had written and it was a real revelation for her and for us because she needed to as part of her process to get that part out, and then it brought her around to an understanding of what her part in the process was. And then after that it was a love fest from that point on. As far as the Academy Awards went, it was a very complicated year in that Fame had come out in the February/March in the year before the Oscars, where you always hoped to come out in Oscar season before the Oscars happened so you are fresh in everybody's head. So not only had *Fame* come out the year before but "Fame" is not the only song nominated from *Fame*, they had also nominated a song called "Out Here on My Own, which Michael Gore had written with his sister, Leslie Gore. So there was this concern—our concern was that it might split the *Fame* vote. Add to that the fact that Willie Nelson was nominated for a song called "On The Road Again," and that Christmas there had been a big hit movie called *9 to 5*, with a big hit song that was still on the radio by Dolly Parton—"9 to 5." So there are twenty five reasons why Fame would have been forgotten, it would have split the vote with the other song from *Fame* and Dolly Parton was fresh in everyone's heads—and we all loved her! I subsequently worked with her, I hadn't worked with her at that point and so it was not a done deal. There was no assurance whatsoever going in, so it was a big surprise. Yeah, it was great. But I had a very funny experience at the Oscars because at first of course, it was the first time that I had ever been in the theatre on the night, and I had never experienced the Oscars that way before. So, it was all very unreal; really? This is what it all looks like and this is what it feels like? And this is how people react? I won. We went back and did the press. We went back and sat in our seats for the rest of the program, and then the cars came and took us to—we went to the Governor's party, and then Michael and Lesley and I and some friends of ours ended up in a restaurant on Sunset, having our own little party. I got home about 2:30 in the morning, and I had taped the show (and in those days we taped the show on the video cassette), and I took off my tuxedo and I was getting ready for bed and I run the tape back, up to the point where the award was being presented to see what it look like; and I sat there in front of my TV, in my underwear, in the middle of the night and suddenly that was what the Oscars looked like, that was real; Oh, my god! That really happened! That really happened to me! And they came to the moment of opening the envelop and my heart was pounding and pounding and they read my name and I jumped up and down and I screamed (I didn't scream in the theatre, I cried and I carried on. I had the whole reaction about 8 hours later because it had not been real until I had seen it (imitates square shape of the TV again) in the context that I had always seen it. It was very surreal.

Lisa being kicked out of the school and told by her dance teacher "I don't think you'll ever be good enough" and this is a harrowing moment. Her dreams smashed, she is ultimately driven to contemplate suicide in the subway while Leroy and Coco sing and tap dance to "Singin' in the Rain" (a brilliant condensation of the "whistling in the dark" musical tropes).

Actress Laura Dean remembers playing Lisa and working on *Fame*:

Alan Parker was very generous to the actors and very warm and friendly. He did want my character to be very vulnerable in the scene when I get kicked out of the school, so he wanted me to do that scene naked in the locker-room, and I was 16 at the time and not interested in doing that, and he literally bought me a book of photography of dancers naked and said, "I'll make you look beautiful and don't worry about it," and I said I understand that they look beautiful but I am 16 and I don't want to do that—Number 1. And Number 2 –if I was being kicked out of the school, the teacher is not going to do it in the locker room—she's going to call me into her office and kick me out there. So that is how the scene went. So, I was kind of proud of myself for sticking to my guns! Barry Miller—he and I—I don't think we had any scenes together but we were on the set a lot of the time at the same time. He and I used to sneak off and he would grab a walkie-talkie, sneak off and go into another room. And people would be scrambling—What does Alan Parker need?! We played little jokes like that! And I also became friends with Lee Curreri—he actually wound up marrying my sister, so he is my brother-in-law and we're still good friends! And of course, Paul McCrane and I knew each other because we did a show together at the public theatre before *Fame*. I have one really distinct moment in my mind, I remember when the film was first in early production, the name of the movie was going to be named *Hot Lunch*, which was a riff on Barry Miller's character in the original script, would sell marijuana out of his lunch box, and on his lunch box it said Hot Lunch, and that was the title of the film. But in 1979 there was a porn movie called *Hot Lunch*, Starring of all people, an actor named Alan Parker, and it was right in Times Square—*Hot Lunch!*—Starring Alan Parker! So, needless to say, the name of the film got changed; and I remember the day they told us that the name was changed to *Fame*. Paul McCrane and I were getting costume fittings and we were sitting together waiting for something, and we found out that the name of the film was *Fame*; and David Bowies 'Fame' came on the radio, and we just started singing it—Fame, Fame—it was so exciting! We thought—What a perfect name! That was fun! One of the wonderful things about the film was that one of my high school class mates was actually in the movie— Gene Anthony Ray, who played Leroy. He and I went to the Performing Arts together. We both started as Freshmen the same year; and we used to go—there was a Burger King on Sixth Avenue, between 45th and 46th Street and we would meet there for breakfast before school. He did not end up staying at Performing Arts but he did end up getting the role of Leroy in the film and so it was great fun; he was lots of energy! He was a little crazy guy: but we had a lot of fun and I miss him, because he has passed away which is sad. But he was a great performer and a wonderful person, so, we miss you, Gene. What I love about the movie that has stood this test of time is Times Square, 1979, pre-disneyfication of Times Square: the grit, the dirt; the orange Julius and the Ho Joes, and all of that stuff. The actual school of the Performing Arts was on 46th Street, between 6th and 7th Avenue, and I mean, I tell my friends and my kids that I went to High School in Times Square, when Times Square was a toilet bowl! I mean, down the block from my high school was an all-male revue which didn't phase us at all. So, I loved that the film captured that moments in time when New York was gritty; you know, you had the 25 cent peep shows next to the Howard Johnsons. I think the film captured, you know, a slice of New York that does not exist anymore. I love Times Square and I am happy that it has had revival; that people go there and spend time there and that it is a playground, but it is not what it used to be. So, I can watch the movie and reminisce about that. The scene in the subway, when my character decides that she is going to kill herself; actually, in the original script, she did—she jumped and died. MGM didn't feel that that was a good way to end a characters life in a musical so they changed it to me just throwing my dance bag in and saying, "Fuck it. If I can't dance, I will just change to the drama department." So, it was kind of a last minute change actually, which is way after that scene you don't even see my character until the very end. I could not believe that I was in a musical and I was not going to be singing in this musical; because I have been a singer since I was born. In fact, the moment I was born, the doctor said to my mother, "What a pair of lungs!" because I came out screaming. That is my mother's story. I don't know. I don't remember it. I was so frustrated! I'm in a musical and I am not singing! And I would always kind of sing on the set. I am a kind of person that I will hear a phrase, it reminds me of a song and I start singing-everything is a musical to me; so I would sing all the time, and I used to sing on the set, and Alan Parker would say to me, "You are not going to be in the finale, Laura!" Because I knew there was one part of the film that hadn't been written yet, and that was the finale. And I would keep singing, and Alan keep saying, 'You're not going to be in the finale, Laura!" Oh, I remember—we were shooting a scene on 46th Street, and I went into the bathroom on the set and I was singing and somebody heard me singing and he said, "Oh, you have a beautiful voice," and I said Thanks, Alan Parker doesn't think so, and he said, What do you mean? And I said, "Oh, I want to sing in the finale and duh, duh, duh," and he said, "Well you have a beautiful voice" and I said "Thank you. Who are you?" He said, "I'm Michael Gore, and I am writing the finale." I was like, "Hi! You're my new best friend!" Anyway, they actually made me audition to sing the finale—they made everybody audition to sing the finale. Everybody who was singing had to learn the whole thing be-cause they had to figure out who was going to sing what part. But Michael Gore, god bless him, fought for me, and when we did the recording session, he had me record all the tracks; I mean, he had me do what we call the basic track. So I sang the whole song through. Eventually all my character does is the first four lines. That is how I end up singing in the finale. And then of course, I kept thinking, So write me a few more scenes, so that my character is seen—but they never did. Oh, well, I get to sing in the finale!

On top of the grimness of the attempted suicide is where a heroin addict beats Ralph's little sister, and there is even a suggestion of rape. This happens while Doris and Ralph play out a scene from *Marty,* a play and film about desperate working class people while Coco's lie about where she lives to Bruno is another great example of a ghetto kid trying to look settled. Coco is ultimately from a lower class than the Italian working class Bruno, and this is something that torments her.

Fame is world of abusive fathers, distant and overbearing mothers, illiteracy, drug abuse, the conflict between generations, art as a means of survival and the possibility of dreams not being realized. It also depicts a throwaway mentality, where talented and gifted naturals seek refuge in narcotics and escapism, rather than honing in on their abilities. The character that truly embodies this is Ralph. He is an intuitive performer and has the makings of a great comedian, but is swamped by an image that he is so desperate to present and besieged by personal anguish, doubt, grief and perpetual sadness. Barry Miller's performance as the tragic clown Ralph should have garnered him an Academy Award nomination for Best Supporting Actor that year. His Ralph is yet another character that would creep into the public consciousness around the time, these tormented young boys driven to self-destruction heralded by troubled existences. These boys would pop up in films such as *Endless Love* (1981), *Ordinary People* (1979), *Christine* (1983) and many more. Following in the 1980s would be a slew of teen-angst pictures that would prove to be massively successful and very popular with audiences for years to come. The films of John Hughes such as *Ferris Bueller's Day Off* (1986) and *The Breakfast Club* (1985), as well as movies such as *Fast Times at Ridgemont High* (1982) and *St. Elmo's Fire* (1985) would present us with more disenfranchised youth of the 1980s. Playing against these films would be endless slasher films and tit'n'ass fare which would mark the 1980s as the decade of excess—both in terms of violence and explicit sexuality. *Fame* would be instrumental in the advent of teen-centric cinema during the decade, and with its freestyle profanity, nudity and dealings with dark concerns such as drugs, parental detachment, attempted suicide, abortion and abuse. It would pave the way for teen films to tackle these themes.

Fame delivers New York in all its grittiness and peepshow glory, the same New York City that is the playground for savage streets that blanket brilliant horror films such as *Maniac* (1980) and street-gang fare such as *The Warriors* (1979). More teen anguish is represented in the guise of the shy and lonely Montgomery who is seen stepping aside for the heterosexual Ralph and Doris to comfort each other and share a kiss. Montgomery may come from a long line of sexless sissies that Hollywood was so good at dishing out, but his strength is his ability to understand his friends. He is a gay-helper character essentially, but he is also someone who lives on a plateau above the others. He observes, understands and quietly disappears. When he sings "Is It Okay to Call You Mine?"—a lovelorn tender ballad that precedes Doris's pot-induced "awakening" at *The Rocky Horror Picture Show* performance—we understand his loneliness and longing for someone to call his own. The film dances with the idea of Montgomery having a quiet crush on Ralph, but never rams it down our throats. Instead, much like the character of Montgomery, it suggests it and then quietly leaves. It's only until the increasingly bleak end of the picture where his crush is outed and turned into something ugly.

Hilary's depressing monologue begins the film's series of dark climaxes: it doesn't work out well for any of these kids, and the lack of closure for some of them further demonstrates the brilliance of Alan Parker and his refusal to tie things up with pretty bows. Parker doesn't want to let us know what happened to Bruno or to Lisa, but instead he throws them into the mix in the finale. Who knows what their lives will entail after that? Missing from the finale are Ralph and Hilary, while Coco seems unscathed by her horrific experiences earlier on. Late in the picture, a sleazy opportunist preys on Coco and offers her a "screen test." It is a distressing scene as Coco is talked into removing her blouse on camera for the lascivious sex criminal that pretends to be a French director. Moments before Coco's ordeal, Mrs. Sherwood's dying husband acts as a platform for her and Leroy to finally understand one another. A final peace is made as Leroy learns compassion and his first moment of selflessness. *Fame* is a gritty picture but its message is that in time we will all be stars.

SUSPENDED IN TIME: *Xanadu* and *Can't Stop the Music*

Roller skates had made an impression in the Linda Blair vehicle *Roller Boogie*, but now in *Xanadu*, the fad had a life of its own. With the Universal logo tributing the 1930s with a biplane circling the earth accompanied by classic 1930s music, and then shifting to a concord ushering the electric guitar jazz fusion of the Electric Light Orchestra, *Xanadu* sets to merge two musical worlds in one fantasy extravaganza about Zeus, his muses and two struggling artists inspired by Olivia Newton-John. Michael Beck, fresh from starring in the incredible *The Warriors* mutters "Guys like me shouldn't dream anyway," and the film quietly invites us into the world of this record cover artist. "I'm Alive" comes crashing in and a strange high concept musical begins. This film is confused, nonsensical and fantastic. The roller skate fad is never absent as excellent songs rise to the surface in this sci-fi/fantasy musical mess that has no steady focus or narrative purpose.

Zeus has sent his muses to work their magic on a record cover artist and a senior swing band musician, and together they are influenced by one of the muses to open up a roller disco. The swing bandsman is legendary Gene Kelly in what would be his last film, and watching him and Olivia Newton-John dance up a storm together is magical. The idea of marrying rock'n'roll with Glen Miller style swing is innovative and charming, but not enough to carry a film. This is not to say that *Xanadu* lacks moments of wonder: for example, the house that Gene Kelly lives in is a Hollywood manor that an old silent movie star once lived in. Kelly's character is a clarinet player from the past—a living legend now lost and forgotten—and introduced like an elfin sand dwelling creature on the beach. Youthful and broad in all his choices, Kelly is a delight to see on screen, and although at times you cringe at the thought of him roller-skating with a bunch of bizarre looking chorus kids, for the most part you are laughing with him. Gene Kelly's involvement in the film is a bit of anomaly: there is a constant question about his participation in such a strange film that came out of nowhere. Regardless, Kelly is watchable and seems comfortable dancing about to E.L.O.

701

Gene Kelly and Zeus's muses at the premiere of *Xanadu* (1980)

Michael Beck is appealing enough as the suddenly inspired album cover artist with his flaxen hair, ambitious glee and overt enthusiasm, but he is not the Beck from *The Warriors* where his subtlety as an actor was showcased in his performance as a gang leader in a dystopian New York City. *Xanadu* doesn't give him much to do but react to the charming Olivia Newton-John who zooms through the film with confidence and sweetness. As appealing as Beck can be, he is also sometimes awkward and lacking in personality, but his is a role that acts as a backdrop to Newton-John and Gene Kelly. Beck famously went on to say "*The Warriors* opened many doors and *Xanadu* closed them all."

Film historian and author Robin Bougie shares his thoughts on *Xanadu*:

> I've watched *Xanadu* more than any movie ever made. I've lost count how many times. A hundred viewings at least. It started as a sort of nostalgia-based revisiting of the ELO and Olivia Newton John soundtrack, which I have all these fond memories of from grade school. Then I'm watching the

movie to unwind from a hard day at work. Something brain-less and fun, and I was sort of laughing it off at first—you know, for the first few viewings. Sort of enjoying it ironically or something, but at some point you can't use that excuse anymore. I had to look in the mirror and accept what and who it is that I am. 'You legitimately love Xanadu. You're still a good person, it's ok. But you can't keep running from this.' I mean, it helped that I have such a crush on 1970s Olivia Newton John, and adore Michael Beck, even though he can't sing and dance worth a shit. But I love him in *The Warriors*, and *Megaforce*, and whatever else I see him in. That was his moment: 1979 and 1980. That was when it seemed like he was gonna be the next big thing for a few minutes. It's too bad it didn't really pan out for him further than that, because he should have been the next John Travolta or something. It's just that he couldn't sing and dance, damn it. But he sure gave it a try in *Xanadu*, didn't he? Gotta respect the effort at least!

Xanadu is not pretentious, nor is it a message movie or even a genu-ine tribute to a bygone era. It is just silly, irreverent fun packed with set pieces that make no sense but at the same time, are wildly entertain-ing. When Olivia Newton-John and Michael Beck morph into cartoon characters care of former Disney artist Don Bluth, we are treated to a sequence reminiscent of major fantasy moments from B-musicals from the 1950s and 1960s. There is no real reason as to why these characters become animated, but it doesn't really matter because the madness that unfolds is validated and the concept is easy to swallow. This is cinema at its most accessible and most anti-elitist: as much as it is anti-intellectual it brims with a bizarre confidence.

Sandahl Bergman played one of Zeus's muses, and remembers the film:

I did Gene Kelly's show in Las Vegas in 1970; it was called "The Gene Kelly Show." It was at the international Hilton where Elvis performed. I did his show there for three months. So I worked with Gene Kelly and would sit every night in the wings watching "Singin' in the Rain" because they actually did have the rain come down, and I grew up watching that movie. So I worked with him back then, and that what was so funny, when I got cast to do *Xanadu*, you know, he was of course on board. I remember we were talking and I said "Gene, I did your show," he said "I remember you. I always thought you were gonna go somewhere" and so it was great. Reconnecting with him almost twenty years later to do *Xanadu*. That was a great experience. I loved Kenny Ortega. That whole movie, even though it was sort of a flop, you know in some way, it was just a great experience. And of course, Olivia Newton-John was just a dear, you couldn't ask for a greater gal. And that was another movie I was on for I want to say almost five months. That's what kept me in Los Angeles. Funny enough, I got evicted from my apartment in New York. I had no reason to stay in LA. I was going to back to New York, but then I didn't have an apartment to go back to, so I ended up staying in Los Angeles, then work begat work, begat work, begat work and I never went back to New York again, basically because I had no apartment to go back to. So that again is another life evolving experience. So what happened to me was *Xanadu* happened, and eviction, no apartment in New York—I guess I will stay here. I guess I need my car, I will just hang here for a little bit, and then all of a sudden, I just started working a lot more, so that is why I never went back to New York. Otherwise I would have gone back to New York in a heartbeat. Oh, it was just so much fun. It was just so out there, and again it was a project that Joel Silvers and Larry Gordon produced. They were the biggest producers at that time in Los Angeles. And they took on this sort of weird project, and they were more known for psychological thrillers. They took on this like, musical, fantasy movie. Funny enough, it was a flop, but it became sort of an underground like...well...I have done a lot of speaking about *Xanadu* at certain times and the fans are like "Oh, we love this movie" and I love the movie because it was a great job, I worked with great people, and again that was my ammo. Great job, great people, Olivia couldn't have been nicer, the producers were great, Gene Kelly, I got to connect with again. It was just sort of a funny situation and that movie kept me in Los Angeles. I went from there into Conan. Robert Greenwald, yes, who was amazing and was a big fan of course of Bob Fosse. He was just as I said...how this musical got made in this point in time in nineteen...I'm not sure what year it was...yeah it was seventy nine. How this film got made...I have no idea. In the movie industry in that point in time, but like I said Joel Silver and Larry Gordon were two of the biggest producers in the industry then and they got it made. You get Olivia and you get Gene Kelly and of course we had Michael Beck who was this dream and a doll, and we get Kenny Ortega, as choreographer, who is just so much fun to work with, and then we have this world of roller skating and this fantasy. I think those that loved it, absolutely loved it, and there were other people like "What?" I just love the movie. It was just so much fun to do and they paid me way too much money because the producers had seen a screening of *All That Jazz* and they said "We just want her in this movie."

Journalist and writer Adam Devlin adds his insight into the film:

Xanadu. A fantasy. A musical. A place where dreams come true. Xanadu has it all—disco, roller skating, romance and a hark back to the good old days with legend Gene Kelly. But all of that was just a background blur to its star— Olivia Newton-John as the muse Terpsichore. Olivia never looked better than she does in Xanadu. She was stunningly beautiful and the camera loved her. Xanadu is one of those rare films that is iconic and important and relevant not because of its success but because it defines a moment in time—the death of disco. It also gives us one of the rare moments when a mainstream Hollywood movie was defined by, and remembered for its female solo lead star! Xanadu *is* Olivia Newton-John! That Xanadu wasn't a hit didn't bother to me—to me it was pure magic; absolute fantasy. To me it was one of the best and most entertaining films I'd ever seen. It is still, some 30+ years later, one of my favorite films! I can't count the number of times I've seen Xanadu—it would have to be in the hundreds. And every time I watch it I get something new from it. But what impresses me most is just how charming Olivia is in this role. Here she had a newfound confidence in front of the camera. And in many regards Xanadu's "Kira" was a much more challenging role than Grease's Sandy. In Xanadu she had to sing, she had to dance—with Gene Kelly, and she had to roller-skate while do all of it! And she never stopped smiling all the way though it! Yes the script is a mess—all over the shop not really knowing what it wants to be. Yes the direction is sloppy at best. Yes there is a wonderful piece of animation half way through that really adds nothing to the film. Yes it missed the roller-disco craze by about 6 months. Yes it is a flawed film. And for me, its flaws make it a masterpiece. And it still has a real charm today, thanks mostly to Olivia Newton-John.

Just as ruthlessly zany and as endearing in its own psychotic way is the Village People vehicle *Can't Stop the Music*. Opening with Steve Guttenberg roller skating out of his dreary day job to follow his dreams of becoming a great composer; he travels through New York to a bouncy and catchy disco song. *Can't Stop the Music* is a thoroughly ridiculous, outrageous and insane movie that doesn't make much sense at all, but, who cares? It is so easy to watch and so addictive that it is really hard to look away. This film, much like its cousin *Xanadu*, is like a sugary treat—it is bad for you and you know it's bad for you, but it tastes so good that it's hard to resist! Similarly to *Xanadu* and *The Apple* (discussed further shortly), *Can't Stop the Music* is a frantic, frenzied mess that jumps around like a speed addict excitedly talking about "the most important thing in the world" but never making sense.

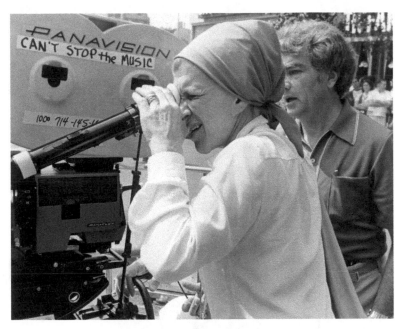

Nancy Walker directs *Can't Stop the Music* (1980)

Valerie Perrine and the Village People on the set of *Can't Stop the Music*
(1980)

Valerie Perrine enjoys the "Y.M.C.A" along with the Village People in *Can't Stop the Music* (1980)

A production still of Valerie Perrine in *Can't Stop the Music* (1980)

Some of the film's set pieces are unfortunately clumsy in their anxious desire to employ a gay subtext, but because the movie is a mess as a whole, this gay agenda sticks out like a sore thumb, rendering it too blatant to say anything really political or witty. Instead, the film bombards us with jokes that run out of steam fast. The movie never pretends to be anything but a screwball gay gag that tailors its heterosexual leads to play along. For example, there is a scene where Steve Guttenberg helps leading lady Valerie Perrine take off Bruce Jenner's pants and then later has him ogling at a stripping and flexing bodybuilder who sings "Wanna feel my body?." This is director Nancy Walker's way of involving even heterosexual male characters in a kind of gay voyeurism focused on an acute appreciation of the male physique. The film is a massive gay joke, but the humour is never remotely offensive (unlike the endless slew of homophobic comedies to come out of the 1970s and 1980s).

During the period, gay jokes were a staple in comedy films of the day and there seemed to be a hushed homophobia that went by without complaint—until activist groups such as Act Up picketed films, but mainly targeted grisly thrillers such as William Friedkin's *Cruising* (1980) rather than comic light films. However, this is a problem. These comedies do something far more dangerous than what a film like *Cruising* (an incredible film with a stark and nasty edge that is all completely necessary and masterfully handled) did—they carry on as if fag jokes are acceptable and this isn't a good thing. However, *Can't Stop the Music* plays out differently. The heterosexual lead in Valerie Perrine becomes a spokesperson for the gay culture that the film celebrates and when she says that she is "accepting of everyone" she becomes the adult version of Dorothy Gale, collecting beloved gay men who help shape her and bring her home.

Perrine is gorgeous in this film, a nymph wandering the streets of New York, meeting her Village People and bouncing through the film as a spirited light beam. Her healthy body is matched by her healthy attitude towards life and ambition, and refreshingly this character is a young woman existing in a silly comedy that gets to do her own thing, make her own rules and run her own show. In a bizarre sense (and also considering the slew of fellow actresses in the film that all have dynamic and strong roles—as strong a role in a nonsensical disco musical comedy can be) *Can't Stop the Music* is relatively feminist in despite its focus on gay men.

Valerie Perrine remembers the film:

Can't Stop the Music was produced by a friend of mine, Allan Carr. What can I say that hasn't been said about him! I think he intended on making a good movie. But I am proud of. Let me put it that way. I also thought it was going to be a big success but they had got a director who had never directed before, and she didn't know what she was doing. It turned out to be a fiasco. Nancy Walker was terrible I had her banned from the set. I said either she goes or I go! She used to sit in her dressing room, watching day-time soaps. Working with The Village People and everybody else was great. But she was awful. I didn't really think about the concept of the film. It was more of a case of Allan asking me to do the film. I was a good friend of his. So, I did it. During the shoot we did used to go over to my house at lunch time. That was fun. We had a good time. Lots of fun. As far as the shoot itself, the milk commercial was fun, doing the milk commercial was the most fun, I think. Once I met the Village People, I became a huge fan and they're wonderful people. We used to go to my house for lunch. That was nice. I actually saw them not long ago in Las Vegas. I went to see their show and it was fun. I ran into them in Vegas. But Nancy Walker was terrible. She would go into her trailer while they were setting up scenes, and she would go in there and watch soap operas. But yes, Nancy didn't know what she was doing. There was one time where Bruce Jenner and I were just outside the stage door. We opened and entered the set. And I was back there thinking Bruce will not be seen or heard if he enters at this mark and all of a sudden Nancy Walker screamed out "If we're shooting, we can't be shooting while you are talking! So, shut the fuck up!" And I opened the door and I looked inside and she was facing the wrong direction. So I was right.

She wouldn't have been able to shoot Bruce correctly. She didn't know where the camera was! A nightmare!

The film loses steam once the Village People form, and post-"Y.M.C.A" (a showcase of male aesthetic) the movie falls flat and is exhausted. Besides some of the silly numbers such as "Do the Shake" (set to make milk more glamorous than champagne—yes, this is a genuine article plot angle of the film), there are no other real highlights. Singing "Liberation" is a clear testament to the spirit of gay liberation and if Nancy Walker's film has anything to say, then this is it.

I AM WHAT I AM: *Popeye*

With its ominous opening featuring a thunderstorm welcoming our beloved comic strip hero to the shores of Sweet Haven, there is already a good indication that this musical adaptation of Elzie Crisler Segar's famous spinach-guzzling sailor will be a rocky and uneven movie. Besides its inspired casting, beautiful outdoors locales and cartoon-style, Robert Altman's *Popeye* is one of the most unremarkable movie musicals of all time. Its major flaw lies in the script itself, where nothing interesting happens. With notorious stories regarding the disastrous shoot, the infamous well-documented anecdotes regarding the amount of narcotics running rampant during production putting the film into start-stop, and concerns about running over budget hanging over the film, *Popeye* was cursed from the beginning when Paramount producer Robert Evans wished to acquire the filmic adaptation rights to the successful Broadway musical *Annie*, directed by Mike Nichols. Unfortunately for Evans (who really wanted to adapt a film based on a comic strip/book character—possibly inspired by the massive success for Warner Bros. with *Superman: The Movie*), Columbia won the rights to the cinematic treatment of everyone's favourite Depression-era orphan, which inspired Evans meet other executives and ask: what comic book characters do we have the rights to? The answer was Popeye, and with great reluctance from Paramount, a musical film based on the muscle-bound, pipe chugging Seabee went into development.

Originally intended for the lead was Dustin Hoffman, with Lily Tomlin in the role of Olive Oyl. When Robert Altman signed on to

711

direct, casting changed and writers changed hands. Into the picture came the versatile and talented writer Jules Feiffer who made a career out of comics for periodicals such as The Village Voice. His script went through the ringer multiple times and became so watered down that the final results are limp and flat. The film relies on the performances of its cast, and thankfully for Robert Altman and Paramount, the choice of character actors to populate the coastal troubled town of Sweet Haven are perfect. Heading the troupe is Robin Williams who had made an impression in the sit-com spin off to *Happy Days, Mork and Mindy*. Williams gives Popeye all the punch necessary: he is a physical actor and therefore the mannerisms and quirks are completely controlled and managed with gusto, he can improvise and this shows in his delivery of certain gags and quips, and most importantly Williams has that innate ability to cross over from broad comedy to robust sentimentality which is necessary in the film's strongest moment where Popeye sings "Swee'Pea's Lullaby" (one of the only moments in the film that truly works).

Robert Altman's mainstay acting troupe have always been an eclectic mix of brilliant artists, and Shelley Duvall is no exception. Here is a gifted actress with intuition and versatility, and she injects the heroine of the piece—the lanky, kooky Olive Oyl—with a perfect amount of wackiness, vulnerability and warmth. Continually "Oh-ing" and "Ooooh-ing" throughout the film (which is something the original cartoon character did and something that polarized her popularity), Duvall is the epitome of a frazzled, ditzy and extremely weird Olive and the annoying elements of this comic strip icon come alive with zeal. But this doesn't make the film easier to watch: rather, it makes it more stressful if anything. Seeing that one of the most positive things about the film is a character who's "Oh-ing" and "Ooooh-ing" will no doubt get on even the most patient of audience members' nerves.

The songs in *Popeye* are written by the talented Harry Nilsson. But much like screenwriter Feiffer, he seems to bring nothing to the end product. Not only are the songs uninteresting and lacking in any insight into character or situation, but they are also poorly presented and staged. *Popeye* sadly misses the point and Altman's direction is flustered and manic, but energy levels are at an all-time low. In this chaotic mess of a movie, nothing happens—at least, nothing interesting or entertaining.

**Shelley Duvall and Robin Williams as comic strip sweethearts
in *Popeye* (1980)**

Plot and song don't marry well at all in this motion picture. The drab narrative is lethargic and tiresome, even with characters frantically jumping around.

Films and television shows based on comic books and comic strips were certainly nothing new by the time of Altman's Popeye, and of course by then the ground breaking *Superman: The Movie* had revolutionized the genre and garnered it a broader appeal beyond hardcore superhero fans. When Christopher Reeve took to the skies, everyone watched.

Musicalizing a comic book character proved to be hit and miss; cementing a book musical within the confines of a comic book movie was something that polarized fans and mass audiences alike. Based on the successful and critically acclaimed stage musical, *Annie* (1982) directed by Hollywood legend John Huston and boasting an incredible cast including Carol Burnett, Albert Finney, Bernadette Peters, Tim Curry, Ann Reinking and a cast of super talented youngsters lead by Aileen Quinn who played the titular loveable orphan was a perfect example of a movie musical based on a comic strip that worked perfectly (although composer Charles Strouse had concerns).

The octopus at the end of *Popeye*—an elemental villain that tries to drown both Sweet Pea and Olive Oyl—is a beautifully designed puppet and its tentacles have all the sliminess one would want from a grumpy malevolent underwater beast. This octopus really should have been used in the Italian made eco-horror killer octopus film from the late 1970s *Tentacles* (1977), but that's another story. The endless mugging from the cast gets to be a nuisance and we kind of wish the octopus turned up earlier and killed them off one by one.

Popeye is sloppy. In theatre we understand and accept the fact that company members are going to be used throughout a musical and swing from role to role (the Argentinian working classes become the aristocracy in *Evita*, the witch hunters in *Wicked* become glamorous citizens of the Emerald City. and so forth) however, in a *movie* musical this is something that stands out and looks clumsy unless it is used in a stylistic manner where it makes sense and adds to the aesthetic and serves the narrative. In *Popeye* this is not the case: characters reappear in swing roles and it is distracting and inappropriate. For example, ladies that are first presented as part of the extended family of the Oyls turn up later as prostitutes that lasciviously approach Popeye during his declaration of "I Am What I Am." There is also a nasty moment in this sequence where Popeye grunts something along the lines of catching a venereal disease if you were to touch one of these "ladies of the night." This kind of morality is ugly (a word repeated in the beginning of the film by Olive Oyl), and there are many moments in the film that are downright just that—ugly. Olive Oyl using Swee' Pea's supposed psychic abilities to choose winning race horses, Popeye's estranged father forcing little Sweet Pea to eat spinach and calling him names, Wimpy kidnapping Swee'Pea and handing him over to the film's core villains Bluto and so forth are good examples—but this ugliness is never countered by the film's imagery.

Shot on location in Malta and using some beautiful areas of the island, Altman does sometimes deliver a visually interesting picture. The romantic Mediterranean is lavish and glorious, with the deep blue and green sea looking seductive and alluring. The set for Sweet Haven, now affectionately known as "Popeye's Village," remains on the coast of Malta and is still a tourist attraction. The art direction for the film is a stand out. It is constructed to look like the angular and misshapen infrastructure as established by cartoonist Max Fleischer who delivered the Popeye cartoons from the 1930s and 1940s.

Bluto's number "I'm Mean" plods along reeking of the unpolished, while the number preceding it "He's Large" as sung by Olive Oyl and friends murmurs through leaving us perplexed and confused by its intention. With all its flaws, there is a freakish element to the film that might appeal to some audience members, but for the most part the best moments in the film are when Popeye shows off his physical prowess and his abilities in the fighting arena. There are inspired moments such as Popeye punching a thug like a boxing bag, Popeye being screwed through a pier, Popeye shooting through the ocean like a submarine and so forth, giving the film a cartoon-edge which is most certainly deserves and needs. The cartoon violence is loads of fun but doesn't come nearly soon enough—this film is desperate for more action, and sadly, it doesn't hit the right notes in that department at all. Instead, the plot is dull (including things such as a secondary villain, outside of the oafish Bluto, in the Tax Man who plots to destroy the Oyl family by repossessing all that they own and being a nuisance overall). Besides the functional plot elements that are plagued with problems, the core theme of the film lies in the concept of fatherhood and forced fatherhood.

Popeye and Olive are forced into parenthood as Swee'Pea somewhat magically appears. The baby is abandoned and gets mixed up with one of Olive's bags, and the duo become her adoptive parents. However Popeye is more dedicated. The original reason he has come to Sweet Haven is to find his long lost father, Pappy (Ray Walston) who had been distant, absent and irresponsible. Films from this period seem to be obsessed with the sins of the father and scrutinized the relationship between fathers and sons. All of this takes a thematic backseat when we are subjected to a boxing match with a grimacing Linda Hunt watching on. She and her co-stars are the product of some inspired costuming and make-up, but their cartoon looks are dwarfed by the indoor settings that they populate. The picturesque imagery of the outdoors is completely otherworldly compared to the very subdued colors and lack of color for the interiors. The imagery is not memorable, but thankfully some of the creepy performances make up for it.

Paul Dooley as Wimpy is terrific, and this gluttonous hamburger obsessive is a sickly opportunistic character, complex with ugliness. His repugnancy is in direct polar opposition to the adorable baby that plays Swee'Pea, who is fantastic and would have been a dream to work with. Popeye and Pappy's estranged relationship, Wimpy's use of Swee'Pea to bet on horses, and Popeye and Swee'Pea's loving connection all play the notion of fatherhood and what it means to have children. At times, this theme is heavy handed because the screenplay doesn't let anything else develop. Violent brute Bluto—a menace and an anti-intellectual—is a thuggish villain and one of the film's strongest points as he is a caricature that works, whereas Popeye seems to be the moral compass, the character who has the most integrity and the way that "I Am What I Am" is presented is a proclamation of all this.

Harry Nilsson is a brilliant songwriter, but for some reason the songs in *Popeye* just don't take off. They fumble through, are riddled with rheumatism. The strongest numbers are the aforementioned "I Am What I Am," "He Needs Me" and "Swee'Pea's Lullaby" which all serve a purpose—one is an epiphany, one a declaration of love and the other an expansion on a theme: the theme of fatherhood. If the rest of the score were to be on par with these three songs, the plot and story structure (as well as the boring set pieces) would be easier to swallow because the songs could carry a worthwhile movie musical. But unfortunately, plot is an issue in Sweet Haven. When Popeye pushes the Tax Man down a chute into the ocean below, the town rejoices and see Popeye as a hero—if this was all that needed to happen to eliminate the tax man, why wasn't it done earlier? And it could have been anyone to do it. But then when Popeye laments the missing Swee'Pea the film picks up in song, as he howls out "Well me I came from heaven...." and the movie's most moving moment is born. If the entire film was made up of more action sequences, great songs and moments of tenderness such as this sequence, than Altman would have had a well-rounded picture. But for some reason, it seems that he is confident enough in his great casting choices, and lets his people do their thing.

Cartoon violence in Robert Altman's *Popeye* (1980)

The casting of Ray Walston as Pappy is a nice homage to his performance in *South Pacific* as Luther the opportunistic Seabee—it's as if Pappy himself could be Luther himself, or how he turned out. As an angst-ridden bad parent, Walston is terrific and highlights Robin Williams's sensitive turn as an adoptive daddy to a lost baby. Forced parenthood pops up in many movies to follow in the wake of *Popeye* and even carry out through into the 1990s with films such as *Terminator 2: Judgement Day* and *Jurassic Park* (1993) employing this trope, however in *Popeye*, the positive father/son relationship come across as far too sanctimonious. As sappy as the film can get, it is also irresponsible and ugly. Overall, the thick cartoon imagery is a highlight and even though there is plenty of room for more of it, when it hits the screen it is a delight to see. Some examples of this include Olive being held captive inside a periscope (directly influenced by Max Fleischer's cartoons) as she cries out for Popeye to rescue her. Unfortunately, Popeye can only really save her—he can't save Robert Altman's picture which is a shambles.

WE WERE POOR, BUT WE HAD LOVE:
Coal Miner's Daughter and *The Jazz Singer*

During the 1970s, Country music trumpeted triumphantly on the small screen with shows such as *The Glenn Campbell Show*, *The Johnny Cash Show* and *The Dolly Parton Show* giving audiences an insight into the story-heavy world of hillbilly and mountain music. This keen interest in this genre kickstarted a love for artists who came from impoverished backgrounds, grew up in large families, struggled all their lives and in the meantime wrote and weaved together a career centred on narrative-driven music. Singers and songwriters who more than often played instruments as well (many of the instruments being indigenously American such as the banjo) such as Loretta Lynn inspired filmmakers to tell their stories. It was in regard to the naturally gifted Lynn that *Coal Miner's Daughter* was born.

The look of the film is crisp and for the most part it is almost colorless. It revels in deep greens and brooding greys and blacks with Kentucky painted up as a drab and dingy landscape riddled with dense mud. Nothing can grow here, except a flower named Loretta Lynne. Sissy Spacek is outstanding as this country music sensation. Coming from *Carrie* in 1976 (for which she was nominated for an Oscar), Spacek gets to play a different kind of character in this musical biopic—and this time she got to take home the coveted Academy Award. Similarly to horror protagonist Carrie White, she feeds her Loretta with fragility, a shy edge, and grants her an introverted inner strength and quiet restraint. Here is a youngster who grows into a complicated and stable woman. Playing against this personal growth is an oppressive sense of desolation in Kentucky, with a seemingly endless depiction of mud and dirt and the smell of poverty.

Because the film's core focus is Loretta's origins and impoverished upbringing and ability to create music, the feel and energy of the film is built around a hillbilly's story, a slice of Americana where the opportunistic are easily shot down and the secret brewing of moonshine, box socials and the world of coal mining play out to the sound of personal insecurity and complacency. Loretta is her daddy's favourite, but also someone he doesn't mind beating up on when she develops a relationship with Tommy Lee Jones's character Duke. The concept of family and personal connections made outside of the constraints of the family is something that *Coal Miner's Daughter* embraces wholeheartedly. It is a simple responsibility and a dedicated one, and this is what makes this phenomenal biopic a masterpiece.

Sissy Spacek as Loretta Lynn in *Coal Miner's Daughter* (1980)

An off-camera still of Sissy Spacek in *Coal Miner's Daughter* (1980)

The world of the American hillbilly has been presented in the movies many times, and these characters are often depicted as stereotypes—yokels who are uneducated cretins, inbred and filthy, and for the most part mean spirited. But here, family is key and Loretta's silent understanding of her position in her large family as caretaker of her siblings and dutiful workhorse to the community that she belongs to is palpable and real. Just like the lyric in her famous song "we were poor but we had love / that's the one thing my daddy made sure of" sums up the duality of Kentucky mountain folk—the depressing reality of poverty goes hand in hand with familial structure and compassion.

When we first hear Loretta sing, it is to nurse a baby and get him to sleep. Spacek's vocal abilities are terrific; she has an authenticity that you just cannot fault. Spacek the musician is just as confident as Spacek the actress. She possesses an earthiness, soulfulness, and has a handle on the storytelling that Loretta Lynne shapes so well. She has a spiritual connection to the lyrics that elevates her performance from great to superb. When she takes on the dramatic elements of the film we get it, because we have seen her do this work before, in the aforementioned *Carrie* as well as equally outstanding films such as *Badlands* (1973). But when she sings, her brilliance is heightened.

Complimenting her performance is her leading man and this is Tommy Lee Jones at his finest. He parades on through the film with such cocky bravado and confidence that it is impossible not to be conflicted by this not-so-perfect man. Jones's performance wears the character with a reassured education—he knows Duke, and he gets Duke. When he wins Loretta's pie at the box social and spits it out because she failed to fill it with sugar and used salt instead, he hurries back carefully to make sure he hasn't lost her. This big tower of a man wants to take on the fourteen year old innocent as his lover, and the naïve Loretta becomes infatuated with him. And so beings the start of their tumultuous relationship, and from this the film's backbone is built into something plausible and solid. The love story is the core of the film, and Loretta Lynn's music is the marrow.

Sweet Dreams (1985) tells the story of Patsy Cline in a brilliant but mean spirited fashion. It would boast a remarkable performance by the talented Jessica Lange, however in *Coal Miner's Daughter*, Beverly D'Angelo's (still fresh from her spirited performance in *Hair*) portrayal of the superstar of country is also fantastic. D'Angelo gives the artist a sense of breathy vulnerability, and the idea of the character being introduced all busted up and bruised after an accident is a brave choice and also an off putting one. Fragility sits in the background of this film—the fragility of the spirit, the fragility of promise and the fragility of success. Loretta's fragility and innocence is centred and beautifully articulated as Spacek plays it with flawless resonance. When her father tells Duke "Don't ever hit her and don't take her too far away from home," we understand that this is a man letting his baby girl go. Duke, of course, breaks both promises—he does hit her (a number of times) and moves her away from Kentucky. Loretta's first sexual experience with Duke is depicted in a very uncompromised way—with her nervous energy and insecurities omnipresent. When he penetrates her she yelps in pain; it is confronting and very real, there is nothing at all romantic about their union. This is the case throughout the film: in many ways, it is a relationship made out of necessity. Loretta cries "You told daddy you wouldn't hit me and look at you already," and instead of this being something healthy and empowering (this angry cry from the abused) it is a little girl's plea to be recognised as an adult. The violent outbursts, the tension and the frustrated egos are welded within the very fabric of the film and Spacek's childlike sincerity is painfully authentic. She is absolutely convincing as a fourteen year old in the early moments of the film, and as she develops, the change and the playing out of the arc is subtle; nuanced and captivating all the way.

Sissy Spacek and Loretta Lynn unite to sing during production of *Coal Miner's Daughter* (1980)

The exceptionally talented Spacek sings her heart out in *Coal Miner's Daughter* (1980)

When she is given a guitar instead of a wedding ring it unlocks something: her desire to play music and create. An artist is born. Loretta is such a likeable character as she goes through life as an innocent without any selfish desires. Every choice that she makes, and every decision that is made for her, breathes more endearing qualities into her. When she discovers that she is pregnant she takes it in her stride, and when she tells her man he responds with "Well I think you've found the one thing that you might be good at." When she sets out to Washington and farewells her father, it is something that she simply must do, rather than give it a sobbing song and dance. When the film moves into second gear, with Loretta saddled with children and singing her heart out in the kitchen while she cooks, cleans, tends to her young and manages an entire household, we get the sense that this is a woman that can accomplish anything without complaint.

There are three great scenes that summarise Loretta's blossoming into the phenomenal musician that she will become. These start with her struggling to find the chords while bashing the prehistoric washing machine that keeps stalling. Next she perfects the chords and is interrupted by her restless kids. Finally in the kitchen she is allowed to complete a song and has her man do the dishes while she plays. Following this sequence, Duke drives her out to a honkytonk to perform in front of hard drinking mountain folk. She wins the audience over in a second and her career takes off from there. When Loretta struggles to record her songs, her husband brings in her children to sing to. It works. A beautiful moment where mamma sings to her babies is where magic is born. Female musicians and male musicians are equals, there is nothing concerning their gender at all, instead it is all about their craft and their storytelling. In *Coal Miner's Daughter*, woman is presented as artist as well as mother, caretaker, daughter and vulnerable warrior.

After Loretta's father dies, the film begins to tailor the morose to its needs; it brings the drama home and embeds it within the fabric of the piece, so when we move onwards to Loretta becoming a singing sensation, we still get the sense of sorrow and a deep rooted melancholy. Here is a little girl lost who still needs her daddy's care and attention, but now suddenly a woman who needs to create. Her sense of loss, her preference for plastic flowers that never die and her estranged connection to her man all makes up for a complex character. There is something so profound in every acting choice that Spacek loses herself in, and an elegance that transcends the ignorance her character embodies.

The friendship between Loretta and Patsy is one of the strongest aspects to the film. Patsy the liberator introduces Loretta to make-up, glamour and a nonchalant attitude towards men. Loretta starts to accept the fact that she was rushed into adulthood and Patsy sees this. Patsy Cline is a hardened woman, someone seemingly tough as nails, but vulnerable deep down. Loretta looks up to her, and these two musicians share a mutual love and admiration for one another. When Patsy is killed in a plane crash, more depressing stabs in the narrative give the film an unnerving sensibility, and this carries through to Duke's growth as a human being. His casual cheating which becomes the inspiration for "You Ain't Woman Enough To Take My Man" and his anger is a shock and drives the movie before settling into a comfortable trough. It also never really takes too much time with Loretta's addiction to pills and her exhaustion, but it does something miraculous visually: the change in color for the film as it chronicles Loretta's rise to stardom is magical, and her performances in various night spots are glamorous events. The mastery of the film depicting her breakdown amongst the most glitz adds a snarl to this animal—an honest moment and a perfect summary of show business can be a thunderous oppressor of the fragile spirit.

The closing moments of the film brings the love story element home as it sets up the compromise and the unity of marriage. An argument between Loretta and Duke ends with them jovially having a joke about their fight and they drive off with the wind blowing in their hair. The freedom that responsibility robs of you, the art that has to be conceived and executed and the desperate longing for affection and family all gets swept away in a hillbilly breeze tainted by the stale smell of moonshine and swamp.

From the sublime to the average, *The Jazz Singer* starring superstar Neil Diamond is a labored and insipid venture. Much like *A Star Is Born*, *The Jazz Singer* is a second remake of the first "talkie" of the same name starring the legendary Al Jolson and its subsequent initial reimagining from 1953 starring comic Danny Thomas. Unlike *A Star Is Born* which features some terrific songs from Paul Williams and a nice critique on the world of rock'n'roll as a battlefield of gender politics and artistic integrity, this take on *The Jazz Singer* is unnecessary and uninventive. It takes the best elements of the Jolson classic and leaves them out to dry as it tries to embrace the idea of generational warfare, and estrangement between fathers and sons. The film is loaded with histrionics, and at times is unwatchable. The screenplay does its job, but it suffers at the hand of the whining characters that populate its world: there are not many likeable people in this film. Barbra Streisand's *Yentl* (1983) some years later would do the same thing, but in a far superior manner. Neil Diamond is a competent actor, and a lot of his methods are refined and nicely articulated. The problem is there are many times—mostly because of his co-stars—where he doesn't really hit the right mark and doesn't seem to be completely at peace with the material. There is this inner-conflict that comes across on screen, and a strain to his abilities as a thespian, which is unfortunate. Luckily, this seems to disappear when he is allowed to do what he does best—entertain on stage as the great musician and showman that he is. The songs add nothing to the film's dramatic elements. There is nothing new about fathers and sons arguing about what is right and what is wrong, but there could have been something innovative and interesting to be done here—with music. But it was not to be.

BIM, SHARPIES, MEATLOAF AND JESUS ITALIAN STYLE:
The Apple, Quadrophenia, Roadie and *White Pop Jesus*

The Apple is crazy. Structurally, contextually and in thematic terms, this mad movie musical is anarchic. And that is just the beginning of what makes it so fantastic! With its chaotic opening as people flock to see the latest Worldvision Song Contest through to a creepy commune situation where renegade hippies lounge around reminiscing about times long gone, the film is a bizarre blend of religious allegory, hyper-sexual flamboyance and an apocalyptic creepshow. Produced by Cannon films who had built their own legacy of motion pictures with a distinct personal flair, this film sought to cash in on the success of the excellent *Tommy*. *The Apple* fumbles in the dark playing with religious themes and the menacing world of organised cults: its numbers are frenzied seemingly unaware of how abrasive they come across, but all this is part of the film's

725

bulldog charm. It bounds and slobbers all over you and it's phenomenal!

The Apple is a wonderfully crazed explosion of ideas and concepts, and while the film is most certainly not *Tommy* (and definitely certainly not *Jesus Christ Superstar, Phantom of the Paradise, Ziggy Stardust and the Spiders from Mars*, or even *Xanadu*), it is its own animal. It is a reckless, mutant beast that stops at nothing to deliver a crazed rampage that doesn't really know what it's doing. The plot is seemingly based on the story of Adam and Eve with the seductive allure of success as its flimsy backbone. The megalomaniac head of the Worldvision Song Contest and the industrial powerhouse that is BIM monitors the heart rate, passion and excitement of his audience. "BIM Is A Power!" and "Hey! Hey! Hey! BIM's on the way!" launch the film into hyper drive as we enter a science fiction dystopia of egotistical characters and monstrous cretins that lasciviously ooze with opportunistic slime. The costumes are outlandish and scream decadence for a new breed of movie goers, and as much as the film is a successful post-apocalyptic science fiction musical, it fails to be a critique on industry and enterprise (which it quite possibly could have been). But Cannon Films are not interested in presenting an underlying subversive edge: they are keen on a frenzied rock'n'roll hybrid musical that sets out to frighten the horses.

It is set in 1994, which would ironically be the year that marked the death of Nirvana's Kurt Cobain and the longevity of possibly the last of the real youth cultures in grunge, riot grrrl, foxcore,—all derivative of punk. *The Apple* sees the young and impressionable Bibi (Catherine Mary Stewart) as a star on the rise, governed and marketed by the BIM maestro Mr. Boogalow (Vladek Sheybal). The film chronicles her involvement in the dark and wild world of BIM and the music industry, and its influence on society as a whole. The ride is inventive and completely off the wall. Musically, the film bounces along from stadium rock and prototype heavy metal leanings right through to the folk stylings of "The Universal Melody" which at first doesn't appeal to the rock hungry audience but soon enough touches the audience which inspires Boogalow to move forward and act on seducing the green Bibi.

"They're just a couple of kids from Moosejaw!" cries a BIM associate, while another suggests "Nostalgia is always dangerous." Lines like this give the film classic narrative tropes, such as backwater kids making it and surprisingly enlightened dialogue. But this didn't help the film in its initial release. It was an incredible flop costing the Cannon group a lot of money and hardly making any back. Sure, the songs are not product of The Who, but who cares? They are sometimes terrific monstrous ditties that power through the film like a steamroller. Grace Kennedy's voice in "Coming" sleazes upon an unsuspecting audience while the title song is an astounding maniacal freak show. *The Apple* presents its musical numbers in a blunt fashion, it is a gimmicky explosion of raucous buffoonery. While Allan Love sings the titular number, mutants and demons parade around an inferno, where he wails "It's a natural, natural, natural desire, meet an actual, actual, actual vampire"—this is a sample of the hilarious lyrics that riddle the film. And hilarious is what *The Apple* is: funny and maddening.

The ad campaign for *The Apple* (1980)

Actress Catherine Mary Stewart remembers *The Apple*:

The story is an Adam and Eve metaphor. Bibi is seduced by "Shake" the snake and takes a bite of the big apple as shown in the fantasy sequence. In other words this innocent young woman is seduced by the glitz and fame offered to her by Boogalow International Music, or BIM. I met Mary

727

Vladek Shaybal in *The Apple* (1980)

to get to know me, and my approach to BIBI. I was with Mary during the recording sessions. Her tone was very well matched to my tone and the character I was playing. It was helpful for me, also, to be involved in the recording sessions. I loved the look of the film. It's always tough to try to predict what the future might look like. Most "futuristic" films tend to go over-board when you look at them in retrospect. They found some very cool locations in Berlin and Hamburg that look futuristic even to this day. Overall, given the sort of satirical/sardonic tone of the film, I think it's appropriate, visually. All the music was original. Some of it may seem dated now, but at the time I thought it was fantastic! There was a lot of work put in to the production to make the sound big and very professional. *The Apple* was my very first professional acting experience so I found it all very exciting and glamorous! Manahem knew what he wanted and didn't beat around the bush. We worked quickly and efficiently. I was prepared for the hard work having trained as a dancer. It truly was a life altering experience. The themes that are explored in the film such as fascist dictatorship, religious satire and the idea of artistic integrity tossed away for instant stardom are as prevalent now as they ever were. The story is universal and timeless. For someone who had never worked in film before it was an honor to work with such luminaries as Vladek Shebal and Joss Ackland. George Gilmour, Grace Kennedy and Allan Love were inspiring musicians/actors. We were all like one big happy family, including the dancers and other actors. We all hung out together off the set as well as on the set. I'm still friends with some of those involved with the movie to this day! I think both performative moments as well as naturalistic numbers are common and necessary in movie musicals. I had a gas performing all the musical numbers. It was like a dream come true! This genre of movie musical was popular at that time but it's like saying different production companies are trying to cash in on super hero genre movies right now. Of course producers are going to try to cater to what they think the audience wants at that time. Having said that I honestly believe Menahem and Yoram were trying to do something unique and awesome. They believed in this movie 100%. *The Apple* was produced during an era of colourful/disco movie musicals. But again I think they were attempting much more than that. For some it worked, for others maybe not so much, but the integrity behind the making of this movie was Paramount. I'm proud to have been a part of it. I have many wonderful enduring memories of the experience. I feel like the situation of my involvement was a great "fairy tale" sort of scenario, being

729

cast as a complete unknown from a cattle call dance audition. I'm happy that for many it's entertaining and has had the longevity that it has had. It continues to be screened all over the U.S. including several times at the prestigious Lincoln Centre in New York, my hometown. I've attended a couple of screenings. It's always very entertaining watching the enthusiastic audience reaction, much of which consists of people dressed up a la *The Apple* and mirroring the words, songs and actions as they appear on screen. Fun stuff!!

Writer Robin Bougie adds his insight into the film:

The Apple is such a unique life-altering experience, and like 9-11, you never forget where you were and what you were doing when you first witnessed it. Personally, I have Kier-La Janisse (the author of *House of Psychotic Women*) to thank. Back in the 1990s she was my local videostore clerk at a shop called Black Dog Video, and one year she had this amazing music-themed cult film festival at a local theater. The Apple was the movie that she most insisted that I'd need to see, and I'm glad she did, because it blew my fucking mind. Being Canadian, right off the bat one of the things I love the most about The Apple is how Alphie is presented to us as being from Moose Jaw Saskatchewan, when he very clearly has a British or Scottish sensibility about him. He's about as Saskatchewan as Al Pacino is from Uganda. I mean, I was born in Uranium City, Saskatchewan. It's so obvious that they just wanted to make Alphie and Bibi from a small town somewhere, and just picked a spot blindly on a globe. "Moose Jaw! That sounds rural!" Plus you have the fact that the movie is supposed to be set in America, and yet it's painfully obvious that it's shot in Germany! I love that. It makes everything seem off kilter. It's a musical, but the real star of this movie is the costuming and the sense of production design. It's that 1970s idea of what the future would look like. 1970s futurism is fucking amazing. *Rollerball, The Apple,*

Westworld, Message from Space, Zardoz—I love that shit, man. It's a very precise look and aesthetic, and it's very specific to the 1970s. It's wonderful. Lots of silver, and triangles, and amazing hair. Just look at that costume that Catherine Mary Stewart wears when she performs "Speed." It's like future-glam! That costume says it all right there.

The Who's musicals were electric and functional, with *Tommy* being a complex and vividly magnetic ride. When they worked on the Sting-vehicle *Quadrophenia*—an explosive and energetic look at the worlds of skins and sharps in working class England during the heyday of those subcultures—it was an effortless job. Done with vigour, integrity and a ruthless unapologetic drive, *Quadrophenia* sets the energy levels to high and keeps its pitch in every fame. Musically the film is very good, and the resonance and power of The Who's music are in the very fabric of the film stock. With its bleak and downtrodden outlook, the film doesn't go overboard on the sombre lethargy, but instead remains upbeat in an agitated kind of way.

A completely different British export is *Roadie*, starring American rock star and concept album creator extraordinaire Meatloaf. Boasting a laundry list of great rock'n'roll acts and punk rockers like Alice Cooper and Blondie (as well as legends of rhythm and blues and country like Roy Orbison and Hank Williams Jr.), *Roadie* does a good job giving these musical giants a platform to act as well as an excuse for token performances. The film never stammers or trips over itself, when there is most certainly room for it to do just exactly that. Meatloaf plays Travis, a Texan truck driver who gets roped into being a roadie for a bunch of touring acts, and along this journey he discovers a lot more about the cult of celebrity and the notions of fandom.

The film is also about leaving comfort zones and experiencing the world outside of the social trappings set up by tradition. Even though the film doesn't do this as interestingly enough as *The Wiz* with its allegorical journey or *Oz* with its dreamlike naturalism, it does give Travis a path paved by opportunity and experience. In fact, *Roadie* is very similar to the narrative landscape of *The Wizard of Oz*—a rural youngster whisked away into a surreal world where he meets friends and establishes an enemy and brings order to a world that is painted by oppression. But in *Roadie*, oppression is blasé. There is no real threat like in *The Wiz* or *Oz*: instead, the fun police are the natural enemy. This is will become part of the fabric of movie musicals to come throughout the 1980s.

Along for the ride with Meatloaf is nymphette groupie Lola Bouilliabase (Kaki Hunter) who proudly proclaims that "rock'n'roll is the greatest energy of our time, and us groupie are the spark plugs of rock'n'roll." More great lines that pepper the film such as "I can't believe you've never heard of Alice Cooper. Don't you read t-shirts?" The film's interest in Travis and Lola's blossoming relationship sits at the heart of the story, but gets in the way of the pleasantly plotted musical moments that movie the movie along. Meatloaf is earnest and engaging on screen. There is nothing he does in the role that is awkward or ill-directed and he manages the green and open hearted pseudo-innocence with tenderness. Even when he unleashes the wild and manic, hyper-theatrical Meatloaf we all know and love, there is a stillness to his high energy which makes the character a bizarre hero. Along with Art Carney as Travis's father, musicians Alice Cooper and Debbie Harry are most notably the stand out performers, showing off their acting chops with swift ease and comfort. Harry would go on to wow critics in David Cronenberg's body horror opus *Videodrome* three years later, and in a sense *Roadie* was a nice bit of practice for the platinum blonde princess of punk. In *Roadie*, it is wonderful to see her front Blondie belting out a great variant of the June Carter song "Ring of Fire" made so famous by Carter's husband Johnny Cash.

In a completely different league is the Italian production *White Pop Jesus*. If *The Exorcist* and *Jaws* saw a cavalcade of imitators popping up in rapid succession, then *Jesus Christ Superstar* would most certainly inspire some as well, most notably is this Euro-style take on a musical about the messiah. Directed by Luigi Petrini and featuring piano and keys work from Goblin's Maurizio Guarini, the film sees the son of God sent down from the heavens to take on the mafia as well as other social ills that plague Rome. Some of his battles include taking on a giant syringe (an overt representation of the heroin problem hitting the streets of Rome at the time) and rampant thieves that have no qualms about stealing in broad daylight.

Instead of the rock score of *Jesus Christ Superstar*, *White Pop Jesus* introduces disco to the mix and delivers a bizarre and yet truly captivating mess that is jaw dropping. Not only does Jesus take on the mafia, but he is also continually chased by sexually charged ladies who want a piece of the messiah. Perplexed by the idea of not being able to commit to a mortal woman, Jesus is has an internal dialogue (or possibly a dialogue with his father) that questions the reasoning behind his stigma and sheds light on his loneliness and eagerness for companionship on earth. It is a wacky and insane concept, but in many ways it works. Musically, the numbers are bouncy and intricately written. These are songs conceived with a great understanding of character, purpose, story and function. Stylistically the film reads like a less flashy *The Apple*, where songs appear with magical dismissal of the organic and whack you over the head with gleeful and unapologetic assault. Throughout *White Pop Jesus*, themes are subtle to make way for the core two plots: the mafia's shady dealings and Jesus's personal dilemma as a superman on earth. *White Pop Jesus* deserves to have a stronger cult reputation than it already has, and the soundtrack is something that is its strongest point: all the things a great musical should have!

SPIC, NIGGER, FAGGOT, BUM , YOUR DAUGHTER IS ONE:
Times Square **and** *The Blues Brothers*

Times Square incorporates teen alienation, mental illness, musical expression and punk feminism in a simply packaged class resentment fable that mostly runs smoothly. But it is not without its problems. The film is not necessarily a musical in a classic sense nor is it diegetic in form, but it does move forward through song (namely songs by punk rock acts such as The Ramones). This angry coming of age movie is a collection of kooky situations strung together by various electric moments shared by two revolutionary girls who continually load the screen with Bechdel Test approved energy. *Times Square* is certainly one of the best of the teen-angst films that will eventually dominate the multiplexes in the 1980s: it is vigorously angst-ridden, it is unapologetic and it is in all meanings of the word "revolutionary," but it does lack direction and focus.

Years before the Riot Grrrl movement (a punk rock feminist movement inspired by incredibly talented and influential musician and

733

feminist Kathleen Hanna of band Bikini Kill), *Times Square* brings a primitive revolutionary riot grrrl style to the foreground and it is presented in an uncompromising and angry manner. By the end of the film, our heroines inspire young teen girls all across New York to don garbage bags, plastic jewellery, trashy make-up and fishnet stockings and to hit the streets and reclaim the night. This is New York for the angry alienated teenage girl and this is the New York that will serve them—at least for one evening. Movies that followed in the late 1980s and early 1990s such as *Pump Up The Volume* (1990), *Mad Love* (1995), *Fear* (1996), *Wild Things* (1998), *Fun* (1994), *Poison Ivy* (1992) and many more would feature mentally unstable teens who either survive and overcome adversity or succumb to violence (spiritual as well as physical). *Times Square* was a perfect predecessor and a healthy option in comparison to the overbearingly safe and sanctimonious teen 'no one understands me' mantra delivered by the likes of directors such as John Hughes.

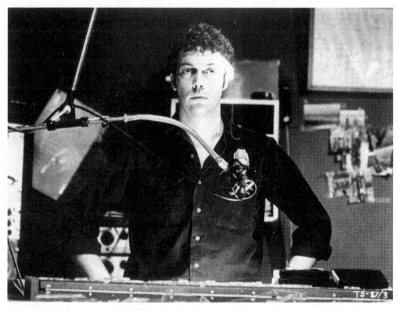

Tim Curry in *Times Square* (1980)

Tim Curry is great as always, but unfortunately when the film closes in and focuses on his character (a DJ that is chasing up on the two girls and following their lives and careers with ratings being the main reason of course) it stumbles. What is far more interesting is the relationship between the two girls who form a bond and try and create a mini-revolution. What happens in *Times Square* is incidental, but what the film is fundamentally about is important—teenage girls needing to find a feeling of self-worth and empowerment. This film, in all its filth and fury, says this with a jagged resentment. When culture continually privileges teen boys (positively and negatively) and excludes teenage girls, there is a problem. The term "youth" itself becomes synonymous with teen boy: even the youth rebellion movement was constantly referring to student protestors as "long hairs" and "beards" which denies the vast numbers of the angry chanting anti-war young women. *Times Square* gives the teen girl a platform to be angry, red faced and revolutionary—if only for a moment.

The angry cry of the outsider in *Times Square* (1980)

A completely different musical from the same year was joyous comedy and a heartfelt tribute to a long-gone era was *The Blues Brothers*. Based on a skit from the long running variety comedy show *Saturday Night Live*, *The Blues Brothers* is a jam-packed, delirious, fun-filled ride propped up by some superb musical performances from some of R&B's forgotten legends, who by the time of this film's release were forgotten and underappreciated. What John Landis's film does is give these artists a platform to showcase their lost talents. His film is a genuine tribute to this period of great blues musicians: Ray Charles, James Brown, Cab Calloway and Aretha Franklin. But on top of that, the film is an irreverent jukebox musical that never loses stops being a love letter to the music it lauds. It fundamentally it keeps its sense of humour liberal and peppered throughout with a steady edge.

Dan Aykroyd and Ray Charles behind the scenes on **The Blues Brothers** **(1980)**

The film tells the story of Jake Blues (John Belushi) who has recently been released from prison, and his brother Elwood (Dan Aykroyd) who comes to collect him. The Blues siblings decide to visit the orphanage they grew up in and discover that the home of their childhood is to be closed down unless a substantial amount of money is paid up. On advice from the janitor (played by the enigmatic Cab Calloway), the duo sets

Aykroyd and Belushi in a publicity still from The Blues Brothers **(1980)**

out to a sermon hosted by preacher James Brown and get inspired to start up their R&B band to raise funds to help save their beloved orphanage. A clean set up is installed. But a streamlined narrative is rejected in favour of a magnetic collage of happenings that are carefully constructed, detailed and steered by John Landis who understands all genres. Here, his grasp of comic language and the movie musical is on show for all to enjoy. Landis would direct the brilliant *An American Werewolf in London* (1981) a year later which would successfully marry horror with comedy

Director John Landis and Ray Charles behind the scenes on The Blues Brothers
(1980)

On the set with Aretha Franklin from The Blues Brothers **(1980)**

in a nuanced and sophisticated manner, and here in his *The Blues Brothers*, he runs with the jukebox musical format and brings it together with slapstick. The comedy is gleefully delivered in subdued stark coolness by Belushi and Aykroyd, and set pieces (including a massive car chase and crash sequence) brings the film a degree of the epic.

1980 set a standard for the movie musical, and for the most part it was a period that championed the gritty and the urban. Movies to follow would focus more on the aesthetic and if they didn't appear to, they subliminally explored dark terrain as well as very unnerving thematic takes on story. *Pennies from Heaven* (1981), *One from the Heart* (1982), *Footloose* (1984), *Flashdance* (1983) and many more would present visions of loneliness, compromise, abuse and apathy, while films such as *The Best Little Whorehouse in Texas* (1982), *Oliver and Co.* (1988) and *Steppin' Out* (1982) balanced the fun with the sentimental. However, the advent of MTV and the rise of the music video would cast a shadow over the success and necessity of the movie musical, and for the most part, audiences—especially young audiences –would much rather see pop stars such as Madonna ape the likes of Marilyn Monroe in *Gentlemen Prefer Blondes* (1953) in her video for "Material Girl" rather than take on the influential Howard Hawks classic. Besides masterfully made and commercially successful films such as *Little Shop of Horrors*, the movie musical became a quiet entity come the 1980s, but were cherished by genuine movie-loving filmmakers who would homage them in their own works, such as John Landis with his incredible "Thriller" (1982) video, with make-up legend Rick Baker (who had invented the Best Make-Up Academy Award for his superb work in *An American Werewolf in London*,1981) turning Michael Jackson into a werecat while decaying zombies danced in a dark alley. Musicals changed shape, and like the 1970s before it, the 1980s embraced this transition wholeheartedly.

Afterword

FILM MAKER AND HISTORIAN RICHARD W. HAINES HAS AN
encyclopaedic knowledge on all aspects pertaining to film stock and the
prints used for the movie musicals examined in this book. Here is his
phenomenal insight:

> The musicals of the 1970s went through numerous
> changes in terms of production formats and presentation.
> The first notable trend was the phasing out of large format
> negatives for principal photography. In the 1950s and 1960s,
> 65mm (Todd AO, Panavision 70) were popular systems
> to shoot big budget musicals in. Among the notable titles
> of that era were *Oklahoma!* (1955 Todd-AO), *South Pacific*
> (1958 Todd-AO), *West Side Story* (1961 Super Panavision
> 70), *The Sound of Music* (1965 Todd-AO) and *My Fair Lady*
> (1964 Super Panavision 70). Early large negative formats like

VistaVision (1956 *High Society*) and Technirama (1962 *The Music Man*) had already been phased out. The only musical shot in 65mm in the 1970s was *Song of Norway* (1970 Super Panavision 70). The advantage of the 70mm format were superior sharpness and resolution in the release prints due to the increased negative area exposed in the camera and improved fidelity with the six track discrete magnetic stereo sound. 70mm print were struck directly from the 65mm negative resulting in a first generation release copy which was optimum quality for an analog format like film. The other advantage the ability to make 35mm anamorphic reduction prints for general release. However, 70mm as a presentation format increased in popularity in the decade. 70mm blow ups were made on many musicals. While not as fine grain as a print derived from a 65mm negative, they still offered first generation quality when they were enlarged directly from the 35mm negative. There was a slight cropping of the image to compensate for the ratio difference between anamorphic (2.35) and 70mm (2.21) Most blow up prints were derived from anamorphic 35mm negatives. Features included *Darling Lili* (1970 Panavision), *Fiddler on the Roof* (1971 Panavision), *Jesus Christ, Superstar* (Todd-AO 35 1974) *Lost Horizon* (1973 Panavision), *Funny Lady* (1975 Panavision) and *Grease* (1978 Panavision). Another trend was making 70mm blow up prints from flat (1:66 or 1:85) negatives. There was a decrease in visual quality in this type of release print compared to those derived from anamorphic negatives. However, the six track magnetic sound remained the major selling point for exhibitors, especially musicals. Some titles blown up to 70mm from flat negatives include *Man of La Mancha* (1972), *The Wiz* (1978) and *The Blues Brothers* (1980). There were also instances of films originating in 16mm being blown up to 70mm release prints including *Woodstock* (1970) and *The Concert for Bangladesh* (1972). The image quality was poor with obvious grain and the six track stereo sound the sole attribute. *That's Entertainment* (1974) was unique in

742

that it utilized multiple aspect ratios in the 70mm blow up print, depending on what format the film clips originated on. Aside from 70mm Roadshow prints, there was a major change in the quality of general release prints beginning in 1975. Technicolor shut down its proprietary dye transfer process which generated excellent quality prints derived from first generation matrices that had a better primary colors, contrast and dye stability compared to the other labs which offered positive printing on Eastmancolor stock. Musicals like *Darling Lili* (1970) *Cabaret* (1972) and *Fiddler on the Roof* (1971) were printed in the dye transfer process for general release. Technicolor replaced its IB process with high speed printing which the other labs adopted over time. The speeds reached 2000 feet per minute which made it difficult to generate a good expose on the general release prints. To offset the substandard quality of the mass produced high speed prints, distributors often made 'EK Showprints' for press screenings and large screen cinemas in the major cities. These were camera negative prints that were of superior quality to what most audiences saw in the multiplexes. A major change in sound was implemented with the introduction of Dolby stereo in 1975. Rather than apply four magnetic tracks inside and outside the sprockets as had been done since 1953 for magnetic stereo 35mm prints, Ray Dolby used a split area optical track. Splitting the track area in half combined with noise reduction created two discrete left and right channels along with matrixed center and surround channels. Although not as discrete as the six track magnetic sound used in 70mm, it offered a good quality alternative on standard 35mm stock. All theaters needed was a Dolby processor and new optical track reader although it could be played as a standard mono track for theaters that didn't want to install the new equipment. Among the early Dolby Stereo 35mm musicals were *A Star Is Born* (1976), *Grease* (1978) and *The Rose* (1979). In the 1980s, Dolby Stereo became standardized for most US releases.

All of the films discussed in this here book: the magical, the monstrous, the maniacal, the misguided, the sublime and the silly, the beautiful and the deranged—all of them sing out an expression of anger or joy, complexity or numbing banality, sincerity or grandiose ego, and all attempt to weave some kind of entertainment or commentary on a decade completely riddled with change and revolution. All in all, these musicals, the good, the bad and the ugly, teach us to dream the impossible dream, embrace divine decadence, challenge tradition and let us know that we can be who we are. So, my advice right here is this: dive into the 1970s and throw on a musical—your senses will never be the same.

Thank You*s*

A massive thank you goes out to the brilliant Alexandra Heller-Nicholas who has been a guiding light in the writing of this book, a huge thanks to Justine Ryan and Hande Noyan who made the job easier with their incredible help and a big yell out to Manoah Bowman, Matt Bauer, Hollywood Book and Poster and Independent Visions who provided the gorgeous pictures, Peter Savieri who did a marvellous job with the Muppets drawing and Darren Cotzabuyucus who did a fantastic job on the cover design.

A grandiose thanks also goes out to...

Cinemaniacs, Fangoria, This Film Is Better Than You, Deal With It.com, Conan McGrath, Marcus Eastop, Lisa Bartolomei, Andrew Martin, Natalie Papak, Sean Sobczak, Ben Hellwig, Camilla Jackson, Anthony Davies, Ryan Clark, Cara Mitchell, Burt Bacharach, Mark Fak,

David Robb, Ben Ohmart, Sam Bowron, Shade Rupe, Rosanna Arquette, Anthony Biancofiore, April Muhl, Sean Patrick Brady, Mark Goldblatt, Antony Botheras, Chris Alexander, Paul Williams, Justin Beahm (and the late Gordon Hessler), Grace Gambin, the American Cinematheque and the Australian Film Archives for all of your incredible help, insight and generosity.

Thank you to my wonderful and very talented contributors…

Howard S. Berger, Robin Bougie, Adam Devlin, Richard W. Haines, John Harrison, Kier-La Janisse, Briony Kidd, Craig Martin, Michael Gregg Michaud, Alexandra Heller-Nicholas, Amy Seidman, Kat Spazzy, Adalita Srsen and Staci Layne Wilson.

And finally, to all the incredibly gifted artists who I had the distinguished pleasure of interviewing for this book. Your stories will always be remembered and honored and I am truly blessed to know you all…

Sandahl Bergman, William Peter Blatty, Herb Braha, John Carpenter, Julie Dawn Cole, Didi Conn, Bruce Davison, Sharon Day, Laura Dean, Eddie Deezen, Lesley Anne Down, Rick Drasin, Bill Feigenbaum, Jack Fisk, Ellen Foley, Sidney J. Furie, Mick Garris, Troy Garza, Deborah Geffner, Ellen Greene, Joel Grey, Archie Hahn, Sonja Hanley, Alan Heim, Norman Jewison, Bill Kerby, Bruce Kimmel, Sally Kirkland, Lynzee Klingman, Robin Lamont, Edgar Lansbury, John LaZar, Jeff Lieberman, Gilmer McCormick, Philippe Mora, Joyce Van Patten, Barry Pearl, Austin Pendleton, D.A. Pennebaker, Valerie Perrine, Dean Pitchford, Ann Roth, Carole Shelley, Scott Simon and Sha-Na-Na, P.J. Soles, Sissy Spacek, Jerry Sroka, Catherine Mary Stewart, Charles Strouse, Maureen Teefy, Twiggy, Lesley Ann Warren, Gigi Williams, Barry Winch and Stuart Wurtzel.

Index

Numbers in **bold** indicate photographs

About the Author

Lee Gambin is a writer from Melbourne, Australia. He is a writer for Fangoria magazine among other periodicals and DVD and bluray releases. His book "Massacred by Mother Nature: Exploring the Natural Horror Film" is a best selling book on the subject on eco-horror movies and he is currently working on a book for Centipede Press as part of their Studies in the Horror Film series all about Joe Dante's werewolf masterpiece "The Howling."

CPSIA information can be obtained
at www.ICGtesting.com
Printed in the USA
LVHW081818180721
693027LV00006B/88

3 1901 04550 5015

9 781593 938543